C000150189

1,000,000 Books

are available to read at

www.ForgottenBooks.com

Read online
Download PDF
Purchase in print

ISBN 978-1-5276-5704-5
PIBN 10878724

This book is a reproduction of an important historical work. Forgotten Books uses
state-of-the-art technology to digitally reconstruct the work, preserving the original format
whilst repairing imperfections present in the aged copy. In rare cases, an imperfection in
the original, such as a blemish or missing page, may be replicated in our edition. We do,
however, repair the vast majority of imperfections successfully; any imperfections that
remain are intentionally left to preserve the state of such historical works.

Forgotten Books is a registered trademark of FB &c Ltd.
Copyright © 2018 FB &c Ltd.
FB &c Ltd, Dalton House, 60 Windsor Avenue, London, SW19 2RR.
Company number 08720141. Registered in England and Wales.

For support please visit www.forgottenbooks.com

1 MONTH OF
FREE
READING

at

www.ForgottenBooks.com

By purchasing this book you are eligible for one month membership to ForgottenBooks.com, giving you unlimited access to our entire collection of over 1,000,000 titles via our web site and mobile apps.

To claim your free month visit:

www.forgottenbooks.com/free878724

* Offer is valid for 45 days from date of purchase. Terms and conditions apply.

English
Français
Deutsche
Italiano
Español
Português

www.forgottenbooks.com

Mythology Photography **Fiction**
Fishing Christianity **Art** Cooking
Essays Buddhism Freemasonry
Medicine **Biology** Music **Ancient**
Egypt Evolution Carpentry Physics
Dance Geology **Mathematics** Fitness
Shakespeare **Folklore** Yoga Marketing
Confidence Immortality Biographies
Poetry **Psychology** Witchcraft
Electronics Chemistry History **Law**
Accounting **Philosophy** Anthropology
Alchemy Drama Quantum Mechanics
Atheism Sexual Health **Ancient History**
Entrepreneurship Languages Sport
Paleontology Needlework Islam
Metaphysics Investment Archaeology
Parenting Statistics Criminology
Motivational

JOURNAL

OF

SACRED LITERATURE

AND

BIBLICAL RECORD.

EDITED BY

THE REV. HENRY BURGESS, LL.D., Ph.D.,

MEMBER OF THE ROYAL SOCIETY OF LITERATURE.

VOL. II.

LONDON:

ALEXANDER HEYLIN, PATERNOSTER ROW.

EDINBURGH: W. OLIPHANT AND SON. DUBLIN: S. B. OLDHAM.

1856.

LONDON :
PRINTED BY WALTON AND MITCHELL,
WARDOUR ST., OXFORD ST.

JOURNAL

OF

SACRED LITERATURE

AND

BIBLICAL RECORD.

No. III.—OCTOBER, 1855.

THE STUDY OF THE BIBLE: IN WHAT SPIRIT SHOULD IT BE PURSUED?

PERHAPS, in the present day and in our own country, there is no question more important than the one we have given above, in relation both to individual advancement in religious truth, and to the interests of the church at large. In the course of Divine Providence the Bible occupies a place in Christendom which it never before held, given to it by the invention of printing and the development of Protestantism. In the earliest periods of the Christian church, the Holy Scriptures had more or less of a fragmentary character, and could not be appealed to as they now are, as an organic whole; and even after the canon was authoritatively settled, and the Bible took substantially the form which it has now, the scarcity of complete copies, and the want of literary culture, placed it in a different relation to the bulk of Christian people from that which it now holds. The influence of these remarkable changes is felt most by Protestants, but they are by no means solely affected by them. The old churches of the Christian world—the Romish, the Greek, and the more primitive Oriental—all participate, in some degree, in the effects of a free circulation of the documentary records of the faith. These are phenomena which demand the attention of thoughtful minds, anxious that the Word of God may have free course and be glorified; for, as no advantage has ever been given to mankind without some measure of mis-direction or abuse

1527588

attaching to it, so the treasures of biblical knowledge have entailed in their general possession a measure of error and danger.

The doctrine that to whom much is given of him much shall be required is universally true, but it has a special certainty in the case of religious privileges. The early churches were required to grow in grace, and in the knowledge of the Lord Jesus Christ; not only when they hung upon the words spoken by apostolic lips, but also when left in a great measure to their own unaided resources, in connexion with the oral teaching they had received, and the gracious and constant guidance of the Holy Ghost. It is difficult to picture to ourselves the exact state of a primitive Christian community, called from heathenism by St. Paul, for instance, and then left by him to the care of a bishop or overseer, chosen from themselves. In faith and hope and charity they were, doubtless, often rich; but in what *we* think necessary for Christian progress they must have been comparatively poor. Literary appliances they probably had none, corresponding to our complete Bibles, our liturgies, catechisms, and hymn-books. Later in the history of the church these means of instruction and of devotion were multiplied, yet they never assumed the place they hold among ourselves, now that printing gives for sixpence what once cost many pounds, not to dwell on designing attempts to keep the people in mental darkness. It must be seen at once that a great responsibility thus rests upon ourselves for the right employment of such decided advantages; and that it behoves us to enquire in what degree we have properly used them.

The full and easy possession of the Bible is, however, only *one* of the talents committed to our trust; the facilities for its elucidation and comprehension constitute another, equally important. We stand in the accumulated light of eighteen centuries, all thrown upon divine revelation, and giving to it therefore a distinctness which it probably never before possessed in minds not supernaturally illumined. History, human discovery, science, knowledge and art, have combined with the evolutions of divine providence to prevent the Bible being a sealed book, and to make the Christians of the nineteenth century specially capable of understanding its contents. There is nothing in the whole compass of human knowledge which has been so enriched with subsidiary aids for its right interpretation as this wonderful book, and, consequently, there is no subject which ought to be so well understood. Our present object is to enquire how far this completeness of biblical attainment is reached by us as a Christian people, and to enforce the temper and spirit in which our theological researches should be pursued.

It will be at once conceded that every biblical investigation should be intended to conduct us to TRUTH. The most conceited preacher, the most novelty-loving commentator, and the most bigoted private Christian will be loud in their declaration that it is *truth* which they have in view in all the fantastic interpretations which they put upon the Word of God; and in all the wayward and eccentric courses into which their fancy or inclination may lead them. Now, however willing we may be to give all these parties credit for sincerity, it is impossible we can concede that they either know what truth is, or that they adopt the most likely course to find it out. That which is true, means, in their vocabulary, that which they *wish* to be true. They are continually acting upon a foregone conclusion, and pretending to seek for that which they are quite sure they have already within their grasp. No one at all acquainted, even slightly, with the religious world, can be ignorant of the fact that the mental occupation of most professing Christians is not a *search* for something, but rather a battling for that which is already possessed; not a laborious and careful weighing of premises, but a dogged defence of a conclusion which has been arrived at *per saltum.* The Psalmist prayed, " *Open thou mine eyes that I may behold wondrous things out of thy law;*" but with these, all is already seen, and there is nothing more to find. Another sacred writer speaks of *digging for wisdom as for hid treasures,* but the satisfied generation to which we are referring has no necessity for such toil, as the jewel is already in their hands.

An attachment to *conventionalism* is the most prominent feature of the *method* of biblical study in England at the present time, and has been so, with some few exceptions, ever since the Reformation. There is a popular theory, or an accustomed and fashionable mode of viewing the contents of the Holy Scriptures, which at once discourages enquiry and stereotypes mere human opinions. Here, we think, is the real danger which truth has to cope with, an obstacle in its way far more formidable than many systems which are thought seriously to militate against it. Let us, for instance, compare what we may call the *Perfectionists* with the *Rationalists,* and we shall find the former more to be dreaded than the latter; although the one class is orthodox and the other heterodox. By the Rationalists we mean those who deny, or at least doubt, whatever cannot be made to square with the deductions of *their* reason; by the Perfectionists those who deny the truth of whatever is not found in *their* pre-arranged and settled ·system. Now the former, vicious in theory and injurious in practice as is their theory, do good by exciting enquiry, and raising up defenders of the truth. They cannot really injure the truth itself, but merely *seem* to endanger it in the estimation of such as have too little confidence in its heaven-born and immortal character; and this apprehension calls forth the resources of piety and learning in defence of the faith. St. Paul declares (1 Cor. xi. 19), "There must be also heresies (αἱρέσεις) among you, that they which are approved may be made manifest;" and it is most interesting and satisfactory to know that the wildest vagaries of the heterodox have always resulted in the yet further establishment of Catholic truth. It would be a most profitable enquiry how far the low Neologism of Germany has subserved the interests of biblical science by call-ing forth the energies of divines and scholars. *If the founda-tions be destroyed, what can the righteous do?* Neology asserted that a buttress was defective, and led to an examination into the fact, to the satisfaction of all candid observers that its strength was firm and impregnable.

But the Perfectionists neither search for the truth themselves, nor give opportunity for the investigations of others. Some council, or divine, or body of divinity, or religious community, has defined for them how Scripture is to be interpreted, and there is an end of the matter. They say to all enquiry, but that which favours their dogmas, *hitherto shalt thou come, but no further, and here shall thy proud waves be stayed.* They look and utter scorn upon the careful and devout students of Holy Writ, who by deep thoughtfulness have elicited a new exposition, if with lynx-eyed jealousy they can discern any possible incom-patibility between it and their creed. They have, doubtless, much truth on their side, but their views admit of no adjust-ment, alteration, or accretion; and (themselves being judges) being already perfect, are to be implicitly received. It may be asked, do not the Perfectionists, like the Neologists, furnish occasion for the advancement of biblical truth by the errors they entertain? But a little reflection will shew that the cases are widely different. Neology attacks the truth—Perfectionism pro-fesses to defend it, and in many respects does so. Perfectionists are in the main orthodox, and sincerely attached to what is most. valuable in Christianity, and therefore cannot be treated as enemies. The consequence is that while no man in England hesitates to reprehend the wild systems of neological and hete-rodox writers or sects, the case is widely different when men of unblemished creed are concerned. An error of excess is more difficult to combat, in religion, than one of defect, for it is an ungracious task to be opposed to the boasted champions of a high estimate of revealed truth. Hence those whom we have called Perfectionists operate like a dead weight upon the interests of a sound and progressive system of biblical interpretation; they defend the waters of life indeed, but by keeping from them the wholesome breezes of a free and enlightened criticism, they make them become stagnant. They are, in relation to biblical truth, in the position of many men with regard to their duties as Christians, whose virtue is wholly negative; and who, while quite free from vice, are yet injurious to Christianity by their entire destitution of any active virtue.

Conventionalism is not *Catholicity*, and while we deprecate the influence of the one, we would pay a marked deference to the other. Catholicity is the form taken by Christianity, doctrinally and practically, in all ages of its history, with regard to all its bold and salient features, apart from the numerous minor variations and shades of social and individual character. Even political government, although so much the creature of human inclinations and passions, takes a uniformity in its grand characteristics in all countries and ages; much more therefore is it to be expected that a system of religion directly revealed by God will have a oneness and harmony through the whole course of its existence, however moulded and fashioned it may be by the human elements to which it is subjected. God made the mountains, the rivers, and the plains, and these grand features of nature are not eradicated because the people who live among them at one time leave the soil uncultivated, and at another sow the fields and plant vineyards; now cultivate the arts of peace, and now fill the vallies with the din and desolations of war. We could not think our holy religion is divine, if a oneness did not run through its history as to essential doctrines, ordinances and practices, and therefore, under a wise and discreet controul, catholic consent is a most weighty consideration in everything relating to the Holy Scriptures. But conventionality is quite a different thing; something fashioned to the varying hour and not permanent like the everlasting mountains. It is the mere local arrangement of a plot of ground, or the occasional turning of part of a river into a new channel, in relation to the magnificent outline of the broad expanse of nature which meets and fixes every eye. What the church has thought in all ages is something to be reverenced and relied on; what religious society now receives as new and untried *may* be proved to be expedient and useful, but it must be weighed and tried before it is to be generally followed. Our readers, we trust, will not misapprehend our meaning, which is not to tie us down to antiquity, nor to urge to the rejection of novelty; but to give to both the place they must relatively occupy in the minds of those who study Scripture in the light of the providence of God.

We have noticed Conventionalism as a foe to an enlightened exegesis of Holy Scripture, not because it is the only one, but on account of its great and almost universal influence. It binds with adamantine chains, not only the bulk of Christian people, but also their ministers, who, as leaders and instructors of others *ought* to be free from its trammels. It operates in the church, as fashion does in society in relation to dress, modes of living and etiquette,—making thousands follow as a leader what has no real existence,—a phantom, a breath, here to-day and gone to-morrow, and yet powerful to compel almost all to bow to its arbitrary laws. As long as a fashion lasts, only the bravely independent dare to question its authority; and as long as some new doctrinal or practical phase of biblical interpretation is in vogue, those who will not be spell-bound by it are looked upon as mere rationalists or something worse. They may be near the mind of Christ and his apostles, and near to the opinions of the early church; but what can all that weigh against the dictum of a Luther, a Calvin, or a Wesley? Other impediments in the way of biblical knowledge will be noticed in the more preceptive and positive form which will now be given to our remarks.

1. In every enquiry concerning the contents of the Bible, a desire to discover truth should be supreme, taking the lead of all other motives and grounds of action. This indeed should influence us in all mental pursuits and investigation, even when the subject leads to no direct practical results, or has no imme-diate bearing on the duties of life. The love of truth, in the abstract conception of it, is a high attribute of intelligent being, and in proportion as it is felt, it approximates us to the divine nature. Whether the question is, How does the sap circulate in vegetable tissues? or, What are the revealed attributes of God? we should not be satisfied with crude or indistinct concep-tions if we can obtain clearer ones. But there is a distinct peculiarity in Scriptural subjects, which raises this general prin-ciple to one of the very highest and most solemn importance; for those subjects concern our present happiness and final destiny in a way in which no other topics can possibly affect them. Our lost condition by nature, and our recovery by grace; the way in which we can be made holy on earth and happy in heaven, are the grand considerations presented in Holy Writ; the in-trinsic importance of which urges us to become thoroughly acquainted with the nature of the heavenly message concerning them. It is true that the substance of the *glad tidings* does not reside in verbal niceties, and may be received by those who can-not read a letter of the written record; but if we can read, and in proportion as we have opportunities to study the Word, it is

evidently our duty to search diligently for its whole meaning. A neglect of what may be called the circumstances of a message from heaven, is scarcely compatible with a reverence for the message itself.

A knowledge of the defects of our own minds gives us an additional inducement to make the law of truth paramount in religious enquiry. One of the first discoveries we make of our own weakness concerns our proneness to mere prepossessions; the tendency to take things for granted; to follow custom and fashion; to be the victims of the conventionalism to which we have just referred. We find also that in religious matters this prejudice is the strongest, and that in the sphere where it is most dangerous, it is likely to wield the greatest power. There are few *thinking* men, if any, who have not been sometimes startled at finding that they have, from childhood, mistaken errors for truths, and treated as divine utterances the mere figments of human imaginations. The detection of *one* such case as this, in our early history, should be sufficient to put us on our guard against the *idola tribûs*, the idols of mere popular interpretations. Yet how little is this candid temper exhibited in theological argument and in biblical enquiry! We feel ashamed when we remember that in the sphere, where, of all others, calm and unprejudiced judgment is most necessary, it least prevails; that *theological* reasoning is the least strict and chastened of any; that if logic runs wild anywhere it is in the walled preserves of biblical knowledge. What foregone conclusions, what unreasonable hypotheses, what demonstrations *per saltum* are exhibited every day in a department of mental research, which especially demands a healthy and manly system of dialectics!

Let us take the current literature of theology and see how far a love of truth seems to influence the vast number of productions which yearly demand our notice. Searchers after truth should be on the alert for new ideas, and as willing to listen to fresh propositions as to reject them when weighed in the balances and found wanting. We do not mean that every wild scheme or new fancy must stop us in our course, to impede our progress until it is logically refuted, for then no progress could be made; but the opinions of divines and scholars, the result of laborious study, are always worthy of respectful attention. Yet more than one-half of the books which issue from the press will be found to treat new ideas with neglect and contempt; to brand them as heterodox or neological; and to attribute to their propounders very unworthy motives. Religious periodicals are very apt to exhibit this unworthy spirit, especially those which take the character of newspapers. In such quarters we often find abuse instead of argument, and a treatment of worthy and learned men which indicates both a bad spirit in the writers and an entire ignorance of the subjects they oppose. This disposition to cry or write down the sentiments which are opposed to our own, without any attempt to comprehend their scope or understand their value, is utterly incompatible with the love of truth which should especially mark the theologian.

2. A regard to the laws of evidence, or the right method of proof, must be inseparably connected with a love of truth, since it is only by their means that it can be discovered. Whatever dangers there may be arising from the use of reason in religion, it is absolutely necessary to employ it in every step of our progress, and we might as well close the eyes when walking as attempt to go on without it. The controversies about reason and faith, or about *fides ante intellectum*, are generally matters of supererogation, as uncalled for as they are useless, since faith not built on the deductions of reason is mere superstition, something unworthy of the name it bears. Intellect, that God-like quality in man, is given us to be a guide and a ruler; to counteract mere instincts or child-like prepossessions, and it is not to be disused or disparaged because it sometimes leads astray. Nothing can exceed the thorough manliness of the sacred writers in this respect, their constant appeals to reason in their inculcation of the new religion they were commissioned to promulgate. The same observation is true of our Lord himself, whose whole ministerial course was a fine compliment to man as rational, a respectful deference to those mental powers which he had given to his creatures. What is a miracle but an appeal to reason? It forms the premises of which faith is the legitimate conclusion. A claim is made upon our confidence; a miracle satisfies the judgment; rational belief follows. This is the process in God's treatment of us, recognizing those laws of evidence which are fundamental principles of our nature.

But we could name more than one popular production *professing* to illustrate the Scriptures, where a course diametrically opposed to that pursued by our Lord and his apostles is habitually taken, and the laws of evidence and proof are constantly violated. With the most solemn gravity, statements are made resting on nothing more than tradition, or the subjective ideas of their propounders, which, when submitted to proof, will be found utterly without any rational foundation. Certain departments of biblical science are more particularly exposed to this unsound method of treatment, of which we may mention, especially, *Prophecy, the Canon of Holy Scripture,* and *Inspiration*. The first of these has always presented a wide field for the vagaries of the shallow school of theologians, because the uncertainty of the meaning of unfulfilled predictions, makes them an appropriate sphere for their aimless assertions and inconsequential reasonings. In proportion as things are obscure, they are thought to be the more fitted for Christian investigation, as though the solving of enigmas, and the explication of conundrums, were the appropriate occupation of a divine and a preacher. Hence Gog and Magog, Armageddon, the number of the beast, and similar intricacies, receive every year new explanations, to be confuted and replaced by others in long yet hopeless succession. It *was* a rule in theology that figurative language should be allowed for, but it is treated literally by the expounders we are now speaking of, so that the allusion by the prophets to fir trees and oaks is made to refer to modern railroads. It *was* once conceded that prophecy remained obscure till after its fulfilment, but a popular doctor of divinity has not hesitated to make Armageddon mean Sebastopol, and to find in the present war abundant fulfilments of passages in the Revelation. Crowds of people, open-mouthed and credulous, receive these *dicta* as gospel, but the thoughtful Christian mourns at the state of ignorance in the Church of Christ, and feels that if prophecy does not lose all its credit as an instrument for establishing faith, it must be because there are some who listen to reason and refuse to confound Scripture declarations with rash expositions. We imagine that the very obscure and difficult nature of the subject of unfulfilled prophecy is thought, by a mental hallucination, to take it out of the pale of the process of induction, and that what is misty in itself, need not be considered in the clear atmosphere of logical rules; a conclusion as absurd as it would be for a chemist to begin to analyze subtile gases in an alembic of cambric or tissue-paper.

No question demands stricter rules in its investigation than that of the Canon; or how, and when, and on what authority, the books of the Bible were made the arbiters in matters of faith and practice. There was, of course, a historical process, although some of its steps may be lost in remote antiquity, and all enquiry should be directed to discover *that;* or, in case of failure, to arrive at some probable certainty as to what it was. That there were relative degrees of importance in the view taken of these books, in primitive times, is a fact which it would be folly to deny. Even in the fourth century, Eusebius classifies some of the books of the Scriptures as of a confessed doubtful authority, without supposing for a moment that the uncertainty prevailing as to these documents endangered the faith, or rendered unstable the goodly fabric of Christianity. It would seem inevitable that we of the nineteenth century could not get clearer light than the Fathers of the fourth; and that the doubts which existed then might be fairly entertained now, without a man being treated, on account of them, as a heathen and a publican. Yet, in the face of all facts, there is in many quarters, a determination to treat the Scriptures as though the whole book came directly from God, like the tables of the law given to Moses on the mount, and to allow of no degrees of evidence as to the canonicity of certain of its parts. Is this fair, is it wise, is it truthful? It may seem to us that a voice from heaven to tell the Church what to receive as of authority would have been the best mode of fixing the Canon; but as no such demonstration has been afforded, it is in vain for us to attempt to supply the place of such an *imprimatur* by any assertion of our own. If men will believe that there is no certainty in the Bible, unless Mark or Luke are received as in every respect on a level with Matthew and John, they will of course invent a theory to make them so; but those who follow *evidence* will still think there may be a distinction maintained between inspired apostles and those who were only their companions and ministers. We confess we are now pleading more for a right method of proceeding in these subjects, than from any wish to alter or lessen the relative authority of portions of Holy Writ. In our own experience we know no difference in our estimate of the several gospels or epistles, but receive them all as equally capable of supplying our spiritual need, and building us up on our holy faith. But then, we do not feel justified in transferring our satisfaction from the actual ground of it to a doubtful one, from moral probability to demonstrative certainty. What has satisfied the Church in all ages satisfies us, and we ask no proof or assurance that could not be attained by the fathers and confessors of primitive times. In a word, we will cling to what is true, not to what we might wish to be so; nor will we give to the infidel impugner of our divine religion a handle or occasion for triumphing, by using a less logical process of reasoning upon it, than we would apply to any other topic of enquiry.

Most of the remarks made on the Canon, will apply to the subject of Inspiration. All we ought to do is to enquire what the Bible *claims;* what the sacred writers themselves *professed* as to the influence upon their writings of the Spirit of God. A thousand theories may be formed on this subject, but they can never be reasonably adopted if they go beyond the rule we have now mentioned. As water cannot naturally rise above its fountain, no more can Inspiration be raised above its quality, as it moulded and moved apostolic men, and all schemes to effect such an object, like pipes and other hydraulic appliances, must be but local and temporary, only capable for a time of disturbing the divinely-appointed level. But nothing is more evident than the efforts made in our day to substitute what men think Inspiration *ought to be*, for what it really *is*. The reasoning is something like the following :—There must be a standard of appeal in matters of faith, and the Bible is confessedly the standard. Unless every word of that book is infallibly true, it cannot be such a standard. How can we receive the evidence of any document on the subjects of God, and salvation, and immortality, if it is not certainly true in its statements of astronomy, geology, or history? Therefore, as the Bible *is* our certain guide to the former subjects, it must be so in the case of the latter, and all others which it treats upon. But here the premises are at fault, for it by no means follows that a·safe religious guide must be equally sure in every other department of knowledge; and, what is far more to the purpose, the Scriptures do not claim to be such a guide. If we are willing to bow to the Bible on any subject, it should be especially listened to as to what are its own assumptions, and the question of Inspiration should be decided by another, What saith the Scripture?

But the confusion prevailing in the departments of biblical enquiry already mentioned, from the neglect of the rules of evidence, is but little compared with that which prevails in the field of interpretation. Dr. John Owen, in his controversial works, often charges the Socinians with making the Bible *a nose of wax*, capable of being twisted and turned any way as occasion may require, and there is too much reason to prefer the charge among ourselves, two centuries later. But we cannot trust ourselves to dwell on a subject which is peculiarly irritating to any one who desires to see a sound exegesis prevailing, and we must pass on with only a slight allusion to the evil of which we complain. If men would confine themselves to the English Version, the evil would be more easily remedied, because plain persons could then judge for themselves; but the Hebrew and Greek originals are always being tortured to deliver utterances unknown to the sacred writers. Let one illustration be *instar omnium*. When the country was recently agitated on the Sabbath question, Dr. Cumming, the author of a mountain of books on various religious subjects, hazarded the opinion in the *Times* newspaper, as a fact, that the word rendered *the* seventh day, might be rendered *a* seventh day. For this he was properly taken to task in the *Guardian*, and informed that in the Hebrew the definite article exists in the phrase in question. But, relying on popular ignorance, or, which is the most charitable construction, made confident by his own, the reverend gentleman replied by asserting that in Hebrew, articles are used very much at random, and may be considered definite or not, *ad libitum !* We much regret that Dr. Cumming is thus evidently shut out from the great pleasure arising from the certainty given to biblical students by the grammatical precision of the Hebrew language.

3. The right spirit of biblical enquiry is a charitable one, disposed to put the best construction upon the opinions of others, and to advance our own with modesty and kindness. Strange proposition this, when theological rancour has passed into a proverb! but though opposed by facts it is yet true. In the New Testament everything like anger or resentment, or undue depreciation of others, in the pursuit of truth, is discouraged by example, and forbidden by direct precept. Our Lord and his apostles knew the fact, and acted upon it, that *the wrath of man worketh not the righteousness of God*, and the former administered a fine reproof to those of his disciples who forbade the casting out of devils by those who did not associate with them. But it is superfluous to endeavour to prove that the *odium theologicum* has no encouragement from the Bible; perhaps all will confess this in words, however much they may act contrary to the admission. If we pass from scriptural authority to expediency and propriety, what can be more adverse to biblical studies than objurgatory and uncharitable temper and language towards those who, in the same pursuit, may differ from us? A knowledge of our own liability to err may well make us tender towards others, even when we are sure they are wrong; but in matters which are not plainly revealed and admit of doubt, uncharitableness is a great crime.

There are such things as orthodoxy and heterodoxy; we are not insensible of the importance of following the one and eschewing the other; and of using all Christian means of bringing about right thinking on all scriptural subjects. But then we must remember that, on many points, orthodoxy is but human opinion after all, and that while we may *fear* our neighbour is wrong, this is not the same thing as proving him to be so. But even if the error could be demonstrated, pity more than hate becomes us, and if this were but once admitted as the rule of action, how many harsh words and bitter reproaches would be spared, to the comfort of the Church, and the removal of a great scandal from the way of those who are without. We are not the judges, much less can we be the inflictors of the penalty; and while we hold fast to what we conscientiously believe to be good, we should leave others to stand or fall to their own master, as he may decide respecting them.   Truth would be far better aided, if, in 'all biblical questions an irritating and depreciating tone were laid aside, and theologians were to reason more like philosophers.

4. Reverence for what we handle is another element which should enter into all biblical enquiry.   Something of this feeling will pervade well regulated minds when they study vegetable and animal life, and endeavour to trace out the divine laws which pervade the profoundly curious substances they are called to analyze; it will even find a place when the gaze is enquiringly fixed on a broken fragment of a rock, separated from the parent stratum of long departed ages.   But seriousness especially becomes us when *religious truth* is the subject of our researches; and lightness and frivolity are never more entirely out of place than when we are treating of the Word of God.   Yet what is it but irreverence when a preacher speaks upon a text which he has not examined; or an expositor gives a meaning to a passage without being *sure* it is the correct one; as far as the use of means can enable him to decide?   We may be wrong, nor would we transgress willingly the rule of charity we have just laid down, but it does appear to us that more than one half of what is written and printed on Apocalyptic subjects would never see the light if a cautious reverence predominated in the authors. So much crude speculation, such inept fancies, such illogical conclusions could surely never be perpetrated, if the minds which frame them approached the Bible with the emotions with which it ought to be read, much more to be studied and explained to others.   So, in the plainer and more trodden paths of ordinary exegesis, could error be so often stated for truth, if a reverential search into the sacred originals were habitually carried on?   We must say, we think not.   The mistake is indeed often committed by such expounders, both of prophetic and didactic Scriptures of thinking themselves inspired, instead of being merely the elucidators of what was written under the guidance of the Spirit, and, in such cases, the feeling of reverence may be compatible with most unwarranted hypotheses.   But this admission is only the same thing as saying that irreverence is escaped by the plea of mental imbecility or insanity.   In reference to such things as are now rife in America, called spiritual manifestations, and which have happily proved harmless in our country, the conclusion seems to us to be inevitable, that their disciples must be either deluders or deluded, rogues or fools.

5. Prayer for divine assistance is eminently demanded of the biblical student.   In every undertaking it is proper to acknowledge our dependence upon God, but the sphere of Scriptural

truth is peculiarly graced by an entire reliance on that aid which is promised to the humble and earnest disciple. There is the book we are to study; it contains *a meaning* which we wish to ascertain, and the question is, how are we to come at it. There are the original languages of the writers, there is the testimony of the church of Christ, and there are the labours of learned and holy men who have preceded us in the same field. All this would seem to be sufficient, but it is not, for the right use of these aids depends on something which man seldom has, but which God can always give him, *a candid and teachable spirit.* The objects around us in nature have one appearance to all men when the vision is in the possession of all its powers, but by various diseases of the eye, such as obliquity of the orb, different degrees of convexity, or an impure state of the blood in the veins, they appear different to different persons. So what we have to work upon is the same with all, the apparatus is equally accessible, and yet the results may be totally different, because the mental eye is jaundiced or distorted. There is no physician who can always rectify the error of the bodily eye, nor can we now expect that it will be miraculously set right, but the eye of the mind can be made "single" by our heavenly Father. Part of the covenant of Grace ensures the Holy Spirit to them that ask it; and we are taught that if any man lack wisdom he is to seek it of God. This divine aid is to be sought by prayer, and it may safely be said that the most devout student will generally be most successful. We say *generally*, for prayerfulness is not the only quality required to make an expositor. Great things are to be expected of the study of the Scriptures when they are approached in the spirit of humble dependence.

We must now leave these considerations to the serious and candid attention of all our readers. This Journal is conducted on the principle that good men, by the use of the gifts which God has conferred upon them, may throw light on the sacred pages, even while they arrive at different conclusions. In our editorial decisions as to admission or rejection we dare not make our own opinions the arbiters, for then these pages would be the organ, not of the church, but of an individual. We would admit nothing which we believe to be of sceptical source or tendency, but we cannot call anything sceptical, or neological, or heterodox, because it does not harmonize with *our* sentiments. We are happy in knowing that our practice in this respect has the sanction and approval of many wise, learned, and good men; and if in any case its propriety is questioned, we can only refer in justification to the remarks now before our readers.

THREE MONTHS IN THE HOLY LAND.

(Continued from the last Number, p. 267.)

CHAP. VIII.—*Tyre—Tomb of Hiram—Hills of Galilee—Halt for the night at Er-Rumāsh.*

I WAS dressed and ready to start when the lark began to sing its cheerful welcome to the morning sun, then rising over the plain. I then woke up Sheikh Achmet, who, rubbing his eyes, looked as if his experiment had failed; and having desired him to come after me, with the servants, I mounted my horse, and at once began this day's journey; according to the advice of Theocritus, which travellers in the East will do well to follow; "To rise with the lark, and with it also to rest at noon."

The day was bright, and promised fair. The breath of morn already scattered the fragrant dew from the leaves of the gum-cistus, and filled the air with its perfume; while it rustled over the waving corn, and sped from the shore the white sail of the fisher's boat, on the surface of the wide blue sea. The crested lark twittered, as it flew tamely along the path; the brilliant bee-eater glittered in the sun with topaz and emerald, as it darted into the air after its winged prey; the beautiful *Argynnis Cynara* flew rapidly by, with expanded wing, suddenly checked itself, and then settled on the purple blossom of the tall lycopsis: while a pair of Egyptian vultures, slowly rising from the neighbouring rocks, soared in concentric spires into the cloudless sky. Before us, the road opened into the Tyrian plain, into those ancient fields which have been the nursery of past kingdoms, and the pride of their own land. Here the son of Semele stood astonished at the beauty of the situation, by land and sea, and at the riches of the soil of these once enchanted shores. For even now they still continue to pour forth from their bosom, the choice gifts of their exuberant soil, as a bountiful reward for the listless toil of the native labourer.

As we passed, there was a man at work in the field. His ill-assorted team, a cow and a donkey, were standing by, waiting to be fastened to the plough. I drew near to look at it, and wished the labourer good morning, to which he replied, "Welcome!"

The plough was rude, and coarsely put together; made entirely of wood, and, although simple in its construction, it was, as it appeared, difficult to manage. The team being harnessed, the

labourer now began his work. Firmly grasping the single handle
of the plough, he leant upon it with all his might, in order to
make it penetrate the soil; while he found it no easy task to goad
his fractious team, and at the same time to guide the plough,
by raising it over the large stones which here and there appear
on the surface of the ground. The man was intent upon his
work, for at the least inattention on his part, the plough would
strike against a stone, and fall from his hand. I called to him,
and he replied; but without turning his eyes from the furrow.
Then I understood the lesson of singleness of purpose, and of
earnestness on our way heavenwards, which our Saviour meant
to give his disciples, when he said, "No man, having put his
hand to the plough, and looking back, is fit for the kingdom of
God."

While observing him, I was struck with the manner in which
he held the goad, while at work. He used it seldom to urge his
team, but he held it with his right hand tight against the share,
resting its handle on his shoulder. I waited until he halted, and
then asked him to let me look at it. This goad was a heavy
stick, eight or nine feet long, pointed at one end, and at the
other furnished with a flat piece of solid iron, about a foot in
length, and from three to four inches broad. This the labourer
kept close to the extremity of the wooden share, during the process of ploughing, in order to assist it in opening the ground,
and for the purpose of scraping the ploughshare, when too much
clogged with earth. A single blow from a powerful arm, with
such a weapon as this goad, would fell a man to the ground.
We can easily, therefore, understand the feat of Shamgar, who
when raised by God to deliver Israel, "slew of the Philistines,
with an ox-goad, six hundred men."

I now stood on the plain of Tyre, about two miles from the
isthmus, on which, at present, lies the small town of Sûr. As
the plague was raging within its desolate walls, I drew no nearer;
but, desiring my servants to go on and wait for me at the fountains of Râs-el-'ain, about a couple of miles further, I climbed
one of the mounds which skirt the plain to the east and south,
from whence I enjoyed an extensive view of the site of ancient
and modern Tyre. The plain on which those two famous cities
stood and flourished in olden times, lay spread at my feet. It
extends north and south, between the sea and a range of hills,
on which I was standing, once the abode of her dead. It is from
three to four miles in length, and two miles or so in its greatest
width, which is between the rock of Palæ-Tyrus and the opposite
Isthmus of Sûr. Watered now, as of old, by the running stream
of Callirrhoë, which ever bubbles among luxuriant groves of orange

trees and oleanders, the plain of Tyre, as I beheld it, in its spring attire, was one rich meadow, chequered with green pastures, fields of corn, and patches of "sweet cane from a far country." Here and there arose like giants over the plain, tall and gaunt masses of ruins, the remains of a broken line of the famous aqueducts, which in days of yore carried the water from the fountains of Tyre to the citadel, and thence to the island city. And among these ruins were enclosed gardens of pomegranates and other pleasant trees, clad in thick and vigorous leaf, and bathed by the transparent wave of the Great Sea. Truly, as the prophet said of old, Tyre was "planted in a pleasant place!"

On this plain, about two miles from the sea, in an easterly direction from the isthmus, stood by itself, apart from this range of hills, a lofty rock. Thither, in days when "the Canaanite and the Perizzite dwelt in the land," and long before Abraham was born, some exiles came from Sidon, attracted by the beauties of this spot and its unrivalled position, and first·built their huts of bulrushes around that rock, the rock Tsûr, "the stronghold of Tyre." There they reared a rude altar to their god Moloch; while the two small rock-islands opposite began to offer a shelter to a few lonely fishermen, the first we are told who ventured their rude and fragile bark over the bosom of the deep. But rising Tyre soon eclipsed the greatness of her mother city, when the huts of her poor seafaring men made way for the palaces of her merchant princes, around the gorgeous shrine of her god Melcart; when Hiram having levelled the rugged surface of the island rock, covered it with large warehouses and stately dwellings; when he built her safe and spacious harbours, and filled them with his famous merchant ships; and then went every year in pomp and state to return thanks for the glory of his kingdom, in the splendid temple of his great patron god. Then was Tyre "of perfect beauty." Her plain, like the garden of Eden, was fresh, fruitful, and rich, well watered by the clear streams of Callirrhoë under a sky that never frowned, and in a climate always mild and healthy. Her citadel was guarded by brave soldiers of Arvad, her "warriors hanged the shield upon her walls round about," and laughed at the enemy from the towers of her fortressed city. The valiant sons of Phut and Lud watched day and night at her gates; and her streets paved with marble resounded with the clatter of her chariot wheels, and with the prancing of her Phrygian horses glittering in polished brass and gay trappings of fine cloth from Dedan. Her merchants were princes and her traffickers the honourable of the earth. Her ships made of fir-wood from Senir, were manned by chosen sailors from Zidon and Arvad; who spread their purple sails of fine linen from Egypt on masts of cedar from Lebanon; or handled the oar of oak from Bashan, sitting on benches inlaid with ivory from the isles of Chittim. Her fleets went forth to carry far and wide the fame of her greatness, to "enrich the kingdoms of the earth with the multitude of her riches, and of her merchandize," and to found kingdoms on the distant shores of the Great Sea; from whence they returned laden with the riches of the world. From Tharshish they brought silver, iron, British tin and lead; and from Javan and Mesech, "vessels of brass and bright iron." In her mart, the mart of the whole world, merchants of Syria and Sheba traded in gold, emeralds, and other precious stones, and in spices and coral; and those of Haran, Asshur and Chilmad exchanged the choice produce of their soil for her broidered work, fine linen, and scarlet cloth. Judah sent hither the finest wheat of Minnith, with oil and balm; and Damascus also traded with her in white wool and in luscious wine of Helbon. Then "Tyre, having built herself a stronghold," became great on land, and "very glorious in the midst of the seas."

But Tyre in all her glory was judged. Her heart lifted up, by reason of the greatness of her wealth and traffic, became her ruin. And the prophet of God was sent to warn her king Eth-baal, of his impending doom.

"Thou hast been in Eden the garden of God, and every precious stone was thy covering," says the prophet. "But, by the multitude of thy merchandize they have filled the midst of thee with violence, and thou hast sinned. Therefore will I cast thee as profane out of the mountain of God, and I will destroy thee, oh, covering cherub! from the midst of the stones of fire. Thine heart was lifted up because of thy beauty, thou hast corrupted thy wisdom by reason of thy brightness; I will cast thee to the ground, I will lay thee before kings, that they may behold thee." "And they that know thee among the people shall be astonished at thee, I will make thee a terror, and thou shalt be no more; though thou be sought for, yet shalt thou never be found again, saith the Lord God."

And so it came to pass. "For I will work, saith the Lord, and who shall let it?" The king of Assyria came with his armies, he "destroyed her walls, and broke down her towers," he laid waste the city, and carried her inhabitants away captive. And after him Alexander the Great finished the work of destruction already begun, and "scraped her dust from her" when he swept from the surface of the plain the remains of the ancient city on land, Palæ-Tyrus; and with those materials raised a causeway to the island city, which he took after an eventful siege. Palæ-Tyrus was now no more; and the island city, which at first

rose from her ruins, gradually fell from her greatness to her present degraded state.   Alas! for the joyous city, "whose antiquity
is of ancient days!"   Where are her three spacious harbours,
scarcely sufficient to hold her fleet of merchant-ships; from which
Elissa left to found her rival city Carthage?   Are yonder reefs
covered with foam the famous rocks of Rhodope; and are those
few fishing-boats all that remains of her ships of Tharshish?
And her splendid suburbs of Eurychorus embellished by the son
of Abibaal, where are they?   Where is the magnificent temple
which Hiram built on the islet of Melcart; or his own gorgeous
palace in the old island city?   What traces have they left?
Look at yonder wretched village of Sûr wasted by time, plague
and famine, and left as it were only to attest the truth of God's
eternal word.   There it lies on one side of the isthmus, while
the other side is as if Tyre had never been, like "the top of a
rock," "a place to spread nets upon, that shall be built no more."
And of the land-city, Palæ-Tyrus, no one standing on her plain
can say of any one spot, "Here was Tyre."   But rather in the
words of the prophet, "How art thou destroyed, that wast inhabited of seafaring men, the renowned city!"

   "Who hath taken this counsel against Tyre, the crowning
city, whose merchants were princes, whose traffickers were the
honourable of the earth?   The Lord of hosts purposed it, to
stain the pride of all glory, and to bring into contempt all the
honourable of the earth," as a warning to other kingdoms, which,
like Tyre, may be lifted up with pride on account of the multitude
of their riches.   For "he that sitteth on the circle of the earth,
before whom the nations are counted as the small dust of the
balance, as less than nothing and vanity," even "God is judge;"
he putteth down one and setteth up another as he pleases.

   But there is yet hope even for fallen Tyre.   For there is yet
life in the dust of that plain, and the days are coming when the
church of Christ shall be established in the earth.   Then the
Gentiles shall come to her light, "and the daughters of Tyre
shall be there with a gift."

   The hill on which I stood is hollowed out into sepulchral
chambers, some of which are open at the top, and apparently of
great depth, while others are still closed.   As I was chasing with
my hat a fine specimen of the *Pieris Daplidice*, I narrowly
escaped falling into one of these openings, which was partly
hidden by the long grass.   I checked myself in time, and the
butterfly escaped; but my blood ran cold when I saw that I had
only just missed falling into the depths below.   My servants
were far away, and had I actually fallen into this hole, I might

have been left there, probably, some time, undisturbed in my meditations on Tyrian catacombs.

But while I was thus musing on the past fortunes of Tyre, the sun had risen high in the sky and warned me to proceed on my journey. I left this spot with regret and descended into the plain. Anon the path led me between the range of hills on which I had been standing, and the rock Tsûr already mentioned. This rock is accessible to the top from the hill side; but falls abruptly towards the sea. It commands a complete view of the plain of Tyre, to the right as far as the Tyrian suburbs on the banks of the Leontes, and to the left as far as the fountains of Rās-el-ain; while it faces the isthmus and overlooks its ruined harbour. There is a *wely* on the top of it; a poor substitute for the "stronghold of Tyre;" and it is by the natives called El Mashûk. From this rock I followed the path in the direction of a broken line of aqueducts, which points to the above fountains, and passing by a few green tents in a field to the left, occupied by Turkish officers of quarantine, I came at last to the celebrated fountains of Tyre, where I found my party waiting for me. To these springs, alike remarkable for the abundance and the clearness of the water, the plain of Tyre owed its amazing fertility. Their stream was carried first to the citadel of Tyre on land, and then to the island city, by means of magnificent aqueducts, some arches of which are still standing. These, however, do not date from a very high antiquity, for they are probably of Roman construction. Yet we read that when Tyre was besieged by Salmanasar under king Elulæus, sentinels were placed at the springs and by the aqueducts, in order to stop the supply of water to the island; so that the inhabitants were obliged during the siege to dig cisterns, and to drink what water they found in them. In order to raise the water of the springs to the level of the aqueducts, a wall of concrete masonry, several feet thick, and about thirty feet high, was built around the largest of the springs; thereby forming an immense reservoir of the purest water, which ever bubbles from below, as if longing to spread over the land its freshness and life. From one of these reservoirs, to the level of which a gentle ascent leads, the view over the plain of Tyre is full of interest. From hence the eye ranges over the remains of the aqueducts, first to the fortress rock of Palæ-Tyrus, and thence towards the isthmus, which appears in the distance beyond the dark foliage of luxuriant trees; thus giving some idea of the probable extent of ancient Tyre. Alas! for the emptiness of all earthly glory! There stood the queen of cities; the noble mother of nations of the earth. Within her walls king after king sat on his glorious throne, and on her soil realm after realm rose and fell, flourished and passed away, like the flowers of her plain. Time was—but how long ago!—when yonder rock was crowned with a kingly citadel, and rose above the din and bustle of busy Tyre; when it smiled on her prosperity and guarded her fabled treasures of silver and gold. But now silence and death seem to brood over the whole. I heard not a sound, not even the click of the miller's wheel; even that lay still and dry. The breeze of noon alone rustled in solemn harmony with the bubbling of these neglected springs, which now no longer flow through the marble streets of "the renowned city," nor abundantly water, as of old, her rich and fertile plain. But now the gurgling fountain of the once life-giving Drosera, and the limpid wave of Callirrhoë, at times only turn a lonely mill, and day and night continue to flow unheeded, and then run to waste into the sea.

After having rested during the hottest part of the day, we left these running streams and the shades around them, and began to ascend the hills in an easterly direction towards the frontiers of Galilee. The scenery changed at once, and became varied. Our path lay by deep and narrow glens, and across fallow fields, covered with spring flowers, or through cultivated ground, already budding forth with promise of abundant fruit. As we gradually rose above the plain, I felt invigorated by the fresh mountain air, blowing gently from the heights before us. And thus ascending, alternately on foot, to gather some of the lovely flowers of these hills, or resting on horseback, I forgot both time and distance, and reached without fatigue an elevated spot, from which a view never to be forgotten lay spread before me.

On the far west, the horizon was bounded by the level heights of Carmel; with glimpses at intervals of the plains of Acre and Aczib, which were partly hidden behind the nearer promontory of Rās-El-Abyād, projecting far out into the sea.. On the shore at my feet, the parched peninsula and white village of Sûr, with the straggling remains of its ruined harbours, and the foaming reefs of Rhodope, advanced far into the deep blue sea, looking like the dismantled walls of the plain. This plain stretched along the shore, in one uninterrupted meadow, edged with a white line of surf, as far as Sarepta, and beyond it to Sidon, until it mingled in the haze, with the faint outline of lower Lebanon, on the distant shores of Gebal and Arvad. On this spot, in sight of the whole coast of Phœnicia, a still perfect, though time-worn monument seemed to command the scene, over which it stands alone; a solemn witness of the past glories of this land. It is a remarkable sarcophagus, about eighteen or twenty feet high, and in pure Phœnician taste. Its massive covering has, apparently, never been removed: but an opening has been made on one side; probably in search of the treasure it was supposed to contain. For it is no less, say the natives, than " Kabr Hairām," " the tomb of Hiram," king of Tyre. He wished, perhaps, to be laid, when dead, on the spot from which he had often looked on the glittering armour and gorgeous uniform of his troops manœuvring on the plain below, under the waving banner of their Tyrian chieftains. Here he sat, may be, in royal pomp and splendour, surrounded by his Tyrian officers, to follow along the shore the sinuous course of the rafts of cedar-wood which his servants, the Zidonians, were taking to Japho, for the temple of God at Jerusalem. Here he came also to view with inward pride his magnificent fleet, as it spread its purple sails of fine linen to the winds, and steered for the distant isles of Elisha, or for the silver land of Tarshish. Here he was laid, perhaps; and his pomp has followed him. The solemn scene before me was altogether one of great interest and beauty; but my own feelings were in strange contrast with the utter indifference of my companions. No sooner had Sheikh Achmet let his donkey loose to graze, than he sat with his face to the wall and his back to the view to smoke his pipe, while Tânûs and Abou Keslân laid down to sleep!

I asked Sheikh Achmet what this monument was. Shrugging his shoulders, he answered, " Hajār," " stones."

Continuing our route, we came to some remains of very ancient buildings, portions of which, consisting of single stones of a large size, were still standing, amid extensive traces of foundations dug in the live rock. Among shrubs of rock-rose and gum-cistus in full bloom flitted the sprightly *Thaïs Hipsipyle,* in great numbers; and a little beyond we reached the brow of a steep hill, the ancient boundary of Phœnicia, on the side of Galilee. Although amid such scenes as those I witnessed at every step, while full of Phœnician recollections, and about to enter the land more particularly consecrated in God's holy word, and sanctified by our Saviour's presence, I needed—

> " No shew of mountain hoary,
>   Winding shore, or deepening glen,
>   Where the landscape in its glory
>   Teaches truth to wandering men,"

yet how gratified I felt when, having cast a last look over the Phœnician coast, which, like a map, lay spread at my feet, I turned round, and my eyes rested on the varied landscape of the hills of Galilee in the tribe of Asher! It was a lovely scene. A group of women dressed in red and blue, with a white handkerchief round their heads, were drawing water at a clear fountain by the side of the path, which wound amid green meadows to the village of Cānāh, surrounded with olive-trees. Immediately behind rose the hills of Galilee, and above them, in the distance, the well-known summit of Mount Hermon covered with snow.

Passing by the village, through a plantation of old olive-trees, we came to the brow of a hill, which commands to the west an extensive view of this undulating country. "High hills the refuge of wild goats, and rocks for the conies:" at their foot grassy slopes, and deep woodland glens densely clad in evergreens, growing by the springs of the vallies, which run among the hills on "these mountains of Bether." We descended into one of these glens, along the slope of a hill covered with young grass, purple orchisses, red and white anemones, and other spring flowers, relics

> "———of Eden's bowers,
> As pure, as fragrant, and as fair,
> As when 'they' crowned the sunshine hours
> Of happy wanderers there."

And there we halted under an evergreen oak, by the side of a running brook. Our steeds were at once set free to range at leisure on the thick herbage of the hill; while I spread my carpet on the turf, and lay down to rest. In this peaceful retreat the wood sounded with the voice of the partridge, and the cooing of turtle doves; while the brown butterfly sauntered in the chequered shade, among the blue blossoms of the iris, growing on the edge of the stream. "For the winter was past, the rain was over and gone, flowers appeared on the earth, the time of the singing of birds was come, and the voice of the turtle dove was heard in the land." And while enjoying the gentle breeze which fanned me to rest, and looking upwards at the blue sky, which peered through the dark foliage of the tree under which I lay, I could not but call to mind the poet's lines—

> "Is not the pilgrim's toil o'erpaid
> By the clear rill and palmy shade?
> And see we not, up earth's dark glade,
> The gate of heaven unclose?"

In a moment Sāleh had picked up some dry sticks, lighted a fire, and made some coffee, which they all sat down to enjoy, Sheikh Achmet with his pipe, and Tânûs without one; for he had none, and patiently waited for a whiff from Achmet's. Meanwhile I opened my provision bag to see what it contained, and I found in it just enough and no more. The leg of a roast fowl, brought from Beyrût, and forgotten at Neby Yûnus; some cheese of sheep's milk; some bread and figs. I felt sufficiently hungry to enjoy the fare, and quaffing a draught of cold water from the brook, I drank it to Pindar's health, and with him said :—

" ἄριστον μὲν ὕδωρ"

" There's nothing like water !"

A steep and narrow path through dense evergreens up the dry bed of the glen, brought us anon to the village of Fiâtar, perched on the top of a hill, from whence the view extends over the ancient territory of Asher, into the land of Nepthali beyond. As far as the eye could reach, it ranged over a succession of undulating hills, literally clad in evergreen oak of various sorts, either cleft by deep vallies and bubbling streams, or separated by rich pasture lands, covered with flocks; over which the summit of Mount Hermon in the distance seemed to preside in peace; while the sun, which was nearing the horizon, cast long shadows and bright gleams of light on the white villages scattered over the landscape. Of a truth, Asher is still blessed, and " is acceptable to his brethren." From hence we descended the hill into the valley immediately below us, and for awhile followed the dry bed of the Wady, at times across rich pasture land, and at other times through ancient forests of oak in which the sound of the axe has never been heard—virgin hills and glens untouched by man, and fresh from their Creator's hand. How thick and green was their foliage ! How cool and refreshing their shade ! Presently we emerged from this dark forest into the meadows of Wady El-Ajân, over which the sun was pouring floods of mellow light; when we parted. Sheikh Achmet and Tânûs left me to go to their home at Tibnin, a village on a hill a few miles off, and I was now left without escort, and unprotected ! to continue my journey through the woods and green pastures of this picturesque valley; until, at sunset, I arrived (although without escort, yet) safe and sound, at the out-of-the-way village of Er-Rumāsh. As this retired village does not lie on the road generally taken, my arrival caused a sensation, first among the dogs, which set up a loud and determined yell, and even shewed their teeth; and then among the villagers themselves, who anxiously rushed out of their houses, fearing nothing less than a dread incursion of Arabs; the terror of the peaceful inhabitants of these valleys. The Sheikh however came to meet me, not like his dogs, but with " Marhabā !" " welcome !" and I was now safe under his care.

"Friend," said he, "my heart is thine, and my house also; come and lodge with me."

I valued his heart and his hospitality too, but I dreaded his house; for Qabb Elyas had left deep and lasting impressions on me. I therefore declined his offer, and invited him in return to come in the evening to my tent. He then, at once, gave orders to some of his men, and helped himself to pitch it on the turf near the village; and after that lost no time in accepting my invitation. My tent was soon full of guests, each of whom I treated to a pipe of tobacco, which they pronounced excellent, and to a cup of coffee, at which he exclaimed, "'Azîm!" "splendid!" while they carried on a brisk conversation, asking many questions, and answering few; until, as it grew late for a traveller, I wished to rest. They rose immediately, and left me with their very best wishes for a good night.

CHAP. IX.—*Departure from Er-Rumāsh—Safad—View of the Sea of Galilee—arrival at Magdala.*

THANKS to their good wishes and to exercise, excitement, and fresh air, I slept sound, till the dawn peering through the tent door beckoned to me to rise and be gone.

"Not yet, Hadjee," said the Sheikh, who was up before me. "My daughter is ill at home, come and see what you can do for her; she is my only child."

"I am not a physician, my good friend," said I.

"Are you not? don't you know of anything that may save her?"

"What is the matter with her?"

"I don't know; we have no one here to tell us; come and see her."

And so saying, he led the way to his house, and brought me in.

"There she is," said the old man in tears, "if you can do anything for her."

She was apparently sixteen or seventeen years old, and was ill with intermittent fever.

Fortunately, I had by me some quinine, which I gave her father, telling him how she was to take it, and hoping it might do her good. Poor child! she could hardly speak; but raising her dark and languid eyes, she said with a faint voice, "Allāh yebārak fîk," "God bless you for it."

No sooner was it known that I had visited the Sheikh's daughter, than I was beset with patients of all sorts. Young men and maidens, old men and children, pressed around me for relief. A man born blind earnestly begged for some physic to restore his sight. Another, a paralytic, cried out for the same thing. In vain did I try to persuade those good people that I could do nothing for them; the more I said it the less they believed it. One of them, who would take no refusal, followed me to my tent. I judged of his complaint by his appearance, and gave him a powerful emetic; but I did not wait to witness its effects.

For it was time to start. The dew had already disappeared in the morning sun, and the flocks were gone to the meadows; and I intended (D.V.) that after this day's journey over hill and dale, I should see the sun set over the sea of Galilee, from the village of Magdala. The Sheikh and his friends accompanied me a short distance on the road, and then wished me a prosperous journey, "mā' salāme," "in peace." So farewell to the people of Er-Rumāsh.

The country was beautiful. At first our path lay through a wide valley of rich pasture-land, covered with flocks, and then by the banks of a clear mountain-stream, which bubbled deep in a glen planted with oak and brushwood; where a covey of partridges was tamely feeding as we passed. A little further the vale opened into a plain covered with luxuriant crops, and surrounded by an amphitheatre of rocky hills, the lower slopes of which were clad in rich verdure. In this sheltered and secluded valley the bees were buzzing at their busy work, while the beautiful *P. Apollo* soared in stately flight over the waving corn, and rested with expanded wing on the downy petals of the purple scabions. The turtle-dove cooed among the branches of the oak; the hawk uttered his shrill cry from the cliffs above; while the splendid roller, clad in turquoise and beryl, spread his brilliant wings to the sun as he flew from tree to tree at the foot of the rocks. The air was of course delicious. The sun was of course brilliant. And the whole of nature seemed to rejoice at this early hour, as on the morning when she came from the hands of her Creator, fresh and fair. If this land be so beautiful even now, while it lies under the frown of Heaven, what must it have been when flowing with the milk and honey of God's own blessing? It is still a good land; "a land of brooks of water, of fountains and depths, that spring out of valleys and hills; a land of wheat and barley, and of vines, and fig-trees, and pomegranates; a land of olive and honey;" a land wherein bread might be eaten without scarceness, and in which, if there were enough inhabitants to till the ground, they would lack nothing. For the "land which the Lord God careth for" must flourish even while it mourns. "His eyes are always upon it, from the beginning of the year unto the end of the year :" now indeed in judgment, but hereafter it will be in favour, and then this land will perhaps blossom afresh, as in her palmy days of old.

I ceased not to look and to admire ; to feel and to be thankful for such enjoyment. And thus beguiled at every step of the road, I reached almost unawares the village of Farâh, situate on the brow of a high hill. At this point the features of the country began to change. Looking east over the territory of Nepthali, it presented no longer the undulating hills of evergreens and rich meadows of Asher, through which I had just passed ; but bare and rocky summits, rising above rich pasture-land, abrupt slopes covered with grass, fertile fields, and deep valleys extending to the northward in the blue morning haze, as far as the range of Lebanon and the waters of Merom, below Mount Hermon. The woods and flowery pastures of Asher here gave place to an apparently more barren and volcanic land. If this be, as it appears from Edrisi's account to have been, the land of Cabul, no wonder if Hiram, king of Tyre, did not admire it much, after leaving the smiling landscape of Asher, through which I had just travelled on my way from Tyre.

From this village we descended into the narrow valley of Mu'addamyeh, which we followed for awhile, until we reached El-Jish, or Giscala, mentioned by Josephus as the last fortress in Galilee to surrender, and which was destroyed by a violent earthquake in 1837. Leaving it on the left, we again followed the path down a rapid descent, and then up a very steep volcanic hill covered with loose rocks, among which grazed a gazelle, which fled at our approach. Then we passed a pond, called Bilket-et-Jish ; perhaps the crater of an extinct volcano, traces of which are scattered over the surrounding country. Before us on the high ground lay the clump of trees and village of Kāditā, from whence I hoped to have had a view of the sea of Galilee. I urged on my horse, but only to be disappointed ; for the high mountain of Safad stretching before us hid from our eyes everything that lay beyond. Leaving Kāditā to the right, we continued our route down a hill covered at that time with white cyclamen, rose-coloured flax, umbelliferous plants of various kinds, and scarlet adonis, to 'Ain Zeitun, at the foot of the mountain of Safad, which had hitherto bounded our view to the eastward, and withheld from my longing eyes the shores—

> " Where Gennesaret's wave
>   Delights the flowers to lave,
>   That o'er her western slope breathe airs of balm."

I knew that from that brow I should first behold a scene, among earthly scenes how much endeared to us! I could not therefore stop to quench my thirst at the clear fountain, which from hence flows into the valley beneath, but I got off my horse in order to climb the quicker. I reached the top of the rock; then turned sharp round to the left, and a view truly like none other on earth opened at once before me, spread, as it were, by magic at my feet. It took me some time to collect my thoughts, and to realize that what I then saw was not a dream. And, for a time at least, I should have forgotten all about dinner, but for Abou Keslân, who, whatever else he did, never lost sight of that, and now left me no peace until I had paid sufficient attention to these earthly matters. Accordingly, we entered the town of Safad to buy provisions.

Passing through heaps of ruins, caused by a late earthquake, we found ourselves at times, following the street, over the roofs of houses, which are built in tiers, one above the other, against the hill, and came to the market-place. There a fair was held, and a busy, bustling scene it was. Squalid Jews, gaily-dressed Syrians, swarthy and wild-looking Bedouins from the plains, and merchants from Lebanon, met, bawled, bargained, bought, sold, cheated, or at least tried to overreach one another, in apparently great confusion. We forced our way with some difficulty through the unyielding crowd, and halted by the side of the castle under an old olive-tree. There I spread my carpet to rest, and to contemplate at leisure the magnificent scene which now lay before me.

From this height, as from an eagle's nest, my eager eyes soared across the whole of the sea of Galilee, which, like a patch of the blue sky itself, set in the surrounding hills, lay deep in the distant plain below; and then over the abrupt shores of the country of the Gadarenes, into the extreme borders of the plains of Botsra, to the wooded hills of Bashan, and beyond them to the higher mountains of Gilead; then across Jordan, and over the naked hills of southern Galilee, Mount Tabor, and Little Hermon, to the far distant heights of Carmel, above Taannach and Megiddo; and immediately below me opened the deep chasm of the Wady Leimon, into which fall the precipitous sides of the mountain of Safad.

Who could stand where I was, and view for the first time, and all at once, spots of such intense interest without feelings of emotion too deep to be uttered? What boon actually to behold the land in which our Saviour lived, the scenery with which he was daily conversant, and to single out, one by one, the scenes of his miracles; the desert place in which he multiplied food for the hungry multitude; the waters on which he trod, and which cowered at his feet; the shores on which he afterwards landed, near his own city—Capernaum; the plain of Gennesaret; the village of Magdala; the town of Tiberias, and the opposite country of the Gergesenes; and to know that these very hills echoed his voice,—that those very fields also bore him from village to village, on his errand of mercy, to seek and to save the lost! And yet, what a contrast between the first impression of this sacred scene and the utter indifference of all around me! I asked a decayed Israelite, who had strolled towards us from the town, what was yonder hill in the distance, pointing to Mount Tabor. He shrugged his shoulders, with a very significant expression of, "I don't know." I tried him on the mountains of Gilead, but he knew no more about them. At last I asked him what that blue tranquil lake in the plain might be? "Tubāriyeh:" and there our conversation dropped.

The town of Safad is not mentioned by name in either the Old or New Testament. Its name first appears in the Vulgate version of the book of Tobit, where it is called "Sephet," although that name is not to be found in any other version of that book. But its high and commanding position, and the mere fact of its being one of the most conspicuous features of the landscape, as seen from the plain of Gennesaret, favours the opinion that it is the town alluded to by our Saviour, when, near Capernaum, and within sight of it he probably pointed in that direction, and said, "A city that is set upon a hill cannot be hid." Safad became celebrated for its school of rabbinical learning, and until very lately still kept up that reputation in some degree. In 1837 it was almost completely destroyed by an earthquake, when a great number of its inhabitants perished in the ruins. The way in which it is built, in tiers like steps, against the side of the hill, rendered the effects of the calamity awful. The upper row of houses fell on the one immediately below it, until the city lay in a heap of ruins, covering hundreds of wretched beings, dead, dying, or miserably bruised and mutilated. It had, however, partly risen from its ruins, and already gave signs of prosperity, and it will probably continue to flourish, until another earthquake, not unfrequent in this volcanic part of the country, bring upon it a fate similar to the last.

The sun was already verging towards the distant hills of Samaria, and light evening clouds were rising, like flakes of wool, from the lake below, when we left Safad. The descent was, at first, steep and rugged, but after crossing a deep ravine the path led us through rich pastures, spangled at that season with bright-coloured flowers, amongst which the scarlet adonis

and large tufts of the purple and of the feathered grape-hyacinth
were most conspicuous.   By and by we came to the summit of
a hill, planted with prickly oak, from whence we saw the sun
sink behind Mount Tabor, and cast his last rays on the cliffs of
Gadara, while the lake before us lay slumbering in the shade.
As I had been unable to obtain really correct information, I
miscalculated the distance from Safad to the plain, which we did
not reach till dark : and as neither of my servants had ever travelled this road, and the muleteer, who professed to know it,
had forgotten all about it, we were for some time unable to discover the track among the tall grass, and still taller thistles,
which grow luxuriantly on every uncultivated spot of this plain.
For, although we were then following the main road, it was
often not perceptible among the tangled weeds that covered it.
For except in the immediate neighbourhood of the larger towns,
the roads in this country are only paths, the beaten track of
travellers on foot or on horseback.   As there had been for some
time few inhabitants at Tiberias, and fewer still at Safad, the
traffic between those two towns was insignificant, and the main
road had in consequence become quite obliterated.   Our position
forcibly brought to mind the passage of Isaiah, in which, speaking of the future kingdom of Christ, he says, " An highway,"
(i. e., a causeway, a made road,) shall be there, and a way; and
the wayfaring man, though a fool, shall not err therein."   Our
situation in this wild and solitary place was by no means envi-
able ; and as the moon shed very little light, and my servants
had tried in vain to discover the path, I quietly resigned myself
to circumstances, and already prepared to pitch my tent for the
night, and wait for the dawn of day, when one of the muleteers,
who had gone a-head, cried out from within a dense crop of
giant thistles, " Here's the Sultan's road," (or the king's highway.)   " All right," thought I, though I was well stung in
trying to join the pioneer.   He proved, however, right ; and
following the path, but not without some difficulty, we passed
by an old building,—a mill, I believe, and by a fountain, which
I heard bubbling among willows and oleanders, for it was so
dark that I could not see it.   Shortly afterwards we descried a
light in the distance, and heard the bark of dogs, warning the
inhabitants of our approach ; and, crossing some marshy ground,
in a few minutes we halted for the night on the shore of the
lake of Gennesaret, and close to the small village of Magdala.
But the land-wind, which I was told generally blows down from
the surrounding hills upon the plain of Gennesaret during the
first watches of the night, all of a sudden blew almost a gale,
and so high, that it baffled all our attempts to pitch the tent.

We succeeded at last, with the assistance of some of the inhabitants of the village; and after a hasty supper, I closed the tent-door, and retired to rest.

CHAP. X.—*Magdala—Capernaum—the Sea of Galilee.*

ON the shore of the sea of Galilee, and at Magdala! I slept, of course, little, but lay awake and watched until the early dawn tinged the clouds which were hovering around the summit of Mount Hermon. I then got up ere my servants awoke, and taking with me my Syriac gospels, I climbed the grassy slope which is at the foot of the rocks immediately above Magdala, and there I sat down to dwell at leisure on the surrounding scene.

The day was ushered in, close and cloudy; and the sun, just peering from behind the snows of Mount Hermon, was reflected in one bright streak of light on the rippled surface of the lake, still as it were asleep in the grey shadows of the morn. Before me, along the winding shore, and extending to the left, lay the fertile plain of Gennesaret, surrounded by naked hills, on which Safad, the city set upon a hill, appeared high and prominent. At the opposite end of this plain from where I sat, the hills rose abruptly along the lake, as far as the place where the Jordan empties itself into it, and where, receding from the water, they surround the desert plain on which our Saviour fed the multitudes. Then closing in, the hills again overhang the lake along the eastern coast of Golan and the steep shores of the Gadarenes, where the river Jordan issues from the lake, and flows between high hills on either side, down its own wide valley of El-ghôr. Thus, with the exception of the town of Tiberias, which lay hidden by the bold line of riven rocks, immediately behind me, I had before me the whole extent of the sea of Galilee, with its surrounding hills. The wind of the night was hushed; not a sound was heard, not even the early twitter of the crested lark, nor the rustling of the morning breeze among the grass: not a voice broke the solemn silence of nature; a white pelican alone, slowly gliding on the glassy surface of the lake, along the shore, by the old fig-tree of Magdala, was the only living object seen.

But when the sun appeared from above the lower range of hills which surround the lake, the scene suddenly changed. Then distant voices from the village were heard, mingled with the bleating of sheep, and the lowing of oxen preparing to accompany the labourer to the field; then the rocks overhead echoed the shrill note of the kite on the wing after his morning chase, and the timid lark skulked among the stones strewed around me, or crept under tufts of the rose-coloured caucalis, on which already flitted the pretty white *Daplidice*, and with it also the buzzing busy bee; and the sun shone, as of old, on the humble dwellings of Magdala, and sparkled, as of old, on the wavelet of the lake, now murmuring on the strand so often hallowed by the footprints of the Son of God. For here he landed from the opposite coast of Gadara, when driven from thence by its hardened inhabitants. There, along the water-side, is the path which he often followed on his way to his own city, Capernaum. On this shore, and perhaps near at hand, he called the poor fishermen from their nets, and preached the gospel to the multitudes who stood on this plain. These waters have borne him on their bosom, either when sailing with his disciples from place to place in their fishing-boat; or, when anxious for their safety, he walked to them on the foaming billows, and bid them be of good cheer, for that he, their Lord, was at hand. Yea, and to think of him here on these sacred shores, and to read in his own language the very words that dropped from his lips when he healed the sick and comforted the sorrowing,—when he won souls for heaven, or looked with pity on the penitent of Magdala; this was a privilege I deeply valued, and I felt that the place where I stood was indeed holy ground.

After having remained here some time, I descended from the hill, and bathed in the clear wave of the lake, out of which I came refreshed and ready for breakfast. That was soon over. I then desired Sāleh and the muleteers to remain by the tent until I returned, and bid Abou Keslân prepare to follow me along the lake. And while he got my horse and his own steed ready, I sauntered among the houses of Magdala. The few inhabitants I saw there were poor. They chiefly lived on the tillage of the neighbouring fields, which yield to them more than even returns for their indifferent toil. Their houses were like those of all the poorer inhabitants of this land through which I had travelled. Each house consisted of a single room, which varied in size from twelve to twenty feet square, built of stone or mud, as the case might be, without windows, and with no other opening than the door, which was low and narrow. The roof, which at times was not twelve feet from the ground, was flat, made of trunks of trees, thrown across from one wall to the other, then covered with small branches or reeds, over which a thick layer of gravel, broken pottery, or tiling was laid, and well beaten together with an outer coating of mud. A flight of steps against the house outside led to the top of the roof. In this house the family lived, surrounded by all they were worth of household utensils, boxes, bins containing grain, and whatever other goods and chattels they might possess. Such were the houses of Magdala; such also was our Saviour's home at Capernaum: for he too was poor and despised, the son, as his own townsmen thought, of a hardworking man, who got his living at the sweat of his brow. We find accordingly that some of our Saviour's parables were taken from his own associations, and from his own mode of living, which was that of his poorer hearers; and as the East knows of no change but that of time, most of the objects I now beheld reminded me forcibly of some of our Saviour's words. As I passed by one of the houses at Magdala, a poor woman was sitting at the mill grinding corn. Anon the same woman would take the flour thus made by her, and mix it with leaven, to make dough for bread, to which our Saviour alludes in St. Matt. xiii. 33, and which he must have seen his own mother Mary do repeatedly. In the next house another woman was actually making bread, while her children still lay in bed. The dough was ready, and she was making it into small thin loaves, to be baked in the village oven close by. Five or six of these loaves would go to a pound weight. The man, therefore, must have been very poor who needed to borrow three such loaves for his friend as poor as himself; while the bed in which the children lay, and the heavy wooden bolt of the door, brought vividly to my mind the words, " The door is now shut, and my children are with me in bed;" and what our Saviour says of the woman, who, having lost a piece of money, lighted a candle, and swept the house, became also more intelligible to me when looking into one of these dwellings. For, having no window, it was comparatively dark even at mid-day, and would require to be examined with a light even at that time, when emptied and swept, in order that so small an object as a piece of money might be found among the household stuff it contained. Some of our Saviour's miracles also became at once much plainer to me while thus looking at these houses, and none more so than the particulars, often misunderstood, in the narrative of the man sick of the palsy, who was let down through the roof and placed before Jesus.

Abou Keslân now joined me. I desired him to lead my horse, while I followed on foot, walking by " the way of the sea," on the road which among oleanders and bushes of agnus castus follows the water's edge. At no great distance on this fertile plain, alike favoured by the riches of the soil, by climate, and by the waters of the lake teeming with fish, there stood, even in the days of the Canaanites, the city Chinnereth (Josh.

xiii. 27); afterwards allotted to the tribe of Nephthali, and
which gave its name to this lake, called in the Old Testament
"the sea of Chinnereth," and in the New Testament, "the lake
of Gennesaret." This plain, once well cultivated by a numerous population, is at present tilled in part only by a few Arabs,
and this strand, once lined with villages and covered with the
fishing-boats of their inhabitants, is now silent and desolate,
overgrown with clumps of prickly dôm, oleanders, and willows,
the safe and lonely retreat of kingfishers, white herons, and
pelicans, which here live and fish undisturbed on these deserted
shores; and on the lake, not a sail, not a boat was to be seen;
but for the swarms of wild fowl which played on its tranquil
surface, it would have appeared a lifeless waste. Yet, amid this
solemn silence, the shore even now whispered the words which
it once heard from our Saviour's lips. I followed the path,
across a stream, which divides the plain in its greatest width,
and which, after fertilizing the soil, empties itself among thickets
of willows and oleanders. Here the shore projects a little into
the sea, and looks like the site of a port long ago filled up, and
now covered with bushes. Beyond, the path leaving the water's
edge, led us through fields and meadows, some already covered
with crops, and others in the act of being ploughed and sown.
A sower was at work, and while he sowed, some of his seed fell
on good ground, and some went to waste. Somewhere, near at
hand, perhaps on this very spot, the multitude stood, and listened
to our Saviour, as he sat in the boat, a little way from this
shore; when he, pointing perhaps to a man at work, like this
sower, on one of the fields this very path crosses, said, "Behold,
a sower went forth to sow :" for here, in the field where that
man was sowing as I passed, there was the "wayside" on which
some of the luckless wheat had fallen, there were "thorns" in
plenty; yonder were "stony places," and elsewhere also was
"good ground." Meanwhile, the "partners of Andrew and
Simon" might have been casting their nets into these very
waters, midway between Capernaum, our Saviour's home, and
Bethsaida, the city of Andrew and Philip, within hail of the
boat in which our Saviour stood; and here, where the clear
green wave so fondly laves the gravelly beach, they might have
drawn their net to land, and then "put the good fish into their
vessels, and cast the bad away." And it was also perhaps on
this shore that the Lord appeared in his glorified body unto his
disciples for the eighth time after his resurrection. Anxious
and sorrowful, they had left the holy city after his death, and as
they were poor, they went back to their fishing-boats. Here the
Saviour met them : he saw the bark in which the poor fisher-

men, his own chosen apostles, had toiled in vain all night long, and for the last time before he sent them to be fishers of men, he bid them significantly to cast the net on the right side of the ship. They did so, and great was the multitude of fishes they caught. Then they knew him; for who but the Lord could thus bring fishes to their net? And they came to land. And here, after he had eaten with them perhaps for the last time on earth, he looked upon Peter, who thrice had denied him, and then thrice asked him, "Simon, son of Jonas, lovest thou me?" And when Peter, inwardly reproved, and grieved at his Lord doubting his love, said, "Lord, thou knowest all things; thou knowest that I love thee;" then the Saviour afterwards, as if to test his apostle's love, said unto him, "Follow me!"

Walking thus slowly along the shore, I had by this time reached the opposite extremity of the plain, a little more than three miles from Magdala, and I came to a few scattered heaps of ruins and mounds of rubbish, partly covered by thick bushes of dôm. Close by, at the foot of the hills, there is an old khan (Khan el Minyeh), in the immediate neighbourhood of which rises, under a large fig-tree near the lake, a spring of water of the deepest blue, thickly lined with moss, and other aquatic plants. This fountain is called "'Ain-et-Tīn," or "the fountain of the fig-tree," which overshadows it; and in Dr. Robinson's map it marks the probable site of Capernaum. After the khan, the path rises above the plain, over the spur of the hill, which there forms a small rocky promontory, planted with trees; and soon after, along the shore, and a little above the lake, it brought us to a copious spring of brackish water, which gushes out of the neighbouring hill, and turns a mill on its way to the lake. There, a large flock of buffaloes were quietly cooling themselves in the water, and unexpectedly reminded me of similar scenes in India.

At this point, the scenery becomes more circumscribed. The hills, at the foot of which our path lay, were girt with oleanders and willows by the water's edge, and adorned with a few stunted oaks and bushes of dôm, scattered here and there over their grassy slopes. They rise abruptly from the shore, as far as the northern extremity of the lake, by the mouths of the Jordan, where they recede a little to make room for the desert plain of Bethsaida, now before me. There, behind that plain, the hills rise higher still, and almost hide the snowy summit of Hermon, and then gradually slope into the bold and abrupt coast of the opposite shores of Golän. Turning round, my eyes fell on the ruined mill I had 'passed, surrounded with trees in the foreground; then on the plain of Gennesaret, and the hills of Magdala, where my tent appeared like a white speck; and beyond, on the distant towers of Tiberias, the opening of the valley of Jordan, and the high shores of Gadara. Here I experienced a great difference in the climate, owing probably to the high hills by which the lake is surrounded, and to its depression below the level of the Mediterranean. It was about noon, and the day was hot and sultry: not a breath of air stirred: nature stood as it were still: even the fish seemed asleep on the glassy surface of the lake, which, like a polished mirror, "stole," as the Indian poet says, "from the shore" the exact image of the surrounding hills.

I went on, and while sauntering along on the rugged and stony shore, I came to a mound of ruins, called by the natives Tell Hûm, where a grim-looking, half-naked Arab on horseback rode up to me, and placing his spear across my path, before my horse's head, bid me stop. I did so, while Abou Keslân behind me muttered some expression of alarm at this unexpected meeting. I bade him hold his tongue, and I wished the swarthy descendant of Ishmael, "Good day!"

"Marhabā, welcome! But what do you want here?" said he gruffly.

"I am come to see your country."

"My country! all that is my country," pointing to the plain beyond. "But who sends you: the Sultan?"

"No,"

"What do you come for, then?"

"To visit your land and your lake, with your leave."

"Be-khātirak! just as you please!"

And with these words he shouldered his spear and rode off. I followed the path a little further towards the mouths of the Jordan, but as I was afraid of risking the exhalations of that locality at this season of the year, I retraced my steps through fierce thistles to a stony hill above Tell Hûm, where I halted, to Abou Keslân's unfeigned delight. For he did not bargain for contemplation at the price of toil, thistles and no dinner. Ever and anon he would grumble, "What are you after?" "Where are you going to?" For the scenery on which I loved to dwell was only to him, "Hajāroobahar,"—stones and sea. He consoled himself, however, with his pipe and an hour's sleep; and left me to study at leisure the features of the scene before me.

Above, heaven was open and clear; below, the lake slumbered in peace—so tranquil and so blue! At my feet, the shore gently curved along the water's edge as far as the mouth of the Jordan, between two and three miles from where I sat; and beyond, it stretched into a sloping plain at the foot of the hills.

> " Here we may sit and dream
>   Over the heavenly theme,
> Till to our soul the former days return ;
>   Till on the grassy bed,
>   Where thousands once He fed,
> The world's incarnate Maker we discern."

It was to that " desert place belonging to the city of Beth-saida " (St. Luke ix. 10) that our Saviour and his disciples " went over the sea of Galilee," " by ship privately." And thither many " ran afoot, out of all cities," from this very one here lying in ruins, " and outwent " the Saviour and his disciples, " and came together unto him." There Jesus was moved with compassion towards them because they were as sheep not having a shepherd. And as the day was now far spent, his disciples came to beg he would dismiss the people. But that plain was, as it now is, a desert place, and the Saviour would not send them away empty, lest they should faint by the way. He there-fore commanded his disciples to make the people sit down in ranks, and they sat down on yonder green grass ; and then, tak-ing his own humble fare—five barley loaves and two small fishes, all that his disciples could get for him and them—he looked up to heaven. Yea, Jesus looked up to thank his Father for the bread which anon his own hands were to multiply abundantly as an emblem of himself, the Bread of Life. But that look was not of thanks alone. The hour was at hand ; only one more passover ere he suffered ; when his body would be broken, when his blood would be shed, and his own flesh would be given for the life of the world. That look was also a look of obedience, " Father ! not as I will, but as Thou wilt !"

Yonder is the shore from which the Saviour constrained his disciples to get into a ship, and go to the other (this) side before unto Bethsaida, while he sent away the people. And when he had sent them away he departed into a mountain—one of yonder grassy hills rising above the desert plain—where

> " All through the summer night,
>   Those blossoms red and bright
> Spread their soft breasts unheeding to the breeze,
>   Like hermits watching still
>   Around the sacred hill,
> While erst our Saviour watch'd upon his knees."

From thence, while praying for his disciples, he saw the small bark in which they were on these waters toiling in rowing, for the wind was contrary to them. Then he came to them, walking on this sea ; and from the midst of the storm his well-known voice cheered them; "It is I," said the Lord, "be not afraid." And with him in the ship they landed safe at the place whither they went; at Bethsaida in the land of Gennesaret, by yonder clump of trees as you look to the right, along the shore towards Capernaum. Hither some of the people repaired the following day, some across these waters, and some along this path; and as they wondered at finding him so soon at Capernaum, he said to them with his wonted love, "Labour not for the meat which perisheth, but for that meat which endureth unto everlasting life which the Son of Man shall give you; for him hath God the Father sealed."

Descending into the path I had left, I followed it back to the old mill, and then over the rocky promontory into the plain of Gennesaret, and then by 'Ain-et-Tīn, and along the shore of the lake. There, as if to multiply sacred associations, I found a fisherman casting his net into the sea. He stood with his casting net slung across his shoulder, up to his knees in the water, and as motionless as his only companion—a white heron on the strand below. With a keen eye the fisherman watched his prey frisking in the transparent wave; then, with unerring aim, cast his net, and drawing it out of the water he extricated from its meshes four fine fishes, while he cast some smaller ones away. I bought the good ones of him, and brought them to Magdala, where, before consigning them to Sāleh's care, I sketched one of them in remembrance of the fish and of the fisherman of Gennesaret.

After my dinner, which consisted of the fish just caught in the Sea of Galilee, an honey-comb, and some bread from Magdala, I went up to the rock on which I had sat in the morning to look from thence over the scenery I had just visited. I had now been backwards and forwards over the most interesting portion of this shore, on which stood some of the places oftenest mentioned in the gospel narrative, and I wished to form my own ideas of the probable site of those towns, from what I had seen myself. There, close by, lay Magdala—undoubtedly Migdal-el, and now called Mejdel or Megdel. This plain, stretching along the shore to the left and surrounded by its amphitheatre of hills, is also certainly the land of Chinnereth, Genesar, or Gennesaret, spoken of by Josephus as well watered and beyond measure fertile and lovely. But where are Dalmanutha, Capernaum, Chorazin and Bethsaida?

Dalmanutha is, as well as Magdala, mentioned only once, in St. Mark viii. 10, while the parallel passage in St. Matthew has "Magdala". "The parts of Dalmanutha" on which our Saviour landed, after having crossed the sea from yonder shores of Gadara opposite, and "the coasts of Magdala appear to have been identical. Of the two names, the latter alone subsists to this day.

As to Capernaum, there are few places mentioned in the New Testament of greater interest than that. For it became our Saviour's own city (St. Matthew), when in the first year of his ministry on earth, after having been driven from Nazareth where he had been brought up (St. Luke), "he came and dwelt at Capernaum" (St. Matthew), and "straightway on the Sabbath-day he entered into the synagogue and taught" (St. Mark), and there cast out an unclean spirit. That same day, our Saviour cured Simon Peter's mother-in-law of a fever; and here in the cool of the evening, they brought him many that were sick, and he healed them; and in the night departed into a solitary place and prayed (St. Mark).

From Capernaum our Saviour set off to preach "throughout all Galilee" (St. Mark); and three months after, on his return, "seeing the multitude, he went up into a mountain near Capernaum and there taught" (St. Matthew). A short time after, being again at Capernaum, "it came to pass that as the people pressed upon him, to hear the word of God, he stood by the lake of Gennesaret, and saw two ships standing by the lake; but the fishermen were gone out of them, and were washing their nets. And he entered into one of the ships, which was Simon's," "and he sat down, and taught the people out of the ship." Shortly after we find our Saviour again at Capernaum, when the following touching circumstances, mentioned with such precision by the evangelist, took place. We read that Jesus having again entered into Capernaum, after some days it was rumoured that he was in the house. His home then, was like other homesteads of the poor of this land. In that humble abode, the Saviour sat preaching the word of God, and the crowd, anxious to hear it, gathered around him and filled the house, "insomuch that there was no room to receive them, no, not so much as about the door." "And behold! men brought in a bed a man which was taken with the palsy, and borne of four," perhaps his own sons. If they could but lay him before Christ who pities the poor, and heals the broken heart, when there, he would be safe! And they sought means to bring him in, and to "lay him before him." And when they could not find by what way they might bring him in, because of the multitude, they went up the outer flight of ten or twelve steps, "on the housetop." Then, having uncovered the roof where he was, *i. e.*, having removed the outer coating of earth and gravel, they afterwards "broke up" the branches or small wood which supported it, and then "let down the bed on which the sick of the palsy lay," "into the midst of the house," "before Jesus." And the compassionate Saviour, who calls the weary and the heavy-laden to give them rest, seeing their faith, said to the sick man, "Son, be of good cheer, thy sins be forgiven thee." Then to shew the Pharisees that he had power to forgive sins, "Arise," said he, "to the sick of the palsy, take up thy bed and go unto thy house." "And immediately he arose, took up his bed, and went forth before them all." That same day, our Saviour, passing through the town, "saw a man named Matthew sitting at the receipt of custom, and he said unto him, Follow me! And he left all, rose up, and followed him."

It was also near Capernaum that our Saviour in the early part of the second year of his ministry, went out into a mountain to pray; and having continued all night in prayer to God, chose and ordained twelve that they should be with him, and that he might send them forth to preach. Then he entered into Capernaum and healed the centurion's servant. From thence our Saviour went again "throughout every city and village" of Galilee, preaching and shewing "the glad tidings of the kingdom of God." And the twelve were with him: and afterwards, again returned home to Capernaum (St. Mark). And after his return from the feast of tabernacles at Jerusalem, he again taught his parables by the seaside (St. Matthew), and being at home at Capernaum, he expounded them to his disciples. While thus occupied in teaching them in the house, his mother and brethren, unable to come at him for the press, stood without desiring to see him (St. Luke). That same day, our Saviour and his disciples took ship, and came over unto the other side of the sea, unto the country of the Gadarenes (St. Mark). And having there cured the man possessed of a devil, "he entered into a ship, passed over and came into his own city (St. Mark). Here Jairus met him and fell at his feet, and besought him greatly for his little daughter, who lay at the point of death. He went, and found the child dead; but, at his bidding the dead arose; for his words are spirit and they are life (St. Mark). From thence he went to Nazareth (St. Matthew), and from Nazareth, having again for the third time gone about preaching the kingdom of God, he returned to Capernaum, when, seeing the multitude, he was moved to compassion on them, because they fainted and were scattered abroad, as sheep having no shepherd. Then saith he unto his disciples, The harvest truly is plenteous, but the labourers are few (St. Matthew), and then he gave them power to go and heal all manner of sickness, and all manner of disease (St. Matthew). And when they returned (St. Mark), he took them apart into a desert place, whither they departed by ship privately (St. Mark); there he fed the five thousand, and the following day he came back to Capernaum and taught in the synagogue: saying, "I am the living bread that came down from heaven: if any man eat of this bread he shall live for ever "— " Lord, evermore give us this bread!"

Then again, in the third year of our Saviour's ministry, we find him at Capernaum; when they that received tribute-money came to Peter, and said, "Doth not your master pay tribute?" He saith "Yes." But they who could only muster among themselves a little bread and a few small fishes, had no money to pay tribute, and he ought to have been free from this tax as Son of God, But being unwilling to offend them needlessly he sent Peter, the only one of his disciples, who was of age to be liable to the tax, to the sea, and wrought a miracle in order to pay it. And a few months after, not long before "the time was come that he should be received up," he appointed other seventy also, and sent them to preach from Capernaum, and there awaited their return.

Thus was Capernaum favored above other cities in Galilee. In it the Son of God lived, and he blessed it with his continual presence. There he taught more parables, there he preached oftener, and wrought more miracles than in any other town or village of this land.

Yet at Capernaum he was without honour, he was despised and rejected of men in whose eyes the brightness of the sun of righteousness had shone in vain: and for that, Capernaum was judged. It had risen higher than other cities. It was to fall lower than they. For Capernaum was to fare even worse than Sodom. Then the Lord, after all he had said and done in Capernaum, came to it once more; but, now no longer to call it to repentance. It was to seal its doom. "Thou, Capernaum, which are exalted unto heaven, shalt be thrust down to hell!" and then he left it. After this sentence, Capernaum could no longer exist. And shortly after our Saviour's ascension, its situation was scarcely known. It is in vain therefore to look anywhere for its ruins; Capernaum was to be utterly destroyed; and of it not one vestige remains.

But we would fain ask, where did it stand? What position did our Saviour's own city occupy on this plain of Gennesaret? The situation of "the village of comfort," for such is the meaning of the word Capernaum, must have been well chosen and fair. So far we may conclude it to have been on this plain of Gennesaret which we read was so rich and fertile, and the testimony of the Gospel is conclusive on the subject. For we find by comparing St. Mark vi. 45, where our Saviour constrained his disciples to get into the ship, and to go unto the other side before unto Bethsaida with St. John vi. 17, where in the same instance they are said to have entered into a ship, and to have gone over the sea towards Capernaum, that these two cities must have been near each other. And we further ascertain from St. Matthew xvii. 24, that Capernaum was upon the sea-coast, and from St. Mark vi. 53, that both Capernaum and Bethsaida lay somewhere on this plain ; for the disciples "having passed over, came into the land of Gennesaret." As to the probable situation of Capernaum on this shore, the only clue of importance we have is the testimony of Josephus. He says that having met with an accident by a fall from his horse on marshy ground, perhaps the same I crossed yesterday on my way to Magdala, he was taken to (of course the nearest town) Caphernome. And elsewhere he says, that the land of Gennesaret owed its wonderful fertility to the waters of the spring called Caphernaoum, which runs through and waters it, and which yield the good fish Coracinus.

Now these particulars cannot apply to 'Ain-et-Tīn, where some travellers would fix the site of Capernaum. First, there is no marshy ground near that spot ; it occupies the most arid and uninviting portion of the land of Gennesaret. Then, although the spring of 'Ain-et-Tīn yields some small fish, it only rises within a hundred yards or so of the lake into which it empties itself through a bed of bulrushes, too insignificant to be mentioned in connection with Josephus' accident. While, on the other hand, the description he gives of the spring of Caphernaoum agrees better with the stream which comes down from the hills, and divides the plain of Gennesaret in its greatest breadth. At its entrance into the plain, this stream is swollen by the gurgling spring of El-Mudawerah, and makes one garden of the land through which it flows, now sluggish in marshy ground, and anon bubbling among fields and flowery meadows, thick herbage, and beds of oleander in bloom. Then it empties itself into the lake, close to a small square promontory, which I have already mentioned, and now overgrown with willows, and inhabited only by the white heron and the brilliant king-fisher. The mouth of this stream teems with excellent fish. It is still the favourite haunt of the native fishermen, one of whom I found at work on this very spot. There, or in this immediate neighbourhood, may have stood of old the city of Capernaum, long since fallen, swept away, or buried in the shifting deposits of its own limpid stream.

As regards Chorazin, mentioned in St. Luke x. 13, as distinct from Bethsaida, but in connexion with it, and with it also denounced, it appears to have been near Capernaum and Bethsaida. Like those cities, it must have lain on this, the principal scene of our Saviour's life in Galilee, in order to have witnessed as many of his "mighty works" as they. In the midst of many different opinions as to the probable site of Chorazin, and in the absence of any data to enable us to fix it with any certainty, we may, at all events, follow the nomenclature of the word. Whether derived from Chourashin or Chareshin, both of which imply a wild, and wooded, or dry and stony place, the word would apply best to the mound of ruins called Tell Hûm, half way between 'Ain-et-Tîn, and the northern extremity of the lake, and within three miles of the probable site of Capernaum. That part of the sea-coast is mostly covered with large and rugged stones; and the shore being rough and shallow is ill adapted for fishing. On the other hand, I should feel inclined to place Bethsaida, the city of Philip, Andrew, and Peter, midway between Capernaum and Chorazin, at 'Ain-et-Tîn in "the land of Gennesaret." There, a strand of fine gravel would of itself invite the fisherman to settle on it, and to ply his precarious craft along the shelving shore. For we must bear in mind that neither Bethsaida nor Chorazin were doomed to the same utter destruction as Capernaum. But the Lord judged and upbraided them for the mighty works that were done in them, and he mentioned them in connexion with Tyre and Sidon. And, as in Tyre and Sidon, so also in Chorazin and Bethsaida, we may expect to find traces of their existence. We accordingly find them in the ruined dwellings of Tell Hûm and 'Ain-et-Tîn. The former on a rugged and stony shore, as Chorazin; the latter on a shelving beach, as the fishing-town of Bethsaida.

Both are still left, but only to warn the passer by that once they were, and that because they repented not, they are now no more.

If an additional proof were requisite to shew that this Bethsaida could not have been further north than the corner of the plain at 'Ain-et-Tîn, it might easily be drawn from the relative position and local features of the scenery. For when, after having dismissed the multitude on yonder desert place, "the disciples took ship to cross over unto the other side," they launched at once into the open sea. There they toiled all night in rowing; for the wind, which as yesterday, often sweeps down the hills and over the plain of Gennesaret, and suddenly raises the surface of the lake, was then contrary to them. Had Bethsaida lain further north, for instance at Tell Hûm, it would scarcely have been " on the other side," and the disciples in thus crossing over to Bethsaida, would not have been " in the midst of the sea " (St. Mark vi. 47), but rather along the shore on which the multitude had been. Then the disciples could have rowed easily in the lea of the high hills, which there rise abruptly from the shore.

But where is the mountain on which our Saviour having "continued all night in prayer to God," chose and ordained twelve, that they should be with him?" And from whence, having come down with them and stood in the plain, followed by a great multitude of people, he lift up his eyes on his disciples, and said, "Blessed be ye poor, for yours is the kingdom of God?" Look around and see. Those hills are the same; their rocks are as high, and their slopes are as green as when they echoed his voice. This plain is the same; as wide and as rich as when it sounded under the tread of countless multitudes which came to hear him, and to be healed of their diseases. Last evening, and until the fourth watch of the night, the wind blew high, and these waters rose and roared, but now they slumber at rest, as when he said unto the sea, "Peace, be still!" "and there was a great calm." The air is as mild as when he breathed it himself. These flowers are as fragrant and bright, this grass as green and as soft, as when they blossomed at his feet. And yonder snows of Hermon are as white in that blue sky; and their image is as fresh and perfect in the lake as when he looked at them himself from the dwellings of Magdala.

I was loath to return to my tent, but the day now began to wear away, and before night I must be at Tiberias. We struck the tent, and casting one lingering look on Magdala, its over-hanging rocks and fertile plain, I left it with great regret, and rode off. Here the path rises from the lake, and passing by a copious fountain of cool and deep-blue water, it continues for about three miles under the brow of steep and rugged rocks, high above the sea. Then it descends again as far as the walls of Tiberias, which is situated by the water-side, on a small plain at the foot of the surrounding hills. The sun was setting when we arrived at the gate of the town. Aware of the high reputation Tiberias enjoys above other towns, for the superior quality of its vermin, I did not feel anxious to pitch my tent for the night within its walls. We sought in vain a suitable spot near the town, and we went a mile beyond, as far as the baths of Hammāth but without success. The shore was everywhere hard, or dirty; and it was dark when we came back to the town. At last, from want of a better choice, we pitched the tent under the crumbling walls of the old castle. Sāleh at once lighted a fire, while Abou Keslân attended to my horse. The kettle anon soon hissed as usual, and my bed being ready, after supper I retired to rest.

CHAP. XI. *Tiberias—and the hot springs of Hammath.*

IN escaping from the fierce bite of ravenous fleas, I fell victim to another plague—

> Nam " cadit in Scyllam qui vult vitare Charybdin."

My tent was pitched in the dark without much choice as to the locality, and on what turned out to be a bed of nettles eaten down by the goats of the town. Once or twice during the night, which was long and sultry, I awoke and felt something creeping over my face, and inside the bed. But I hoped for the best, and again fell asleep. Great however was my horror when I awoke in the morning to find my bed, my clothes, my books, my food, myself, in short everything I was worth, literally covered with black caterpillars. My first feelings were certainly far from agreeable; but as I recognized in these little crawlers the future form of the *Vanessa Io* (peacock butterfly), the thought of a flight of those beautiful insects reconciled me in some degree to the unwelcome inroad of their grubs. I destroyed as few of them as I could, and shaking them off into the open field, I wished them well.

The morning, like the night, was very close and sultry, and the difference in the air of this place, which lies low at the foot of volcanic hills, was even at this early hour sensibly felt. As the sun rose higher, the tent began to afford but a poor shelter from the heat, which soon became oppressive when the clouds disappeared, and the sunbeams fell on the glassy surface of the lake, as on a brazen mirror. Not a breath of wind in this hollow; not a tree in sight, but one or two stunted palms, with branches as if immoveable from want of air to fan them; and a withered acacia growing among the ruined walls of the town, was all the verdure I could see. After breakfast, I sat on the shady side of the tent, until the heat obliged me to take shelter inside it. But there I found the flies so troublesome, that I was obliged again to rush out into the open air. Thus alternately driven in by the heat, and driven out by the flies, I spent a part of the morning in reading out of the Syriac scriptures, the incidents in our Saviour's life, which took place on these shores; and after that I heard both Sāleh and Abou Keslân read out of the Arabic gospels. They did it, poor fellows, as attentively as they could, with the noise of Albanian soldiers quartered in the castle close by, and the heat, beggars, flies, and a flock of goats, which taking the tent probably for a rock, began one after another to run up and down its limber canvass. I grew weary of this at last, and leaving the tent in charge of my servants, I strolled out.

First, through the town, if the sad remains of a late earthquake lying in confused heaps deserve that name. The greatest
part of the houses had fallen, or were falling. The streets were
encumbered by mounds of rubbish, or entirely blocked up. Side
by side with the houses that had escaped the general overthrow,
a few miserable dwellings were beginning to rise from the dust,
scarcely better than the ruins around. The walls of the town
were almost all thrown down, and the few towers still standing
were already tottering and ready to fall. The soil which is volcanic, was everywhere parched and dusty. The inhabitants, for
the most part Jews, were few, and how filthy ! Melancholy descendants of their learned ancestors ! What would R. Judah
think of them, few of whom could read, in this too, their holy
city ! If we are to believe their account, Tiberias must once
have been a fair town to behold. But what others say seems
infinitely more probable, that even in its palmy days, few would
live in it, that were not obliged ; for Herod and Antipas brought
thither inhabitants from all parts, and bid them reside there
under a heavy penalty if they left. For who would live at Tiberias if he could help it? Whatever the Gemara may say, and
whether Tiberias be Rakkath or no, it was assuredly no compliment to Tiberius to call such a place as this after him. But he
deserved it perhaps, and Herod no doubt must have done it on
purpose.

I made my way among heaps of rubbish, putrid carcases of
horses and dogs, and then through a breach in the town walls
on to the road that leads to the hot springs of Hammāth. On my
way thither, I passed a few broken pillars of grey granite, the
remains, although certainly few and far between, of former splendour, which shew that of old the town probably extended as far
as the hot baths. From hence I climbed a hill which rises immediately above the town, and was then covered with flowers
and aromatic shrubs ; delightful contrast to the filth and effluvia
of the town. As I walked along, numerous quails fluttered in
all directions. The air was pure, and the view from this height
was beautiful. The lengthened shadows of the mountains
stretched over

> " The lake's still face,"

which "like a liquid looking-glass " already lay in the shade,
and slept

> " Sweetly in th' embrace
> Of mountains terraced high with mossy stone,"

while a single bright ray of light fell on the town of Tiberias,
and detached it from the hazy distance, where the snows of

Hermon appeared in the mellow tints of an evening sky. Immediately below me lay motionless at anchor, and close in shore, a boat into which men and women in varied costume were preparing to enter.

I descended a steep ravine, and came to the baths. I entered; but was soon obliged to go out again, for the heat was insufferable. There are several springs of different property; and all of a high temperature. In the hottest of those springs I could not keep my hand an instant; for its temperature is above 140° Fahrenheit. But I had no opportunity of ascertaining whether, as Ibn-el-Wardi says, it could boil a kid, a fowl, or an egg in an instant. These springs supply two distinct baths; one for the poor, and another, built by Ibrahim Pasha, for the wealthier inhabitants. These waters were famous in olden times. They still· retain some of their celebrity, and are frequented by numerous rheumatic and other patients from the neighbouring country. But whether, as the Arabic author above quoted says, they cure in three days all those that make use of them, I cannot tell. They are called the baths of Emmaus, which has nothing to do with the village of Emmaus, where our Saviour appeared to his disciples. This name is a corruption of "Hammath," which means "hot springs;" and by this name they were known in ancient days, and thus mentioned as probably allotted to the tribe of Nephthali. In later times they were reckoned as a part of Tiberias itself.

Although the clumsy flat-bottomed boat moored here was a poor matter-of-fact apology for the apostles' fishing boat, I had a great desire to sail in it, for it was the only craft of any kind on the lake. No sooner, however, had I expressed my wish, than the owner, an elderly looking Jew, came forward and asked, in broken German too, of all things! where I should have looked for pure Syriac or Hebrew, an exorbitant sum for a short sail on the lake. I felt annoyed at this vexatious imposture; here too, and at such a time. For, as I did not share the feelings of a traveller I once met, who said "he knew he was being imposed upon, and liked it," I would not give in; but waited till a number of people from Tiberias, who were in the baths, should return home, and I got into the boat along with them. But if the "ship" itself was unscriptural, what was the motley crew that sailed in it? Noah's ark over again! There was an aged man, not a patriarch assuredly, though old enough for that, who had, probably, never washed since the day of his birth, with long clotted ringlets, and covered with squalid and tattered garments. And with him his wife, apparently no kinder to him than Vahela is reported to have been to Noah. There were, besides, men, women and children, to say nothing of other creeping things of various kinds, and innumerable. In short everything for the time combined to drive all sacred romance from me; except indeed, danger from the water. For our crazy vessel leaked so much, that three or four of the crew constantly baling, could scarcely keep it afloat; and we had a fair chance of swamping during a passage of a mile, and within hailing distance of the shore. And then the screams of the women, the dirt of their husbands, although just out of the bath; the cries of their children, and the creaking of our unwieldy oars, were altogether a sad come-down from my long-cherished hopes of a romantic sail at sunset on the tranquil bosom of the sea of Galilee.

And at landing, instead of the boat gently running ashore on fine gravel, near St. Peter's Church, (where he is said to have made fast his own boat!) our steersman rudely bumped against the ruins of an old wall, and tumbled us out on a filthy landing-place at the foot of one of the towers. I extricated myself as well as I could, and passing through a drain, and then by the little church of St. Peter, I reached the tent, where I left directions for dinner and supper all in one. While it was preparing I strolled along the shore out of sight, and by a retired clump of oleanders I undressed, and plunged into the tempting wave. I came back to the tent refreshed; and my spirits improved as I ate my supper of fish at the tent-door, and watched the last rays of the setting sun lingering over the snowy summit of Mount Hermon, which they seemed unwilling to leave. Till at last the hoary mountain itself stood pale and lifeless in the purple tints of the distant horizon.

Then cool evening followed; and with it silence and repose spread over the scene. And as the moon, from behind a bank of fleeting clouds, shone in streaks of silver on the rippled waters of the sea, a gentle breeze began to rustle through the leaves of the old mimosa tree;—how welcome and refreshing after a day so hot and so close! I stood for some time at the door of the tent, looking at the flitting shadows of the clouds on the lake, as it were asleep at the foot of its own hills. I could fancy the moon shining of old, as it now did, on the wake of the fishing-boat in which our Saviour and his disciples crossed over to the opposite shores of Gadara. The hills, the lake, the moon were the same; and heaven too is unchanged. For he is there. And I listened, but nature was hushed. The last flock had come down from the hills, it was folded for the night, and the shepherd was at rest. The breath of evening alone wafted at intervals the distant cry of the wild fowl sporting on the moon-lit sea; while it waved the branches of the palm growing by the ruined old mosque, and softly fanned to sleep the drooping flower of the plain.

M.

CHRIST's death was voluntary. He had the free choice of avoiding it. Wielding omnipotence, he might have called legions of angels to his assistance; but he preferred to succumb before the consequences of sin, or his human brethren would be unsaved. As he hung on the cross, the taunt of the priests almost expressed the truth. They said, "He saved others, himself he *cannot* save;" while it was a fact that though he saved others, himself he *would* not save.

The conclusion seems unavoidable, that the terrible agony he endured in the garden of Gethsemane is to be explained by the consciousness he had, that *he might, or might not*, submit to the tortures that were preparing for him.

And herein this temptation, at the close of his ministry, is separable from that which occurred at its commencement. At that earlier trial the choice was, not whether he would abandon men, or help them, but whether he would set up the *glorious* kingdom at once, or defer it. He could not take possession of earthly powers, so long as sin remained unatoned for, without himself sinning, and worshipping Satan. Hence during this first temptation, there was no struggle, no *agony*; he did not, even for an instant, dwell upon the possibility of inclining away from the one path. The sufferings he then underwent were merely corporeal: his body was weakened by hunger, and angels came and *ministered* unto him, but there are no traces in the narrative of his struggling in prayer for spiritual support.

But when, as in the temptation of Gethsemane, the choice was, whether he would suffer dreadful anguish, or leave the world in its misery, he could contemplate both sides of the alternative. Whatever loss *we* should have undergone, he might have forsaken us, and been still perfectly sinless. Had he regarded himself alone, he might have refused to taste the bitter cup, and yet have retained, without damage, his own holiness and his own felicity; and when his human mind, thus tempted to be happy, revolved the fearful insults and torments he must otherwise bear, it is not surprising that he (the man Jesus) was in an *agony*, and sweated blood, and began to be sorrowful and very heavy, praying that, if it were possible, if it could be made to agree with the divine requirements, he might be spared. But while he would have avoided the pain, *if possible*, and could have done so without sin, yet when he thought that but for that pain, other men who were not sinless must be destroyed, he bowed his head with meek submission to this, his Father's will, and drained the proffered cup without a murmur ; and the *agony* (that is, the struggle) was completed in the garden. Never afterwards did he pray to escape those torments. His groans and cries were produced only by bodily pain, not by mental distress.

From this, therefore, it immediately follows that no afflictions, however acute, of an imperfect man, can be compared with those of Jesus ; for no other man can suffer voluntarily and meritoriously : either he will be vain-glorious, as the pagan, and *seek* his pains, and then be not only without merit, but positively sinful, or he will be submitting to chastisement from the Lord, or bearing testimony to the truth ; in which he has no choice. In no conceivable case can an imperfect man be *ago-nized* with respect to his sufferings ; for if the *undergoing* them be not sinful, then the *refraining* from them must be so. And this consideration, while reprobating that endurance of torture for its own sake (which is altogether pagan), also prevents any thought from rising up within us, that martyrs and victims have sustained *bodily* anguish equal to that of our Lord,—a thought whose pressure is sometimes avoided by supposing that God, not man, suffered, than which nothing can be more unreasonable or unscriptural.

Hence, let us be sure that, as Jesus was not upheld by the reflection that he *must* submit, so he had not that inhuman glorying in his tortures which has been sometimes mistaken, at the most trying scenes, for divine support ; and then we arrive at the conclusion, to which this history has been leading,—that Christ bore all this *out of love to us.* There was no other motive whatever inducing him thus to die ; no yielding to chastening discipline, as in other men ; but simply and purely, *because he so loved us.*

The only comparison that occurs, is that which St. Paul mentions in the beginning of the 5th chapter of his epistle to the Romans, though that soon glides from an analogy into a contrast. When we wish to form a notion of Christ's love, we imagine, as the highest instance of human affection, that a man might possibly be found to die *for his friend.* But this love sinks into insignificance by the side of Christ's, since he died *for his enemies.*

And it seems that, in order to bring this latter truth vividly forward, the narrative represents Christ's death as caused by his adversaries. It was necessary that he should be willing to meet death, but, at the same time that he should not have died, unless they had been so extravagantly malignant. If we were to suppose for a moment the atonement to have been effected by Christ descending from heaven and suffering on Calvary, without the intervention of human enmity, we might, indeed, have been *struck* by the love displayed, but we should not have *felt* it; for we might have thought that this display was not needed,—that we could have done tolerably well without it. But, when we learn that the foes of Jesus acted precisely as other men would have acted, with the same prejudices and under the same circumstances *(if not spiritually directed)*, and that he would not have suffered had men been only a little less sinful; then we are persuaded that, great as was his love, it is matched in extent by our sins, and that the love and the sins mutually enhance each other.

People are apt to ask, when they read of Christ's death being accomplished by a peculiar concurrence of wickedness, "What would have been the case if these Jews had not been quite so malignant? How then would the atonement have taken place?" They forget that, upon this supposition, men would not have been so sinful as they actually are; and that then, for aught we can say, no atonement *of this kind* would have been required.

The moral effect which this atonement is to work upon us, is due to the contemplation of the great love of our Master and only Saviour; and, as was before intimated, we lose the chief part of this effect when once we slacken our hold upon the true catholic doctrine, that he died *as a man*, as any one of us would have died. We were once much impressed with the excessively pernicious consequence of forgetting Christ's humanity in the atonement, when conversing with a poor man, who (like Job) had sunk himself into a desperate state of mind because he was in such affliction. He urged that God could not love him; for, if he did, he would not abandon him to poverty and hunger. We rejoined that God has never promised to keep us from temporal afflictions, and that Christ endured much more than we could undergo. "Ah!" replied he, "but Christ could work miracles, and the only reason why he did not use his divine power to save himself, was because he knew the end of his afflictions." It was in vain that we pointed out that Christ never performed a miracle for his own benefit. The murmurer departed, with a persuasion that our Lord's sufferings were nothing to his, because, by his divine foreknowledge, he was assured that he should shortly be happy.

Is this persuasion a common one? Experience shews that it is; and that, wherever it lurks, the *moral* benefit of the atonement is nullified. For, if this atonement has been *revealed,* for the purpose of convincing us that Christ's love was so great, that nothing conceivable can be compared with it; and if the *docetic* views, which are secretly afloat, produce an impression that, after all, it was no such stupendous display of love; is it wonderful that this love is so coldly returned by men?

Although the bond of union in Christ, between the divine and the human, surpasses the comprehension of the wisest of mankind, yet sorrow, suffering, and death, cannot touch the divine. Jesus certainly had the same dislike to the pangs of the cross as we should have; he shrunk with the most sensitive apprehension, from them. His obedience to the supremacy of truth, and the commendation of his spirit into the hands of his Father, were of the same kind (however intensified in degree) as our submission and trust would have been; and *the superior nature* of his afflictions consisted in the unparalleled circumstance that he *could* have avoided them had he chosen. His agony or struggle against this awful choice has no meaning whatever, unless he really suffered in *fear* of death, as well as in the death itself.

We see, then, what the atonement means, as far as we are *morally* concerned. We dare not venture to explain how God was actuated so as, by it, to allow the effect of sin to be wiped away from human trangressors, though we can partially understand that the *voluntary* death of a *perfect* man, out of love to his brethren, was so singular a thing, that it must have accomplished what nothing else could. But with regard to the mode in which *we* are to be actuated by it, the explanation is clear and intelligible. We are hereby persuaded that our sinfulness is so deeply rooted, that no less a sacrifice could avail for its remedy, and that our turpitude not only rendered the sacrifice necessary in the divine counsels, but was the very instrument for effecting it; and we are further persuaded that Jesus Christ, the holy and immaculate incarnation of Deity, so loved us, that, although he had the free choice of meeting, or of avoiding, that terrible death, he underwent it all for the sake of those whose hatred crucified him.

And, by this revelation, we are not only convinced that our sins are so grievous as to demand and to enhance such amazing love, but that we may now, having been justified by his blood, go at any time to God, with unimpaired assurance that he, who gave up his Son to die for us, regards us with affection; that he, who did so much, is ready to do all things else; and that he who loved us while enemies, will more certainly love us when he has made us friends.

Again: a reflecting man feels but little hesitation in believ-

·ing that truth is superior to error, justice to iniquity. We are assured that whatever is false and wicked is an opponent of God; and must therefore, in the end, give way before him who is above all. And yet, looking to the narrative of Christ's death, we find that God permitted a sinless man to endure exquisite tortures. Is it conceivable that this should have been so, unless there had been evils otherwise irremediable? unless he chose to suffer, only because no lighter or more tolerable plan of escape was opened, even by Infinite Wisdom.   .

The case is altogether different when any other man is afflicted, though he be as righteous as imperfect man could be. For we cannot view our afflictions but in one of three lights: 1st, as the consequence of our own sin; or 2ndly, as the result of the vicious system with which we have become entangled; or 3rdly, as a discipline to *prepare* us for holiness. But in neither of these lights can we contemplate *Christ's* sufferings without charging him with sin. If they were due to his own life, or because he lived among iniquitous men, he must have been sinful if a just God made him suffer for them; whereas, being *sinless*, he was not *constrained* to die.

Moreover, he wanted no discipline. His will had never been estranged from God's, and required no educational process for bending it back. He was born, independent of the generative chain which binds all other men together in a mass of evil; and he came, confessedly, for the purpose of dissipating this mass. How could he have effected the design of his mission if he were himself linked with the system as we are, and must, in like manner with us, have awaited God's time to be released from it?

One word more on this subject. While we allow that Christ came to save us from evil, and that such overpowering love was exhibited in the effort, we do not find the majority of men entertain very acute apprehensions of this evil, or fervent sense of this love. And why? Because their sinfulness is so firmly seated, that even Omnipotence is scarcely able to overturn it; and if any Christian desire to form a true conception of his own sin, let him pass in review the story of Christ's suffering and death, and ponder well those words, "Greater love hath no man than this," and then discover how slowly and how coldly his affection is excited.

Or among a less yielding set of professed disciples, we see, daily, numbers of intelligent men, not unusually wicked, perhaps kind and orderly men, listen to the account of Christ's death, and of his love,—of his dying request, "This do in remembrance of me;" and yet without so much as a blush upon their face, or anything more than a transient pang at their heart, depart from his abode, and fling his words to the winds. Truly there must be a frightful amount of wickedness in human nature if this is commonly witnessed.

We cannot doubt, from the constant language of Scripture, that this atonement was, literally and unreservedly, for all men. Every man living,—the degraded savage crouching before a bloody idol, no less than the gifted saint hymning praises to the Eternal,—can always, with perfect assurance of success, find an approach to God, and receive pardon for his sins. The limitation, to be placed on the universality of this benefit, comes not from God, but from man himself.

When we announce Christianity to the heathen, we have no authority for telling him of any change in the means of salvation, but we enlarge his knowledge of God. We shew him a scheme, wherein his deep cravings are satisfied, his suspicions raised into certainties, and we hold out to him, what was never held out to him before, a powerful moral suasion to turn him after God. It is in this information alone that the Christian's position is so immeasurably superior to that of the heathen. It is called the *gospel, or good news*, because it is an announcement to all who hear, that they *can* be saved if they *will;* and to those who are seeking after religious truth, and are hesitating about the way of discovering it, this announcement is verily a gospel, and by them it is so regarded.

Whereas, on the other hand, the wearing of the badge of Christ's service, and the partaking of the outward benefits of Christianity, are of not the slightest moral good to any who are not wishing for God. Unless the gospel be felt as an answer to some earnest want, the heathen might just as well remain a heathen, as *know* God and not *find* him in Christianity.

It was with immediate reference to the *moral* effect of the atonement upon man's will, that Christ instituted those two ceremonies which his disciples were to observe, and which would distinguish them from the rest of the world. The offices of Baptism and of the Lord's Supper are called sacraments, and separated from all other rites, not only because Christ with his own lips instituted them, but because they pointed especially to the atonement. In the one sacrament we are said to be baptized into his death (Rom. vi. 3) ; and in the other, we are urged to exhibit it (1 Cor. xi. 26).

The effect intended to be wrought upon us by the Supper, is seen directly from what we have been contemplating. We obtain no remedial benefit from the atonement, unless the will consents to it. But, in order to turn so perverse a thing as a corrupted will, there is demanded a frequent and a profound meditation on the circumstances accompanying the death; and we meet together with the express purpose of reminding each other of them in the celebration of a simple communion feast. When a moral suasion is fully exercised, our spirits rise to meet God's; we are drawn up to ghostly union with him; and then Christ, whose person comprehends God's nature, has assured us that he in spirit is present, and pours upon us such blessings as we cannot utter.

There is no room, in this view, for that singular notion that the sacrament, when duly administered, brings down God, without reference to the consciousness of the individual, said to be thus *objectively* inspired. God's grace cannot exist as a saving, sanctifying grace, but where the moral powers are *subjected* to God. The sacrament of the Lord's Supper is an empty form, if not a daring profanation, with all who do not find their minds reflecting deeply on Christ's love in his death, and their hearts in consequence loving him in return.

It was also, evidently, because man's *will* was to be actuated, that, as soon as the atonement was *revealed*, every Christian was enjoined to publish it to his neighbour. All who agree to and receive it, are to be marked off from other men by the rite of *baptism*; and it seems scarcely necessary to say, that those who are not induced to seek God through Christ obtain no good whatever from the atonement, whether it is presented to them in the sacrament of baptism or not.

To suppose that the passing through a ceremony, however correctly performed, can by itself put God's spirit into man's heart, is in direct contradiction to the teaching of the Bible,— that the gift of the Holy Ghost means the spiritual union of man's whole moral being with God; and the supposition has obviously arisen from not sufficiently distinguishing between the *subjective* effect of the Holy Ghost upon our wills, which alone causes a cessation of sin (*i. e.*, disunion from God), and the *objective* use which God makes of men's organs and powers (as in the case of a miraculous inspiration), and which does not imply personal holiness, or even one step towards sinlessness.

Here, as elsewhere, Christ's death is the all in all. We are informed that, in its *judicial* aspect, it was a mysterious transaction, in consequence of which our sins are forgiven whenever we turn to God; and it acts *morally*, by leading us to accept the union with the divine Sanctifier, and become persuaded of his love and care.

For, though I may be satisfied, from the mere contemplation of the world and of providence, that it is *right* for me to discover this love, and thereupon love him in return, yet, in fact, it is hard, if not impossible, to make this discovery by such means alone, and I feel that I am not joined to him. Nay, even could I know and experience all that is right, what guarantee would there be that the wages of sin, which has certainly been committed, shall not hereafter overtake me? At the best, I should never rise, from natural reflection only, above the condition of the pagan devotee, who is fearfully looking for judgment. It is therefore essential for us to have an assurance that, as soon as we are joined to God, all our sins are repressed, and ineffective for death; and so we have free and joyous access to the Father, unalloyed by fear, which hath torment, and is cast out by love (1 John iv. 18).

It is the appreciation of this gospel that, at any time of our lives, makes us truly religious. How many incidents occur, almost every day, tempting us to doubt God's presence and care! If the temptation succeeds we are drawn away from him and are consequently in sin. But then enters the saving reflection, " God has given his Son to die for me: and if he, who knew no sin, *chose* to suffer, in order to make a complete atonement, how dare I murmur that his providence disciplines me, *for my own good*, with much less afflictions, even though I may not fully perceive their value! I know in whom I have trusted: I cannot leave God !"

W. H. J.

THE STATE OF INNOCENCE.

THE original condition of man is certainly one of the most attractive and suggestive of subjects to an imaginative mind: poets and others have consequently delighted to describe it in glowing terms, and " have strained their imagination and exhausted nature for images to picture its felicity." Our readers have only to remember Milton's celebrated description of our first parents in the fourth book of his *Paradise Lost,* and the Morning Hymn in the sixth, as instances selected from many they could no doubt easily enumerate.

But there are some who are of opinion that the original state of man was not such a condition as to justify Milton and others to describe it as one of " unmingled enjoyment." For instance, Mr. Wm. McCombie in his *Moral Agency* maintains :—" It is generally assumed, but unphilosophically we think, *and certainly without any authority from Scripture*, that the original state of man must have been one of unmingled enjoyment; and preachers and poets have strained their imaginations, and exhausted nature for images to picture its felicity" (p. 117). That this opinion was also held by the late Dr. Pye Smith, is evident from a communication of his in the *Journal of Sacred Literature* for January, 1848.

When we consider the present constitution of things, how universal experience and observation attest that the human race has been, and still is, in a very corrupt and fallen state, it does appear rather paradoxical to assert, that there was a time when man was at peace with God, and received continual proof of his favour. That the race of Adam, without exception, are guilty of violating more or less those moral precepts, the observance of which has always been considered as the cause of true happiness and enjoyment, is a fact corroborated by the experience of all ages. The corruption of our nature is maintained by all sects of Christians, and the facts which prove it none can deny. Berkeley tried to prove that matter does not exist, and Hume questioned the existence of mind itself; but where is the man, not altogether deprived of reason, who will maintain that the violence of human passions can be completely restrained? Has the country been named where war is unknown? Has the birthplace been pronounced of that race which never heard of fraud, falsehood, injustice, or cruelty? Have even the pleasures of men been mentioned which do not give us proof of the utter depravity of our nature? Do not the immoral games and lascivious religion of the ancients, the gaming table and theatre of the moderns, prove that the doctrine of universal depravity is not only tenable but incontrovertible? But independent of human experience, we have the testimony of Holy Writ. In it do we find the total and universal depravity of the human race, asserted in terms the most explicit. Its declarations in general are that there is none righteous, no not one, that we live without God in the world, that both Jews and Gentiles are under sin, and that the whole world is guilty before God (Rom. iii. 9; Gen. vi. 5; Matt. i. 21; ix. 12). Thus we see its charges are universal, implicating the whole race of Adam, and declaring that all have come short of the approbation of God, and are consequently exposed to his wrath. Both divine revelation and human experience, therefore, prove that we do not act up to the dictates of right reason, and that the conduct of all, in one degree or other, falls short of that standard which it is their duty to follow. Although we admit the existence of evil in human nature to be a universal fact, it does not follow that this evil always existed. It is the object, then, of this article, to

shew that from divine revelation, the only authority admissible
on the subject, it *can be proved* "philosophically," and with authority from Scripture, that the "original state of man must
have been one of unmingled enjoyment," and consequently that
there was a time when evil did not exist in this world.

In verses 26 and 27 of the first chapter of Genesis we find
these words : " And God said, Let us make man in our image,
after our likeness; and let them have dominion over the fish of
the sea, and over the fowl of the air, and over the cattle, and
over all the earth, and over every creeping thing that creepeth
upon the earth. So God created man in his (own) image : in
the image of God created he him; male and female created he
them." To understand properly the information which is here
given, we must define the meaning of the terms, " man" and
" image of God." (1.) אָדָם and הָאָדָם; Adam and the Adam. Is
Adam a proper name, or is it the name of a race or particular
people? That it is the name of a race is maintained in the January number of this Journal; but as we are of opinion that the
arguments in favour of its meaning a proper name or individual
are conclusive, and more in accordance with the principles of
just reasoning, it will be necessary to state them briefly, shewing
their nature and the only conclusions which can be drawn from
them. Our first argument is the fact, that although the term is
often used in Scripture to denote mankind, it is never once considered as "a name applied *to a race of men.*" It is never found
in the plural number; and in the nineteen instances in which it
occurs in the second and third chapters of Genesis, the article is
always used, *the Adam.* The fact that we ought to find it in the
plural number if it applied to a race, and that it is erroneous to
affirm " whenever ' man' is meant collectively, the Adam is
adopted," is surely sufficient to prove the correctness of our
opinion. In the third verse of the twelfth Psalm, we get *aish*
as a term applied to mankind in general : " They speak vanity
man, *i. e.,* every one" (see also Exod. xvi. 29). The whole of
the second chapter of Genesis proves that Adam means an individual; and it is impossible to understand otherwise the narrative
as there related, unless we believe it to be "an allegorical description of the temptation of *all* men, which always *was,* and
is still going on, and would apply equally to every one at the
present day."[a] This is certainly a very easy way of getting rid
of a difficulty, and a direct denial of the truth of the wise remark
uttered by the celebrated Selden : " Make no more allegories in
Scripture than needs must."[b] We have, however, a positive

---

[a] *J. S. L.,* Jan. 1855, p. 451.   [b] *Table Talk.*

statement in the first verse of the first chapter of Chronicles, which gives us Adam's line to Noah, &c.,—"Adam, Sheth, Enosh;" to affirm that Adam is here the name for a race, is to make the Scriptures of no authority whatsoever. Can those who maintain that Adam is only the name for a race, produce such a positive statement as this? We think not; and until they can, they ought not to expect many to accept of their hypothesis. It is true the seventh verse of the sixth chapter of Genesis has been considered as conclusive: "The denunciation may be strictly rendered thus:—'I will destroy the Adamites whom I have created from the face of the land; from Adamite to beast, to creeping things, and to the fowls of the heaven.' "[c] But it is evident that however harmonious such a translation may be with the theory of the holder of the opinion we are refuting, its correctness must be tried by some other test. In a case like this, it is inevitable that such an interpretation, if true, must have found its way into some ancient version of the Old Testament, and been traceable in ancient tradition. But, as far as we are aware, no version gives the least countenance to the doctrine which the text is now made to confirm. The terms of the text are as general as they well can be, and until some stronger reason can be given of the language really meaning a particular race; all that is said about the verse proving the existence of a race called the Adamites, is surely incorrect, if not absurd.

It is also maintained that the words in Gen. i. 27, "male and female created he them," are to be understood not as meaning "two single beings, but the race under the collective name Adam equivalent to our word ' man.' "[d] As we believe that the *complete* work of creation was carried on and *finished* in six days, we must conclude that Eve could not have been created after the seventh day because we are informed that on this day God rested "from all his work which he had made." The male and female means Adam and Eve, two single beings, called "in the day when *they* were created Adam," because the *genus homo* consists of man and woman, and both are included in the proper idea of man. The Rev. B. Powell[e] has asserted, that "other races besides the family of Adam seem to be almost unavoidably implied in several particulars of the scriptural narrative," and he quotes Gen. iv. 14, 17, as proof. Although it is difficult to explain the events there narrated, yet we are of opinion that to

---

[c] *Ibid.*, l. c., p. 440.
[d] *Ibid.*, l. c., p. 449.
[e] Kitto's *Cyclopædia*, art., " Creation."

do so, it is not at all necessary to imagine "the existence of other races distinct from the Adamic race." Seth was Adam's third son; in the seventh verse of the fifth chapter it is stated that this Seth "begat sons and daughters;" and in the fourth verse of the same chapter, we learn also that Adam begat "sons and daughters;" now one of Seth's or Adam's daughters was Cain's wife. To affirm that the latter event could not have taken place, because it would be contrary to the express law of God as stated in Lev. xviii. 9.*f* is most fallacious reasoning,—are laws binding long before they are promulgated? There is certainly an allusion to the existence of human beings in the fourteenth verse; the curse, however, may not have been uttered until after the birth of one or two of Cain's children; if so, nothing could be more natural than Cain's terror, lest some one should slay him; or, it is *possible* that "Cain may have expected the increase of Adam's posterity, and feared the vengeance of a kinsman:" there is nothing improbable in the supposition.*g* We of course consider that the events related in the seventeenth and twenty-fifth verses of the fourth chapter, occurred before those mentioned in the sixteenth verse, and when it is remembered that the division into chapter and verse is of modern origin, there is every probability that we are correct in our opinion.

Our second, and; as our space is limited, last argument, is that the term Adam is understood as a proper name in the New Testament, &c.; and the creeds of Christian Churches are founded on such a fact. Luke iii. 38; Rom. v. 14; 1 Tim. ii. 13, 14; and Jude 14, are passages at once most convincing; and as if anticipating objections, St. Paul in 1 Cor. xv. 45, plainly says, "*the first man Adam;*" Josephus also nearly states the same fact in the apostle's words: "The first man was called Adam" (Ὁδ' ανθρωπος οὗτος Ἀδαμος ἐκλήθη*h*); in the Apocrypha it is used without exception in the same sense.*i* If Dr. Pye Smith and his followers are correct in asserting that "the

---

f Ibid., l. c., p. 436.

g If any of our readers are not satisfied with the view taken of the difficulties mentioned in the text, we would call their attention to the following facts, which alone ought to make them at least hesitate in believing the hypothesis of separate races. It is stated by Bishop Patrick, that in eighty years, 367 children sprang from two individuals in England. Blumenbach, Prichard, Lawrence, and others have proved the descent of mankind from one stock, and that too, independent of the Old Testament.

h Ant., i. 1. 2.

i The words of our Saviour in Matt. xix. 4, are, independent of other arguments, sufficient to prove that only one male and one female were at first created. It has, however, been said (*J. S. L.*, p. 435) that *'αρσεν και θῆλυ* ought to be translated " a

origination of all mankind from a single pair cannot be proved from Scripture;" then we who live in the nineteenth century, have made the grand discovery that ancient fathers, as well as modern divines, have been teaching as well as preaching what has no foundation in Holy Writ, and are consequently liable to be considered as less than worthless authorities in biblical lore!

(2.) אֱלֹהִים צֶלֶם; Image of God. The likeness or image of God in the created is, in our opinion, nothing else than the spirituality of the soul; it cannot possibly mean his external form, as the Almighty cannot be represented by any material substance; nor can we imagine it to be a part of the divine essence, for this is incommunicable to any being which has been created. The resemblance to the Creator must, therefore, mean the soul's immaterial and immortal nature, in other words, its spirituality. God is described in the Scriptures as a Spirit, *i.e.*, an *immaterial* and immortal being; the soul of man is also described as a spirit, therefore there must be a resemblance of the Creator in the created being. But although the spirituality of the soul is seen in its being immortal, we must remember, however, that this spirituality chiefly consists in the soul's capability of maintaining uninterrupted communion with the Creator. Adam's body it is true was also immortal: does it not, therefore, follow that our definition ought to include the body as well as the soul? This is done by some writers,[k] but we think they are scarcely justified in doing so, for the body was just *matter* made immortal (Gen. ii. 7), whereas the soul, or living principle, came direct from God, as it is stated he "breathed into his nostrils the breath of life, and man became a living soul." Consequently the resemblance was not in outward form or external aspect, but in that which lies concealed from mortal view, the mind or soul. Our definition also excludes the idea of sovereignty or dominion which is generally included.[l] It is true that the soul or mind of

---

male and a female," and not " male and female;" now unless our Greek copy of the New Testament is very corrupt, we think that there is nothing to authorize such a translation; the article is not used. The theory maintained by some, that St. Paul when alluding to the first man, only intended to represent human nature as seen in any individual, has been clearly refuted by Neander (*Plant. &c.*, Eng. Trans., vol. 1., p. 424). See also the Rev. J. F. Denham's art. on " Man," in Kitto's *Cyclopædia.*

[k] For instance, Justin Martyr says : " Does not the Scripture say, let us make man after our image, and after our likeness ? what man ? evidently a material man is intended; for it is said, and God took dust of the ground and made man; it is evident then, that the material man was formed after the image of God."—Semisch's *Justin Martyr ;* Eng. Trans., vol., 2, p. 273.

[l] This is done by Dwight, Shaw, &c., Justin Martyr, and Ephraem Syrus are also of the same opinion ; the latter says : " By the power and dominion which he received over the earth, and all that it contains, man is the image of God, who rules over all above and all below."—Dr. Burgess' *Syriac Hymns*, p. 57.

Adam enabled him to possess dominion over every created thing, but believing as we do, that by the fall man lost the image of God, then we cannot include dominion in our definition, as man has still in his fallen state unlimited power over everything terrestrial.

Having ascertained in what sense the terms man and image of God are to be understood, it remains for us to consider the original nature or condition of the individual thus created in the image of God; was it such a nature as to warrant us to believe that the possessor of this image must have enjoyed "unmingled" happiness? The following considerations prove that it was. As man is a compound being made up of body and soul, we will consider their condition when originally formed. The state of the body :—Although Adam's body was made out of the dust of the ground, and can, therefore, claim no higher origin, yet as a piece of the most exquisite workmanship it may well be called a microcosm, "a little world," seeing that the operations and uses of the various parts of which it is composed, are in comparison with the rest of creation equally declaratory of the power and greatness of the Almighty. That such a body was at first formed for endless duration is evident from the fact, that like the mind, it was originally incapable of decomposition or decay. For disease and its attendants, death and decay, could not then claim man as their victim; the loveliness in death, which is observed,—

> "Before decay's effacing fingers,
> Have swept the lines where beauty lingers;"

was a sight never seen in that earthly paradise; where pain and suffering, fear and sorrow, were things unknown.[m] But Mr. Mc Combie and Dr. P. Smith in the works already mentioned, maintain that pain did exist and was felt by our first parents; if so, then felicity of a limited nature must have been their lot, for it is impossible to conceive of a state of supreme happiness where pain exists. The former makes the following statement: Adam's body "was sound and healthful, without any predisposition to disease and decay; yet it was possible enough for him to have

---

[m] We mean by "unknown to man," that death could have no effect on him; some maintain the existence of death before the creation of man, such belief being founded on the supposed facts of geology. There are two considerations which hinder us from giving our assent to such a theory, although we do not deny that it may be perfectly true. (1.) Is it likely that the Almighty created animals, &c., only to die? May they not have been intended for another purpose? (2.) In the *secondary* rocks human bones have been found, and as the science of geology is only in its infancy, may they not also be found in the *primary?*

injured it; there were trees for example, in Eden, against which by carelessness or rashness he might have run himself, and produced fracture or contusion " (p. 114), and of course must have felt pain.   Such a circumstance, however, could not happen to an *immortal* being, for we are not to imagine that because it might happen to a *mortal* body, it might also to one that was *immortal*.   It is useless to try to imagine what might, could, would, or should happen to the body or soul of an immortal being, as such a creature never has been seen since a divine revelation was given to the world.   To such speculations belongs the celebrated problem of the schoolmen, " How many angels can stand on the point of a needle ?"   The state of the soul :— A soul created in the image of God must have made its possessor perfectly aware of his duty to and dependence upon the Creator, as he could not but have a perfect knowledge of the glory and excellence of the Almighty in spiritual things.   That Adam's understanding was one possessed of all necessary knowledge, that his will was a righteous will, and his affections holy affections, is inferred from two passages in the epistles of St. Paul. In the twenty-fourth verse of the fourth chapter of Ephesians we read :—" And that ye put on the new man, which after God (or as some translate it, ' after his image '), is created in righteousness and true holiness ;" and also in the tenth verse of the third chapter of Colossians we find :—" And have put on the new man, which is renewed in knowledge after the image of him that created him.   Possessed, therefore, of a will acting always in conformity to the will of his Creator, and of pure and holy affections, Adam could not but obey the continual communications of his great High Priest, although he was perfectly free to act for weal or for woe.

Such then was the last and the greatest of the Creator's works.   In full harmony with the animate and inanimate creation must have been the body and soul of him who alone was created in the image of God : and it was not until such a being was created, that the Almighty looked down " and saw everything that he had made, and behold it was very good."   Then " the morning stars sang together, and all the sons of God shouted for joy ;" then " the trees of the wood rejoiced before the Lord, the floods clapped their hands, the little hills rejoiced on every side, the valleys laughed and sang."   We the degenerate and guilty posterity of Adam, who possess no longer the image of the Creator, must find it difficult to understand such a harmony, for the lovely and glorious scene on which the morning of creation dawned, will never again be observed in this our world ; for—

"——— while this muddy vesture of decay,
   Doth grossly close ———."

in our immortal souls we cannot, without a strong faith in the truth of a divine revelation, believe that there ever was a state of innocence. We have imperfectly described, from facts stated in such a revelation, what this state must have been. Our deductions, however, cannot be correct, if we admit that pain or sorrow existed in the mind of Adam, and that in his constitution there was "a tendency to evil." Both of these propositions are maintained by Mr. Mc Combie in his *Moral Agency* (p. 130), while the former is also advocated by Mr. Newman :—"As for susceptibility to pain, it is obviously essential to every part of corporeal life, and to discuss the question of degree is absurd. On the other hand, human capacity for sorrow is equally necessary to our whole moral nature, and sorrow itself is a most essential process for the perfecting of the soul." We admit that "a being gliding on the stream of undisturbed enjoyment— nothing desirable denied him, and nothing to regulate or restrain, —could not be a moral being :"⁰ but such a being only exists in the realms of fancy; as there was something denied Adam, the forbidden fruit, he must have been a moral being. But we do not, therefore, admit that the fact of being denied what we consider desirable must cause pain and sorrow; *e. g.*, I may have a great desire to possess a beautiful estate belonging to my neighbour, but being aware at the same time that it is impossible to gratify such a desire, I feel no pain or sorrow. Mr. Mc Combie's reasoning cannot at all apply to Adam, for what was denied he did not consider desirable until he was tempted and disobeyed, and consequently ceased to be the immortal being he was before. Nor does the fact of our first parents disobeying and refusing to submit to the will of God, compel us to conclude that they had "a natural tendency towards evil;" or that "a tendency to evil is shewn in the constitution of man" in the state of innocence.ᵖ If sin, or what is just the same, evil, existed in the original constitution of Adam, St. Paul would surely never have made the statement, "By one man sin entered into the world, and death by sin," &c. It has been well said that a transition from sinlessness to sin is inconceivable; how then do we account for the origin of evil? We cannot, we dare not, make God its author; nor can we maintain it to be the product of necessity, much less eternal; for such theories made antiquity feel the dreadful practical effects of which they were the cause. Grant the truth of such

---

ⁿ *Soul*, pp. 43, 44.   *M. A.*, p. 117.
ᵖ *M. A.*, pp. 130, 131.

doctrines and you cause a disorder which will continue without end; they make the law of crime to be a law which came down to man, and thus enable him to find the justification and the apotheosis of all vice. Evil then is nothing more than the effect of created free-will, which fact will always make it a mystery to the greatest human intellect. "The origin of evil," says Neander, "can only be understood as a fact, a fact possible by virtue of the freedom belonging to a created being, but not to be otherwise deduced or explained. It is not the limits of our knowledge which make the origin of sin something inexplicable *to us,* but it follows from the essential nature of sin as an act of free-will, that it must remain to all eternity an inexplicable fact."[q]

We have now proved that the state of innocence must have been one of unmingled enjoyment, and have shewn how it is that the heart of man now affords slight trace of that image in which he was at first created; and how, consequently, it cannot hold communion with his Creator independent of a mediator. The heart of man, however, has been thought to resemble a palace built at first with magnificence and art, but now plundered and destroyed; and yet retaining amidst its ruins some fragments of its ancient splendour. As we believe that we have the authority of divine revelation and human experience, in maintaining the heart of man to be, since the fall, totally and utterly depraved, we must reverse the simile and consider the present state of man, not to resemble a stately ruin which retains remnants of its ancient grandeur, but on the contrary, that it resembles more one of those tottering towers which ever and anon meet the eye of the traveller, shewing little, if any, of its former splendour, or of its origin.

P. S.

---

[q] *Planting,* &c., Eng. Trans., vol. i., pp. 423, 424.

THEOLOGY, PHILOLOGY, GEOLOGY.

THE central place has been designedly given to philology in our title, because it seems now to be principally concerned in reconciling the claims of theology and geology. Before commencing to trace out a connected scheme for harmonizing the two, we would advert shortly to an unreasonable prejudice against geology. Since men have turned their attention to the fossils in the different strata of the earth's crust, and been driven to the conclusion that the globe which we inhabit must be far older than our race, certain views of the first chapter of Genesis become necessary in order to establish harmony between the word and works of God, although previously such views had been more generally discarded than adopted. Geology demanded an interpretation which theologians had for the most part not acknowledged. But at this point some men became jealous for the honour of Scripture. That sacred volume—the Bible—in their estimation stands independent of science. They are alarmed that any science should afford even the shadow of an argument against *their* doctrine of the self-sufficiency of Scripture; and thus a principle which is in itself most important was driven to an unnecessary—an unreasonable length. The following considerations remove all our scruples as to receiving the assistance of geology in the interpretation of the first chapter of Genesis. The Bible was originally written in foreign languages, and we gladly avail ourselves of the acquisitions of the linguist to interpret the sacred oracles into a language which we understand. The Bible was written originally for people whose manners and customs differed greatly from our own, but we gladly avail ourselves of the researches of travellers who can throw light on numerous allusions, otherwise obscure, if not unintelligible. The Bible was originally written for people whose country differed materially from ours in physical geography, yet we avail ourselves of the information of the man of science on other passages which would also be involved in obscurity were it not for this information. And lastly, the Bible contains a brief account of the history of the earth anterior to the appearance of man : the geologist comes into contact with this period, and upon what ground shall we reject his information ? If we reject the information of the scientific traveller and the philologist, do we not thereby ensure our remaining in ignorance of what might be made clear to us ? May we not anticipate the same undesirable result if we neglect or reject the information of the geologist?

We proceed now to see how the claims of the theologian and the geologist have been harmonized. It was very soon evident that the space of six thousand years was utterly inadequate to account for the phenomena brought into notice by geology; a far longer period was seen to be necessary for the deposition of strata ten or fifteen miles thick, and for the appearance and subsequent extinction of whole races of vegetables and animals. After some opposition, it was allowed that the words, "*in the beginning*" (Gen. i. 1), might as easily refer to a period six thousand millions of years distant as to a period only six thousand years distant from the present. Thus geology came in to shew that there was an immense vista of ages which separated the period of creation from the period of man's appearance—that the verse describing the origin of the world is separated by immense epochs from the verses which describe the work of the sixth day. What farther conclusions are pointed out by geology in reference to the first chapter of Genesis will appear in due time.

Let us proceed now to the *six days*. In the first chapter of Genesis we have a brief summary of the work which God accomplished in six successive days. Reference is made to these six days in the fourth commandment, and more especially in the reason annexed to it (Exod. xx. 8—11), "For in six days the Lord made heaven and earth," &c. Now the six days of the fourth commandment are *six days* of the usual duration of twenty-four hours each; and does not the connexion which they have with the six days described in Genesis indicate that these last are also of the usual duration of twenty-four hours each? The permission is, to work six days, but to refrain from working on the seventh, not because the Lord made the earth and the heavens, &c., in six epochs of indefinitely long duration and rested the seventh, but because he made the heavens and the earth in six days and rested the seventh. There may be a mysterious connexion between the literal days and lengthened periods, but the six days of Genesis viewed in their connexion with the reason annexed to the fourth commandment must, so far as we can see, be taken as six literal days. We shall afterwards consider how geology has given rise to the theory that the six days of Genesis are in reality periods of indefinitely long duration. Meanwhile we shall advert to some peculiarities in the Hebrew text deserving of notice.

It is an important fact that the verb *to create*, ברא, of Gen. i. 1, never occurs in the statement of the fourth commandment or the reason annexed (Exod. xx. 8—11; xxxi. 17). Thus we have room left us for separating the primeval creation of Gen. i. 1, from the subsequent work of the six days. Moreover there is an important relation of subordination in which the verb *to make*, עשׂה, of the fourth commandment stands to the verb *to create*, ברא, of Gen. i. 1. In the kal and niphal conjugations, ברא is never used but in reference to God. Ex. 9; Ps. li. 10, "*Create* in me a clean heart;" Ps. cxlviii. 5; Is. xliii. 7; xlv. 12; lxv. 17, &c. On the other hand, the verb עשׂה, *to make*, is far more extensive in its signification, as it is also in regard to the frequency with which it is used: ברא occurs only about fifty times altogether, but עשׂה upwards of two thousand. עשׂה is used indiscriminately in reference to God or man, and extends even to inanimate objects. It describes the changes or modifications produced by arrangements and collocations of existing materials, or the dedication of a thing to a purpōse. Within the space of a few chapters it is used upwards of thirty times (Ex. xxv.—xxx.) in regard to the furniture of the tabernacle, &c.

We have been somewhat disappointed at the way in which these verbs have been viewed by some writers. There are certain cases in which two words may be used interchangeably, while at the same time it is equally certain that each has a domain into which the other ought not to intrude. This we think is precisely the case with ברא and עשׂה. There are cases in which both are used in reference to the same fact; *e.g.*, the creation of man. It is written, "Let us *make* man," &c. (Gen. i. 26), where עשׂה is used; and in the next (ver. 27) it is added, "And God *created* the man," &c., where ברא is used. Here the historian uses both verbs in describing the same fact. Nevertheless taking the six days' work as a whole it was a work of arrangement and distribution of already-existing materials, or the dedication of completed arrangements to a purpose; and accordingly when it is referred to as such the verb עשׂה is used, as we find in the reason annexed to the fourth commandment. Not only so, but when we take the initial step, and where, so far as we are informed on the subject, there are no pre-existing materials to work with, we have the verb ברא used, as in Gen. i. 1. In the view of the foregoing, then, we plead that an examination of the Hebrew text *favours* the interpretation hitherto followed; whereas some writers have seemed content to go no farther than the conclusion that the Hebrew verbs in question may be used interchangeably. It is to be noticed that we treat the six days in Genesis as six ordinary days: other views on this point will be referred to in the sequel.

We proceed now to another point. While we think theology demands that the six days in Genesis are *not* six indefinitely long periods, geology, it appears, comes in to determine where the work of the six days commences. At one time it had been supposed that the second verse of the first chapter of Genesis indicated the earth was a chaotic mass of ruins and desolation when light was brought upon the scene six thousand years ago. However, it is now decided by the geologist that the present or human period is not cut off from the previous by any period of desolation; accordingly the work of the six days commences with the third verse.

Let us now examine the grounds on which the geologist would make the six days in reality six periods of indefinitely long duration. The six days may be ranked under a twofold division : 1st, those which have an astronomic aspect; and 2nd, those which have a geologic aspect. The latter includes days 3, 5, and 6. Now it is very wonderful that the development of the geologic phenomena exhibits an agreement with the leading characteristics of those days. On the third day, as described by Moses, the prominent characteristic is the clothing of the earth with vegetation. The carboniferous era in geology exhibits strata nearly three miles in thickness, at least in this country, containing immense deposits of vegetable substances. On the fifth day, as described by Moses, reptiles and birds appear; and geologically, the second of the three great leading features, characterizing the fossiliferous strata, is the prevalence of extraordinary reptilian monsters and gigantic birds. On the sixth day we have the account of the beasts of the earth, or mammalian animals, and after them man is created—still on the sixth day. Geologically the third of the three leading features of the fossil remains is the prevalence of mammalian animals, and at a period distinctly subsequent are found the remains of man. The agreement between these two accounts is remarkable. The geologist is disposed to conclude that the days in Genesis must be periods of great duration in order to meet the demand for *time* sufficient to account for the formation of strata several miles in thickness, and containing the remains of whole generations of plants and animals which have successively appeared and disappeared. Here then we must discuss the whole question of the *days* and the *periods*.

1st. We may consider the position as above described, shewing the coincidence between the scriptural days and the geologic periods, as the first argument advanced by the geologist in favour of periods. It appears so far quite unanswerable. The three days of Genesis, viz., the third, fifth, and sixth, correspond with three epochs in geology. We are disposed to consider it equally unanswerable on the theologic side of the question, that the six days of the fourth commandment are so connected with the six days in Genesis that in both cases six literal days are to be understood. Admitting these two positions, it is evident that we are not at liberty to adopt any explanation which proceeds according to the one, while it neglects or does not satisfy the demands of the other. There appears to be some mysterious connexion between days and periods which must be brought to light. If the claims of geology must be reasonably satisfied, so must those of theology. We must admit periods of immense duration and still hold fast by the six literal days. The more we examine the Mosaic account of the third, fifth, and sixth days in connexion with the carboniferous, the reptilian, and the mammalian eras of the geologic account, the more we are driven to the conclusion that there is a connexion between days as days and periods as periods.

2nd. The geologist proposes to maintain the correspondence between the six days of the fourth commandment and the six epochs of his science by considering them *both* as reducible to the category of *periods.* He pleads that the word *day* may mean an indefinitely long time. Thus Gen. ii. 4, it is written, "In the *day* that the Lord God made the earth and the heaven." We intend to concede this point : let it be granted that the word *day* may indicate an indefinite amount of time—an epoch of myriads of years, as required by geology; but though we grant that the word *day* or *days* may be used indefinitely at times, yet we do not consider Gen. i. as affording any examples. But the explanation applicable to the geologic epochs must be extended to the six days of the fourth commandment. Here the geologist proposes the reading, " six periods shalt thou work, and on the seventh period shalt thou rest." We are unable to admit such an explanation, so of course we must adopt another. We cannot see that a man is following the requirements of the fourth commandment by saying, " I shall work continuously for six weeks, and rest on the seventh week." *Day* is the word used in the fourth commandment and *day* in Genesis; *six days* are mentioned in the fourth commandment and are expressly referred to the *six days'* work of Genesis, " For in six days the Lord made heaven and earth, the sea and all that in them is," &c. (Exod. xx. 11). One might at first think that this was a most comprehensive passage, referring to far more than the work of the six literal days. But not so. Compare the contents exhibited in the quotation with Genesis; " And God called the *firmament heaven* " (Gen. i. 8). This is evidently the atmosphere, in which the fowl fly (Gen. i. 26). " And God called the *dry land earth* " (Gen. i. 10) : " And the gathering together

of the waters called he seas" (Gen. i. 10). Atmosphere, dry
land, and sea, is a most accurate threefold division of our planet
in the present connexion. As to the remainder, "All that in
them is," in the reason annexed to the fourth commandment,
we at once see the propriety of making it comprehensive of the
generations of plants and animals which were destined for the
air, the dry land, and the sea. The oftener we compare the six
days of the fourth commandment with the six days of Genesis,
the less are we disposed to consider them anything else than six
literal days in both cases.

Granting the six days of the fourth commandment to refer
to six literal days in Genesis, the question therefore arises, how
are we to harmonize these six literal days of Genesis with the
great epochs indicated by geology? We request the reader to
notice the orderly law of progression which characterizes the first
chapter of Genesis. We have first the grand announcement
that as to the material universe, consisting, 1st, of the heavens
beyond us, and, 2nd, of the earth which we inhabit, they were
created by God in the beginning. But the historian's chief
object is in connexion with the earth, so turning immediately to
it he makes a triple statement; 1st, as to its being without form
and void; 2nd, as to darkness being on the face of the abyss;
and, 3rd, as to the spirit of God moving on the face of the
waters. We now reach the precincts of the six days, and commentators have already remarked that they are divisible into
two triads: 1st, there are the arrangements in regard to light;
2nd, in regard to the connexion between the waters in and under
the atmosphere; and, 3rd, in regard to the permanent appearance of dry land and its being clothed with vegetation. The
reader will readily observe the progression here. Light was a
stage in advance of preceding arrangements; the atmospheric
arrangements bring us a step still nearer the vegetable and
animal races that were destined to live in the atmosphere; and
lastly, the production of grasses, herbs, trees, &c., is in advance
of all former arrangements. We come now to the second triad
of the six days. Here we have, 1st, arrangements for the alternation of day and night, for the periodical recurrence of months,
seasons, and years—an appropriate antecedent to the creation of
animals; 2nd, we have reptiles and birds; and, 3rd, we have
mammalian animals. Keeping the end in view from the beginning, it is at once evident how each step is directly in advance
of the preceding and nearer the conclusion aimed at. The
following tabular view will set before the reader the plan of
arrangement followed :—

| ETERNITY. | HEAVEN and EARTH. | 7. CREATION. | 4. Voidness. 5. Darkness. 6. Motion. | 1. Light. 2. Water and Air. 3. Vegetation. | 4. The Lights. 5. Reptiles and Birds. 6. Mammals. | 7. REST. | EARTH and HEAVEN. | ETERNITY. |

Commentators have already noticed, independently of geological controversies, that the concluding triad in the above series is parallel with the preceding. On the fourth day the arrangements are described which refer to the two great luminaries ; on the first day there is light simply. On the fifth day we have the account of reptiles and birds ; on the second day we have the arrangements for their respective elements—water and air. On the sixth day we have the highest forms of animal life ; on the third day the most remarkable era of vegetable life, which, so far as geologists know, has ever existed on our planet. Just as the third, fifth, and sixth of the Scriptural days run parallel with the carboniferous, the reptilian, and mammalian epochs of geology, so do the days of the third triad run parallel with the preceding. In other words, days 4, 5, and 6 have a *retrospective* aspect to days 1, 2, and 3. May not the three geologic days—viz., 3, 5, and 6, have a retrospective aspect to three geologic epochs of vast duration ? We have here three epochs exhibiting retrospective relationship to other three epochs—making six ; may we not have six epochs with retrospective relationship to the whole six epochs ? It is an extension of the same principle. The first three periods are immensely greater than the succeeding, so that we have thus the smaller looking back upon the greater. In the same way, the latter three are immensely greater than the concluding six. So we have the six small periods retrospective of six great epochs—six days of six cycles.

But we may illustrate the principle of *retrospection* still farther. The last important creation which took place on the earth was man. The scale of being up to him was graduated as follows :—Fish, reptile, bird, mammal. These four belong to the vertebrate, or higher division of animated organisms. Moreover, it is curious enough that they appear in the strata in the same order, according to the geologist. Now, according to anatomists, the early development of the human brain exhibits in order the shape of the brain of the fish, the reptile, the bird, and the mammal, before reaching its characteristic development. In other words, we have in the early history of the human brain a *retrospective* glance at all the orders of vertebrate animals hitherto created—that is, the history of a few weeks' looking back upon the history of vast cycles of time. Is not this remarkably analogous to the six literal days having a retrospective aspect to six great epochs?

May we not, in view of the foregoing, suppose that six days were devoted to the dedication of the arrangements which had been in course of preparation during six great cycles, and that the order of the days indicates the order of preparation, just as the four epochs in the history of the human brain point to the four gradations of vertebrate animals previous to man; and that any new arrangements were inserted in accordance with the general plan? For example, if new reptiles were created, they were introduced on the fifth literal day; if any mammals, on the sixth literal day, as we believe was the case with man.

By adopting the explanation, let us see how it will apply in solving difficulties.

1st. It allows six literal days in Genesis corresponding with the six literal days of the reason annexed to the fourth commandment, and so satisfies the theologian.

2nd. Though six literal days, yet being also epitomes of vast epochs, the explanation should satisfy the highest demands of the geologist.

3rd. The retrospective aspect of the days affords a very fair explanation of the apparently anomalous position of the work of the fourth day. It was always a troublesome knot to undo: How have we an account of three days without the sun? In giving an epitome of the great epochs that were past, it pleased God to adhere to the natural order which characterized these epochs. Is it, indeed, extravagant to suppose that He who sees the end from the beginning, and who has given *all* Scripture for the manifestation of his own glory in its bearing upon man, has given to the race the historic epitome in Genesis that his intelligent creature—man—might recognize the more strikingly the agreement between his word and works, and that it was a God of order, of knowledge, and wisdom who presided over both? And that the heart of man might be urged to greater gratitude as he became aware of the extensive preparations which were making for him myriads of years before his arrival? But this leads us to another consideration; for

4th. The six days were *prospective,* as well as retrospective. The six days in Genesis were intended as a basis for the weekly division of time which was to prevail during the human period. Thus, by one arrangement, two important objects were accomplished. We thus get the six literal days of Genesis into an intermediate position between the past and the future. As regarded the past, they gave a condensed account in chronologic order of the history of the earth up to that point. Perhaps as yet we have read only half of this history, brief as it is, for astronomy has not yet demanded the identification of days 1, 2, and 4,ᵃ with any cycles of vast duration. As regarded the future, the work of six successive days and the rest of the seventh formed the foundation of a most important institution which was to characterize the coming age.

5th. The explanation by which we obtain six literal days applies, so far as we can see, quite satisfactorily to the first chapter of Genesis. According to the stricter meaning of the word *day*, it means the period of light, as the historian takes care to mention (Gen. i. 5). When the period of light is past—then comes evening—then comes morning, and with it the commencement of a new day. For it is to be noticed, the rendering at the end of each day's work would be literally "and there was evening, and there was morning—day first, second, third," &c. The work that is done, the arrangements that are made, naturally and appropriately occupy the *day* time—the period of light; when all that is over, evening and morning pass in succession, but the period intervening is not devoted to work, and therefore they are simply mentioned to carry the reader on to the work of the following day. The date is put at the end, instead of at the commencement; and, unhappily, the way in which our version connects, or rather identifies, the "evening and morning" with each date has tended apparently to destroy the obviousness of the consecutive relationship between day-time, evening and morning.

But we may proceed still farther to develop the harmonious relation between geology and genesis, and let us advert for a moment again to the sacred narrative. Notwithstanding the little advantage taken of the difference between the verbs *to create* and *to make*, there is a peculiarity in the work of the fourth day which compelled the theologian to look more favourably on the distinction between these verbs as helping him out of difficulties. It is not said that God *created* the sun and the moon on the fourth day. It is the verb of arrangement, *appointment* (Ps. civ. 19), dedication, that is used. The psalm here referred to is a poetical paraphrase of the first chapter of Genesis.

But there is another peculiarity in regard to the fourth day. Commentators have already noticed that the rendering "Let there be light" (Gen. i. 14), is not quite accurate. The substantive verb is singular, the noun is plural. The passage may be rendered thus—"Be it: the lights in the expanse of the heavens for dividing between the day and between the night; and let

---

a It is curious enough that meteoric stones, which are supposed to come from the moon, are found as far back as the secondary formations, about which time the moon is introduced into the arrangements of the fourth day.

them be for signs," &c. The result is, that there is no objection
to believing that the sun and moon may both have been in existence before the time when they are specially introduced to our
notice. Now, geology comes in also to shew that what are the
characteristic existences of given epochs had not their commencement within the proper limits of such epochs. It is during the
third epoch that vegetation clothes the earth—*i.e.*, becomes a
characteristic, or reaches its highest point of development; but
it were no contradiction to the words of the third day, "Let the
earth bring forth," &c., were the geologist to demonstrate that
plants existed long anterior to the great carboniferous era.
Similarly, in regard to the fifth day, "Let the waters bring forth
abundantly the moving creature," &c. (Gen. i. 20). In regard
to the creatures here referred to, geology informs us when they
reached their most remarkable epoch, but it also informs us that
that epoch did not see their commencement. In regard to the
great epoch succeeding the reptiles and birds, geology tells us it
was characterized by the most remarkable development of mammalian animals; but this does not imply that mammals first
appeared, and reached their highest point during the same era;
on the contrary, geology informs us that some mammals existed,
at least, towards the close of the preceding epoch.

So far, then, we have no difficulty in regard to the relationship subsisting between the days as six epochs retrospective of
six great cycles. The characteristic of the day indicates what
was characteristic of the cycle, but which characteristic did not
necessarily *commence* during the same cycle in which it reached
its maximum,

We have next to point out how these six days are significant
as six literal days of dedication. We are now supposing that
almost all the preliminary arrangements have been completed.
Light has been shining upon the earth, may be for millions of
years preparing all things, so far as its influence extended for the
great end kept in view from the beginning; but will light be required any longer? The atmosphere has performed its office; will
it be required any longer? The earth has had its chambers filled
with coal, the vegetable kingdom has declined, will it be required
at all in the theatre of events about to appear? The sun and
moon have ruled the day and night respectively for ages, will
they be required in the new order of things? Reptiles have held
sway on the earth, but their empire has long since decayed, will
they be required at all under the new monarchy? The mammal,
too, has been great in the earth, but his greatness has dwindled
down considerably, shall he be permitted to exist at all during
the coming age? These are the questions about to be decided as

the result of the review of his works taken by Jehovah. Shall they continue as they are, or shall they not ? On the first day, Jehovah says of light, It shall continue. On the second day, of the atmosphere, It shall continue. On the third day, of the earth, It shall continue to bring forth grass, &c. And so on. The verb in every case is in the future.

We have just seen that neither philologically, nor geologically, are we driven to the necessity of assigning the *first* appearance of plants or animals to the particular epoch or day on which they are noticed. They are mentioned only when they become *characteristic* existences on the face of the earth. But now we have one more point to explain. We have separated the spheres of the verbs *to create* (ברא) and *to make* (עשה). What is the full extent of the verb *to make* in connexion with the six days' work ? Granting that, in point of form, we have six literal days in Genesis to correspond with six literal days in the reason annexed to the fourth commandment, the question may be asked, how is it true that the earth, &c., were *made* in six days ?

In the reason annexed to the fourth commandment two verbs are used to which we request attention. " Six days shalt thou *labour* (עבד) and *do* (עשה) all thy work. For in six days God made (עשה) the heavens," &c. We have already seen that the expression, "heavens and earth," sea and all that in them is," refers to the work of the six days, commencing with Gen. i. 3. Six days shalt thou *labour* and *make*, for in six days God *made* the heavens, &c. It is not said that during six days the Lord bestowed *labour* upon, and finally *made*, the heavens, &c. Geologically, we believe that, for myriads of years, God was bestowing labour upon the preparation of the earth for its final destination as the abode of man. What, then, was done during the six days referred to by the verb *to make* (עשה) ? The following uses of the word in Scripture may help us to a conclusion on this subject. In 1 Ki. xii. 31, it is said that Jeroboam *made* priests of the lowest of the people. In 1 Sam. xii. 6, it is said that the Lord *advanced* Moses and Aaron. In Jer. xxxvii. 15, it is said that the princes smote Jeremiah, and put him in prison in the house of Jonathan the scribe : for they had *made* that the prison. Now, the real meaning of the verb עשה in these passages is *to appoint* as given by Gesenius. The priests were already in existence, but were now *appointed*, whether by formal act or not, to a particular office ; Moses was already in existence, but at a particular time he was *appointed* to the office and duty of leader of the Israelites ; and, lastly, the building spoken of, which was converted into a prison was in existence before, but was now *appointed* to be used as a prison. In the same way, may we not refer the verb *to make*, in Gen. i., to the *appointment* of the heavens and the earth, the sea and all that in them is, to the purpose kept in view regarding them from the beginning? When the six days of inauguration began, the light, the atmosphere, &c., were in existence, but were now formally appointed to be subservient to the wants of the intelligent creature—man, who was shortly to be created; just as the rainbow had made its appearance often enough before the flood, but after the flood was appointed by the Lord to be a sign of a covenant between himself and mankind that he would not again overwhelm the earth with a deluge. The same verb, used with regard to the appointment of the rainbow (Gen. ix. 12, 13), is used with regard to the appointment of the two great lights on the fourth day (Gen. i. 17). It is, in both cases, the verb *to give* (נתן) in our version rendered by *set*.

We have now given a brief exposition of a scheme of harmony applicable to the solution of the difficulties which have arisen in consequence of the apparent discrepancy between the revelations of geology and the interpretation of Scripture. The leading idea upon which our scheme is founded is contained in the hypothesis of six literal days intermediate between the past and the future with distinct relationship to both. The relationship of the six days to the future is made known to us by sacred history; the relationship of the six days to the past is made known to us by geology. It is quite certain, historically, that six literal days constitute the period concerned in the fourth commandment; and, if so, there must be six literal days involved in the first chapter of Genesis by reason of their connexion. That six literal days are involved is quite as certain as it is that, geologically, the world has been myriads of years in its progress to its present state. The two verbs to *create* and to *make* enable us to separate between the parts of the narrative which refer to the primeval creation of matter, and the subsequent appointment of arrangements to a purpose respectively. The six literal days of the fourth commandment determine six literal days for Genesis; and *vice versâ*, the meaning of *to make* (עשה) in Genesis determines the meaning of the same verb in the fourth commandment. Here, then, we can see how the balance can be preserved between the six days of the fourth commandment and the six days of Genesis. "Six days shalt thou labour and *appoint* all thy work, for in six days the Lord *appointed* the heavens and the earth, the sea and all that in them is," &c. The great objection to the former explanation was, that it destroyed the balance between the *command* and the *reason*, "Six days shalt thou labour, &c., for in *six periods* the Lord made," &c. We notice that recently another explanation has been proposed, founded on the probability that Moses saw in vision the past history of the earth. The *visions* are liable to the same objection as the *periods*. Thus, " *Six days* shalt thou labour, &c., for in *six visions* the Lord made known to Moses the previous history of the earth, extending over myriads of years." It is evident that both the *periods* and the *visions* destroy the relationship between the six days of the command and the six days of the reason.

So far, then, our plan of reconciliation appears to extend to all the important difficulties involved. However, there is a peculiarity in regard to the fifth day, and its bearing upon our plan of harmony of which we wish to apprize the reader. It is said, " And God *created*," &c. (Gen. i. 21), in regard to reptiles and birds. Now, the verb of arrangement or dedication is not here used, so that our hypothesis requires that it should be geologically true that numerous reptiles and birds were introduced for the first time on the day previous to man's creation. What we mean will be clear after considering shortly the work of the sixth day. The characteristic of the sixth great epoch was the predominence of the mammalian animals. The characteristic of the sixth day is its reference to mammalian animals. Existing arrangements were ratified. As regards these animals, the decree went forth, " Let the earth continue to produce them " (Gen. i. 24). And in the following verse, " And God *appointed* the beast of the earth after its kind," &c. But, in addition to all this, besides ratifying existing arrangements in regard to the propagation of mammalian animals, a new species is to be introduced—namely, man; and of him it is said, " And God *created* man," &c. (Gen. i. 27). This binds down the event to the sixth day. In the same manner, does not the statement, " And God *created* " (Gen. i. 21), in regard to reptiles and birds, imply that, at least, several species of each of the above were introduced for the first time on the fifth literal day? On this subject we must await more definite information from the geologists.

We shall embody the substance of the foregoing in the following paraphrase of the whole passage in Genesis relating to the creation.

" As to the material universe comprehending, 1st, the heavens beyond us; and, 2nd, the earth which we inhabit, they were created by God in the beginning. Now as to the earth : its history on to the time of man may be ranked under three leading divisions, each division consisting of three subdivisions. The leading characteristics of the first division or triad of epochs may be described as follow : 1st, the earth was without form and void ; 2nd, there was darkness on the face of the abyss ;

and, 3rd, the spirit of God was moving on the face of the waters. When these ages were past there began a new series of two connected triads which were destined to have more prominent reference to man. The first triad may be characterized, 1st, by the introduction of light; 2nd, by the arranging of a proper balance between the quantity of water in the ocean and in the atmosphere; and, 3rd, by clothing the dry land with a plentiful vegetation. When this triad of ages had passed, the second of this connected series began; for, 1st, on the fourth epoch more detailed arrangements were made regarding light, thus having reference to the first epoch; 2nd, more complete arrangements were made on the fifth epoch as compared with the second, for the waters and the atmosphere prepared on the second epoch were now on the fifth stocked respectively with their inhabitants, Saurian reptiles and birds; 3rd, on the sixth epoch arrangements of a more advanced nature as regards the dry land were made, for as the third epoch was the great era of vegetable life, so the sixth epoch was the great era of animal life, inasmuch as it witnessed the dynasty of the mammal, the highest form of animal life. Thus the fifth and sixth were the great epochs of animal life. All these great epochs are preparatory to the introduction of man. It is time for his appearance, and the work of the six great cycles is reviewed and solemnly ratified. But ere we pass in review the six days of inauguration of the past, we must take a glance at the future. During the human epoch there is to obtain, according to the plan of the Eternal, a weekly division of time. Six days man is to work and on the seventh he is to rest, and this septenary arrangement is embodied in a great fact. The six days of work are to correspond with six days of solemn inauguration and completion; and these latter are to be the six days of inauguration of the six great cycles just closing—day and cycle mutually corresponding. On the first day God reviews the work of the first epoch. His voice is heard ratifying the arrangement regarding light—as to its continuance and its alternation with darkness. This refers to the *day-time* of the first day; when it is past, then comes evening, and after that morning; their succession in time alone is indicated, for work is to characterize the *day-time*, not the *night-time*. So closes the first day of inauguration. The second day begins and the work of the second epoch is reviewed. The voice of God is heard, ratifying the atmospheric arrangements regarding the waters on the earth and in the atmosphere. Thus the work of the second epoch is ratified on the second day. So ends the day-time of the second day. Then comes the evening —after it the morning which ushers in the third day. The dis-

tribution of air and water was ratified the day before. The
voice of God is heard, and the distribution of land and water is
reviewed and ratified on this day; that is, the work of the third
day was the ratifying of the work of the third epoch. The day-
time of the third day passes; the evening comes, and the morning comes, and with it the beginning of the fourth day. The
resemblance between the first and second triad of epochs is
faithfully preserved, though in miniature between the first and
second triads of days. The day-time of the fourth day is spent
in reviewing the arrangements regarding the sun and moon for
the periodical recurrence of smaller and larger cycles of time.
The voice of God is heard ratifying the arrangements. The
evening comes and the morning comes—their successive occurrence alone being indicated, for the space between them is not
the period characteristic of work; and so we reach the commencement of the fifth day. During the second epoch of the
first triad the waters and atmosphere were prepared; during the
second epoch of the second triad they were respectively stocked
with reptilians and birds: so far the great scale. As to the
small scale: on the second day of the first triad of days the
aqueous and atmospheric arrangements were ratified; and now
on the second day of the second triad of days—the fifth of the
whole series, the second epoch of the second triad of epochs is
reviewed, and the voice of God is heard ratifying the arrangements in regard to it. The work of inauguration, completion,
and ratification of the fifth epoch thus occupies the day-time of
the fifth day. Evening comes, and morning comes, and ushers
in the memorable sixth day. The third epoch of the first triad
saw the dry land covered with vegetation; the third epoch of
the second triad saw the dry land inhabited by the highest order
of vertebrata: so far the large scale. As to the small scale of
days—the third day of the first triad saw the ratification of the
work of the third epoch, and now the third day of the second
triad brings us to a review of the work of the third epoch of the
second triad. The characteristic existence of the epoch was the
mammal; and God chooses to signalize the day corresponding
to the epoch by the *creation* (ברא) of another mammal. Man is
created and made lord of all the inhabitants of the air and the
ocean as well as of the plants and animals of the dry land. The
voice of God is heard, for " God saw *all* that he had done, and
behold—*very good!*" (Gen. i. 31). So ratifying on the sixth
day and up to that moment the arrangement of the sixth epoch."
So far the paraphrase.

At this precise point the two scales coincide. The benedic-
tion of man marks up to that moment the last event of the

sixth day; it was also the last event of the sixth epoch. That
other lines intersect at the same point and that other harmonies
may be developed by geology and astronomy, is very possible.
We have reached the close of the work of appointment and
creation with which the six days were occupied—what of the
seventh day? God wrought during six days and rested on the
seventh: the six days referred to six epochs of work, does not
also the seventh refer to an epoch of rest? If so, did the sixth
epoch close with the sixth day; and the seventh epoch, that of
rest, commence with the seventh day? or is the sixth epoch still
in progress, and is the seventh epoch yet future? The six days
referred retrospectively to six cycles, do the seven days refer
prospectively to seven cycles—to six thousand years of toil and
a millennium of rest? If so, will not the cycles of human and
divine rest correspond, and does not such correspondence indicate that the present is still part of the sixth great epoch which
ushered in man? These questions are more easily asked than
answered, and we do not intend to enter upon them now. We
remind the reader, in conclusion, that the tabular view given in
the foregoing pages is not affected by a decision either way as to
whether the present be the period of divine rest. That table
exhibits an introverted parallelism, one of the commonest arrangements in Scripture. At each extremity we have eternity
—past and future. Next, at the beginning of the introverted
series, we have *creation;* 1st, in regard to heaven; 2nd, in regard
to earth. Occupying its appropriate place towards the close we
have *rest;* 1st, on earth; 2nd, in heaven. In the centre are
the three triads already described.

M.

OBSERVATIONS ON MATTHEW xxiv., xxv.—ITS ANALYSIS AND INTERPRETATION.

IN the fields of sacred literature there is perhaps no fact more certain than this, that grammar and philology, with all their recognized aids and appliances, have not prevailed hitherto in modern times to explicate the construction and signification of our Lord's great prophecy on the Mount of Olives. The lovers of biblical research may be expected, in such a case, to welcome any co-operative method of enquiry, which, while submitting itself to the analogy of the faith, shall explore for landmarks of truth in other walks of observation than those so familiarly trodden in our days. The tangled confusedness that has seemed to pervade the prophecy, is mainly referable to two patent facts; in that, first, we have not seen the mind of the disciples, as Christ saw it in their query; and, secondly, we have not heard Christ's instructions as the disciples heard them in his reply. There is no proof that the peculiar obscurity which our Lord's prophecy presents at this day, was existent to the minds of his actual hearers. To them every pause of his, every look, tone, gesture, emphasis, and the like, would be an expressive comment upon the sense. Every clause, period, paragraph, as indeed the whole structure of this discourse, would be marked distinctly to their ear. Every transition as to subject, every repetition and cumulation of ideas, together with the entire texture of the thoughts expressed, would be mapped to their mind's eye; and in that manner the form, force, and gradual progress of the statements would be obvious to their perception. Now the same assistance which the disciples derived from our Lord's oral analysis, we must obtain if possible through other channels of information. And such means have been provided to our hand. There are three general bearings in which the prophecy offers itself with a suggestive aspect,—as a *Composition*, as a *Record*, and as a *Reply*. In the exceedingly systematic method of his *composition*, our Lord himself has provided us with an efficacious key or clue to the proper analysis and interpretation of his discourse. In the *variations* of the three synoptical *records* (Matt. xxiv., xxv.; Mark xiii.; Luke xxi.), the inspired evangelists have supplied us with another sufficient key to the same just analysis and interpretation. Those two keys will be found to support and verify one another, while they also concur in giving results which present the prophecy as an exact and complete *reply* to the recorded query of the disciples.

In proceeding to treat of these matters with a view to the true sense of the prophecy, it will be convenient to give our attention in the first instance, to the *variations* of the three *records*. We receive with reverence those several documents, just as they come down to us; and we are satisfied that they all are of divine authority, both in their agreements and in their differences. It is not material to our present object, whether such variations may have been owing to Christ himself, or to the Holy Ghost moving his inspired witnesses, *i. e.*, whether the divergencies of statement be owing to a difference of deliveries on the part of our Lord, or of recensions on the part of the evangelists. We have no difficulty in persuading ourselves that in whichever way, and in whatever degree, such variations may have been of divine causation,—they cannot have been ordered without a purpose. To us, then, they will be notable phenomena; and it will be no very wonderful surprise to us if the practical effect of them upon our own minds should ultimately be guidance and instruction.

For brevity's sake, it will be convenient to use a notation of this sort, viz. :—

$$\text{Matt. xxiv., xxv.} \quad = \quad \text{M}$$
$$\text{Mark xiii.} \quad = \quad \text{M}$$
$$\text{Luke xxi.} \quad = \quad \text{L}$$

The general drift of the earlier part of our argumentation will be much as follows. Those three records divide themselves and one another respectively into two several portions, viz. :—

$$\text{M into } M_1 \text{ and } M_2$$
$$\text{M ,, } M_1 \text{ ,, } M_2$$
$$\text{L ,, } L_1 \text{ ,, } L_2$$

in such manner that M_1 and M_1 and L_1, the anterior portions, are mutually equivalent to one another, while also M_2 and M_2 and L_2, the latter portions, are mutual equivalents in another way; so that the distinct separateness (when seen) of M_1 from M_2 and of L_1 from L_2, shall exhibit the distinct separateness of M_1 from M_2 (*i. e.* of Matt. xxiv. 4—36, from 37—xxv. 46). Our course will be to first analyze and synthesize M_2 as the easier portion of St. Matthew's record; and this will give us vantage ground for analyzing and synthesizing M_1—the anterior and more difficult portion. By such expedients the interpretation will evolve itself as a kernel. Our immediate aim may be represented to the eye, thus :—

$$M_1 = M_1 = L_1$$
$$M_2 = M_2 = L_2.$$

I. Repetition (quasi).

On comparing *Matt.* xxiv., xxv., with *Mark* xiii., we find that down to a certain point, and no farther, they agree manifestly together, either as it were *verbatim*, or in *full equivalence;* i. e., *verbatim* (I use the word as it will apply) in M. xxiv. 4—8, and M xiii. 5—8; *in equivalence of sense and extent* in M xxiv. 9—14 and M_1 xiii. 9—13; again *verbatim* down to the end of M xxiv. 36—with the exception of three verses, xxiv. 26, 27, 28, to be remembered in the sequel. With such exception to be so remembered, the whole M xxiv. 4—36, and the whole M xiii. 5—32 *agree together*, either verbatim or in full equivalence. The reader will verify the fact.

But in the after portions of the two records such agreement *ceases*. For though the two remainders do accord in the same practical character, and more particularly in the injunction *to watch*, which is thrice repeated in Matt. xxiv. 42, 44, xxv. 13, and four times in Mark xiii. 33—35, 37, yet not one of St. Matthew's *parables* in xxiv. 37—xxv. is found in Mark, as also St. Mark's *parable* in xiii. 33, 34 is not found in Matthew.

The case, upon the whole, is as if the two records took one another, or as if one of them took the other, and divided it into *two portions*, and then gave the former of the two verbatim or in full equivalence, but abstained from giving the latter portion in any such manner. I am not anxious to theorize upon the phenomena thus observed. My argument does not affirm that either this one or that one of the two records, was anterior to the other in point of time, nor that either of them in particular makes reference to the other. I do but note the fact, that there is really such agreement and such difference within the limits pointed out. And I observe that the phenomena are *suggestive* of this *primary position*, viz., that the two records M and M, when compared together, do divide one another into *two portions*, which we will call M_1 and M_2, M_1 and M_2 respectively.

The reader will form his own opinion upon the division thus suggested. My own object is not to dogmatize either for or against opinions, but to initiate a

M	Matt.	Mark.	M
M_1	xxiv. 4—36.	xiii. 5—32.	M_1
M_2	37—xxv.	33—37.	M_2

cumulative argument in proof of that *primary division*. If its truth can be shewn, the fact must plainly be of importance, as an aid to analytical investigation. In particular, two results will follow. First, we shall be freed from the temptation of taking some latter part of the anterior portion M_1, and adding it to some anterior part of the latter portion M_2, and thereby making a false combination of words, the effect of which must be to mislead attention and embarass the judgment. In the next place, this immense advantage will accrue, that our labours of observation will not have to extend themselves vaguely over the whole prophecy as one and indivisible; but they will be restricted to the narrower limits of the two component and separated portions.

Our road *bifurcates*. We have M_1 before us; and we have M_2 before us. Each must be examined. But the student will be pleased to observe, that M_1 is precisely that portion in which the peculiar difficulty of the prophecy almost wholly dwells, while M_2 is comparatively easy of interpretation. It will be a discreet thing, therefore, and an allowable, to *reserve the consideration of M_1*, till we shall first have made some proof of our method of investigation in the analysis of the easier portion M_2. Various facts will evolve themselves for notice as we go on. But still the primary point to be kept in view, is that primary division which has been suggested as subsisting between M_1 and M_2.

II. PERORATION.

It is obvious in St. Mark's record, that M_2 is of a distinctly practical character in its relation to M_1, and in that respect is constructively distinct from

	Matt.	Mark.	
M_1	xxiv. 4—36.	xiii. 5—32.	M_1
M_2	37—xxv.	33—37	M_2

M_1, to which it is the *practical conclusion*. Therefore, if thus M_2 is distinct from M_1, and M_1 from M_2, the idea suggests itself, whether M_1 (the equivalent to M_1) may not also be a distinct portion with reference to M_2, and have its practical conclusion therein, just as M_1 is seen to have its practical conclusion in M_2. If analogy of reasoning holds anywhere, I do not see why it should not hold here, as yielding a presumptive argument for that great division. The reader will form his own opinion. I have no wish to lay undue stress upon separate and independent points. My object, as I said, is to build up a proof by cumulation. If the great extent of M_2 xxiv. 37—xxv. 46, should seem to remove it from the category in which M_2 xiii. 33—37, may well appear to stand as a peroration,—the objection or difficulty (should it be either the one or the other), will not be extremely difficult to remove. Our next argument will have a bearing upon that point.

III. COMPENDIUM.

We are led to a more minute comparison of the portion M_2 with the portion M_2. It is natural to consider that, in the nature of

	Matt.	Mark.	
		xiii. 5—32	M_1
M_2	xxiv. 37—xxv.	33—37	M_2

things, while there is a verbatim agreement, and an agreement by full equivalence in substance and extent, there are also other kinds of agreement, such as the *synoptical* and the *abbreviated*. St. Mark's record can bear such relation to St. Matthew's. For instance, the temptation in the wilderness, which extends through Matt. iv. 1—11, is given in a remarkably concise manner in Mark i. 12, 13. The question then presents itself, whether we can discover anything of this sort in M_2 as compared with M_2. In order the better to trace the fact, we must observe the leading features in M_2 and in M_2.

St. Matthew's record, in this respect, resolves itself very easily into portions not more than eight in number; thus :—

$$
\text{xxiv.} \begin{cases} 37\text{—}39\ldots\ldots\ldots \text{found apart in Luke xvii. 26, 27.} \\ 40,\ 41\ldots\ldots\ldots \text{found apart in } \quad\text{,,} \quad 35,\ 36. \\ 42 \quad\ldots\ldots\ldots \text{of disputed connexion.} \\ 43,\ 44\ldots\ldots\ldots \text{parable of the thief.} \\ 45\text{—}51\ldots\ldots\ldots \quad\text{,,} \quad\quad\text{,,} \quad\quad \text{pastorate.} \end{cases}
$$

$$
\text{xxv.} \begin{cases} 1\text{—}13\ldots\ldots\ldots \quad\text{,,} \quad\quad\text{,,} \quad\quad \text{virgins.} \\ 14\text{—}30\ldots\ldots\ldots \quad\text{,,} \quad\quad\text{,,} \quad\quad \text{talents.} \\ 31\text{—}46\ldots\ldots\ldots \quad\text{,,} \quad\quad\text{,,} \quad\quad \text{sheep and goats.} \end{cases}
$$

On the other hand, the latter portion of St. Mark's record, after representing the Master of the house on his far journey, presents these five *leading ideas* with reference to persons on earth, viz. :—

$$
\text{xiii.} \begin{cases} 34. \begin{cases} \textit{Authority to servants} \\ \textit{Every man's work} \\ \textit{Porter to watch} \end{cases} \\ 35,\ 36.\ \textit{You to watch} \\ 37.\ \textit{You and all to watch.} \end{cases}
$$

On thus comparing M_2 and M_2, we perceive a sort of compendious or expansional agreement beginning to appear. We have plainly—

$$
\text{xiii.} \begin{cases} 34.\ \textit{Authority to his servants} \\ 34..\ \textit{Every man's work} \end{cases} \text{in} \begin{cases} M_2 \text{ xxiv. 45—51. [pastorate.]} \\ M_2 \text{ xxv. 14—30. [talents.]} \end{cases}
$$

As for the "porter to watch," this particular idea does not seem to present itself very obviously in M_2. But the idea, *you and all to watch,* is to be seen there :—

$$
\text{xxiv.} \begin{cases} 37\text{—}39,\ \text{the case of } \textit{all.} \\ 40,\ 41,\ \text{the case of } \textit{you the few.} \\ 42, \quad\quad \text{to } \textit{watch.} \end{cases}
$$

Thus of those five leading ideas in M_2, three at least are found in M_2.

Looking further into the matter, we readily observe that the leading terms and ideas in St. Mark's *you to watch*, xiii. 35, 36, are given in the parable of the *virgins*. For instance, the *preceptive opening* in M_2 xiii. 35, is distinctly found in M_2 xxiv. 12. So the time of *midnight* in xiii. 35, is in xxv. 6: so the *coming suddenly* is in xiii. 36, and in xxv. 5, 6: so the state of *sleeping* is in xiii. 36, and in xxv. 5: and generally the *you* (the disciples) in xiii. 36, may be seen under the apt designation of *virgins* in the whole xxv. 1—13. Thus there is a relation between the parable of the virgins and St. Mark's xiii. 35, 36, precisely similar to that which we noticed between St. Matthew's narrative of the temptation in the wilderness and St. Mark's more concise and cursory reference to some of its broader features. We use no arbitrary violence, then, when we take M_2 xiii. 35, 36, as a *concise equivalent* for the parable of the virgins. Observe now where we are in the comparison of M_2 and M_2.

34. { Authority to servants	=	xxiv. 45—51 [pastorate]
{ Every man's work	=	xxv. 14—30 [talents]
{ Porter to watch	=	(?)
35, 36. You to watch	=	xxv. 1—13 [virgins]
37. You and all to watch	=	xxiv. 37—42
	(?)	=	xxiv. 43, 44 [thief]
	(?)	=	xxv. 31—46 [sheep]

Thus in four points out of those five, the portions M_2 and M_2 agree well together. The question arises, then, whether they may not be wholly equivalent to one another. Plainly, the parable of the *sheep* and *goats* (M_2 xxv. 31—46) is *every man's work external;* just as the contiguous parable of the *talents* is *every man's work internal.* I say internal, for a good reason, because all the talents and all their gains are taken indentically into the other world; and therefore are not, and cannot be, time, money, opportunities, and the like,—all which perish in the using, and are not taken into the other world. The talents in the parable claim another character, according to which they are found to be inward and spiritual, and to be gifts, graces, and the like. The one talent would seem to be humility, which though it may continue to exist alone in some degraded form, is useless when alone, and is most needed by the most advanced and excellent of God's servants. Upon that idea, however, we do not here dwell, because our proper work at present is analysis, which in its earlier stages is perhaps not favourable to homiletics. It is more important at this moment to observe that *every man's work*, internal *and external*, is set forth in M_2.

... ... in our analysis is now as

			XIV. 45—51
			XV. ...—34
			XV. ...—49
			XV. —..
			XV. ..—..

... ... that the ... ... of the ... If ... ... Master of the ... ... that Christ, ... a ... upon ... ... make himself ... ... clearly may ... ... with respect to the ... ... external. And if he ... ... the masterdom of a... ... repentance, to be de- ... argument thus briefly touches ... ... who was to watch is iden- ... ... (dominator) in the *parable of* ... ... in the light of one of the ... ... in Holy Writ :—

...	=	XLV. 45—51	
...	=	XXV. $\begin{cases} 14—30 \\ 31—46 \end{cases}$	
...	=	$\begin{cases} \text{Goodman doomed} \\ \text{XLV. 43, 44} \end{cases}$	$\Big\}$ M: XXIV. 37 —XXV.
...	=	XXV. 1—13	
... to watch	=	XLV. 37—42	

... ... between M$_2$ and M$_2$ presents ... of the ... of M$_2$ from M$_1$. It is as ... ... St. Matthew's record of the prophecy; ... ... into two portions M$_1$ and M$_2$, and ... ... it further gave the latter ... ... manner, *i. e., concisely, synop-* ... ... The fact of such division is equally ... ... that M$_2$ gives M$_2$ in the way of ex-

... INTERLOCATION.

... ... is made further observable by another ... ... not to be passed over in silence; viz., ... which occur and recur in M$_2$ and

M_2, are so ordered in M_2 as to be separated from the statements which are in M_1 and in M_1, by the introductory ideas which are interlocated in M_1 xiii. 33, 34. For the separateness of M_2 argues the distinctness of its equivalent M_2.

If any one should question the conclusiveness of the phenomena above set forth, he will at least note the facts; and we will proceed to the further development of phenomena.

V. ALIBI.

On comparing St. Luke's record with St. Matthew's, we cannot but be struck with the apparently inexact manner in which L_1 xxi. 8—33 gives the substance of M_1 xxi. 4—36. Those divergencies, great and numerous as they are, claim an especial measure of attention. They are of exceeding interest and importance, and we shall be led to observe upon them in the sequel.

Our present purpose requires us to notice the immediate fact that St. Luke, in his record of the prophecy, does not give any of the various parables or illustrations contained in M_2. The reader will verify what is here said.

It will be observed further, that Luke xxi. 34—36, which claims comparison with M_2, though omitting all St. Matthew's parables, yet does not

M	Matt.	Luke.	L
M_1	xxiv. 4—36	xxi. 8—33	L_1
M_2	37—xxv.	34—36	L_2

fail to give what is at least equivalent to the part M_2 xxiv. 37—42, the *you and all to watch;* thus :—

$$\text{L. xxi.} \begin{cases} 34. \text{ The case of } you. \\ 35. \text{ The case of } all. \\ 36. \text{ To } watch. \end{cases}$$

Will the reader take these three verses as an equivalent for the whole of M_2? Hardly, I think. Must we say, then, that St. Luke ignores the parables in M_2? This is an idea to be examined into. St. Luke is partial to parables.

Every attentive student of the three synoptical gospels ought to be familiar with a certain class of facts by which infidels and harmonists have been alike perplexed,—I mean, facts of repetition. Let dulness be privileged to count it a dull thing, and a thing not allowable, for a matter to be repeated in religious instruction. Our Lord's taste and judgment were of another kind. His apples of gold and jewels of silver were not so meanly thought of by himself and his evangelists, as to be deemed unworthy of repetition under different circumstances of time, place, and auditory. St. Luke's gospel takes its most dis-

tinguishing complexion from its varying repetitions of our Lord's
sayings. What St. Matthew records as spoken in private to the
chosen disciples, St. Luke loves to record as uttered on a different occasion in the audience of all the people, that so Theophilus (as a layman doubtless) might know the reliability of
those things wherein he had personally been catechized. The
Creator of the grass and of the worlds did not disdain the employment of repetition.   In the case of the bread-miracles
(Matt. xiv. 13—22; xv. 29—39), which in xvi. 9, 10, he distinctly
himself affirms to be two, he seems to have exerted his providential power over the acts and wills of men, in order to produce
phenomena of repetition in the circumstances accessory to those
miracles. In like manner, he was accustomed to pronounce his
parables also on more occasions than one. The parabolic statements concerning Noah and concerning the field and the mill
(with their respective work people of the masculine and feminine
character, in the world and in the house of the church respectively) are found *verbatim* in Luke xvii., as we have already
noticed.

	Matt.	Luke.
Noah and the world ..	xxiv. 37—39	xvii. 26, 27
Field and mill	—— 40, 41	—— 35, 36

But of all the succeeding parables in M_2, not one is given in
Luke xvii. Our search is more successful in Luke xii., where
we find two parables recurring *verbatim*.

	M. xxiv. 43, 44	L. xii. 39, 40
Parable of the thief......	M. xxiv. 43, 44	L. xii. 39, 40
Authority to his servants ...	—— 45—51	—— 42—46

Continuing the line of our observations, we come (in M_2) to
the parable of the virgins. This we do not find in Luke xii., nor
elsewhere in Luke. But we must observe that it is a parable of
the bridegroom and virgins; just as the parable of the thief is one
of the thief and master. In which cases, the virgins and the
usurping master are secondaries and accessories to Christ the
primary character. And as the parable of the thief and master
may be correctly and sufficiently designated as the parable of the
thief; just so the parable of the bridegroom and virgins may be
regarded properly as a *parable of the bridegroom*. A parable of
the *bridegroom*, then, contiguous to that of the thief, we plainly

find in Luke xii. 35—38; the primary idea being the same as in M₂ xxv. 1—13, although the accessories be different.

Proceeding onwards (in M₂) we come to the cognate parables of the *talents* and *sheep*, which set forth, as we saw, *every man's work, internal and external.* Neither of these two beautiful and solemn parables is found in Luke xii., nor elsewhere in Luke at all. But in Luke xii. 47, 48, we find *every man's work* distinctly recognized, thus—

> And that servant which knew his Lord's will,
> And *prepared not himself,*
> *Neither did according to his will,*
>   Shall be beaten with many stripes ;
> But he that knew not,
> And *did commit things worthy of stripes,*
>   Shall be beaten with few stripes.

Wherein the committing of things worthy of stripes has respect to *every man's work* and duty ; and it stands responsive to that twofold idea of *not preparing himself* and *not doing according to the Lord's will :* in which twofold idea, the former part is clearly to be understood with regard to *work internal*, leaving the latter part (if it is no mere tautology) to be further expressive of *work external*. Thus, while the above passage expresses *every man's work* simply as such, it also regards that work as being partly *internal* and partly *external*. That is, while it expresses the simple idea in accordance with M₂, it also gives the complex form of the idea as conveyed by M₂ in those two concluding parables of the *talents* and the *sheep*.

Now, let us observe the position where we are. First, however, we may notice that in Luke xii., between 35—40 and 42—48, there stands the verse 41, which, under the form of a query on the part of St. Peter, contains the idea of the *you and all to watch.* Christ assents to that idea, and adopts it. For the Divine Wisdom can adopt human thoughts, just as the Divine Providence adopts human actions—the good thought and the action being both alike from the Lord. We have no difficulty, then, in observing the following harmony :—

$$
\text{Luke xii.} \atop (= L_2)
\left\{
\begin{array}{ll}
35\text{—}38 & = \text{Christ as a bridegroom,} \\
39,\ 40 & = \text{Christ as a thief,} \\
41. & = \text{You and all to watch,} \\
42\text{—}46 & = \text{Authority to his servants,} \\
47\text{—}48 & = \text{Every man's work.}
\end{array}
\right\}
= M_2 = {\scriptstyle M_2}.
$$

To indicate this equivalence, we will designate that portion, Luke xii. 35—48, by the symbol L₂. And we remark upon it further, that, besides those five leading ideas found previously in M₂ and M₂, no other leading idea in M. xxiv., xxv., or in M. xiii.

is associated in L_2 with those five leading ideas which a third time we have found grouped together. It is but a truism to say that those five leading ideas, as they stand in L_2 xii. 35—48, have a distinctness in themselves apart from L_1 xxi. 8—33. The inference is less obvious, but perhaps not less certain, that, by analogy, the same five leading ideas in M_2 and in M_2, claim a similar distinctness in themselves apart from M_1 and from M_1; so as that again M_2 shall be seen distinct in its own unity apart from M_1.

VI. Constellation.

The same thing stands out more clearly by reason of the circumstance that L_2 xii. 35—48, is quite another discourse from L_1, or M_1, or M_1, in that it is delivered, according to St. Luke's rule, in the audience of the people, and not to a few disciples on the Mount of Olives or elsewhere. So that those five leading ideas present themselves in a divinely reiterated constellation of truths or instructions, which, while not starting away from all relation to other separate or constellated truths, does yet assert its own collective unity, and claims to be viewed as one. It stands as a compound unit, in the wider unity of the universe of Christ's doctrine. Such constellations are frequent in Holy Writ.

VII. Arrangements.

Those five leading and consociated ideas are tied together by the combined testimony of the three evangelists. The three synoptical records, taken as the testimony of one Divine mind, perfectly refuse to concur in regarding those ideas in any other light than as five units and one quinternion. For, observe the diversity of the arrangements—

1.	You and all to watch,	xxiv. 37—42.
2.	The coming as a thief,	— 43, 44.
3.	Authority to his servants,	— 45—51.
4.	Coming as a bridegroom,	xxv. 1—13.
5.	Every man's work,	— $\left\{ \begin{array}{l} 14—30. \\ 31—46. \end{array} \right.$
	Order in Matt.	1, 2, 3, 4, 5.
	Order in Mark.	3, 5, 2, 4, 1.
	Order in Luke.	4, 2, 1, 3, 5.

It is seen that no one and no two of those five ideas stand together apart from the rest, nor can be separated from them in all the records; as also, that no four and no three of them stand together apart, or can be so separated. The five ideas admit of being taken no otherwise than as five in their individuality, and as one in their constellation.

VIII. Connexion.

That constellation is more obviously compacted together in L_2 on the combined principle of connected unity in itself, and of distinctness from the contiguous statements on each side of it.

1. Its unity is seen in these considerations—viz., that the particular ideas of *bridegroom* and *thief* are agnate as applied to Christ; while the particular ideas of *authority* and *work* are cognate as applied to his servants; and those two pairs of ideas are connected, rather than separated, by the link *you and all to watch.*

2. The distinctness of L_2, *in situ*, is a matter of simple observation; the drift of the discourse being thus:—

Luke xii. $\begin{cases} 13—34 = \text{Covetousness rebuked:} \\ 35—48 = \text{Watching for Christ:} \\ 49—59 = \text{Oppositions illustrated.} \end{cases}$

Such covetousness is bad, 13—21; needless, 22—30; to be supplanted, 31—34. Also, such opposition is inevitable, 49—53; to be incurred, 54—57; to be evaded, 58, 59. Manifestly L_2 xii. 35—48, is of a different character, and is seen therein to be distinct *in situ*. Therefore, being so connected and so distinct, it is in distinct unity as a system of ideas. And if the five ideas are such in L_2 they claim to be such in M_2 and M_2.

IX. Interweaving.

Those five constellated ideas are not thrown together without an internal law, by which the Divine mind would interpret its instruction. We have seen those two pairs in L_2—

Watch for the *bridegroom*, ..	xii. 35—48.
Watch for the (as a) *thief*, ..	— 39, 40.
Authority to his servants, ..	— 42—46.
Every man's *work*, ...	— 47, 48.

It is an obvious thing to see those ideas of *thief* and *authority* contiguous to one another in M_2 43—51. But mark the combination or interweaving of those pairs in M_2:—

Watch for the (as a) *thief*, ...	xxiv. 43, 44.
Authority to his servants, ...	— 45—51.
Watch for the *bridegroom*, ...	xxv. 1—13.
Every man's *work*, ...	—$\begin{cases} 14—30. \\ 31—46. \end{cases}$

The combined pairs are to this effect:—that Christ's coming, which will be as a *thief* and as a *bridegroom*, is to be *watched* for in the use of *authority*, as well as in *every man's work*, without exception. That wisdom is but blind, halt, and withered, which is alive to other men's work, but dead to the realities of its own authority, which yet Christ instituted and has conferred in his household.

Those pairs which are so combined in M_2 have the same mind in L_2. They stretch toward one another, and enclose in their strong embrace that fifth idea in L_2 xii. 41, *We and all to watch*. Thus, again, the five ideas, like five stars of light, are seen to be constellated together in L_2; and if in L_2, then also in M_2 by an analogy which approaches to a demonstration. And if thus M_2 is a constellation apart from M_1, then there is a great division between those two portions of St. Matthew's record, however much the said portions M_1 and M_2 may otherwise be connected.

The student who can reverence the development of God's works in the natural world, may be interested to observe similar phenomena in the utterances of Christ. When St. Peter (in Luke xii. 41) enquired, "Lord, speakest thou this parable (of watching) unto us, or even to all," the Lord met the query with a silent or indirect affirmative. But in L. xvii. 26—30 and 34 —36, he openly illustrates the case of the many or all by that of Noah's contemporaries [and Lot's], and the case of the few or us by the parables of [the bed] the house and the field; in neither of which passages, however, does he expressly append the injunction to watch. Subsequently, in Mark xiii. 37, he affirms the idea fully, as Peter himself might have desired, "What I say unto you, I say unto all, watch." In Luke xxi. 34—36, he gives the same idea, but in an expanded form. Lastly, in Matt. xxiv. 37—42, he gives it in a form yet more expanded, adopting now his own previous words and illustrations recorded in L_1 xvii. 26, 27, and 35, 36, and in xii. 39—46. Interpreters are too rash when they affirm that the same utterance is represented in L. xii., xvii., xxi., Mark xiii., and Matt. xxiv., xxv. Whether the three records, Matt. xxiv., xxv., Mark xiii., and Luke xxi., represent one utterance, or two, or three, is a matter open to discussion.

X. Doctrine.

The distinct constellation of the five ideas is strongly corroborated by the very body of their doctrine, which is to this effect: *You and all must watch* for him who is coming as a *thief* to some and as a *bridegroom* to others; you and all must watch for him, *they who are in his authority,* in the use of that authority, and *every man,* in the performance of his proper *work* which is to be done first *internally for himself,* and next *externally,* with not less care *for Christ in his disciples.* In this instruction, which does not spring out of the earth, we see distinctly the distinct unity of M_2 as complete in itself and apart from M_1, though not unconnected with that previous portion. The ecclesiastical and discipular complexion of M_2 accords well with the same ecclesiastical and discipular character which pervades St. Matthew's Gospel.

XI. Ruling Idea.

Our argument is a cumulative one, to establish the collective unity, in which those five great ideas are presented by M_2, and L_2 and M_2. In L_2 as we have seen, four of them are paired two and two together—viz., *thief* and *bridegroom, authority* and *work;* between which pairs the fifth idea, *We and all to watch,* is collocated. Again, in M_2 as we have seen, those two pairs are woven into a quaternion—*thief, authority, bridegroom, work;* and at the head of the quaternion stands the fifth idea, *They and we to watch.* Again, in M_2, as we have seen, the five ideas recur together; and here the last of them is that idea, *You and all to watch.* This idea is the beginning of the five in M_2; it is the middle in L_2; it is the end in M_2. It is the *beginning, middle,* and *end* of those consociated ideas. It is as a purple thread woven in and out. Compare it as we may, it compacts the whole system into unity, in the several cases of M_2, and L_2, and M_2. It does this in two ways; by its varied position, and by its relation to its four secondaries.

XII. Implication.

We may now perceive the *rationale* of St. Luke's concluding statement in xxi. 34—36. What goes before it in 8—33 answers, of course, to M_1, and to M_1, and may be called L_1. The part 34—36, then, stands in a position analogous to that of M_2 and of M_2. By position it claims to be L_2, standing, as it does, where we might have expected to find such a body of instruction as that which we have designated L_2 in Luke xii. 35—48. The obvious force of that remainder, L_2 xxi. 34—36, is, as we saw, *You and all to watch.* And this is the beginning, middle, and end, as we have seen, of all those five great constellated ideas in M_2 and m_2 and in L_2 xii. 35—48. In that system it is as a kind of central sun, to which the other four kindred ideas are subsidiary and secondary. It may be regarded as carrying them with it by implication and by suggestion. And when we consider how the parables of M_2 are given elsewhere in Luke :—

	Matt.	Luke.	
Noah and the world ..	xxiv. 37—39.	xvii. 26, 27.	Verbatim.
The field and mill.. ..	— 40, 41.	— 35, 36.	Verbatim.
The thief	— 43, 44.	xii. 39, 40.	Verbatim.
Authority	— 45—51.	— 42—46.	Verbatim.
The bridegroom	xxv. 1—13.	— 35—38.	Equivalence.
Every man's work ..	$-\begin{cases} 14\text{—}30. \\ 31\text{—}46. \end{cases}$	— 47, 48.	Compendium.

And when we further consider that St. Luke's record is not accustomed to repeat upon itself; and when we remember that the said record has already, in L_2 xii. 35—48, given those five great ideas in constellation; and that the essence and sense of the five is contained virtually in the central idea, *You and all to watch;* and that this idea has not hitherto been developed in Luke xii., nor in Luke xvii., nor (so far as appears) elsewhere in Luke—we may conceive the rule of the particular gospel (and the rule of doctrine too), to be well observed in what is written in L. xxi. 34—36, which is, as we have seen, a full development of that central idea, *You and all to watch.* Thus, by implication, L. xxi. 34—36, is equivalent to L_2—*i.e.*, to M_2; and its distinct unity which is sufficiently obvious as the practical conclusion to L_1 xxi. 8—33, argues the distinct unity of m_2 and of M_2.

XIII. REMAINDER.

Yet another argument for the primary division that subsists between M_1 and M_2 will be seen in the sequel, when it will plainly appear, by strictest investigation, that M_1, the anterior portion of St. Matthew's record, has, in itself, its own principles of coherence and unity, in a way peculiar to itself, but not less distinct and certain than is the case with the remainder M_2.

At present, our general conclusion from the facts already exhibited amounts to this—that the whole prophecy in Matt. xxiv., xxv., is divided by a great division into two portions :—

$$\text{Viz.} \begin{cases} M_1 = \text{xxiv. } 4\text{—}36. \\ M_2 = \text{xxiv. } 37\text{—xxv. } 46. \end{cases}$$

and that M_2 consists of eight, or rather of six, or rather of five sub-divisions :—

$$\text{Viz.} \begin{cases} \text{xxiv.} & 37\text{—}42. & = \text{You and all to watch;} \\ — & 43, 44. & = \text{Christ's coming as a thief;} \\ — & 45\text{—}51. & = \text{Authority to his servants;} \\ \text{xxv.} & 1\text{—}13. & = \text{Christ's coming as a bridegroom,} \\ — & \begin{cases} 14\text{—}30. \\ 31\text{—}46. \end{cases} & = \text{Every man's work;} \end{cases}$$

the combined force and particularity of which lessons we do not further go into in this place.

Our next field of observation will be M_1—*i.e.*, Matt. xxiv. 4—36. Its analysis and interpretation will be made good by a threefold course of investigation, and by a threefold chord of argument, that will not easily be broken. The results will clash not a little with the undemonstrative English exegetic, and with the unregulated speculation of the Germans. We shall evolve a clear testimony to the church's doctrine as to her Lord's coming, however much her sons and her enemies, and the Millenarians too, may be found wrong at this day, in the multitudinous variety of their conjectures touching the proper interpretation of this prophecy.

E. Dodd,

Magdalene College, Cambridge.

QUOTATIONS IN THE NEW TESTAMENT FROM THE OLD.

No intelligent student of the New Testament needs to be told that very important questions are connected with the quotations it contains—questions both of criticism and of interpretation. The following table has been drawn up with the view of aiding inquiry on this subject, and is now presented as a small contribution to this department of Biblical science.

DIRECT quotations from the Old Testament are, in all, about 263 ; references or allusions less direct 375 : together, 638. The former (to which in this table our attention is confined) may be arranged as—

PROPHETIC, of which class some are *immediate*, referring exclusively to Christ or the Gospel (see Matt. iv. 15, 16) ; and others are *typical*, referring primarily to some typical event or person, and then to some event or person under the Gospel (see John xix. 36). These are marked in the following table p. i. and p. t. respectively : x. indicates that the prophecy is applied to our Lord ;

DEMONSTRATIVE, quoted to *prove* some statement (see John vi. 45), marked dem. ;

EXPLANATORY, quoted to *explain* or confirm some statement or fact, marked ex. ; and

ILLUSTRATIVE, where expressions are borrowed from the Old Testament with new force (see Rom. x. 18), marked ill.

Some passages are both dem. and ex.—that is, they explain and demonstrate by example some general principle. Others are prophetic also.

Quotations introduced by—" that it might be fulfilled," are, in the following table, marked ([1]) ; " then was fulfilled," ([2]) ; and " as it is written," " Scripture saith," &c., ([3]). These formulæ of quotations are important.

The numbers appended to each book of the New Testament indicate how many quotations from the Old Testament each book contains ; the numbers appended once to each book of the Old, how often each book is quoted in the New.

After each quotation we shall indicate whether the passage is *ad sensum* or *ad verba*, and whether taken from the Hebrew or the Septuagint.

New Testament.	Old Testament.	
MATT.—37.		
1. 23.	Is. 7. 14. (58.)	Sense of H. and S., p. t. or i.[1] x.
2. 6.	Mic. 5. 2. (1.)	Sense of H. and S., p. i.[3] x.
2. 15.	Hos. 11. 1. (6.)	H., p. t.[1] x.
2. 18.	Jer. 31. 15. (7.)	H. and sense of S., ill.[2]
2. 23.	Is. 53. Ps. 22.	Sense of various p. i. x.
3. 3.	Is. 40. 3.	Sense of H. and S., p. i.[3] Jno.
4. 4.	Deut. 8. 3. (Pent. 93.)	H. and sense of S., ex.[3]
4. 6.	Ps. 90. 11, 12. (72.)	S. and sense of H., ex.[3]
4. 7.	Deut. 6. 16.	S. and sense of H., ex.[3]
4. 10.	Deut. 6. 13.	N. v. S., sense of H., ex.[3]
4. 15, 16.	Is. 9. 1, 2.	H., p. i.[1] x.
8. 17.	Is. 53. 4.	Sense of H., p. i.[3] x.
9. 13.	Hos. 6. 6. (6.)	H. and sense of S., ex.
11. 10.	Mal. 3. 1. (5.)	Sense of H. and S., p. i.[3] Jno.
12. 7.	Hos. 6. 6.	H. and sense of S., ex.
12. 18—21.	Is. 42. 1—4.	H. (sense of), p. i.[1] x.
13. 42.	Is. 6. 9.	N. v. S., sense of H., ex. or p. t. x.
13. 35.	Ps. 77. 2.	H., sense of S., p. t.[1] or ill. x.
15. 4.	Ex. 20. 12 ; 21. 16.	Sense of S. and H., ex.
15. 8, 9.	Is. 29. 13.	N. v. S., part of H., ex.
19. 4.	Gen. 1. 27.	Ex.
19. 5.	Gen. 2. 24.	N. v. S., sense of H., ex.
19. 18.	Ex. 20. 12.	Sense of S. and H., ex.
19. 19.	Levit. 19. 18.	H. and S., ex.
21. 5.	Zech. 9. 9. (6.)	Sense of H. and S., p. i.[1] x.
21. 13.	Is. 6. 7. Jer. 7. 11.	Sense of H. and S., ex.[3]
21. 16.	Ps. 8. 2.	H. and S., strength=praise, ex.
21. 42.	Ps. 118. 22, 23.	H. and S., p. t. or ex.
22. 24.	Deut. 25. 5.	Sense of H. and S., ex.
22. 32.	Ex. 3. 6.	Sense of H. and S., dem.[3]
22. 37.	Deut. 6. 5.	Sense of H. and S., might=mind, ex.
22. 39.	Levit. 19. 18.	H. and S., ex.
22. 44.	Ps. 110. 1.	H. and S., p. i.[3] x. dem.
26. 31.	Zech. 13. 7.	Sense of H. and S., p. i.[3] x.
27. 9, 10.	Zech. 11. 13.	Sense of H. and S., p. t.[3] x.
27. 35.	Ps. 22. 18.	H. and S., p. or i.[1] x.
27. 46.	Ps. 22. 1.	H., sense of S., p. i. x.
MARK.—17.		
1. 2, 3.	Mal. 3. 1. (5.) Is. 40. 3.	Sense of H. and S., p. i.[3] Jno.
4. 12.	Is. 6. 9.	Sense of H. and S., ex. or p. t. x.
7. 6, 7.	Is. 29. 13.	N. v. S., part of H., ex.
7. 10.	Ex. 20. 12 ; 21. 16.	H., sense of S., ex.
10. 6.	Gen. 1. 27.	H., S., ex.
10. 7.	Gen. 2. 24.	S., sense of H., ex.
10. 19.	Ex. 20. 12.	Sense of H. and S. ex.
11. 17.	Is. 56. 7. Jer. 7. 11.	Sense of H. and S., ex.[3]
12. 10, 11.	Ps. 118, 22, 23.	S., H., p. t. or ex.
12. 19.	Deut. 25. 5.	Sense of H. and S., ex.
12. 26.	Ex. 3. 6.	Sense of H. and S., dem.
12. 29, 30.	Deut. 6. 4, 5.	Sense of H. and S., ex.
12. 31.	Levit. 19. 18.	H. and S., ex.
12. 36.	Ps. 109. 1.	S. and H., dem. p. t. x.

H 2

New Testament.	Old Testament.	
MARK.		
14. 27.	Zech. 13. 7.	Sense of H. and S., p. i.[3] x.
15. 28.	Is. 53. 12.	H. and sense of S., p. i. x.
15. 34.	Ps. 22. 1.	H. and sense of S., p. i. x.
LUKE.—19.		
1. 17.	Mal. 4. 5, 6.	Sense of S. and H., p. i. Jno.
2. 23.	Ex. 13. 2.	Sense of H. and S., ex.[3]
2. 24.	Levit. 12. 8.	Sense of H. and S., ex.[3]
3. 4—6.	Is. 40. 3—5.	Sense of H. and S., p. i.[3] Jno.
4. 4.	Deut. 8. 3.	Sense of H. and S., ex.[3]
4. 8.	Deut. 6. 13.	Sense of H. and S., ex.[3]
4. 10, 11.	Ps. 90. 11, 12.	Sense of H. and S., ex.[3]
4. 12.	Deut. 6. 16.	S. and sense of H., ex.[3]
4. 18, 19.	Is. 61. 1, 2.	Sense of S. and H., p. i.[3] x.
7. 27.	Mal. 3. 1.	H. and sense of S., p. i.[3] Jno.
8. 10.	Is. 6. 9.	Sense of H. and S., ex. or p. t.
10. 27.	Deut. 6. 5. Levit. 19. 18.	Sense of H. and S., ex.
18. 20.	Ex. 20. 12.	Sense of H. and S., ex.
19. 46.	Is. 56. 7. Jer. 7. 11.	Sense of S. and H., ex.[3]
20. 17.	Ps. 117. 22, 23.	S. and H., ex. or p. t.[3] x.
20. 28.	Deut. 25. 5.	Sense of S. and H., ex.[3]
20. 42, 43.	Ps. 110. 1.	S. and H. p. i.[3] x.
22. 37.	Is. 53. 12.	H., n. v., S., p. i.[3] x.
23. 46.	Ps. 31. 6.	Sense of H. and S., ex. or p. t. x.
JOHN.—15.		
1. 23.	Is. 40. 3.	Sense of H. and S., p. i.[3] Jno.
2. 17.	Ps. 68. 9.	H. and n. v., S., p. i. or t.[3] x.
6. 31.	Ps. 77. 24.	Sense of H. and S., ex.[3]
6. 45.	Is. 54. 13.	Sense of H. and S., dem.[3]
7. 38.		Sense of Is. 44. 3; 55. 1; Zech. 14. 8; p. i.[3] ill.[3]
8. 17.	Deut. 19. 15.	Sense of S. and H., dem.[3]
10. 34.	Ps. 81. 6.	H., n. v., S., dem.[3]
12. 14, 15.	Zech. 9. 9.	Sense of H. and S., p. i.[3] x.
12. 38.	Is. 53. 1.	S., sense of H., p. i.[1] x.
12. 40.	Is. 6. 10.	Sense of S. and H., ex. or p. t.
13. 18.	Ps. 41. 19.	H., p. t.[1] x.
15. 25.	Ps. 109. 3, or 68. 4.	Sense of S. and H., p. t.[1] x.
19. 24.	Ps. 22. 18.	S. and H., p. i.[1] x.
19. 36.	Ex. 12. 46.	Sense of S. and H., p. t.[1] x.
19. 37.	Zech. 12. 10.	H., p. i.[3] x.
ACTS.—31.		
1. 16.	Ps. 41. 9.	p. i. or t.[2] x.
1. 20.	Ps. 69. 25.	Sense of H. and S., p. t.[3] or ill.
1. 20.	Ps. 109. 8.	H., and sense of S., ex.[3] or ill.
2. 17, &c.	Joel 2. 28. (2.)	N. v. S., sense of H., p. i.[3]
2. 25, &c.	Ps. 16. 8, &c.	S., and sense of H., p. i. or t.[3] x.
2. 34, 35.	Ps. 110. 1.	S. and H., p. i. or dem.
2. 36.	Is. 61. 1.	p. i. x.
3. 22, 23.	Deut. 18. 15, 19.	Sense of H. and S., p. i. x.
3. 25.	Gen. 22. 18.	Sense of H. and S., p. i.[1] x.
4. 11.	Ps. 118. 22, 23.	Sense of H. and S., ex. or p. t. x.
4. 25, 26.	Ps. 2. 1, 2.	S. and H., p. i. or t.[3] x.
7. 3.	Gen. 12. 1.	S. and H., ex.

New Testament.	Old Testament.	
ACTS.		
7. 6, 7.	Gen. 15. 13, 14.	Sense of S. and H., ex.
7. 26.	Ex. 2. 13, 14.	Sense of S. and H., ex.
7. 32.	Ex. 3, 6.	Sense of S. and H., ex.
7. 33, 34.	Ex. 5. 7, 8, 10.	H., n. v., S., ex.
7. 35.	Ex. 2. 14.	H. and S., ex.
7. 37.	Deut. 18. 15.	Sense of H. and S., p. i. x.
7. 40.	Ex. 32. 1.	Sense of H. and S., ex.
7. 42, 43.	Amos 5. 25.	Sense of H. and S., with variation, ex.
7. 49, 50.	Is. 66. 1, 2.	Sense of H. and n. v., Sept., ex.
8. 32, 33.	Is. 53. 7, 8.	Sense of H. and S. ; apparent variation, p. i.[3] x.
13. 22.	1 Sa. 13. 14. (1.) Ps. 89. 21.	Sense of H. and S., ex.
13. 33.	Ps. 2. 7.	S. and H., p. i.[3] x.
13. 34.	Is. 55. 3.	Sense of S. and H., p. t. or dem.
13. 35.	Ps. 16. 10.	H., S., dem. p. i. or t. x.
13. 41.	Hab. 1. 5. (4.)	Sense of S. and H., ex.
13. 47.	Is. 49. 6.	Sense of S. and H., dem. p. i. x.
15. 16, 17.	Amos 9. 11, 12. (2.)	Partly S. and partly H., dem. p. i.
23. 5.	Ex. 22. 28.	S. and H., ex.
28. 26, 27.	Is. 6. 9, 10.	Sense of S. and H., ex. or p. t.
ROMANS.—52.		
1. 17.	Hab. 2. 4.	Sense of S. and H., ex.
2. 24.	Is. 52. 5.	N. v. S., sense of H., ex.
3. 4.	Ps. 51. 4.	S., H., dem. ex.
3. 10—12.	Ps. 14. 1, &c.	N. v. S., sense of H., dem. ex.
3. 13.	Ps. 5. 10.	S., sense of H., dem. ex.
3. 13.	Ps. 140. 4.	S., H., dem. ex.
3. 14.	Ps. 10. 7.	Sense of H. and S., dem. ex.
3. 15, &c.	Is. 59. 7, 8.	Sense of S. and H., dem. ex.
3. 18.	Ps. 36. 2.	H., n. v., S., dem. ex.
4. 3.	Gen. 15. 6.	S., sense of H., dem. ex.
4. 6, 7.	Ps. 32. 1, 2.	S., sense of H., dem. ex.
4. 17.	Gen. 17. 5.	S. and H., dem.
4. 18,	Gen. 15. 5.	S. and H., dem.
7. 7.	Ex. 20. 17.	S., H., ex.
8. 36.	Ps. 44. 22.	S., H., ex. or ill.[3]
9. 7.	Gen. 21. 12.	S., H., dem. ex.
9. 9.	Gen. 18. 10.	Sense of S. and H., dem. ex.
9. 12.	Gen. 25. 23.	S., H., dem. ex.
9. 13.	Mal. 1. 23.	S. and H., dem. ex.
9. 15.	Ex. 33. 10.	S. and H., dem. ex.
9. 17.	Ex. 9. 16.	H., sense of S., dem. ex.
9. 25.	Hos. 2. 23.	Sense of H. and S., p. i. dem. ex.
9. 26.	Hos. 2. 1.	H. and S., dem. ex.
9. 27, 28.	Is. 10. 22, 23.	Sense of S. and H., dem. p. t.
9. 29.	Is. 1. 9.	S. and H., dem. p. t.
9. 33.	Is. 8. 14 ; 28. 16.	Sense of H. and S., ex. p. i.[3] x.
10. 5.	Levit. 18. 5.	Sense of S. and H., dem. ex.
10. 6, 8.	Deut. 30. 12.	Sense of H. and S., ill.[3]
10. 11.	Is. 28. 16.	Sense of S. and H., ex. dem.
10. 13.	Joel 2. 32.	S., sense of H., ex. dem.
10. 15.	Is. 52. 7.	Sense of S. and H., ex.
10. 16.	Is. 53. 1.	S. and H., dem. p. i.[3] x.
10. 18.	Ps. 18. 5.	S., H., ill.

New Testament.	Old Testament.	
ROMANS.		
10. 19.	Deut. 32. 10.	S., H., dem. p. i. or t.
10. 20, 21.	Is. 65. 1, 2.	S., H., dem. p. i.³ x.
11. 3.	1 Ki. 19. 14.	Sense of S. and H., ex. dem.
11. 4.	1 Ki. 19. 18. (2.)	H. and sense of S., ex. dem.
11. 8.	Is. 29. 10.	Sense of H. and S., ex. dem.
11. 9, 10.	Ps. 69. 23, 24.	N. v. S., sense of H., ill. or p. t.³
11. 26, 27.	Is. 59. 20, 21 ; 27. 9.	N. v. S., sense of H., with variations. dem. p. i.³ x.
11. 34.	Is. 40. 13.	S., sense of H., ex.
12. 19.	Deut. 32. 35.	Sense of H. and S., dem. ex.
12. 20.	Prov. 25. 21, 22. (6.)	S., sense of H., ex.
13. 9.	Ex. 20. 13—17. Le. 19. 18.	S., H., ex. dem.
14. 11.	Is. 45. 23.	Sense of S. and H., dem. ex.
15. 3.	Ps. 68. 10.	S., H., dem. p. i. or t.³ x.
15. 9.	Ps. 18. 50.	S., H., dem. p. i. or t.³ ex.
15. 10.	Deut. 32. 43.	H., dem.
15. 11.	Ps. 117. 1.	S., H., dem.
15. 12.	Is. 11. 10.	S., sense of H., dem. p. i.³ x.
15. 21.	Is. 52. 15.	S., H., p. i. x.
I. COR.—18.		
1. 19.	Is. 29. 14.	N. v. S., sense of H., with variations, ex.
1. 31.	Jer. 9. 24.	Sense of S. and H., ex.
2. 9.	Is. 64. 3.	Sense of H. and S., with variations, ex. dem.
2. 16.	Is. 40. 13.	Sense of S. and H., ex. dem.
3. 19.	Job 5. 13. (1.)	H., sense of S., ex. dem.
3. 20.	Ps. 93. 11.	S., H., ex. dem.
6. 16.	Gen. 2. 14.	S. and sense of H., ex. dem.
9. 9.	Deut. 25. 4.	S., H., ex. dem.
10. 7.	Ex. 32. 6.	S., H., ex.
10. 20.	Deut. 32. 17.	Sense of S. and H., ex.
10. 26.	Ps. 24. 1.	S. and H., dem.
14. 21.	Is. 28. 11, 12.	Sense of H. and S., ex.
15. 25.	Ps. 110. 1.	Sense of H. and S., dem. p. i. x.
15. 27.	Ps. 110. 1.	Sense of H. and S., dem. p. i. x.
15. 32.	Is. 22. 13.	S. and H., ill.
15. 45.	Gen. 2. 7.	Sense of S. and H., dem. ex.
15. 54.	Is. 25. 8.	H., ex. p. i.³ x.
15. 55.	Hos. 13. 8.	Sense of S. and H., with variations, p. t. x.
II. COR.—9.		
4. 13.	Ps. 116. 10.	S., H., ill. ex.
6. 2.	Is. 49. 8.	S., H., ill. ex.
6. 16.	Levit. 26. 11, 12.	Sense of S. and H., dem. ex.
6. 17, 18.	Is. 52. 11, 12. 2 Sa. 7. 14.	Sense of H. and S., with variations,
8. 15.	Ex. 16. 8.	N. v. S. and H., ill. ex. [dem. ex.
9. 7.	Prov. 22. 8.	N. v. S., sense of H., ex.
9. 9.	Ps. 112. 9.	H., S., ex.
13. 1.	Deut. 19. 15.	Sense of S. and H., ex. ill.
GALAT.—9.		
3. 8.	Gen. 12. 3.	Sense of S. and H., dem. p. i.
3. 10.	Deut. 27. 26.	Sense of H. and S., dem. ex.

New Testament.	Old Testament.	
GALATIANS.		
3. 11, 12.	Hab. 2. 4. Levit. 18. 5.	Sense of H. and S., dem. ex.
3. 13.	Deut. 21. 23.	N. v. S., sense of H., dem. ex.
3. 16.	Gen. 22. 18.	S., H., dem.
4. 27.	Is. 54. 1.	S., H., p. i. dem.
4. 30.	Gen. 21. 10.	Sense of S. and H., p. t. or ill.
5. 14.	Levit. 19. 18.	S. and H., ex.
EPHES.—4.		
4. 8.	Ps. 68. 19.	Sense of H. and S., with variations, dem. p. t.^{3} x.
5. 14.	Is. 60. 1.	Sense of both, dem. ex.
5. 31.	Gen. 2. 24.	N. v. S., sense of H., dem.
6. 2, 3.	Ex. 20. 12.	N. v. S., sense of H., ex.
I. TIM.—1.		
5. 18.	Deut. 25. 4.	S., H., dem. ex.
II. TIM.—1.		
2. 19.	Num. 16. 5.	H., n. v., S., ex.
HEB.—33.		
1. 5.	Ps. 2. 7. 2 Sa. 7. 14. (2.)	S., H., p. i. and dem.
1. 6.	Ps. 97. 7.	N. v. S. and H., p. i. dem.
1. 7.	Ps. 104. 4.	N. v. S. and H., dem.
1. 8, 9.	Ps. 45. 7, 8.	N. v. H. and S., dem.
1. 10, &c.	Ps. 102. 25.	S., H., dem.
1. 13.	Ps. 110. 1.	S., H., dem.
2. 6, &c.	Ps. 8. 5, &c.	S., H., ex. p. t. x.
2. 12.	Ps. 22. 23.	S. and H., dem. p. i.
2. 12, 13.	Ps. 16. 1. Is. 8. 17, 18.	S., H., dem. p. i.
3. 7, &c.	Ps. 95. 7, &c.	N. v. H. and S., ex.
3. 15.	Ps. 95. 7, 8.	S., H., ex.
4. 3 & 5.	Ps. 95. 11.	S., H., ex.
4. 4.	Gen. 2. 3.	Sense of S. and H., ex.
4. 7.	Ps. 95. 7, 8.	S., H., dem.
5. 5.	Ps. 2. 7.	S., H., p. i. and dem.
5. 6.	Ps. 110. 4.	S., H., dem. ex.
6. 14.	Gen. 22. 16, 17.	S., H., dem. ex.
7. 17, 21.	Ps. 110. 4.	S., H., dem. p. i. x.
8. 5.	Ex. 25. 40.	H., n. v., S., dem.
8. 8.	Jer. 31. 31.	N. v. S., H., with one variation, dem. p. i.
9. 20.	Ex. 24. 8.	N. v. S. and H., dem.
10. 5.	Ps. 40. 7.	N. v. S., H., one variation, dem. p. i.
10. 16, 17.	Jer. 31. 33, 34. (7.)	Sense of S. and H., dem. p. i.
10. 30.	Deut. 32. 35, 36.	Sense of S. and H., ex.
10. 37, 38.	Hab. 2. 3, 4. (4.)	N. v. S. and H., one variation, ex.
11. 21.	Gen. 47. 31.	S., sense of H., one variation, ex.
12. 5, 6.	Prov. 3. 11, 12.	N. v. S., H., dem.
12. 20.	Ex. 19. 12, 13.	Sense of S. and H., ex.
12. 21.	Deut. 9. 19.	Sense of H. and S., with variations, ex.
12. 26.	Hag. 2. 6. (1.)	N. v. S., sense of H., p. i.
13. 5.	Jos. 1. 5. (1.) Deut. 31. 8.	H. and sense of S., ex.
13. 6.	Ps. 118. 6.	S., sense of H., ex. or ill.

New Testament.	Old Testament.	
JAMES.—5.		
2. 8.	Levit. 19. 18.	S., H., ex.
2. 11.	Ex. 20. 13, 14.	N. v. S. and H., dem.
2. 23.	Gen. 15. 6.	S. and sense of H., dem.
4. 5.		Sense of Ge. 6. 5, 11; Nu. 11. 29, &c., ex.
4. 6.	Prov. 3. 34.	N. v. S. and H., dem. ex.
I. PETER.—10.		
1. 16.	Levit. 11. 44.	H., S., ex.
1. 24, 25.	Is. 40. 6.	N. v. S. and H., ex.
2. 6.	Is. 28. 16.	Sense of H. and S., p. i. x.
2. 7.	Ps. 118. 22, 23.	S., H., p. t. or ex.
2. 9.	Ex. 19. 6. (Pent. 93.)	S., H., ex. or p. t.
2. 22.	Is. 53. 9.	N. v. S., sense of H., ex. p. i. x.
2. 24.	Is. 53. 5, &c.	N. v. S., sense of H., p. i. x.
3. 10.	Ps. 34. 13, &c.	Sense of S. and H., ex.
3. 14, 15.	Is. 8. 12, 13. (58.)	N. v. S., sense of H., ex.
4. 8.	Prov. 10. 12.	H., ex.
II. PETER.—1.		
2. 22.	Prov. 26. 11. (6.)	Sense of H. and S., ex.
REV.—1.		
2. 27.	Ps. 2. 9. (72.)	Sense of S. and H., p. i. or t. x.

In the foregoing tables, the letters H. and S. imply that the Hebrew text is literally translated and that the LXX. is copied *verbatim* in the New Testament: the words " Sense of H. and S." imply that the sense is preserved, but that there is a difference of phraseology : the letters N. v. imply that the passage is nearly *verbatim*.   The quotations, it will be seen, are sometimes strictly verbal, and sometimes widely paraphrastic or greatly abbreviated : but no violence is done to the meaning of the original.

A.

THE AUGUSTINIAN DOCTRINE OF PREDESTINATION.[a]

THE prayer of our blessed Lord, " that they all may be one as thou Father art in me and I in thee," finds its responsive echo even among those who seem but feebly to realize its import, and every attempt to promote the unity of the church of Christ merits at the least an impartial and deliberate, if not a favourable, consideration in the columns of a theological review. This seems to be the object of the present work, and on this account it commends itself to notice.

Before entering upon a detailed examination of a book which professes to prove that the predestinarian question is incapable of more satisfactory solution, and which attempts to consign it finally to the list of mysteries in the higher sense of the term, it may be well to make one general observation upon a much humbler line of argument than Mr. Mozley's. We believe that the reasoning which exerts the widest influence in repelling many from farther examination of the predestinarian question is this, not that they believe it to be absolutely incapable of solution, but that so much of human thought has already been lavished upon it that the chance of its being ever solved by human minds is doubtful, and the chances against its solution by each of the many thousands of enquirers to whom it is open are almost incalculable. It is regarded something in the light of a lottery, in which there are tens of thousands of drawers and but one doubtful prize. To counteract the natural aversion to expend time and thought on a subject so little likely to prove a profitable mental or theological investment is a difficult undertaking. We trust however that it is not impracticable; and, if our readers feel strongly disposed to refuse to accompany us, we would humbly submit, that if very serious errors and contradictions can be pointed out, not only in the reasonings of those who profess to prove that the subject is beyond the human grasp, but of many of those who have been regarded as high authorities, a corresponding encouragement is held out that some of the difficulties which surround the enquiry may be diminished, if not removed.

In his first chapter Mr. Mozley thus briefly states the object of his book :—" The design of this treatise is to give an account

---

a *A Treatise on the Augustinian Doctrine of Predestination.* By J. B. Mozley, B.D., Fellow of Magdalen College, Oxford. London : Murray. 1855. 8vo. pp. 432.

of St. Augustine's doctrine of predestination, together with such comments as may be necessary for a due examination of and judgment upon it." This seems to us a statement which scarcely does justice to the range of thought and argument which the author embraces. These might have warranted the appropriation of a wider and more general title than *The Augustinian Doctrine of Predestination.* The different extremes of Pelagian and Supralapsarian doctrine are largely noticed; their conflicting arguments are examined, and if the degree of truth and error on both sides is not definitively recorded, it is shewn to exist in such measure as to call for the exercise of mutual forbearance. The scales are held, if not impartially in each item, yet with something more than impartiality on the whole. The balance of power is rigidly maintained, and, if a little favour is shewn where any weakness is detected on the one side, it is sure to be counterbalanced by an equal amount of favour when it is called for by a corresponding amount of weakness on the other.

After setting forth the design of the treatise, the author in stating the argument for predestination begins with drawing a just distinction between the predestinarian and the necessitarian :—

"The predestinarian and the fatalist agree, indeed, in the facts of the case, and equally represent mankind as acting necessarily, whether for good or evil, in distinction to acting by original motion of the will. But the fatalist goes to philosophy for the reason of this state of things, the predestinarian to a truth of revelation."[b]—p. 1.

He then proceeds to describe what he calls religious necessitarianism, and to state the argument by which it is supported :—

"There is another kind of necessitarianism, again, which takes for its basis, instead of a physical assumption, like the one just mentioned,

---

[b] "On this, as upon every other question, two extremes have prevailed, which, like many other extremes, have met in the establishment and maintenance of the same error. Identifying moral with mechanical questions, and illustrating voluntary agency by physical phenomena, one class of enquirers has arrived at the belief of a necessary chain, every link of which is absolutely and entirely dependent upon its predecessor. Overlooking the intermediate agencies and instrumentalities, and detaching and insulating each link entirely from its connexion with its distant predecessors, and from the great chain, in order that they might link it more effectually with an original fiat of the Creator, another class has arrived at the doctrine of fato-predestination. The one class arrived at their conclusion through a spurious philosophy, and their doctrine has been appropriately termed ' philosophical necessity;' the other derived theirs from an equally spurious interpretation of revealed truth, and designated it by a term which gave a semblance of a distinction. The only difference between them, however, was in the steps by which they reached their conclusion."—*Doctrine of Scriptural Predestination*, p. 10. London and Oxford. 1854.

a religious one—the attribute of the divine power, and argues downwards from the First Cause, instead of backwards from human action.   To the metaphysician who believes in a Creator or First Cause, and who contemplates man in relation to that Being, one great and primary difficulty presents itself in the question how a being can be a creature, and yet have free will and be a spring of action to himself, a self-moving being.   Our very notion of cause and effect is of the cause as active, the effect as passive; and therefore if man is an effect, how is he an active being?   A tool or instrument that we make issues inert out of our hands, and only capable of that motion which the maker of it gives it.   To make a machine is to cause the whole series of motions which it performs.   Our idea of creation is thus at variance with the idea of free agency in the thing made.   Man as a self-moving being and the originator of his own acts, is a first cause in nature; but how can we acknowledge a second first cause—a first cause which is an effect, a created originality."—p. 2.

In this passage we have a striking illustration of that species of argument which rests on a confusion of terms and a want of discrimination, and in Mr. Mozley's answer an equally forcible illustration of the great defect which pervades his whole work and train of argument, namely, a love of paradox, which leads him to delight in combatting an exaggerated statement or a sophistry on one side by introducing a positively contradictory or equally sophistical statement on the other.   For such a proceeding we see no necessity in the present case, nor in any one of the instances which he has adduced.   Instead of admitting even the apparent conclusiveness of the religious necessitarian's reasoning, as Mr. Mozley does, and combatting it negatively by the fact of moral evil, we would admit that there cannot be two first causes, nor two absolute powers of origination; and that the same thing cannot be, in one and the same relation, both a cause and effect.   But what does this prove?   Not that a power of origination on the part of a creature is impossible; for such a power is itself neither a creation nor an effect.   All power of origination must properly belong primarily and exclusively to God, but self-action is what we regard as a divine attribute.   To say that God under any circumstances creates the power of origination, or that a power of origination is an effect in the strict sense of the term, is to suppose that God creates one of the essential elements of his own nature; and that a thing is, in one and the same relation, a cause and an effect.   Man is created, but his power of origination is not created, but delegated from him to whom all power of origination primarily and exclusively belongs.[c]   Its essential nature is

---

[c] Does not the language of Genesis i. 26, suggest a similar distinction ?   " And God said, Let us *make* man :" here we have an act of creation : " and *let* them *have* dominion :" here we have an act of delegation.

not altered by delegation; but it is in man, to whom it is delegated, what it was in God who delegated it—a cause and not an
effect.   It is a gift bestowed, which may be perverted, but which
retains, in the hands of its recipient, the intrinsic nature as an
originating power which it had when in possession of the donor.
This seems a very clear and satisfactory distinction, and one
which will permit the Christian to entertain a belief of man's
power of origination without prejudice to the omnipotence of
God, and to retain a conviction of the existence of moral evil
without impugning God's goodness.   The believer is thus enabled to hold, as a most certain truth, the power of origination
on man's part, while the[d] "necessitarian believes freewill not
only to be false but impossible," and the predestinarian, who
confounds, under the head of creations and effects, that divine
attribute which may be delegated, but can neither be created
nor effected, "is excluded on this question, from the ground of
philosophy, from the perfect and consistent theory of the fatalist,
and draws his conclusion from the revealed doctrine of the
fall."[e]

Mr. Mozley thus takes for granted a conclusion for which
there seems no just ground, namely, that the argument of the
necessitarian against man's power of origination is logically and
philosophically unanswerable; whereas it seems to us to rest
entirely upon the very great fallacy of designating as an effect a
power of which the essential principle is that it is a primary
cause.   To call a power of origination an effect, and then to
reason from such an assumption that it cannot be a cause, is
neither more nor less than begging the question.   There seems
therefore no reason for adopting the circuitous course of proving
man's possession of a power of origination, by adducing the
existence of moral evil, and still less for maintaining that the
only way in which we can hold the truth on this point is paradoxically, or by the belief of two extreme opinions so stated as
to be made irreconcilable with each other.

The doctrine of original sin as the basis of predestinarian
views forms the next subject of consideration, and the argument
for irresistible grace, and for a dispensation independent of man's
will for its results, is stated.   On this subject great stress is laid
upon the necessity for a difference between the dispensation
under which man fell and that by which he is to be restored.
This is an argument of great force, but not much to the point,
as between the maintainers of an absolute predestination and
their opponents.   All may admit the necessity for a wide differ-

---

[d] p. 3, l. 11.   [e] p. 3, l. 18.

ence between a system under which man forfeited God's favour and one by which he is to regain it. This is not the point at issue. The question is, whether the difference between the systems is such that man was left entirely in the one to his own unaided powers, to stand or fall simply in his own strength; while, by the other, his own strength and will are entirely superseded. Was Adam the sole agent in his state of probation? Is God virtually the sole agent in the salvation of those who are under the covenant of grace? These are the points of contrast between the Adamic and Christian dispensations upon which absolute predestinarians naturally and consistently rest their views and their arguments, and to these alone Mr. Mozley directs his attention. This however is altogether a one-sided aspect. If we admit that the difference between the two dispensations is exclusively one which has reference to their relation to man's strength and will, then the doctrine of irresistible grace naturally if not inevitably follows. There are however other admitted points of contrast, and, in proportion to the number and importance of the other differences between the Adamic and Christian covenants, is the necessity for so total a disparity in reference to man's will destitute of foundation. In illustrating this statement we will endeavour to make the subject as popular as possible, and will avail ourselves of the simile adopted by Mr. Mozley:—

"Suppose a man carried away by a torrent, to master which he has proved himself unequal, would it be a reasonable or consistent act to take him out only to recruit his strength for a second resistance to it? So, after man in the exercise of freewill has fallen and lost freewill, is it not a mockery to save him by giving him freewill again? What will he do with the gift but fall again? On such a mode of divine dealing, the fall may be repeated indefinitely, and the divine purposes for the salvation of man may remain in perpetual suspense, and never attain completion." —p. 6.

Now, as an illustration of the respective positions of men under the Adamic and Christian dispensations, this seems a very imperfect and partial statement. In the first place it exhibits that confusion of power and will which is so prevalent an error of the absolute school. It supposes that Adam fell, not through a defect of will, but of power, and that he " was carried away by a torrent to master which he was " not unwilling but " unequal." This erroneous view is then farther supported by supposing, that the only alternative of an absolute and irresistible grace, virtually superseding man's power of origination and even agency, is an amount of gracious assistance which would place him in a position of no greater advantage than what Adam enjoyed. Let us suppose, however, that instead of merely re-cruiting the strength of a man who had been carried away by a torrent, we were, after due refreshment of his wearied body, to provide him with an iron-pointed staff, with which he might stay his steps, and which would enable him to bring his bodily powers more largely into action, would he not be more favour-ably circumstanced than before, although his own exertions would be equally necessary? Or, if it were desirable to afford him still greater facilities, a rope might be thrown to him with promises of assistance if he would only lay hold of it; or, he might be still more effectually assisted, by requiring him not to depend entirely on a continued exertion in holding the rope, but to tie it around his middle, in order that he might, when wearied, pause, and recover his strength, without incurring the danger of being carried away in the interval. All these additions to our author's illustration are so many varieties of a doctrine of grace, each giving to man effectual assistance, without super-seding or even interfering with his power of will; and they are all intermediate positions between a state in which man is left entirely to his own unaided strength and one in which his own exertions are entirely superseded as a necessary element of his success.

But this is not the only defect of this description. It prac-tically ignores other points of contrast between Adam's condi-tion and that of Christian believers.*f* If the sole and entire disparity between the two covenants consisted in the measure of strength and assistance respectively vouchsafed, there would be strong reasons for magnifying the difference in this one respect; but, in proportion as the other discrepancies are numerous and important, the necessity for a wide difference in any particular one is diminished. This truth may be embodied in the illustra-tion already referred to. If the man struggling against the torrent had in prospect a rich reward if he overcame it, and a corresponding loss if he were carried away, this consideration would be an important element in the issue. If, on the one

---

f " A dispensation which left the salvation of man dependent on his will, was highly suitable as a first one; suitable alike to the justice of the Creator and the powers of the untried creature, and such as we should naturally expect at the begin-ning of things; but such having been the nature of the first, the second must, for that very reason, be a dispensation of a different kind, effecting its design not by a conditional, but by an absolute saving act."—*Augustinian Predestination*, p. 6., l. 27.

" Moreover, it has been always held that man had grace in addition to free-will, even under the first covenant. Then in what are the two opposed, except in the nature, quality, and power of that grace which they respectively confer, that in the one grace was, and in the other is not, dependent on any original motion of the will for its effect."—*Ibid.*, p. 10, l. 24.

hand, as in Adam's case, a single failure precluded all future trial; and if, as in that of the Christian, repeated trials are vouchsafed, this difference alone would place the latter in a vastly more favourable position. If, in addition to this, Adam's probation was interminable; (and there is no intimation in Scripture of its period), and the Christian's probation is comparatively limited, while renewed trials are not only permitted but encouraged; this variety alone, without any difference in the communication of encreased and continued strength, would be sufficient to constitute a very wide contrast. Fresh and continually renewed exertion on man's part, and gracious and supernatural aids on God's part, are both of them elements of the superiority of the Christian over the Adamic dispensation. The Pelagian may ignore one; the Augustinian may ignore the other; but both of them, in so doing, prove that they are partial and one-sided in their representations. St. Paul, in the fifth chapter of his Epistle to the Romans, gives us an inspired statement of the contrasts between the two covenants; and, while he directs our attention to gracious aids, as well as to renewed efforts supported by renewed forgiveness, the latter is evidently the predominant feature of distinction. A ruin resulting from one offence is the great distinguishing feature which is contrasted with a salvation resulting from the forgiveness of multiplied transgressions; and those who maintain that Adam himself had gracious aids, while they cannot find a shadow of ground for asserting that he enjoyed any corresponding forgiveness for actual offences, practically and virtually admit, that the forgiveness purchased by Christ, but of which there is no trace in the covenant with Adam, must be the principal point of difference between the two dispensations. The conclusion, that "the Gospel aid to salvation" if fundamentally different, is different in the way which is mentioned in the treatise on *Augustinian Predestination,* that is, in its reference to the internal aids afforded to man's will and strength, is not only built on insufficient grounds, but, if it means that this is the exclusive, or even principal fundamental difference, it is in direct opposition to the language of St. Paul, both in Rom. v., which makes the forgiveness of many sins, in opposition to the punishment of one offence, the principal fundamental discrepancy, and in Rom. vi., where the prospect of future mercy as well as the sense of past forgiveness is brought forward as the great motive to an interminable resistance of sin.

The argument for the consistency of an arbitrary selection with God's moral government is one of the points next discussed, and is thus expressed—

" The doctrine of predestination being thus reduced, as its essence or distinctive part, to an absolute saving act on the part of God of which man is the subject, we 'have next to consider the particular nature and character of this act. The doctrine of predestination, then, while it represents God as deciding arbitrarily whom he saves and whom he leaves for punishment, does not by any means alter the conditions on which these respective ends are awarded. His government still continues moral —pledged to the reward of virtue and punishment of vice. It follows that in ordaining those whom he does ordain to eternal life, God decrees also that they should possess the qualifications necessary for that state— those of virtue and piety."—p. 8.

This is an evasion, and not a very acute evasion of the difficulty. No one except a thorough Antinomian ever imagined that God would receive to heaven persons destitute of that holiness without which no man shall see the Lord. The question is not of God's regard for morality in the case of persons actually saved, but of the possibility of reconciling with his wisdom, his distinguishing where there is no shadow of difference ; with his consistency, his dealing with persons, equally the creatures of his hand, and in every respect in the same condition, so differently, that he absolutely decrees the one to eternal happiness, and the other to eternal misery. The question is of the possibility of harmonizing with God's mercy, his withholding from any creature those aids which, depending entirely on his own will, would be as efficacious in every case, as in those in which they are vouchsafed, and which might have been vouchsafed in every case without in any way prejudicing God's justice or his moral government. To vindicate God's moral government in any other aspect, and by attaching to a selection of individuals absolutely and arbitrarily made, qualifications as absolutely and irresistibly bestowed, is mere trifling.

The narrowness of the field on which so momentous a doctrine as that of absolute and arbitrary predestination has been built, must have struck more than one thoughtful mind ; and it has not escaped Mr. Mozley's notice ; but from the weakness in this respect assistance is sought, by attempting to identify the doctrine of absolute predestination with the doctrine of grace, and thus to enlist in its support the whole of those passages in which reference is made to the gracious assistances vouchsafed under the covenant of mercy.

" The mode in which the doctrine of predestination is extracted from the doctrine of original sin being thus shewn, it may be added that by thus reducing, as we have done, the former doctrine to its pith and substance, we evidently much widen the Scripture argument for it, extending it at once from those few and scattered passages where the word itself occurs to a whole field of language. The whole Scripture doctrine of grace is now appealed to as being in substance the doctrine of predestination, because there is only the divine foreknowledge to be added to it in order to make it such."—p. 9.

For an absolute predestination an irresistible grace is necessary; for a predestination depending in any way on man's will, as to who shall be its subjects, a proportionately modified doctrine of grace is all that is required. To say therefore that the doctrine of predestination may appeal to the whole Scripture doctrine of grace is nothing to the point, so far as the different views of predestination are concerned. The absolute and arbitrary predestinarian holds an absolute, arbitrary, and irresistible doctrine of grace; the person who advocates a predestination, the personal issues of which depend on man's will, holds a corresponding doctrine of grace. Both appeal to Scripture for their views of predestination, and both appeal to Scripture for their doctrines on the point of grace. To identify predestination and grace does not therefore, in any degree, promote a solution of the difficulty, nor does it afford an exclusive ground or even any measure of advantage either to the Augustinian on one side, or to the Arminian on the other. Predestination may be said to be "no more than the gospel doctrine of grace with the addition of the divine foreknowledge," but this is as applicable to the Arminian as to the Augustinian doctrine. The question remains, does the foreknowledge take cognizance of man's acceptance or rejection of grace, and thus, in conjunction with grace accepted, become predestination; or is God's foreknowledge, an absolute foreknowledge of individuals whom he has absolutely decreed to save?

We have thus examined the first chapter to enable our readers to judge of the amount of depth of thought and closeness of reasoning which have been brought to bear upon the subject. The grave defects on these points which have been pointed out afford little promise we fear of the present book exhausting the subject, or placing it in any respect on new or more satisfactory ground. We now proceed to point out the great object of the work, and the nature of the argument adduced to promote it. The object is to promote peace on latitudinarian principles, to urge the opposite parties to agree to differ, not only on the doctrine of predestination but on those other doctrines which are so intimately connected with it, as for instance, that of baptismal regeneration.

"A slight consideration will be enough to shew how intimately this doctrine is connected with the general doctrine of grace; and that one who holds an extreme, and one who holds a modified doctrine of grace in general, cannot hold the doctrine of baptismal regeneration in the same sense. If a latitude of opinion, then, may be allowed on the general question, it seems to follow that an equal latitude may be allowed on this further and more particular one; and that if an extreme predestinarian, and a maintainer of freewill can maintain and teach their respective doctrines within the same communion, they need not exclude each other when they come to give their respective doctrines their necessary and legitimate application in a particular case. I cannot therefore but think, that further reflection will, on this and other questions, modify the opposition of the two parties in our Church to each other, and shew that their disagreement is not so great as in the heat of controversy they supposed it to be."— p. 342.

The arguments by which our author advocates this manner of reconciliation are, that the question of predestination is one " which can never be settled absolutely in the present state of our capacities," that it is one which can only be held paradoxically or by maintaining each of two extreme truths, which are supposed to be irreconcilable with one another.

The desire to promote doctrinal peace by exertions proportioned to its inestimable value, and by means consistent with its heavenly character is one thing, the attempt to secure it by an indolent retractation of the eager, and intense, and continued pursuit by which alone it can be hoped to be attained, and by the sacrifice of truth and consistency is another. To allay the heat of religious controversy is a necessary step, not only to the attainment of peace, but to the successful pursuit of truth. But heat and animosity are not essential elements of the discussion of even fundamental religious doctrines, but the adventitious accretions of human infirmity, ebullitions of that wrath of man which worketh not the righteousness of God. While therefore we would appreciate at its full value the desire to promote peace, exhibited in the treatise on *Augustinian Predestination*, we entirely dissent from the means adopted, and deny the validity of the argument adduced.

The following is one of those passages in the treatise which while they exhibit a philosophical aspect are defective in its most valuable requisite, a nice discrimination.

"Predestination comes before us in Scripture as a feeling or impression upon the mind of the individual. All conscious power, strength, or energy, when combined with a particular aim, tend to create the sense of a destiny—an effect with which we are familiar in the case of many remarkable persons. A man who feels in himself the presence of great faculties which he applies to the attainment of some great object, not unnaturally interprets the very greatness of these faculties as a providential call to such an application of them, and a pledge and earnest of a successful issue. Thus, in proportion to the very strength and energy of his own will, he regards himself as but a messenger from, an instrument of, a Higher Power; he sees in himself but a derived agency, an impulse from without.   It seems necessary that he should refer those extraordinary forces, which he feels working within him, to some source beyond the confines of his own narrow existence, and connect them with the action of the invisible Supreme Power in the universe.   He is in a sense, in which other persons are not, a mystery to himself; and to account for so much power in so small and frail a being, he refers it to the unknown world in which reside the causes of all the great operations of nature. This is the way in which he expresses his own sense and consciousness of remarkable powers; he would have regarded an ordinary amount of power as his own, but because he has so much more, he alienates it, and transfers it to a source beyond himself.   Thus heroes and conquerors in heathen times have sometimes even imagined themselves to be emanations from the Deity.   But a common result has been the idea of a destiny, which they have had to fulfil.   And this idea of a destiny once embraced, as it is the natural effect of the sense of power, so in its turn adds greatly to it. The person as soon as he regards himself as predestined to achieve some great object, acts with so much greater force and constancy for the attainment of it; he is not divided by doubts, or weakened by scruples or fears; he believes fully that he shall succeed, and that belief is the greatest assistance to success.   The idea of a destiny in a considerable degree fulfils itself.

"The idea of destiny then, naturally arising out of a sense of power, it must be observed that this is true of the moral and spiritual, as well as of the natural man, and applies to religious aims and purposes, as well as to those connected with human glory." . . . . "And it is evident that one whole side of Scripture encourages Christians in this idea."—pp. 40—42.

In this passage the author manages either intentionally or unconsciously to blend and confuse two very different and distinct principles.   A strong hope or even assurance of the attainment of a *definite* object grounded upon a conviction of the possession of adequate and well-known means, is very different from that vague, and indefinite notion of a destiny, which has occupied the minds of many men in all ages.   The one is the hope of the Christian, the other the prospect of the ambitious and imaginative dreamer.   The godly consideration of predestination is a strong trust or assurance of an appointed end, resting on a well grounded calculation of the means placed at the disposal of him who entertains it.   It is the common property of all true believers, and is offered to all who profess the name of Christ.   The end in view is clearly known, the means to its attainment are distinctly realized; and both means and ends are such that they may be realized by thousands and millions, without in any way prejudicing individual expectations.   The sense of destiny which Mr. Mozley confounds with this principle is the very reverse in all these prominent and essential characteristics.   Its object is enveloped in the mists of an unknown futurity, and the destiny of the individual can only be known by its actual fulfilment. He may turn out a sage, a lawgiver, or a conqueror; but, whatever his destiny, it is peculiar : it depends, for its very existence, on a distinction from those by whom he is surrounded. Whatever the nature of his destiny he must be one among millions, among thousands, or at least among hundreds, or else his expectation of a destiny is frustrated. The two principles which are thus confounded in the passage above quoted are as different as day is from night. No Christian believer whose earnest hope or humble assurance is grounded on a conviction of the sufficiency of the power, wisdom, and goodness, engaged in his behalf, and on a sober estimate of his own determination to cleave to God, ever has been, or ever can be disappointed of his expectations; thousands and tens of thousands could be found, not only among the aspirants for heroic honours in ancient times, but among the astrologer-mongers of the middle ages, and the novel readers of the present day, who have cherished a sense of destiny which has proved a delusion and a dream. Two of the most objectionable features of absolute and arbitrary predestination are, that, like the heathen sense of destiny, it rests on preferential grounds,*⁹* and that it can be known only by its actual fulfilment. True scriptural predestination grounds its thankfulness in the greatness of the blessedness placed within its reach, on the rich, and abundant, and overflowing sufficiency of the means of obtaining that blessedness, on the innumerable hosts who shall participate in the enjoyment of it, on the conviction that its enjoyment is increased, instead of being diminished, in proportion to the number of participants. The objectionable doctrine on the contrary seems to rest its thankfulness, not on the absolute blessedness of its inheritance, but on the complacency of being the favourite of a partial heavenly parent. Its trust rests, not so much on an intelligent and deep penetration of the all sufficiency of the means provided by a God of infinite power, wisdom, and goodness, but on a comparatively self-willed and capricious appropriation of a correspondingly capricious but absolute promise of eventual success, which throws all intermediate agencies and instrumentalities into the back ground, as mere shadows and not realities. Heaven's anthems delight not from their intrinsic harmony but from their contrasts with the discords of hell; the note

---

⁹ The perfect type of such a doctrine of destiny would be one who could add to the absolute blessedness of an eternal weight of glory the heightening consideration, that he alone had been plucked as a brand from the burning, that, like the heathen hero or conqueror, he was not only one of thousands, but that none but himself could be his parallel.

of heaven's most extatic strain is not that, in which the full chorus of innumerable hosts, like the voice of many waters swells upon the ear, but that which is mixed with the distant wails of those who have been arbitrarily and capriciously excluded for ever from its precincts.

The artifice or error, conscious or unconscious, by which the amalgamation of two principles so widely different is attempted, consists in blending a sense of destiny, dependent for its existence on preferential grounds, with one which is altogether independent of any such consideration. The notion of destiny is one which can only be entertained by "remarkable persons." It is built on a belief that they possess powers beyond what are enjoyed by those around them. It is a "sense and consciousness of remarkable powers," of more than "an ordinary amount of power," of an amount of power so far beyond the ordinary, that the possessor is compelled to ascribe it to some other source, as proving him in some cases to be an "emanation from the Deity," and as "destining him to achieve some great object." How this definition of destiny can be reconciled with the subsequent declaration that such a sense of destiny "need not be confined to remarkable and eminent Christians," is more perhaps than any of our readers will be able to point out, and we think that they will conclude with us that the author has commenced with a description of one subject and ended by substituting its contrast.

The statements already referred to in reference to the fundamental difference between the Adamic and Christian dispensations, which was maintained to consist in the different position in which man's will was placed under the respective covenants, may serve as another example of inconsistency. The difference in the relation of man's will is described as the *fundamental* difference between the two dispensations, and yet the differences between those who hold that man's salvation is the result of an absolute and irresistible act of grace, and those who maintain that his own acceptance or rejection of Divine aid is the turning point in the issue, do not appear to be sufficient to justify either party in supposing, that it *differs* from the other *fundamentally*. We believe with Mr. Mozley that these differences are not such as should interfere with Christian fellowship, but we do believe it because we also believe, in the first instance, that, in his anxiety to uphold the Augustinian doctrine at a weak point, he has unduly magnified one difference between the Adamic and Christian dispensations, and merged what St. Paul describes as their great distinguishing characteristic. The prominent fundamental point is not the different relation of man's will to his salvation, but the provision of a Saviour, through whom not only aid and strength, but forgiveness for failures past is vouchsafed, and mercy for future—and morally speaking unavoidable—short-comings is hoped for and expected.

To notice all the similar inconsistencies *seriatim* would occupy much more time and space than can be given in an article in a review, and we must therefore satisfy ourselves at present with pointing out the defects of the work on *Augustinian Predestination* in its large features. It takes as its groundwork the theory of indistinct ideas. These the author designates by a new name, rather opposed to their indefinite nature. "A half conception," though imperfect, is very definite in its limitation, and, when it has been associated with the other half, the point at which the two parts meet is very distinctly pointed out; and the whole conception becomes complete and perfect. Admitting that there are vague and indistinct conceptions which, from the nature of the subject, must ever remain such to the human mind, this does not prove that the human will or divine power are among them. Granting that there are in theology para-doxical truths, does it follow that predestination and the pre-sence of both human will and divine agency in the work of salvation are of the number? If we concede to the author of *Augustinian Predestination* all that he manages by a confusion of terms, and by other similar artifices to assume, his conclu-sions might perchance follow, although even this is doubtful. But we altogether disclaim, for reasons which we have already given, the want of discrimination which confuses a real power of origination with effects strictly so called ; we deny the assertion that "nothing short of a characteristic of will which comes into collision with our ideas of the divine power meets the demands of our consciousness;" and we repudiate, not only as rash, but as dishonourable to God and to his word, the statements that—

"Some truths of religion cannot be stated without contradiction to other truths, of which reason or the same revelation informs us, and therefore cannot be stated positively and absolutely, without becoming in the very act of statement *false.*"

With respect to the combination of human will and divine agency in the work of salvation, we also maintain that the language of Scripture is contradictory only to those who hold either of the opposite extremes ; and that our author's proposed remedy, of holding both extremes at once, instead of a middle position in which they meet, instead of obviating only doubles the supposed amount of contradiction. So far as that Augean sub-ject, the question of the human will, is concerned, the treatise on *Augustinian Predestination* has left it where it found it, and the author, in common with many others, who are not strangers to Edwards's unanswered work, has thought proper to ignore that section of Edwards's book which meets and qualifies the argument from consciousness, on which all the conclusions in the Augustinian treatise rest, on this point, for support. Had the author satisfied himself with endeavouring to foster and confirm that spirit of moderation on the predestinarian controversy, which we are happy to believe now prevails, and which affords such strong encouragement to bring forward any approximations to a more satisfactory elucidation of the difficulties with which it is beset, he would have done the church good service. But he has not satisfied himself with this; he has gone much farther, and, in so doing, he seems to have exceeded his province.

A treatise which maintains that the question which it discusses is incapable of being absolutely settled in the present state of human capacities, shelters itself, by such a statement, from many of the consequences which it might incur if it proposed to solve the question. Of this statement it is but fair to give the treatise all the benefit, and we think it may be shewn that it requires it. All that has been or can be proved by any person in reference to the solution of a question like that of predestination, is, that it has not yet been satisfactorily settled by any proposed theory or train of arguments. The nature of the subject may be such as to suggest strong presentiments *à priori* of its being beyond human grasp; or, it may have baffled the human intellect in so many instances as to render the prospect of its future adjustment chimerical; but presentiments are not proofs, and no number of failures however great absolutely precludes the possibility of ultimate success. If those who maintain that the question is incapable of adjustment can be shewn to have failed in depth of thought, in logical consistency, in impartiality, or in the extent of their acquaintance with all the theories and arguments which have been proposed, then little dependence can be placed on their conclusions. While the Augustinian treatise exhibits, in many places, indications of a very high order of intellectual power, we do not think that the predestinarian question is one for which that power is either of adequate strength or particularly adapted. The work is written in a philosophical spirit, but it frequently betrays a serious deficiency in the first principle of true philosophizing, " *Bene distinguere est bene philosophari.*" Many of its arguments are well stated, but there is frequently a change of terms in its process of reasoning, and much consequent confusion, and sometimes contradiction; and it confines its attention in a great measure to the two long established, opposite, and extreme theories, over-looking those which are intermediate, and which have in their favour the motto, that truth lies between extremes. It must however be confessed that the treatise on *Augustinian Predestination* possesses a certain kind of impartiality; but it is of a character so peculiar that it is not likely to commend itself to either of the conflicting parties in the controversy, or to the church at large. It is the impartiality of a capricious and arbitrary judge, who treats two contending parties with equal injustice at one time, and equal favour at another.

It is doubtful whether Mr. Mozley's tenderness for some of the weakest points of supralapsarian doctrine, and his vague and general charges of subtlety and evasiveness against all interpreters who do not take the Augustinian view of those passages of Scripture which bear upon the subject, will be regarded as an equivalent for his designating the Augustinian as an "aspect of Christian truth which simply erred in a pardonable obliquity," and "a cherished error of the minor and pardonable class." And neither Augustinians nor the Church of England at large will feel disposed to have the admiration of her judgment on this point to rest upon such statements as would insinuate, that our formularies and 17th article merely tolerate predestinarianism as a pardonable obliquity. To speak of "allowing a place" for a doctrine which is, in the same work in which this expression occurs, declared to have, not only some scattered passages which cannot be otherwise interpreted without evasiveness in its favour, but to be supported by "the whole Scripture doctrine of grace" seems to us an extraordinary and inexplicable proceeding. While we would accord to it the credit of good intentions, and of much thought upon the subject, we regard the present work as a failure, so far as it professes to place the question upon more satisfactory ground, or to exercise a powerful influence upon the Christian mind. To prove to contending parties, unduly confident of the exclusive correctness of their own views, and of the total erroneousness of those of their opponents, that there is much to be said upon both sides of an agitated question, is one thing; to profess to prove that the question is one which never can be satisfactorily solved is another. Every element of persuasion and argument which can be employed to moderate the heat and animosity of theological controversy, and to induce Christian men to examine the points at issue between them in that spirit of calm, peaceful, and dispassionate enquiry, so becoming a lover of truth, is of inestimable value, because it invites mutual conference and explanation. The attempt to prove that a controversy is not only incapable of satisfactory solution, but that the doctrine to which it refers contains within it, as its essential elements, conflicting and inconsistent statements, is however a very different undertaking. Such a position is calculated to exercise an influence of the very opposite character, and to discourage all investigation of a subject thus admitted to be more than difficult, because absolutely contradictory.

Having thus examined Mr. Mozley's work in its general bearing upon the predestinarian question, we proceed briefly to notice it as professing "to give an account of St. Augustine's doctrine on the point, together with such comments as may be necessary for a due examination of, and judgment upon it." The treatise of Augustinian doctrine regards St. Augustine's views, as the result of a philosophical and rigid series of inferences from the supremacy and irresistibility of the divine power. In this conclusion, Mr. Mozley differs from many whose opinion is entitled to some weight, and who regard St. Augustine's extreme statements as partly the result of the circumstances of his personal conversion, but still more largely of the pressure of Pelagian opponents. It is however comparatively of small importance whether St. Augustine arrived at his conclusions in a philosophical spirit, and by a strictly logical and close train of reasoning, or whether his latter statements were influenced partly by his personal experience, and still more largely by a desire to combat with greater success the errors of Pelagius; and we will therefore content ourselves with stating, that there are strong reasons to believe that the latter was the true process, and that Vossius, and those who agree with him, may be proved to be justified in saying, "Moreover, Augustine, that he might press Pelagius harder, added to the common opinion of the fathers, and that defended by himself while a bishop, this appendix, 'that grace was offered to one in preference to another, and was more efficacious in one than in another owing to an absolute decree of God.'"[h]

What we are more anxious to examine in connexion with this treatise is, whether it has given a correct and discriminating view of what St. Augustine's doctrine really was, whether it has pointed out the lights and shades with a nicety and precision in any way superior to that of those who had previously handled the subject. We question whether it has done so, and we support our challenge on the ground that the author of the Augustinian treatise has followed the common track of those who have preceded him, in a gross error, that he has failed in discrimina-

---

[h] Voss. *Hist. Pel.*, lib. vi., Thes. x.

tion on what is the very essence of the controversy, and that he has in doing so done injustice to the father whose doctrine he professes to elucidate.

The great point at issue is, whether God's election and pre-destination are arbitrary and capricious, or not; and Mr. Mozley assumes throughout his work, and that without hesitation, that St. Augustine's doctrine was that of an arbitrary and capricious predestination. Let us then hear what St. Augustine says on the point. Speaking of his conversion, that event which, as of the greatest personal interest, is so likely to tinge all a man's views of Christian truth with its own peculiar colouring, he says,

"Did you despise the tears of her who sought from you neither gold, nor silver, nor any changeable good, but the salvation of the soul of her son? By no means, O Lord, but you were indeed present, and effected it *in the order* in which you had predestined it to be done."[i]

Even when he speaks of God's will in the most absolute terms, and of predestination as the absolute result of that will, he not only does not exclude from the guidance of God's will those attributes of justice and wisdom on which all order and law and distinction of things that differ rest, but his language is such as most emphatically disclaims any such separation. He guards even in his strongest statements against the imagination of there being any respect of persons with God, any shadow of injustice or of want of wisdom in his judgments. It is "the just and merciful God who prepares those whom he foreknows, not from respect of persons, but in the irreproachable judgment of his equity."[j] The will of God is exercised according to law, and justice, and wisdom, and there is in predestination itself a law and order of proceeding. Now the exercise of strict justice and perfect wisdom, and their development of general laws of dealing, and of perfect order and arrangement, according to which all God's dealings and judgments, even the most inscrutable, are guided, are altogether inconsistent with an arbitrary and capri-cious dispensation. Justice and wisdom, law and order, and arrangement, are all elements of a systematic dispensation. And a systematic dispensation is unjustly designated as either arbitrary or capricious.

In a treatise entitled, *On the Augustinian Doctrine of Pre-destination*, it was reasonable to hope for a clear discrimination of St. Augustine's views, and full and satisfactory proofs of what the author maintains to have been St. Augustine's doc-trine. But in both these points the treatise has failed. The author has fallen into the common error of imagining, that,

---

i *Confess.*, lib. v., c. ix.   j *Contra Pel. Hyp.*, lib. vi.

because St. Augustine maintained an "inscrutable predestination" and an "occult justice," he consequently *held* that God's predestination was inscrutable and his justice *occult*, because they were arbitrary and capricious in their character. Now this by no means follows. It may be proved that direct individual and absolute decrees are entirely inconsistent with predestination according to any law whatever, and that St. Augustine in holding the former could not consistently hold the latter also; but that St. Augustine directly maintained an arbitrary, capricious predestination, Mr. Mozley has not proved, although he without hesitation or qualification continually applies those epithets to St. Augustine's doctrine.

We now proceed to bring forward some remarks on the subject both of the combination of human will with divine agency in the work of salvation, and in the collateral question of predestination, which will, we trust, be found not altogether uninteresting to the general reader, nor altogether beneath the notice and consideration of persons who, like Mr. Mozley, profess to prove that the subject has not only been met by no theory, but that it is incapable of being so settled. The principles which it advocates are to be found in a work published in 1854,[k] and therefore, some months before the treatise *on Augustinian Predestination* made its appearance.

It appears to us, that most of those who have hitherto written on the controversy have either missed altogether, or not attached sufficient importance to the great source and subject of dispute. The great question is, Does God in the work of salvation deal with men through laws, and by fixed principles, or does he act without law or fixed principle of any kind, that is to say capriciously? Those who suppose that God terminates his dealings to individuals simply as such, and without any regard to classification, maintain, by virtue of such a supposition, that God does not in the kingdom of grace guide himself by any laws or principles whatever; for a relation to many is defined by the most eminent authorities on jurisprudence to be of the very essence of law; principles of treatment inevitably lead to classifications of subjects. If it be admitted, that a relation to many is of the essence of law, and that principles of treatment involve classifications, truths which we think no person will venture to deny, we are prepared to shew upon these simple and concise data, which are not, we trust, open to the charge of being "fine trains

---

k *The Doctrine of Scriptural Predestination, briefly stated and considered in its tendency to promote Unity, and in contrast with the theories which have been substituted for it. With some remarks on the Baptismal Question.* Bagster and Sons, London; J. H. Parker, Oxford.

of inferences or endless distinctions spun out in succession," that those who maintain an absolute, individual, and direct predestination, not guided by law and fixed principles, in so doing have no alternative but an arbitrary and capricious election—that those who invariably assert such a doctrine are *Augustino multum Augustiniores*, and that, if St. Augustine at any time has done so, he has propounded a doctrine altogether at variance, both with particular statements at other times, and with first principles of the highest order which he has himself unhesitatingly admitted.

As to the first proposition there seems little difficulty. Salvation may depend upon one or many of innumerable laws or principles within the divine choice; but, between a dispensation proceeding by law and by fixed principles, and one guided by no law or fixed principle, and, therefore, both arbitrary and capricious, there seems to be no alternative.

The second proposition may be very promptly disposed of. Whatever St. Augustine may have said under the pressure of controversy with Pelagian opponents, he was far from invariably maintaining an election or predestination apart from law or fixed principle. He frequently maintained that the reasons of God's selection of one and rejection of another were inscrutable, and his indiscriminating followers and admirers have concluded that in so doing he left no alternative but a capricious and arbitrary election, because they were unable to distinguish things that differ. Now the dealings of God may be inscrutable and his justice may be an "occult justice" from various causes. God's judgments may be absolutely and entirely inscrutable, because the principles on which God acts are so completely hidden from our view or opposed to our conceptions that we cannot form the most distant idea of what those principles are. Justice, wisdom, and goodness in God may be so opposed to, and different from our notions of these attributes, that we have no clue to guide us to any conception of them as they really exist in him. Of such an imagination, a predestination and election to the principles of which we have no guide is the natural correlative. But God's dealings may be inscrutable from reasons which do not in anywise conflict with our belief, that the divine justice, wisdom, and goodness, though in their fulness infinitely transcending our conceptions, are similar in character to what we designate by these names. They may be inscrutable because, although the principles upon which they proceed are well known, God's dealings are so extensive and complicated that man is completely lost in the expanse. The kingdom of grace may be guided by principles as rigidly fixed and by laws as universally prevalent as the kingdom of nature, and it may be impossible to tell the reasons of the particular moral complexion of each moral and intelligent unit, for the very same reason that it would be impossible for any man to analyze all the minute details which have exercised an influence, through successive reproductions from the day of the first generation of its primitive parent, and all the variations of sunshine, and shade, and moisture, and warmth, which have combined in giving to any one oak-leaf its particular size, shape, and shade.[i]

An inscrutable election and predestination are not therefore by any means necessarily an arbitrary one, but is as consistent with the most general laws and the most invariable principles of action on God's part as with an entirely capricious mode of dealing.

Whether St. Augustine has, in any passage, directly or indirectly asserted that God's dealings on the salvation of one man and the rejection of another are inscrutable, because they proceed upon no law or fixed principle, or upon laws and principles altogether unknown or opposed to our conceptions, we will not undertake to say; but we believe that we will be fully born out in maintaining that he generally at least declines or hesitates to qualify the inscrutability in such a way as to lead to this conclusion. So far is he however from invariably if ever directly maintaining a predestination, apart from law and fixed principle, that, while he declines to trace that himself, he does not forbid others from investigating its operative principle even in individual cases; and, in one instance at least, he admits the possibility of its being traced out and comprehended by man.[m]

We now come to the last proposition to be proved, namely, that if St. Augustine has in any instance propounded an election apart from law and fixed principle, such a theory is at variance both with other particular statements and with principles of the first and highest order which he has laid down as of universal

---

[i] Ordinem rerum Zenobi consequi ac tenere cuique proprium, tum vero universitatis quo coercitur ac regitur hic mundus vel videre vel pandere dificillimum hominibus atque rarissimum est. (*De Ord.*, lib. i., c. i.) Quia sicut ipsi mali homines in terrâ, sic etiam illi non omnia, quæ volunt facere possunt, nisi quantum illius ordinatione sinuntur cujus *plene judicia* nemo comprehendit, juste nemo reprehendit. *De Civ. Dei*, c. xxiii. See also following note.

[m] Hæc autem vocatio quæ sive in singulis hominibus, sive in populis atque in ipso genere humano per temporum opportunitates operatur, altæ et profundæ ordinationis est, et comprehendi non potest, ni forte ab eis qui diligunt Deum ex toto corde, et ex tota anima, et ex tota mente sua, et diligunt proximos sicut ipsos. Tanta enim charitate fundati possunt jam fortasse cum sanctis comprehendere longitudinem, latitudinem, altitudinem, et profundum. Illud tamen constantissima fide retinendum, neque quicquam Deum injustè facere, neque ullam esse naturam quæ non Deo debeat quod est."—*Octoquitatrium Quæst. Lib.*

application. The particular statements are familiar to all who have studied the question, and we therefore proceed to point out the general principles to which we refer. Not only does he maintain that all things are governed by eternal and immutable laws," but he admits, that by a knowledge and inspection of these laws men may partially comprehend God's judgments and angels may foresee future events.º Again, order is the arrangement of *equal* and *unequal things*, assigning to each its place,ᵖ and order so rules the universe as to embrace all things without exception.ᵠ Now such a definition of universal order cannot be reconciled with a procedure in so important a province as the salvation of mankind, by which thousands who are absolutely equal and intrinsically undistinguishable are so differently disposed of, that some are carried to the highest pinnacle of heavenly glory, and others consigned to the lowest depths of perdition. Law and order, as defined by St. Augustine, and admitted by him to be of universal application, are altogether inconsistent with decrees directly terminated to individuals, and with distinctive positions where there is no difference. His statements upon these broad and universal principles warrant us in giving his particular assertions as to God's discrimination between individuals an interpretation which will harmonize with them, where the language permits it; and his declaration that the distinction between individuals depends entirely on God's will, and that the reasons are inscrutable by us, are no proof that he regarded God's will as not proceeding by laws of the most general character, or that his judgments in this respect were inscrutable for any other reason than that the moral events to which these judgments had reference, were of so intricate and complicated a character, embraced so vast an extent of time and space, and such a wide interdependence of human agencies and divine interpositions, as completely to baffle human investigation in their minute details. On the contrary, his statement that the calling of men, whether as individuals or nations, or as a race, was-

---

ⁿ Dicebamus nobis ipsis: Ubi non lex? Ubi non meliori debitum imperium? Ubi non umbra constantiæ? Ubi non modus? *De Ordine*, lib. i., c. ix.

º Aliud autem in æternis atque incommutabilibus Dei legibus, quæ in ejus sapientia vivunt mutationes temporum prævidere, Deique voluntatem quæ tam certissima quam potentissima est, Divini Spiritus ejus participatione cognoscere quod sanctis angelis recta discretione donatum est. *De Civitate Dei*, c. xxii.

ᵖ Ordo est parium dispariumque rerum sua cui loca tribuens dispositio. *Ibid.*, c. xiii.

ᵠ Quid saltem censes, inquam, ordini esse contrarium? Nihil ait ille. Nam quomodo esse contrarium quicquam potest ei rei, quæ totum occupavit, totum obtinuit? *De Ordine*, lib. i., c. vi. Unde enim solet, inquam, oboriri admiratio præter *manifestum* causarum ordinem? Et ille: Præter manifestum, inquit, accipio: nam præter ordinem nihil mihi fieri videtur. *Ibid.*, c. iii.

guided by the opportunities of times and seasons, and was a matter of lofty and profound arrangement *(altæ et profundæ ordinationis)*, naturally suggests an inscrutableness not of the absolute but of the vast and complicated character.

The controversy between the opposite parties on the question of predestination may be summed up under three heads:—I. Does God in grace and predestination proceed by fixed and general laws? II. Are these laws in any measure revealed to man for his guidance? III. If so, what are these laws? If those who call themselves Augustinians will be satisfied to go no further than St. Augustine did, they will admit that in grace and predestination (which is only according to St. Augustine the preparation of grace,) God does proceed by laws. When this has been conceded, the most objectionable feature of the extreme and fatalist doctrine on the subject is struck out, and the *virus* of the controversy is expelled. But St. Augustine not only admits that God proceeds by laws in grace, but he himself lays down six general rules respecting it, thus proving that he believed these laws to have been made known for man's guidance. If his followers, or those who designate themselves such, will be guided by him on this point, the field of controversy will be still farther narrowed. The remaining question, namely, What are these laws in the aspect in which that question points to and defines the ground of distinction between one man and another, would require a separate article for its elucidation; because on this point, not only the Super-Augustinians, but Augustine himself, require to be convicted of that subtle and evasive mode of explanation which would endanger the meaning of all Scripture, and with which Mr. Mozley unhesitatingly charges that interpretation of these passages which bear on the controversy, wherever that interpretation runs counter to the light in which they were viewed by St. Augustine.

We would only observe, at present, that if divine and human agency combine in any measure or degree in the work of salvation, that measure and proportion are as definite as any physical proportions in the natural world can be. Should it be asked, Why then are not that measure and proportion as definitely revealed by God as they are certainly and definitely known to him? we would assign, as a reason, what has appeared to our own mind satisfactory beyond the reach of cavil. If the amounts of human and mediate divine agency, and of direct and immediate divine agency, were exactly the same in every individual case, and in every individual exercise in each case, then it might well be asked why a measure and proportion of such universal application were not definitely described in Scripture. But if, on the other hand, the proportions of human and mediate divine agency, and of immediate or internal divine agency, or of grace in this limited sense, are all but infinitely diversified in their combined operations, then the question is not, "Why were not these proportions revealed?" but, "How could they have been embodied in the word of God?" And the answer is, "Such a revelation is as morally impossible as it would have been utterly useless in man's present state. It could not be vouchsafed without converting that Scripture which contains a general history of God's dealings into a universal biography, embracing the whole series of acts in every man's life, nor without changing a discovery of the general principles of grace into a narration of all its individual and separate exercises. The wisdom and goodness of God have adopted a course of greater simplicity and of corresponding value and usefulness. The relation of human and divine agency is generally stated, and the particular application is left to every individual's own opinion and experience, with a stimulus of the most powerful kind to excite men to humility on the one side, and diligence on the other. While the man who overrates his own strength and disparages God's grace is sure to be made to feel his own weakness and to suffer an enforced humiliation, for his want of voluntary humility; the professor who depreciates the advantages and natural powers with which he has been gifted, and thus accuses God of wishing to reap where he has not sown, will be condemned out of his own mouth. He will perish because he *would* not be saved: his destruction will lie at his own door."[r]

R. K.

MATTHEW ii. 15.

'Εξ Αἰγύπτου ἐκάλεσα τὸν υἱόν μου.

THE quotations in the New Testament from the Old have been a fruitful source of perplexity to those who have devoted themselves to the critical study of the Scriptures, partly on account of the diversity of the manner in which they are made,—some being taken from the Hebrew, others from the Greek; some being

---

r Qui vocatus non venit, sicut non habuit meritum præmii ut vocaretur, sic *inchoat* meritum supplicii, cum vocatus venire neglexerit. Ita erunt duo illa misericordiam et judicium cantabo tibi, Domine. Ad misericordiam pertinet vocatio, ad judicium pertinet supplicium eorum qui venire neglexerint.—*Quæst.*, lib. iv., quæst. lxiii.

given verbatim, others *quoad sensum* merely,—but still more from the difficulty in many cases of determining the purpose for which the citation is adduced.

Of these, not the least embarrassing is the quotation by Matthew, apparently of the second clause of Hosea xi. 1, "Behold the angel of the Lord appeareth to Joseph in a dream, saying, Arise, and take the young child and his mother, and flee into Egypt, and be thou there until I bring thee word: for Herod will seek the young child to destroy him. When he arose he took the young child and his mother by night, and departed into Egypt: and was there until the death of Herod: that it might be fulfilled which was spoken of the Lord by the prophet, saying, 'Out of Egypt have I called my son'" (Matt. ii. 13—15).

Two explanations of this quotation have been attempted; according to some, it is to be referred to the principle of *accommodation* or *allusion*—all that Matthew means to say, being, that the language employed by the prophet to describe a fact in the history of the Israelites might, without impropriety, be applied to a similar event in the history of our Lord, viz., his being brought up out of Egypt; while others consider that the evangelist proceeds upon the ground that the one event was designed to be *typical* of the other, and that the words of the prophet have a *twofold reference*.

To the former of these views, it may be objected,—1st, that it reduces the statement of the evangelist to a paltry play upon the words (for it would be nothing more), alike unsuited to sober narrative, and inconsistent with the gravity and simplicity of the writer's character; and 2ndly, that it is directly at variance with the formal and solemn announcement of the inspired penman, that the event related by him took place "in order that (ἵνα) what was spoken by the Lord through the prophet might be fulfilled." Those, again, who hold the other opinion, find it no easy matter to point out the *rationale* of the alleged typical connexion betwixt the two events, or to shew wherein lies "the moral fitness" (as Bishop Marsh expresses it) of the one to foreshadow the other; and so are compelled to rest the stress of their argument on the formula with which the quotation is introduced. This, however, is scarcely satisfactory, especially as the force of that formula (ἵνα πληρωθῇ, κ.τ.λ.) has been disputed.

It may be worth while, therefore, to look once more at the connexion in which this puzzling citation occurs. Now, upon a careful review of the whole chapter, especially of the verses which we have set down at length, it will, we think, be evident to any one who will use his own eyes, and exercise his own judgment on the case, that Matthew ·*does* not say that the words of the prophet were fulfilled when the infant Saviour was *brought up from Egypt,* but when he was *carried down into Egypt.* Had the former been the intention of the evangelist, it would certainly have answered his purpose much better (whichever of the foregoing theories we adopt) to have deferred his citation until he came in due course to speak of the return from Egypt (see ver. 21), and we may therefore conclude that he would have done so. Instead of this however, he expressly affirms that "Joseph took the young child and his mother, and *departed into* Egypt; and *was there* until the death of Herod, that it might be fulfilled which was spoken, &c.;" words which intimate, one would imagine, distinctly enough, that not only the *descent into Egypt,* but also the *sojourn* there, were the means by which the Scripture was fulfilled.

This observation, at first sight, may appear to remove us farther than ever from the settlement of this *quæstio vexata;* but we venture to think, it will be found to be in reality the key to its solution. Indeed, if the fact alluded to by Hosea was *typical,* the current notion as to Matthew's application of his words assigns far too literal a fulfilment of the type. Typical events and symbolical actions are seldom *identical* with the events or actions which they symbolize, but rather resemble the language of prophecy in dimly shadowing forth what they are intended to teach. The opening verses of the sixty-third chapter of Isaiah in which the question is put, "Who is this that cometh from *Edom,* with dyed garments from Bozrah?" are generally admitted to refer to the Messiah, and yet there is no evidence that our Lord ever was in the *literal* Idumea, nor does any body conceive that this was necessary to the accomplishment of the prediction. Why then should we think of a *literal Egypt* here? For our own part, we believe the words would have been as exactly fulfilled had the infant Saviour been conveyed to Arabia or any other region *where his life would have been safe.*

It is scarcely necessary that we should stop to prove that *Egypt* as well as Edom was one of the Old Testament symbols for *the enemies of God and of his church.* We may, however, refer to Psalm lxxxix. 10 (where "Rahab" in the first parallel answers to "enemies" in the second); Joel iii. 19; Zech. x. 10, 11; xiv. 18, 19; and, inasmuch as the symbols of the old Testament are revived in the Apocalypse, Rev. xi. 8. Such were the sufferings indeed, of Israel in "the land of bondage," that "to bring down into Egypt" seems to have become a sort of proverbial expression for the *infliction of chastisement,* as in Deut. xxviii. 68; while "the bringing up of the Israelites from that country" is the symbol of the *deliverances* which the Lord had yet in store for his people, especially for the spiritual Israel in Messianic times, as in Hos. xii. 9; Is. xi. 15, 16; li. 9—13. *Judea*, then, in the mind of the evangelist was "Egypt" to the youthful Jesus. If to any this appear harsh, we would remind them, that such a mode of speaking is not only common in Scripture, but occurs even in profane authors, as when Livy says—*Capuam Hanibali Cannas fuisse* (xxiii. 45). In particular let it be observed, that in the passage in Revelation above referred to, it is to "the great city where our Lord was crucified" that the appellation in question is given ("which spiritually is called Sodom and Egypt") a circumstance equally in favour of the view for which we are pleading, whether with some of the latest and most eminent commentators, we take the words ("where our Lord was crucified") *literally* as denoting the capital of Judea, or *figuratively;* for if the term "Egypt" could be applied to a place where our Lord was only *virtually* crucified, *much more* might it be said of the place where he *actually* suffered. This is confirmed by the manner in which the sojourn in the land of Ham is limited, viz., by the *death of Herod,*—"and was there until the death of Herod,"—plainly teaching that it was essential to the "fulfilment" spoken of, that the child should be shielded from the fury of the cruel prince who at that time held sway over *Judea*. We do not consider it necessary, in order to complete the analogy, to shew as some have attempted to do, that Israel was a type of Christ, a position which we fear can scarcely be made out. It will not be disputed, however, that that nation besides the symbolical character of its ritual was, both in its polity and history, a type of the true *church of God*.

We must then remember the intimate union between *Christ* and his church, which is such, that not only are they represented under various figures as constituting parts of one whole, but are even referred to under one and the same designation; *e.g.* in Is. xlix., under the title of "Israel" "God's servant" (comp. ver. 1 as quoted in 2 Cor. vi. 1, 2); and in Gal. iii. 16, under the denomination of "Christ," "the seed of Abraham" (comp. ver. 29). But without insisting upon mere *phraseology*, it is sufficient for our present purpose to know, that so close is the union referred to, that whatever affects the one for weal or for woe affects the other (see Matt. xxv. 40, 45; Acts ix. 4, 5). In the case before us, it is easy to see on the one hand, that upon the successful accomplishment of the Redeemer's mission, and therefore on his safety until his hour should come, all the hopes of the church were suspended. On the other hand, it is clear that the enmity of Herod was not and could not be directed against the Saviour *personally* at so tender an age, but *officially*, as him to whom the voices of the prophets and inquiries of Eastern sages pointed as the future "King of the Jews," and whom he consequently regarded as his rival. The blow therefore which he struck was aimed not so much at Christ himself as at his *kingdom*, and therefore at the *church* of which he was to be the Saviour and head. Thus, both in the nature of things, and even with reference to the *animus* of the persecutor, it was the *church* that was imperilled, and the deliverance recorded was therefore an interposition in *behalf of the church*.

In this view it is impossible not to be struck with the appositeness of the quotation, so that Matthew might well have cited the verse entire—"When Israel was a child, then I loved him, and called my son out of Egypt." For when *Herod* slew all the children in Bethlehem and its vicinity from two years old and under, that he might thereby ensure the death of the infant Jesus, and so extinguish the expectations of the nascent *church*, did he not re-enact the part of *Pharaoh*, when that monarch sought to crush the hopes of the youthful *nation* of Israel, by commanding all the males to be destroyed as soon as they were born? Even though we could not trace so close an analogy as that which has been pointed out, there is perhaps enough to justify the assertion of Matthew in the fact already hinted at, that the event described by Hosea, as the most striking manifestation of the power and goodness of God which had occurred in the history of the Israelites, is again and again held up to view in the writings both of Moses and the prophets, as at once the converging point of their gratitude for the past, and a solid ground of confidence for the future, as the *exponent* in short *of a great general principle*, viz., Jehovah's faithfulness to his promises, and care of his chosen people, of which, as it affected the *spiritual* Israel, the incident related by the evangelist was only another and a remarkable example.

But as the evangelist does not say merely that the exode of the Israelites had at length found its counterpart, or that the principle which it involved had met with another illustration, but that *what was spoken by the mouth of Hosea* concerning that event was fulfilled, it still remains to enquire into the intention of the *prophet* in penning the words, or rather of the Holy Spirit in directing him so to write. Shall we say that they contain no more than a mere *historical* allusion such as might have been borrowed from the Pentateuch, or that the passage as it stands in Hosea is *prophetical?* Both suppositions have been maintained with great plausibility; the one, we need scarcely say, by the advocates of the accommodation hypothesis; the other by those who hold that the exode was typical. And it is very difficult to decide in favour of either; for so long as we look only at the *original* source of the citation, we are constrained to agree with Dr. Henderson, when he says—"that these words are a description of what Jehovah had done for Israel ages before the prophet wrote, and not a prophecy of any future event, is so evident, that no person who impartially examines the preceding and following context, can for a moment call it in question;"[a] but while we confine our attention to the language of *Matthew*, in spite of all that has been said of the latitude of the introductory formula, we can scarcely help conceding to Dr. Davidson, that the words " have a twofold reference," or " one sense realized by two events."[b]

In this dilemma, it will not be presumptuous to surmise that perhaps the truth may be found to lie betwixt the two extremes. It is evident, on the one hand, that the New Testament writers had a decided *partiality* for expressing themselves in the language of the Old Testament. Hence Paul in Rom. xi. 4, instead of simply stating that there was a remnant in the days of Elijah who did not worship Baal, quotes the answer to the complaint of the prophet recorded in the first book of Kings; again, in chap. ix., he quotes from the writings of the very *last* of the prophets in reference to a well-known fact in the family history of the *founder* of his nation; and so John xix. 36, in place of saying that the treatment of our Saviour's body was prefigured by the treatment of the paschal lamb, speaks of it as a fulfilling of the language used at the institution of the rite. On the other hand, we can generally if not in every case, discover a *substantial* reason for such reference to the ancient Scriptures. This is especially true of those instances in which Jehovah is himself the speaker, as in the passages which we have adduced. Thus, in connexion with Rom. xi. 4, we must consider that the number of the faithful few was *known to God alone*; chap. ix. 13 relates to the ground of the different treatment of the sons of Isaac, which *only God could explain*; and in John xix. 36 the propriety of the reference is seen by remembering that, if any rite or event was typical, it was so in consequence of *divine appointment*.

Now what has been said of the last example equally applies to the case in hand; for it is " that which was spoken *of the Lord* by the prophet" in reference to a *typical* event, which Matthew says was fulfilled. Then it should be observed that

---

[a] See *Comment.* in loc. cit.
[b] *Sacred Hermeneutics*, p. 490.

"the Scripture" which John appears to quote is nowhere to be found as he expresses it; but that, in point of fact, he turns into *a prophecy* concerning Christ, a *command* given respecting the keeping of the passover (Ex. xii. 46 or Numb. ix. 12).[e]

And if a divine command in relation to the treatment of a typical sacrifice could fairly be taken as equivalent to a prophecy regarding the antitype, why might not an appeal by Jehovah himself to his dealings with the typical Israel, be cited as tantamount to a prediction of what they were intended to foreshadow? This will be the more readily admitted, if we remember that the prophecies of Hosea are addressed throughout to *the typical people*, and therefore have a legitimate applicability to New Testament times, to which there are occasionally more marked and striking allusions, as in chap. ii., ver 15 and following, where the *very same figure* is employed as in the passage in question— "Therefore, behold, I will allure her, and bring her into the wilderness *(q.d.*, out of Egypt) and speak comfortably unto her; and I will give her vineyards from thence (like those of Canaan), and the valley of trouble for a door of hope; and she shall sing there as in the days of her youth, and as in the day when she came up out of the land of Egypt."

If any apology be thought necessary for differing from so many learned and distinguished interpreters as to the circumstance in our Lord's history to which the evangelist refers, we have only to say, that the *origin* of the common opinion is easily accounted for by the coincidence of "Egypt" being mentioned both in the citation and in the narrative, while its *currency* is to be ascribed to the proneness with which all are more or less affected, to follow in the beaten track without inquiry.

Edinburgh.   W. S.

---

[e] We are aware that there is another source which may occur to some, namely, Ps. xxxiv. 20; but a very little reflection will shew that that passage would not have suited the purpose of the evangelist, the language being poetical and *figurative*, as in Psalm li. 8.

ON THE VERB ζωογονέω, AS IT OCCURS IN LUKE xvii. 33, AND ACTS vii. 19.

Luke xvii. 33.—" Whosoever shall seek to save his life shall lose it ; and whosoever shall lose his life shall preserve it."—ζωογορήσει αὐτὴν (sc. ψυχήν.) Cf. Matt. x. 9, and xvi. 25 ; Mark viii. 35 ; Luke ix. 24 ; John xii. 25.

Acts vii. 19.—" The same (king) dealt subtilly with our kindred, and evil intreated our fathers, so that they cast out their young children, to the end they might not live."—τοῦ ποιεῖν ἔκθετα τὰ βρέφη αὐτῶν, εἰς τὸ μὴ ζωογονεῖσθαι.

THERE seems to be peculiar force and beauty in the word ξωογονέω here employed, which, like so many other delicate touches in the New Testament, altogether escapes us in our English version. In Greek authors, ζωογονέω means " to bring forth alive, to engender living animals."[a] In the New Testament it occurs in no other passage than the two quoted above, unless, indeed, we accept it in 1 Tim. vi. 13, where it is offered as a various reading. It will be convenient to consider first the verse taken from the Acts.

And without lengthened discussion (which space forbids), we would submit to the consideration of our learned readers, whether the following rendering may not express the sense of the original in this place more accurately than our English version, " so as to expose their offspring, in order that it might not be born alive." We are aware that this is awkward English, but we cannot find a better sentence.

Our common version implies, as it seems to us, that the children of Israel, by reason of the cruelty of Pharaoh, themselves exposed their infants, in order that (with the express purpose that) these infants might perish. Now, such conduct, besides being most unnatural, seems inconsistent with what is narrated in Ex. i. 15, 22, where we read that " Pharaoh charged *all his people*, saying, Every son that is born (τοῖς Ἐβραίοις the LXX. add, to avoid all mistake) ye shall cast into the river, and, every daughter ye shall save alive." The king's command was given to the people of Egypt, and not to the children of Israel. And accordingly, the mother of Moses concealed him, lest some of the Egyptians should seize and expose him. And when she herself was compelled to that sad necessity, surely it was not " to the end he might not live," that she deposited him with such anxious care at the river-side.

---

[a] Robinson's *Lex. to Gr. Test.*

In order to ascertain the meaning of these words of Stephen, we must bear in mind the course of conduct which the tyrant actually pursued towards the Hebrews. First, he directed the midwives to kill the male children, and to preserve the females alive. " But the midwives," we read, "feared God, and did not as the king of Egypt commanded them, καὶ ἐζωόγονουν τὰ ἀρσενα." Now, here the word ζωογονέω is clearly used, not in its primary meaning of " to bring forth alive," but in some meaning closely connected with, and naturally flowing from this ; not generally as if synonymous with σώζω, but specially, and as a causative, signifying " to cause to be born alive." The two women were commanded, when presiding at a birth, as soon as they had discovered the sex of the child—if a male, to kill it,—if a female, to preserve it. In their piety they disobeyed the monarch, and suffered the males, equally with the females, to be born alive into the world, to be presented as living infants to the parents.

When Pharaoh saw that his plan of extermination had failed, he issued other instructions, this time to his people generally,—viz., that they should cast all Hebrew children as soon as born into the river. This was commanded, Stephen says, in the words quoted, εἰς τὸ μὴ ζωογονεῖσθαι—that is, either (1) that the male offspring being exposed might not be preserved alive ; or (2) that the Israelites, seeing the cruel fate that awaited their new-born, might consent, as to an alternative, to the barbarous edict before issued by the tyrant—viz., that their male infants be dispatched immediately that their sex be ascertained—*i.e.*, that they be killed in the very birth.

Against (1) there are two serious objections : the first that it would make εἰς τὸ μὴ ζωογονεῖσθαι equivalent to εἰς τὸ ἀπολέσθαι, and thus rob it of its peculiar force ; the second, that even thus it would be but a poor platitute to affirm that the infants were exposed *in order that they might perish*, since the idea of exposure necessarily includes that of death.

We are thus driven to adopt (2) and discover in this part of the address of the first Christian martyr a new light thrown upon the page of Old Testament history. We learn, what we could not have known certainly before, that Pharaoh put forth his second edict—*that* concerning exposure—to the intent that his prior edict concerning infanticide which was then unheeded might thereafter be observed.

————

The exact meaning of the word ζωογονέω in the passage taken from the Acts is, perhaps, of little importance ; not so, however, in the verse from St. Luke's Gospel. A right understanding of it, then, will help us, if we mistake not, to a just appreciation of

the pregnant truth which the verse contains.   The reports given
us by the other evangelists of this saying of our Lord do not
contain the word in question.   Luke himself, when delivering it
in another place (ix. 24), substitutes for this remarkable expression the more ordinary σωζω.   All which seems to indicate that
there is an exact propriety in the word which, though it be so
often missed and passed over, the careful historian has not failed
to notice and preserve.   Let us first of all glance briefly at this
saying of our Lord, as reported by the other evangelists.

St. Matthew has (x. 39)—" He that findeth his life shall lose
it : and he that loseth his life for my sake shall find it"—a para-
doxical saying, delivered in a form common in Eastern aphorisms,
and in its character of paradox conveying, in a striking manner,
most weighty truth as to the relationship of "heavenly" to
"earthly things."   In the *loss* of the first clause (ἀπολέσει) we
cannot fail to perceive the ὄλεθρος αἰώνιος (2 Thess. i. 9), the
damnation (from *damnum,* loss), which shall be the terrible doom
of those that "have their portion in this life."   In the *finding* of
the second clause is equally evident the happiness of that man
who, forsaking all worldly gains, has found the pearl of great
price; who, letting go his hold on the vanities of earth and de-
positing his treasures where neither moth nor rust can corrupt,
shall find a goodly store awaiting his arrival in the heavenly man-
sions—friends ready to welcome him to "everlasting habitations."
This same evangelist has preserved for us this most beautiful
word of Christ in a form slightly different (chap. xvi. 25),
"Whosoever will save his life shall lose it : and whosoever will
lose his life for my sake shall find it," where it must not escape
our notice that the "whosoever will save" is in the original, ὃς
γὰρ ἂν θέλη,—*i.e.*, whosoever shall desire to save.   Here the
meaning would appear to be some such as this :—for expressions
containing general principles are not to be applied in their full
breadth to particular cases; he that inordinately desires, with
more than lawful earnestness, to preserve his life shall suffer the
loss of it in the death eternal; and he that deliberately, and after
counting the cost, shall stand to his Christian profession, though
death be the inevitable consequence, and thus, in a sense, be
accessory to his life's destruction, shall find his life preserved to
him in that world where all is life and love.

St. Mark repeats this latter version of St. Matthew with no
variation, except that, as is his wont, he adds to "for my sake,"
"and the gospels," and substitutes for "shall find it," "the same
shall save it."   With him the more general idea of salvation takes
the place of that other, more particular and personal, of the
Christian's finding anew what he had lost.

St. John's statement is characteristic of its author. He loves
to deal with abstract principles, and with these in pairs—love and
hatred, life and death; as in his first epistle especially, but, indeed, in each one of his writings; "He that loveth his life shall
lose it: and he that hateth his life in this world shall keep it
unto life eternal."

St. Luke, like St. Matthew, has the saying twice. His first
version of it (chap. ix. 24) is similar to those of St. Matthew and
St. Mark, as given above. His second is the passage quoted at
the head of this article, and which we come now to discuss.

With the circumstantial accuracy of the historian, for which
his gospel is throughout distinguished, he seems to have apprehended the *ipsissima verba* of the Saviour. Not that it need be
inferred from such an opinion that the other evangelists are in
this instance incorrect and faulty; for, from its frequent repetition (six times, as we have seen in the four Gospels), we doubt
not that this was one of those heavenly maxims which often
passed the lips of the Lord, as in his daily ministrations he came
daily in contact with the same ignorance, sorrow, and sin; the
same in their source and essence, but with some variation of form
and aspect. His earthly course was not, so to speak, that of the
rushing meteor which, flashing by in dazzling splendour, leaves
to the awe-struck crowd vainly to gaze and wonder; rather of
the great luminary, which, with all its wonders of radiance inexhaustible and healthful influences innumerable, is in nothing
more glorious than in this; that day by day, unwearied and
laborious, he fulfils the task of the Great Creator. Each morn
as he comes forth, arrayed in all his strength and majesty, re-
joicing as a giant to run his course, he may well remind us of
Him, who, the true light of the world, sums up in himself all
honour, and glory, and power, and might, and who, possessed of
all magnificence, delighted to bestow it on his sinful creatures
(alas! how often heedless of the boon), and in his own person,
invested with the glory of the Godhead, did service to the needs
of man.

But we must refrain. We wished to suggest that our Lord
probably uttered, on many occasions, the portion of truth we are
now considering; that he did this, not always in precisely the
same words, but, the general meaning the same, with slightly
altered expression; and that the different records of the evangelists have preserved to us these minute differences, interesting
as revealing to us the lights and shades of thought which crossed
the mind of the Saviour, no less than the several utterances which
his several followers were careful to retain.

St. Luke's phrase, " whosoever shall *seek* to save his life," is peculiar to himself, and is a mark of the professed historian, who notes the outward, rather than the inward acts, deeds rather than feelings, efforts rather than desires. In the latter of the two clauses, we have the remarkable word ζωογονέω, whose meaning we have already considered. "Whosoever shall lose his life shall make it to live" (or, quicken it) is the literal translation (the loss of life being suffered, as the Greek implies, at the hands of the destroyer). But here, by reason of the exceeding subtlety and philosophic beauty of the Greek language, our idiom must utterly fail to convey, in a single sentence, the full and exact meaning of this profound truth. St. Luke employs two words, one simply, the other in composition, both of which we are compelled to render "life." But there is a most important difference between them. For the "life" (ψυχή, *anima)* of which a man may be mulcted by his fellow-man is no more than the mere animal life which he has in common with the brutes, which he surrenders at the dissolution of soul and body, and which the malice of his cruel fellow may expel from his quivering frame.

Whereas the life (ζωή) that shall be imparted to the Christian martyr is that mysterious, heaven-born principle, of which, indeed, there is much that we know not, but which, the Scripture tells us, animates even now the new-born soul; and shall hereafter be communicated to the body, the partner of that soul, by that Divine Spirit who shall "quicken the mortal bodies" of all the saints. This is that true life which the first man lost in his woeful fall: in that same day he died; thus the heavenly principle quitted the creature who himself had rent asunder his connexion with the God of heaven, and returned to its glad abode. But life could not for ever be confined to heaven while love was there: together, hand in hand, they left the realms on high, and, embodied in him who, himself God, was yet himself man, they came to seek a resting-place once more among the sons of men. Yet mournful to tell, few received that life which ever has for its companion, love. They killed the Lord of life and glory. But though dead as they, some were quickened into newness of life (ζωῆς not βίου, Rom. vi. 4); alienated from the life of God they had been (ἀπηλλοτριωμένοι τῆς ζωῆς τοῦ Θεοῦ), now behold them new-born with a heavenly birth; death is no more for them; the primeval curse is for them repealed; the higher law of ζωή from heaven in them shall supersede the lower of ψυχη, which is of earth. They seem indeed to live as do others: men would say the same fate awaits them,—"A few short years, and the great enemy of mankind shall make an easy conquest." But no! it shall not be. The man of this world shall be indeed compelled unwillingly, after years of struggle and fond delusion, to that awful doom : yea, and when he wakes from restless slumber, what is it he can find beneath him but another deep of miseries ; and that how awful !   But on the child of heavenly birth a new being has dawned ; he has within him " the power of an endless life," no malice of the wicked one nor of *his* children can quench that deathless flame.   True, he is but *in part* new-born ; he still must carry the former carcase wearily to the grave : but there, lightsome he shall drop his load, and his eager spirit ascend to his Father, God !   And more ; the burden he has left shall rest awhile ; and anon, as the precious grain in much corruption, so shall the heavenly germ even of that vile body put forth its hidden life, and grow into strength and beauty, and wax yet stronger and stronger till, as a goodly harvest, it greet the longing of its heavenly fellow.   Then in full fruition shall be known by the new-born man the bliss, and joy, and glory of the life eternal.

And thus the words of Jesus have peculiar beauty—" Whosoever shall lose his life at the hands of the destroyer shall quicken it."   When the last breath has fled the house of clay, one moment instinct in all its faculties with the wondrous principle of life, the greatest mystery to man ; the next, inert and motionless, waiting the havoc of corruption that even now silently steals in to do its work : truly it seems as if that goodly fabric were destined for nought but ruin and oblivion.   Yet a little while, and there shall come a messenger from heaven to claim it from the spoiler, a lord more princely than the former tenant, a life (ζωή) yet more wondrous than the life of nature (ψυχή) ; and entering that same body shall fill it with a new, a higher life, and rear it up again as of old, yet transfigured with exceeding glory, to take its portion in the realms of day.

Then, Fellow-Christian, take courage !   Thine is a high and glorious calling.   Foes may gather around thee and stand thick on every side ; many may think thee a defenceless victim for their prey ; the wicked may wreak on thee their bitterest revenge : yet what hast thou to fear ?   Let them take thy life ; they have no more that they can do.   Trust thou in God ! Thou must leave *at last* that frail tenement to the cold tomb ; take heed, that leaving it in his service thou prove thyself born again of his Spirit who shall also quicken thy mortal body.

G. F. H.

ON ASSYRIAN VERBS.

Sect. IV.—*Examples of the Aorist of Qal.*

33. It appears so contrary to what might be expected, that a tense which corresponds in its form to the Hebrew future should have the signification of a preterite, that I have thought it right to commence with examples from Achæmenian inscriptions, of which we possess translations in a language cognate to the Sanskrit and Zend. I begin with that already quoted in par. 16, from the Behistun inscription. Here the verb is *akunawam* in the Persian (ii. 91). The Babylonian (line 63) has ⊫ (45) ⧠ (113) ⊫𝍦 (256) ⌡ (19) ⤪ (211), *as.ku.u'n.su.nu.* The Persian verb is in the imperfect, the root being *ku* (for *kri* Sanskrit) and *naw* being a conjugational addition. This tense corresponds to the simple preterite in English. "I placed them" is the literal translation of the Babylonian verb; and the same tense may be always used for the Babylonian tense that we are considering.

34. I must here make a few observations on the manner in which I have written the above word, and in which I will write words that may occur hereafter. In the first place, I substitute the Assyrian forms of the characters for those actually used in the inscription. Reference to the published copies of the Behistun inscription will shew that there is a difference in the second and third characters of this word; and there are many other characters also which were differently formed. I choose the Assyrian form of each character; and where the Assyrians used a variety of forms I choose that which appears the best to be taken as a standard. In the second place, I have placed a number after each character. When I have occasion to write a character more than once, I will use the number alone; and at the conclusion of the article I will give a list of all the characters I have introduced, their numbers being in numerical order, and the values of each being annexed. Thus each character will appear twice, and twice only,—when it first occurs and in the list at the end. In the third place, the syllabic value of each character is given at the end of the word, where there will always be found as many values as there are syllables, these values being separated by points. The word formed of these syllabic values will occasionally be added. In the present instance it is *áskun-sunu*, the hyphen separating the affix from the verb.

35. In iv. 35, the Persian inscription has *akunaush*, which is

the third person singular of the same verb in the same tense. The Babylonian (line 96), has here ⟨cuneiform⟩ (25) ⟨cuneiform⟩ (268) ⟨cuneiform⟩ (140).45.19.211 ⟨cuneiform⟩ (105), *in.da.na.a's.su.nu.u't*, *inda-nás-sunut*. In both these instances, all the radical letters appear; the roots being *sakin* and *nadin*. The latter verb signifies " to give:" in the present context it is said that Ormazda *gave* certain persons into the hand of Darius. Locomotion is here implied, and the augment is consequently inserted (par. 16). When the first radical is נ, it is usual to assimilate it in this tense to the following consonant. It is so in the present verb in other instances where it occurs; and the reason why it is not so here (unless it be an error of the writer of the inscription, whose grammar is not always to be depended on) was that by the addition of the augment the accent was drawn away from the first syllable. The short vowel, it will also be observed, is dropped at the end of the affix. Contractions of this nature are sometimes required by euphony. When a verb terminates in an unaccented vowel, *su* is generally shortened to *s*, and the enclitic *va* to *v*. We have also in certain cases *sun* for *sunu* and *sin* for *sina*.

36. The same Persian verb *akunaush* is translated in the Persepolitan inscription over the figure of Darius, which Lassen and Westergaard call B, by ⟨cuneiform⟩ (12) ⟨cuneiform⟩ (59) ⟨cuneiform⟩ (262), *i'.bu. us*; *sa bit hagd i'bus*, equivalent to *hya imam tacharam akunaush*; " who this house made." The first character, which for the most part denotes the simple vowel *i*, here represents that vowel followed by the guttural *'ayin*. This character is invariably used in the Babylonian and Persepolitan inscriptions to represent the first syllable of the third person masculine, singular and plural, of the aorist, when the root begins with *'ayin*. In the Assyrian inscriptions, on the contrary, the third person masculine singular of these verbs is, in most instances, identical with the first person singular. It is a fair inference from this that the Babylonians did not in general express the sound of this letter, but confounded it with *aleph* or *he*, while the Assyrians distinguished it from these. In the inscription C, where the Persian has " what I made and what King Darius my father made," which is expressed by *kartam* followed by the genitive, the Babylonian translation has in the first instance, ⟨cuneiform⟩ (135).59.262 ⟨cuneiform⟩ (48), *a'.b'u.u's.su*; and in the second, 12. 59.262.48, *i'.bu.u's.su*; *a'bússu* and *i'bússu*; see par. 19, 20. The proper value of 12 was *i* and of 135 was *a'*, יֵא. There being no character which properly denoted *i'*, יִ, the Assyrians extended the latter to express it, which they considered to

represent its sound most nearly, while the Babylonians preferred the former.

37. We may now consider the question as settled that this
tense of the verb really denotes the past. In the historical inscriptions of the Assyrian and Babylonian kings it is perpetually
used for what they did, and what others of whom they spoke did.
On the Nimrûd obelisk we have repeatedly after the name of a
river, 135 ⟨cuneiform⟩ (199), *a'.bir,* "I crossed," from עבר; after
that of a mountain preceded by the preposition "to," 135 ⟨cuneiform⟩
(295), *a'.li,* "I went up to," from עלה. In line 80 the last word
is in the third person *i'.li* (see last par.), and in line 117 we have
in the plural, 135.295 ⟨cuneiform⟩ (46), *i'.li.hu,* "they went up."
In lines 124—126, we have a series of verbs in this tense.
"Their males" (literally, what they had slayable), ⟨cuneiform⟩ (4) ⟨cuneiform⟩
(223), *a.duk.* "I slew," from חיק. "Their females (or spoil),"
45 ⟨cuneiform⟩ (119) ⟨cuneiform⟩ (188), *ash.lu.la,* "I carried away," from שלל.
"The towns," ⟨cuneiform⟩ (79) ⟨cuneiform⟩ (33), *ap.pal,* "I threw down,"
from נפל; ⟨cuneiform⟩ (40) ⟨cuneiform⟩ (78), *aq.qur,* "I dug up," from נקר;
"with fire," 45 ⟨cuneiform⟩ (51) ⟨cuneiform⟩ (209), *as.ru.u'p,* "I burned,"
from שרף. "An image of my majesty," 45 ⟨cuneiform⟩ (63).209, *ash.*
qu.u'p, "I set on high (?)" from שקף, "Yanjuhu," 4 ⟨cuneiform⟩ (126)
⟨cuneiform⟩ (165), *a.tsu.kha,* "I removed," from נסח; [other instances
have ⟨cuneiform⟩ (214), *ats,* in place of 4, *a,* which would be more
correct;] "to Assyria," 209.188, *ub.la,* "I brought," from יבל
= Hebrew יבל. The two last verbs have the augment of locomotion, and the last omits the vowel of the second syllable of the
aorist, as generally happens when it is an *i.* This would be
written in Hebrew characters, אֻגְלֶה. Without the augment it is
written, 46 ⟨cuneiform⟩ (225) ⟨cuneiform⟩ (277), *u*(or *yu).bi.i'l.* This
might be either אֻבְל or יְבֵל, * úbil* or *yúbil,* the first person singular
or the third person masculine singular; for these persons are
written, alike in the qal of verbs in *pi-vaw* as well as in the third
and fifth conjugations of all verbs. 46 expresses indifferently
א, ה and ע, and occasionally even ש and simple י. It thus differs
from ⟨ (21), which had the last of these values only, and if preceded by a character terminating in *u* must necessarily coalesce
with it.

38. The form *áppal* is perhaps incorrect. In earlier as well
as later inscriptions, we have for the last syllable ⟨cuneiform⟩
(127), *pul.* On the great bull at Kouyunjik, Sennacherib says,

79.59 ⟨⊏Υ⌄ (222), *ap.pu.u'l.* The last verb is here 40 ⧽⨯ (15), *ak.vu*, from נכה. Subsequently, he says of his enemies ⌐⊏ΥΥ (263) 59.119, *ip.pu.lu,* "they threw down;" ⊢Υ⌄Υ⌄ (283).63.51, *iq.vu.ru,* "they dug up." The remaining word is illegible after the first character, 283; but analogy would require 283.15.46, *ik.vu.hu,* "they burned." In the Khorsabad inscriptions (153.7), we have in the singular 253.33, *ip.pal,* "he threw down;" 283. 78, *iq.qur,* "he dug up;" ⊏⌄ΥΥ (90).51.209, *is.ru.u'p,* "he burned. The character 33 certainly denotes *pal;* but it remains a question whether it was extended to *pul* by writers who were not acquainted with the proper character for this syllable, or whether the verb *napil* admitted the two declensions, with *u* and with *a.* I suspect that it did so, but with different significations, —the former declension properly signifying "to throw down," and the latter "to fall down." It seems certain that the verb *shakin,* when declined with *u,* signifies "to place;" while its proper value is "to lie;" and Hebrew analogy would lead us to think the same of *napil.* If this view be correct, the form *áppal* is incorrect; the Assyrian writer having committed a like error, but in an opposite direction, to that of those who say "lay" for "lie," or "set" for "sit." I have already spoken in par. 15 of another impropriety, which frequently occurs on the obelisk, and indeed in this very verb; *ápal* is written where the correct form would certainly have two *p*s and probably *u* after them.

39. Examples of this tense in other persons than the first person singular and the third person masculine singular and plural are by no means common. The following must suffice. In the great inscription of Nebuchadnezzar, he says to Marduk (ix. 49), ⊏⊏ΥΥΥ (272).79.140 ⊢⊢Υ (287) ⋤⋢⋤ (192) ⌐Υ (238), *ta.a'b.na.a'n.ni.va,* "thou formedst me, and." The root is, בנה; and it should be observed that in this, as in other verbs defective in *lamed-he,* the last radical completely disappears before the augment. In the bull inscriptions of Sargon (Botta, 45, 34), we have ⊏⊏\⌐ (116).48.268, *tak.su.da,* "his hand (fem.) attained to much." The verb here precedes its accusative, and the augment is consequently added. On Bellino's cylinder (l. 7), we have the plural form corresponding to this 283.48.268, *ik.su.da,* "my hands (fem. pl.) attained to." The regimen here precedes the verb, and the augment is accordingly omitted.

40. In describing in par. 19 the cases where the subjunctive enclitic was used, I omitted the cases in which it is annexed to a verb having the relative *sa* for its subject. To such verbs it seems optional whether it be or be not annexed. In the example

in par. 36 it is omitted; but in the acknowledgment of the deity of Ormazda, which begins so many inscriptions at Persepolis, it is invariably inserted. For *hya imâm bumim adâ,* &c., "who made this earth," we have *sa irchitiñ hagatâ,* 253.211.46, *ib.nu.hu, ibnúhu;* this subjunctive enclitic not displacing the third radical, as the augment would have done. In the same connexion we have ⬚⬚⬚ (269) ⬚⬚ (172).211, *id.din.nu.*

41. Two classes of forms connected with this tense are especially deserving of notice from their utility in proving the connexion of characters as including in their values the same consonant. The inscriptions of Sargon, published by Botta, contain the same text in the first and in the third persons. M. Botta himself, overlooking this distinction, assumed that the different words used in these inscriptions ought to be read alike; and he thus most erroneously inferred the equivalence of their initial characters. I perceived the distinction; and I thus established the syllabic values of a whole series of characters. Two difficulties, however, lay in my way, and for a long time puzzled me. Some verbs were alike in both inscriptions, beginning with 46. It was a long time before I satisfied myself that this was in Assyrian the representative of ש and ר indifferently. The other difficulty was, that in the third person the plural appeared to be used. It was not "I" and "he," but, as I supposed, "I" and "they," which occurred before the verbs of the two inscriptions; and this, though the pronominal affixes were *ya* and *su,* clearly "my" and "his." At last I perceived that the *u,* which I took for the plural termination, was in reality the subjunctive enclitic.

42. This being premised, I think it right to give such of the verbs occurring in these Khorsabad inscriptions as are in the aorist of qal. Of the first we have four varieties—two in the first person and two in the third; viz., 4 ⬚⬚ (28) ⬚⬚⬚ (68). 238, *a.bi'.'il.va;* 4 ⬚⬚⬚ (150).238, *a.bi'l.va;* 12.28.119.238, *i.bi'.lu.va,* 12.150.119.238, *i.bi'l.lu.va.* " I (or who) made myself master of, and." The root is בעל; and I think that the characters 28 and 68 differ from 225 and 277 (see par. 27), in that the former includes the sound of *'ayin,* which I denote by an apostrophe. For the above four forms reference may be made to Botta 10.12, 145.10, 13.20 and 1.27. I read them, omitting the enclitic, *ábi'il* or *ábi'l, ibî'lu* and *ibî'llu* (see par. 20.) At the end of the shorter pavement inscriptions, we have in all the inscriptions 135.28.126.211 ⬚⬚⬚ (34), *i'.mit.tsu.nu.ti.* The first character *might* be read *a'* or *i'* (par. 36). I think, however, that in all the inscriptions it should in this word be read *i'* ; the subject of the verb not being "he" or "who," indicating the king, but *nir*

bi'luti-ya (or *su*), "the yoke of my (or his) dominion." The next character is of uncertain value. It probably represents *mit*, but it is also used for *bat*. The substitution of 126, *tsu*, for 48 or 19, *su*, shews that the value of 28 in the present word terminated in *t*, which, however, may stand for *d*. The root is probably מוש; but it has a transitive sense here, which it does not appear to have ever had in Hebrew. "The yoke of my dominion kept them quiet." Though I give this, as what appears to me the preferable reading and translation, I admit its uncertainty. Perhaps, we should read the first two syllables *a'.bat* or *i'.bat*; and translate the clause, "I (or he) imposed on them the yoke of my (or his) dominion." It is certain that the very puzzling character (28) had all the values *ba'*, *bi'*, *bat*, and *mit*.

43. In Botta, 9.29, we have 214.113 ⟦symbol⟧ (95), *aj.ku.ra*; where 2.21 has ⟦symbol⟧ (77).113.95, *ij.ku.ra (nibittsu)*, "I (or he) called (its name)." The root is קר. This verb is beyond the influence of the relative, and the enclitic is accordingly absent. The augment is due to the verb preceding its accusative. In 9.39 we have 79.192.238, *ab.ni.va*; in 2.25, 253.192.238, *ib.ni.va*, "I (or he) made, and." In 15.33 we have 40 ⟦symbol⟧ (73).238, *aq.ri.va*; in 16.125, 283.73.238, *iq.ri.va*, "I (or he) invoked, and." The root is קרא; 9.35 and some other inscriptions insert 135 after 73. This is *iv*, which value 135 admits as well as *i'*; *iqrivva* for *iqriva*. In 9.37 we have 40 ⟦symbol⟧ (163), *ak.ki*; and in 16.126, 283.163, *ik.ki*, "I (or he) slaughtered (victims)," from נכה.

44. The other class of verbs which it will be advantageous to notice specially, is that of verbs which are connected with accusatives that are nouns derived from them. Such are ⟦symbol⟧ (227).48 ⟦symbol⟧ (154) ⟦symbol⟧ (31) ⟦symbol⟧ (32).154.272, *am.su.u'kh, mi.si.i'kh.ta*, "I measured the dimension." The root is משח (Hebrew משח, Syriac ⟦Syriac⟧, but Arabic ⟦Arabic⟧). Here it may be observed that the character 154 was the only representative which the Assyrians had for ח.ה. and ה.; and that before a consonant it was often omitted, so that these terminations of syllables were represented by the vowel alone. Thus, in Bel. 33, we have *Madaya*, 51.63.34, *ru.qu.ti*, "distant Medians," from רחק. It is pretty evident also that 4 ⟦symbol⟧ (162), *a.di*, "together with," "as far as," is from אדה, and that ⟦symbol⟧ (96).34, *qa.ti* as it is sometimes written before *ya*, is properly *qakhti*, from לקח. This signifies "a hand;" and the word was also represented

before the affix, and always when without it, by the ideograph (125), consisting of the figure of a hand, 48, with the sign of duality, as in par. 29. For this ideograph 48 alone is frequently used in the older inscriptions; and it represents *qat* as a syllable, as well as this word. A like confusion existed in the Assyrian inscriptions between ה, ח, and ח, all of which might be expressed by (153); which, however, was more frequently omitted. In this instance, indeed, the confusion was greater; for this character seems to have been used also for ה, *hi;* whereas ח, *khi*, had a distinct character, (151), to represent it. This defect of characters to represent the gutturals, as well as the peculiar Semitic letters ט and ק, had great weight with me in leading me to the conclusion that the syllabary of the Assyrians could not possibly have been of native origin.

45. A similar instance occurs on a pyramid recently arrived at the British Museum, we have, lines 13, 14, of the second column of the only side that is legible, 32 (37). 283......45. 59 (64), *shi.pi.i'k....ash.pu.u'k,* "a heap of.....I heaped up." Again, obelisk 101, 102, we have (61).188.126.211 45.119.188, *shal.la.tsu.nu ash.lu.la,* "their spoil I carried away, or spoiled." In the instance given in the last paragraph, the accusative was definite, and terminated in *a*. In these two instances the theme is used without addition, and this denotes the accusative indefinite as well as any case in construction. The use of 126, ס, to represent the union of the ת of the theme with the שׁ of the affix, deserves particular attention. I consider it to prove that the Assyrians pronounced ס as *ts*, and that they gave the sound of *s* in *sore* to the ש of the affixes and preformatives.

46. In connexion with the last clause, we generally find another, the noun of which is written ideographically in most inscriptions. In those of Tiglath Pileser II., however, it is written phonetically. We have, for instance, BM.50.2.10, 162. 283.272.184.223, *di.i'k.ta.su a.duk*. The meaning is "his males I slew;" but *dikta* is a feminine noun in the accusative definite; literally "that which was slayable of his." *Shallat* sometimes signifies "spoil," generally "what was carriable away;" but it sometimes signifies "women," as in the above inscription BM.50. 1.8, when a number precedes it, "457 women;" and 61, *shal*, is constantly used as the determinative for females. The root of *áduk* and *dikta* is דוך, a defective in *kaph-waw*.

47. An ideograph denoting "bricks" is used with the verb (278).225.25, *al.bi.i'n,* Oct. 7. 54; and in BM.38.7 with

277.225.211, *il.bi.nu.* The word here expressed ideographically occurs written phonetically on the Khorsabad bulls. In Botta, (49, 52,) we have, after the causative form of this verb, *usalbiná,* "I caused to be made," 295 ⊨𝍣 (182) 𝍧𝍫𝍠 (290), *li.bit.tu,* "bricks." The root is פֿב; and the final *n* is changed to *t* before the *t* of the afformative. This form is the accusative plural. I may here observe that the standard form of these feminine nouns are *p.kl.t* for the accusative singular indefinite, and for the singular in construction in every case; *p.k.ltu* for the nominative singular, and for the accusative plural indefinite, and the plural is constructive in every case; *p.k.lta* for the accusative singular definite, and *p.k.lti* for the dative singular. The vowels vary in different nouns. The theme of the noun last mentioned would be *libnit.*

48. I will give one more instance of a verb and noun thus related. In the great inscription of Nebuchadnezzar (vi. 30) we have 151.73.77.126.154.73.135.238, *khi.ri.i'ts.tsu akh.ri.i'v.va,* "its ditch I dug, and." On Grotefend's barrel 2.7, we have the first word without 77; and in vi. 60 we have 269, *it,* in place of 77, *its.* Either character may be inserted, though neither is absolutely necessary. The root of these words must, I think, be חרר; though the last radical is somewhat uncertain. Other forms belonging to this tense are 154.95.4, *akh.r'a.d,* R.388; and 154.51.46, *ikh.ru.hu,* Baviân inscription. The former may be read *akhrá,* and the only difficulty is, why it should have the augment as it follows the accusative. Probably, "I conducted its conduit" would be a better translation than "I dug its ditch;" or the verb and derived noun may in the earlier inscriptions have had the primary signification of *making a passage for drawing anything off,* which would suit the Hebrew sense of the root; while the secondary meaning of *digging* may have supplanted this in later times. In the Baviân inscription, the plural form 151.95.4.34, *khi.r'a.d.ti,* replaces the singular *khirit.* This is the accusative (or dative) plural definite, "the ditches, or conduits." The standard form would be *p.kláti,* and the nominative definitive would be *p.klátu.* *Ikh.ru.u* of the Baviân inscription is in the third person plural, as the context proves;

I would write it in Hebrew characters יחרו, or in Arabic يَخْرُؤُ *ikhru'u.*

49. The above examples seem sufficient. I will now specify the irregularities of the different classes of verbs. It will suffice to take the four forms which are regularly *ápkul, tápkul, ípkul,* and *ípkulu,* as all the rest may be derived from these. If the first radical be *aleph,* these become *ákul, tákul,*

íkul, íkulu; if *he* or *nun, ákkul, tákkul, íkkul, ikkulu;* if *waw, úkil, túkil, yúkil,* and *yúkilu, u* and *yu* being written alike; I have not met with *u* between the second and third radical, when the first was *waw*. The augmented forms are *uklá,* &c., *yukluni'*; provided that the second and third radicals can be brought together with euphony. *Ublá* is in actual use. If the first radical be *kheth* or *'ayin,* the tense is regular as respects pronunciation; but in Assyrian, 154 is used for both *akh* and *ikh,* and 135 for both *a'* and *i'*; while in Babylonian *ikh* is represented by 12.154 and *i'* by 12 alone. I may add that *ta'* in verbs of this sort is represented by ⟨cuneiform⟩ (275), and *na'* by 192. But few Assyrian verbs begin with *yod;* most of those which have this for their initial in Hebrew having *waw* in Assyrian. I do not recollect having met with any of these verbs in this tense of qal; but in the fifth conjugation they seem to follow the analogy of those which have *'ayin* for their first radical.

50. Some verbs which have *sin* for their first radical are irregular in this tense in a way to which there is nothing similar, I believe, in any of the cognate languages. When the second radical is a dental, or one of the compound letters which begins with a dental, that is, when it be ד, ז, ט, ס, צ, or ת, the *sin* is frequently changed in *lamed*. Thus, we have 278 ⟨cuneiform⟩ (247), ⟨cuneiform⟩ (252), *al.dhu.u'r,* Oct. 8. 45, or 278 ⟨cuneiform⟩ (201), *al.dhur,* R. 68; Bm. 16, 48. The root is certainly שׁטר; and in other forms when a vowel separates the *sin* from the dental the former is preserved. Nay, in many inscriptions (though not in the most ancient ones), *s* is retained in the aorist of qal. The Vau inscription of Xerxes seems to have 90.247.252, *is.dhu.u'r;* and, in several places, we have 45 ⟨cuneiform⟩ (175), *as.tur.* (Ob. 72). Here the following rule supersedes that just given.

51. When *sin* immediately precedes certain letters, it changes them into others which harmonize with it better. Thus, in the aorist of qal of the verb שׁקל, the third persons masculine, singular and plural, are 90.113.222, *ish.ku.u'l,* and 90.113.119, *ish.ku.lu.* I have not found these words in any of the historical inscriptions; but they are given in a grammatical tablet in the British Museum. I take *ástur,* for *ásdhur,* to be a similar instance, in which this rule of euphony supersedes the former one. Other instances of its application should be looked for. Like changes may also occur with other letters. I am nearly certain that פ converts a ת, which immediately follows it into ט.

52. There is no irregularity in this tense caused by the identity of the second and third radicals. When the second is *Waw,* the forms are *ákul, tákul, íkul, ikulu;* not differing, I believe,

from the forms of verbs with *pe.aleph.* Both of these classes of
verbs are, however, rare; and I have not seen a sufficient number
of examples to enable me to pronounce with certainty. If the
second radical be *waw*, and the third *weak*, the *waw* is generally
treated as an ordinary letter. I have met no verbs with *i* for the
second radical. If such there be, I presume they would follow
the analogy of those last named. *'Abi'il*, or *ábi'l*, and *ibi'lu*,
already given in par. 42, indicate, as well as can yet be done,
the forms where the second radical is *áyin*; as 12, ⟨⟩ (17) ⟩
(260), *i.mih.du* (Beh. 14), does, where it is *aleph* or *he*. Hebrew
analogy would induce me to consider ⟩ as the root; but the
Assyrian form is rather ⟩, the derived adjective being written
238.153.260, *ma.a'h.du*, when not written 238.260, *ma.du*; 17
is often confounded with 31; but the former is sometimes equated
to 31.135, *mi.i''*, and may also represent 17.153, *mi.i'h.*

53. When the third radical is *he*, the usual forms are *ápki*,
tápki, *ípki*, *ípku*; sometimes *u* replaces *i*, and then the plural
form is *ípkuhu*; but, in both cases, the augmented forms are *apká*
and *ipkuní*. When the third radical is *aleph*, I believe that *u* is
never used at the end; but when the first person singular terminates in *i*, this *i* is changed into *u* in the third person plural
masculine. The standard forms would then be *ápki* (and with the
augment *apká*), *tápki*, *ípki*, *ípku'u*. This class of verbs, however,
admits also the *a* declension, *ápka*, *tápka*, *ípka*, *ípka'u*. To the
i of the former declension, 135 *i'* is sometimes added; but I believe that this always represents *iv*. It is not always added when
the third radical is *'ayin*, and it is added when the final radical
is *aleph* or *he*. In a word, verbs in *lamed 'ayin* are confounded
with those in *lamed he*. Thus, in Botta 153.4, we have 90.15.
238, *ish.mu.va*, for " they heard, and." A more correct form
would be 90.31.46.238, *ish.mi.'u.va.* In the singular, it is 90.31
ish.mi; and, with the enclitic, 90.31.135.238, *ish.mi.i'v.va*
(II. 4); or 90.31.238, *ish.mi.va* (Ob. 144). Where the third
radical is *Kheth.* the only irregularity is in the writing; and
I have already explained it in par. 44.

SECT. V.—Other Tenses of Qal.

54. The preterperfect, which also expresses the pluperfect,
is formed from the aorist by adding *u* to the forms which end in
a radical letter; or if the verb be defective in *lamed-he* by substituting *u* for the final vowel. I believe the addition made to
those forms which terminate in a vowel is a syllable beginning
with *n* and terminating with the same vowel. This tense does
not admit of an augment.

55. The clearest example which I know of this tense is in the great inscription of Nebuchadnezzar X. 3, which is a complete sentence, 182 135.59.48, *bit a'.bu.su,* "A house I have built." In this instance, it is impossible that the *u* at the end can be a subjunctive enclitic, as the sentence is unconnected with what precedes it. Another very clear instance has been already given in par. 20. The verb and its regimen are Ⱳ (6).4.37.119. 32.140.192, *sa a.pi'.lu.si.na.ni, sa ápi'lu-sina-ni,* "which (fem. pl.) I have made myself master of." *Ni* being here the subjunctive enclitic, it is clear that the *u* before the affix cannot be another, but must be a part of the verb. It is the same which we had in par. 42; only that 37, *pi'*, is here substituted for 28, *bi'.* Perhaps this was occasioned by the uncertainty of this last character; but the Assyrians preferred *p* to *b*, while the Babylonians preferred *b* to *p*. The Babylonian roots שנב and פרנ seem to have been always שנב and פרנ in Assyrian; *bal,* "a son," at Babylon, as in Marduk-bal-iddin, was *pal* in Assyria, and in Greek transcriptions which have come to us through it, as Sardanapalus. The use of פל for בל ought not, therefore, to surprise us. The course which I would recommend, in all instances where it is practicable, is to consider the form which corresponds to the Hebrew or Syriac as the correct form, and the other a corruption.

56. In V. 1—10, we have a series of verbs in this tense, where it has a pluperfect signification. The king had spoken of works which his father made, but did not complete. These verbs are in the aorist with the subjunctive enclitic. A new sentence then begins. ("Its ditch") 12.154.51.208, *i.i'kh.ru.va,* "he HAD dug, and (with two new walls of bitumen and bricks)," 283 ⫷⊏Ⴌ (124).51, *iq.ju.ru,* "he HAD closed in (its mound)." Other verbs follow in the same tense; 12.59.48.238, *i'.bu.su.va,* "he HAD made, and," and two others in the third and fifth conjugations. The reality of this tense and its peculiar signification seem very clear from these examples. In other passages of this inscription the second verb is written with 126, *tsu.* This character, and 124, resemble one another, and one of the two readings must be incorrect. The translation which I have given is by no means certain. "He had constructed" would make as good sense. What, however, I think most probable is that the root is קצר; that *iqjuru* is substituted for *iqchuru*, on the euphonic principle of par. 51; and that 126 is a mistake of the writer for 124. The root קצר, قصر, has in Arabic the sense I have given above, "to close in."

57. Instances of the plural of this tense are rare. I suspect, however, that there are two in the Behistun inscription. One is in line 7, where we have first the conclusion of the sentence,

"These are the provinces which obey me." This verb is in the
present text, and will soon be quoted as an illustration of it.   He
then proceeds, "by the help of Ormazda they *have* become subject to me."   The verb is 269.290.51.211, *it.tu.ru.nu*, which corresponds to no form of the aorist.   This is evidently from the
same verb as ⟨cuneiform⟩ (204).201, *at.tur*, in line 5 and 269.201; *it.
tur* in line 12, "I became (their king)," "he became king."   In
the former passage, 19, *su*, is printed, and, it may be, cut on the
rock, in place of 32, *si*.   The affix "their" being *sina*, and not
suna.   Whatever be the root of *altur*, it is the first person singular of the aorist; and *itturunú* is the third person plural of the
preterperfect of the same verb, *nu* being added to the aorist form
itturu, to which syllable I give a secondary accent, required by its
distance from the chief accent.   The correctness of adding this
accent will presently appear.   The other place in which I think
this tense occurs in the Behistun inscription is line 50, when we
read that ("the enemy") 253 ⟨cuneiform⟩ (71).51 ⟨cuneiform⟩ (274).238,
ib.khu.ru.nuv.va, "had come together, and (advanced)."   The
Persian has *hagmatá paraitá*, the first word being a preterperfect
participle passive, and the second a verb in the tense usually corresponding to the aorist.   Col. Rawlinson's translation is "con-
gregati rediêre."   It appears from this that there is good reason
from the Persian to consider the two verbs in this sentence to be
in different tenses.   The form is the same as before, and the
secondary accent on the last syllable causes the *v* of the enclitic
to be doubled (see par. 15).   I read *ibkhurunúvva*.   In the other
instance, the verb which corresponds to *itturunú* is *áhatá*.   The
aorist would be *áha*, and this must be a different tense, which I
take for the perfect or pluperfect.   It only occurs in this place
and in a sentence which occurs several times, after the name of a
conquered enemy "and the chief men who *had been* his followers."
Here I ought to observe that I formerly valued 274 as *niv*.   Dr.
Oppert objected to this, alleging that its value was *nuv*, and saying that he had proof of this.   I replied, that if so, it must admit
both values, as *I* had proof that it was *niv*.   Curiously enough,
we were, not long after, together looking over an Assyrian sylla-
bery in the British Museum, and we found the character with the
two values actually attached to it, 192 ⟨cuneiform⟩ (57), *ni.i'v*, and
211 ⟨cuneiform⟩ (143), *nu.u'v*.

58. The present tense is of very rare occurrence in the inscriptions; but its form may be inferred in various ways in many
verbs where it is not found.   The future is derived from it in
the same manner as the preterperfect is from the aorist.   There
is an augmented form, which is in general the present with *t* in-

serted after the first radical. There are also the forms of this tense in several verbs given in a grammatical tablet in the British Museum. From combining all these sources of information, I think that the forms of the present tense can be established with nearly the same certainty as those of the aorist. I give below a table of the four tenses which take the preformatives, arranging them in the order, aorist, preterperfect, present, and future; and I give for comparison the Ethiopic contingent, which I omitted in the table in par. 13, because it did not resemble the aorist.

1. c. s.	ápkul	ápkulu	apákal	apákalu	epakel
2. m. s.	tápkul	tápkulu	tapákal	tapákalu	tepakel
2. f. s.	[tápkuli	tápkuliní	tapákali	tapákaliní]	tepakeli
3. m. s.	ípkul	ípkulu	ipákal	ipákalu	yepakel
3. f. s.	tápkul	tápkulu	tapákal	tapákalu	tepakel
1. c. p.	nápkul	nápkulu	[napákal]	[napákalu]	nepakel
2. m. p.	[tápkulu	tápkulunú	tapákalu	tapákalunú]	tepakelu
2. f. p.	[tápkula]	tápkulaná	tapákala	tapákalaná]	tepakelâ
3. m. p.	ípkulu	ípkulunú	ipákalu	[ipákalunú]	yepakelu
3. f. p.	ípkula	[ípkulaná]	ipákala	[ipákalaná]	yepakelâ

I have already observed that the second radical in this tense is frequently doubted. I believe that it is invariably so in the Achæmenian inscriptions; but this is by no means the case in the older ones, and it ought to be considered an abuse (see par. 15). Several verbs have *i* in place of *a* before the second radical. The vowel after the second radical seems to have been almost always *a* in regular verbs; but there are a few exceptions; and defectives in *weak lamed* have *i*, which disappears when a syllable is added, whether by inflexion or by augment.

59. The examples of this tense which actually occur are very few. We have 12 ⫯𝍢⫯ (229).79.225, *i.qu.a'b.bi*, or, as it is more frequently written, 12 ⫰⫯⫯ (228).225, *i.qab.bi*, in all the Achæmenian inscriptions; and it is uniformly rendered in Persian by *thátiya*, a present tense. The translation of the sentence at Behistun, where it occurs so often, is clearly, "King Darius says also." The ordinary value of 229 is *ga*; but it is always used in the Babylonian and Achæmenian inscriptions for 96, *qa*, the Assyrian form of which was not in use among the Babylonians. In the Assyrian inscriptions we have several times 6 12.96.59.19 (or 32).192, *sa i.qa.bu.su*(or *si*).*ni*, for "which they call;" the affix *su* being used where the object named is masculine, and *si*

where it is feminine. This gives us the true third person plural *iqábu*, shewing that the root was נקב, or perhaps נקי; for the following example will shew that נ, when it is the third radical, may disappear as completely as ח, نَبِ, among many meanings, is said to have that of *clamavit*. I can find no other verb in any of the cognate languages between which and this I can trace the slightest analogy.

60. In line 7 of the Behistun inscription, we have 12. ⟨⟨ (26).57.238.153.25.192, *i.shi.i'm.ma.hi.i'n.ni*. I write this *ish-imma-hi-'nni*; and it is evidently a verb in the third person feminine plural, with the augment of regimen, and the affix of the first person singular. The same verb occurs in line 48 with ▷▲▷▷⟨⟨ (167), *shim*, in place of 26.57. It is not so obvious from what verb it comes, and in what tense it is; but I have no doubt that it is the present of שמע. The meaning would thus be, " These are the provinces which hearken to me, or obey me;" or possibly, " which are called mine." In Persian *agubatá*, which is properly " had heard," is used to signify " had been called;" and it is possible that this may be the meaning here. It is against this view that where *agubatá* occurs in the Persian, the Babylonian paraphrases it by *iqbu* (or *iqbu'u) umma anaku*, " who had said thus, I am," in place of " who had heard;" and that in the present passage the Persian inscription paraphrases the text, reading *patiydisha* " (the provinces which) came to (me)." On the other hand, this latter interpretation is countenanced by the Median (or as some call it, the Scythian) text, which reads here *appa yunina tiris-ti*, " which they called mine." It appears to me evident that *ti* is a subjunctive enclitic, like that of the Assyrians. The system of enclitics seems common to the two languages, the Assyrian and the Median, or Elymæan, or whatever it may be; *tiris-sa* would be "they called, and," corresponding precisely to *iqbu-va*.

61. An example of the present tense with augment and affix appears to occur in line 24 of the Nakshi Rustam inscription, though the necessity for the affix is not very evident, nor is its form exactly what might be expected. The word which occurs is 4.228 ⟨⟨ (111).45.32.140.4.105, *a.qab.ba.a's.si.n'a.á.tu*, " I commanded them." Perhaps, *sinátu* is a separate pronoun, before which *aqabbá*, with the augment, would be regularly used; and the two words have been blended together by the euphonic insertion of 45, *as*. Unfortunately, this important inscription has been much injured. Westergaard's copy was but badly copied; but, such as it is, we should feel grateful to him for having published it. A more accurate copy which has since been taken remains private property.

62. These are all the verbs that are *certainly* in the present tense, which I have met with. They are all presents of two verbs, defective in the same manner; so that from these alone, it would have been impossible to exhibit the regular conjugation. An Assyrian grammatical tablet in the British Museum here comes to our aid. It gives the third person masculine, singular and plural, of several presents, compared with those of their aorists; and for these I have constructed the paradigm of the whole tense. The examples of regular verbs in qal are aor. sing. 90.51.64, *is.ru.u'k*; pl., 90.51.113, *is.ru.ku*; pre. sing., 12 𒀭𒁹𒌋 (273) 𒀸𒈾𒋻 (291).61, *i.sa.a'r.rak*; pl., 12.273.95.113, *i.sa. ra.ku*. Afterwards the tablet gives 12.273.61.48, *i.sa.rak.su*, for the third person singular of the present joined to an affix. This shews that the duplication of the second radical was not necessary; and in the next example it does not occur at all. Aor. sing., 90.113. 256, *ish.ku.u'n*; pl., 90.113.211, *ish.ku.nu*; pres. sing., 12.273 𒈾𒋛 (243).287, *i.sha.ka.a'n*; pl., 12.273.243.211, *i.sha.ka.nu*. A third instance exhibits an irregularity, already noticed in par. 51. The root is שׁקל. Aor. sing., 90.113.222, *ish.ku.u'l*; pl., 90.113.119, *ish.ku.lu*; pres. sing., 12.273 𒂍 (39), *i.sha.qal*; pl., 12.273.96.119, *i.sha.qa.lu*. These forms are also given before the affix; and then we have 229 in place of 96. The former is properly *ga*, but it is often used for *qa*, of which the latter was the proper representative; *gal* was also represented by 39. I think, however, that in this place the second radical was ק, because the character 𒀹 (3) is here given as the monogram for the root; whereas the monogram for שׁקל was 𒉿𒌍 (128).

63. I may as well digress here to explain the nature of these monograms which occur pretty frequently in the inscriptions from the north-west palace at Nimrûd, and occasionally in others. A certain character, which had for the most part one or more syllabic values, represented also a root. It was sometimes used for it alone; but a character was often added to it for the purpose of indicating the tense or other form of the root. To give one example out of many, 𒀹 (24), in addition to its syllabic values represented the root שׁקל. If 105, *ud*, were added to it, it was to be read as some form of the aorist in qal, which the context would define; if 204, *ad*, were added, it was to be read as *aktashad* or some other form of that tense, or of the present. If 34, *ti*, or as I believe 290, *tu*, were added, it was to be read *ki-shitti* or *kishittu*. The former of these two words is certainly to be read as I have written it, for it is so transcribed in inscriptions to the same purport; it means "acquisitions." The latter means

"mines," being followed by the words for "silver" and "salt" (Obel. 106, 107); and this may very well be the same word. Some of these monograms, I must add, express two verbs. It is expressly stated in the tablet that I have been quoting that 6 denotes both שם and שיר. 6.211 is indeed interchanged with 6.40.211, *sha.a'k.nu*, in different copies of the same inscription; as is 6.256 with 90.113.211, *ish.ku.nu*. Other instances of a monogram having different values are 211=נב and שוֹא, and 128 =שוּל and שיר.

64. The forms of this tense in several classes of irregular verbs are not obtainable from any of the examples adduced. Verbs in *pe-nun* are quite regular Verbs in *pe-waw* are, I believe, declined, *úkkal, túkkal, túkkali, yúkkal*, &c.; the first person and the third person masculine being written in the singular alike. If the first radical be *'ayin*, the forms would be *íkkal, tíkkal, tíkkali*, &c., those for " I " and " he " being again identical. If it be *aleph* or *he*, I should suppose that they would be *ákkal, tákkal, tákkali, ikkal*, &c.; while *apál, tapál, tapáli, ipál*, &c., would probably represent those of defectives in the second radical. See what will presently be said of the future of irregular verbs.

65. In the Achæmenian inscriptions there are three verbs which I believe to be futures; but it cannot be proved from the translations that they are not presents with the subjunctive enclitic. These are 272.37.77 ⊱𝕀𝕀 (107).211, *ta.pi.i'ts.tsi.nu*. (Beh. 102). The translation is *apagudaydhya*=Sanskrit *apagûhaydsi*, which is in the tense called by Benfey the conjunctive present. The sense, however, is future, "If thou shalt conceal;" and I think that the present with the enclitic would have been *tapit-si'nnu* in place of *tapi'tstsinu*. The root is שם. In the same inscription, l. 97, we have 272.228.59, *ta.qab.bu*; and in the Nakshi Rustam inscription, l. 25, we have the same word with the addition of 21, which I take to be a simple ו, *u*, necessarily forming one syllable with a preceding character, the value of which terminated in *u*; and therefore differing from 46, which is thus used but rarely (see par. 37). In both these places the Persian translation is mutilated; but Col. Rawlinson has supplied *maniydhya* from a parallel text. This is the same tense as the preceding. The meaning, however, is alike future; and the same argument may be used for this being a future. The present with a subjunctive enclitic would terminate in 59.46, *bu'.hu* (see par. 40).

66. In Bellino's inscription, line 62, there is a passage which I translate, "When this palace shall grow old and decay." The two last words are 12 ⊱𝕀𝕀𝕀 (47).225.51.238 ⊢𝕀𝕀 (285).140.71,

i.lab.bi.ru.va in.na.khu, ilábbirúva innákhu. The last verb occurs frequently in the aorist, where it is written 135.140.154, *i'.na.a'kh.* The root must be נשׂא. I believe it does not exist in any of the cognate languages any more than נבא, which is very common, and of which a great variety of forms h^ave been found in the inscriptions. In an inscription which I copied from a tablet in the British Museum, there are two other verbs evidently in the same tense as those last produced. "(When) thou crossest, or shalt cross," is expressed by 275.253.225.51, *ti'.i'b.bi.ru;* and "(when) thou goest, or shalt go," by ➤𝖄𝖨 (73) 188.113, *tal.la.ku.* In the 24th line of the Nakshi Rustam inscription there is a word which I am disposed to read 254.59.262.6, *ib.bu.u's.sa,* and to take for the present of qal in the third person feminine plural, "they do." A comparison of the words, *ibbússa, tibbíru,* and *innákhu,* has led me to the conclusion that verbs with '*ayin* for the first radical double the second radical in the present and future, pre-fixing always the vowel *i* (see par. 64). The future follows the law of the present in all verbs which have not a *weak lamed.*

67. Many verbs which are by the context unquestionably future occur on the octagon of Tiglath Pileser the First, and on the stone of Michaux at Paris. Neither of these inscriptions has been published; and the copies of them which I have are imperfect. I can therefore only give a few detached futures. "He shall write," of which the root is שׂטר, is expressed by 12. 24(or 6).268.51, *i.shad.*(or *sha.)da.ru;* "he shall dwell," from שׁכן, is 12 ➤𝖄𝖨𝖃 (241).243.211, *i.shak.ka.nu;* "he shall burn," from שׂרף, is 12 ⦚⦚⦚◻ (27).95.59, *i.sar.ra.pu.* Other futures occur, the meaning of which is less certain; 12 ➤𝖛 (181).44. 211, *i.tsa.pa.nu,* is from צפן; 12.140.260.46, *i.na.d'u.u,* as it must be read here, may be from נתן or from נדה; 209.111.290, *yub.ba.tu,* can only be from נבת; and it determines the form of the future when the first radical is *waw.* This appears also from a tablet in the British Museum, which gives for the aorist 46.275.194, *yu.ti.i'r,* "he restored;" and for the corresponding present 105. 272.291, *yut.ta.a'r,* "he restores." The same tablet gives 269. 172, *id.din,* for "he gave;" 12.140.204.172, *i.na.a'd.din,* for "he gives." When the aorist takes the augment, it is written 269.162.140, *id.di.na;* so that the Assyrian root is certainly נתן, not נדן.

I do not recollect having met with this tense in the plural. I can only judge of its probable forms by analogy of those of the preterperfect.

68. Of the imperative there are but few examples; 32.17, *shi.mi',* "hear," and with the augment 32.238.4, *shi.m'a.d* (or

shi.ma.'a; but I prefer the former reading), occur in the inscriptions of Nebuchadnezzar. At Behistun we have 278.243, *hal.ka,* "go ye," from ⊤⊓. This is joined with 260.243.153, *du.ka.a'h,* "smite ye," from ⊓⊤. The feminine plural is given here in an unusual form, with the addition of *he.* It appears to us strange that the feminine gender should be used in a case like this; but the nouns for "provinces" and "armies" were feminine; and there are frequent instances of the feminine being thus used, which can admit of no doubt. If it were not so, although the Persian translation has *paritá* and *jatá,* I should take the terminations to be the augment attached to the second person singular. Elsewhere we have 4.252.238, *ha.lik.va,* followed by 260.46.113, *d'u.u.ku.* This seems to be "go thou and . . . smite ye." The inference which I draw as to the form of the imperative from these few examples, is that in ordinary verbs it was the same as the second person of the present, omitting the preformative *ta.* The typical forms would be *pákal, pákali; pákalu, pákala.* In the comparatively few verbs in which *i* is substituted for *a* after the first radical of the present (of which ⊓⊔⊔, our example, *happens* to be one), the first vowel of the imperative is *i* also. In like manner the vowel between the second and third radicals is the same in the present and in the imperative; and when this vowel is *i,* it is generally omitted in the feminine singular, and in the plural. The imperative of verbs whose second radical is quiescent *vaw,* is of the form *duk, dúki, dúku, dúk;* and it is probable that similar forms with *a* and *i* in place of *u* were used when it was *aleph* or *'ayin.* It may be conjectured also that where the first radical was *aleph, 'ayin,* or *vaw,* the imperative would in the masculine singular differ in the final vowel only from the first person singular of the aorist, that vowel being the same as in the present.

69. Of the optative, precative, there are numerous examples in the first person singular and in the third person masculine singular and plural. The standard forms are *lúpkul, lípkul, lípkulu.* Examples in the Achæmenian inscriptions are 295.77 ⟨⊥ (231), *li.i'ch.chur,* translated by *pátuwa,* "may he defend," from the root ⊔⊓ (D of Lassen. 20). In the 18th line, 287.192, *an.ni,* is added, making *lichchuránni,* "may he defend me;" where the Persian has the same verb, preceded by *mám.* In Beh. 108 we have 295.51 ⊓⊤ (252), *li.ru.u'r,* translated by *jatá biyá,* "may he be an enemy." The literal meaning of the Babylonian word is, "may he curse," from the root ⊤⊔. In Beh. 102 we have 295.73.113.153, *li.ri.ku.u'h.* The Persian translation is *daragam jivá,* "mayest thou live long." The Babylonian paraphrases this; it has apparently (for the text is incomplete), "may

(thy times) be long," from אַרך. The 153 at the end of this verb can scarcely be an augment; and as it never appears in such a position in Assyrian or native Babylonian inscriptions, I cannot but think that it would have been better omitted.

70. In the inscriptions of Nebuchadnezzar we have 119.64. 48.105, *lu.u'k.su.u'd*, "may I obtain;" 119.143.71. ⸱⸱⸱⸱⸱ (239), *lu.úm.khu.úr*, "may I receive;" we have also with less certain meanings, because the contexts contain words which are not understood, by me at least, 295.225.135.119, *li.bi.i".lu*, "may they have possession of," from בעל; 119.262.111.4, *lu.us. b'a.d*, before its accusative, "may I be satisfied with," from שׂבע, and 119.262.225.57, *lu.u's.bi.i'v*, which I take to be the same verb, after its accusative, and therefore without the augment, but with the copulative enclitic contracted (see par. 35). In Grotefend's barrel inscription, which contains a similar text, we have in this word 227, *av*, in place of 57, *iv*. Supposing this to be correct, it can only be attributed to a euphonic law, similar to that which produces the Hebrew *patakh furtivum*. The word to which the *v* of the enclitic is attached is לושׂביע *lúsbia'*, in place of *lúsbi'*.

71. The older inscriptions contain many additional optatives; and these are very useful in the construction of syllabaries, as they determine the values of several characters commencing with *l*. Examples of such optatives are ⸱⸱⸱⸱ (18).247.252, *lil.dhu.u'r* "may he write," from שׂטר (see par. 50). The initial character in this word represents a quiver, the Assyrian name of which was לל *lil*. The root was לל, which signifies "to put up, as in a quiver." The Assyrian kings, speaking of the termination of their expeditions, were in the habit of saying "my arrows (or the arrows of Assur)," 46.18, *u.lil*, "I put up in their quiver." When the latter form of the accusative is used, the verb ought, I believe, to be read *yulíl*, "*he* (*i.e.*, Assur) put up." The sculptures represent the king and Assur over his head, having, *both* in the same manner, either bows charged with arrows in their hands, or their arrows in their quivers, and the bows out of use. It will be shewn hereafter that *ulíl* אלל, is the aorist of the third conjugation of לל. I cannot dismiss this word without the observation that it is the most natural derivation of the noun ליל "night," the time of things being put up. Other examples are ⸱ (2).113.211, *lish.ku.nu*, "may they place," from שׂכן, ⸱⸱⸱ (123).48.262; *lib.su.u's* "may he cleanse?" from בשׂם or בשׂם, which I believe is not known as having been used in any of the cognate languages; 252 ⸱⸱⸱ (87), *lik.kih*, "may he slay (victims in sacrifice)?" or perhaps *liq.qi* "may he purify?"

from נמה or נקה. The two last verbs occur in similar connexion in the first person of the aorist; and here 79 and 40 replace 123 and 252. The latter verb is evidently the same which is elsewhere written with 163 *ki* (see par. 43). Indeed, in another inscription we have 252.163; but 163 and 87 can scarcely be identical, and if the latter be *qi*, the former may have been used for it by a license of which there are frequent instances. I will add another example of this tense, which occurs at the end of the main part of the Nakshi Rustam inscription. It is a form which I cannot but consider anomalous, and peculiar to this late age. We have 295.269.172.211, *li.i'd.din.nu*, which I take to be for *líddin-su*, "may he give it!" An object to the verb is required, and *liddín* is the entire of the third person singular of this tense. It may be questioned whether we are to consider this as a new affix or as a peculiar instance of the assimilation of concurrent letters.

72. The examples given illustrate the forms of the leading persons of this tense in every kind of verbs but those which begin with *waw*. The first and third persons of the aorist of these verbs are of the forms *úkil* and *yúkil*, the initial syllable being in both expressed by 46. That 119, *lu*, would replace 46 in the first person of the optative was to be expected; but it appears that it does so in the third person also. Tiglath Pileser first says that the tablets of his ancestor (" to their places") 46. (76), *u.tir*, "I restored;" and he then prays that when his place shall decay, some of his descendants may rebuild it, and his tablets to their places, 119.76, *lu.tir*, "may he restore," and write his name with his. I have reasons, which I cannot here explain, for considering the root of these forms to be חדר; although they might be from חור in Pihel, as in the instance adduced in the last paragraph. I have only met one instance of a second person of the optative; the root and the conjugation may be doubted; but it may nevertheless be considered satisfactory evidence that *lu* was prefixed to *t*, and of course to *n* also, when they were preformatives of the aorist. The instance in question occurs in the great inscription of Nebuchadnezzar, II. 1; it is 119.275.253.37. ⟨⟨⟨ (22), *lu.ti.i'p.pi.i's*, "mayest thou ———." The third person singular feminine in the optative is not the same as this; but, as I have observed in several instances, is of the form *lipkul*, like the masculine.

Some forms analogous to those of the Assyrian optative exist in most of the cognate languages; but they are not sufficiently developed to make it worth while to institute a comparison between them. I therefore pass on to the last regular tense of Qal.

73. To the tense which I am about to consider I give the name of continuative. I have already mentioned that it resembles the Hebrew preterite in having all its additions at the end. In this it differs from all the preceding tenses except the imperative. I have only met with this tense in the first person singular, and in the third person in both genders and numbers; I can, therefore, only complete it from the analogy of the cognate languages and of the pronouns of the first and second persons, which I have explained as being verbs in this tense, forming complete parenthetic sentences, as "it is I," "it is thou," &c. I will content myself with giving the separate personal pronouns in a line with this tense.

1. com. sing.	*pakláku* or *paklak*	4.140.113, *a.ná.ku.*
2. masc. sing.	[*pákiltá*]	204.272, *at.tá* for *antá.*
2. fem. sing.	[*pákilti'*]	[*atti'* for *anti'*].
3. masc. sing.	*pákil* or *pákal*	48.46, *su.u*, *sú'u.*
3. fem. sing.	*páklat*	32.12, *si.i.*, *si'i.*
1. com. pl.	[*pákilnú*]	[*annú*].
2. masc. pl.	[*pákiltúnu*]	[*attúnu* for *antúnu*].
2. fem. pl.	[*pákiltína*]	[*attína* for *antína*].
3. masc. pl.	*páklu*	48.211, *sú.nu.*
3. fem. pl.	*pákla*	32.140, *si.na.*

74. A few examples of these forms must suffice. I have already mentioned in par. 20, the words for "I was stopping," with and without the subjunctive enclitic. The simple word is ⟨⟨–⟩ (300).111.113, *uch.ba.ku.* The enclitic, added after 163, *ki*, "when, or while," is 192, *ni.* The root is מן. A comparison of the inscription on the frame of the statue in the British Museum, lines 34, &c., and of the other inscriptions which contain the same text, gives the five following verbs in this conjugation; and all these verbs have ideographs belonging to them, which may be used with 113 for the forms here given (see par. 63): 27. 95.113, *sar.ra.ku*, "I am a king;" 28.188.113, *bi'.la.ku*, "I am a master;" 140.153.268.113, *na.a'h.da.ku*, "I am glorious;" 77.95. 113, *'ich.ra.ku*, "I am able" (or powerful? מצי;) ⟨⟨⟨ (108).272. 113, *kap.ta.ku*, for *kabdaku*, from מב, "I am honourable." The ideographs which represent these five verbs are ⟨⟨ (20), which is phonetically *man* or *nish*; 285, phonetically *in*, or something like it, which might be expressed by *iñ*; 12, phonetically *i*; ⊢𝔼‖ (267), phonetically *makh*, and ⟨𝔼⊢ (215), of which I know no syllabic value.

75. The meaning of the name Nabunahid is evidently "Nabu is glorious," the latter part being a verb in this tense. It is written 140.153.269, *na.a'h.id*. Of one of the people mentioned in the annals of the builder of the north-western palace at Nimrud, it is said ("who like women") ⪤ (85).51.192, *chap.ru.ni.* from ־סר, "were in the habit of dancing," as I suppose the word to mean. We read in the same annals of mountains, ("which for the passage of armies") 188.6.40.211, *la sa.a'k.nu*, "were not fit." The same word is used of cities which "(among mountains) lay, or were situated." In these inscriptions this verb is generally written 6.211, on the principle of par. 63, which must still be read *saknu;* of a single town 6.87 *sakin* is used. When the position of cities is described as on the near or far bank of the Euphrates, or in the middle of it, the word for "lies" is ⼁ (5).295, *cha.li*, from ־חלה. The second vowel may however be *a*. We read "(the city) was very strong," 47.287, 47.20, *dan.an, dan.nish*. These are from the same root as adjectives which we constantly meet with in the royal titles *sarru rabu, sarru dannu*, "the great king, the strong king." *Ish* is an adverbial termination. It is added to nouns as well as adjectives; thus *sallátish* is equivalent to *ana sallati*, "for a spoil." It must not be supposed that *dannish* is here used because it is from the same root as the verb which it qualifies. It is the equivalent of *valde*, which would be used with any adjective as well as with *validus*. The concurrence of the two words is accidental. Instances of the feminine are rare. I have met, however, with 85.272.204, *chab.ta.a't*, which is evidently from the common verb ־חבת, and is the feminine singular of this tense. It occurs BM.44.26, and again 33. The exact translation of the clause is by no means certain. If it be what I suppose it, *chabtat* here governs an accusative case, as this verb always does in its other tenses. This would be important, could it be established, as in all the other instances I have adduced the verbs in this tense are intransitive. They shew, however, that the tense is used to express a permanent or at least a long continued state, or habitual action, as opposed to transient action, whether past, present, or future.

I ought to add that the subjunctive enclitic, when it is added to the third person singular of this tense, takes the form *i*, instead of *u*. Thus, we have 188.225.194, *la.bi.i'r*, "it was old;" but 163.188.225.73, *ki.la.bi.ri*, "when it was old."

E. Hincks.

CORRESPONDENCE.

*** The Editor begs the reader will bear in mind that he does not hold himself responsible for the opinions of his Correspondents.

THE DIAL OF AHAZ AND THE EMBASSY FROM MERODACH BALADAN.

Sir,—In the last number of *The Journal of Sacred Literature* (pp. 407—413), is a paper[a] entitled *The Dial of Ahaz, and Scriptural Chronology*, in which the writer speaks of ascertaining the year of " The

---

[a] Near the end of this paper (p. 412), the writer tells us that he regards, as "a hopeless contradiction," the notion "that Darius, the son of Ahasuerus, of the seed of the Medes, was identical with Cyaxares the son of Astyages." Now, if such a hopeless contradiction can be satisfactorily proved to exist, and if it can also be shewn that Darius, the son of Ahasuerus, was (as your correspondent thinks) *identical with Darius Hystaspes;* I shall willingly, as well as of necessity, retract all that was advanced by me upon this subject, at p. 171 of the April number of *The Journal of Sacred Literature.* In the meantime, I venture to trespass upon your indulgence by requesting the favour of your inserting the following attempt to defend my view.

In p. 413 your correspondent gives a " genealogical table to make more intelligible" the impossibility of identifying Darius the son of Ahasuerus, with Cyaxares the son of Astyages. I proceed to offer a few objections to the statements in this table.

1. The reign of Nebuchadnezzar in Babylon is there said to have commenced, 578 b.c. This date appears to me to contradict the Egyptian chronology.

The prophet Jeremiah tells us that "Nebuchadnezzar smote the army of Pharaoh-Necho king of Egypt, "in the fourth year of Jehoiakim, son of Josiah king of Judah" (xlvi. 1, 2). Now the generally received dates of the accession and death of Pharaoh-Necho are 619 and 603 b.c. Dr. Hincks, however, thinks it certain that the first year of Nechao II., corresponded to 612 b.c., and that he died in the sixteenth year of his reign, 597-6 b.c. Hence the death of Nabopolassar, and the commencement of the sole sovereignty of his son Nebuchadnezzar, are not to be dated *later* than cir. 595-4 b.c.

We also thus learn that the *nineteenth* year of Nebuchadnezzar, and the destruction of the temple at Jerusalem, must not be dated *later* than cir. 576-5 b.c.

And, as the fourth Ptolemy (Philopater) began to reign cir. 222-1 b.c., he ascended the Egyptian throne about *three hundred and fifty-four* years before the destruction of the temple at Jerusalem. Hence, Demetrius the Jewish historian is in error, when (p. 409) "he places the last captivity of the Jews, which was in the nineteenth year of Nebuchadnezzar, 338 years and three months before the reign of the fourth Ptolemy; *i. e.,* in 560 b.c."

Again Psammiticus, the predecessor of Pharaoh-Necho, ceased to reign in 612 b.c. But Herodotus assures us, that it was in the reign of Psammiticus, that the Scythians established themselves in Asia. Thus it was *not* (p. 409) in 606 b.c., but *before* 612 b.c. that the twenty-eight years of Scythian dominion commenced in Asia.

2. In his genealogical table your correspondent makes 511 b.c. to be the date of the commencement of the reign in Babylon of Cyrus the son of Cambyses and Mandane. Now it is generally believed to have been fairly proved from certain recorded eclipses

going back of the shadow on the Dial of Ahaz," and of the possibility of thence deducing the third year of the reign of Sennacherib, and the fourteenth year of the reign of Hezekiah.

I remember reading with much interest the following passage in the *Journal of Sacred Literature* for October, 1854, p. 218: "It is well known to Hebrew scholars, and noticed in the margin of our authorized Bibles, that the exact meaning of the word translated ' sun-dial' of Ahaz,· is ' degrees' or steps of Ahaz." By an ingenious astronomical argument, aided by diagrams, but unintelligible without them, Mr. Bosanquet shewed that upon such steps as appear to have been used for exhibiting the sun's meridional altitude, any very large partial eclipse, almost but

---

in ancient times (*J. S. L.*, Jan., p. 459), that the fifth of Nabopolassar (the father of Nebuchadnezzar) was 621 B.C., the seventh of Cambyses 523 B.C., and the twentieth and thirty-first of Darius Hystaspes respectively 503 and 492 B.C.

But if the seventh of Cambyses was 523 B.C., then it follows that Cyrus, who was the son of Cambyses and Mandane, and also the father of Cambyses, Smerdis, and Atossa (who was first the wife of her brother Cambyses, and afterwards of Darius Hystaspes), must have died cir. 530 B.C., and therefore could not have reigned at Babylon in 511 B.C.

Also, if 621 B.C. was the fifth of Nabopolassar the father of Nebuchadnezzar, then it is utterly inconsistent with the testimony of ancient history to suppose, with your correspondent, that this Nabopolassar (p. 409) ceased to reign on the joint thrones of Babylon and Nineveh 606 B.C., on account of the Scythian irruption into Asia, and that he was afterwards again reigning at Babylon in 579 B.C., in conjunction with his son Nebuchadnezzar.

And if the reign of Cyrus at Babylon commenced not (as in the table) in 511 B.C., but earlier than 530 B.C., then must the reign of Nebuchadnezzar have commenced, not in 578 B.C., but earlier than 597 B.C. ; and his nineteenth year must have been at least *three hundred and fifty-seven* years earlier than the accession of the fourth Ptolemy in 222.1 B.C.

3. In the table in question, two things are stated concerning Darius Hystaspes, (*a*) that he married a daughter of Ahasuerus, *i. e.*, of Cyaxares the son of Astyages ; and (*b*) that he began to reign in Babylon in 493 B.C.

The table states correctly that Cyrus married a daughter of Ahasuerus or Cyaxares ; but if we are to receive the testimony of ancient writers, viz., that this Cyaxares had only one child, and that a daughter, who was married to Cyrus, we cannot admit that Darius also married a daughter of this Cyaxares.

And are there not insuperable difficulties in the way of our believing that Darius Hystaspes *began* to reign in Babylon 493 B.C. ? For unless we can fairly disprove the statement of Herodotus, we seem bound to receive his assertion, that the Babylonians revolted from the Persians, early in the reign of this Darius, who did not succeed in taking the rebellious city until after a protracted siege of about twenty months, when he put to a cruel and ignominious death three thousand of the vanquished inhabitants, removed the gates of brass, dismantled the fortifications, and so greatly reduced the height of the lofty walls, that they were no longer fitted to protect rebels against a besieging Persian army. That all this took place early in the reign of Darius, is evident from the fact that this conquest of Babylon was prior to the expedition against the Scythians. If, therefore, we are to follow Herodotus, *the city and territory of Babylon were already a province of the Persian empire*, when Darius ascended the throne in 521 B.C.

I have elsewhere observed in a paper on Darius the Mede and Darius Hystaspes, that the latter, in his inscription at Behistun, does not speak of Babylon as if he had been the first Persian monarch who had conquered Babylon and annexed it to the Persian empire. On the contrary, the language of the royal annalist seems plainly to indicate that the Babylonians were defeated and punished as *rebels*, who, having

not quite total, on the northern limb of the sun, occurring about ten or a few more days from the winter solstice, near the hour of noon, would produce the effect described by Isaiah, and in the book of Kings. He then stated that by the kindness of the Astronomer Royal, he was enabled to shew that such an eclipse did take place at the very time deduced from the chronological argument, viz., on the 11th of January, fourteen days after the winter solstice of 690 B.C. The only difficulty was about the time of the day. Mr. Airey calculates the time of the central eclipse to be soon after eleven o'clock ; which is too early for the phenomenon on the steps to be produced. But a letter was read from the well known mathematician and astronomer, Mr. Adams, shewing that the received

---

already been in lawful subjection to the Persian empire, had revolted from their rightful sovereign.

Thus the combined testimony of Herodotus and the Behistun inscription, would seem fully to justify the historian Mitford in telling us that " *Assyria*, Media, Lydia, Armenia, Egypt, Tyre, with their dependencies, were now (*i. e., at the beginning of the reign of Darius Hystaspes*, cir. 521 B.C.) united under one vast empire."

And if Darius was the mighty king of Persia, and monarch of the vast Medo-Persian empire, from 521—486-5 B.C., it seems clear beyond all question that Cyrus could not have been king of *Persia* and Babylon in 511 B.C., and that he would not have ventured in that year, when Darius Hystaspes had already held the Medo-Persian throne ten years, to send forth throughout the kingdom a written decree (which he could not doubt would meet the eye of Darius), commencing with the following arrogant, not to say treasonable assumptions, "Thus saith Coresh king of Persia, The Lord God of heaven *hath given me all the kingdoms of the earth*" (Ezra i. 2).

4. It is stated in the table that Darius Hystaspes was born in 555 B.C., and died in 485 B.C., aged seventy years. That Darius lived to the age of 70, is asserted by Ctesias ; and this view is really necessary to your correspondent's argument, which requires that this king should have been about 62 years old in the sabbatical year of 493 B.C. I do not wish to dispute the point, but would observe that it is not so certain as to leave no room for doubt. Herodotus, I believe, represents this Darius as 21 years of age when Cyrus went on his expedition against the Scythians 530 B.C. On this view, the year of Darius' birth would be cir. 551 B.C., and 493 would have been about his fifty-ninth year, and 489 B.C. his sixty-second.

Your correspondent identifies Darius the Mede with Darius Hystaspes; and, as the former was "about threescore and ten years old when he took the realm of the Chaldeans" (Dan. v. 31), the latter, if really identical with the former, must have begun to reign in Babylon cir. 493 B.C. (if we follow Ctesias), or cir. 489 B.C. (if we follow Herodotus).

It is not, however, difficult to prove from Scripture and authentic secular history (what has already been shewn from Herodotus) the impossibility of this identification. No one will doubt that Darius Nothus ascended the Persian throne cir. 423 B.C., when the title of King of Assyria must have become utterly obsolete, while that of " king of Persia" had long previously obtained, and still possessed, a world-wide renown. If he had been the Darius of the second temple, we cannot offer any satisfactory reason why in his sixth year, cir. 417 B.C., he should have been styled by the returned Jews, " king of Assyria" (Ezra vi. 22). On the contrary, the very application of this title, by the united assembly of the returned Jews at the celebration of their first passover, after the dedication of the second temple, appears to me to be strong presumptive evidence, almost amounting to demonstration, that the Darius of the second temple must have been the son of Hystaspes.

The readers of Ezra (v. 13) are not surprised to find that Tatnai, the governor of Samaria and the adjacent countries, should style Cyrus king of Babylon, but many of them must think it strange that Ezra designates the Darius of the second temple,

secular variation of the moon was slightly erroneous, and that the time of the eclipse in question might perhaps be advanced half an hour; adding, however, that in his opinion the error was not quite so large, but that he hoped to arrive at more complete results.

It did not, however, appear to me that the correctness of your correspondent's chronological argument would be decisively established, even should Mr. Adams succeed in removing all uncertainty with reference to the actual occurrence of the phenomenon in question, on the 11th of January, 690 B.C.

In duly considering this point, we must first carefully weigh the language of the Lord, through his prophet, to the sick king of Judah.

---

by the title of "king of Assyria." The apparent difficulty, however, may seem to be wholly removed, if we follow the received chronology. We have only to suppose (and surely the supposition is highly probable) that Ezra, when compiling his history, had before him a contemporary record of the first celebration of the passover after the dedication of the second temple, wherein the very words were recorded which were employed by the returned Jews who were present at the feast. And when he found there how these Jews, in their gladness and exultation, praised the Lord for making them joyful, and turning the heart of the *king of Assyria* to them," Ezra would deem it his duty, as a true and accurate historian, to retain the language of the contemporary document, and not to change the elder Assyrian title into the more recent title of "king of Persia," although he himself elsewhere employs the latter title when speaking of this Darius.

But why did the Jews, on that interesting occasion, designate their royal Persian benefactor as king of Assyria, a title which doubtless belonged to him? It may be replied that, of the restored Jews present at this first passover after the dedication, all who were above twenty-two years of age, must have been born under a king of Babylon. For it was with this title that Darius the Mede became the sovereign of the exiled Jews; and, indeed, it was not until Cyrus became king of Babylon, that he became also lord of the captive descendants of Abraham, and issued his decree for the rebuilding of the temple at Jerusalem. The conduct of Cambyses, the son and successor of Cyrus, had not been such as to make the comparatively recent title of king of Persia popular in Judea. Above all, this new regal title *had no connexion with those earlier national recollections and associations* which would naturally fill the hearts of the restored exiles on the solemn occasion of the first passover in the second temple.

There remained, therefore, two regal titles by which, in the fervent outpouring of the national gratitude to the Lord, they could designate their illustrious benefactor Darius, viz., king of Babylon, and king of Assyria. To the former of these there were two objections; it would serve to recall the humbling recollections of their long captivity, while it would scarcely be, at that particular time, either an honourable or acceptable designation for Darius.

What, then, had occurred to make it unsuitable to select for Darius Hystaspes, in the sixth year of his reign, the title of king of Babylon? Ancient history informs us that the Babylonians revolted from this Darius in the fifth year of his reign. The city, as has been already remarked, was invested by the Persians; and thus the siege, which lasted nearly twenty months, may have ended shortly before the close of the *sixth* year of the son of Hystaspes. The Jews would, therefore, according to the received chronology, be busily and successfully employed in finishing their second temple (which was completed in the *sixth* year of Darius), while the Persians were prosecuting the siege of Babylon, and Darius, exasperated at the obstinate resistance of the rebels, was meditating their speedy humiliation and punishment. Accordingly, past national recollections, combined with the state of public affairs at that particular time, would effectually incline the restored Jews, when joyfully offering their public thanksgivings unto the Lord, to exclude all mention of the

"And Hezekiah said unto Isaiah, What shall be the sign that the Lord will heal me, and that I shall go up into the house of the Lord the third day? And Isaiah said, This sign shalt thou have of the Lord, that the Lord will do the thing that he hath spoken: shall the shadow GO FORWARD ten degrees? or *go back* ten degrees? And Hezekiah answered, it is a light thing for the shadow to go down ten degrees: nay, but let the shadow return backward ten degrees. And Isaiah the prophet CRIED UNTO THE LORD: and he brought the shadow ten degrees backward, by which it had gone down in the dial (degrees or steps) of Ahaz" (2 Kings xx. 8—11).

It seems plain from this brief narrative, that the Most High left it

---

proud and rebellious city, and to speak of their earthly sovereign and benefactor, *not* as king of Babylon, but as KING OF ASSYRIA.

And if the Darius of the second temple was, as seems almost (or rather, altogether) certain, the son of Hystaspes, the Scriptures must be understood as positively forbidding us to identify the Darius Hystaspes with "Darius, the son of Ahasuerus, of the seed of the Medes." For the prophet Haggai informs us (i. 1—4), that *in the second year of the Darius of the second temple,* the Jews had not only returned into Judea, but were already dwelling in cieled houses. They must therefore have already been residing a few years in their own land, before they had built and furnished comfortable houses for themselves. But, *in the first year of Darius the son of Ahasuerus* (Dan. v. 31; ix. 1), we know that the Jews were still in their exile beyond the Euphrates, nor had the decree been yet promulgated, which permitted them to return to the land of their fathers, and rebuild the temple at Jerusalem.

The testimony of the Jewish historian Josephus is important. He makes Darius the Mede to be contemporary with Cyrus the illustrious conqueror of Babylon, and plainly teaches us that the Darius of the second temple was Darius Hystaspes.

Accordingly, it was in the second year of Darius Hystaspes (cir. 521-0 B.C.), that the angel said, "O Lord of hosts, how long wilt thou not have mercy on Jerusalem, and on the cities of Judah, against which thou hast had indignation *these threescore and ten years?*" (Zech. i. 12). Ascending through seventy years from this date, we have cir. 590 B.C. (about which time the army of Nebuchadnezzar finally invaded Judea, and did not return to Babylon until they had destroyed both city and temple) as the commencement of *the threescore and ten years of indignation,* of which the angel speaks. We cannot thus make the *nineteenth* year of Nebuchadnezzar, in which the temple was to be destroyed, to be later than cir. 590—586.

I am not aware that there is any satisfactory reason for supposing that Jeremiah alludes to this particular period of threescore and ten years, mentioned by the angel in Zech. i. 12. The prophet appears to speak of only two periods of seventy years, which were almost entirely coincident with each other. According to the received chronology, one of these periods, that of the subjection of the nations to the Chaldean dynasty, began with the victory at Carchemish in 606 B.C., and ended 538 B.C., when Babylon was taken by a Medo-Persian force under the command of Coresh (Cyrus); the other, that of the service of the exiled Jews under the Chaldean yoke, terminated also (in strictness of speech) in 538 B.C. But the last remnant of the Chaldean yoke, viz., the dwelling as exiles in Babylon, did not end until two years later, when the decree of Coresh (Cyrus) allowed them to return into Judea, and rebuild their temple (536 B.C.).

At p. 408 is the following important statement: "That no system of Scripture chronology can ever be satisfactory which is not based upon the division of time into sabbatical weeks, or seven year periods, into which it was prospectively laid out by Moses, by decree from mount Sinai, and which must, therefore, be involved in the history of the chosen people, from the time of their entrance into the promised land."

This assertion seems to imply that we already possess, or are able to discover

absolutely to the choice of Hezekiah, whether the shadow should *advance* or *recede;* and that if the sick king had declared his desire that the shadow should advance ten degrees, the Lord would assuredly have granted this desire, *by causing the shadow to* GO FORWARD *ten degrees.*

Unless, therefore, it can be proved that during some part of the duration of the eclipse in question, the shadow would also *be advanced* ten degrees on the steps of Ahaz, it follows that if Hezekiah had desired (as he was fully permitted to do) the going forward of the shadow on the steps, such an advance could only have been accomplished by the special exertion of the miraculous power of God, and not by any event occurring in the appointed order of nature.

---

something like a true and regular list of the sabbatical years from the time of the entrance into the promised land. But your correspondent, when attempting to shew that 493.2 was sabbatical, states that it is one in regular series, calculated from three known Sabbaths mentioned by Josephus. Yet how can we feel fully assured (even if we believe the Jews to have retained a correct reckoning of their sabbatical years until the days of Vespesian) that these sabbatical years in Josephus are accurately represented by the particular years B.C. which have been assigned to them? The mistake of a single year might vitiate the computation.

It may be inferred from your correspondent's arguments that there is more or less uncertainty and perplexity on this subject. He compares (p. 409) the regnal numerals of Scripture with what is called "the eight-eighty year period of the Chaldean historians," and makes this admission, "There is an *interval, therefore, of three years* to be accounted for in the scriptural account." And we are told that it is not improbable, from the book of Judith, that there was an interregnum of a few years before Josiah reigned. If, as appears to be the case, the recently discovered Assyrian inscriptions prove the book of Tobit to be a fictitious tale, we shall hesitate to appeal to the apocryphal book of Judith as if it were an authentic historical document. An opportunity may hereafter be offered of discussing the question of the authenticity of the contents of the latter book.

It is stated (p. 408) that "the canon of Ptolemy places the last year of Asaradinus or Esarhaddon, at Babylon, in 668 B.C.; which year, therefore, we may reasonably conclude, was that of the death of his father Sennacherib at Nineveh." This can scarcely be considered to be a reasonable inference, if we bear in mind that the canon teaches us that 668.7 B.C. was the year of the death of Esarhaddon himself, and *not* of the death of his father Sennacherib.

I would, however, especially notice the inference which your correspondent draws from this conclusion, viz., *that Sennacherib reigned twenty-five years.* One of the Greek historians, I believe, assigned eighteen years to Sennacherib's reign. Col. Rawlinson has discovered an Assyrian inscription referring to the *twenty-second* year of Sennacherib, and seems to think that this king reigned only twenty-two years. It may be quite impossible, at present, to decide this question. But, surely, your correspondent, who supposes Sennacherib to have reigned *twenty-five* years, cannot, consistently with such an opinion, appeal to the book of Tobit *as an authentic document,* and say that "from the last verse of the book of Tobit, we learn that Ahasuerus with the Jews was equivalent to Cyaxares with the Greeks" (p. 411).

It is true that at the close of this apocryphal book, we read that Tobias, the son of Tobit, "died at Ecbatane in Media, being an hundred and seven and twenty years old. But before he died he heard of the destruction of Nineveh, which was taken by Nabuchodonosor and Assuerus; and before his death he rejoiced over Nineveh." If, however, we have reason to believe this book to be an idle fiction, we cannot feel altogether assured of the truth of this (supposed) historical statement.

Now, if the Assyrian inscriptions shew that the reign of Sennacherib extended into the *twenty-second* year, and the writer of the book of Tobit does not allow that reign to exceed even five or six years, we have strong reason for regarding the book

And when I read how "Isaiah *cried unto the Lord*," i. e., *prayed fervently* that the shadow might recede ten degrees, it seems difficult to believe that the going back of the shadow was not a miraculous event—a miracle wrought by omnipotent power in answer to the prophet's prayer, and in fulfilment of the Lord's promise—but only the necessary result of an eclipse, occurring in the appointed order of nature.

Too much stress must not be laid on the visit of the Babylonian ambassadors sent to Hezekiah by Merodach-Baladan, who had heard "that Hezekiah had been sick and was recovered." It seems, however, quite reasonable to suppose that the going back of the shadow ten degrees on the steps of Ahaz, in connexion with Isaiah's prophetic announcement,

---

as a tale of fiction. But it may be reasonably proved from Assyrian inscriptions, that the return of Sennacherib after the defeat of his forces was not *later* than his *fourth* year. Let us compare with this statement the following passage from Tobit.

"And if the king Sennacherib had slain any, when he was come, and fled from Judea, I buried them privily; for in his wrath he killed many; but the bodies were not found, when they were sought for of the king. And when one of the Ninevites went and complained of me to the king, that I buried them, and hid myself; understanding that I was sought for to be put to death, I withdrew myself for fear. Then all my goods were taken forcibly away, neither was there anything left me, beside my wife Anna, and my son Tobias. *And there passed not* FIVE AND FIFTY DAYS, *before two of his sons killed him*, and they fled into the mountains of Ararath, and Sarchedonus his son reigned in his stead; who appointed over his father's accounts Archiacharus my brother Anael's son" (Tobit i. 18—21). If we suppose Sennacherib to have reigned even *seven* years, then must this king have been occupied during two or three years in occasionally killing Jews, and Tobit must have occasionally exerted himself in burying them. The fair inference from these verses would, perhaps, be that about five or six months may have elapsed after the return of Sennacherib from Judea, and that, between the commencement of Tobit's concealment and the murder of Sennacherib, there did not occur *five and fifty days*.

Many will suspect that the writer of this apocryphal tale obtained from his own inventive imagination, not only this interval of fifty-five days, but also the name, parentage, and advancement of Achiacharus the son of Tobit's brother Anael, as well as the unusual facts that Tobit and Tobias died, the former at the advanced age of an hundred and eight and fifty years, and the latter when one hundred and seven and twenty years old.

It has been generally thought that Nineveh was taken by Cyaxares and Nabopolassar, and thus the writer of Tobit may have had as little authority for writing Assuerus as he had for inserting the name of Nabuchodonosor instead of that of his father Nabopolassar. Nor are we warranted, by adding an unfounded conjecture to the (supposed) historical testimony of the writer of Tobit (evidently a tale of fiction), to assume as certain, "that Ahasuerus was with the Jews equivalent to Cyaxares with the Greeks; and that, in some way, Darius Hystaspes must have been the descendant of Cyaxares."

With reference to Tobit's strange blunder concerning the length of Sennacherib's reign, I venture to offer the following suggestion in the way of inquiry. Where did the writer of this apocryphal work obtain his information concerning the shortness of the period which he supposed to have elapsed between Sennacherib's return from Judea, and his murder by his sons?

Now I find in Lodge's Josephus, the following version of a quotation made by the Jewish writer from the Chaldean historian Berossus: "Sennacherib retired himself (from Judea) into his city, where, *after he had lived for a time*, he was traitorously slain by Adrammelech and Selenar, his two eldest sons." I think that, in Whiston's translation, the language is still more favourable to the idea of a short interval. Is it, therefore, possible that even so early as the age of Berossus, an

would be as much talked of in Jerusalem as even the sudden and unexpected recovery of the king from the very brink of the grave. It would, therefore, appear to be almost certain that the tidings of these wonderful events which preceded the removal of the malady, would be conveyed to the court of Babylon; and that it was with special reference to the remarkable astronomical phenomenon, which may have been observed at the time by the Chaldeans at Babylon, that ambassadors were sent to Jerusalem " to inquire of *the wonder* that was done in the land" (2 Chr. xxxii. 31). Yet this embassy would have been equally sent, whether the observed phenomenon had been caused by a special interposition of Divine power, or by an eclipse occurring at a particular season of the year.

---

erroneous tradition may have prevailed among the Chaldean historians that the interval between Sennacherib's disastrous return and death was short? If a Jew had read in Berossus or any other Chaldean writer that the interval in question was comparatively brief, he could not correct his error from the indefinite language of Holy Writ (2 Ki. xix. 37 ; 2 Chr. xxxii. 21). It was not the object of the sacred writers to give an account of Sennacherib's subsequent career, but merely to state that, in fulfilment of the divine prediction (Isa. xxxvii. 7), he finally perished miserably by the murderous hands of his own sons, in the temple of his god Nisroch.

I confess myself to have been surprised at the following attempt to shew that Darius the Mede, son of Ahasuerus of the seed of the Medes, was the Persian king Darius Hystaspes: " The only objection which remains to be disposed of is, that Daniel, who so well knew the age of the king, and who must have been equally well acquainted with his genealogy, speaks of him as the son of Ahasuerus, and of the seed of the Medes. This at first sight appears to be a serious difficulty. . . . No one, of course, would venture to deny that the father of Darius was Hystaspes, for this is indelibly graven on the rock at Behistun, by direction of Darius himself. Daniel, therefore, whose record I take to be as trustworthy as that of the rock, in speaking of Ahasuerus of the seed of the Medes, can only have referred to the maternal ancestry of Darius as being derived from the Medes. . . . There is no difficulty in believing, if Daniel has declared the fact, that Darius the son of Hystaspes, was either descended from Cyaxares, the father of Astyages, through his mother, or that he may have married a daughter of Cyaxares the son of Astyages, another daughter of whom was married to Cyrus" (pp. 411, 412).

Certainly, *if Daniel has declared the fact*, that the Persian Darius, son of the Persian Hystaspes, was the son of a Median princess, or son-in-law of the second Cyaxares, it would be our duty to submit at once to such a declaration. But I find no such declaration in that prophet's book ; and it has already been noticed that Xenophon states that the second Cyaxares had only one child, a daughter, who was married to Cyrus. Nor does Herodotus give any encouragement to the conjecture that the mother of Darius was descended from the first Cyaxares. He tells us that it was only under the strong influence of superstitious fear that Astyages condescended to give his daughter in marriage to the Achæmenian Cambyses. It is not, therefore, probable that the first Cyaxares would, without any apparent political motive, have consented to accept the Achæmenian father of Hystaspes as a son-in-law.

Your correspondent, in endeavouring to remove what he acknowledges to be a serious difficulty, proceeds to ask and answer a question in terms which again frankly admit the grave obstacle which the language of the sacred writer opposes to his view : " But why should Daniel adopt this most unusual and unnatural mode of designating this prince by his maternal ancestor Ahasuerus the Mede, instead of the ordinary mode, and that adopted by Darius himself, in the inscription at Behistun, of tracing his ancestry in the paternal line, through Hystaspes to Achæmenes the Persian ?"

" The answer to this question I believe to be that, in one case, he was desirous

The view of your correspondent is undoubtedly consistent with the most devout reverence for the Word of God, as it fully recognizes, on the occasion in question, a special and miraculous interposition on the part of the Most High God of Israel. For we may safely feel an assured conviction, that the Jews of Hezekiah's time possessed no astronomical knowledge, such as to enable them to announce accurately the time of an approaching eclipse, still less could they be aware, that a certain kind of eclipse, occurring near the hour of noon, and a few days from the winter solstice, would have the effect of causing the shadow to recede on the steps

---

of gratifying that portion which preferred to be governed by a Mede, in the other, that portion which vaunted the superiority of Persia."

Both the supposition and explanation are unsatisfactory. In p. 411, Darius Hystaspes, who is there erroneously identified with Darius the Mede, is supposed to have taken the kingdom of the Chaldeans in 493 B.C., being then about sixty-two years of age. Darius had already been reigning nearly thirty years over Media and Persia. Is it not very improbable, that in this late period of his Medo-Persian reign, the Babylonians should so greatly prefer a Median to a Persian sovereign, that the son of Hystaspes should deem it politic to meet the supposed prejudice, by designating himself as a Median, on account of a (supposed) connexion, by marriage or maternal descent, with the royal house of Media. And is it not also most improbable that the mighty and renowned king Darius Hystaspes, who was proud of his Persian descent from Achæmenes, and who would naturally desire to maintain the pre-eminence of the Persian name throughout his empire, should condescend in 493 B.C., after having been, nearly thirty years, the illustrious Persian sovereign of Persia and Media, to designate himself as a Mede in his province of Babylon, where it must have been so long notorious that he was a Persian and son of a Persian; especially when we remember that about twenty-three years previously, he had taken the city of Babylon after a siege of twenty months, impaled three thousand of its inhabitants, removed its gates, dismantled its fortifications, and so reduced the height of its lofty walls, that they were no longer adequate to protect the city against a besieging army.

If then the Darius of Daniel really was (as Darius Hystaspes doubtless was) a Persian, and son of a Persian, why should the prophet so plainly and distinctly designate him as a Mede? And we are to bear in mind that Daniel is not alone in employing this designation; it is also expressly used by an angel or heavenly messenger from God. For we read that "in the third year of Cyrus (Coresh) king of Persia (and surely after Darius the son of Ahasuerus of the seed of the Medes, had ceased to reign in Babylon), a heavenly messenger from the Most High, thus speaks to Daniel: 'Also I, in the first year *of Darius the Mede*, even I stood to confirm him' (Dan. xi. 1). This is not less decisive than 'what is elsewhere read in the same book, 'And *Darius the Median* took the kingdom'" (ver. 31).

Now we have no reason whatever for supposing that the words either of Daniel, or of the heavenly messenger, were intended to be made known to the heathen contemporaries of the prophet. It must not be forgotten that the prophet Daniel was not composing a history which should be read by Darius or Cyrus, by Medes or Persians. He was drawing up, as a competent witness, a true statement of certain facts for the instruction of the church of God. Hence, it would seem to be scarcely possible to draw any other reasonable and probable conclusion from the three passages, which have been quoted from the book of Daniel, than this, viz., that Darius the Mede, the son of Ahasuerus of the seed of the Medes, was a Mede and the son of a Mede, and *not* a Persian and son of a Persian.

Upon the whole, therefore, it appears to me that the Darius of the second temple was Darius Hystaspes; that the Coresh of Ezra was the Cyrus of Herodotus, and that the Darius and Ahasuerus of Daniel were contemporary, and therefore identical, the former with the Cyaxares of Xenophon, and the latter with the Astyages of Xenophon and Herodotus.

of the dial. Isaiah, therefore, at the time of his interview with Hezekiah, could have derived his knowledge of the near approaching phenomenon of which he spake so confidently only through a direct and express revelation from the Omnipotent and Omniscient God. Infidelity may deem the view of your correspondent to be a less offensive and repulsive (though to her equally incredible) way of explaining the narrative of Hezekiah's recovery, than that which supposes the earth, not only to have been arrested in her diurnal rotation by the Omnipotent Will of God, but also to have been constrained by the same Supreme Will to revolve upon her axis in the opposite direction, so as to cause the shadow to return ten steps upon the dial of Ahaz, and then to resume its rotatory movement in its previous and proper direction. Yet, if it should prove, upon investigation, that the latter view is the only possible way of accounting for the occurrence of the phenomenon in question, at the particular time of Hezekiah's sickness, the devout and humble believer in the Divine revelation would reverently receive it. He would say, " Is any thing too hard for the Lord ?" and would feel convinced that the miracle of which we are speaking would not be a difficult task for the Divine Omnipotence to execute—and that he who caused the iron axe-head to rise and float upon the water in the days of Elisha (2 Ki. vi. 6), and the waters of the Jordan " to rise up upon a heap," when Joshua led the children of Israel into the Promised Land, and then proceed onward in their appointed channel when the chosen people had passed over—could, with equal ease, cause the shadow to go backward ten degrees on the steps of the dial of Ahaz, through a sudden and miraculous change in the direction of the earth's diurnal rotation, and then, having accomplished his purpose, restore that rotatory movement to its original direction. Such a miracle, however awfully grand and marvelous to our conceptions, would not produce the slightest interruption in the earth's annual and the moon's lunar revolution; it would not necessarily cause fearful agitations and convulsions on the surface of our globe, —these the omnipotence of God could effectually prevent,—its only perceptible result in Judea would be to prolong, for a short space of time, on that particular day, the continuance of the sun's appearance above the horizon.

There is yet another point to notice. Can we infer from the Scriptural narrative, a reasonable probability that the third day previous to the recovery of Hezekiah was so late in the winter season (whatever be the date of the year) as the 11th of January—*i.e.*, that the shadow went backward upon the steps of Ahaz on the 11th of January; and that, on the 13th or 14th of January, Hezekiah being recovered from his sickness, went into the house of the Lord, according to the Divine Promise ?

If we examine the marginal chronology in our authorized Bible, we shall find (Isa. xxxvi. 1, and 2 Ki. xviii. 13) the date of 713 B.C. attached to the first entrance of Sennacherib into Judea, when he received tribute from Hezekiah, and that the date of 710 B.C. is attached to the advance of Tartan and Rabshakeh from Lachish against Jerusalem. When these dates were first admitted into our Bibles, it was supposed by many that Sennacherib, after receiving Hezekiah's submission and tribute, led his army into Egypt, and passed some time in the conquest of that country.

That, on his return from Egypt, he sent a large force under Tartan and Rabshakeh against Jerusalem in 710 B.C., in which year occurred the miraculous destruction of the 185,000, and Sennacherib's return to Nineveh.

In the present day, however, it has resulted from the discovery and examination of the Assyrian inscriptions, that Sennacherib did not invade Egypt in his third year, but that he returned to Nineveh with the tribute which he had gathered from Judea; and it is supposed that the destruction of the 185,000 occurred in the same year. I shall assume the correctness of this view in the following remarks.

In this eventful third year of Sennacherib, there are three special periods with reference to Hezekiah.

The first period was when the fear of man entirely prevailed over pious trust in God, and when Hezekiah, alarmed at the rapid successes of Sennacherib, and apparently without consulting Isaiah, and asking counsel from God, sent, of his own will, to the Assyrian king at Lachish, to proffer unconditional submission and such tribute as Sennacherib should impose. And it was then that, in part payment of the appointed tribute, Hezekiah gave the Assyrian " all the silver that was found in the house of God, and cut off (the gold from) the doors of the temple of the Lord " (2 Ki. xviii. 13—16).

The second period was that of the dangerous sickness of the king of Judah, from which he was miraculously restored. This serious malady (which might have partly originated in Hezekiah's distress of mind, and anxious fears lest Sennacherib, after having received the tribute, should violate the terms of agreement) would seem to have been a judicial visitation from the Lord to rebuke and punish the king's want of confidence in the God of his fathers, and to chasten him for having culpably neglected to ascertain, through Isaiah, the Divine will and counsel. In consequence of the earnest prayers and tears of the king, God consented to spare his life and restore him to health. Two promises were at the same time given. The first—" I will add unto thy days *fifteen years*" (Is. xxxviii. 5), proves that, as Hezekiah reigned twenty-nine years, the sickness and recovery occurred in his fourteenth year—*i.e.*, in the year in which Sennacherib invaded Judea. The second promise—" I will deliver thee and this city out of the hand of the king of Assyria, and I will defend this city" (xxxviii. 6), proves that the sickness and recovery occurred before the destruction of the Assyrian force.

All inferences from these Scriptural facts must, of course, be more or less conjectural. I am, however, inclined to think that the rapid successes of Sennacherib make it probable that Hezekiah sent in his submission and paid his tribute before the end of the summer.

It seems to me also probable that, as no valid reason can be assigned why there should be a long interval between the offence and the punishment, or why there should be a protracted season of sickness—Hezekiah fell sick shortly after the payment of the tribute, that his sickness lasted but a few weeks at the utmost, and that it is more probable that the going back of the shadow on the steps of the dial of Ahaz occurred before the end of September, than that it took place so late as the 11th of January.

The third period was that in which confidence in God was lively and strong, not only in Hezekiah himself, but also in the hearts of his people. This we learn from 2 Chr. xxxii. 6—8. "And he set captains of war over the people, and gathered them together to him in the street of the gate of the city, and spake comfortably to them, saying, Be strong and courageous, be not afraid nor dismayed for the king of Assyria, nor for all the multitude that is with him : for there be more with us than with him. With him is an arm of flesh ; but with us is the Lord our God to help us, and to fight our battles. And THE PEOPLE *rested themselves upon the words of Hezekiah, king of Judah.*" The sacred historian seems here to assure us that the inhabitants of Jerusalem felt an inward confidence that the words of Hezekiah were true, and that the Lord would certainly deliver them, and their king, and their city, from the Assyrian invader.

And how are we to reconcile this spirit of confidence in God, and universal determination to resist to the utmost, with the feelings of distrust and apprehension of the final issue, which constrained Hezekiah to proffer, in humble, not to say abject, terms, submission and such tribute as the enemy should himself impose? It seems scarcely possible to think that, even if, while the enemy were pursuing a rapid career of triumphant success, and Jehovah seemed to have given up Judah, as he had already given up Samaria, into the hands of the Assyrian, Hezekiah had used words of confidence and encouragement, the people could, in spite of the melancholy tidings and rumours of each successive day, have trusted in, and rested upon, the assurances of their king. The difficulty, however, will at once vanish, if we suppose that, at the time in question, the tribute had already been paid, and that Hezekiah had just recovered from his sickness. For the fact that, only a few days previously, God had, through his prophet, expressly promised to deliver his people and city from the king of Assyria —that the shadow had gone backward ten degrees on the steps of Ahaz, in strict agreement with the word of Isaiah—and that Hezekiah, miraculously restored from the brink of the grave, had, according to the promise of the Lord, gone up, on the third day, into the house of God—would alike account for the confident expectation, both of king and people, of effectual deliverance from the Assyrian king.

Now, on looking at the earlier part of 2 Chr. xxxii., we find that, after the hostile entrance of Sennacherib into Judea, when Hezekiah saw that the Assyrian was purposed to fight against Jerusalem (and he would, doubtless, discover this very soon), he consulted with his princes, and the Jews at once proceeded to stop the waters of the fountains without the city, to repair the broken wall, and make weapons and shields in abundance. But his courage failed him when he beheld the unchecked career of Assyrian success, and doubting his own ability to resist Sennacherib successfully, and moved, perhaps, by a compassionate wish to deliver his suffering people from a cruel foe, whose marauding bands were busied in plundering, slaughtering, and leading into captivity, he humbled himself to offer submission and tribute, which were accepted, not, it may be presumed, without a pledge that Sennacherib would desist from farther hostilities.

If, then, we think that the above-mentioned preparations may have been carried on with less energy during the short sickness of Hezekiah, yet, when we bear in mind that in a season of imminent peril the work of months may be done in a few weeks, we may readily believe that the greater part of the defensive measures mentioned in 2 Chron. xxxii. 3—5, were executed during the time that Sennacherib was making himself master of the defenced cities and probably of Lachish, and also during the short sickness of Hezekiah. Thus, if we believe that the period of confidence, described in ver. 6—8, occurred between the king's recovery from sickness and the advance of Tartan and Rabshakeh against Jerusalem, it is neither necessary to crowd into that interval all the defensive preparations named in ver. 3—5, nor to suppose the interval itself to have exceeded two or three weeks.

The fourth period commences with the departure of Tartan, Rabsaris, and Rabshakeh from Lachish against Jerusalem, probably with the 185,000, who soon after perished suddenly. Rabshakeh, on their arrival from the city, proceeds to summon Hezekiah to surrender; but in vain. God, through his prophet, renews the promise of deliverance, and declares that "he will send a blast upon Sennacherib (marg., *put a spirit into him,* probably of fear and terror,) and cause him to hear a rumour and return into his own land" (Isa. xxxvii. 7). After having failed to terrify the Jews into a surrender, Rabshakeh returned to inform his master, who had, in the mean time, removed from Lachish, and was now encamped before Libnah. Sennacherib, having heard that Tirhakah King of Ethiopia was advancing against him, determined to delay marching in person to Jerusalem, but sent back a blasphemous and threatening message to Hezekiah. The latter having received and read the impious letter, carried it into the house of God, where he prayed fervently for immediate deliverance.

It would appear that, on the very same day, Hezekiah received from the Lord a promise that (although Tartan and Rabshakeh with their host had been permitted to encamp near Jerusalem) Sennacherib himself should not come in person "before the city with shield, nor cast a bank against it. For (saith the Lord) I will defend this city, to save it for mine own sake, and for my servant David's sake" (xix. 32). Accordingly we read how "it came to pass *that night,* that the angel of the Lord went out, and smote in the camp of the Assyrians, 185,000; and when they arose early in the morning, behold they were all dead corpses" (2 Ki. xix. 35).

This fourth period was the (probably) brief space of time, during which, as we have just seen, Tartan marched from Lachish to Jerusalem —Rabshakeh summoned Hezekiah to surrender—returned to his master at Libnah—a blasphemous message was again sent to Hezekiah—almost immediately after the 185,000 were cut off in one night—and, in which period, Sennacherib removed with the vast power that remained with him, from Lachish to Libnah. When we take into consideration the facts, that it was but a short distance from Jerusalem to Lachish or Libnah, and that Tartan would meet with no opposition on his march from Lachish to the metropolis, we shall readily admit that a fortnight or three weeks, (or even a less interval) would be fully sufficient for the occurrence of these events.

Before I conclude, it is necessary to notice that striking part of the last divine message to Hezekiah, in which it is said—"And this shall be a sign unto thee, ye shall eat this year*b* *such things as grow of themselves*, and in the second year that which springeth of the same; and in the third year sow ye and reap, and plant vineyards, and eat the fruits thereof" (Isa. xxxvii. 30).

I do not here dwell upon the apparent connexion between these words, and the divine ordinance of the jubilee. It is enough to say that if we are to understand the divine message as a command to the Jews not to sow that year—(there does appear to be an implied injunction not to sow *the second* year)—then the fair inference would be that the destruction of the Assyrian host and the flight of Sennacherib occurred before the arrival of the seed-time of the fourteenth of Hezekiah. The words of the prophet, would, however, rather appear to agree with another view, viz., that the Assyrians had already remained so long in the land, that the seed-time of that year was altogether gone by. Great scarcity and dearth would be the natural consequence of this, but God graciously removes Hezekiah's fears, by promising a sufficient supply from the spontaneous produce of the earth. This may incline us to believe that the Assyrian host remained in Judea through a portion, or even through the whole of the month of December. But if so vast a host should continue too long in the land, then, under the treading of the men, and the trampling of the horses, the spontaneous produce of the soil would be so seriously injured, as to be insufficient to meet the wants even of that reduced population which had escaped the slaughter and captivity inflicted upon so many by the enemy. Accordingly, the divine message seems to imply an assurance from the Lord that the flight of Sennacherib should be sufficiently early to permit the secure growth of the spontaneous fruits of the soil.

Hence, if the shadow went backward ten degrees upon the steps of Ahaz, on the 11th of January, and Hezekiah, having been miraculously restored to health, went up into the house of the Lord on the 13th or 14th of January, then the (probable) five or six weeks' interval between this event and the flight of Sennacherib, would allow the trampling of the Assyrian horses and the treading of the men to continue in the land, even through the greater part of the month of February—a supposition which seems too inconsistent with the terms of the divine promise, to be admissible, unless we can prove that the letter and the spirit of the sacred narrative positively require such an admission.

It must not be forgotten in this discussion, that the reign of Hezekiah appears to have commenced at the beginning of the month of Abib (2 Chron. xxix. 3), and that thus his fourteenth year may have been nearly coincident throughout with the third of Sennacherib. And we must remember that, at the time of which we are speaking, the Assyrians had already been masters of Syria and Samaria for some years. Sennacherib, therefore, had not, in his third year, to set out from Nineveh in search of a remote and almost unknown region, and fight his way thither through hostile tribes. The way was familiar to many of his generals, and it

---

b From the Tisri of the 14th to the Tisri of the 15th of Hezekiah. The years of Hezekiah's reign appear to have been dated from the first day of Abib.

passed through nations subject to his power, and obedient to his will. He would therefore be early in the field. If, indeed, the Assyrian annals tell us that in his third year he attacked Sidon, Askelon, and Ekron, we may believe that these cities made but a short and feeble resistance. For the Most High thus describes the rapidity of Sennacherib's successes, until his vast detached host was destroyed before Jerusalem. "Now have I (saith the Lord,) brought it to pass, that thou shouldest be to lay waste defenced cities into ruinous heaps. Therefore their inhabitants were of small power, they were dismayed and confounded: they were as the grass of the field, and as the green herb, as the grass on the housetops, and as corn blasted before it be grown up" (Isa. xxxvii. 26, 27).

I would draw the following conclusions from what has already been advanced.

1. It seems from the computations of astronomers not to be certain that the eclipse of the 11th of January, 690, was sufficiently near to the hour of noon to cause the shadow to recede on the steps of the dial of Ahaz.

2. The sacred narrative, while it appears to favour the idea that Hezekiah may have recovered from his sickness before the end of September, may be regarded as unfavourable to the notion that the Assyrian host was not destroyed before the end of January.

3. The fact that it was left to the choice of Hezekiah whether the shadow should go forward or backward on the dial of Ahaz, discourages the supposition that the going backward of the shadow in the 14th of Hezekiah, was caused by any event, such as an eclipse, occurring in the appointed order of nature, and seems to teach us that the phenomenon in question was the result of a special interposition of the power of the omnipotent God of heaven and earth.

Before I conclude this letter, it may appear almost necessary to offer a few observations upon a difficulty connected with the embassy from Merodach Baladan to the King of Judah.

This difficulty is thus stated in *The Journal of Sacred Literature* for July, 1854 (p. 404), "In the third and fourth years of Sennacherib, Merodach Baladan was not King of Babylon. Though he might be desirous of strengthening himself by acquiring fresh allies, it could not be from Babylon that he would send ambassadors; and yet it is expressly stated by Hezekiah (2 Kings xx. 4) that the ambassadors came from Babylon."

In endeavouring to meet this objection it is requisite to give a sketch of the previous history of Merodach Baladan, borrowed from the same instructive and interesting paper (pp. 408—410).

It was in the year[c] 722 B.C., that Merodach Baladan, with the help of the King of Elam, made himself master of Babylon. He continued to be the sovereign of this city until 710 B.C., when Sargon conquered Babylon; driving out Merodach Baladan, who however retained the king-

---

c I here give the dates as they are written by the learned author of the paper in question, but feel myself quite incompetent either to assert, or object to, their correctness.

dom of Chaldea, bordering on the Shât el Arab and the Persian Gulf. At the close of 704 B.C., Merodach Baladan again regained the sovereignty of Babylon; but at the end of six months, Sennacherib, in his first year, defeats the Elamites and Babylonians, and expels Merodach Baladan, who still retained possession of Chaldea; Belibus having been placed upon the vacant throne of Babylon by Sennacherib.

But "in the fourth year of Sennacherib, Belibus having thrown off his dependency on Assyria, on hearing of the reverses sustained by Sennacherib in Judea, Sennacherib attacks him, and takes Babylon for the second time. He then advances against Merodach Baladan, who abandons Chaldea, and takes refuge in an island."

We are thus taught that Merodach Baladan was still living in the fourteenth and fifteenth years of Hezekiah, and that he continued master of Chaldea, until Sennacherib, in the year after his disastrous campaign in Judea, had taken Babylon, and dethroned Belibus. It was therefore quite possible for Merodach Baladan to have received the news of Hezekiah's miraculous recovery (especially if we suppose that recovery to have taken place previous to the end of the month of September) in sufficient time to have sent ambassadors to Jerusalem before Sennacherib advanced against the revolted Babylonians.

It is also highly probable, or rather almost certain, that the restless and ambitious Merodach Baladan was careful to have secret emissaries at Babylon, from whom he could receive early information of all events of importance which occurred there, and of all interesting tidings from other countries, as soon as it reached that city.

The fact that Sennacherib advanced against Merodach Baladan, and compelled him to abandon Chaldea, and take refuge in an island, after the Assyrians had dethroned Belibus, makes it probable that Belibus, on determining to revolt from the King of Nineveh, had entered into amicable relations with Merodach Baladan; and thus we are at full liberty to suppose that the ambassadors from the latter may have actually visited Babylon on their way to Jerusalem.

At all events, we may easily believe that Merodach Baladan directed his ambassadors to speak of him as King of Babylon to Hezekiah, and expressly to state that they came from the King of Babylon. And this is all that Hezekiah may have intended to state when he said to Isaiah, "The ambassadors are come from a far country, from Babylon" (2 Ki. xx. 14; and Isa. xxxix. 3).

G. B.

P.S. I have incorrectly stated above, that Tatnai, Governor of Samaria and the dependencies west of the Euphrates, styled Coresh "King of Babylon." The fact is that this Tatnai, writing in the *second* year of Darius, states that himself with others had recently visited Jerusalem, to demand of the Jews, why they presumed to proceed with the rebuilding of their temple; adding that, on questioning the Jewish elders, the latter had replied to him as follows—"In the first year *of Cyrus the King of Babylon*, the same King Cyrus made a decree to build this house of God" (Ez. v. 13). Now it certainly seems a fair inference from this fact that, in the second year of Darius, and about *four* years before the celebration of the first passover after the rebuilding of the second temple, the title of King of Persia (although in his memorable decree Coresh had expressly designated himself by this very title,) was not yet in use among the returned Jews—for even the Jewish elders, persons of official respectability, in their reply to Tatnai styled Coresh King of Babylon. It would, therefore, have been somewhat inconsistent with this fact if only four years afterwards, at a public religious festival, when old national feelings are most apt to prevail, the popular voice of the Jews should have, in their thanksgivings to the God of their fathers, employed the title of King of Persia—a title so utterly unknown to their fathers, and still so strange and unfamiliar to themselves. And as Babylon was in a state of open rebellion and defiance against Darius in his sixth year, it was natural and reasonable, under such circumstances, that the title of King of Babylon should give place to the more ancient designation of ' *King of Assyria.*'

These facts are also decidedly more favourable to the idea that the Ahasuerus and Artaxerxes whom Ezra places between Coresh and Darius, were Cambyses and Smerdis, whose united reigns did not amount to nine years; than that they were Xerxes and his son Artaxerxes Longimanus, whose united reigns amounted to sixty years. If we add the eight years during which Cyrus was King of Babylon to the eight of Cambyses and Smerdis, it is not at all unlikely that at the end of sixteen years the Jews should still employ the title of King of Babylon; but it is very far less probable, under all the circumstances of the case, that this title of King of Babylon should still remain in use, after the Jews had been sixty-eight years under the sovereignty of the kings of Persia.

May I be permitted to add another remark upon this letter of Tatnai. This governor of Samaria and his associates the Apharsachites (a portion of the Gentile colonists planted in Samaria by Esarhaddon,) thus express themselves in their letter to Darius—"Be it known unto the king that we went into the province of Judea, to the house of the Great God" (v. 8). Why should these men designate the God of Israel as *Great God?* It may be replied that their employment of such a title is in thorough accordance with (and is therefore an indirect testimony to) the fact, that the motely assemblage of Gentile colonists (Ez. iv. 9), even if they had not yet altogether forsaken the idols of their fathers (2 Ki. xvii. 41), unanimously and sincerely acknowledged the supremacy of that God whom the Jews worshipped, even while they sought, from selfish motives, to prevent the rebuilding of his temple.

THE LOST TRIBES OF ISRAEL.

IN your last number is a short notice of Mr. Kennedy's paper on the *Question of the supposed Lost Tribes of Israel,* in which he endeavours to shew that the popular notion of "the supposed loss of the ten tribes of Israel," in "consequence of their subjugation by the Assyrians, is an illusion, without any reason or authority in its favour."—p. 3.

In this letter it is not my intention to speak of the apocryphal dream of the apocryphal Esdras, nor am I to write about the North American Indians, or the Afghans[a] of Asia. I shall endeavour to prove: (1) that the plain predictions and historical statements of Holy Writ altogether forbid us to believe "that the main body of the ten tribes cannot be supposed to have been taken away by the Assyrians;" (2.) That the great passover of Hezekiah was celebrated in the second month of the *first year* of his reign; (3.) That the exceedingly glorious promises of universal and permanent holiness, peace, and prosperity, which it was foretold should be bestowed upon Israel and Judah at their predicted reconciliation and final restoration to their own land, have never yet been fulfilled; and, therefore, that the promised final restoration is yet future.

A. Mr. Kennedy very properly assigns the first place to the testimony of the Word of God, and says (p. 40), "we have it in our power to correct Josephus and St. Jerome by more ancient, and, *what is the highest*, by Scriptural authority." To that highest authority I would now appeal, and commence my task by requesting your readers to weigh well the following prophetic denunciations. The first was pronounced by the Lord through his servant Ahijah, against the kingdom of the ten tribes, in the reign of Jeroboam, the son of Nebat: "*For the Lord shall smite Israel,* as a reed is shaken in the water, and HE SHALL ROOT UP ISRAEL OUT OF THIS GOOD LAND which he gave to their fathers, AND SHALL SCATTER THEM BEYOND THE RIVER (Euphrates), because they have made their groves, provoking the Lord to anger. *And he shall give Israel up*, because of the sins of Jeroboam, who made Israel to sin" (1 Ki. xiv. 15, 16). Let the students of this deeply interesting question also read and consider the Divine denunciations given through Amos and Hosea. " Therefore will *I cause you to go into captivity beyond*

---

a I here transcribe the following judicious remarks extracted from a letter written by Major Edwarde's to an old friend of the London Jews' Society, who had requested from Major E. further information with regard to the Bene-Israel of Afghanistan. These extracts are published in the *Jewish Intelligencer* for April of the present year. " Almost immediately after you wrote, you must have seen Captain James' paper upon the Afghans being of Jewish descent, as published in the *Church Missionary Intelligencer*. Captain James has been deputy commissioner (or in other words civil administrator) of the district of Peshawar for four years, and his duties, magisterial, judicial, and financial, placed him in daily and hourly communication with the common people, the tribes and classes about whom you inquire. I do not hesitate therefore to say, that, being a man of great research and study, he has had better opportunities of forming a judgment than any other man living. In the course of those four years he has acquired the language of the Afghan tribes (Puûsht), collected many of their old books and genealogies, and made himself master of their own traditions and feelings upon the subject. His deliberate opinion, therefore, that the Afghans are *what they say they are*, "sons of Israel," is entitled to very great respect. It is impossible, also, to consider the resemblance of customs and manners, which he adduces, without being carried very much to the same conclusion. But I think that the subject is plunged into such divinely-purposed darkness, that it would be rash to pronounce that the lost tribes are found. Thus they have been found in Africa, Australia, and the depths of the Hindoo Himalayas: and each discoverer is convinced that he is right. All I would say is, that there is an exceedingly strong and interesting case made out. Decidedly more is to be said in favour of their Jewish descent than against it. But the subject still wants more sifting than Captain James has had time to give it."

Damascus, saith the Lord" (Am. v. 27). "*Israel shall surely go into captivity forth of his land*" (Am. vii. 17). (These two predictions may, perhaps, have reference to the whole of Israel, but the ten tribes are certainly included.) "*My God will cast them* (Ephraim) *away*, because they did not hearken unto him, and *they shall be wanderers among the nations*" (Hos. ix. 17). And with these predictions should be compared the clear and concise *historical summary* of their fulfilment, as declared by the Lord himself, through his servant Jeremiah, in one short sentence addressed to the rebellious Jews, not long before the invasion of Judea by Nebuchadnezzar : "And I will cast you (Judah) out of my sight, AS I HAVE CAST OUT ALL YOUR BRETHREN, even THE WHOLE SEED OF EPHRAIM (Jer. vii. 16).

We do not, indeed, doubt that the prophetic denunciations of Ahijah, Amos, and Hosea, became, in due time, corresponding historical facts. Can we, however, bring ourselves to believe that the facts which fulfilled those denunciations, are fairly and correctly set forth in the first three of Mr. Kennedy's conclusions, which are here transcribed, for the reader's convenience, by the side of the statements of the sacred historian.

I. "That the numbers of those taken away in the different captivities (of the ten tribes) have been much over-estimated ; for that only the principal people were taken as hostages, with the men of war, and others available as slaves."—p. 49.

"In the ninth year of Hoshea, the king of Assyria took Samaria, *and carried away Israel into Assyria,* and placed them in Halah and Habor, by the river of Gozan, and the cities of the Medes " (2 Ki. xvii. 6).

II. "That *the main body* of the ten tribes cannot be supposed to have been taken away, but left in their ancient possessions, when they became subjected again to the kings of Judah."—p. 49.

"And they (Israel) rejected his statutes . . . . Therefore *the Lord was very angry with Israel,* AND REMOVED THEM OUT OF HIS SIGHT ; there was none left but the tribe of Judah only " (2 Ki. xvii. 6.

III. "That *the only tribes* that can be supposed to have been taken away in any considerable body, with regard to their relative numbers, were the Reubenites, the Gadites, and the half - tribe of Manasseh, and that of Naphtali, who being located in the open plains on the north, and on the east of the Jordan, were the first and most exposed to the attacks of their enemies ; while the other tribes living in a more hilly country were not so easily overpowered.

"The above-named tribes also having lived more contiguous to the heathen, pro-

"*And the Lord rejected all the seed of Israel,* and afflicted them, and delivered them into the hand of spoilers, *until he had cast them out of his sight.* For he rent Israel from the house of David ; and they made Jeroboam the son of Nebat king : and Jeroboam drave Israel from following the Lord, and made them sin a great sin. For the children of Israel walked in all the sins of Jeroboam which he did ; they departed not from them ; *until the Lord removed Israel out of his sight ;* as he had said by all his servants the prophets. SO WAS ISRAEL CARRIED AWAY OUT OF THEIR OWN LAND TO ASSYRIA, unto this day " (2 Ki. xvii. 20, 23).

"And they (all Israel) left all the commandments of the Lord their God, and made them molten images, even two calves, and made a grove, and

bably⁵ yielded 'most to their customs, and thus when taken away among their conquerors, have become most absorbed among them.' "—p. 50.

worshipped all the host of heaven, and served Baal. And they caused their sons and their daughters to pass through the fire, and used divinations, *and sold themselves to do evil in the sight of the Lord,* to provoke him to anger. *Therefore the Lord was very angry with Israel,* AND REMOVED THEM OUT OF HIS SIGHT " (2 Ki. xvii. 16, 18).

And what are we to understand by the emphatic expression of God's removing Israel out of his sight? This question is easily and satisfactorily answered by consulting again the passage which has been already quoted from the prophet Jeremiah, through whom, shortly before the Babylonish captivity, the Lord addressed to the impenitent Jews this menace : " And I will cast you (Judah and Benjamin) out of my sight, as I have cast out all your brethren, even the whole seed of Ephraim." And surely these words would appear to prove, beyond reasonable question, that God fulfilled his threat " to root up Ephraim and his fellow-tribes of the kingdom of Israel out of the good land which he gave to their fathers, and to scatter them beyond the river (Euphrates)"—*as truly, and as literally,* as he fulfilled his subsequent threat to cast out of his sight Judah and Benjamin, whom he caused Nebuchadnezzar to carry into captivity beyond the Euphrates. And if it had been the Divine purpose (as the writer believes that it was) to teach us that the main body of the ten tribes was not left by the sovereign of Nineveh in their own possessions, but that, on the contrary, it was carried away into the Assyrian territories, could predictions and historical statements be more plainly and expressly to the point

---

⁵ The tribes of Simeon and Dan were probably, from their close neighbourhood to the depraved Philistine cities, as wicked as were the Reubenites and Gadites. And it was no doubt of Ephraim and Manasseh, of Simeon and Dan, as well as of Reuben and Gad, that it was written—" they sold themselves to do evil in the sight of the Lord, to provoke him to anger ; and therefore the Lord was very angry with Israel, and removed them out of his sight." The forms of expression—" sold themselves *to do evil in the sight* of the Lord," and " he removed them *out of his sight*" are nearly related to each other. It was not possible for Israel to be removed out of the sight and knowledge of the omnipresent and omniscient God. But the children of Israel were God's peculiar people, towards whom, in the promised land, Jehovah was not only their God and moral Governor, but also their political Lord and King. While located in the promised land, they " were in the sight of the Lord," in a sense in which this expression could be used of no other nation upon the face of the earth. Accordingly when they were removed from Canaan into a distant region, they were said to be removed out of the sight of God, as King of Israel. The language of Scripture does not lead us to think that Shalmaneser carried as many or as few as he pleased into captivity, but rather that he was as clay in the hands of the potter, the unconscious instrument in the fulfilment of the divine denunciation to remove Israel out of the Lord's sight. When it is said (2 Ki. xvii. 18), "There was none left but the tribe of Judah only," it is plain that the tribes of Judah and Benjamin, having together formed the kingdom of Solomon's successors, are here spoken of under the name of one tribe, Judah. In like manner God makes this promise to Solomon : " I will not rend away all thy kingdom ; but will give *one tribe* for David my servant's sake, and for Jerusalem's sake, which I have chosen " (1 Ki. xi. 13); but in 2 Chr. xi. 12, Rehoboam is spoken of as " having Judah and Benjamin on his side."

than are those which have just been placed before the reader from the Old Testament?

B. And when we have examined the grave error into which Mr. Kennedy has fallen with reference to the date of the great passover of king Hezekiah, we shall be still more deeply convinced that the historical statements of the Old Testament seem altogether to forbid us to think with Mr. K., "that the main body of the ten tribes cannot be supposed to have been taken away, but (rather must be supposed to have been) left in their ancient possessions, when they became subjected again to the kings of Judah." I proceed to extract some of Mr. K.'s observations connected with the date of the passover in question; "Samaria was taken by Shalmaneser in the ninth year of Hoshea, which was the sixth year of the reign of Hezekiah, king of Judah (2 Ki. xviii. 10). It must have been after this event, and in apprehension of a like fate impending over Judah, that Hezekiah took counsel of his princes and all the congregation to keep a solemn passover (2 Chr. xxx. 2). He then ' sent to all Israel and Judah, and wrote letters also to Ephraim and Manasseh that they should come to the house of the Lord at Jerusalem to keep the passover.' From this and the following verses, it is apparent that a considerable portion of the people of Israel had been left behind by the Assyrians, and *we may conclude even the larger portion of them.*"—p. 17.

Here, then, we have one of the strongest (supposed) arguments in support of the view, that "the main body of the ten tribes cannot be supposed to have been taken away by the Assyrians." When Mr. K. wrote thus, he evidently believed that the great passover of Hezekiah was celebrated *after* the destruction of Samaria, and *not earlier* than the seventh year of Hezekiah. Is not this view directly contrary to the statements of Scriptural history?

Let the reader bear in mind the two following facts: "The passover was appointed to be slain on the fourteenth day *of the first month;* on that day all the congregation of Israel were to keep the passover." There was one exception to this strict law. For we read in Nu. ix. 10, "If any man of you, or of your posterity, shall be unclean by reason of a dead body, or be in a journey afar off, yet he shall keep the passover unto the Lord. The fourteenth day *of the second month* at even they shall keep it. But the man that is clean, and is not in a journey, and forbeareth to keep the passover (on the fourteenth day of the first month), even the same soul shall be cut off from among his people." Here we have a gracious provision made for those persons who should be prevented from keeping the passover at the appointed time through accidental impediments—*i.e.,* through impediments not caused by wilful misconduct.

Now, on turning to the history, we find that Ahaz, the father and predecessor of Hezekiah, "had cut in pieces the vessels of the house of God, and shut up the doors of the house of the Lord; and he made him altars in every corner of Jerusalem." And, doubtless, during the closing years of his reign, the celebration of the passover and other great religious feasts was openly discountenanced. But we read that, immediately after his death, his pious son, "in the first year of his reign, *in the first month*, opened the doors of the house of the Lord and repaired them" (2 Chr.

xxix. 3). He also commanded the priests and the Levites to sanctify themselves and the house of the Lord. "They began *on the first day of the first month* to sanctify . . . . and in the *sixteenth day* of the first month they made an end." As the cleansing of the temple was not accomplished before the fourteenth day of the first month, the passover for that year could not, perhaps, be duly kept. Hezekiah, however, proceeded without delay to offer burnt-offerings and a sin-offering. And, on this occasion, the king did not confine his thoughts and prayers to Judah and Benjamin; for it is expressly stated that Hezekiah commanded that the burnt-offering and the sin-offering should be made *for all Israel—i.e.,* for the ten tribes also; although, before that time, Reuben and Gad, Naphtali and the eastern half-tribe of Manasseh had been carried away into captivity. Had the death of Ahaz occurred two or three months sooner, Hezekiah would, doubtless, have been able to celebrate his first passover on the fourteenth day of the first month. But as he appears to have ascended the throne, very little, if at all, before the first day of the first month, it was not possible to cleanse and sanctify the house of God in time for the due celebration of the passover on the appointed day in the first month. This, and this alone, was the reason why Hezekiah "took counsel with his princes and all the congregation in Jerusalem to keep the passover *on the second month.*" And we may thus feel thoroughly assured that after the first year, the zeal and piety of Hezekiah never allowed the temple to be again neglected and ceremonially defiled during his reign, and that the passover was never again celebrated in the second month while he remained on the throne of Jerusalem.

Your readers will thus be assured that the following extracts from 2 Chr. xxx. have all reference to the state of Israel *five years before* the final captivity of Ephraim, and *while Hoshea was yet king of Samaria,—* viz., "Hezekiah sent to all Israel and Judah, and wrote letters also to Ephraim and Manasseh, that they should come to the house of the Lord at Jerusalem, to keep the passover unto the Lord God of Israel. For the king had taken counsel, and his princes, and all the congregation in Jerusalem, *to keep the passover in the second month* " (verses 1, 2). " So they established a decree to make proclamation throughout all Israel, from Beersheba even to Dan, that they should come to keep the passover unto the Lord God of Israel at Jerusalem" (ver. 5). "The king commanded, saying, Ye children of Israel, turn again unto the Lord, and he will return to the remnant of you that are escaped out of the hand of the kings of Assyria" (ver. 6). "So the posts passed from city to city through the country of Ephraim and Manasseh even unto Zebulun" (ver. 10). "Divers of Ashur, Manasseh and Zebulun humbled themselves, and came to Jerusalem" (ver. 11). "Many of Ephraim, and Manasseh, Issachar and Zebulun, had not cleansed themselves, yet did they eat of the passover otherwise than it was written" (ver. 18).

These several Scriptural statements are quoted in Mr. Kennedy's paper, p. 18; and your readers must be now aware how thoroughly erroneous is the following inference which Mr. K. has drawn from them. " From these passages it is indubitable that even immediately after Israel is said to have been carried away captive by the Assyrians, there was still a large remnant of them left in their own land, among whom we have particularly specified six out of the ten tribes, namely, Dan, Ephraim, Manasseh, Asher, Issachar, and Zebulun, which tribes at least may therefore be presumed to have been mainly left to become amalgamated with those of Judah and Benjamin."—p. 19.

Having, I trust, successfully appealed against Mr. Kennedy's conclusions to the highest of all authorities, the Word of God, it may be added, the celebrated Jewish historian Josephus evidently supposes the celebration of Hezekiah's great passover to have occurred *before* the destruction of Samaria by Shalmaneser.

It is said in Ki. xvii. 3, that "against Hosea came up Shalmaneser king of Assyria; and Hoshea became his servant, and gave him presents;" or, as in the margin. From the well-known character of Assyrian invasion and conquest, we may believe that on this occasion the Assyrians would carry away some of the Israelites into captivity.

At length the king of Assyria came throughout all the land, and went up to Samaria, and besieged it three years. We cannot say accurately, how long the siege continued. It may have occupied a portion greater or less of Hezekiah's fourth year, the whole of his fifth, and a portion of his sixth. But even if the Assyrians spent only eighteen months in the siege, what disastrous calamities must have been inflicted on the Israelites during that period. About five years *after* the great passover of king Hezekiah, who in his invitation to that festival, addresses the Israelites "*as the remnant of you that are escaped out of the hand of the kings of Assyria,*" the army of Shalmaneser advances in order to destroy this remnant. Many, especially of those who had kept the passover with Hezekiah, would take refuge in the dominions of Hezekiah. During the long siege, the merciless Assyrian marauders would sweep over the whole of the devoted country, bent upon slaughter and upon obtaining booty and slaves. As these warriors consisted of hardy and active mountaineers, as well as of tribes of the plains, the Israelites of the hill country would find no secure refuge in their fastnesses and strongholds. Almost every[c] town and village would be discovered, assaulted and taken, and the inhabitants who survived the sword, would be doomed to captivity. And it is not improbable that during the siege of the city of Samaria a number of captives was sent into Assyria exceeding that which was finally carried away from Samaria. The fearful cruelties which were perpetrated at the capture of this city may be learned from Hosea xiii. 16. And when, after the work of desolation had been accomplished, the Assyrian army had withdrawn, and the fugitives returned, these would form only the miserable remnant and wreck of that population which six years before Hezekiah had described as "the

---

c We read in Jer. xxxiv. 7, "When the King of Babylon's army fought against Jerusalem, and against all the cities of Judah that were left, against Lachish, and against Azekah; for these defenced cities remained of the cities of Judah." We thus see that while besieging Jerusalem, the Babylonians took in succession the other cities and towns of Judah. And probably they thus sent beyond the Euphrates a larger number than all those who were carried away by Nebuchadnezzar from Jerusalem. And it is probable that in the final siege of Samaria, the Assyrians pursued a similar course in the kingdom of Israel.

remnant escaped out of the hands of the king of Assyria." This wretched remnant which survived Shalmaneser's triumph, would better be described in the language of Isaiah : " Yet gleaning grapes shall be left in it, as the shaking of an olive-tree, two or three berries in the top of the uppermost bough, four or five in the outmost fruitful branches thereof, saith the God of Israel " (Is. xvii. 6).

From this scanty remnant we may believe to have descended that "remnant of Israel" who are spoken of as living during the reign of Josiah, in 2 Chr. xxxiv. 9.

C. I have now to shew that the glorious results of universal and permanent holiness, peace, and prosperity, which are to be bestowed on Israel and Judah, at their great predicted restoration to the land of their fathers, have never yet been accomplished, and that therefore, the great and final restoration of Judah and Ephraim predicted in the Old Testament is yet in future. Mr. Kennedy thus quotes from Ezekiel (p. 11), " Thus saith the Lord God; Behold, I will take the stick of Joseph, which is in the hand of Ephraim, and the tribes of Israel his fellows, and will put them with the stick of Judah, and make them one stick, and they shall be one in mine hand. And say unto them, Thus saith the Lord God; Behold, I will take the children of Israel from among the heathen, *whither they be gone*, and will gather them on every side, and bring them into their own land ; and I will make them one nation in the land upon the mountains of Israel, and one king shall be king to them all : and they shall be no more than two nations, neither shall they be divided into two kingdoms any more at all " (Ezek. xxxvii. 19, 22).

I would ask a few questions here.

When the captivity returned from Babylon and formed *a dependent Persian province*, was this the fulfilment of Ezekiel's words, " I will make them one nation in the land upon the mountains of Israel, and one king shall be king to them all ;" or, of the prediction in the twenty-second verse of the same chapter : "And David my servant shall be king over them ; and they all shall have one shepherd ?"

When we read the rebukes of the selfishness of those who had returned from Babylon, delivered through Haggai (i. 4, 11); when we read Malachi's complaints of the profane disrespect shewn to God's worship (Mal. i. 6, 10), is this the fulfilment of those promises to sanctify Israel, and give him a new heart, which we read in Ezek. xxxvi. 23, 28 ?

When we read what the Jews suffered from some of the Ptolemies, and from Antiochus Epiphanes, and of their desolation and dispersion by the Romans under Titus the son of Vespasian—does all this fulfil the predictions of Amos—" And I will bring again the captivity of my people Israel, and they shall build the waste cities, and inhabit them ; and they shall plant vineyards, and drink the wine thereof; they shall also make gardens, and eat the fruit of them. *And I will plant them upon their land, and they shall no more be pulled up out of their land*, which I have given them, saith the Lord thy God ?"

Let the reader carefully study the prophetic books of Haggai and Malachi, and the historical books of Ezra and Nehemiah, and remember the rejection and crucifixion of Jesus Christ the true Messiah ; and let him judge how far the glorious predictions concerning the reconciliation of Ephraim and Judah, and their final restoration in holiness, security, and prosperity to the land of their fathers have yet been fulfilled.

29th May.   G. B.

I may add that the numbers implied in Esther (and very many of whom were doubtless of the ten tribes) would lead us to expect that in the days of Josephus, there should be vast multitudes of the descendants of the ten tribes living in the dominions of the Parthian sovereign of that day.

LORD ARTHUR HERVEY "ON THE GENEALOGIES OF OUR LORD."

To the Editor of " The Journal of Sacred Literature."

SIR,—In the article entitled "The Book of Jasher," in the last July number of *The Journal of Sacred Literature*, there occurs the following passage :—"*The Genealogies of our Lord and Saviour Jesus Christ*, by Lord Arthur Hervey, is here quoted (*i. e.*, in Dr. Donaldson's work) with approval, as when he says that the period between Joshua and Samuel was much shorter than is stated in the common chronology. *We recommend him to explain* 1 Ki. vi. 1, *compared with* Acts xiii. 20." Now I believe that a complete answer to the criticism contained in the words I have underlined would be to retort upon the writer his own words, and say, " We recommend him to explain 1 Ki. vi. 1, compared with Acts xiii. 20." For, unless these two passages give *the same* chronological calculation of the period in question, it is obvious that their *united* force cannot be objected to the calculation adopted by me. I think too it must be admitted that, if the two passages are quite irreconcilable, and in fact contradictory, the authority of each of them, considered as a decisive statement, is materially shaken. But that the two calculations are irreconcilable is not merely my private opinion, but is so manifest that scarcely a single commentator of note, as far as I am aware, either ancient or modern, has even attempted to reconcile them. Ancient and modern interpreters of this portion of sacred chronology are mainly divided into two classes, those who adopt the longer calculation which the historical books seem by their present arrangement to indicate, and which the statement ascribed to St. Paul expressly adopts, and who consequently reject or ignore the calculation of 1 Ki. vi. 1; and those who, following the last-named shorter calculation, reject or explain away, as an accommodation to Jewish prejudices, the statement of St. Paul. In the first class may be mentioned Demetrius, Josephus, Africanus, Clemens Alexandrinus, Theophilus, Georgius Syncellus, &c., &c., of the ancients; and Scaliger, Jackson, Hales, and many others among the moderns. In the second class, Eusebius among the ancients holds the chief place, and he expressly rejects St. Paul's calculation. Among moderns it may suffice to quote the opinion of the late Dr. Faussett, Lady Margaret's Professor of Divinity in the University of Oxford, who following the calculation of

1 Ki. vi., also expressly rejects St. Paul's computation as "incidental" and "vague," and classes it with other "familiar instances of this kind of inaccuracy which appear to leave the rigid advocates of universal and plenary inspiration without a reply."[a]   Evidently then the united authority of these two passages, of which one assigns 480 years to the whole interval between the Exodus and the foundation of the temple, and the other assigns 450 years to the times of the judges alone,—which added to 40 years in the wilderness, + the times of Joshua, + the times of the elders, + the days of Samuel's government, + 40 years of Saul's reign, + 40 years of David, + 3 years of Solomon, make up between 600 and 700 years,—cannot be pleaded as a reason for stifling inquiry into any other evidence that may be found, to assist us in determining the true chronology of this important period.   Such evidence, of no obscure or doubtful kind, I believe may be found in the Holy Scriptures.

I will describe as briefly as possible the steps by which I was led to this conviction.   When my genealogical inquirers brought me to that part of our Lord's genealogy which covers the time between the Exodus and David, my attention was of course at once rivetted by the discrepancy between this part of the genealogy and the received chronology.

I found that the genealogy, four times repeated without variation, interposed only *three* generations between Salmon and David, while the chronology interposed some four or rather five hundred years between the entrance into Canaan and the birth of David : a discordance which was heightened by observing, that to a period of about equal length immediately *after* David, the genealogy assigns *nineteen* generations.

I found further, that ALL THE OTHER GENEALOGIES in Scripture covering the same period, of which there are seven, agree exactly with the genealogy of David, when allowance is made for the recorded age of Judah, Boaz, and Jesse, but are absolutely irreconcilable with the received chronology.   I found that the recorded high priesthoods agree with the genealogies, but that, according to the chronology, some ten or twelve high priests must have passed away without the faintest record of their existence.

I found that in the historical transactions recorded in the closing chapters of the Book of Judges, which ought, according to the chronology, to be separated from Moses by some four or five hundred years, the grandson of Moses and Phinehas the son of Eleazar were still alive.   I found that the Book of Ruth, which comes after the Book of Judges, relates to the old age of the son of Salmon.

I observed that 1 Sam. i. 1 contains a strong indication that the fifth generation above Samuel was that of the ancestor who settled at Ramathaim-zophim at the time of the conquest of the land ; an indication of which I afterwards found a full confirmation in the genealogy which represents that ancestor as the grandson of Korah.

I observed a great number of minuter circumstances, for which I would refer the reader to the ninth chapter of my book on the genealogies,

---

[a] *Sacred Chronology*, pp. 79, 74, &c.   The curious reader may further consult Petavius, *De Doctrinâ Temporum*, lib. ix., cap. xxxiv., xxxv.

which, immediately my suspicion was awakened as to the shortness of the interval in question, lent themselves with unanimous testimony to confirm that suspicion, and seemed to be utterly inconsistent with the longer interval of the received chronology.

On the other hand, I could not find a single incidental statement or circumstance which was unfavourable to the shorter time; a negative evidence of no little weight: while of the two direct chronological statements, the one, viz., 1 Ki. vi. 1, is at variance with the other (Judg. xi. 25, 26), and with the chronology which the historical books themselves evidently suggest, and which the Jews, including Josephus and St. Paul, adopted from them; the other (Judg. xi. 25, 26) cannot possibly be made to construe, and bears plain and decisive marks of corruption upon the face of it.

The result of all this was to produce a strong conviction upon my mind that the view of the length of the interval from the Exodus to Solomon given by the genealogies is the true one, and not that given by the chronology; and the conclusion I came to, still reasoning exclusively from the Scriptures themselves, was that about 280 years is the true length of this interval.

But it was obvious to enquire further how this alteration of Jewish chronology, by which about two hundred years are deducted from the times between the Exodus and the foundation of the temple, and the Exodus brought down about two hundred years later in the world's history, would affect the relation of Jewish to profane history; in other words, whether the history of other nations is compatible with such an alteration. The only two foreign histories which I had the means of referring to for this purpose were the Edomitish and the Egyptian, and the result in both cases was most remarkable. The fragment of Edomitish history preserved in Gen. xxxvi. and 1 Chron. i. gives a list of kings of Edom who reigned before the reign of Saul over Israel. This list contains the succession of eight kings. Eight reigns therefore is the largest number that could have intervened between the Exodus and the reign of Saul. Now allowing 30 years to a reign, this gives $8 \times 30 = 240$ years.

As regards Egyptian history, I found, on referring to Sir Gardner Wilkinson's *Ancient Egyptians*, that the only obstacle to assigning the events connected with the Exodus to that period of Egyptian history, to which alone they correspond, and to those reigns of Egyptian kings to which both the internal evidence and the oldest historical notices, Egyptian and Greek, actually assign them, is that the Exodus, according to the received chronology, took place about two hundred years earlier than those Egyptian reigns and events are proved by the astronomical ceiling of the Memnonium to have occurred. Consequently the bringing the Exodus about two hundred years later immediately produced an entire harmony with Egyptian history, and got rid at once of endless perplexities, anachronisms, and other difficulties. I found further, when my book was almost through the press, that Lepsius had contended upon Egyptian grounds, and with unanswerable arguments, for shortening the period in question by about a hundred and eighty years, and had also shewn that the oldest Jewish tradition had actually preserved the date of the Exodus in accordance with such shortening, viz., B.C. 1313.

Such are some of the principal considerations which have led me to the conclusion, that the interval between Joshua and Samuel is shorter than is stated in the common chronology. For further details I refer those, who care to go into them, to the ninth chapter of my book, on the genealogies of our Lord. But I trust that enough has appeared, even in this outline, to shew that I did not advance the opinion without some fair grounds, and that the reasons in favour of it are at all events too strong to be smothered by a bare comparison of two conflicting statements. The subject is not a little interesting and important, though, as Petavius fully acknowledges, it is not a question which trenches upon faith. If the views which I have put forth can be satisfactorily refuted, and the present chronology for those times defended and reconciled with the genealogies, by all means let it be done. There is a fair field for candid discussion by those whose only object is to get at the truth. But in the mean time I cannot think that I have done disservice to the cause of sound and reverent Biblical criticism in calling attention to certain phenomena which exist in fact, whether they are observed or not, and in drawing from those phenomena the conclusions which, in the careful exercise of my reasoning faculties, alone appear to me to be warranted by them.

I remain, Sir, your faithful and obedient servant,

ARTHUR HERVEY.

Ickworth, August, 1855.

THE NINEVEH INSCRIPTIONS.

SIR,—I am sure that all your readers, especially those of them who may be addicted to philosophical pursuits, must feel greatly indebted to Dr . Hincks, for his interesting communication in the last number of the Journal on the language of Ancient Assyria.

The appearance of that paper revived in my mind a desire which I had long cherished, and in which I have no doubt that many participate along with me, that Dr. Hincks or Colonel Rawlinson would favour the public with the details of the process by which they consider that they have succeeded in decyphering the famous arrow-headed inscriptions, just as Messrs. Layard and Botta have already described the manner in which the monuments on which they are engraved have been exhumed.

To the uninitiated, the interpretation of these mysterious legends appears like what is called in Algebra an indeterminate problem, or a single equation containing two unknown quantities, which admits of an indefinite number of solutions. Given, the *language*,—it is easy to see how the *characters* might be discovered; or if the characters be given one might hope at length to master the language; but when we are equally ignorant of the language and its symbols, where shall we find a limit to assumption and conjecture?

There are two considerations which seem to justify us in expecting some more minute information on this head. The first is, the confidence which the discoverers evidently repose in their conclusions; which is such, that one of them has not only presented us with the first of a series of sketches of Assyrian Grammar, but has even ventured to employ his assumed knowledge of that language to the criticism of other cognate dialects which have been known and studied ever since they ceased to be spoken. The second is, that—without venturing for a moment to question the profound learning and acute sagacity of discoverers—the more tentative the process, the more conjectural the result, and the smaller the number of witnesses (at present not much above the Mosaic minimum) by which the soundness of that result is attested, or who are competent to give evidence in regard to it, the more ample we naturally desire their testimony to be, that we may be put as much as possible in a position to judge for ourselves.

The paper of your correspondent, T. M., does not throw much light on the subject, although his account of the system which he defends is sufficient to raise the greatest doubts in one's mind as to its correctness. For (1.) the interpretations which the system of Mr. Forster yields startle us at the very threshold by their *inanity* and *puerility*. The Assyrian sculptors must have been distinguished by a rare amount of humility if they thought so little of their own handiwork, as to deem it necessary that their sculptures should be explained by having the *names* of the objects represented written over them. Is there any well-authenticated instances of a similar practice on record, save when the ingenuous modesty of some infantile limner has supplied a verbal interpretation of the efforts of his "'prentice hand?" (2.) The application of the *Arabic* language to the interpretation of Persian inscriptions is about as reasonable as it would be to apply the Zend to the re-solution of Assyrian legends (which your correspondent leaves us to suppose is done by the other party); or if Mr. F. adopts the hypothesis of a primitive and universal language, why should that be *Arabic*, rather than Hebrew or Sanscrit, or some other of their cognates? (3.) His assumption (for this is manifestly taken for granted) that the characters are *alphabetic* is belied, as it seems to me, by their appearance. Their complicated structure affords a strong presumption that, if not verbal like the Chinese, which they somewhat resemble, they are at least syllabic, as Dr. Hincks conjectures. Yet I think the suggestion of your correspondent about a comparison with *known alphabets* is deserving of further attention. For admitting the *syllabic* value of the cuneiform characters, and even that they may have been originally, like the Egyptian and Chinese, *idiographic*, we should still be warranted to expect that if the language, *e.g.*, of the Persepolitan inscriptions, is related to any known dialect (such as the Sanscrit or Zend,) some analogy between the symbols of the one and the alphabet of the other should be discoverable. There can be no doubt that the Hieratic and Demotic characters are abridged and more cursive forms of certain hieroglyphs; and even our own Roman alphabet can be traced (in some cases at a glance) through the ancient Greek, Phœnician, and old Hebrew to the same source.[a] It is of course easy to suppose that different *languages* may have been expressed by the same characters, a practice which has been abundantly exemplified in more modern times (as with the Arabic and Roman).

In conclusion I have only to add, that the wish that I have ventured to express must not be interpreted as implying incredulity, but rather as indicative of a leaning towards the system of Dr. Hincks and his indefatigable coadjutor, and a craving to be able to share in their assurance of its accuracy.

I am, Sir, your obedient servant,

SCRUTATOR.

ON "THE RESULTS OF TEXTUAL CRITICISM," BY MR. SMITH.

DEAR SIR.—Quite concurring in the general statements of Mr. Smith in his remarks on textual criticism,[b] I venture to note that his suggested solution of the difficulty as to the cure of the blind men near Jericho is *not* admissible. Both Matthew and Mark say EKΠOPEYOMENΩN, and that may easily have been a misreading of EICΠ, as Mr. Smith suggests; but then both add ἀπὸ Ἰεριχώ, with which the supposed reading EICΠ cannot agree. Moreover, Luke does not say, "as they were going in to Jericho," but as they drew near (ἐν τῷ ἐγγίζειν). May I call the attention of your critical readers to the rendering of De Wette, "As he drew near (to Jerusalem) at Jericho," &c. This rendering is favoured by the whole strain of this part of Luke's narrative, who seems ever to keep in view the termination of our Lord's course (see chap. xviii. 31; xix. 29, 37, 41) though I confess it seems a little forced. In the last quoted passages, however, forms of ἐγγίζω seem used in the same way.

J. A.

THE NINEVEH INSCRIPTIONS.

To the Editor of "The Journal of Sacred Literature."

SIR.—Having read with great interest the article on this subject in your July Number, I made an attempt to test the accuracy of the method recommended, by trying to decypher some *medallion inscriptions*. With

---

[a] I will cite as examples the letter M, which is evidently a rude representation of the undulations of *water* (Hebrew, *Ma-yim*), and our O which is as clearly an outline of the *eye* (Hebrew *A-yin*).

[b] *J. S. L.*, July, p. 325.

your permission I send you a few examples which are taken from Layard's last publication, *Nineveh and Babylon.*

On page 606 a cylinder occurs, representing a combat between a man and a human-headed horse on one side and a griffin on the other. The legend by the side of this device is not in the arrow-headed but in the cursive character of Assyria, and this is more nearly identical with the old enchorial alphabets and with the Hamyaritic. The first word is AH, the equivalent Arabic letters for which are ظ ذ, *zat.* Looking out for the root of this word كزظ, *i.q.,* كذظ, I found the sense to be *curvam habens maxillam,* and also the epithet *distortam.* This initial word stood beside the crooked-jawed griffin, and revealed to me the manner in which I might comprehend the "Illustrated News" of Ancient Nineveh. Again; take an arrow-headed example from the opposite page (607). This inscription consists of single, isolated words,—one in each line. The subject is plain enough. A squat dwarf receives upon his head the winged globe, let down upon him by two human figures who support it. I find every circumstance in this device explained word by word in the accompanying legend. The isolated word |⟨𝕋𝕋⊨|, كور, is *brevis corpore, latusque humilis,* thus describing the figure of the dwarf as graphically as the picture. The other words are equally descriptive of the scenes transacted in this curious device, but I omit details because I wish simply to send you specimens, and to make my letter a short one.

On page 539 a sacrificial scene is depicted. We observe a priest, two altars, and a bird resembling a cock with a naked neck and a mitred crest. The monogram on the gem becomes legible by finding the Arabic letters equivalent to the Assyrian. The bird becomes thus distinctly ascertained: it is the حبيش —the *mimida vitrata,* the mitred-guinea fowl: and you may observe the mitre as perfect as if it had just issued from the herald's office.

Whenever the gem contains any remarkable feature, it is sure to be defined in the legend. Thus in one of the gems published by Mr. Forster, a winged figure is seen grasping two ostriches by their necks. The last word may be termed "the characteristic." It is دغ, *compressit arctavitque guttur, et strangulando necavit.* Thus the word suits the action completely, for the winged figure holds the ostriches by that part of the neck anatomically called the *guttur.*

As I only desire to elicit the experience of others rather than to detail my own, I will refer to a gem of Mr. Layard's with an heraldic looking engraving of two animals rampant on each side of a palm tree. Mr. Layard calls them "goats." I took them for "zebras," and was curious enough to try to find out what the inscription, in three words beneath them, would say. The first I read by Forster's alphabet, "wild ass;" the second, "an ass marked with bi-coloured stripes;" and the third, "disporting" or "at play." The two zebras with beautifully-marked stripes are playfully rampant, as the legend leads us to expect.

As this is a game which every orientalist may play for himself, I will conclude by hoping that some one else will pursue it with vigour : as the questions which will be settled by it are vitally important with reference to the illustration of Old Testament history.

Believe me, ever yours,

York, August, 1855.   AN INQUIRER.

THE TWO FRIENDS.

THE friendship of David and Jonathan has long been proverbial, and indeed, is one of the most charming episodes in the Old Testament history. But it has perhaps escaped the notice of most readers of the Scriptures, that the records of the New Testament are adorned by the exhibition of a friendship, which, for its depth of reality and uniform consistency, will vie in interest even with its older and more acknowledged counterpart. That David and Jonathan were friends, is directly asserted by the sacred writer; it was impossible, therefore, to be unaware of the fact. The friendship of Peter and John (for it is of them we speak) is nowhere asserted in so many words; there exists, nevertheless, an amount of material which enables us to arrive at the conclusion that these two apostles were intimately attached friends, with a moral certainty little if at all inferior to that which obtains in the former case.

We do not profess to start any novel hypothesis; the friendship of Peter and John has been already noticed, from time to time, in some of its more prominent indications. Our aim is simply to bring together into one view the several particulars which contribute, more or less, to establish the subject on a firm and satisfactory basis, and to put into tangible form that which may be floating in many minds only as a vague impression.

1. The first mention of John is in connexion with Peter's brother (John i. 35—40).

2. Peter and John were partners (Luke v. 1—10).

3. We find John in Peter's house (Mark i. 29; see this reciprocated in No. 12).

4. In the several lists of the apostles, Peter, Andrew, James and John are mentioned together (Matt. x. 2; Mark iii. 16—18; Luke vi. 14; Acts i. 13).

5. They were together at the raising of Jairus' daughter (Mark v. 37).

6. They were together at the transfiguration (Mark ix. 2).[a]

7. They were together on the Mount of Olives (Mark xiii. 3).

8. They were jointly commissioned to prepare the Passover (Luke xxii. 8).

---

[a] It is more than probable that they were the "two disciples" sent to procure the ass on which our Lord rode into Jerusalem (Matt. xxi. 1; Mark ix. 1; Luke xix. 29): St. Mark's account, so evidently the production of an eye-witness, points clearly to Peter as one; and who so likely to be his companion as John? Cf. Mark xiv. 13, with Luke xxii. 8.

9. It was through Peter that John was prevailed upon to ask our Lord who should betray him (John xiii. 21—25).

10. They were all together in Gethsemane (Mark xiv. 33).

11. Together, they followed Christ after his apprehension, and John obtained admission for Peter into the high priest's palace (John xviii. 15, 16,—Cf. Acts iv. 13).

12. They were evidently living together after the crucifixion (John xx. 2, 10.—Cf. xvi. 32; xix. 27).

13. "They ran both together" to the sepulchre of their risen Lord (John xx. 3, &c.)

14. They were together at the lake of Tiberias (John xxi. 2).

15. It was to Peter that John first communicated his recognition of the Saviour, although his own brother James was present (John xxi. 7).

16. As the converse of the last, Peter, when informed of his own future destiny, immediately betrayed his anxiety to know what would befall, not Andrew his brother, but John his friend (John xxi. 20, 21).

17. "Peter and John went up together into the temple of the hour of prayer" (Acts iii. 1).

18. They were associated in the mission to Samaria (Acts viii. 14).

19. As an appropriate close to this long series of coincidences, so suggestive of the minute truthfulness of the inspired writings, the last time John is mentioned in New Testament history is in connexion with Cephas (Gal. ii. 1, 9.—Cf. No. 1).

We are now prepared to expect in the *writings* of these two apostles similar indications of mutual interest and affection to those which their *actions* have afforded.

Accordingly we find both St. John, in the gospel which bears his name, and St. Peter, in that of St. Mark (which was virtually his own), delighting to do honour, the one to the other, and each availing himself of every opportunity of exhibiting his friend's conduct to the greatest advantage.

If we turn to St. Mark (*i.e.*, St. Peter), we cannot but observe how delicately he vindicates James and John from the imputation of neglecting their aged father which might seem to rest upon them from the concise manner in which St. Matthew, as usual, condenses his narrative. The latter (iv. 18—22), in relating their call to the apostleship, conveys the impression that Zebedee was left altogether alone by his sons. St. Peter, however, takes care to add that "they left their father Zebedee in the ship *with the hired servants*" (Mark i. 19, 20).

Then again, St. Peter, when enumerating the twelve apostles, passes slightly over his own precedence, and altogether omits to explain the circumstances under which he himself received the surname of Peter, or what that name imported;—while he fails not to record, and interpret too, the honourable title of Boanerges, conferred on the son of Zebedee (Mark iii. 16, 17).

St. Matthew (xvii. 1, &c.), describing the Transfiguration, tells us that Jesus took "Peter, James, and John his brother" to be witnesses of that memorable event. St. Peter, in relating the same occurrence (Mark ix. 2), naturally omits the words "his brother;" for he knew and loved John too well to think it necessary to designate him at all in connexion with a scene so familiar to them both.

On the other hand, St. John is particular in explaining how and why Simon was surnamed Cephas or Peter, thus pointing attention to the leading part which St. Peter was destined to take in the publication and establishment of Christianity (Cf. John i. 42 with Matt. x. 2; Mark iii. 16; Luke vi. 14).

Moreover, it is interesting to observe how tenderly St. John narrates the painful story of his friend's fall (a story nowhere so fully detailed as in the gospel dictated by the offender himself); while John alone, of all the evangelists, is particular in informing us that it was Peter who bravely drew sword against such odds in defence of his master, and he only describes the deeply interesting occasion on which our Lord gave his erring but repentant follower the opportunity of thrice expressing his ardent love and devotedness to him, and then, in the most solemn manner, renewed his apostolic commission (Cf. John xviii. 10, 15—18, 25—27, with xxi. 15—19).

St. John omits all reference to St. Peter's unsuccessful attempt to walk on the water to meet his approaching master (Cf. John vi. 16—21, with Matt. xiv. 22—33), but is careful to relate a similar exploit, which redounded so much to his honour (xxi. 7—11).

Finally, it is to St. John's friendly pen that we are indebted for the record of that noble confession of the Messiah which St. Peter uttered in the face of an almost general defection (vi. 66—69);—as well as of that characteristic burst of mingled emotions with which Peter at first deprecated the washing of his feet by his Lord and Master, but which, on his further enlightenment, constrained him to cry out, "Lord, not my feet only, but also my hands and my head (xiii. 6—9).

THE GENESIS OF THE EARTH AND OF MAN.

DEAR SIR,—May I beg the favour of your inserting the following observations on a review which appeared in the last number of your Journal, of a notice of a pamphlet which I contributed to the previous number.

The writer of the review in question commences by remarking that "the paper of R. S. P. is properly a notice of a pamphlet, the title of which he gives; but, inasmuch as he adopts the views broached by the author of that pamphlet, it may be more convenient to meet the communication as if it were entirely his own." While I do not hesitate to admit the "convenience" of this mode of attack, I must enter my protest against its fairness. I stated indeed distinctly that I adopted the opinion of the writer in question as to the " Genesis of the Earth," but I as distinctly refrained from expressing any judgment as to his view of the " Genesis of Man." My words as to that view were, " It may be an erroneous belief, yet it deserves a careful and candid examination."

In combating the theory that the Mosaic account of the creation is the narrative of a revelation by means of a vision or a series of visions,

B. H. C. observes: "The revelation of *future* events may have been by vision, but where can we find a revelation of *past* events of which this can be said and proved?" Remarking, by the way, on the strange sound of that "may," I would observe that the principle of doubting every statement in the Bible which has not its exact parallel would lead to dangerous results, and further, that to make a distinction between visions of *past* and visions of *future* events seems to me a mere quibble.

Again, he remarks, "To assume that the record is one of *appearances* and not of *facts* is to strip it of its historical character, and to deprive some other portions of Holy Writ of their truthfulness." It is argued, however, in the pamphlet that the revelation is perfectly true as a representation of the events, and no doubt is therefore cast upon its truthfulness. B. H. C. proceeds, "How can we say, for instance, that 'in six days the Lord made heaven and earth,' if we mean that in so many days he revealed by vision to some one the fact of his creating them?" Here again is a misrepresentation, since it is supposed by the writer of the pamphlet that the six visions corresponded to the six days of creation. My reviewer regrets that I make "the same misapplication of the words, 'one day is with the Lord as a thousand years, and a thousand years as one day,' which is so common and so alien from their true intention. That the word 'day' is often used indefinitely in the Bible, as in most languages, is admitted; but it has a definite meaning, and we believe it has in this very passage of Peter (2 Peter iii. 8)." The application or misapplication of the word "day" did not originate with the author of the pamphlet, and I wait for an explanation more consistent with good criticism before I abandon this one. If the meaning B. H. C. would give to what St. Peter says respecting the time of our Lord's advent be founded on the notion of six days of work followed by a millennial seventh, I can only regret that he has adopted a view based upon a cabalistic explanation of the commencement of the Book of Genesis according to the numerical value of the letters, and has fallen into the "common" error of attempting to fix that day of which our Saviour said none knew save the Father. The reviewer next observes, "Equally unfounded do we believe the opinion to be, that Exod. xx. 11 is interpolated, of which there is not, so far as we are aware, even the shadow of a proof." The reason why some critics have held this passage to be an interpolation I stated in the notice of the pamphlet, and I quoted its author's remark that his view rendered such a supposition unnecessary. In the concluding part of what relates to the geological question, the reviewer remarks, "We must confess that we do not see how 'this explanation admits the most literal interpretation of the biblical narrative.' Why does it not reduce it to a dream, a waking dream if you will—but still a dream?" Are the visions of the holy seers, I would ask, and such books as that of Daniel and the Revelation of St. John, the bulwarks of Christianity and of Protestantism to be thus disparaged? The criticism that places history before "the sure word of prophecy" is, I am not afraid to maintain, simply neologian, and more to be feared than that which in my case B. H. C. so loudly condemns.

I must now make some observations on what the reviewer has remarked concerning the second subject of the pamphlet—"the origin of the human race." He says, "I believe .... Adam to have been the first of his species, for it is said, 'There was not a man to till the ground' prior to his formation." If however it is supposed that agriculture and civilization began with Adam, as the author of the pamphlet holds, this argument loses its force. I cannot here enter into the doctrinal question, since its discussion would occupy several pages. I do not deny that it presents considerable difficulties; but many divines, such as Dr. Pye Smith, as well as those who have held the other planets of our system to be inhabited, have not considered such difficulties insuperable, and I do not think that B. H. C. has acted fairly in ignoring the observations on this head which I quoted from the pamphlet. The reviewer continues, "Adam's calling his wife Eve because she was the mother of all living is diluted into this, 'that she should bring forth children.' We submit that this is not criticism." As the writer of the pamphlet has not done what is here supposed, but has shewn his belief that the meaning must be that Adam called his wife Eve because he prophesied that she should be the mother of many children, I submit that this is not criticism. After elaborately shewing the comprehensiveness of the term "all living" by reference to the different ancient versions, and to the *Talmud*, the reviewer adds: "To make matters worse, the verb היתה 'she was,' or rather 'she became,' is imagined to be an emphatic future." Ridicule of the use of the preterit as an emphatic future would cast ridicule on many prophecies in the Bible, and would shew a real or assumed denial of the first principles of Hebrew grammar. In two previous places does B. H. C. make observations which can only tend to the disparagement of prophecy. I am not surprized therefore to meet with such a remark as the following treading on the heels of that first quoted. "The question, where did Cain get his wife from? has been a favourite one with infidels; and his building a city has also furnished the same party with objections." This I again submit is not argument, except in the sense that the Inquisition used arguments with Galileo. So long as the church refuses to admit an explanation that is contrary to tradition, the infidels will make the most of truths that oppose that tradition, but it does not follow that an opinion is false because it has been so put forth. Moreover the present is not the time in which it is any longer safe or wise to raise an outcry of infidelity in the place of sober logic and common sense. I am inclined to think that no more dangerous example of the lengths to which traditionary teaching carries its uncompromising followers can be afforded than in the following passage. "We believe that Cain married his sister, and broke no laws by so doing; the degrees within which marriages are prohibited not having been then fixed." If we suppose, with the author of the pamphlet, that Adam's sons married into another race, or that wives were created for them, this difficulty disappears. Yet in order to maintain the dogma of the unity of the human race in its strictest sense, and by clinging to a Jewish tradition that Adam's sons married their sisters, the whole human race is made of incestuous origin. This will be regarded as a strong expression, but why are we to apply the term incestuous to all marriages of the kind but the supposed one in question? Abraham's cannot be adduced as a parallel since it is more probable that Sarah was his niece than his half-sister, and it is certain that she was not his uterine sister.   The belief in the *horror naturalis*, the very keystone of ethics is abandoned, and the immutability of God's laws denied.   We should not forget who said that the Jews made the commandment of God of none effect by their tradition.

The calculations of B. H. C. to shew what neither I nor the writer of the pamphlet called in question, the sufficiency of a single pair to popu-late the world, must not be passed unnoticed.   He says, "Adam may have had sons and daughters, and doubtless had such, whose names have long ago perished; and in the course of five or six hundred years the possible descendants of a single pair may have been a number which will startle those who look at it for the first time.   In this Journal for July, 1852 (p. 498), we furnished a calculation based upon a fact, from which it appeared that in sixty years two had become eighty, or increased forty times; and yet among their children there had been probably an average amount of mortality.   I now find that in 600 years the actual descendants of those two persons may reach the astounding total of 20,971,820,000, 000,000 !   I trust that this will serve to set at rest the question as to the capabilities of the race for increase.   At the end of 360 years from the creation of Adam, or of a "year of years," according to our reckoning, the number of the world's inhabitants may have been 8,192,000,000, or about ten times its present population, and this on the supposition that all sprung from a single pair."   Since the author has just before admitted that men then lived to near a 1,000 years, and this admission includes that of *long* generations, his calculation based upon *short* generations is self-contradictory; but I am prepared to maintain its impossibility, while I do not doubt that all mankind can have sprung from a single pair.   It is worthy of remark however that the Hindus have been accused of extra-vagance in assigning to Krishna so numerous a progeny that 30,088,100 schoolmasters were needed to instruct his grandchildren.

"It is said," observes the reviewer, "that the word Adam, אָדָם, 'whenever it occurs after the death of the man to whom the name of Adam is first applied, properly signifies the Adamites, just as Israel in the like case properly signifies the Israelites.'   To this we object, as not fairly representing the *usus loquendi* of the Hebrew text; and affirm that, to render the word by *Adamites* would frequently be both inconsistent and absurd.   If R. S. P. will take the pains to try the experiment with those passages, for instance, which are alluded to in Gesenius' *Lexicon*, he must see that his view cannot be defended."   If B. H. C. had examined, not alone Gesenius' *Lexicon*, but Fürst's *Concordance*, as carefully as I have done, he would not affirm so boldly anything of a language with which we are so imperfectly acquainted as Hebrew; and in the present case my examination, undertaken long before he counselled it, has not invalidated the view of the writer of the pamphlet.   If the Bible never mentions any but descendants of Adam, except incidentally, Adam may very properly sometimes be used to signify man or men.   Again, B. H. C. objects to the word with the prefixed article being used specifically in like manner as Israel is used for the descendants of Israel.   But if it primarily means, as indeed few will question, the red man, we can easily understand that it should often receive the article.   If, however, B. H. C. will consult the syntax of any Hebrew Grammar, he will see this remark of his to be utterly untenable. Respecting the giant races, supposed by the author of the pamphlet to be of a non-Adamic stock, the reviewer says, "Now one word about these Nephilim. It is very likely that, in the time of Moses, the name was given to some *fancied* race of great stature who existed before the flood, and whom superstition still consigned to lands which were but imperfectly known. These were the ghosts and the hobgoblins with which the weak and the ignorant were terrified. One thing, at least, is certain ; that the statement of the spies, in Nu. xiii. 33, was untrue, and it is scarcely safe to build a theory upon a lie." The "theory" is not built upon a single statement, much less upon a lie, but upon a number of statements, the truth of which none but infidels have ever called in question. The spies spoke of the stature of the Anakim in the usual Oriental phraseology, but that they were a people of great stature is proved by passages which are referred to in the margin of this very text. The might of Goliath and his kinsmen, the size of Og's bed or coffin, and the like, prove the existence of a giant people (the Rephaim) who were connected with the antediluvian Nephilim.

Without entering in detail into the arguments adduced by B. H. C. to shew that all mankind, instead of simply all Adam's descendants, except Noah and his family, perished by the flood, I cannot omit noticing what he says of physical differences. "There is, however, another argument alluded to which would prove more than R. S. P. wishes. I allude to the ambiguity of diversities of complexion, &c., in man. Those physical diversities do not prove difference of species, nor even disprove a common origin." Thus summarily is the great ethnological question disposed of in a sentence. "If R. S. P. will look again at Genesis x., he will find that from the sons of one man have descended tribes in whom all extremes of difference may be traced." I would ask B. H. C., however, if a predominant race does not often give its name to a larger one subject to it, and whether all Scythians, or all Russians, can be called the same people. "And let it be remembered that, at the early period when the chapter alluded to was written, those variations were as marked as they are now." On what authority is this stated? "The production of varieties of any race is not a mere question of time, as will appear by a glance at our domesticated animals, and cultivated fruits, vegetables and flowers. So far as the human complexion is concerned, it is unjust to suppose that the change in any case has been from white to black, or from black to white; more probably it has been from an intermediate hue. However, this is certain,—that the Jewish race at this moment exhibits every variety of colour." The last statement is, *primâ facie*, correct, but will not bear examination; for, except in the first generation after intermarriages with negroes, when do we find any negro characteristics in a Jew? and who has detected in any one race the cranial peculiarities of the whole human species?

The Reviewer, though he is convinced that the philological argument for the common origin of man is of great weight, yet forbears to touch upon it. This I regret, for I think it is a most important point of the controversy, and will ultimately tend to its settlement.

The last argument brought against the views which were noticed in my paper is that our Lord assumed the nature of the race he came to save, and that if all men are not descended from Adam, Christ came to save races to which he was not allied. But if there existed but one race before Adam, the marriages of his sons and daughters with persons of that race (for which the writer of the pamphlet argues) would make all his descendants to be allied to the supposed Pre-Adamites.

.   The reviewer concludes with a compliment to me and another writer. "The candour, piety, and ability of those whose opinions we have ventured to canvass disarm criticism of its severity, and assure us that they have no end in view but the elucidation of truth." Since the article calls in question my orthodoxy and scholarship, I am at a loss to understand any part of this strange eulogy, though I am quite aware that criticism which is not distinguished by those qualities disarms itself.

In conclusion, let me offer my most sincere thanks to another contributor to your pages, who signs his letter H. H. B., and in that communication shews that he does not misunderstand my motives, although he does not accept the results to which I have partly given my adhesion. Would that I could have writtten this letter in the same mild tone that he has adopted; but when one who has devoted very much of his time and energies to the elucidation of God's Word finds his motives called in question, and his well-meant criticism condemned as infidel, he cannot be expected to vindicate himself in honeyed words. And I shall ever maintain that the principle I have laid down in my former communication, that the safest interpretation of Scripture is the most literal, cannot be denied, that so long as we hold in the highest reverence its inspiration, differences in interpretation can lead to no ultimate evil, and that to shut our eyes and stop our ears to what suits not preconceived opinions is no small sin.

R. S. P.

British Museum.

NOTICES OF BOOKS.

Who is God in China, Shin or Shang-Te? *Remarks on the Etymology of* □יהוה *and of* Θεός, *and on the rendering of those terms into Chinese.* By the Rev. S. C. MALAN, M.A., of Balliol College, Oxford, and Vicar of Broadwindsor, Dorset. London: Bagster, 1855. 8vo. pp. 318.

THE first and most important object of missionaries, in endeavouring to convert heathens to the knowledge of the true God, is assuredly to find, in the language of the people among which they work, an appropriate substitute for the term GOD. They have to consider both what idea the term already in use conveys to the people, and what the idea is which they wish to impart to those whom they teach. In most languages there may be a choice of terms to render " God," dependent on the dialects of that language, or on the extent of country over which it is spoken; and in some cases the choice of a proper term may prove more difficult than at first appears, owing to the more or less confused state of religious forms and ideas among the people.

It can be no matter of surprise, therefore, to hear that those who first went to Christianize China, found some difficulty in choosing a fit medium to convey the idea of the God they preached from among the various terms in use among the people of that archaic and peculiar land. Their choice, however, lay between *three* terms in particular— *T'heen*, Heaven; *Shang-Te*, Supreme Ruler; and *Shin*, Spirit. As far back as the middle of the seventeenth century the Jesuits, the Dominicans, and the Lazarists were at issue on the point. They agreed in rejecting *T'heen*, " Heaven," as too indefinite. Some few were in favour of *Shin*, " Spirit;" but by far the greater portion of them chose to adhere to *Shang-Te*, " Supreme Ruler," as representative of the Christian term, " God." The difference of opinion on this subject gave rise to so much altercation that it called for the intervention of the court of Rome, and legates were sent by the Pope to quell the religious excitement of his missionaries. A compromise was then entered into, and the term *T'heen-Choo*, " Lord of Heaven," was substituted for *Shang-Te*, as likely to please all parties.

The choice of a term by the Romanists was not likely to dispose Protestant missionaries in its favour. We find, accordingly, that a very warm discussion has been carried on, chiefly, of late years—and, we regret to say, not always in the best spirit—by Protestant missionaries in China, respecting the term to be adopted by them for " God." Drs. Marshman, Morrison, and Milne, who published the first translation of the Bible in Chinese, chose *Shin*. But when it became necessary to revise their more or less defective versions of the sacred texts, and to bring to bear on that work the increase of knowledge and of Chinese scholarship acquired since the days of those eminent men, the question was asked very naturally, " Shall we retain *Shin*, or adopt some other term for ' God?' " Some decided at once in favour of retaining *Shin*. Others contended that this term, not being appropriate for its object, they would adhere to *Shang-Te*, while others tried in vain to coin new terms of their own making, an attempt which, we need hardly say, failed utterly. The question at issue then was, which of the two, *Shin* or *Shang-Te*, shall prevail? and on that question the Protestant missionaries in China and their friends split. They then referred the matter to their respective Bible Societies at home. The American Bible Society decided on retaining *Shin* for " God," in all books printed at her expense in China; but the British and Foreign Bible Society, and the Church Missionary Society chose, we believe, more wisely, to refer the matter to their missionaries and agents in China, who, by their learning and long residence in the country, were likely to be the best judges in the matter. And they, as it appears from their latest accounts, have almost unanimously determined to adopt *Shang-Te* for " God," and to retain *Shin* for " Spirit" only, in the million copies of the New Testament which are being printed for distribution in China. This resolution (and not the use of *Shang-Te* by the insurgents, as erroneously stated in the *Literary Churchman*, for August 11, p. 177) bids fair, we hope, to prove a practical settlement of the question.

As a matter of course, a great deal has been written by missionaries in China on both sides; but the principal publication on the subject in this country was, until Mr. Malan's work appeared, the small anonymous pamphlet, " *Shin v. Shang-Te*," written by a strenuous advocate for *Shin*, who professes to give an impartial summary of the controversy, and calls upon all who have at heart the glory of God and the spiritual good of China, to require that *Shin*, and no other term, be adopted for " God" in the Chinese Scriptures. He rests the main strength of his argument on the fact that the majority of the missionaries in China are in favour of *Shin*, which they consider an appropriate term for אֱלֹהִים and Θεός, as being, like these, a generic term; whereas *Shang-Te* is, in their opinion, (like *Jupiter*) only the *proper name* of one of the chief deities of China; and as a proper name of such a deity, it ought, they say, no more to be found in the mouth of Christians than the names of Canaanitish gods were to be mentioned by the Israelites.

The object of Mr. Malan's work is to refute that pamphlet, and to shew that, judging by analogy, the nearest and fittest equivalent the Chinese have for " God " is *Shang-Te*; whereas the use of *Shin* must inevitably lead to Polytheism and to Pantheism, since it is understood in China in that sense alone.

He first of all shews that the plea of " a majority" in favour of *Shin* carries with it very little weight, since the best scholars, that is, those likely to be the best judges in such an important question, must of necessity be found in the minority. He next proceeds to examine the grounds for preferring one term to the other—by searching into

the etymology of the terms אֵל and אֱלֹהִים, Θεός and ὁ Θεός, which are to
be rendered into Chinese, and into that of the Chinese terms *Shang-Te*
and *Shin*, which are proposed as substitutes for the Hebrew and Greek
originals. Mr. Malan does not *rest* his argument on etymology alone,
since he maintains that *Shang-Te*, which means one thing, is an appropriate substitute for " God," which means another. But he justly
considers it of the greatest importance to ascertain, first, whether there
be anything in the literal meaning of either of the Chinese terms,
that may render that term inadmissible as a substitute for " God."

First comes אֵל, which Mr. Malan proves to mean " powerful," and
as such, " first," and " foremost." Then אֱלֹהַ, as an intensitive of אֵל,
which adds the idea of " worship" to that of " power" and " priority,"
in אֵל. Next is אֱלֹהִים, the plural of " virtues," or of " majesty," of
אֱלֹהַ; which adds " majesty" to the " worship" of אֱלֹהַ, and to the
power of אֵל. After that, Mr. Malan examines the derivation of Θεός,
and its use with and without the article. Mr. Malan believes that
Θεός is but a dialectic (Attic) difference of Δεύν, Deus or Θεῦς, derived
from the Sanscrit root Div or Diu, masculine, feminine, and neuter,
which implies " brilliancy," and means " light," " day," the " sun,"
and the " bright expanse of Heaven." Accordingly " Jupiter," i.q.,
Ιου Πατερ in the Iguvinian tables, is itself a dialectic pronunciation of
Dius (or Deus) pater, or Diespiter, both of which are the Sanscrit
Dius-piter or Diaus-piter, that is, " Heaven-father," and shews that
Jupiter, like Jehovah or Shang-Te, are not in themselves *proper
names*, but *common names*, used as appellatives of One only Being,
whether he be considered as the " One protecting Source of Light and
Life" (Diuspiter) or as " Eternal Essence" (Jehovah), or as Supreme
Ruler (Shang-Te). Whatever the *Literary Churchman* may think to
the contrary, Mr. Malan's position must hold good, until the number
of examples he brings forward to substantiate it be disproved.

He next examines the Chinese word *T'heen*, " Heaven," and shews
that it would be inadmissible as a substitute for " God."

Then comes *Shin*. Mr. Malan brings forward the highest authorities in Chinese to shew that *Shin* as a *collective* term, which means
" Spirits" in general, of Heaven, man, or beast, and vivifying Spirit
or " Spirits," emanating from the " Sun," in particular, is taken practically to mean " Deity," only because the Chinese, believing that
" Shin" pervades all things, and gives them their entity, they single
out a certain number of those things as special objects of worship. So
that they give the name " Shin" to many *evil* spirits even, and to
certain beings which, although worshipped, are thought much inferior
to their so-called " Gods."

Mr. Malan tells us that, wishing to approach the subject with his
mind free from bias, he abstained from reading anything written on
the subject except the pamphlet he refutes, so as to form his opinion of
the case from the Hebrew, the Greek, and the Chinese texts alone.
Accordingly, as the pamphlet, *Shin* v. *Shang-Te*, does not give in detail
the reasons for which *Shin* is preferred by some, Mr. Malan is left to

judge of those reasons from the internal evidence of that publication. He notices that *Shin* is held out by the author of *Shin* v. *Shang-Te* as a fit rendering for "God, gods," (always coupled together), because "God, gods" is a "generic" term, they say.   Mr. Malan replies, that "God" is not a "generic" term, since he is alone of his kind : for that "gods" is the plural not of "God" but of a "God"—a name given by figure of speech only to beings which are "no gods."   That, therefore, "God, a god, gods" is not as the author of *Shin* v. *Shang-Te*, says a *genus* like to that of "man, a man, men," all made by God, and born of the same man.   Therefore, since "God" is not a "generic" term, *Shin* which is both *generic* as "Deity," and *collective* as δαίμων, δαίμονες, spirits in general and in particular, is not a fit substitute for the "One God."   For its collective meaning cannot be restricted to any one individual in particular, by means of the article, which does not exist in Chinese.   Even adjuncts leave its meaning undetermined ; for *T"heen-Shin* means, in classical Chinese, either *Shang-Te* alone, the host of his attendants together with him in heaven, or the vivifying influence said to repose in the sun and to give life to the earth.

2ndly. If *Shin* is chosen because, being a *collective* noun, it seems to bear some similarity with the plural אֱלֹהִים, Mr. Malan replies that this plural is that of "majesty ;" for when taken in a *plural* sense, it then applies to God and to the Heavenly Hosts also.   *Shin*, therefore, is not a fit word even then, for its advocates do not wish to imply the "Heavenly Hosts" whenever they make *Shin* stand for the one God.

3rdly. If Shin is thought to claim the precedence over *Shang-Te*, because it means "Spirit," and God is a "Spirit," Mr. Malan answers that it is the very reason why *Shin* should not be used for "God," for "God" is a *Personal* God.   Nowhere in the Bible is he spoken of as a "Spirit" only, with *Spiritual* attributes alone; but he is spoken of as a *Person*, with *personal* attributes.   Therefore, to predicate *personal* attributes of a *spirit*, called by no other name than "Spirit," (for *Shin* means nothing else, whether of heaven, of man, or of beast, good and bad), bears a contradiction on the face of it.   Not only are *personal* attributes incongruous with "Spirit," but to make *Shin*, "Spirit," stand for "God," because "God is a Spirit," is, in fact, to say, that since "God is a Spirit," a "Spirit or Spirits is God;" it is drawing God from Spirit, and not Spirit from God.

Having thus disposed of the probable arguments in favour of *Shin*, Mr. Malan next proceeds to consider the meaning of the term *Shang-Te*. This he shews, also, by a multitude of examples, to be both the *Supreme* and *Personal* God of China.   His name, "Supreme Ruler," is a personification of heaven, from whence, and at his will, the vivifying Spirit, *Shin*, which emanates from the sun, comes down upon earth to give life to the world.   He is Father—for his eldest son is the Emperor—like Indla, or Heaven, in the Naidic Hymns.   He is Ruler—like the Heavens (in Dan. iv.) identified in the same chapter with the "Most High."   He is Judge, who rewards and punishes, blesses and curses, as the case may be. But he is *alone;* for Mr. Malan shews that the five or six *Shang-Te's* said to be worshipped (in *Shin v. Shang-Te*) were declared by Confucius to be only theological terms for the five primary elements; while *Shang-Te* reigned over them supreme.

Exception is taken by the writer of *Shin v. Shang-Te* at the term *Shang-Te*, because it is, he says, a proper name of the Chinese Jupiter. To this Mr. Malan replies that *Shang-Te* is no more a proper name than *Jupiter*, or *Jehovah*, for instance. They are common names, which become proper names in so far, and no further, as they belong to the only Being who has a right to bear them. And as regards *Jupiter* in particular, Mr. Malan remarks that *Shang-Te* bears no resemblance to the Jupiter of popular mythology, which is probably what its adversaries mean, although it naturally bears great affinity to " Jupiter," in its real and original meaning of " Heaven Father," and as Father, " Ruler " and " Protector," also.

Mr. Malan, therefore, concludes that the *emanation* SHIN answers best to the δαίμων of the Greeks, to their δαίμονες, to the neuter " Sarvagatam Brahma " of Brahminism, to Deity in its practical acceptation, and that it is a good and fit rendering for " *Spirit*" in the Bible, according to its literal meaning; but that, on the other hand, *Shang-Te*, from whom *Shin* emanates, is the only and fittest substitute the Chinese have for the Christian term God, both from the similarity it bears to אֵל, אֱלֹהַּ, אֱלֹהִים and Θεός, in their literal sense, and from the relative position occupied by God and *Shang-Te* in the minds of their respective worshippers.

Having thus explained his reasons for choosing *Shang-Te* for " God," and *Shin* for " Spirit," in the Chinese version of the Bible, Mr. Malan next proceeds to examine which of those two terms suits best, by critical remarks on a great number of passages both of the Old and of the New Testament, in which he establishes a comparison between *Shin*, as used for " God," by Drs. Marshman, Morrison, and Milne, and *Shang-Te*, as it has been adopted by the latest translators at Shanghaë. We are of opinion that Mr. Malan is entirely borne out by the proofs he brings forward; and we also think it must be gratifying to him to find (see an extract from a letter of Dr. Medhurst in the *Clerical Journal* for August 8th), that the result of his own unaided researches in the Chinese originals coincides entirely with the opinion of so great a Chinese scholar as Dr. Medhurst.

The work is distinguished by a surprising amount of real learning, but it also has the quality of presenting the argument lucidly to readers of ordinary scholarship. We recommend it, not only in connexion with the question at issue, but also as an admirable summary of information on the subject of the Divine Names. It is some time since we had the opportunity of presenting to our readers so important a contribution to sacred philology as this treatise, and we thank Mr. Malan for it.

The Third Part of the Ecclesiastical History of John, Bishop of Ephesus. Now first edited by WILLIAM CURETON, M.A., F.R.S., Chaplain in ordinary to the Queen and Canon of Westminster. Oxford: at the University Press. 1855. 4to. pp. 420.

A MYSTERY hangs over many portions of the annals of the church, which like a dark mist obscures our vision, and prevents us from gazing distinctly upon it. This uncertainty in reference to many of the most important persons who have taken part in the Church's affairs has left the Christian world at large in comparative ignorance of their existence : and the same is true of not a small number of events which in their day caused a thrill of emotion to run through every member of the Church, and raised the Christian public upon the tiptoe of expectation or of anxiety. True, there have been some men and some events whom the world has "not willingly let die," and they stand forth in bold relief in every sketch of Church history. Every one is familiar with some of every century whom it seems to have been necessary to preserve in memory as the landmarks of religious history, serving to shew the position and relation of successive ages. But this is not enough; and we believe that if the history of God's dealings with the Jewish Church was so important that he set inspired men to write it, and bid every mother's son make it his study, it cannot be unimportant for us to chronicle and to become familiar with the dealings of God towards the church of Christ in every age and country. We do not say this is more important than the other, but that it has an interest and a value which no difficulties can justify us in undervaluing or neglecting. From time to time events and persons which had been long dead and buried have a kind of resurrection, and come forth from their sepulchres with all the charm of novelty, and with all the freshness of life. From time to time some long-lost fragment of the Church's chronicles is brought to light, and men read with new interest what their forefathers lost sight of, and what their fathers did not and could not know. Every now and then some ancient chapter of the Church's records is brought up from some gloomy recess or far distant repository, where it had not only escaped observation, but had been in danger of complete ruin. As it is, it has suffered from the damp of ages, and the long series of atmospheric changes ; parts of it are all but illegible, parts of it are completely gone, yet what remains is precious in the eyes of the Christian scholar, and he feels within a glow of grateful emotion to that Providence which has preserved for him these lessons of the past. It is by such means that additions are being gradually made to the materials of church history, and that every new compiler from those materials is able to introduce something for the first time, necessary to the completeness of the record. There is much reason to fear that many highly valuable and instructive documents are hopelessly gone, but there is perhaps equal reason to hope that what we possess already will be materially augmented from sources yet undiscovered or but partially explored.

Now we have been led to make the preceding observations because it is not every day that we have the privilege of introducing such a name as John, Bishop of Ephesus, and such a book as this valuable relic of his church history. We venture to say that till this work was published, some even of our readers had scarcely heard of him. He comes before us therefore as to us a new man, and as such we must say a few words about him : and his book comes before us as a new book, about which also a few words must be said.

When we turn to the usual authorities on such matters, we find them well nigh silent concerning the subject of our sketch. It would be very difficult to extract from Cave anything definite or certain except this, that he was born at Epiphania in Syria, he was the fellow-townsman and kinsman of Evagrius ; that he flourished about the year 591 A.D., and wrote a history reaching from the end of the reign of Justinian to the time of Maurice. He also blames Vossius, and no doubt justly, for confounding this John with John Rhetor, who also wrote a history, which concluded in the reign of Justin I. The learned editor of this work agrees that John of Ephesus is the same as John Asiaticus or of Asia, and was the historian to whom Evagrius alludes in his own book. The writer last named says that from the times of Justinian the history of events was written by Agathias Rhetor and "John my fellow-citizen (πολίτης) and relative," not only till Chosroes the younger took refuge at Rome, but on to his restoration by Maurice, who shewed no dilatoriness in the work, but took it up right royally, very soon setting him up again by liberal supplies of money and of men. He adds, however, that these histories were not then published. To this scanty notice Assemanni endeavours in his great work to make considerable additions. Some of the facts he names are not without value, but the account as a whole seems to be very inaccurate. Had Assemanni possessed the book now before us, he must have rejected several of the statements to which he gives credence on the faith of some (not very ancient) Syriac authors. Thus one of his authorities places the death of John in the year of the Greeks 889, that is, in A.D. 578. That this cannot be correct is unquestionable, because one of the facts of the history before us to which a date is attached by the author is related to have occurred in the year 896, *i. e.*, in A.D. 585. In other instances our book contradicts the biographer, as when he says that the chronology adopted by John deviates by no less than ten years from the ordinary computation. He makes John bring down the life of Justinian to the year 885, *i. e.*, to A.D. 574, when it is proved by all other testimony that that emperor died ten years earlier, or in 875, *i. e.*, in A.D. 564. And he proceeds to affirm that on the same principle most of John's dates differ by a decade of years from the received chronology. We are happy to be able to shew that Assemanni's authority is one upon which in this case no reliance can be placed. It is only necessary to turn to the book before us, and look for the record of the death of Justinian, to which particular allusion is made ; we must however premise that the history does not profess to begin till about the year A.D. 576, or the sixth of Justin II. At p. 320 of this volume (book v., chap. xiii.) we find the object of our search. John speaks of "the decease of Justinian the king, which was on the 14th day of the month Tishri the latter *(i. e.,* Nov. 14) in the year eight hundred and seventy and six, when he had reigned thirty and nine years. Now Justin, his sister's son, reigned after him thirteen years wanting forty days." This instance alone is sufficient to point out the substantial agreement of John with recognized historians on the matter of dates, to which he pays (for the times) minute attention. Still farther to illustrate this question, it may not be amiss to give two or three others of John's dates. Tiberius, the successor of Justin, was installed Cæsar, Dec. 7, A.D. 575. Tiberius again constituted Maurice the Cappadocian, Cæsar, Aug. 5, A.D. 582. Tiberius was crowned, Sept. 26, A.D. 579. Justin died, Oct. 4, of the same year. Chosroes the Persian died in the year A.D. 579, after a reign of forty-eight years. To save trouble, we have regularly deducted 311 years from the author's dates, which belong to the era of the Seleucidæ.

It is time, however, that we leave this dry subject of chronology for other matters of more general interest, and enquire if anything is known of the life of John himself. Although he is called John, Bishop of Ephesus, it is highly probable that he had no direct spiritual jurisdiction in that city, which was the metropolis of that part of Asia Minor which peculiarly claimed the appellation of Asia. Several of the facts of his life seem to indicate that he was rather a "missionary bishop," on whom devolved the duty of seeking converts from among the heathen who still remained in those parts, and of introducing them to the church. Invested with this wide commission, he is termed Asiaticus, Bishop of Asia, the image-breaker, and he who is over the heathen. This latter title is very similar to one which has been given to Hippolytus, George (of Cappadocia?), &c. In his missionary character, John is to be met with at Constantinople, where in the nineteenth year of Justinian he was honoured with a special royal commission to enquire after the heathen who still secretly practised their religion there. This commission he executed with great energy, and with much satisfaction to his masters, though *we* should think with too much rigour. However, great numbers acquiesced in the demands of the constituted authorities, went to church, became the catechumens of John, and were baptized by him. We are not surprised to find him again commanded by Justinian to enquire after the heathen of various provinces of Asia Minor with a view to their conversion. On this occasion perhaps he received his title as Bishop of Ephesus, or of Asia. On this last occasion, says the historian, "Seventy thousand pagans were detected and converted in Asia, Phrygia, Lydia, and Caria; ninety-six churches were built for the new proselytes, and linen vestments, Bibles and liturgies, and vases of gold and silver, were supplied by the pious munificence of Justinian.'[a]　There is one error in this account of Gibbon's of the ninety-six churches; the new converts themselves erected forty-one; the emperor provided the rest.　The zeal of John was not merely directed against paganism: he was more than an iconoclast; he is said by Bar Hebræus to have disinterred the bones of the heretic Montanus, and of Carata, Maximilla, and Priscilla, his three prophetesses, which were burnt.　"Toleration was not the virtue of the age."

How long John of Ephesus retained his influence at court is uncertain.　Most likely, as he belonged to the Monophysite party, among whom, indeed, he was a distinguished leader, his fortunes fluctuated with those of his sect.　There is abundant proof that he shared largely in the sufferings which befel those who held the same views with him in particular, at the instigation of John of Sirimis in the reign of Justin II.　The work before us gives us a good deal of his personal history and experience in the time of his misfortunes, which, however, we must unwillingly pass over.　The period, and circumstances, and place of his death are uncertain.　The only date which has been assigned to this event, so far as we know, is incorrect as shewn above.

Having no further knowledge of his life upon which we can rely, we now come to his writings generally, and to this history in particular. We regret that we are unable to present a list of his works to our readers; we can only say, that he was the author of various biographies, some of which are contained among the Syriac MSS. in the British Museum; and that he wrote a great historical work, which was divided into three parts.　This is his *Ecclesiastical History*, which he tells us commenced with the reign of Julius Cæsar, and was continued down to his own day.　The first part appears to be totally lost; and of the second, nothing remains but the few fragments quoted by Assemanni in the account of John, to which we have alluded.　They are copied by him from a work by Gregory Bar Hebræus, a Syriac writer, whose authority is Mar Michael.　The greater part of the third division of John's work is contained in the volume before us, now for the first time printed from a Syriac MS. in the British Museum.　It is unfortunately incomplete.　Not only are the beginning and end wanting, but also various portions from other parts.　Yet incomplete as it is, we gratefully accept what remains, as a precious relic of a highly valuable and important work.

With a few words upon the plan and period of this book we must conclude the present notice.　Properly speaking, the history reaches from about the year A.D. 570 to about A.D. 575,—that is, it embraces a period of about five years.　The author divides his work into six books, and these again are subdivided into chapters—viz., Book I. into 42; Book II. into 52; Book III. into 56; Book IV. into 61; Book V. into 23; and Book VI. into 49.　The first and second books

---

[a] *Decline and Fall of the Roman Empire*, chap. xlvii.

are chiefly occupied with matters relating to the persecution of the Monophysites under Justin, at the instigation of John of Sirimis, bishop of Constantinople. The third book contains a record of various circumstances in the closing years of Justin, and in the reign of his successor Tiberius. The fourth book gives a very full account of the conversion of certain remote African tribes, and of events connected therewith. The fifth book introduces us to the Tritheists, and the former part of the reign of Maurice. The sixth book is a collection of narratives of striking occurrences in the wars with the Persians, the Avares, and other enemies of the Romans at that period.

In the 418 pages of which the volume before us consists, there is very much useful and interesting information, and not a little for which we may elsewhere search in vain. If it should be objected that it is the production of a Monophysite, and therefore of a partizan, we ask what histories will stand if such a test is to be supplied? Few, indeed, are the written histories of great periods of the church which are free from party spirit. If we find it we must make allowance for it. The same may be said of our author's credulity, as the one shews that he was endowed with the same human nature as others; this may serve to shew that he partook of the weaknesses of his age. The readers of the church historians of the fifth century will understand this.

We hope that Mr. Cureton will find leisure to present the British public with his promised translation of a book which he has edited with so much care, ability, and success.

----

1. *General History of the Christian Religion and Church.* From the German of Dr. AUGUSTUS NEANDER. Translated from the last Edition by JOSEPH TORREY, Professor of Moral and Intellectual Philosophy in the University of Vermont. Vol. IX. Published from the Posthumous Papers by K. H. TH. SCHNEIDER. Edinburgh: T. and T. Clark. 1855. 8vo. pp. 584.

2. *A Compendium of Ecclesiastical History.* By Dr. JOHN C. L. GIESELER, Consistorial Counsellor and Ordinary Professor of Theology in Göttingen. Second Edition. Translated from the German by the Rev. WINSTANLEY HULL, M.A., Vicar of North Muskham. Volume V. Edinburgh: T. and T. Clark. 1855. 8vo. pp. 412.

WE have at length, in English, the last instalment of the Church History of the great Neander. It embraces a period whose importance can scarcely be overrated, extending from Boniface the Eighth to the Reformation. This space includes the Councils of Basle and of Constance, and the lives and labours of our own Wicklife, and of Huss and Jerome of Prague. The biographies and opinions of those great men are sketched with the same masterly skill which has so long furnished life-like portraits of the great actors in church history, and a great treat is in reserve for our readers who intend to make themselves ˙rsonally acquainted with this volume. Perhaps, in a semi-political point of view, and as bearing on the Reformation, the history of the Popes will be perused with the greatest interest. Their own ambition and folly brought about the great papal schism, which presented to Christendom the startling and scandalous spectacle of two heads of the Church, both pretending to be infallible and divine, and by its results hastened the Reformation. While we regret that Neander did not live to portray the moving scenes of the age of Luther, we are glad that he lived to bring his history down to a period when writers became more numerous, and make his loss less deeply felt.

Gieseler also is no more, and his history is associated, like Neander's, with the idea of the loss to the Church which the death of such pains-taking men produces. This volume reaches from the Council of Pisa to the rise of the Reformation in Germany and Switzerland. The German work extends to the Peace of Westphalia, A.D. 1648, and would occupy two more volumes of the English edition. Messrs. Clark will be guided by the wish of their subscribers whether they shall proceed or not; and, for our own part, we beg to express a strong hope that so valuable a text-book will be completed by them. We must mention that both these volumes are parts of the "Foreign Theological Library," which deserves the extensive patronage of the religious and learned public.

A History of the Christian Church. By Dr. CHARLES HASE, Professor of Theology in the University of Jena. Translated from the Seventh and much-improved German Edition. By CHARLES E. BLUMENTHAL, Professor of Hebrew and of Modern Languages in Dickinson College, and CONWAY P. WING, Pastor of the first Presbyterian Church in Carlisle, Pennsylvania. London: Trübner and Co. 1855. Large 8vo. pp. 756.

ONE peculiarity of this work is its bringing into a small compass the whole history of the Church, down to the sects and parties of the present age. It may appear at first sight, that so comprehensive a survey could not be well taken in so limited a space; but Dr. Hase has succeeded in his design most admirably, and given, not a mere series of dry details, but very graphic and spirited accounts of the various ages of the Christian era. The translators say properly, in reference to this subject, that "a miniature representation of a vast mass of facts, in which each personage and event shall appear in their individual freshness and relative proportions, requires for its execution peculiar talents and rare opportunities. The Germans appear to possess these in a greater degree than most other people. Their learned men highly appreciate the value of such manuals, and their literature abounds in them." From this general observation they proceed to furnish a character which we must give entire, as conveying far better than we can do the style and character of the book:—

"From the letters we have received, and from public journals, we might present many testimonies, not only that such a work was needed, but that nothing in the literature of the present day was so likely to supply the deficiency as a translation of the work we had announced. The style of our author is especially adapted to the Anglo-Saxon mind; his astonishing power of condensed expression; his æsthetic, if not religious sympathies with every variety of intellectual and moral greatness; his skilful daguerreotypes of character by means of the transmitted light of contemporary language; the delicate irony and genial humour which pervade his descriptions; the picturesque liveliness with which a single character or incident brings out the manners and spirit of an age; the precision with which his scientific arrangement is preserved; the critical judgment with which the minutest results of recent investigation are introduced, and the graceful proportion and animation with which the whole stands out before us, render his history attractive to all kinds of readers. He throws away every name or event which has no historic utility or organic life. He appreciates an heroic spirit wherever it appears, and each period is estimated as nearly as possible in its own light. This is not merely a history of the hierarchy, of the nobility, or of great men, but of *the Church*. His descriptions, therefore, embrace especially traits of common life, the progress of the arts, and indications of advancement in social freedom. If his theological opinions do not quite coincide with our own, he seldom, at least in this work, obtrudes them upon our attention. His object seems to have been to maintain historical accuracy, rather than to exhibit his own opinions; and if sometimes our favourite characters or views do not appear in the light in which we have usually contemplated them, his uniform impartiality and intelligence make us suspect our earlier judgments. None but those who observe the structure rather than the particular dogmatic experiences of this work, will be likely to detect the author's peculiar views, and such readers can afford to give them whatever consideration they deserve. A striking comparison has been drawn between him and a living English historian and essayist; but the reference can be only to the liveliness and brilliancy of his historical scenes, and not to the minute space in which the picture of more than eighteen centuries is presented."

When speaking of space, we must not let our readers infer that this work is a small one. The volume is very large, and the pages well filled with compact type, so that it is really a substantial monument of skill and erudition.

---

1. *The Ecclesiastical History of New England; comprising, not only Religious, but also Moral and other Relations.* By JOSEPH B. FELT. Vol. I. Boston: The Congregational Library Association. 1855. Large 8vo. pp. 668.

2. *New England's Memorial.* By NATHANIEL MORTON. Sixth Edition. Also, *Governor Bradford's History of Plymouth Colony, &c. &c.* Boston: Congregational Board of Publication. 1855. 8vo. pp. 538.

THESE volumes will naturally excite more attention in America than in England; yet they have a general interest as the records of very exciting times, the events of which have had a mighty influence on Christendom. The way in which the language and institutions of England have been spread over the western world, is a dispensation of Providence, the immediate results alone of which are now seen. The time will come when the ultimate developments of American politics and religious tendencies will make all the particulars of the early settlements of the New World of great importance.

The Church Historians of England. Vol. III. Part II. Containing the Works of Simeon of Durham. Translated from the Original Latin, with Preface and Notes, by the Rev. JOSEPH STEVENSON, M.A., of University College, Durham, Vicar of Leighton Buzzard. London: Seeleys. 1855. 8vo. pp. 380.

THE series of which this volume is a portion well deserves the support of Englishmen, especially of those who take an interest in the early religious history of their country. There have already appeared Beda, the Saxon Chronicle, Florence of Worcester, Ethelwerd, Alfred, Hyde, Wallingford, Ingulf, Gaimar, and William of Malmesbury; and the present volume contains Simeon of Durham. Of the life of this author little is known. It appears that he was present at the disentombment of the body of St. Cuthbert, in the year 1104, at which time he was an inmate of Durham Cathedral. He probably died at the time the Chronicle terminates, A.D. 1129. His works now presented to the English public are as follows:—His "History of the Kings," extending from A.D. 616 to 1129; "History of the Church of Durham," which gives a full account of the fortunes and migrations of the monks of St. Cuthbert, from the introduction of Christianity into Northumbria to the year 1096. Of this work Mr. Stevenson says: "Although professing to deal with ecclesiastical history only, it furnishes us with many important illustrations of the secular affairs of the northern districts of England. Simeon was well informed upon the incidents which he narrates, although it must be admitted that he is sometimes betrayed into serious errors. He loses no opportunity of magnifying the dignity and importance of his patron saint, by recounting instances which draw largely upon the credulity of his readers; but these narratives for the most part so well illustrate either the history, or the manners, or the faith of the age to which they relate, that we are no losers by their introduction." This is the right way to estimate the value of works like these. They took the form of the times when they were written, and their very absurdities are often their best commendation.

Then follow—"The History of the unjust persecution of the first Bishop William;" "A short History concerning the Intruder during the time of Bishop William the Second;" "Chronicles of the Angles;" "History of the Siege of Durham," and some shorter pieces. Mr. Stevenson speaks highly of Simeon as an accurate and credible writer, a truthful and honest historian. The series is well edited, and great credit is due to Mr. Stevenson for the great care bestowed by him on every portion of it. We shall watch the work as it proceeds, and make our readers acquainted with its consecutive portions.

———

1. *A Historical and Critical Commentary on the Old Testament, with a New Translation.* By M. KALISCH, Phil. Doc., M.A. Exodus. London: Longmans. 1855. 8vo. pp. 656.

2. *The same work, adapted for English readers, without the Hebrew text.* 8vo. pp. 488.

FOR a long time past we have expressed a wish, in the pages of this JOURNAL, that some competent scholars would undertake a learned comment on the Hebrew text of the Holy Scriptures, corresponding in plan to those of Bloomfield and Alford on the Greek of the New Testament. Such a work presents itself to our notice at last, but from a quarter where we did not look for it, and we are happy to be able to say it is well done. The only anxiety we now feel is for the completion of what has been commenced with so much credit; because, judging from the size of the volume before us, the whole Commentary must be of considerable extent. Yet there is nothing we could wish curtailed, and we shall be glad to hear that the learned author is amply encouraged to finish his labours in the same careful and earnest spirit in which he has begun them.

Exodus was allowed to precede Genesis, because "it forms the centre of Divine revelation, and is best calculated to convey a correct idea of the spirit and tendency of the Commentary." The explanation of the Jewish laws is treated with more copiousness than in any existing Biblical exposition, because the people of Israel was distinguished by its laws from other nations. "By its theology it became the holy, the chosen people; whilst by its manners and customs it is only a member of the common family of the oriental nations." The spirit in which the task has been undertaken is pleasingly described in the preface. "The author, by endeavouring to sum up, as it were, the previous researches, in order to promote, however modestly, the Biblical exegesis by calm and impartial combinations, has, at the same time, established his claim to the indulgent examination of the learned public. He has undertaken the arduous work strengthened by his love for the sacred and earliest sources of human civilization, and he willingly confides it to the benign influence of Divine grace." An Introduction of thirty pages discusses some preliminary questions, such as—"Importance, name, contents, division, and unity of Exodus;" "Chronology of Exodus;" "Accounts of ancient profane writers of the Exodus," &c., &c. M. Kalisch is everywhere conservative in his opinions, and a healthy tone pervades all his remarks. In reference to the unity of the book, he says:—

"Its unity has been questioned, not only by that school of Biblical critics which dismembers the sacred writings quite as arbitrarily and blindly as many hypercritical philologists of the last century dissected Homer's songs into incoherent fragments; but even more moderate interpreters believe that our book is disfigured by spurious interpolations. We have, in all such passages, tried to refute this very questionable opinion. *We see the completest harmony in all parts of Exodus; we consider it as a perfect whole, pervaded throughout by one spirit, and the same leading ideas.*"

In the body of the work the Hebrew text occupies the right hand page, and the new translation the left, while the very copious notes are placed in the lower margin. The English version is adhered to strictly wherever it is practicable, only necessary alterations being admitted, the variations being always marked. The Commentary itself is the result of great reading, and lays under contribution every learned source both ancient and modern, from Aben Ezra to Gesenius and Ewald. It is impossible to read a chapter without feeling that the writer is worthy of confidence, while there is a freshness and spirit in his style which makes pleasure the handmaid of edification. We hope the work will excite the attention of all our readers. The English edition is for those who are not able to read the Hebrew, and contains the substance of the larger volume.

The great importance we attach to this work makes us anxious that nothing may prevent its completion. We know that the zealous and learned author is prepared to consecrate his best energies to a service which he regards as the noblest he can be engaged in, but we cannot presume that he is prepared to sustain heavy pecuniary loss, in addition to the outlay of labour which it entails. On this account we would speak plainly to our readers, and urge them to encourage Dr. Kalisch, by procuring for themselves this first volume. Biblical scholars, and all who are solicitous for the explanation and illustration of the Holy Scriptures, have often a generous duty to perform, leading them to patronise what they may not exactly want for the good of a common cause : and thus to help on enterprises which would otherwise fail. All our readers may be suited by one or the other of the editions of this Commentary : the learned by that with the Hebrew text and the more erudite notes ; and those whose studies do not extend beyond their native Saxon, by that which is simplified for their especial use.

A Hebrew and English Lexicon of the Old Testament, including the Biblical Chaldee. From the Latin of WILLIAM GESENIUS, late Professor of Theology in the University of Halle-Wittemberg. By EDWARD ROBINSON, Professor in the Union Theological Seminary, New York. With corrections and large additions, partly furnished by the author in manuscript, and partly condensed from his larger Thesaurus, as completed by ROEDIGER. Fifth Edition, revised and stereotyped. London : Trübner and Co. 1855. Large 8vo. pp. 1170.

THIS is decidedly the most complete edition of Gesenius's Manual Hebrew Lexicon. No former one could contain the last additions of the learned author, since his Thesaurus has only recently been finished. Everything of importance has been incorporated in this volume, and its size and price, as well as the clearness of its typography, will make it a boon to students of the Hebrew language. It is a subject for grateful reflection that the sacred tongue is yearly receiving more earnest attention, and that the apparatus necessary for the prosecution of the study is more easily procured.

Gesenius's Hebrew Grammar. Seventeenth Edition. With numerous Corrections and Additions. By Dr. E. ROEDIGER. Translated by T. J. CONANT, Professor of Hebrew in Rochester Theological Seminary. With Grammatical Exercises and a Christomathy by the Translator. New York : Appleton; London: Trübner. 1855. 8vo. pp. 374.

GESENIUS's valuable labours on Hebrew philology have never received a better dress than the present. The paper and type are admirable. The educational appliances at the end of the volume are well adapted to give to the learned a thorough knowledge of the language by a sure graduated process. In this respect Hebrew literature may be expected to make rapid strides in the coming generation; for while, by the old method, students were expected only to *translate*, they are now encouraged to *compose* in the language, which has thus applied to it the method which makes such efficient classical scholars.

Uhlemann's Syriac Grammar. Translated from the German by ENOCH HUTCHINSON. With a course of Exercises in Syriac Grammar, and a Christomathy and brief Lexicon, prepared by the Translator. New York: Appleton; Edinburgh: T. and T. Clark. 1855. 8vo. pp. 384.

IN the translator's preface we are informed that this Grammar is acknowledged by all to be a manual of rare excellence, and we are glad to welcome it in an English dress. " Some of our helps of this kind in the study of Syriac are too brief, and others too voluminous. Uhlemann has aimed to present, within moderate limits, a work sufficiently extensive for ordinary purposes of instruction." We hope this work will prove another stimulus to many to enter upon a study which promises to bring to the competent scholar both mental treasures and literary fame. The stores of Syriac learning are yet far from exhausted, and in our own national Museum they lie like fields white to the harvest, ready to yield their sheaves to the earnest labourer. The beauty of the typography of this volume almost incites to progress in the study of it, and it deserves to be well known and used among us. The Christomathy and Lexicon are valuable additions to the Grammar.

Cyclopædia of Biblical Literature, Abridged from the Larger Work. By JOHN KITTO, D.D., F.S.A. Illustrated by numerous Engravings. Edinburgh: A. and C. Black. 1855. Medium 8vo. pp. 808.

THE larger work alluded to in the above title occupies a very high place in the department of Biblical science, and has had a very large circulation. It is now out of print, and a new edition is being prepared by the Rev. Dr. Burgess, with numerous alterations and additions. But the price (three guineas) necessarily keeps this work out of the hands of many who wish to avail themselves of it; and for their use this abridged edition has been prepared. It will be found an excellent compendium of the great Cyclopædia; is a beautifully printed volume; and is decidedly one of the cheapest books now asking for public patronage. This is a new and revised edition.

The Christian Cyclopædia; or, Repertory of Biblical and Theological Literature. By the Rev. JAMES GARDNER, M.D. and A.M. Edinburgh: Johnstone and Hunter. Large 8vo. pp. 900.

THIS large volume contains an immense mass of information, collected and arranged with considerable care. The work contemplates the profit of the private Christian more than of the Biblical scholar, and surveyed within this more humble, though useful, range of operations, we can give it our cordial approval. The compiler says, " In its place this Cyclopædia embraces the general features of both a Biblical and theological dictionary, along with a comprehensive digest of the literature and biography connected with Christianity; the idea having been suggested by, as the volume is founded on, a work which was published in America nearly twenty years ago." In the theological articles there is a leaning to a certain side, as was to be expected, yet the arguments *pro* and *con* are stated with fairness and candour. The book will form a valuable addition to a Christian library.

Specimen of a Revision of the English Scriptures of the Old Testament, from the original Hebrew, on the basis of the common English version, compared with the earlier ones on which it was founded. Prepared for the American Bible Union by THOMAS J. CONANT, Professor in Rochester Theological Seminary. In Three Parts: I. The common English Version, the Hebrew Text, and the Revised Version, with critical and philological notes. II. The Revised Version, with explanatory notes, for the English reader. III. The Revised Version, by itself. New York: American Bible Union; Louisville: Bible Revision Association; Cincinnati: American Christian Bible Society; London: Trübner and Co. 1855. 4to. pp. 32.

OUR American brethren are proceeding with some earnestness in their efforts to make translations of the Holy Scriptures represent the originals as closely as possible. The care taken will be shewn by the advertisement prefixed to this specimen, which we copy entire.

" The plates having been prepared for the following sheets, they are sent out for the satisfaction of those who are interested in the work of revision. From this specimen, they will learn the plan of the work for the Old Testament, and the manner of executing it.

" The following rules of translation shew the general principles followed in this work, without entering into minute specifications.

" 1. Give the author's meaning. To this object every other is to be sacrificed, if necessary.

" A perfect translation is an exact expression of the author's meaning, in his own manner. It should, as far as possible, be to the original writing what the image reflected from a perfect mirror is to the object.

" 2. Translate *word for word*, by the corresponding literal equivalents in English, wherever English idiom will allow it. Where this cannot be done, translate *phrase for phrase*, by English equivalents, as near the original form as possible.

" 3. Give the sense of the author, in the author's own manner.

" If a literal translation, word for word, would be ungrammatical, awkward, harsh, obscure, or feeble, where the author's expression is correct, clear, graceful, vigorous, and animated; then the mere verbal correspondence is no just representation of the original.

" 4. Preserve faithfully the general characteristics and costume of the original work.

" A translation should make no false impressions, in regard to the *age*, the *country*, and the *people*, to which the book belongs. The scenery, natural history, climate, productions, the manners, usages, opinions, state of knowledge and of the arts, &c., should all be faithfully mirrored in the version. In regard to style also, a *modern air* should not be given to an ancient writing.

" 5. Use literal translation, where more than one construction or interpretation of the original words is possible, and both can be conveyed by the literal form.

" Where this cannot be done, the different constructions should be put in the text and margin. The reader of the translation should have the same opportunity, for judging of the possible interpretations of the passage, as the reader of the original.

" 6. Use no superfluous words.

" A translation should contain no words which are not necessary for the exact expression of the sense of the original, in the form best adapted to it. There is no use, therefore, for *italicised* words.[b]

" 7. In this work, the phraseology of the Common English Version is to be used, so far as is consistent with fidelity to the original, and a proper regard to the present usage of the English language.

" *Editions of some of the works, to which reference is made :*

" *The Ancient Versions*, in the Complutensian, Antwerp, Paris, and London (Walton's) Polyglotts.

" *Septuagint Version :* the text of the Vatican MS. in the Editio Romana, one vol. fol. Rome, 1587 ; Bos' ed. one vol. 4to. 1709 ; Holmes and Parsons' ed. four vols. fol. Oxford, 1798 —1827 ; Tischeudorf's ed. two vols. 8vo. Leipz. 1850 ; Jager's ed. two vols. 4to. Paris, 1839 ; the text of the Alexandrine MS. in Baber's Fac-simile, six vols. fol. London, 1816—28 ; Breitinger's reprint of Grabe's ed. four vols. 4to. Zürich, 1730—32.—Tischendorf's Fac-simile of the Codex Ephraemi, two vols. 4to. Leipz. 1843—5, and of the Codex Friderico-Augustanus, one vol. 4to. Leipz. 1846.

" *Other Greek Versions*, in Bahrdt's Hexapl. Orig. quæ supersunt, two vols. 8vo. 1769—70.

" *Syriac Version*, in Lee's ed. two vols. 4to. London, 1823.

" *Vetus Itala*, in Sabatier's ed. three vols. fol. 1743 ; Jerome's revision of it, in Vallarsi's ed. of his Works.

" *Vulgate*, Erhard's ed. one vol. fol. 1748.

" *Versions of later date :*

" *Sante Pagnino*, Biblia Sacra (1528) 2d ed. one vol. fol. 1541.

"   "   as revised by Arias Montano (in the Antwerp Polyglott).

" *Luther*, die ganze heilige Schrift (1534), in *Steir* and *Theile's* Polyglotten-Bibel, 1847—

---

b " If a translation contains words which have been improperly added to the original, they should of course be *italicised*, to put the reader on his guard. But this is not the case in view here."

" *Castalio*, Biblia Sacra (1551), two vols. 8vo.   Leipz. 1738.

" *Junius & Tremellius*, Biblia Sacra (1579), one vol. fol. 1607.

" Biblia ; de gantsche Heylige Schrifture (by an order of the Synod of Dort, 1618 ; published by authority of the States-General, 1637); one vol. fol. 1741.

" La Sainte Bible, traduite par *Lemaistre de Sacy* (1667); four vols. royal 8vo. 1841.

" *Old English Versions ; and as revised in the Common Version :*

" *Wycliffe*, (about 1382—4 ; revised, about 1388); ed. by Forschall and Madden, four vols. 4to. Oxford, 1850.

" *Coverdale*, (1535); Bagster's Reprint, one vol. 4to. London, 1847.

" *Tyndale*, (published by Rogers, under the name of Matthew, 1537) one vol. 4to. London, 1549.

" *Cranmer*, (1540), one vol. fol. 1540.

" *Genevan Version*, (1560), one vol. fol. 1583.

"   "   (with Tomson's Version of N. T.) one vol. 4to. 1606.

" *Bishops' Bible*, (1568), one vol. fol. 1595.

" *King James' Revision*, (1611), 2d ed. one vol. fol. 1613.

"   "   as restored by the American Bible Society, one vol. 8vo. 1854.

" *Other Versions consulted, including Commentaries with Versions.*

" *Pineda*, commentarius in Jobum, two vols. fol. 1612.

" *Drusius*, nova versio et Scholia in Jobum (in the *Critici Sacri*, vol iii.) 1636.

" *Codurcus*, libri Job versio nova ex Hebr. cum Scholiis (*ibid.*) 1651."

As we wish our readers to form a judgment of the results of the labour thus bestowed, we will quote the revised translation of the first chapter of the Book of Job.

" There was a man in the land of Uz, whose name was Job.   This man was perfect and upright, and one who feared God and shunned evil.   There were born to him seven sons and three daughters.   His substance was seven thousand sheep and goats, and three thousand camels, and five hundred yoke of oxen, and five hundred she-asses, and very many servants.   And this man was great, above all the sons of the east.

" Now his sons went and held a feast, at the house of each, on his day ; and they sent, and invited their three sisters, to eat and to drink with them.   And when they had let the feast-days go round, Job sent and purified them.   And he rose early in the morning, and offered burnt-offerings, according to the number of them all : for Job said, It may be that my sons have sinned, and have forsaken God in their hearts.   Thus did Job continually.

" Now it was the day, when the Sons of God came to present themselves before Jehovah ; and Satan also came among them.   And Jehovah said to Satan : From whence comest thou ?   And Satan answered and said : From roaming over the earth, and from walking about upon it.   And Jehovah said to Satan : Hast thou observed my servant Job, that there is none like to him on the earth, a perfect and upright man, one that feareth God and shunneth evil ?   And Satan answered Jehovah, and said : For nought doth Job fear God ?   Hast not thou hedged him about, and his house, and all that he hath, on every side ?   The work of his hands thou hast blessed, and his substance is spread abroad in the earth.   But, put forth now thy hand and touch all that he hath,—if he will not renounce thee to thy face !   And Jehovah said to Satan : Lo, all that he hath is in thy power ; only, against himself do not put forth thy hand.   And Satan went out from the presence of Jehovah.

" Now it was the day, that his sons and his daughters were eating, and drinking wine, in the house of their brother, the first-born.   And there came a messenger to Job, and said : The cattle were ploughing, and the she-asses were grazing beside them ; and Sabæans fell upon and took them ; and the servants they have smitten with the edge of the sword, and only I alone escaped to tell thee.

" Whilst he was still speaking, there came another, and said : The fire of God fell from heaven, and burned the flocks and the servants, and consumed them; and only I alone escaped to tell thee.

"Whilst he was still speaking, there came another, and said: Chaldæans formed three bands, and set upon the camels and took them; and the servants they have smitten with the edge of the sword, and only I alone escaped to tell thee.

"Whilst he was still speaking, there came another, and said: Thy sons and thy daughters were eating, and drinking wine, in the house of their brother, the first-born. And lo, there came a great wind from beyond the wilderness, and struck upon the four corners of the house, so that it fell on the young men, and they died; and only I alone escaped to tell thee.

"Then Job arose, and rent his garment, and shaved his head; and he fell to the earth and worshipped. And he said: Naked came I forth from my mother's womb, and naked shall I return thither. Jehovah gave, and Jehovah hath taken away; blessed be the name of Jehovah!

"In all this Job sinned not, nor uttered folly against God."

———

Roberts's Sketches in the Holy Land, Syria, Idumea, Arabia, Egypt, and Nubia; reduced from the Lithographs by Louis Haghe. With Historical and Descriptive Notices, and an Introductory View of Jewish History, by the Rev. GEORGE CROLY, LL.D. Part VI. London: Day and Son.

WE noticed the commencement of this valuable work in our last number, and it has since appeared regularly every fortnight. In every respect it answers to the conditions put forth by the publishers, and we have much pleasure in again bringing it under the notice of our readers. This part contains the following illustrations;—Church of the Annunciation, Nazareth—The Fountain of Cana—Cana, general view—Town of Tiberias, looking towards Lebanon—The Sea of Tiberias, looking towards Bashan—Tiberias from the walls, Safed in the distance. The literary department, by Dr. Croly, is well executed,—combining correct descriptions of the places with a graphic brevity. The Holy Scriptures and the works of the most approved travellers are constantly appealed to, and the result is an account of each engraving —brief but satisfactory.

———

1. *Christian Theism. The Testimony of Reason and Revelation to the Existence and Character of the Supreme Being.* By ROBERT ANCHOR THOMPSON, M.A. London: Rivingtons, 1855. 2 vols. 8vo. pp. 876.

2. *The First Cause; or, A Treatise upon the Being and Attributes of God.* In Two Parts, viz.,—I. The Proof from Reason. II. The Proof from Revelation. By J. C. WHISH, M.A., Incumbent of Trinity Church, East Peckham. London: Seeleys. 1855. 8vo. pp. 464.

3. *An Essay on the Existence and Attributes of God.* By the Rev. PATRICK BOOTH, A.M., Minister of Innerleithen. Edinburgh: Paton and Ritchie. 1855. 8vo. pp. 308.

ALTHOUGH it is our intention to enter more fully on Mr. Thompson's argument than the present notice will permit, we think it right to him and our readers to refer to it without any delay. Already it stands at the head of six treatises which the Burnett competition has called into existence,—three noticed in our last number, and three now under review. It is a satisfaction to ourselves at least, that our judgment coincides with that of the examiners as to the relative merits of the works to which the prizes were awarded. Mr. Thompson's essay is the largest, and we think it is in every respect the best of those which have yet appeared. What unknown mental treasures may yet be destined to see the light we cannot possibly predict; but, if nothing more comes of the rejected papers, there is little fear of the critical sagacity of the judges being questioned by posterity. We do not mean by this observation to disparage the five other essays,—far from it: they are all good in their respective spheres and aims, but we merely mean to intimate that Mr. Thompson's is—what it ought to be —the best of the six.

Mr. Thompson has chosen for the motto of his first volume, but without stating its source, " Μία μὲν οὖν ἡ τῆς ἀληθείας ὁδὸς, ἀλλ' εἰς αὐτὴν καθάπερ εἰς ἀένναον ποταμὸν ἐκρέουσι τὰ ῥεῖθρα ἄλλα ἀλλοθεν," " There is one path of truth, but into it, as into a perennial river, streams flow from various sources,"—an idea which the whole essay beautifully illustrates. The supremacy of revelation—the way of truth—is everywhere maintained; but at the same time, all other sources from which we derive the knowledge of God are recognized. The *first* volume treats of the existence of the Supreme Being, and is divided into two books; the *first*, on "The first principles of knowledge, and their misapplication in systems of Atheism and Pantheism;" the *second*, on "The direct evidences of Natural Theism." Book the *first* discusses these topics,—Of terms and method, modern systems, including those of Descartes, Locke, Berkeley, Hume, Kant, &c.;—Elementary principles of knowledge;—Speculative theories of existence, such as Idealism and Materialism;—Atheism, dogmatic or positive, and sceptical or negative;—Pantheism, physical, intellectual and semi-pantheism. Book the *second* treats of the character of the evidences; —On space and time;—Knowledge of the soul and of the world;— Evidences of an incomprehensible, infinite Being in the limiting conditions of all knowledge;—*à priori* proofs;—God is a Spirit;—The personality of God;—The revelation of God in the aspirations of the soul. An Appendix treats of Causality as a universal principle of judgment, and of its objective validity. Under these heads a vast amount of information is afforded, classified in a very luminous manner. Apart from the immediate object of the essay, the history of speculative philosophy is presented in a very popular manner in its bearings on the great questions at issue in a system of religion.

The second volume is " On the character of the Supreme Being," and likewise consists of two books. The *first* book is on " The manifestation of the Divine Character in Nature;" and includes the following particulars in successive chapters:—The wisdom, unity and infinity of the Author of Nature;—The Divine Wisdom is unsearchable; the Plurality of worlds;—The Divine Holiness;—The Law of God;— Evil not chargeable upon the Creator;—The Divine attributes. The *second* book comprehends the following important subjects, under the general head, " Scriptural revelation of the Divine Character. Objections of modern Deism ;"—Evidences and interpretation of Scripture; —Dogmatic Theism of the Sacred Scriptures ;—On Miracles, and their relations to the Divine Wisdom ;—Modern Infidelity and its claim to sit in judgment upon God ;—The Scriptural doctrine of human sinfulness with reference to the Divine perfections ;—The development theory of human nature ;—The Divine Wisdom and Goodness in the revelation of the Old Testament ;—Redemption : the great manifestation of Divine Wisdom, Holiness, and Love ;—The final consequences of evil, considered with reference to the Divine perfections ;—Fulfilment of the Divine purpose in the perfection of the life of Christ. The conclusion then surveys the whole subject in some of its practical tendencies. We must rest satisfied at present with this general outline of the work, and express our admiration of it as the production of a Christian scholar and gentleman. Some objections to parts of the argument we reserve for a future occasion.

Mr. Whish informs us that he does not agree with those who think that the subject he is about to discuss has been worn threadbare, but rather agrees with Dr. Skinner, that "a day will come when in respect to these matters which have more divided mankind than all others, one judgment will be formed by all rational beings, when conviction of the rectitude of the Divine Government shall perfectly pervade the intelligent universe." He then develops his purpose in the following passage, which we feel sure will dispose our readers favourably towards the book :—

"Even though we should feel that such a hope is too sanguine, and that among our fallen race there is little probability of perfect unanimity before that time when the truth will have more than its own inherent power to support it, when it will be as persuasively taught by the majesty of the judge as by the unquestioned accuracy of the judgment ;—yet we must all agree with Dr. Skinner when he says, ' If the religion of Christ be not defensible by sober reasoning, it is not capable of being successfully defended. If it be not founded in reason, it is not founded in truth. But if it is founded in truth and reason, then may it safely challenge investigation, and not fear the penetration and strength of the weightiest understanding.' It does thus challenge all mankind ; and every human mind which has the requisite knowledge is instinctively compelled to accept that challenge, and through the appeal of anxious questioning, if not of doubt, to test its genuineness and authenticity. The history of such an investigation, by whomsoever made, could scarcely fail to be of interest to those who are similarly engaged ; and the following pages may be taken as a record of the kind, arranged in the order which seemed best suited to the subject. It may, however, be necessary to remind the reader that he must not consider himself to be in possession of the writer's opinions until the views stated in the *first* part, and supposed to be formed by reason alone, have been compared with the modifications and corrections deduced from Scripture in the *second* part. It is the sincere hope and belief of the author that the tendency of all he has written is to give repose to the mind, and to induce the most perfect confidence in the wisdom and love of our heavenly Father; and he earnestly prays that as his labours have been very profitable to himself, so the perusal of them may, by God's blessing, be beneficial to others."

The small volume of Mr. Booth is a very modest production, treating of the following subjects, which are discussed in a very sensible.

and pious manner:—Cause and Effect;—Self-existence: Dr. Clark's argument;—*à posteriori* argument;—Power, Wisdom, and Goodness of God. Introductory chapter. *A posteriori* arguments; human conscience and will; unity of God;—Power, Wisdom, and Goodness of God, as shewn by the light of nature;—The same, as shewn by the light of nature and revelation;—The same, as shewn by the Gospel of Christ;—Practical inferences and reflections.

The Poetical Works of William Lisle Bowles, Canon of St. Paul's Cathedral, and Rector of Bremhill. With Memoir, Critical Dissertation, and Explanatory Notes, by the Rev. G. GILFILLAN. Edinburgh: Nichol. 1855. 2 vols. 8vo. pp. 722.

THE poetry of Canon Bowles has been long before the public, and its general correctness and the purity of its sentiments have procured for it very general acceptance. We think Mr. Gilfillan overrates the author when he says that he was " the father of modern poetry;" but his works are well worthy a place in Mr. Nichol's very handsome edition of the English Poets, to which these volumes belong. We like Mr. Bowles's Sonnets better than his more lengthened pieces, and introduce one of them as a specimen of the whole.

"THE HOUR-GLASS AND THE BIBLE.

" Look, Christian, on thy Bible, and that glass
    That sheds its sand through minutes, hours, and days,
    And years; it speaks not, yet methinks it says
To every human heart,—So mortals pass
On, to their dark and silent grave! Alas
    For man! an exile upon earth he strays,
    Weary, and wandering through benighted ways;
To-day in strength, to-morrow like the grass
That withers at his feet! Lift up thy head,
    Poor pilgrim, toiling in this vale of tears;
That book declares whose blood for thee was shed,
    Who died to give thee life; and though thy years
Pass like a shade, pointing to thy death-bed
    Out of the deep, thy cry an angel hears,
And by his guiding hand thy steps to heaven are led!"

A Selection of Psalms and Hymns, arranged for the Public Services of the Church of England. By the Rev. CHARLES KEMBLE, M.A., Incumbent of St. Michael's, Stockwell. London: Batten; and Simpkin and Co. 1855. Various sizes.

WE should not be disposed to notice the numerous hymn books which yearly issue from the press, as a rule; but we make an exception on account of the great value of this selection, both as to its contents, and as to the extreme cheapness of its smaller editions, which adapts it so well to the poor, and to children in schools. The volume contains above eight hundred pieces, arranged in two departments; first, the Psalms are given from the versions of various authors, the aim being to select those which best convey evangelical sentiments. Then follow the Hymns, not disfigured by professed improvements, as is too often the case, but as they proceeded from their authors, the only alteration made being their reduction to four or five verses. We know of no collection more adapted to public or private use. For the closet it is about the best book of devotional Psalmody which has ever come under our notice.

INTELLIGENCE,

BIBLICAL, EDUCATIONAL, LITERARY, AND MISCELLANEOUS.

The Anglo-Biblical Institute.—This modest, but really learned and useful society, contemplates the purity and correctness of the sacred texts of the Holy Scriptures as its sole aim; and the object is sought to be attained by papers read at its meetings, and *vivâ voce* discussions. Its transactions are now before us, and from them we present the following selections to our readers. Information respecting the society may be obtained of the secretaries, Dr. Joseph Turnbull or John Hamilton, Esq., F.R.A.S., at the rooms 22, Hart Street, Bloomsbury Square, London.

May 1st.—John Lee, Esq., LL.D., F.R.S., in the chair:—The ordinary transactions were commenced by Dr. Brunn, a visitor, reading, in Hebrew, and translating the 100th Psalm.

Dr. Jolowicz then read a paper on "Biblical Astronomy," in continuation of the discussion on that subject at the last meeting. He remarked with regard to a letter written by the Chief Rabbi, S. J. Rapoport to Ch. Selig Slonymski.

The term כסיל, occurring in Job ix. 9, and xxxviii. 31, was further shewn, as at last meeting, to be properly rendered by "Orion." The Syriac having sometimes given גיורא for כסיל, and also for עיש and עש, the author concluded that the idea of *strength* was included in them all; and that this agrees with the character attributed to the constellation Orion, as originally designed for star of Nimrod, who, according to the oriental mythology, was chained to heaven.

The term כימה, rendered in Job xxxviii. 31, by Pleiades, and so interpreted by Gesenius and others, Dr. Jolowicz considered to be more properly rendered by Scorpio; quoting the authority of Rabbi Samuel, in the Babylonian Talmud, who says, "The constellation Scorpio lies in the נהר דנור, the milky-way." The same phrase is found in Dan. vii. 10, נהר דינור ונו, "*a fiery stream* issued and came forth," &c. The astronomer, Rabbi Samuel, therefore, so understood the phrase; and the Hebrews seem to have had no other term for the milky-way; unless the term שחקים, Job xxxviii. 37, be so understood, which is highly probable, for the "numbering" must there relate to *stars*, not *clouds*.

A learned and animated discussion arose on the reading of this paper; and the subject was further adjourned to next meeting, when Mr. Black engaged to bring a paper on Job. xxxviii. 37, "Who can number the clouds in wisdom," &c., and Dr. Jolowicz to bring his work on "The Ascension of Isaiah," in illustration of the phrases, "*the third heavens*," and "*the seven heavens*."

June 5th.—Same chairman:—Dr. Turnbull, read, in Hebrew, and translated the second Psalm.

The Rev. A Löwy gave a critical reading of the 49th Psalm, which elicited some important remarks and suggestions on several difficult portions of the text, particularly verse 14th, on which it was proposed to read כמשרים instead of כצ שיתו, as harmonizing better with the context; and it was unanimously agreed that מות ירעם should be rendered with the LXX., θανατος ποιμανει αυτους, and not, as in the received version, "death shall feed on them."

The Rev. Mr. Whitford, Rector of Dunton, Essex, favoured the meeting with an account of the new critical edition of the Septuagint, which he has in the press, and of which he presented a specimen in type. It is intended to comprise the whole *corpus criticum* of the chief editions of the LXX. The learned editor gives considerable importance to the Complutensian. The work is in quarto, with the various readings and authorities in the form of foot-notes.

Dr. Lee concluded the transactions by reading, in Greek, and translating the eleventh chapter of Luke, verses 14—36.

July 3rd.—Dr. William Shroud in the chair:—The Rev. Mr. Löwy read, in Hebrew, and translated the thirty-eighth chapter of Isaiah from ver. 9 to 21.

The originality of the learned member's translation of some passages gave rise to an instructive discussion on the meaning of several Hebrew words presenting difficulties. The expression שמים עוף, in verse 14, was thought to require further investigation; and the translator undertook to present, at a future meeting, not only the result of his researches in this instance, but a more extended inquiry into the Hebrew words expressive of the various kinds of birds mentioned in the Bible.

A further discussion arose on the meaning of שאול, in verse 10, and on the question whether it could be properly translated by any English word. The term "hell" was considered to be the best term regarded only in itself; but the conventional ideas associated with that term are a powerful objection to its use as an equivalent meaning. "Hades" was thought unsuitable, as conveying no idea to the English mind; though more suitable, perhaps, than any other word, as an equivalent for שאול. On the whole it was concluded that it would be best to leave the word in Roman letters, "sheol;" and to explain its literal meaning by a glossary appended to any particular English version.

The Rev. Mr. Whitford read a rhythmical version of the whole aforesaid passage, made by himself, as a specimen of his translation of the Odes of Scripture, which he has some intention of publishing. He also read a portion of a paper "On the true value of the Septuagint version, and the necessity of its immediate critical revision." This great work, as was briefly noticed last month, Mr. Whitford has commenced. If he could obtain adequate support, his researches would extend to all the great libraries of Europe for critical materials, in addition to those already published or known to the learned world. But, for the present, his labours are confined to an exact reprint of the Complutensian Text. "This will be, for the first time, printed separately, uncorrected, save misprints, &c. (all carefully recorded); the marks of Origen will be restored; there will be, in the foot-notes, a synopsis of the Aldine, the Roman, and the Alexandrian editions, and of the versions of Aquila, Symmachus and Theodotion, also of the Cotton MS. and the Codex Alex., where they vary from the text as printed." The work is in the press; to be published by subscription, at One Guinea, when a sufficient number of names are obtained.

Mr. Whitford concluded by reading, in Greek, and translating the eleventh chapter of the gospel by Matthew from verse 2 to 8; and the business of the session terminated.

Researches in Babylon.—At the Asiatic Society, July 7th, a paper containing the concluding portion of Col. Rawlinson's "Memoir on the Birs-i Nimrúd," was laid on the table, and portions of it were read to the meeting. It traced the history of the City of Borsippa, as distinguished from Babylon, from the earliest times to the present day, collecting all the notices of the place which occur in the cuneiform inscriptions, whether Chaldæan, Assyrian, or Babylonian, and comparing them with later statements in the Greek and Latin writers, with various passages of the Talmud, and Sabæan Sidr, and with a copious array of early Arabic authorities. In connection with this subject, the comparative geography of all northern Babylonia was discussed in more or less detail. The hydrographical system of the country was described at some length, and the innumerable changes to which the courses of the Tigris and Euphrates and their subsidiary network of canals had been subject during a period of forty centuries, were explained and verified. Translations accompanied this paper of all the passages referring to Babylonia and Chaldea which occur in the Assyrian annals; and there were further, literal English versions of most of the native Babylonian records, such as Nebuchadnezzar's great inscription on the East India House slab; his cylinders from Senkereh, from Birs-i Nimrúd, and from Babylon; and the various legends of the time of Nabonidus. Among the many sites described and identified were the following:—1. *Hit*, answering to the 'Is of Herodotus, Αειπολις of Isidore, Ιδικαρα of Ptolemy, *Ahava* of Ezra, *Ihidakira* of the Talmud, and *Dacira* of the historians of Julian. The real name of the city was *Ahi*, or *Ihi*; and the adjunct *Da-Kira* simply meant, in Chaldee, "of bitumen," referring to the famous bitumen springs peculiar to the place.—2. *Nearda*, the seat of the famous Jewish Academy identified in the immediate vicinity of Perisabor, or Aubar.—3. *Pombeditha*, near Maiozamalcha, the modern *Khân-i-Saad*.—4. *Heliopolis*, or " city of the sun ;" *Sepharvaim* of Scripture, called in the inscriptions *Sippara*, or *Agana*, (with the latter compare *Naragam* of Pliny; Ακρ-ακανον of Abydenus; *Akra d'Agana* of the Talmud), Σιππαρα of the Greeks, and Sura of the Jews and Arabs (through the intermediate forms of *Sifra* and *Sivra*), at the modern Mosaib on the Euphrates.—5. *Cutha* of the Bible, the city of *Nergal*, known to the Arabs as *Cutha*, the city of *Nimrud* (*Nergal*, as the god of the chase, being always confounded with *Nimrud*): in the Inscriptions *Kuté* or *Tiggaba*; Διγυα of Ptolemy; *Digba* of Pliny; *Tigubis* of the Peutingerian Tables at the modern ruins of Ibrahim.—6. *Bilua* of the Inscriptions; Βιλβη of Ptolemy, at Hymar.—7. *Borsippa*, or Birs-i Nimrúd.—8. *Akkad* at Niffer.—9. *Erech*, or Orchoe at Warka.—10. *Ellasar* of Genesis; *Larsa* of the Inscriptions; and *Nars* of the Arabs at Senkereh.—11. *Ur* of the Chaldees, *Hur* of the Inscriptions, at Mugheir, &c.

Another paper was laid on the table, which contained the second chapter of Col. Rawlinson's memoir " On the Early Babylonian History." This chapter referred to the Semitic period of the history; and contained copies and translations of the legends of twenty-five different kings of the primitive Chaldean empire,—such legends having been found upon the bricks, tablets, cones of clay and cylinders which had been recently obtained in Chaldea. These names were in almost every case unknown to history; and many were exceedingly difficult to read. It seemed quite certain, however, that the line ascended at least as high as 2000 B.C. Among the earliest kings were two whose names were doubtfully given as *Urukh* and *Ilgi*, and who appeared to have been the first great and general builders in Chaldea, their legends being found in the foundations of all the most ancient ruins throughout the country; that is, at *Mugheir*, at *Senkereh*, at *Warka*, and at *Niffer*. Another king was *Kudur-mapula*, who had the title of " ravager of Syria," and thus seemed to represent the *Chedorlaomer* of Scripture. In his father's name, indeed, the last element was *khak*, which was peculiar to the names of the Scythic or Æthiopian kings of Susa, and thus seemed to indicate his Elamite descent. (*Tirkhak*, for instance, is found in the bricks of Susa, identical with *Tirkakeh* of Scripture, who belonged to the African Æthiopians, and was thus of cognate origin with the Susians; *khak* is, in all probability, the *hak* or *hyc* of the Egyptian Shepherds, and the *khakan*, or king, of the Turks at the present day.) *Ismidagon*, again, who was proved by the inscriptions of Assyria to have lived before 1900 B.C., was often found on the Mugheir bricks, as were also the names of his son and grandson, *Ibil-anu-duma* and *Gurguna*. Lower down in the series occurred *Durri-galzu*,—a trace of whose name is still preserved in the title of *Zergul* applied by the Arabs to one of the cities of his foundation. He repaired the famous temple of *Sin*, or " the moon," at Ur of the Chaldees, as appears by his bricks; and he is honourably mentioned on the cylinder of Nabonidus. The great city of Northern Babylonia, now called *Akkerkuf*, was built by this king. The bricks of *Purna-puriyas* are also found at Senkereh; and he is mentioned among the early kings on the cylinder of Nabonidus. *Khammurabi*, a still later king, has left many traces of his power. He built a palace at *Kalwada*, near Baghdad; and his bricks are found both at Mugheir and Senkereh. A hoard, also, of clay tablets, obtained by Mr. Loftus at Tel Sifr, in Southern Chaldea, are dated in the reign either of *Khammurabi*, or of his son *Samshuiluna*. A stone tablet, moreover, belonging to this king, *Khammurabi*, was one of the first Babylonian relics deposited in the British Museum. It is not easy to affiliate these kings, or to determine their chronological succession. For the convenience, however, of arrangement, Col. Rawlinson has classed in one series, and placed at the end of the list, a number of monarchs who seem to have been especial devotees of the " Moon God,"—their titles containing the name of " *Sin*" as one of their component elements. Thus occurred in succession, *Sin-shada*, the builder of the great palace at Warka, opened by Mr. Loftus; *Zur-sin*, the founder of the city of *Abu Shahrein*,—an account of which, by Mr. Taylor, is printed in the forthcoming number of the Asiatic Society's Journal; *Rim-sin*, of whom a fine stone tablet was lately dis-.

interred from the ruins of Mugheir; and *Naram-sin*, who is also mentioned, on the cylinders of Nebonidus, as the repairer of a temple in ancient times, and whose name again appears on an alabaster vase obtained by the French Commissioner at Babylon. The number of inscriptions relating to these primitive Chaldean kings which were translated and analyzed in the paper laid before the Meeting amounted to thirty-five; and it was shewn that a very solid foundation had been thus laid for building up our historical knowledge of Western Asia into what we have hitherto been accustomed to call the patriarchal ages. The period over which, indeed, Col. Rawlinson's paper professed to extend was from B.C. 2234 to 1273, the latter being the supposed date of the commencement of the Assyrian empire.

Publication of Assyrian Inscriptions.—Surprise has been often expressed that, whilst ample funds have been provided, both by Parliamentary grants and by private subscription, for carrying on excavations in Assyria and Babylonia, so little should have been done towards utilizing the results. On this head, however, there will soon be no longer room for reproach; for the Trustees of the British Museum, as we are informed, convinced of the great importance of the matter, have now decided on applying to the Treasury for a special grant, in order to enable them to publish all the most valuable cuneiform inscriptions which have been discovered during the course of the recent excavations. The documents which it is thus proposed to render available for general examination are as follows :—

1. A series of legends (thirty-five in number), from bricks, stone tablets, cones of clay, &c., belonging to the primitive Chaldæan Empire, and dating B.C. 2000—1500.

2. Brick legends of the early Assyrian kings, from B.C. 1273 to about 1100.

3. Annals of Tiglath Pileser the First, about B.C. 1120, completed from three cylinders found at Kileh Shirgat.

4. Annals of Sardanapalus, about B.C. 850, from four independent texts at Nimrúd.

5. Annals of Shamas-Phul (father of the Biblical Pul), from the new Nimrúd Obelisk, about B.C. 800.

6. Short legend of Pul and Semiramis, from a statue of the god Nebo, about B.C. 760.

7. Annals of Sargon, from the new Khorsabad cylinders, about B.C. 705.

8. Annals of Sennacherib, from the famous cylinder of Col. Tayler's, recently acquired by the Museum,—B.C. 694.

9. Selections from the annals of *Asshur-bani-pal*, the son of Esar-Haddon, from fragments of cylinders in the Museum,—B.C. 660.

10. A set of new types of brick legends, belonging to the later Assyrian kings,—Pul, Sargon, Sennacherib, and Esar-Haddon.

11. Cylinders of Nebuchadnezzar, from Birs-i Nimrúd, Senkereh, and Babylon, and cylinders of Nabonidus, from Mugheir; and

12. A series of brick legends, of Nebuchadnezzar, Nereglissor, and Nabonidus, from Babylon, Warka, Senkereh, and Mugheir.

Under these twelve heads a series of historical documents will be brought together, ranging over a period of about 1500 years, from the Patriarchal ages to the taking of Babylon by Cyrus. The inscriptions will be lithographed; and, wherever the originals can be consulted, will be exhibited in fac-simile : the whole for[m]ing a quarto volume of about 200 pages.

Anoth[er] [v]olume, of the same dimensions, will be devoted to miscellaneous matter, colle[cted] for the most part, from the clay tablets, which once formed the library of t[he ki]ngs of Nineveh, and which are now deposited in the British Museum.

The [inscr]iptions in this volume will be arranged under the following heads:—

1. S[yll]aries and vocabularies, together with all the tables, which are very numer[ous] explanatory of the system of cuneiform writing and of the grammatic[al] [s]tructure of the Assyrian language.

[2.] [S]pecimens of mathematical tables, astronomical formulæ, calendars and regi[ste]rs of observations.

[3.] A selection from the mythological tablets, exhibiting the names and attributes of the gods and goddesses worshipped by the Assyrians, and explaining the general system of the Pantheon.

4. A series of passages referring to the wild sports of the Assyrians, and illustrating the hunting scenes sculptured on the walls of the Nineveh palaces.

5. Architectural descriptions of great importance for the due understanding of the ruins, as recently uncovered; and

· 6. A miscellaneous series comprising dynastic lists, catalogues of the seas, rivers, mountains, and countries known to the Assyrians, classifications of birds and beasts, &c., &c.

Col. Rawlinson, assisted by Mr. Norris, of the Royal Asiatic Society, will be appointed, we understand, to edit this collection of inscriptions; and it is calculated that two years will suffice for the completion of the undertaking.

We are further informed that the Trustees, in this publication of the inscriptions, have declined to sanction interlineary readings in the Roman character, with literal Latin translations. They have thought it better to limit their official guarantee to the faithful reproduction of the cuneiform texts,—throwing on the editors in their unofficial capacity the responsibility of interpretation; nor are we much inclined to quarrel with their decision in this respect, for, on the one hand, as the Trustees of the British Museum do not constitute a critical tribunal like the Council of the French Institute, it would be unwise to commit themselves to a verdict on so complicated a question as the reading of the cuneiform character; and on the other hand, as the Royal Asiatic Society, relieved of the cuneiform lithography, which is the only expensive part of the publication, will be able to issue in its journal, at a remunerative price, Col. Rawlinson's readings and translations simultaneously with the issue of the cuneiform texts by the Museum, the public will not be losers from the division of labour and expense. —*Athenæum.*

At the Society of Antiquaries, June 21st, Mr. Henry Stevens, the agent of the Smithsonian Institution, exhibited an octavo Bible of the authorized version, called *The Wicked Bible*, on account of the very great number of gross typographical errors, among which is the remarkable one of the omission of the negative "*not*" in the seventh commandment. When Charles the First was made aware of the fact by Bishop Laud, the king's printers, Robert Barker and Martin Lucas, were fined by the Star Chamber three hundred pounds. Though this book has been sought for the last hundred years, no copy until now has been discovered, and this is probably unique.

A trophy.—General Pelissier lately presented to the library of Algiers a volume of the "History of the Life of Christ," which was taken in the chapel of the cemetery of Sebastopol. It is in the Slavonian language, and in the folio form, is bound in the ancient style and gilt, and has two clasps in copper. On the top cover, in a gilt wreath, are the three personages of the Trinity. On one of the blank leaves is written in Russian, "This book belongs to the Church of the Saints in the Cemetery;" and lower down, "Month of December—the priest Altin Bringin was here the 27th December, 1827." The whole life is divided into twelve parts, one for each month; and the volume in question comprises the part for the month of December. The book was printed at Moscow, and the paper is of a grayish colour. The titles of the chapters and the first letters of each paragraph are in red ink, and this gives it the appearance of the earlier productions of the typographic art. The bottoms of the pages are worn from constant use, and some of the pages are so dirty as to warrant the belief that the Russian clergy are not rigorously required to officiate with clean hands; while other pages are stained with drops of yellow wax which evidently fell from the candles which it is the custom to burn in honour of the saints. General Pelissier, in transmitting the book to the library of Algiers, wrote the following lines, and they have been pasted in one of the fly leaves :—" Head quarters before Sebastopol, 9th of June, 1855. 'History of the Life of Christ.' Taken in the chapel of the cemetery of Sebastopol, where victory carried us. The sacred objects and several other things were conveyed to the monastery of St. George, but this book was reserved by him who had the discretionary power, in order that it might be presented to the library of Algiers. It is in the Slavonian language and printed in the Slavonian characters.—PELISSIER."

Ancient Libraries.—Your learned correspondent may probably look for the formation of public libraries earlier than the deposit of the Theograph copy of the law in the ark. It is certain that the Tables engraved by the finger of God (Exod. xxxi. 18; xxxii. 16), were not the first example of writing, as has been hastily concluded; since the sin and discomfiture of Amalek were commanded to be " written in a book," before Israel had yet approached Sinai (Exod. xvii. 14); and Job, whose era there seems no reason to doubt was prior to that of Moses, speaks familiarly of books: " O that mine adversary had written a book !" (Job xxxi. 35.)

But there is an allusion which seems to imply that the Canaanitish nations —those illustrious rivals of the ancient Egyptians in arts and arms—not only used books, but collected them in public libraries, long before the Hebrew conquest. For Caleb, after expelling the Anakim from Arba (=Hebron, "went up thence to the inhabitants of Debir, and the name of Debir *before* was *Kirjath-sepher* " (Josh. xv. 15; Judg. i. 11).

Now Kirjath-sepher was evidently the ancient Canaanitish name, but this signifies " the city of books." Debir signifies " an oracle ;" and whether this latter appellation was bestowed on the city on its conquest by the Hebrews, or had been used by the Canaanites themselves in displacement of the more ancient title, there appears in the double nomenclature sufficient warrant to conclude that this city was a renowned seat of learning, a college or university. Of what nature the literature and science of those days was, we can scarcely conjecture; and the Egyptian papyri have as yet thrown little light on the inquiry; but they may not have been theological, or rather idolatrous, and, if not, I suppose the Israelites would be under no obligation to destroy the books which they found. In that case, the title " Debir" might continue to be appropriate after the inheritance.—*Notes and Queries.*

The Zend Language.—At the Asiatic Society, June 16, the secretary read some notes upon the Zend language, by John Romer, Esq., in addition to those already published. Mr. Romer maintained that the Zend and Pehlevi languages of the Parsi books were mere inventions, and were never spoken languages. The present notes were in answer to some objections brought against his former notices, and the merits of his arguments cannot be fairly appreciated without going deeper into the question than space will allow. The grounds upon which he mainly rests these last objections, are the great similarity of Zend to Sanskrit, and, more especially, to the Gujarati idioms and corruptions of Sanskrit, a resemblance which it could not have had if it were an ancient language brought to India, as alleged by the Parsis. Moreover, when it is stated that the language of the Zend Avesta contains within it some forms resembling the archaisms of the Veda, he could not believe that, of two languages of equal antiquity, one should have produced the Rig Veda, and a highly polished literature, while, in the other, there were only writings of the most insignificant value when they are not absolute nonsense.

Eclipses and Chronology.—At the same place and time, J. W. Bosanquet, Esq., read a paper " On the Subject of certain Corrections required in the Canon of Ptolemy," in order to bring it into harmony with the eclipse at Jerusalem in 689 B.C., and the eclipse of Thales in 585 B.C. He observed that the antiquity of the canon is much exaggerated, when it is supposed that it was compiled in the time of Berosus; and supported his opinion by shewing that Demetrius, who was nearly contemporary with Berosus, placed the reign of Nebuchadnezzar twenty-six years lower than the canon; that Josephus, with Berosus in his hands, did not adopt its dates; and that Clemens Alexandrinus in the second century, Africanus in the third, and Eusebius in the fourth, had no such authentic list of reigns with dates before them to refer to. Mr. Bosanquet stated that the validity of the canon rested upon a series of lunar eclipses, observed at

Babylon, the particulars of the most important of which he quoted from Ptolemy's Almagest; and considered that the following dates in the canon might be taken as thereby established—viz., first of Nabonassar, B.C. 247; first of Mardocempadus, B.C. 721; fifth of Nabopalassar, B.C. 621; seventh of Cambyses, B.C. 523. As regarded the five last Babylonian kings, however named by Berosus—viz., Nabocolassar or Nebuchadnezzar, Ilverdam or Evilmerodach, Nereglissar or Nergalsharezar, Laborosoarchod, and Nabonidus, no eclipse, or other astronomical observation, had been recorded by Ptolemy to fix the date of either of their reigns. On the contrary, in order to place them in harmony with the two solar eclipses of B.C. 689 and B.C. 585, it was necessary, he stated, that the years of the accession of Nebuchadnezzar to the throne of Babylon, should be placed below the latter date, at least twenty years lower than in the canon, Nineveh having fallen after the eclipse of Thales, and Nebuchadnezzar having come to the throne after the fall of Nineveh. Mr. Bosanquet then observed that the only trustworthy authors to be consulted on the question were Herodotus and Berosus, to the exclusion of ecclesiastical writers, who are of a much later date; and pointed out that Berosus, when carefully studied in the fragments of his work preserved by Polyhistor, Josephus, and Abydenus, leads us, with great exactness, to the year B.C. 578, as that of the first of Nebuchadnezzar, that is to say, seven years after the eclipse. For Berosus tells us that Nabopalassar reigned twenty years *in Nineveh;* and Polyhistor, who copied from Berosus, says that he was the king called Sardanapalus. From another extract it might be collected that he became either vassal or ally of Saracus, who succeeded him at Nineveh; and from an extract in Josephus, given in the words of Berosus, it appeared that he died at Babylon, after having reigned twenty-nine years, or forty-nine years in all. An eclipse recorded at Babylon during his reign as lord paramount at Nineveh, marks his fifth year as B.C. 621. His forty-ninth, therefore, was B.C. 578. Now this is the very year which Demetrius, who must have seen the work of Berosus, makes the first year of Nebuchadnezzar, his son and successor. Exactly the same result, he observed, was deducible from Herodotus, who states that there were twenty-eight years of Scythian domination over Asia after the subversion of the last Assyrian king (Sardanapalus), at the end of which twenty-eight years Nineveh was finally taken by the Medes and Babylonians. Counting, therefore, twenty-eight years from the last of Nabopalassar in Nineveh, B.C. 606, brings us to the year B.C. 579 for the fall of that city, which immediately preceded the accession of Nebuchadnezzar. By lowering thus the reign of Nebuchadnezzar to B.C. 578, it appeared that the last year of Nabonidus, the last Babylonian king, would fall about the year B.C. 510, instead of 539, where it is placed in the canon; and Mr. Bosanquet pointed out that this was the date of the fall of Babylon, as stated by some, in the time of Clemens Alexandrinus, and as emphatically contended for by Orosius, in the fifth century. He then handled the three copies of the Babylonian canon, called the ecclesiastical, the astronomical. and the canon according to Theon, shewing how the same difficulty existed at the time of their compilation as now—viz., how to reconcile the date of the capture of Babylon by Cyrus, in B.C. 510, with the reign of Cambyses, his successor, beginning in B.C. 529. The ecclesiastical canon, he observes, solves the problem by placing the first year of Cambyses in B.C. 507, in defiance of the eclipse of B.C. 523, in his seventh year. The astronomical canon solves it by throwing up the reign of Nebuchadnezzar forty nine years above the date deduced by Berosus, thus setting at nought the eclipse of B.C. 621, in the fifth of Nabopalassar. All three copies adopt the year B.C. 538 as that of the first year of Cyrus; and Mr. Bosanquet considers this to be the traditional and true date of the victory of Cyrus over Astyages, and that it was so viewed by the compilers of the canon appears from two of the copies expressly stating that Nabonidus, the last king of Babylon, was Astyages himself—a tradition which may be traced back as early as the writing of the apocryphal book called Bel and the Dragon. He considers that the third copy was framed on the same false assumption; and that thus having raised the reign of Nabonidus twenty-eight years in the scale of time, the same process was applied to his four predecessors, by ignoring the twenty-nine years of Nabopalassar during which he reigned at Babylon. Mr. Bosanquet then briefly alluded to an hypothesis of his own, to be treated more fully at some future time—viz., that Cambyses, son of Cyrus and Cassandane, was the father, not the son, of Cyrus the Great, by which all fixed dates might be preserved, and the conflicting accounts of Cyrus contained in Herodotus, Xenophon, Ctesias, and the Book of Daniel, might be reconciled; and concluded by shewing, from three different historical sources, that the interval between the fourteenth year of Hezekiah, or the third year of Sennacherib, and the first year of Nebuchadnezzar, was 110 years. So that if the year B.C. 689 was the fourteenth of Hezekiah, the year B.C. 578 must have been the first of Nebuchadnezzar, and *vice versâ*; and that as both these dates are fixed with reference to the unerring data of two solar eclipses, producing thereby a double confirmation of their correctness, it becomes necessary to lower the five last Babylonian kings in the canon in conformity with these dates, as proposed.

Cuneiform writing.—At the Syro-Egyptian, June 12th, a paper was read "On the Origin of the Cuneiform Character," by L. J. Abington, Esq. The peculiar form of the literal character, properly called wedge-shaped, the author argued, had its origin in a locality to which such a manner of writing was suited rather than any other. It was first used in an alluvial region, and never passed beyond the limits of that empire, the throne of which was first fixed in the plains of Shinar, where men had "bricks for stone, and slime for mortar." The form of the letters indicates the material upon which they were written, and would never have been adopted for inscriptions upon any other substance than clay. The earliest writings upon stone are linear, either straight or curved scratches, without any ornamental expansion of the extremities, or such swellings of the lines as give elegance to the characters formed originally by the pen or the brush. Such plain-lined petrographic writing, if inverted, would be difficult to read for want of a well-marked difference between the top and the bottom of the words; therefore, when men began to write upon loose tablets of clay, which might be taken up in any direction by the reader, it became necessary to use a character which at the first glance would shew him how it should be placed for reading. It would be difficult to devise a form of letter better suited for clay writing than the cuneiform. Mr. Layard has given us an idea of the pen, or rather stamp, which was used, and nothing could be better adapted to the purpose; it does not require the scratching or cutting of the tablet, but produces the characters by impressing them. The broad end of the type or stamp was first applied, and the triangular point pressed in to produce the head of the letter, then the edge being turned down would produce the tapering body of it. The author said he had found a very little practice, with a well-made tool, sufficient to copy the inscriptions in Botta's work with accuracy and facility. The wedge-shape character is essentially ceramographic, and would never have been chosen for petrographic work; it had its birth on the plains of Shinar, but when in the embellishment of public buildings, sculptured slabs of gypsum required descriptive inscription, the established character was of necessity engraven on the stones, and in a later period was cut in the limestone rocks of Behistun, &c. The hammer-headed character is also clay-born, but each letter was produced by two separate stamps—one to make the body-line, and the other to impress the head, or crossbar. It could not be written with the facility of the wedge, and therefore seems to have been but little used.

The Exodus.—At the same time and place, Dr. Benisch read a paper in which he critically examined the Hebrew texts referring to the Exodus, and from the passages analyzed arrived at the following conclusions:—1st. The oppression of the Israelites commenced under an invader who came from a foreign country, in all likelihood from or through Palestine. 2nd. The Exodus took place in the reign of his grandson. 3rd. The Pharaoh of the Exodus had a son, who was fellow-king. 4th. That son being the first-born, perished at the Exodus. 5th. The conquest, or subsequent submission of Egypt, was gradual, and was at first attended with wars. 6th. The conquerors ultimately coalesced with the native population.

Coptic Papyrus.—At the Royal Society of Literature, June 27th, Mr. Vaux read a paper by C. W. Goodwin, Esq., "On a Coptic Papyrus in the British Museum." Mr. Goodwin proved, by a careful examination of the fragments still remaining of this document, that it must have been a grant of land to some monastery, the name of which is now lost, and that it was written in all probability at Thebes, between the eighth and ninth centuries A.D. It is well known that all Coptic MSS. are extremely scarce; hence this one—though much injured by time, and imperfect both at the beginning and the end—has considerable interest and value. Appended are the names of several witnesses to the deed.—The Rev. Mr. Porter, of Damascus, subsequently gave to the Society a very interesting oral account of the present state of the neighbourhood of that city, and exhibited a map, beautifully executed by himself, of the district now called the *Hawrán* (anciently Auranitis.) Mr. Porter expressed it as his opinion that there were numerous sites around Damascus which would well repay a careful excavation.

Egyptian Discoveries.—We read in the American papers, that Mr. John B. Greene has succeeded in discovering the celebrated Egyptian calendar of which Champollion could only copy the first lines. A cast of this monument was taken on the spot by means of a particular kind of composition, photography not reproducing it properly. Different colossal figures, the upper parts of which were only visible, have been now cleared, and brought to light; one of them, in excellent preservation, shews the features of Ramses the Third, and is about nineteen mètres high. Mr. Greene, in clearing round this colossus, was able to discover and take drawings of the inscriptions of the pylone, or grand portal, erected between the two courts; and he has also proved the existence of a pavement in granite, which probably covered the whole court, and above which rose a passage, which appears to have led into a second court. The excavations of Mr. Greene, add the newspapers, which have just completely made known one of the most important edifices of Pharaonic Egypt, will, by the numerous inscriptions which they furnish, throw fresh light on different points of Egyptian philology.

Discovery of Saxon Coins.—A party of drainers have been employed during the past week in draining some fields in the neighbourhood of Scotby. While engaged in their laborious occupation in a meadow belonging to Mr. Sutton, one of the men turned up a number of coins and some bars of metal, the real value of which he had no conception of. The soil in which they were found was almost like that of peat moss in a saturated state, and from the low situation the water seems to have accumulated and remained there for centuries. The articles discovered soon passed from the hands of the finders to those of persons who better appreciated their worth, not from their intrinsic value, but from their rarity and the interest attached to them from the age which originated them. All the coins were of Saxon origin, reaching almost as far back as the time of Alfred the Great. They are of silver, and in an excellent state of preservation, Some bear the name of "Edward the Elder," others that of "Athelstan," or, as the impression has it, "Adelstan," his son, and first king of Britain, There is some dispute as to the justice of this title among historians, but upon these coins, which were discovered on Monday last, there is proof positive that Athelstan himself considered he had a right to the honour, and consequently styled himself King of Britain. Alfred the Great, the father of Edward the Elder, died on the 26th of October, A.D. 901, in the fifty-third year of his age, and the thirtieth of his reign. He was succeeded by his son Edward the Elder, so that it seems the coins in question are nearly 1000 years old. In appearance they look as if they had just emerged from the mint, except that the metal is blackened by age. The impressions are as perfect as on the day they were struck. Athelstan was the natural son of Edward. In addition to the coins were found, in the same field, in close proximity, several bars of pure silver, which seem to indicate that they were there for the purpose of coinage. It is known that favoured subjects in early times received licenses to coin money, under heavy penalties in case of abuse of the privilege. It is not improbable that the coins and silver discovered at Scotby may have been last in the hands of one of these persons. It appears almost certain, from the distinctness of the marks on the die, that the money had never been in circulation. Besides the coins and silver, an iron instrument of the shape of a small billhook, and answering to the description of the ancient Saxon weapon, the "bill," was thrown out of the drain, having been dug up from a depth of upwards of six feet. It is in an excellent state of preservation, and the rude workmanship of the age and the roughness, though genuineness of the metal, are no bad proofs of its antiquity.—*Carlisle Patriot.*

Discovery of Greek MSS.—The following letter, from that earnest and intelligent scholar, A. C. Harris, Esq., of Alexandria, is so full of interest that I have no hesitation in communicating it to you, with a few remarks explanatory of the very valuable discoveries to which reference is more especially made :—

"Alexandria, June 21.

"My dear Friend,—On my return from Upper Egypt, I received your very acceptable note, dated 17th of February last, and afterwards I had the pleasure of a visit from the Rev. Mr. Mills, who brought me your two other notes of 30th of March and 16th of April. This gentleman I saw but once, for when I went to look for him to offer him some civilities, I found he had gone to Cairo. Our joint visit to Hartwell often comes into my head as a most agreeable recollection. . . . I wrote a short time ago to Dr. Lee, thanking him for his very kind present of a book. . . . I sent the Doctor some novelties in the way of hieroglyphical cyphers which I thought interesting, and proved by them that the characters represent the city of Ashmouneyn. Mr. Babington has been so good as to send me a copy of the Ὑπερίδου Λογοι (Orations of Hyperides) of Mr. Arden, and I have been in correspondence with him. I found this year at Gornou a number of other minute fragments, all in the very same handwriting as that of the Orations, to which I supposed them to belong; but upon subjecting them to a little scrutiny I find that they belong to another roll, the conclusion of which I secured, and which contained Book 2 of the Iliad, so that I have the same book written at Thebes, and in Middle Egypt, perhaps in very different ages. There is, however, very little of the former—it may be that the Arabs will offer me some more next season. I picked up a very handsome little roll, written in Hieratic, and bearing a king's name I cannot read. . . . I should be quite delighted to have the two small pamphlets of Mr. Birch, if he would give them to me. It is a charity to furnish a little food for the mind of one so remote as I am, and who knows nothing of what passes in the literary world unless he finds it in the *Athenæum.* George Gliddon has sent me a copy of his work, 'Types of Mankind.' I have not had it long enough to read it through. I am delighted to hear that Mr. Sharpe continues at his usual labours,—they will be more useful to the student than the long dissertations I see upon Moses, and the passage of the Israelites, which is but one fact in a great history—certainly a very interesting one,—but Egyptian matters may be studied for themselves alone. We want more work upon the language, and a more diligent collection of materials. . . . I wish Mr. Sharpe would look up all the astronomical matter to be found, for the *savans* on the continent seem to be rushing into calculations upon very uncertain data. We found an American gentleman, Mr. Greene, of Paris, occupied at Medinet Haboo in uncovering and copying the half of the calendar that was untouched by Champollion; I do not know if it possesses any value. He undertook to teach my daughter to photograph, and she has made some progress. Next voyage, which we shall commence next November, will be enlivened by this occupation. The piece of the cubit is in my possession; the black stone that belonged to Mr. Traill is in my house. He gave it to me long ago, upon my paying the expenses he had incurred upon it. I had the pleasure to see Col. Rawlinson in his passage through Alexandria. He read off to me some arrow-headed inscriptions with great facility, and told me he was carrying home a great quantity of new and important objects. I am sorry to say that Egypt has been invaded by the cholera from Constantinople. It passed at once by the railroad to Boulac, without stopping here, and at Cairo has carried off up to 350 per day. I regret that Mr. Todd's brother, a very excellent person, and very good friend of ours, was amongst its victims. He had but recently settled at Cairo from Australia. I trust, in the end, the cholera will not return upon us here. We are not very easy about it. The Hadjees (pilgrims) carry this scourge about with them. . . . All sorts of projects are on foot for making ship-canals, railroads, &c.,—in which the projectors make no account of the person and interests of the poor Fellah (cultivator), who is to do all this work for nothing. . . .

"Yours, &c.,   A. C. HARRIS."

The allusion in the foregoing letter to the discovery of "fragments in the very same handwriting as that of the Orations" must, of necessity, be unintelligible to those who are not already acquainted with the curious matter to which it refers, and I therefore, beg to offer a few words of explanation.

In the winter of 1847, Mr. Harris was sitting in his boat, under the shade of the well-known sycamore, on the western bank of the Nile, at Thebes, ready to start for Nubia, when an Arab brought him a fragment of a papyrus roll, which he ventured to open sufficiently to ascertain that it was written in the Greek language, and which he bought before proceeding further on his journey. Upon his return to Alexandria, where circumstances were more favourable to the difficult operation of unrolling a fragile papyrus, he discovered that he possessed a fragment of the Oration of Hyperides against Demosthenes, in the matter of Harpalus, and also a very small fragment of another oration, the whole written in extremely legible characters, and of a form or fashion which those learned in the Greek MSS. consider to be of the time of the Ptolemies. With these interesting fragments of orations of an orator so celebrated as Hyperides, of whose works nothing is extant but a few quotations in other Greek writers, he embarked for England. Upon his arrival here, he submitted the precious relics to the inspection of the Council and Members of the Royal Society of Literature, who were unanimous in their judgment as to the importance and genuineness of the MS.; and Mr. Harris immediately set to work, and with his own hand made a lithographic fac-simile of each piece. Of this performance a few copies were printed and distributed among the *savans* of Europe,—and Mr. Harris returned to Alexandria, whence he has made more than one journey to Thebes in the hope of discovering some other portion of the volume, of which he already had a part. In the same year (1847), another English gentleman, Mr. Joseph Arden, of London, bought at Thebes a papyrus, which he likewise brought to England. Induced by the success of Mr. Harris, Mr. Arden submitted his roll to the skilful and experienced hands of Mr. Hogarth; and upon the completion of the operation of unrolling, the MS. was discovered to be the terminating portion of the very same volume of which Mr. Harris had bought a fragment of the former part in the very same year, and probably of the very same Arabs. No doubt now existed that the volume when entire consisted of a collection of, or a selection from, the orations of the celebrated Athenian orator Hyperides; and Mr. Arden, with a liberality and energy that cannot be too highly commended, forthwith gave to the world a beautiful fac-simile of his portion of the treasure, edited by the Rev. Churchill Babington; and this is the book to which Mr. Harris alludes in another part of his letter.

The portion of the volume which has fallen into the possession of Mr. Arden contains "fifteen continuous columns of the 'Oration for Lycophron,' to which work three of Mr. Harris's fragments appertained; and likewise the 'Oration for Euxenippus,' which is quite complete and in beautiful preservation." Whether, as Mr. Babington observes in his preface to the work, "any more scraps of the 'Oration for Lycophron' or of the 'Oration against Demosthenes' remain to be discovered, either in Thebes or elsewhere, may be doubtful, but is certainly worth the inquiry of learned travellers." The condition, however, of the fragments obtained by Mr. Harris, but too significantly indicate the hopelessness of success. The scroll has evidently been more frequently rolled and unrolled in that particular part—namely, the speech of Hyperides in a matter of such peculiar interest as that involving the honour of the most celebrated orator of antiquity—it had been more read and had been more thumbed by ancient fingers than any other speech in the whole volume; and hence the terrible gap between Mr. Harris's and Mr. Arden's portions. Those who are acquainted with the brittle, friable nature of a roll of papyrus in the dry climate of Thebes, after being buried for two thousand years or more, and then coming first into the hands of a ruthless Arab, who, perhaps, had rudely snatched it out of the sarcophagus of the mummied scribe, will well understand how dilapidations occur. It frequently happens that a single roll, or possibly an entire box, of such fragile treasures is found in the tomb of some ancient philologist or man of learning, and that the possession is immediately disputed by the company of Arabs who may have embarked on the venture. To settle the dispute, when there is not a scroll for each member of the company, an equitable division is made by dividing a papyrus and distributing the portions. Thus, in this volume of Hyperides, I should conceive that it had fallen into two pieces at the place where it had most usually been opened, and where, alas! it would have been most desirable to have kept it whole; and that the smaller fragments have been lost amid the dust and rubbish of the excavation, while the two extremities have been made distinct properties, which have been sold, as we have seen, to separate collectors. So, at all events, such matters are managed at Thebes.

Mr. Harris mentions fragments of the *Iliad* which he had purchased of some of the Arab disturbers of the dead in the sacred cemeteries of Middle Egypt, most probably Saccara. I should be disposed to differ from the inference that these copies were written in Middle Egypt, or that the copies found at Thebes were written in Upper Egypt; as I cannot but think it probable that all Greek manuscripts found in Egypt, in whatsoever part, were written or copied at the great emporium of literature, the Library of Alexandria, and thence carried into remoter districts by the learned, and ultimately, as a valuable treasure, buried with them.   I remain, &c.,

JOSEPH BONOMI.

" The black stone " is not that of the Caba that has become black by the sins of Moslemeen, but a black granite plinth of a statue with an inscription on it bearing the names of the king and queen of that race of sun-worshippers whose monuments occur in various districts of Egypt.—Mr. Traill, a horticulturist of great eminence, who had been in the employment of Ibrahim Pasha more than twenty years, and had converted the southern extremity of the island of Rhoda, an island in the Nile opposite Cairo Vecchio (Fostat), into a beautiful garden.— Boulak, the port of Cairo, from which city it is distant about half an hour's ride. —*Athenœum*.   .   J. B.

A pension of £50 a year from the Civil List has been granted to Dr. Dick, the author of some excellent works on Christian Philosophy. We only regret that a larger sum was not at disposal for recognition of the literary services of so estimable a man and useful writer.

The Life of Dr. Kitto, by Mr. Ryland, of Northampton, is nearly ready. It promises to be a work of no ordinary interest. Subscribers' names are received by Messrs. Oliphant and Son, Edinburgh.

A new edition of the *Cyclopœdia of Biblical Literature*, edited by Dr. Kitto, is preparing for publication under the editorship of the Rev. Henry Burgess, LL.D., &c.; Editor of the *Journal of Sacred Literature*.

William Stroud, Esq., M.D., author of a *Greek Harmony of the Four Gospels*, is preparing for publication a new translation of the Gospels, with notes.

Messrs. Clark, of Edinburgh, are preparing for publication, in a large volume, royal 8vo, Theological Essays, reprinted from *The Princeton Review*. Second Series.

NEW WORKS PUBLISHED DURING THE LAST QUARTER.

FOREIGN.

Arnoldi.—Commentar zum Evangelium des heiligen Matthäus. 8vo.

Arvèlk ("The East"), a journal published twice a month in the Armenian Language. Paris, 8vo.

Blaubach.—Das Hohe Lied. Uebersetzt and erläutert. 16mo.

Bohlen (Dr. P. von).—Die Genesis historisch kritisch erläutert. Königsberg, 8vo.

Breslau (M. H.)—A Compendious Hebrew Grammar. London, John Weale. 12mo.

Bunsen.—Die Zeichen der Zeit. Briefe an Freunde über die Gewissensfreiheit und die Rechte der Christlichen Gemeinde. Pt. I.

Chassay (F. E., Professor of Scripture in the Sorbonne).—Jésus, lumière du Monde. Histoire de la Prédication de Notre Seigneur. Paris, 8vo.

Chateaubriand (le Vicomte de).—Le Genie du Christianisme. 16mo. Paris, Hachette. Bib. des Chemins de Fer.

Delitzsch (Dr. F.)—System der Biblischen Psychologie. 8vo.

Dillmann (Augustus).—Veteris Testamenti Ethiopici: Tomus primus, sine Octoteuchus Ethiopicus. Lipsiæ, 4to., pp. 346.

Friedrich (E. F.)—Quæ Cantici canticorum Salomoni esset Poetica forma. Königsberg, 4to.

Gesenius's Hebrew Grammar, by Roediger. A new edition, with Chrestomathy and Exercises. London, Trübner. 8vo.

———— Hebrew Lexicon, by Dr. Robinson. A new and complete edition. London, Trübner. 8vo.

Gieseler (Dr. J. C. L.)—Kirchengeschichte der neuesten Zeit. Bonn and London, Marcus.

Hahn (Auct. A.)—Commentatio de Superstitionis natura ex sententia Patrum Ecclesiæ priscæ. 4to.

Heppe.—Bekenntnissschriften, die, der altprotest-antischen Kirche Deutschlands. 8vo.

Kahler (C. H.)—Auslegung der Epistel Pauli an die Philipper, in 25 Predigten. 8vo.

Lengercke (Dr. C. von).—Volks-und Religions-Geschichte Israëls. Bd. bis zum Tode Josuas. Königsberg, 8vo.

Low.—Praktische Einleitung in die heilige Schrift und Geschichte der Schriftauslegung. Vol. I., 8vo.

Mone (J. F.)—Hymni Latini medii ævi; e codd. MSS. edidit et adnotationibus illustravit. Tomus Tertius. Hymni ad Sanctos. Freyberg, 1855. 8vo., pp. 584.

Mooren (von J.)—Nachrichten über Thomas à Kempis nebst einem Anhang von meistens noch ungedruckten Urkunden. 8vo.

Nadal (l'Abbé). Histoire Hagiologique, ou Vies des saints et des bienheureux du diocèse de Valence, accompagnés de notes historiques, géologiques et critiques sur les églises, monastères et antres établissements religieux de ce diocèse. 8vo.

Polyglotten Bibel zum praktischen Handgebrauch. Bearbeitet von R. Stier und K. G. W. Theile. Bielefeld, 8vo. (Last part of the work.)

Saalschütz (Dr. Jos. L.)—Archäologie der Hebräer. Part I. Königsberg, 8vo.

Saint-Martin (Menard).—Conferences Apologétiques sur Jesu-Christ, prechés à Nîmes en 1854. 12mo. Toulouse, Societé des Œuvres Religieuse.

Samuel ben Meïr, Commentar zu Kohelet und dem Hohen Liede Herausgegeben von A. Zellinek. 8vo.

Sardinoux (A.)—Le Christ et l'Eglese: Recueil d'études theologiques et practiques.

Seyffarth.—Berichtigungen der Römischen, Griechischen, Persischen, Ägyptischen, Hebräischen Geschichte und Zeitrechnung, Mythologie und Religionsgeschichte auf Grund neuer historischer und astronomischer Hülfsmittel. 8vo.

Sigwart (Ch.)—Ulrich Zwingli. Der Charakter seiner Theologie mit besonderer Rücksicht auf Picus von Mirandula. 8vo.

Soldan (Dr. W. G.)—Geschichte des Protestantismus in Franckreich. Leipsig, 8vo.

Stier (Dr. Rudolf).—Die Reden des Herrn Jesu. (Now complete in seven volumes.) Leipzig, 8vo.

Vesson (Auguste).—Calvin consideré comme Exégète. Montaubon, 8vo.

Warnkönig (L. A.)—Die staatsrechtliche Stellung der Katholischen Kirche in den Katholischen Ländern des Deutschen Reichs besonders in 18 Jahrhundert. 8vo.

Williams (Monier, M.A.)—Sakoontalá; or, The Lost Ring. A free translation from the Sanskrit, in prose and verse, of Kalidása's drama. Hertford, Austin. Fcp. 8vo., pp. 300.

ENGLISH.

Alford (Rev. H.)—Divine Love in Creation and Redemption: a Course of Sermons. 18mo., pp. 320.

Babington (Rev. Churchill).—The Benefit of Christ's Death; probably written by Aonio Palesrio, reprinted in fac-simile from the Italian edition of 1543, with a translation and introduction, &c., &c. Small 4to.

Baines (Rev. John).—Life of William Laud, Archbishop of Canterbury. 18mo., pp. 282.

Barrett (Rev. W. G.)—Geological Facts; or, The Crust of the Earth; What it is, and what are its uses. 12mo., pp. 302.

Bartlett (J. S.)—A brief History of the Christian Church. 18mo., pp. 186.

Bohlen (Dr. P. von).—Introduction to the Book of Genesis, with a Commentary on the Opening Portion. From the German. Edited by James Heywood, M.P., F.R.S. 2 vols. 8vo., pp. 668.

Burton (Lieutenant R. F.)—Personal Narrative of a Pilgrimage to El-Medinah and Mecca. 8vo.

Constable (David).—Letter of John Calvin, compiled from the original manuscripts, and edited with historical notes by Dr. Jules Bonnet. Translated into English. 8vo., pp. 484.

Dymoke (Sir Henry, Bart.)—Reflections on the Sabbath. 12mo., pp. 32.

English Bible, The, newly divided into Paragraphs, &c. Part VI. I. and II. Samuel. 4to.

Huidekoper (Frederic).—The Belief of the First Three Centuries concerning Christ's Mission to the Underworld. Boston and New York. 12mo., pp. 200.

Joyce (Rev. James Wayland).—England's Sacred Synods. A Constitu-
tional History of the Convocations of the Clergy, from the earliest records of Christianity in
Britain to the date of the promulgation of the present Book of Common Prayer. 8vo.,
pp. 756.

Kalisch (Dr. M.)—A historical and critical Commentary on the Old Testament: with a new translation. Vol. II. Exodus. 8vo., pp. 656.

———. The same; English edition. 8vo., pp. 488.

Laing (David).—The works of John Knox, collected and edited. Vol.
IV. 8vo., pp. 580.

Malan (Rev. S. C.)—Who is God in China, Shin or Shang-Te? 8vo.,
pp. 318.

Norton (Andrews).—Internal Evidences of the Genuineness of the Gospels.
Part I. Remarks on Christianity and the Gospels, with particular reference to Strauss's
"Life of Jesus." Part II. Portions of an unfinished work. Boston. 8vo., pp. 326.

———. A translation of the Gospels, with Notes. Boston. 2 vols.
8vo., pp. 960.

Ogilvie (John, LL.D.)—Supplement to the Imperial Dictionary. Imperial
8vo., pp. 500.

Oliphant (F. W.)—A Plea for Painted Glass; being an Enquiry into its
nature, character, and objects, and its claims as an art.

Real Presence, the Doctrine of, as set forth in the works of Divines and
others in the English Church since the Reformation. Part II. 8vo., pp. 146.

Reichel (Rev. C. P.)—The Christian Ministry: a Sermon preached in the
Parish Church of Holywood. 8vo., pp. 40.

Rose (Rev. H. J.) and Burgon (Rev. J. W.)—History of our Lord Jesus
Christ exhibited in a series of seventy-two highly-finished and beautifully-coloured engravings.

Taylor (Rev. J.)—The True Doctrine of the Holy Eucharist, as instituted
in Scripture, and received in the Catholic Church in all ages, in refutation of Archdeacon
Wilberforce's Book, "The Doctrine of the Holy Eucharist," and the Popish Views of that
sacrament in general. 8vo., pp. 576.

Thompson (Rev. Robert Anchor).—Christian Theism, the testimony of
Reason and Revelation to the Existence and Character of the Supreme Being. (Burnett
Prize Essay.) 2 vols. 8vo., pp. 876.

Tucker (Miss).—The Southern Cross and the Southern Crown: or, The
Gospel in New Zealand. 18mo., pp. 272.

Waldegrave (Hon. and Rev. Samuel).—New Testament Millennarianism;
or, The Kingdom and Coming of Christ as taught by Himself and his Apostles; set forth in
Eight Sermons preached before the University of Oxford, in the year 1854, at the Lecture
founded by the Rev. John Bampton. 8vo., pp. 702.

Whitford (Rev. R. W.)—Prospectus of a Synoptical or Critico-Historical
edition of the Hellenistic Version of the Old Testament; being an exact reprint, for the first
time, of the Greek LXX. text of the Complutensian Polyglott.

Winkworth (Catherine).—Lyra Germanica: Hymns for the Sundays and
Chief Festivals of the Christian year. Translated from the German. 12mo.

Yonge (C. D.)—The Works of Philo Judæus, the contemporary of Josephus. Translated from the Greek. Four Volumes, 18mo.

THE

JOURNAL

OF

SACRED LITERATURE

AND

BIBLICAL RECORD.

No. IV.—JANUARY, 1856.

EARLY ECCLESIASTICAL WRITERS.[a]

FROM the New Testament we discover that even in the days of the apostles, Christianity called forth a controversial mental activity. While St. Paul lived, this appears to have been mostly confined either to the Judaizing teachers, or to gross heretics who turned the grace of God into licentiousness; but before St. John left the earth, a more refined form of religious error seems to have crept over portions of the Church. This is precisely the course which we should have expected things to take in the peculiar historical circumstances of Christianity. When the Church was yet young, and wanted the form and consistence which it soon attained, it required a strong principle to keep men uniformly attached to its varying fortunes, and those who apostatized in heart would be likely to relapse into Judaism or into Gentile idolatry, and to pave the way for their return to the world by a practical questioning of vital and peculiar Christian truths. But before the first century terminated, the reproach of the Cross had in some degree ceased, because it was seen that those who gloried in it became and continued numerous and

[a] 1. *A General Survey of the History of the Canon of the New Testament during the first Four Centuries.* By Brooke Foss Westcott, M.A. Cambridge: Macmillan and Co. 1855. 8vo., pp. 618.

2. *Spicilegium Syriacum: containing remains of Bardesan, Meliton, Ambrose, and Mara Bar Serapion.* Now first edited, with an English Translation and Notes, by the Rev. W. Cureton, M.A., Canon of Westminster, &c., &c. London: Rivingtons. 1855. Imperial 8vo., pp. 170.

strong. As soon therefore as Christianity came to have a past history, and began to appeal to documentary evidence for its doctrines, it had to grapple with the subtleties of dialectics, and the more refined forms of heathen and metaphysical abstractions.

The example was set by the apostles and evangelists, of employing the pen in defence of the faith. Two of the gospels, at least, owed their existence, as surveyed from their merely human side, to an exigency demanding literary means to satisfy it; while the epistles, for the most part, were spontaneous and unpremeditated efforts to explain what was misconceived, or to supply what was wanting in the case of special communities. While their mental productions were overruled and sanctioned by the Spirit, and conserved by the providence of God for all time, it is difficult to conceive that the writers themselves were aware of the ultimate tendencies and immortal results of their literary labours. We are of opinion that had any party, in the Church of Corinth, for example, taken upon him to reply to St. Paul, that holy and humble man would have paid attention to his arguments, and rested little on his own conscious inspiration in a dogmatic form, provided the objecter or questioner had been holy and devout, and not conceited and captious. That his epistles would become the *law* of the Church, perhaps never entered into the mind of the apostle. He knew that the truth which they all contained would be a perpetual foundation for the Church until Christ's coming again, but that his words would be the documentary archives for its maintenance, was more, as far as facts reveal the matter, than he probably contemplated. We have a very strong conviction that we mistake the character of the early Church, and the relation of the apostles to its growth and edification, because we throw the circumstances of our position around the very different one occupied by Christians eighteen hundred years ago. The truths of the Gospel were then all revealed, preached, and in various degrees received and understood, but they had not been formally committed to paper, and consequently could not be appealed to as a fixed and completed collection. How often has it been asked by the Christian, when harassed with doubts about matters of government and practice not clearly revealed, How did it happen that neither St. Paul nor any of his coadjutors compiled a body of divinity for the use of the Church, but rather left its laws and statutes in a form so fragmentary? *Why* they did not must be referred *ultimately* to the wisdom of God, preferring to leave the care of His truth as much to providence as to written revelation: to develope the Church historically, as well as to lay its foundations dogmatically; *proximately*, however, we believe the cause is to be

found in the fact that the apostles did not contemplate so large
an addition to the Holy Scriptures as they finally received,—did
not imagine that their own productions should, as the New
Covenant, go hand in hand through all time with those writings
which they appealed to as "given by inspiration of God, and
as profitable for doctrine, for reproof, for correction, and for
instruction in righteousness."

We make these observations not only because of their bearing
on the object of this paper, but also on account of the very
general prevalence of a contrary view, which, we think, in
several ways operates unfavourably on the interests of Christian
truth.   A short time back a company of Christian ministers met
together to read the Scriptures, and to expound a portion in turn
for mutual benefit, and on the occasion referred to, the passage
for consideration was 2 Timothy ii., but especially the second
verse,—"And the things that thou hast heard of me among
many witnesses, the same commit thou to faithful men, who
shall be able to teach others also."   The question was diligently
discussed : What were *the things* delivered to Timothy, and which
he was to commit to others ?   The view we took was that the ἃ,
rendered *the things*, meant the substance of the Gospel, delivered
probably to Timothy by St. Paul in a public charge, an explanation which also accounts for the διὰ πολλῶν μαρτύρων, the many
witnesses, mentioned at the same time.[b]   This meaning was,
however, zealously controverted.   Stress was properly laid on
the verb παράθου, which was collated with the frequent use of

---

[b] This is not the place to enter into a disquisition upon the difficulty of this passage
arising from the peculiar use of διά ; if the rendering of the English version, *among*,
is to be received.   In all ages the text has employed the sagacity of critics, and led to
not a little controversy.   A few *excerpta* may be given.   Theodoret explains : ἅπερ
ἤκουσάς μου πολλοὺς διδάσκοντος. Theophylact : οὐ λάθρα, ἀλλὰ μετὰ παῤῥησίας,
πολλῶν παρόντων. Of old, a various reading seems to have been attached to the
passage, since Hippolytus (lib. De Antichristo, § 1) reads for μαρτύρων, παρακλήσεων,
by many exhortations ; that writer either quoting from memory and committing a
blunder, or from a codex with a variation, all traces of which have since been lost.
But Mill has shewn that Hippolytus has other spurious readings.   A different pointing
and construction have been attempted to solve the difficulty, καὶ ἃ ἤκουσας παρ' ἐμοῦ,
διὰ πολλῶν μαρτύρων ταῦτα παράθου, What thou hast heard of me, do thou, testifying
in many words, commit, &c.   This gloss has been adopted, with a dogmatic purpose,
among others by Wotton, in his book on *The rights of the Clergy in the Christian
Church.* The Vulgate has *per*, the Peschito, Syriac ܒܝܕ, *by means of, through.*
On the whole it seems most probable that St. Paul refers to the presbyters spoken of,
1 Tim. iv. 14 ; and we would suggest that the use of διά may be harmonized with this
view by the passage in Homer *(Il.,* xii. 104), ὁ δ' ἔπρεπε καὶ διὰ πάντων, *he excelled
among all ;* on which Liddell and Scott remark, "The notion of pre-eminence is obtained from his *standing out from among them,* and thus being distinguished," that
being involved in διά.   The only passages in the New Testament which Schleusner
can find with the meaning of *inter, among,* to διά, are very doubtful : Gal. iii. 19 ;
Heb. ii. 2.

cognate words in the two epistles, especially παραθήκη, *a deposit,* and it was argued that what St. Paul had committed to Timothy was something documentary, *since it could not be that mere oral tradition was the thing meant,* a matter safe in the hands of St. Paul and Timothy, but no further. This step being reached, it was next concluded that the gospels and epistles, as far as then written, were intended by St. Paul, and that his words might be paraphrased : "The things which thou hast heard of me, and which are delivered to thee in writing, commit thou to faithful men," &c.

We adduce this case as a good illustration of the way in which a doctrinal or dogmatic bias influences the interpretation of the Scriptures. The defenders of the view we have just given could not conceive of Gospel truth being left to preaching or oral teaching alone, but believed it must, even in the apostolic times, have been entrusted to documents, and that then, as now, the New Testament had a referrible existence as the voucher for the truth delivered. Thus the passage in the Epistle to Timothy became complicated ; while to us, who were free from the trammels of that opinion, it seemed perfectly plain and simple. There are but very slight indications through all the New Testament, of any portion of it being looked to as a standard of reference ; the Old Testament was quoted and recommended to the study of the believers, and the doctrines and acts of Jesus Christ were orally stated and commented upon by inspired men, who, when churches were founded, ordained others to transmit the precious deposit. The observations of Olshausen on this subject are worthy of attentive consideration, and we shall make no excuse for quoting them : " So long as the apostles were upon earth, and the power of the Spirit from on high was in lively action in every member of the Church, so long there was no sensible necessity of a book to serve as the rule of faith and practice. Whenever any uncertainty arose in regard to either, application was made to one of the apostles, and his advice was taken. The epistles of the apostle Paul owe their origin in part to such enquiries. Hence in the lifetime of the apostles, though their writings were highly valued, they were naturally not regarded as sacred writings which were to be the rule of faith ; because there was a more immediate guarantee of truth in the living discourse of the apostles and their first companions, as also in the Holy Spirit, which was so powerfully exerting its influence upon the Church. The apostolic writings, therefore, were indeed read in the public assemblies, but not alone and not regularly."[c]

---

[c] *Proof of the Genuineness of the Writings of the New Testament.* Edinburgh, 1847.

If the view we have given be incorrect, it can surely be made to appear so, and we shall be happy to relinquish it when evidence is produced against it. Our simple desire, we trust, is to know what was the actual state of the early Church in relation to the New Testament, and we would quite as readily adopt the opinion that it was to them, as to us, *the rule of faith*, if sufficient grounds can be shewn to support it. But we confess we are by no means to be driven from our own view by any cry of neology on the one hand, or of semi-popery on the other; those two formidable bugbears which have been set up in modern times to frighten timid souls into the fold of a conventional orthodoxy. As nothing is so unfavourable to a correct estimate of what is ancient in the history of mankind, as the habit of throwing the thoughts and manners of the present upon the past, so, on the contrary, it tends much to the discovery of the truth in such matters to approach their consideration with no prepossessions of our own. It is, perhaps, impossible to do this completely, but if we aim at it, we shall at least approach such a desirable state of mind; while; if we are determined to enter the precincts of far distant ages with all our prejudices upon us, we shall discover there, not the truth, but our own subjective notions of what it ought to be. The former plan will secure us some of the light of day, while the latter will compel us to grope in the dim beams of the dark lantern of our own ignorance.

As Christianity mainly depended, during the first century, on oral teaching for its promulgation, so the heresies which arose in that period were propagated in the same way. We can only thus account for the fact that, while, as we have before said, mental activity was displayed against apostolic truth, no literary remains have come down to us. But when the apostles had all departed, and the Canon began to be formed as a security against error, it became more and more the case that church questions were discussed on both sides in written documents, which thus sought the whole Church for the sphere of their influence, in contradistinction from the mere local boundaries of oral teaching. But as the Canon of the New Testament was not formed at once, but was the gradual accretion of long successive years, so it was long before controversial writings acquired a permanent value, and were treasured up as documents to be referred to. There was first a destitution of any perception of the necessity of a written rule of faith; then something like a norm was presented in the gospels and apostolic letters; afterwards arose a desire to collect all that could be discovered of these precious documents; lastly, a decision, tacitly at least, of the whole Church as to what constituted the Canon. This process is described in few words, but it took ages fully to perfect it, and to give to the New Testament the form and authority we now concede to it.

If we wish to know why so few of the writings of the Early Church have come down to us, either in substance or traditionally, we may find an answer to the question in the fate of the autographs of the gospels and epistles, written by the hands of men around whose brows from that time to this the Church has delighted to entwine the halo of sanctity. This is an age which, perhaps more than any other, can estimate the value of relics of the past, especially when associated with historical renown, high mental attainments, or eminent writers; and our eagerness to become possessors of but a few words written by our poets or heroes, will at once indicate to us the priceless worth of an autograph epistle of St. John or St. Paul. An historian of the Library of the Vatican, tells us that " St. Peter, when he would set up the see of the truth, brought the Holy Gospel to Rome ; and that Paul the Apostle when he called Timothy thither, was careful that literary monuments should be brought with him : For *bring with thee*, he says, *the books, and especially the parchments*. Behold the beginnings of the Vatican Library. *En Vaticanæ Bibliothecæ primordia !*"[d] But, except by a figure of speech, the learned Assemani could not indicate, in that depository of glorious remains, the least fragment of papyrus or parchment which apostolic eyes had looked upon or fingers touched. Yet there was a time when all that those holy founders of the Church had written in their public capacity existed and was handled, read, and copied from. What became of those wondrous productions, or by what strange fate have they refused to unfold their glorious characters to posterity ?

Perhaps we might justly reply, that the age was too intent on great things to care for little ones; that it had such a high perception of THE TRUTH itself, that it failed to appreciate the casket. The unsettled state of the kingdoms of the world also tended to depress mere sentiment, and to deprive things of a conventional value. Upon earth there was great " distress of nations and perplexity, the sea and the waves roaring," and if amidst the din of arms and the destruction of great cities such things as the Ark of the Covenant with all its precious contents were entirely lost to the Church of God, we cannot well wonder that the autographs of apostles should share the same fate. But a deeper reason than any of these operated, we believe, to deprive

---

[d] See J. S. Assemani *Catalogus Codicum MSS. Bibliothecæ Apostolicæ Vaticanæ*, tom. i. (all published), Romæ, 1756.

succeeding generations of those intensely interesting literary monuments of Christianity. Before the value we now attach to these documents had grown up in the early Church, it is probable the autographs had ceased to exist, and that it was from copies of them that the Canon of the New Testament received its authoritative completion. We know that various readings were appealed to very early by polemical writers, and had the original gospels and epistles then been in existence, such a fact could not have occurred. We cannot say when the vast importance of having the very manuscripts in which the laws and regulations of the Church were deposited, first revealed itself to those anxious for a standard of the faith, but we may be sure of this that the desire was only awakened to find that it was fruitless, because they had perished, either by the carelessness of their possessors, or by the wear and tear to which they had been subjected.

Believing as we do that the Church has always had the watchful care of its great Founder, we cannot see anything accidental or unimportant in the fate of the documents which evangelists and apostles either wrote or dictated for the benefit of their contemporaries. If not a sparrow falls to the ground, nor a hair of the head of his people, without the knowledge and permission of our Father, how can it be possible that the history and final destruction of these precious remains should be without his controul? Perhaps we should not be wrong if we were to state that these manuscripts were permitted to perish lest they should be almost idolized in after generations, but we may affirm with more certainty that such destruction has wrought well for the Church, by eliciting the research and skill of its members, and developing to a high degree their intellectual powers in its service. However specious may be the arguments brought forward to prove the necessity of an *infallible* appeal in matters of Christian doctrine and practice, we are convinced that a *moral certainty*, the result of deduction and reasoning, is far to be preferred, both as to its bearing on individual training, and on the welfare of the Church at large. Had the original manuscripts of the Scriptures survived to our day, with their characters too legible to allow of one textual doubt, a certain class of difficulties would certainly have been unknown; but would this have compensated for the mental activity and prayerful effort to discover the truth, which a measure of documentary obscurity now occasions?

If nothing availed to preserve the autographs of apostles, it cannot surprise us that the literary productions of ordinary men have altogether perished, when their preservation was not secured by any important relation to the interests of the Church at large.

The way in which, humanly speaking, the gospels and epistles would have been in danger of neglect and disuse, if controversial considerations had not rendered a standard of divine truth necessary, may shew us how uninspired productions of a mere local or temporary bearing would be forgotten and die, and be only known as once existing by a passing allusion in the works of more fortunate authors which have come down to us. Although, as we before observed, a literary tendency in the Church was not very quickly developed, there are indications that, even in apostolic times, many committed to paper what they knew of Christ's history, or endeavoured to gain currency for their own doctrinal opinions by the same means. St. Luke tells us that before he composed his gospel, "*many* had taken in hand to set forth in order a declaration (διήγησις, *narration, history)* of those things which are most surely believed among us." It is well shewn by Alford that neither the writers of our present Gospels nor the Apocryphal Gospels can be exclusively intended in this passage, but histories which have perished. "That such narratives should not have come down to us," says the same author, "is no matter of surprise, for they would be absorbed by the more complete and sanctioned accounts of our present evangelists; and Church tradition has preserved very few fragments of authentic information of the apostolic age. It is probable that in almost every church where an eye-witness preached, his testimony would be taken down, and framed into some διήγησις, more or less complete, of the life and sayings of the Lord." We have not the same precise information of the existence of mere doctrinal or controversial writings of so early a date, but there are intimations that such were in circulation. St. Paul, for instance, alludes to a forged letter or letters when he says to the Thessalonians (2 Thes. ii. 2), "That ye be not soon shaken in mind, or be troubled, neither by spirit, nor by word, *nor by letter as from us,* as that the day of Christ is at hand." We are aware that the passage admits of a different interpretation. "Patrum nonnulli, v.c. Chrysostomus, Theophylactus, Œcumenius, et Origines confecerunt, fuisse tum à falsario epistolam sub Pauli nomine ad Thessalonicenses scriptam; alii vero cavere potius Paulum voluisse censent, ne, si quid ejusmodi inposterum fiat, Thessalonicenses abripi se patiantur; quo fine in epistola hac extrema ἰδιόγραφον σημεῖον exhibuerit. Ita præter Theodoretum alii."[e] Still later, in the state of the Church which gave rise to the epistles of St. John, we can

---

[e] Wolfius, *Curæ Philologicæ,* sub loco.

scarcely doubt that the pen was made to subserve the heretical teaching which then had so extensive an influence.

The earliest post-apostolic literature which has been handed down to us, consists of the epistles of the apostolic fathers, and the form they bear confirms all we have said on the subject of the early documents of the Church.

"The form of the earliest Christian literature," says Mr. Westcott,*f* "explains its origin and object. The writings of the first fathers are not essays, or histories,· or apologies, but letters. They were not impelled to write by any literary motive, nor even by the pious desire of shielding their faith from the attacks of its enemies. An intense feeling of a new fellowship in Christ overpowered all other claims. As members of a great household, as fathers or brethren, they spoke to one another words of counsel and warning, and so found a natural utterance for the faith, and hope, and love, which seemed to them the sum of Christian life."

These remains bear conclusive evidence that the New Testament as a whole did not then exist, for while some of its separate portions are referred to or quoted, this is done in a very different manner from that employed some years after when the Canon was completed. Christianity is rather spoken of as a great historical fact, exhibited in living and loving hearts, and in a number of communities subject to the same oral or traditionary laws, than as a system dependant on a book, or provided with a sufficient code of documentary statutes. As Mr. Westcott well says, "the earliest references to the Canon are simply incidental." We ascertain from them that some of the New Testament writings were then in circulation, but nothing more.

Reasoning from analogy then, and from the scanty data with which we are furnished, we come to the conclusion that far more has perished than survived of the mental productions of the early Christians. This brings naturally before us the question, Have we all that was ever written by the apostles and evangelists, or did their literature, in part, suffer the same fate as that of their contemporaries and successors? We propose to give this enquiry our calm and serious consideration, as being highly interesting in itself, and having important relations to other matters concerning our common Christianity.

On the very threshold of the subject we meet with a dogmatic objection, which, if we were accustomed to be daunted by such opposition, would prevent our proceeding further. It is said, How can inspired truth ever be lost?

"The supposition of a lost epistle of St. Paul is still unpalatable to

f A General Survey of the History of the Canon of the New Testament, p. 24.

many. They argue against it as if it were derogatory to the wisdom of the supreme being. . . . In concluding that some of Paul's epistles have been lost, a class of Christians may suppose that the perfection of Scripture is impaired; for the notions which once prevailed respecting *the nature* of inspiration and of the Canon are not obsolete. In combating the Roman Catholic Church, it was formerly usual among Protestants to abide firmly by the idea, that nothing inspired has been lost."[g]

The writer now quoted confines his attention principally to the case before him, the discussion of the text, Col. iv. 16, "And when this epistle is read among you, cause that it be read also in the Church of the Laodiceans; *and that ye likewise read* the epistle from Laodicea" (καὶ τὴν ἐκ Λαοδικείας ἵνα καὶ ὑμεῖς ἀναγνῶτε). After a careful and learned consideration of the subject he comes to the conclusion that "the allusion of St. Paul can only be to a lost epistle: such was the opinion of Calvin, Beza, Grotius, Wetstein, and Bengel; and almost all recent expositors hold the same view." He alludes to the subjective origin of the prejudice now under notice, and for that purpose we have extracted the passage. The *overthrow of an opponent, or the defence of an opinion thought to be essential to the views of a party,* in this case, as in so many others, has led to a doctrine which, we think, has no foundation either in reason or in truth. We do not say that party-spirit alone has led to the adoption of this view; *à priori* reasons of various kinds have been adduced on its behalf. Thus Hottinger, in his *Thesaurus Philologicus,* affirms that God in his providence would not permit a canonical book to be lost, and that the Church, the faithful depository of the divine records, cannot possibly have been so deficient in its duty as to suffer the loss to take place.

First, we may observe that every inspired production of the ancient Jewish Church was not preserved in the Canon. Mention is made of the lost works of prophets whose predictions form part of the Canon of the Old Testament; and this fact can only be met by the assertion that their prophetical character in some things is no guarantee that all they wrote was inspired; or by the *petitio principii,* that the fact of their being lost is a proof that they were not inspired. Moses Stuart, in his *Critical History and Defence of the Old Testament Canon,* has a section entitled, "Lost books of the Hebrews, some of which appear to have been canonical," which is well worthy attentive perusal. We do not agree with him in thinking that anything *canonical*

---

[g] *An Introduction to the New Testament,* by Samuel Davidson, D.D., vol. ii., p. 143.

is lost, because we understand by the Canon, the books which the ancient Church preserved, and which existed entire at the time of our Saviour; but we think he clearly shews that we have every reason to believe that the works lost were, some of them, inspired.

"Plainly," he says, "the writers, as a body, were of the order of the prophets. And were not books written by Nathan the prophet, and Gad the prophet, and Iddo the seer, and Isaiah the prophet, and by others of the same office, counted *sacred* by the Hebrews? We can hardly imagine the contrary. But if any one should hesitate to acknowledge this, on the ground that prophets might write other books than those which were inspired, still *the manner of appeal to the works in question which are now lost, both in Kings and Chronicles, shews beyond all reasonable doubt that they were regarded as authoritative and sacred.* For how could a writer remit his readers for fuller authentic information to those books which he did not regard as standing on the same basis as his own work, in respect of being worthy of credit? Had we now those fuller narratives which are so frequently appealed to in the present books of Kings and Chronicles, who can well doubt that many a seeming difficulty in these abridgements of Jewish history would be solved to our entire satisfaction."[h]

In this we quite coincide, and are sorry that Mr. Lee, after quoting it, should so far beg the question as to remark, " That these 'lost' writings were regarded as *veracious annals* is no doubt evident; but the mere fact of their *not* having been even preserved by the Jews 'shews beyond all reasonable doubt' that they were *not* 'regarded as authoritative and sacred.'"[i] Does Mr. Lee imagine that any care the Jews could have taken of their sacred writings would have been sufficient to preserve them in the calamitous periods of their history? Must not the *selection* and *preservation* of what did survive be ascribed to the special providence of God?

Secondly, the history of the MSS. of the canonical books of the New Testament supplies us with an argument bearing on the subject before us. In these, various readings are granted,[j] and as these often arise from repetitions and superfluities, it is almost demonstrable that some are caused by omissions and defects. He must be a hardy devotee to system who would attempt to maintain that amidst all the variations of the text of the New Testament no loss has been suffered of a letter, word, or sentence

---

h Lorimer's edition, London: 1849, p. 163.

i *The Inspiration of Holy Scripture, its nature and proof.* London: 1854.

j "Dari Lectiones Variantes, non tantum in Scripturæ Versionibus, præsertim antiquis, sed etiam in ipso textu Hebraico Veteris et Græco Novi Testamenti, a nemine negari potest, cum hoc testentur tot varietates ex codicibus MSS. et impressis a viris doctis annotatæ." *Waltoni Prolegomena,* vi.

of the inspired autographs. Since divine providence has not interfered to prevent transpositions, repetitions, mistakes of spelling, and the exchange of words of similar sound and meaning, the reasonable conclusion is that there have also been words dropped out in the process of transcription from age to age, which nothing but a miracle could now recover. If the care and oversight of the Church have not prevailed to hinder *additions* being made to the sacred text, what right have we to conclude that no *omissions* have occurred under her vigilant eye? We think therefore it may be conceded that while the Canon of the New Testament remains substantially the same as it was at its first formation, some small portions have been lost in the course of transcription, either altogether, or, which amounts to the same thing, by the substitution of a word or phrase of similar sound or meaning.

But with this concession the principal argument against inspired writings being lost falls to the ground. It cannot be for a moment reasonably maintained that it is derogatory for divine providence to allow an epistle of St. Paul or St. James to perish, while yet it permits any small portion of their surviving productions to suffer that fate. Such an affirmation would be the same as to say that while God cares for his Church, he does not regard its members; that while he protects the main interests of his believing people, he is regardless of their minor affairs. Much more consistent is it with the whole analogy of God's proceedings to say, that he gave the Spirit plenteously to his apostles for the instruction and edification of the Church, and that under its influence they frequently employed the pen on behalf of those who could not hear the word from their lips; that a portion of these written documents were selected to serve as the rule of faith through all time, while the others, having answered their purpose, were allowed to perish, like the millions of words uttered by the same apostles and by our Lord himself, of which the Church has always been deprived. Indeed, what real difference is there between inspired words uttered by the lips, and the same written by the pen? If we are required to believe that none of the latter could be lost, consistency demands that we should place the former in the same category. This is a *reductio ad absurdum*, quite defensible from the declaration of St. John, "And there are also many other things which Jesus did, the which, if they should be written every one, I suppose the world itself could not contain the books that should be written."

Thirdly, the hypothesis we are combating demands that we should believe that many of the apostles never wrote at all; but that while all were equally anxious for the edification of the Church, only a few committed their thoughts to paper, to send to their distant friends and disciples. Why should the Holy Ghost move Sts. Paul, Matthew, John, James, Peter and Jude, to write to the Churches, and omit to employ the others of the twelve in the same efficient mode of doing good? We are aware that it may be said, that this is prying into reasons which are hid in the divine mind, and that we are exceeding our province in entering upon it. We reply, No, we are only forming a reasonable conclusion, and that those are guilty of presumption who affirm that nothing inspired could possibly perish. Several apostles have left letters, called forth by ordinary exigencies in special churches, and the plain inference is that their fellow-apostles did the same, although they have not survived. Against this nothing can be alleged but a subjective notion that it is inconsistent with inspiration that such should be the case; and to maintain a figment of the imagination, one half the apostles are presumed never to have written to those whom they converted to the faith! If it be said that we have no proof that they were men of education sufficient to write a letter, the plain retort is that the inspiration which gave them the power of speaking new tongues, could quite as readily have enabled them to write down their divine conceptions.

Fourthly, as St. Paul and St. John, to mention no others, *could* write, are we bound to believe that they, on no occasion, committed to paper more than has come down to us? Both these inspired preachers of the Gospel wrote fluently, and both lived many years in the active service of the Church which they benefitted by their mental productions. Whatever others may do, we confess ourselves to be utterly unable to think that they employed their pens no oftener than on the occasions commemorated in the New Testament. St. Paul was "in prisons oft;" and St. John was, during a long life, removed very far away from large sections of the Church for which he felt a deep regard. We have no doubt whatever that both took every opportunity of writing, where they could not preach, and that only a small portion of their epistles have been chosen to instruct the Church in all ages of its checquered existence.

If, on the presumption of our opinion being the correct one, we enquire, Is it probable that any apostolic writings may yet be brought to light? we are obliged to reply in the negative. The vast importance of all such remains was too early seen to allow of any of them escaping the public eye, in that season of anxious controversy contemporaneous with the settlement of the Canon. What treasures of various kinds may yet turn out from old libraries or buried cities it is impossible to predict. The Vatican itself, under more favourable auspices may deliver up to our admiring gaze literary remains of an antiquity now not suspected to exist; but we must feel pretty certain that whatever such documents may be, they will be very remote in interest from the "books, especially the parchments," of which the learned Assemani discoursed. Whatever has been lost of inspired productions, we are allowed to speculate upon; but of any future discovery of such inestimable relics, not the faintest whisper of hope is breathed to the most sanguine heart. To the Canon may be applied the words of Ezekiel, "Thou art the confirmed exemplar of measures, full of wisdom and perfect in beauty."[k]

Our aim in all that we have said on this very interesting subject is one of a very practical character. We think that as an enquiry connected with sacred archæology only, it may be pursued profitably; but our present design is far more serious, and concerns the great question of the relation of the Bible to the Church, and the popular notions of the inspiration of the sacred Scriptures. In the present day there is a tendency to treat the Bible as *an organic whole,* without any recognition of its widely varied contents, or of the gradual, and in some respects incidental manner in which the Canon was completed. It is too frequently thought that the book as we have it came bodily from the hands of holy men, a statute book for the Church complete and entire, and that it has been recognized and used as such from the very times of the apostles. That it has this character in relation to ourselves we at once and fully admit. We take the Holy Scriptures as our rule of faith, in their present form, and as a whole, and believe that it is now the will of God that they should be our standard in all doctrinal questions, from whose decisions there can be no appeal, where they are rationally deduced and understood. But this opinion cannot be held safely, without the admission that it was not always thus in the history of the Church; that in its earliest origin it had no New Testament to appeal to, but derived its rule of faith either from apostolic lips or apostolic tradition; and that a case of necessity apparently not foreseen by the sacred writers themselves led to the collection of their surviving works and the formation of the Canon. The admission of this fact is only adding another instance to the numerous indications we have that God works out his own purposes in ways different from those which our *à priori* reasonings would approve of. The

---

[k] Ezekiel xxviii. 12; a translation we have quoted from memory, but have forgotten the author.

Old Testament Canon was formed in the same way;—prophets and historical and didactic writers contributing to an edifice the final proportions, or indeed the very existence of which, was hidden from them. Thoughtful readers will easily see how much of practical import results from the recognition of these facts of history. Into the distinct points we hope to enter fully at some future opportunity, and for the present only mention two. A right perception of the relation of the Scriptures to the early Church will lead, first to a higher appreciation of the Church itself, and, secondly, to a more *rational* and less slavishly *literal* use of the New Testament in the conduct of controversies.

Before we leave the subject of the bearing of a dogmatic bias on the question of lost inspired productions, we will allude briefly to a remarkable instance of its influence on questions of archæology, in relation to the Old Testament. It is observable that in all the enquiries which are made into the early history of mankind, as illustrated by existing phenomena, the sphere of investigation is limited to this side of the Noachian deluge. This is the case, whether the researches concern ancient art and architecture, or manners and customs, as attested by the extant remains of public or private life; a stop being put to the most prying curiosity by the period when the flood of waters overthrew the world of the ungodly. But when we examine the Bible narrative, we do not find anything to lead to the conclusion that the deluge destroyed man's handiwork, or that the cities, temples, private dwellings, arms, and furniture of the antediluvians should not be as much discoverable as those of Nineveh and Babylon and Persepolis, their greater age alone excepted. From what we may reasonably conclude respecting the attainments of those who lived before the deluge, we might expect them to be advanced in art, and capable of carrying out great enterprises; while the flood, although potent to destroy life, did not even uproot the olive tree, by "a branch plucked off" of which Noah knew that the waters had subsided. What is the reason then that enquirers into the past should limit their field of view to post-diluvian history? Simply the fact that it has been concluded, on supposed Biblical authority, that the flood must have thrown the whole crust of the earth into irrecoverable confusion, and left no trace of man or his works upon it. How many errors exist even now, based entirely on some unfounded, and often perverse, interpretation of passages of the Word of God!

But it is time we approach the consideration of the post-apostolic remains now presented to the literary world in the volume of Mr. Cureton, which have beguiled us into the discussion now presented to our readers. The manuscripts from which the Syriac text now before us is taken are of a very high antiquity, as appears from the following account given by the learned editor.

"The manuscript from which the materials for the present volume have been chiefly derived, is one of those which were obtained by Archdeacon Tattam, from the Syriac convent in the desert of Nitria, in the year 1843. It is now numbered 14,658 among the additional manuscripts in the British Museum. Several leaves were added in 1847 from fragments subsequently acquired by M. Pacho, and four more were again supplied from other fragments procured also by him from the same source in the year 1850. At present the volume consists of one hundred and eighty-eight leaves. Originally it must have had more than two hundred and twenty; for the last gathering as it now stands is numbered the twenty-second, and each gathering consisted of ten leaves; it is imperfect both at the beginning and the end, and has suffered mutilations in several parts of the volume, and some of the leaves are much stained by oil. It is written in a large bold hand in two columns; and the headings of chapters, and the titles of separate works are distinguished by red letters. It appears to have been transcribed about the sixth or seventh century of our era."

The first work printed from this antique relic is the *Treatise on Fate*, by Bardesanes, the celebrated Gnostic Christian,—a production which early Church writers say was addressed to the Emperor Marcus Antoninus, although, as Mr. Cureton remarks, there is no internal evidence of this in the work now discovered. The title of the treatise is, *The Book of the Laws of Countries*, and it is a dialogue. The subject treated of is Fate, and exhibits the doctrine which has always been ascribed to the treatise of Bardesanes. "The author declares himself to be fully acquainted with the science of Chaldæan astrology, and gives abundant proof of the same; and further, all those passages which have been quoted as extracts from Bardesan's treatise, are found in this. Moreover, it is written in Syriac, in which most of his works were composed, although he was well skilled in the Greek tongue, as Epiphanius informs us. There can be no doubt, therefore, that we have now in our hands, in the original language of the author and in a complete form, that celebrated dialogue of Bardesan on Fate, written about the middle of the second century, which has been so often referred to by subsequent writers, but of which only a comparatively small portion has hitherto been known to us." He lived and taught at Edessa, and furnished much work afterwards to the great Church preacher and writer, Ephraem Syrus, in counteracting the heresies there inculcated by him among the people. From Ephraem's controversial writings more can be known of this man and his doctrines

than from any other source, although this is not referred to by
Mr. Cureton. Ephraem says of his antagonist (between whom
and himself, however, about two centuries intervened),

> "I found the book of Bardesanes,
> And was distressed by it continually;
> For it defiled my ears and my whole nature
> With its offensive blasphemies.
> For I heard in his homilies profane things,
> And things execrable in his songs.
> For if the body rises not
> It will be equal with things accursed!
> If He created the body for corruption
> And it shall not rise for ever,
> Behold, he blasphemes the Just One,
> And contemns Divine Providence;
> Ascribing hatred to the Loving One,
> And repressing the hope of immortality.
> I have therefore read again, my brethren,
> The writings of the Holy Ghost;
> And my ears were quickly closed
> Against the impurity of that sinner!"

The treatise on Fate occupies about twenty-four pages in Mr.
Cureton's translation, and we shall give a pretty long extract to
excite the curiosity of our readers to the whole.

"I say to him, After this manner again was this Avida saying, 'That
it is from his Nature man acteth wrongly; for if he had not been formed
naturally to do wrong, he would do no wrong.'

"Bardesan saith, If all men did one deed, and acted with the one
mind, it would then be known that it was their Nature governed them,
and they would not have the Free-will of which I spake to you. Nevertheless, in order that ye may understand what is Nature and what is Free-
will, I will proceed to inform you. The Nature of man is this; that he
should be born, and grow up, and rise in stature, and beget children, and
grow old by eating, and drinking, and sleeping, and waking, and that he
should die. These, because they are of Nature, belong to all men, and
not to all men only, but also to all animals which have a soul in them;
and some of them also to trees. For this is a physical operation which
performeth, and produceth, and establisheth everything as it hath been
ordained. But nature also is found to be maintained by animals too in
their actions. For the lion eateth flesh by his Nature; and on this
account all lions are eaters of flesh. And the sheep eateth grass; and for
this reason all sheep are eaters of grass. And the bee maketh honey by
which it sustains itself; for this reason all bees are honey-makers. And
the ant layeth up for itself a store in summer, that it may sustain itself
from it in winter; and for this reason all ants do likewise. And the
scorpion striketh with its sting him who hath not hurt it; and so likewise
all scorpions strike. And all animals maintain their Nature, and those

who feed on grass do not eat flesh; nor do those that feed upon flesh eat grass. But men are not governed in this manner; but in the things belonging to their bodies they maintain their nature like animals; and in the things which belong to their minds they do that which they wish, as being free, and with power, and as the likeness of God. For there are some of them that eat flesh, and do not touch bread; and there are some of them that make a distinction in the eating of flesh; and there are some of them who do not eat the flesh of any animal in which there is a soul; and there are some of them that have connexion with their mothers, and with their sisters, and with their daughters; and there are some that never approach women at all; and there are some that avenge themselves like lions and like leopards; and there are some that injure him who has not done them any harm, like scorpions; and there are some that are led like sheep, and do not hurt those who govern them; and there are some who conduct themselves with virtue, and some with righteousness, and some with vice."—pp. 7—10.

All this might be said by a heathen philosopher;—let us hear his opinion of the followers of Jesus Christ. After enumerating the customs of various countries, mostly selected with reference to sexual matters, he goes on to enquire,

"What then shall we say respecting the new race of ourselves who are Christians, whom in every country and in every region the Messiah established at his coming? For lo! wherever we be, all of us are called by the one name of the Messiah—Christians. [Rather, by the one name of the Christ—Christians.] And upon one day, which is the first of the week, we assemble ourselves together, and on the appointed days we abstain from food. Neither do the brethren which are in Gallia take males for wives; nor those which are in Parthia take two wives; nor those which are in Judea circumcise themselves; nor do our sisters which are amongst the Geli and amongst the Cashani have connexion with strangers; nor do those which are in Persia take their daughters for wives; nor those who are in Media fly from their dead, or bury them alive, or give them for food to the dogs; nor do those who are in Edessa kill their wives that commit fornication, or their sisters, but withdraw themselves from them, and commit them to the judgment of God. Nor do those who are in Hatra stone the thieves. But wherever they be, and in whatever place they are, the laws of the countries do not separate them from the laws of their Messiah. Neither does the fortune of the governors compel them to make use of things which are impure to them; but sickness and health, and riches and poverty—this which does not appertain to their freewill, befals them wherever they are."—pp. 32, 33.

The second ancient piece in this volume is ascribed to Melito or Meliton of Sardis, but as a translation of this, and notes, have already appeared in *The Journal of Sacred Literature*,[1] we

---

[1] See the Numbers for January and April, 1855.

shall not now refer to it. There are also some fragments of the same author. Then follow "*Hypomnemata,* which Ambrose, a chief man of Greece wrote: who became a Christian, and all his fellow-senators raised a clamour against him; and he fled from them, and wrote and shewed them all their folly; and at the beginning of his discourse he answered and said," &c. This is the short work which, in substance, is the same as that known in Greek as the *Oratio ad Gentiles,* and was generally received as Justin Martyr's. Mr. Cureton says, this Ambrose "can hardly be understood to be any other than the friend and disciple of Origen, whom Epiphanius designates as one of those illustrious in the palaces of kings, and whose wealth enabled him to supply his master with all the necessary expenses for completing his Hexaplar edition of the Scriptures, and who also himself suffered martyrdom for the Christian faith." The last piece is, "*The Epistle of Mara, Son of Serapion, to Serapion my Son, Greeting,*" and is a highly interesting document. The editor thinks that it ought to be assigned to a period when the Sibylline verses were frequently cited, the age of Justin Martyr, Meliton, and Tertullian.

We thank Mr. Cureton for these highly interesting and important remains of the early Church, and hope that he will soon furnish some further contributions from the same source. These spoils from the decayed monasteries of the East whet our appetite for more, and give us some hope too that the desire may be gratified. Next to the writings of Apostles themselves, the mind attaches a high value to the mental productions of those who lived near their times, and were the professed followers of their life and doctrine.[m]

---

[m] We are unwilling to add to the already long chapter of the "quarrels of authors," but we are compelled to refer to the way in which Mr. Cureton has marred his labours, in this instance, by what appears to us a petty and almost morbid sensitiveness, unworthy his name and his exertions on behalf of ancient literature. In the numbers of our Journal for January and April, 1855, we presented our readers with the Apology of Melito of Sardis, and various illustrative notes, furnished by a valued and learned correspondent signing himself B. H. C., in whose knowledge of Syriac, and earnest and studious application to the MSS. of the Museum we placed great confidence. To his surprise and our own, Mr. Cureton has given much space in his new volume to a measured and continuous attack upon B. H. C. and his contributions, comparing his translation of Melito with his own, and making very disparaging and, in some instances, insulting observations. On the general question between B. H. C. and Mr. Cureton, we have allowed the former to defend himself in the department of *Correspondence*—to which we refer our readers, who will see that Mr. Cureton's criticisms are partly well-founded, but also partly captious and unsustained. He has also attacked, but with less severity, M. Renan, "a young Orientalist," who has also translated the Epistle, and whose renderings often coincide with those of B. H. C., which Mr. Cureton thinks incorrect. It is easy for the latter gentleman, occupying a high position, to attempt to frown down younger and less favoured disciples of the

On the subject of the Canon, we can direct our readers with full confidence to the valuable work of Mr. Westcott, from which we have briefly quoted. His researches are most painstaking and complete, while the spirit which guides his use of his materials is all we could wish it to be—thoughtful, free from bigotry, and full of affection and reverence for the venerable records of Christian truth. We look upon the work as an important addition to the literature of the subject it treats, and we shall be glad if our recommendation induces our readers to make it their own.

---

same studies as his own; but it must be remembered that it only requires one willing to do it, to make out a pretty long list of matters in which Mr. Cureton might be set right. In a pursuit with few competitors, and rendered very difficult by comparatively few appliances and by past neglect, it is no reflection on a man that his translations are not perfect, or that *one coming after him* may point out errors. After all, the corrections proposed by Mr. Cureton but little affect the general sense of the earlier version of the epistle, for which our readers are indebted to B. H. C,

We are sorry to be obliged to conclude that Mr. Cureton's ire against B. H. C. is caused by the fact of his having preceded himself in introducing the Epistle of Melito to English readers. He says the translation "appears to be the attempt of some young man, who at present has but a very imperfect acquaintance with what has been done in Syriac literature of late, or he could hardly have been ignorant that my volume was in the press." On this point, B. H. C. can speak for himself; we can only say that *we* had no idea that a translation of Melito was forthcoming from Mr. Cureton's pen. Besides, we cannot assent to the proposition that Mr. Cureton's announcement of an intention to translate a Syriac MS. is to place it under seal until he chooses to do so. In conclusion, we assure our readers that B. H. C. is far more than a tyro in these recondite studies. Some years ago, the late Dr. Kitto shewed us a Syriac Lexicon to the New Testament most carefully compiled and beautifully written by this " young man," which only awaits a liberal publisher to be given to the world, since his labours are pursued without those honours and pecuniary emoluments by which Mr. Cureton's more fortunate course has been properly rewarded.

Since writing the above we have received quite incidentally, the following observation from a very competent authority at Oxford:—" I think Mr. Cureton has been unfairly severe on the Melito Articles. Certainly the article in the April number argues for the genuineness much more fully than Mr. Cureton does; and the translation professed to be a free and readable one." The latter qualities cannot always be predicated of Mr. Cureton's version.

VERIFICATION OF CHRISTIAN EPOCHS.

THE received opinion as to the length of our Lord's ministry "the almost universal agreement," according to Dr. Macknight, "is, that it lasted more than three years. Although," says that eminent harmonist, "the Sacred Historians have not said that our Lord was at any of the feasts, which happened in the course of his ministry, except four Passovers, one Feast of Tabernacles, and one Feast of Dedication, we cannot from thence conclude that he was at none but these. For anything we know, our Lord's ministry may have comprehended more than three years and a half, the term commonly assigned to it. Gerhard, Mercator, Joseph Scaliger, Newton and others, were of this opinion; supposing there were traces of at least five passovers in the Sacred History. What I am to say may perhaps shew, that these learned men, though they have extended Christ's ministry a year beyond the ordinary limits, may yet have confined it within too narrow bounds."[a]

It may not be very important to the great ends for which that sacred ministry was undertaken, whether its labours extended over two years or ten, but the adoption of an excessive estimate is attended with the inconvenience of disturbing the true chronology of the Christian age, and by giving its commencement a necessary approximation to the established date of the Julian epoch, which is an impossible approximation according to the facts of history, has induced an opinion that the commemoration of the Christian times has been negligently observed, and some certain years been suffered to lie hid, and uncounted by the keepers of its chronicles.

The opinion delivered by Dr. Macknight is however wholly opposed to the best authorities of the early Church; and notwithstanding the great modern names quoted in support of a lengthened ministry by our Saviour, we think there is a preponderance both of authority and argument in favour of a shorter period even than that which the common and " *almost universal agreement* " has assigned to it. For Dr. Macknight's own particular notion—that it exceeded even the five Passovers, which he says Sir I. Newton and the other great names discovered in the Gospel history—we confess we can only feel an extreme surprize;

---

[a] Macknight's *Harmony*, Prelim. Obser. ii., § 3, and iv., § 1.

the more, because the learned commentator appears to have referred to those true sources of information on the circumstances and period of Herod's death and the preaching of John the Baptist, which are to be found in the account of Josephus and the succession of the Roman consulates; and from which he has drawn what seems to be very correct conclusions on that point of history; but with which it is impossible to associate under any circumstances a period of more than 33 years, as the length of our Lord's life. For these consular lists shew the death of Herod to have happened in the 32nd year from that to which our Lord's death is ascribed by these commentators, and Dr. Macknight amongst others; and the utmost interval which can possibly be contended for between the birth of our Lord and the death of Herod, can only be the two years to which it is supposed the visit of the eastern sages to Bethlehem might have been postponed, after the nativity.

Our great harmonist fixes, by a very correct argument, the death of Herod in the early part of the year A.U.C. 750, which was the consulate of Lentulus and Messalinus, the seventeenth before the two Sexti in whose consulate Augustus died; and the fourteenth before that of Lepidus and Taurus, in which Tiberius received his last adoption by Augustus, and from which St. Luke and many other writers have dated the commencement of his reign.

As these intervals are perfectly well established, one is at a loss to reconcile Dr. Macknight's admission, that the death of Herod was in A.U.C. 750, with an hypothesis that under any possible circumstances our Lord's sacred life could have been extended to an age which would approach to 38 years. There is great laxity, it must be confessed, in the whole reasoning of this writer upon this subject; and it is difficult indeed to agree with him in such a postulate as this—"that though our Lord were really 33 years of age at his baptism, St. Luke might express his age in round numbers, and say he was about 30,"[b]— for such an application of round numbers to such a subject was surely never before heard of:—and how, consistently with his own hypothesis, can he refer to the authority of Scaliger, who makes our Lord's birth to have happened in the year A.U.C. 751; of Archbishop Usher, who makes it fall in A.U.C. 747; and of other commentators of whom there is none that places it earlier than that year?[c]

Under such a state of the question the door appears to be fairly open to a new investigation of this subject, as well as of

---

b Macknight's *Chron. Dissert.* iii., § 7.   c *Ibid.,* § 8.

the matters generally connected with the date of the Christian epoch; and having entered upon it with what diligence we are able, we shall endeavour to lay before our readers some circumstances, which we believe are sufficient to give a more accurate fixture to the dates and events, that bear upon this subject; and such as, at least we hope, may call up a spirit of enquiry among the readers of this Journal, to whose scrutiny and further investigation we heartily commend the subject.

For ourselves we will say, at once, that in our opinion the year named by Archbishop Usher, as that of our Lord's birth, is the true and correct year—that is, the year A.U.C. 749, according to the common assignment of the consular dates; and that his death occurred A.U.C. 781, being in the thirty-second year of his age. The best authors agree, that the nativity occurred in the consulate of *Sabinus and Rufinus*, on the 8th of the calends of January, answering to our 25th December; and his crucifixion occurred in the consulate of the *Two Gemini*, on the 8th day before the calends of April, answering to our 25th March. These consulates stand at an interval of 33 numbers from each other; but the time between the dates assigned comprehends only the age we have named,—viz., to the thirty-second year; for the first of these consulates, that of Sabinus and Rufinus, continued only six days after the birth, that is, from 25th December to the new year ensuing; and the last extended only 85 days into the current year of our Lord's death, viz., from 1st January to 25th March. The first and last consulates together, therefore, made only 91 days, or an exact quarter of a year; which space exhausts two of the 33 consulates, and leaves 31 entire consular years and a quarter.

The same result follows from the reckoning of the A.U.C. For the day of the nativity being eight months and four days after the Parilia, or anniversary of the building of the city, which was kept on 21st April, and the death happening 27 days before the Parilia, the years being A.U.C. 749 and 781, our Lord must have lived 32 years by that shewing, minus those fractional parts which together amount to nine months—making his age as before, 31 years and 3 months. It appears to us also, that the year in which John the Baptist began his ministry was either at the end of the consulate of *Lepidus and Taurus*, or in the first 9 or 10 months of that of *Germanicus and Capito*; for these answer to the fifteenth year of Tiberius from his final adoption by Augustus, as we shall shew. Our readers will find these names in the annexed lists of the Roman consuls of this period. This adoption of Tiberius has been the subject of much discussion, and the cause has probably been that there were several acts of adoption of a partial kind, to the last of which only the reckoning ought to belong. Of this the account is given by Dion Cassius in this way,—that in the consulship of *Marcus Æmilius* with *Statilius Taurus* (No. 55 of the annexed list), Tiberius, in company with Germanicus, made an invasion into Germany, but without encountering an enemy, and not advancing beyond the immediate precincts of the Rhine. There they remained till the autumn, and there they celebrated the birthday of Augustus on 23rd September, immediately after which they returned to Rome. In the next year Germanicus received the consulate, which he held all that year; and this was effected, as it appears, by a recommendation from Augustus to the senate; for Dion relates that Augustus commended Germanicus to the senate, who was not qualified to be elected consul, from not yet having served the office of prætor; and at the same time the emperor "*commended the senate to the favour of Tiberius.*" This was a form of adoption, afterwards used by the emperors towards their sons, and clearly indicating that act towards Tiberius.[d]

The only question that can be raised as to the exact year of the adoption is, whether these two acts were simultaneous, as is certainly to be inferred, by their connexion in the narrative; or whether possibly the recommendation of the senate to the protection of Tiberius might not have taken place after Germanicus was consul: for the other act, the recommendation of that prince to the senate, under which he was elected consul in spite of his disqualification, must certainly have preceded his election to that office, and so have happened in the same year as the two generals returned from Germany. Taking these dispositions to have been the final arrangement of Augustus, as to his family and the succession he proposed, we can hardly doubt, we think, that the events happened together, and that the same policy which made the senate receive Germanicus for their consul elect, obliged them also to bow the knee to Tiberius as their emperor. The earliest period, however, in which this adoption could have happened was the month of October in the consulate of *Lepidus and Taurus*, and the earliest date which would reckon as the fifteenth year from that accession would consequently be the month of October, in the consulate of *Agrippa and Lentulus*—3 years and 5 months before the 25th March in the consulate of the *Two Gemini*, under which our Lord suffered. Further back than that, before our Lord's death, the ministry of John the Baptist cannot possibly be dated. It might have begun any time within a year later from that date, up to which the 15th year

---

[d] Dion Cass. *H. R.*, lib. lvi., c. 26.

of Tiberius would have extended. If our Saviour were baptized, as was probably the case, about December of the consulate of *Gætulicus and Sabinus,* John's ministry might have begun 14 months before that event; but it might have begun only 2 months before our Lord's baptism, and still have been within the year assigned by St. Luke as the fifteenth of Tiberius. It is quite allowable, therefore, to conjecture that John's ministry may have lasted a year, as a proper introductory dispensation to the greater ministry that was to follow; but it is equally allowable to suppose that it might have preceded our Lord's entering upon his ministry only by 6 months, as his birth did that of our Saviour's. There is no clue to the solution of this question, and we must be content therefore to have fixed the possible limits within which the Baptist's mission might have commenced.

The disagreements of early Christian writers appear in a great measure to have proceeded from confounding the dates of the accession of Tiberius under his adoption, and his accession upon the death of Augustus; which last happened on the 19th August in the consulate of the *Two Sexti,* the third consulate from that of *Lepidus* and *Taurus,* and about 2 years and 9 months after the last adoption of Tiberius. These diversities of reckoning are very obvious: thus, when St. Luke says that John the Baptist began his ministry in the fifteenth year of the reign of Tiberius, he reckons, we know, from the year of his adoption under the consuls *Lepidus and Taurus;* but when Origen, St. Jerome, and Orosius say that Christ suffered in the fifteenth year of Tiberius, it is plain they reckon from the death of Augustus; and, in the case of Orosius, this is rendered the more certain by the additional statement that his death happened in the consulate of the two Gemini; for that consulate was clearly in the fifteenth year from that event. But Epiphanius makes the death of our Lord to be in the eighteenth year of Tiberius; where it is equally clear his reckoning began from the year of his adoption, to which that interval corresponds, though he has mis-named the consuls: while Eusebius makes the event to have happened in the nineteenth year of Tiberius, no doubt taking his computations from the same event, but inserting the consulates instead of the years themselves; for the consulates are 19 in number, but the period only to the eighteenth year. The same error may be traced in the statements of Clemens of Alexandria and Origen, when they state that there were 42 years and 3 months between our Lord's death and the destruction of Jerusalem; for that time added to the 31 years and 3 months of our Lord's age, as we have shewn it from the consular lists, would make that event fall at an interval of 73 years and 6 months from the date of the nativity. But if the mistake of 2 years and 9 months between the adoption of Tiberius and the death of Augustus have entered into this account, that will reduce the 42 years, 8 months, to 39 years, 6 months; and make the total years, 70 years, 9 months, as the date, A.D., of the fall of that city,—which is the true account. And that such was the case is evident, because Clemens counts only 15 years of Tiberius Cæsar in the life of our Lord. "The 15 years of Tiberius," he says, "and 15 of Augustus, make up the 30 years to the time that he suffered."[e] The number of years that are deficient is just that which lies between the adopted succession and the death of Augustus, and the source of the error cannot be mistaken: it is plain, that too little is counted of the years of the two emperors in our Lord's lifetime, and that the deficiency is made up by an excessive number of years after his hallowed death, to the events spoken of.

In proceeding to investigate anew the grounds of the different computations regarding the Christian epoch and its events, we must in the first place direct our readers' attention to the annexed tables of the Roman consulates of the period we have to treat of. Of these lists the first two are those of Dion Cassius and Cassiodorus, which are historical records, properly speaking, and of high authority. In particular, the authenticity of Dion Cassius is quite unimpeachable, who lived at the end of the second century, and being himself of consular rank, was able to refer to original sources of information and public records, which gives his statements a stamp of the highest authority. The third table is from the Fasti Siculi, called so from being found in that island, but better known as the *Chronicon Paschale*, by which title it is preserved in the Byzantine collection. This has the marks of an original provincial register, but corrupted by its keepers;—to which point we shall recur in a later page. These lists are numbered in the margin consecutively for convenience of reference, from the first year of the Reformed Calendar of Julius Cæsar, which is the fourth number from the head of the list; the three antecedent consulates being introduced for a reason, which will appear in the course of this discussion.

In entering upon this subject we will first advert to some circumstances connected with the dates assigned to the consulates: and on this point we may observe that the consular date of the first year of Cæsar's Reformed Calendar was certainly A.U.C. 708: that was the date on the 1st January of that year, and so continued to the Parilia, or anniversary on the

---

e Strom., lib. i., 130.

succeeding 21st April. The year of confusion, or that which preceded the first of the new calendar, bore the consular date A.U.C. 707 ; but the triumphs of the latter part of that year are dated also A.U.C. 708, as is shewn by the memorial of them in the Fasti Capitolini, to which we will presently refer. That, therefore, should be the consular date of the first Julian year— No 1 of the annexed list;—but by writers in general that year is taken for the year A.U.C. 709 ; and it appears to us, that much confusion has arisen from a want of due observance on this point. Perhaps it may have been the case, that after the reformation, the A.U.C. was not confined to the consular date, but applied to the events, as they actually occurred before or after the Parilia ; and such was probably the case with the memorials of the Battle of Actium, which is uniformly ascribed to the A.U.C. 722, but which, being fought after the Parilia of that year, may bear that date, not as of the consular year, but by reference to the time the event happened.   We find a different reckoning of the year which succeeded the death of Tiberius, since that is stamped with the date of A.U.C. 789—the consulate being No. 82 of the Julian years ; and so only concurring with the date of the first Julian year, by making that year to be A.U.C. 708 ;—for there are 81 consulates between that year and the one spoken of, which, added to 708, gives the year 789.   So again, we are told that the Emperor Philip celebrated the 1000th year of the city in the 292nd year of the Julian reckoning ; by which the first year of that reckoning is again shewn to be of the A.U.C. 708.   But the death of Herod is held by several authors to have happened in the consulate of *Lentulus and Messala*, and yet on the eve of a pass-over which fell in the A.U.C. 750 ; which, as that consulate stands 42nd of the Julian years, can only agree with the first year of that series by making that first year to be A.U.C. 709 from its beginning.   This is Archbishop Usher's version, and it is plainly an error ; because the latest date assigned to the passover of that year is the 12th April, according to the computations of Petavius ; and so, being within the Parilia, it should be counted A.U.C. 749.   The date of that event was no doubt A.U.C. 749, being the same year of the A.U.C., as is assigned to the event of our Saviour's birth in the preceding consulate ; for that birth occurred at the end of the year and after the Parilia, and was, in that way, of that date.

There is much confusion upon this subject, which seems to have grown out of the Cæsarian reformation, and probably formed a subject on which mankind were divided for many years, and chronologers still may be so.   It seems to ourselves, as if the numbering of the consular year had been changed in that refor-

mation from the Parilia which had preceded the consular accession
to office to the one that succeeded it; making the date of the
year proleptical, between the January of the accession and the
anniversary of the city in April. It is certain that the reform-
ing year, which comprehended 81 intercalated days, or 3 additional months as Suetonius reckons it, must have carried on
the reckoning of the A.U.C. within a month of two full years from
the last anniversary, if the consular date of that year were continued through the whole of the new intercalations; for the
consular reckoning of that year of confusion, as we have said,
was A.U.C. 707 by reference to a Parilia of the antecedent year;
and when the natural year of 365 days had expired, that yearly
reckoning would exist by reference to an anniversary, a year and
8 months gone by; and then the additional 3 months which were
intercalated would make the same anniversary extend its counting up to a year and 11 months. It seems probable, therefore,
that the year may have been altered,—the year of confusion ab-
sorbing in it the A.U.C. 708,—and the consular year of the new
calendar been dated prospectively, as of the A.U.C. 709, though
the old reckoning would be still preserved by some writers. The
discrepant year, which so often occurs in the succeeding accounts
to this period, can only, we think, find a true explanation in
this way, and it appears to us it is a very sufficient one.

A further proof of this, perhaps, is found in the Olympic
year assigned to this first of Cæsar's reformation by the Chronicon Paschale, which year we shall see is the fourth of the
182nd Olympiad; for that registry, being immediately at the time
that Cæsar was correcting the dates generally, may, we think,
be trusted as correct; but the subject is rather a difficult one,
and we must go into it a little analytically.

Let us suppose then that Rome was built upon a supposititious
Parilia, or 21st April, next before the first celebration of the
Olympic Games; which would have happened in the ensuing
June, the period of their celebration. Then we may ask, could
the foundation of the city have been reckoned of that year (consular year from 1st January to 1st January) in which the Olympic epoch arose? The answer appears to be, No! Because if the
building of the city had taken place on 21st April of the succeeding consular year, it would still be within the first Olympic year;
and if the former April could be reckoned as in the first Olympic
year, there would be two Aprils able to be reckoned in that year.
It seems clear then, that the A.U.C. must have been associated
from the beginning with the Olympic reckoning by reference to
the games of the preceding year; while the consular year itself
would count with the Olympic epoch, or as one year older.

This may appear more plain in the table annexed :—

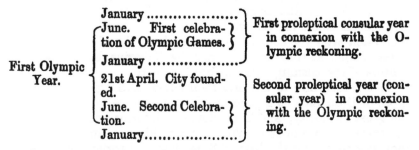

The foundation of the city, although within the first year of the Olympic reckoning, yet is in the second consular year from the Olympic epoch, and so in the second consular year of the Olympic series; and the city being founded in the 23rd Olympic year, that will be in the 24th consular year of the epoch. We must add 24 years, therefore, to the A.U.C. 708 to get the corresponding Olympic year of that A.U.C., which will make the number 332 years; and that, divided by 4, will make the Olympic year of that A.U.C. to be the 4th of the 182nd Olympiad; which is what is ascribed by the Chronicon Paschale to the first year of Cæsar's reformed calendar; and which we have shewn from other sources, is the date that year ought to bear.

The certainty as to these years is fixed also by the registry we have already referred to, of the Capitoline marbles. The two Triumphs there recorded were celebrated in the same year, in which Cæsar returned from Spain and named C. Caninius as consul in the room of F. Maximus (one of the triumphing generals), who expired suddenly on the last day of the year; and in whose place Caninius presided for about 6 hours only of that last day; and that year was certainly the year before Cæsar's death. The entries of these dates are very important, and we copy this of the Triumph as it is recorded, and still may be viewed on the walls of the modern Capitol in Rome. To this we subjoin the other inscription we have before referred to.

C. IVLIVS. C.F.C.N. — CAESAR IIII SINE CONLEGA
EODEM ANNO
Q. FABIVS. Q.F.Q.N. MAXIMVS
MORTVVS EST. IN EIVS LOCVM
C. CANINIVS. C.F.C.N.

Q. FABIVS Q.F.Q.N. MAXIMVS. COS. EX HISPANIA AN. DCCVIII.
III IDUS. OCT :

Q. PEDIVS. M.F. PRO. COS. EX HISPANIA. AN. DCCVIII. IDIB. DEC.

The other Inscription is preserved by Frontinus, and is as follows,—"M. Aquillio Juliano, P. Nonio Asprenate: Coss: anno Urbis Conditæ DCCLXXXVIIII."[f] The succession of these last consuls closes the list we have subjoined, and their period of succession after the consular year, in which Tiberius died, is unquestionable, as they were named by Tiberius himself as the consuls of the ensuing year, before his death.

We return now to the lists themselves, and repeat that upon those of Dion Cassius a general reliance may be placed. He is the great authority, and Cassiodorus, Victorius and others shew the great reliance of later writers upon his accounts, so far as they extended; for the lists of those later historians are essentially the same as his, and it is with the loss of his authority, that all the future accounts of the consular successions become confused and uncertain; for his lists cease soon after the period of our Lord's death.

The *Chronicon Paschale*, however, is certainly the most valuable of these records, since it associates its lists with the Olympic reckoning, and preserves an original register also of the first "*Imperial Indictions.*" Its corruptions, it is true, give it a questionable appearance, but as these can be corrected by the help of the more authentic lists which are ranged in collateral order with it, they are of little consequence; and the causes being disclosed of its interpolations, we shall find ground for concluding that these alterations were made by the keepers of the Chronicon in later times, solely as we may conjecture, to meet the anomalies of a new chronology, which had authority on its side and threatened to destroy the *Indictions*, by which alone a landmark could in future be found for the epochs of the Christian age.

The process of a new compilation of this list was evidently effected in a place and age remote from classical sources, and from the apprehension of any immediate comparison with more authentic records. The interpolated names are not difficult to detect, and they all are found between the 1st year of Cæsar's reformed calendar, and the 41st number of the lists, which is the consulate to which the year of the nativity is ascribed. The marks of ignorance in the transcribers are more generally diffused, —such misnomers as Varius for Varus, Crassus for Flaccus, Brutus for Drusus, and Scipio for Capito, shew very distinctly the uninformed conditions of its keepers. But the intrusive consulates are as follow, and consist of four numbers:—

1st. The consulate of *Octavianus and Cicero*, between the

---

f Frontinus, *De Aquæduct.*, art. 13.

11th and 12th numbers of the list, to which we beg the reader to refer. The true consuls of this year are placed by this Chronicon in the next year, which is the 12th of that list; while the consuls of that year, who are *Œnobarbus and Sosius*, are transposed to a place 3 years lower, being found between the 15th and 16th numbers, where they are entire supernumeraries. The names of Octavianus and Cicero refer clearly to a supplementary consulship, in which Augustus did honour to the son of his former friend, in that year when himself and Crassus were consuls, marked No. 75 in the list, and the year after the battle of Actium. This consulate, therefore, of *Octavianus and Cicero* must be wholly expunged, and those of *Augustus and Corvilius* and *Œnobarbus and Sosius* be transposed,—the former to No. 12, and the latter to No. 13 of the list.

2nd and 3rd. Between the 24th and 25th numbers we find the names of *Celsus and Tiberius*, which also are clearly spurious; and between the numbers 33 and 34, those of *Rubellius and Saturninus*, also spurious; for these two consulates are the mere names of substituted consuls of the next antecedent years, whose names are found so registered in the Chronicon of Idatius—a Spanish list of good authority, of the beginning of the 5th century; in its later years keeping an order very nearly the same as the Sicilian Chronicon, and differing as that does from the historical lists of Cassiodorus and the later writers. Of these provincial records, it may be confessed that they appear to be the best authorities as to those later periods.

4th. Again, between the numbers 27 and 28 are found the names of *Lentulus and Cornelius*, which is a mere repetition of the preceding consulate of Cornelius Lentulus and Publius Lentulus.

These four consulates are not noticed by Dion Cassius, and are introduced plainly for an object of some kind; for which we shall endeavour to find an explanation. But there is, moreover, between the consulship of *Sabinus and Rufinus*, the presumed year of the nativity, and that of the *Two Gemini*, the presumed year of the crucifixion, one consulate omitted in the Chronicon Paschale; and one excessive in that interval also, so that the number is equal in the whole to that of the two historical lists. Of these the omitted consulate is that of *Lentulus and Messala*—No. 42 of the list, being the reputed year of the death of Herod; and the supernumerary one that of *Pompeius Magnus and Apuleius*, between the 58th and 59th numbers, and plainly spurious.

But notwithstanding these obvious corruptions, in respect of which this list differs from the historical, we conceive the Chroni-

con Paschale to be, as we have said, by far the most valuable
chronological record, that the casualties of 1800 years have left
to our hands.   The cycle of the indictions, which are retained
in connexion with the Olympic reckoning and the other historical data, gives a peculiar value to it, which no unclassified
register can possibly possess, however high and elevated the
conditions to which the names are attached.   The broad and plain
marks, afforded by those numbers which move in sequences of
15 years, impress so prominent a mark upon the course of years,
as must be sufficient with proper research to correct any errors,
and elucidate the doubts of all succeeding periods; if dependence
can be at all placed upon the indictive numbers at the epochal
points.   Like the seams of a rumpled garment of fine gauze,
these broad marks must always afford a means of discovering
the true dimensions and form of the whole texture, and of re-
adjusting a proper disposition of its parts.   As regards the Indictions in this *Chronicon*, therefore, it remains only to find some
grounds for assurance, that those of the Nativity and Crucifixion
have not been altered; and this we think the circumstances enable
us to do.

To ourselves then, Now as to the Indictions themselves, the Chronicon Paschale,
under the title *Beginning of Indictions* informs us, "that they
first began to be used in the first year of Caius Julius Cæsar,
in the consulate of Lepidus and Plaucus,—No. 3 of the list,—and
from the month of September."   And although we may conclude
with certainty that this is a mistaken statement, since the consulate of Lepidus and Plaucus was not the first year of Julius
Cæsar, but two years after his death; yet it seems equally clear
that the mistake can only have been a misapplication by the
Chronicon or its compiler of the consulate of *Lepidus and
Plaucus*, for that of *Lepidus and Cæsar*, four years earlier.
And this mistake is sufficient to account at once for the insertion
of the four spurious consulates, under any circumstances wherein
the enumeration of the indictive numbers became of importance.

To ourselves then, it appears very certainly, that those four
spurious names were inserted, with a view to keep these landmarks of the true times intact by the emendatory spirit of the
declining years of the Empire: which under a notion that the
beginning of those cycles was in the consulate of Lepidus and
Plaucus, might reasonably enough require the succession of the
years to be amended, and the indictions altered.   For if that
commencement were true, the indiction of our Lord's birth,
which is now found to be 13, would properly have been 9.   To
meet the present danger of such a disturbance of the true indiction, the Christian keepers of the Chronicon introduced the four

spurious names, which made the number of consulates between that of *" Lepidus and Plaucus "* and *" the Nativity "* of such an amount as preserved the epochal indiction intact; for the corrupted list, by the addition of those names, is made to contain the same number between the consulate of *Lepidus and Plaucus* and the year of the Nativity, as are found between that event and the true commencing year of the Indictions, or consulate of *Lepidus and Cæsar.* There is sufficient complexity in the exact epochs of the Cæsarian power, to make such an error probable; and if we take it into account, that a strong opinion might have prevailed, as to the origin of that cycle, or that an existing authority or prevailing theory of the historical schools insisted upon its being so received, that the consulate of Lepidus and Plaucus should be held as the true commencing year of the indictions; we can hardly conceive anything more judiciously contrived to save the Christian *"Mark"* intact by such an error, than the plan adopted. We shall observe that the five consulates, preceding that of Lepidus and Plaucus, are also numbered; but of that enumeration there is no account. We may notice however, that the period comprehends the 5 years of that continuous Consulate which was conferred by the senate on Cæsar after the Battle of Pharsalia, in conjunction with the dictatorship which in event became perpetual : and we may conclude perhaps, that those numbers denote that Consulate. And if true indictive numbers were there, the compilers of the Chronicon may have made that alteration, which should make them appear as the enumerations of those 5 consular years, which terminated with the first triumvirate after the Battle of Mutina. That was truly the beginning of the Augustan power, and from that probably arose the error in the Chronicon that it was from the origin of Julius Cæsar's power that the indictions were dated. And, is it not possible, that that enumeration may have been made by the authority of Augustus himself, as a stroke of policy; which, by keeping alive the record of that 5 years permanent consulship of his uncle, would make the accession of the triumviral power appear as a legitimate succession to that original grant by the senate; and so prevent any appearance of a return of the State to its old Constitution, even for a single day.

Of this one thing we may be quite assured, that the interpolations of the four consulships in this particular interval, and of a period when the consular Fasti were preserved with care and certainty, could not have happened without some very strong biasing cause: and we think, that that cause cannot be attributed to any fact so probable as the stress, arising from a traditional reverence by the early churches for all matters relat-

ing to the events of our Lord's history : of which the memorial
of the indictive numbers must have formed a part. For it is not
to be forgotten, that in whatever way we count the lists, they
yield the same indictions of 13 and 15 to the two important
epochs of the birth and death of our divine Lord. The very
obviousness of the interpolations also seems to imply that their
fabricators made them to answer a temporary object only, in a
time of barbarism ; and to be such as might be easily got rid of
in a more enlightened age. The introduction of the supplementary consulships, as independent annual consulates, we think
fully supports this observation.

Of the correctness of the historical lists at this date, numerically, we think there is also abundant proof in the events of the life
of Augustus, the dates of which are perfectly well authenticated,
—For the death of that emperor, it is well known, happened in
the consulship of the " *Two Sexti*," No. 58 of the list ;—that he
was, at his death, in his 76th year, and of his reign from the
Battle of Actium, in the 44th consular year ; but wanting one
month of 43 full years. He was also, as Velleius relates, 19
years and six months old at the Battle of Mutina, in which the
two consuls, '*Hirtius*' and '*Pansa*' (No. 22 of the list,) both
fell ; who succeeded to the consulship the year after Cæsar's
death :—and Augustus completed his 20th year, a month before
he took his first consulship (his birthday being on the 22nd
September), in the same year.[g]　Now all these particulars agree
perfectly well with the lists of Dion Cassius and Cassiodorus,
but not at all with that of the Chronicon Paschale ;—as may be
ascertained by simply counting back the years from the consulship of the " *Two Sexti*," in which Augustus died, to the several
assigned periods. For the Battle of Actium was fought in the
consulship of '*Augustus and Messala ;*' the 14th on the list ;
which is the 44th year back from that of the " *Two Sexti :*" and
the consulship of '*Hirtius and Pansa*' (No. 2 of the list) ; which
was the year Augustus was 19 years old, is 56 years before that
of the " *Two Sexti*," and deducted from the 75 full years of
Augustus' age, gives the required 19. Of course the additional
four spurious consulates, which lie between these epochs of the
emperor's life in the Chronicon Paschale, will entirely destroy
these coincidences. There can be no doubt, then, as to the
numerical correctness of the two historical lists ; nor equally of
the corrupt and interpolated state of the Chronicon Paschale,
to the extent we have pointed out.

The same conclusion, however, is arrived at by referring to

---

[g] Vel. Pat. *H. R.*, lib. 2, c. 65.

the events of Herod's history, to which we will now refer. For Josephus relates that Antigonus, the last of the Asmonean kings, was declared an enemy to Rome by the senate, and a decree passed to make Herod king in his room, *on the* 184*th Olympiad when " Caius Domitius Calvinus"* was consul the second time, and *" Caius Asinius Pollio"* was his colleague.[h] We shall find this consulate numbered ' 5 ' in the annexed list; and the Olympiad is truly stated by Josephus, who speaks of the season of the Olympic Games, that the event happened at the Olympiad itself; for the Olympic year of the consulate was the 4th of the 183rd Olympiad, as the list gives it.   From that year to the death of Herod, Josephus again informs us, there was an interval of 37 years. He died, says the historian of the Jews, the fifth day after he had put his son Antipater to death, having reigned since he was declared king by the Romans 37 years :[i] referring to the aforesaid consulate of ' *Calvinus and Pollio.*' From that date, 37 consulates will take us to No. 42 of the list; being the Consulship of ' *Lentulus and Messala,*' and that which next follows the consulship of " *Sabinus and Rufinus,*" under which the birth of our Lord is held to have taken place. We must here observe, that the length of Herod's reign was a matter of so public a kind, and the affairs of Judæa had been so intimately associated with the fortunes and families of the Cæsars from their very commencement, that it is quite impossible there could have been any misinformation on the part of Josephus, on that subject. This then is also in accordance with the historical lists, but the Chronicon Paschale makes the 37 years allotted to Herod's reign terminate 4 years earlier. For there are 37 years between the consulates of *Calvinus and Pollio,* and that of *Nero and Piso* (No. 38 of the list); and if Herod survived the year of the Nativity two or three years, as Dr. Macknight holds, that would make the Nativity date back as far as the consulate of *Drusus and Crispinus* (No. 36 of the list), which is 9 years earlier than the chronologers of the time of Censorinus assigned to that event. The effect of the four interpolated consulates would be also to make the death of Herod happen in the 23rd year before the death of Augustus, from which to the date of what is called the 15th of Tiberius there will be 12 years; so that that computation would bring the preaching of John the Baptist to at least the 35th year of our Saviour's age. For the death of Herod must have been 24 years before that year by this shewing, and our Saviour's birth preceded that event, Dr. Macknight says, by two years. The impossibility of these intervals is so obvious, that

---

[h] *Antiq.* b. 14, c. 14, § 5.   [i] *Ib.* b. 17, c. 8, § 3.

we think our readers will be satisfied with the statement of them, without our commenting further upon the subject.

But the death of Herod is signalized also by an eclipse of the moon, which, by Josephus, happened shortly before his death, and which is computed by Petavius to have occurred about 3 o'clock in the morning of the 13th March A.I.P. 4710; just a month before the Passover of that year in which Herod died. But what is extraordinary is, that within that month Herod had died and been buried, Archelaus been proclaimed king, and a great sedition which had arisen after his succession been allayed by that king. In the same month, Herod visited the baths of Callirhoe for a course of medical bathing, and did several acts of government and settled matters relating to his succession, which must ordinarily have occupied much time. And as all this seems impossible, the commentator on Josephus, in order to obviate the difficulty, informs us in a note that the Passover, in which the sedition took place under Archelaus, was 13 months after the eclipse spoken of, and not one month as is supposed. But that explanation seems open to as much objection as the other; for it can only be true, on the supposition that Archelaus suffered 13 months to elapse before he set forward on his journey to Rome, to solicit the government of his father's kingdom from Augustus—which cannot be credited. Moreover, as Archelaus met the envoy of Augustus, who was dispatched from Rome upon the news of Herod's death to secure his effects, at Cæsarea, immediately after the same Passover; the mission of the envoy must also have stood over for above a year, if the notice of Mr. Whiston is true.[j] The course of history therefore shews that this eclipse could not have happened within a month of either of the assigned Passovers, if Herod's death happened before the same festival: it could not have occurred within so short a time before, as a month, or so long a time after as 13 months, of any Passover, which marked the period of his death. But Josephus connects this account of the eclipse with a story respecting the disqualification of the high priest on a solemn fast day, and the appointment of another priest to fill the office for that single day; and this event is particularly related by the Jewish commentaries of the Mishna and Talmud, as Dr. Hudson informs us, to have happened on the great day of expiation.[k] An eclipse then in the month of March could hardly answer the description of that one, which Josephus refers to. But the fact of there being one in March, as Petavius affirms was the case, is very good ground for believing that there might have been one also in the September previous; for the planets would have been in the same opposition. We find a similar case in the year A.D. 1848, where an eclipse of the moon on the 5th of March, was followed by an eclipse of the same body on the 13th of September following :—and taking Petavius' calculation to be correct, an eclipse on the 13th of March might very well be the concomitant of an eclipse on the 10th of September antecedent: *and that was the day of expiation,* in which the concomitant event to the eclipse mentioned by Josephus, took place. This being six months before the Passover of Herod's death, would afford a reasonable time for all the events which are mentioned, and it makes the history consistent.

The period of Herod's death, is one of the great battle-fields of Christian chronologers, and has occasioned discussions corresponding to its importance. " Some are of opinion, that he died a little before the Passover A.U.C. 750, in the Julian year 42, and before the vulgar æra 4—others fix his death to 25th November following : others place it a little before the Passover A.U.C. 751. Dr. Lardner refers to these three opinions, and concludes from Josephus and Dio, that he did not die before the year 759 nor after the year 751, and that his death happened a short time before the Jewish Passover of one of those years."[l] All agree that the year A.U.C. 750, and the 42nd Julian year, designate the consulate of *Lentulus and Messala* (No. 42 of the list), and that that answers to the year A.I.P. 4710. And Dr. Lardner concludes his argument by alleging, "that, it follows, if Herod died in 750, he died 3 years and 9 months before the vulgar æra, which commences January, A.U.C. 754."[m] This A.U.C. 754 answers to the consulate of *Varus and Vinicius* (No. 46 of the list) ; and is the year to which the chronologists generally assign the error of the Christian counting : for the year of the Nativity being taken as that which precedes the year of Herod's death, —No. 41 in the list,—the interval between the years will be four consulships, and this, one would think, should answer the hypothesis of those who place the Nativity at an earlier period.

This present year A.D. 1856 answers to the A.I.P. 6569, and, being deducted from that number, leaves a residue of 4713 : but the year before Herod's death would be 4709 ;—wherefore there are 4 years short of a full number in the Christian years, to reach the true A.D. :—for 1860 years deducted from 6569, would leave the proper residue 4709.

But this determination of the A.I.P is an arbitrary adjustment

---

[l] Macknight, *Chron. Dissert.*, 2—vol. i., pp. 87 and 90.   [m] *Ibid.*

and determines nothing of a necessary truth. The interval assigned
may be too great, and the Christian enumeration the true one.
Before we proceed therefore with an examination of the later
fasti of the imperial consulates, as we propose doing, it will be
advisable to say a few words upon the nature of the *Julian period*,
by which the epochs of our chronology are now commonly
referred to.   For an authority is sometimes attached to that
reckoning which does not belong to it; since that mystical period
is, in effect, no more than a common guage or dividing ruler,
upon which the events of history are marked and so arranged by
one common measure.   To such a ruler, it is evident the marks
must have been adjusted by reference to the opinions of those
who applied them: and if the opinions of Dionysius and his
Saxon amplifier Bede, from whose computations the present
reckoning was drawn, erred from any cause in assigning a true
interval between their own times and the Nativity of our
Lord, the adaptation of the measuring rule to the wrong interval
by Scaliger would not correct that error; though it may have
done much to perpetuate any that had existence.

Now, that the old computations were extremely defective,
before and up to the time of Dionysius, cannot be questioned;
for the channels through which the public reckoning was derived
were of a kind, on which no dependance ought to be placed.
The foundation of the whole of those computations rests, in
truth, upon the fag-end of an Alexandrian calendar of the fifth
and sixth centuries.   This was the calendar of Cyril of Alexandria, who calculated a paschal cycle of 95 years, from the reputed
year 436; which terminated consequently A.D. 531.   But in
what way Cyril got his data for associating the A.D. of his cycle
with the imperial reckoning we are quite ignorant; and it is quite
possible therefore that he thought the Christian reckoning of his
age to be the true one, though somewhat opposed to the imperial
computation: for we shall shew presently that the reckonings of
the profane and Christian chronology were quite at variance 150
years before his time and could not be depended upon.

This calendar of Cyril's however, was continued by Dionysius
Exiguus for another five of the metonic cycles of nineteen years;
extending it therefore to the year A.D. 626.   But Dionysius differed from his predecessor in this; that instead of dating his
years from what was called the year of the Martyrs, corresponding with the received A.D. 284, and having its anniversary on
29th August, he adopted the more Christian epoch of our Lord's
conception; taking the initial point from the annunciation, or
25th March in the 531st year; which was the year preceding
the first of his own calendar.

This method of computing the years was partially adopted in the century when Dionysius wrote, but it was not till the English Bede adopted the cycle, and enlarged it, two centuries later, that the date A.D. was generally adopted in Europe; and it is one of the distinctive features of the Carlovingian kings to have given that honourable pre-eminence to the Christian year, which it now generally holds. If H. I. Majesty of the new Regime of Frankish power would please to distinguish his reign in a similar manner, the way is before him by correcting the public misapprehension on this subject. For if we are not mistaken, the fault is in the consular lists, by which the Roman historians reckoned their time; which, by interpolations in their registers, have extended the period from their consulate of Sabinus and Rufinus, 4 years beyond its true measure; and if we prove this, it would be worthy of a new dynasty, which is in future to move the destinies of the Christian world, to correct the long fostered error of the Julian reckoning, by making the A.I.P. 6569 of the present year, to be reduced to its proper number of years, which is clearly A.I.P. 6565. If with this could be established a cycle of indictions corresponding to the periods of the lunar nodes, we think a calendar would be made of such a kind, as no future times could touch with uncertainty. It is said, that in an interval of 557 years, 21 days, 18 hours, 12 minutes, the conjunction and opposition of the moon coincides so nearly with the node, as not to be distant more than 11 seconds. In that period every eclipse returns to its former place, and their succession follows in the same order after that period;[a] surely therefore it could not be difficult, if that is true, to have a correct cycle without such possible mistakings as happened a few years ago, when the falling of the Easter Festival was publicly miscalculated. Upon the cycle of Dionysius, however, and the computations of the venerable Bede, the Julian year was established, and the epochs of history arranged upon their assumed "*Pegs*" by Scaliger, who was its projector. But if the Alexandrine Chronicles of the 5th century were under any mistake upon the relation of the Christian epoch to the imperial reckoning, it is certain the cycle of Cyril would not have corrected that error, and it must be found in the descendant chronological fixtures.

The old church calendars, in effect, afford no reliable aid to the chronological question in themselves; yet their traditional testimony is extremely valuable. For as they were made after the Church was associated with the Imperial Government, and when they were, of course, subject to the Imperial reckoning,

---

[a] Cavallo's *Philosophy*, vol. iv., p. 261.

and to the public opinions on the subject of their epochal adjustments, their yet maintaining their own reckoning and submitting to the imputation of the historical chronologers, that their counting was wrong, proves only that they suffered a wrong with patience which they were not able to rectify; and the wrong has been unhappily made permanent by the later chronologers. We think this is shewn by the authority, both of the Chronicon Paschale and Athanasius, who date the Christian years rightly, but have coupled them with indictions that belong to the Roman reckoning. Thus the Chronicon couples the year A.D. 238 with an indiction of 14, which, under a continuous reckoning from 13 in the consulship of *Sabinus and Rufinus*, the year of the nativity, as the emendators require it to be, ought to have an indiction of 10; the 4 years are too much, but they follow the number of the consulates. So Athanasius cites the indiction of the year A.D. 341, as also 14;[o] whereas by the same process of continuance from the indiction of the Christian epoch, the indiction of that year should be 9. There are 5 excessive in that indiction, and they indicate that excess in the Imperial reckoning.

So the question was fairly kept at issue by these authorities. The Christian and profane dates could not both be right, and the indictions follow the order of the consular lists. What was the cause of error is nowhere canvassed, but if it had been admitted by the subordinate party in the State that the error was with them, can it be conceived that such a mistake would not have been corrected? Neither the authority of the emperors, who at that period were putting the Church upon its permanent foundation as an associate of the state, nor the principle of Christian truth in the public assemblies of the Church, would have suffered such an anomaly to exist for a moment. Its continuance, under such circumstances, appears a conclusive proof that the question was held not to be truly on the side of the state authority, and it is still open to correction. We are still at liberty to search into the matter, and say that the error imputed to the Christian chronology belongs in fact to the Imperial, and may be corrected; and that the Christian year is rightly held by the Christian Churches.

In entering upon a new investigation of this subject by a scrutiny of the consular lists, we will take the statement of Censorinus the grammarian as the thesis of our commentary. The treatise of this author, *De Die Natali*, was written in the first year of the Emperor Gordian, and the 238th of the com-

---

[o] Athan. *De Synodis*, 25, Ed. Bened. vol. i., pt. 2, p. 737.

puted years of the Christian age; and in that, he fixes the year of his writing in the following way.—" If I am not mistaken, this year which is marked by being the consulate of *Ulpius and Pontianus* (in which consulate the accession of the Emperor Gordian occurred), is the 1014th from the first Olympiad, the 991st year from the building of the city; and of those years which are called Julian, the 283rd, reckoning from the first January, which Julius Cæsar constituted."[p] A similar testimony to the date of this same period is afforded by Zosimus, who states that the Emperor Philip, the successor of Gordian, celebrated the 1000th year of Rome in the 5th of his reign. For the Emperor Gordian reigned only 5 years, and Philip succeeded him; in whose 5th year the civic commemoration occurred; being an interval of 9 full years from the date of Censorinus' book, and added to the A.U.C. of that statement, bringing in the 1000th anniversary. This celebration by Philip is therefore reckoned by the Christian writers as of the year A.D. 247; and they shew specifically the computation of that age, long before the computation of Cyril of Alexandria, which we have seen was made so late as A.D. 436.

These different civic computations of Censorinus preserve their proper relations, as they appear in the Chronicon Paschale; making the foundation of Rome appear of the 23rd Olympic year. But we must repeat that such agreement in the associated dates of the consular reckoning does not prove the consular reckoning to be correct; or that the consulate of *Ulpius and Pontianus* was, in effect, in the 991st year of the city, or the 1014th of the Olympic reckoning :—for if the consular lists were interpolated, they might yield more years than there ever had passed in reality. A deficiency in the Christian years, or an excess in the consular years at that date is, one or the other, quite certain; for deducting the 238th Christian year, or the number 237, from the Julian 283, the remainder 46 would shew the Julian year of the Christian epoch; that is, it would refer back to No. 46, of the annexed list, being the year assigned to the common error on this subject, as we have before seen; 4 years later than the true epoch. But is that error with the Christian or the Imperial chronologers? Now, for examining the question as to the consulates of the Imperial reckoning, we have three lists before us, though our space here does not permit our introducing them, and our readers must trust us for a true exposition of them. That of Victorius, an author, who wrote about the year A.D. 460, or about 50 years sooner than Cassiodorus, and who

---

was engaged under the pontificate of Leo the Great in reconciling the Paschal computation of the eastern and western
churches. But his consular lists were evidently drawn from
common sources, and are vehemently corrupted, from which his
successor Cassiodorus has purged them a little. Besides this,
we have our former list from the latter writer, and the Chronicon
Paschale.

In all these we find the consulate of *Ulpius and Pontianus*,
referred to by Censorinus, as falling in with the Christian year
238 of the common computation. As to the lists themselves,
we may affirm at once that they are utterly worthless as chronological guides, for they all differ in the order and number of
their consulates :—they all shew, for instance, a different interval
between the 2nd consulate of the Emperor Titus, (which we
select for a reason that will appear shortly) and this year of
Ulpius and Pontianus; and that difference is so great, that,
between the reckoning of Victorius and the Chronicon Paschale,
it amounts to no less a number than seven consulates. Upon
the simple question of a reliance upon these registers, or upon
the Christian traditions one would think, under such a display,
there ought not to be a moment's hesitation. For, if we take
into consideration what extraordinary methods were used by
the early churches to preserve every circumstance relating to
our Lord's history, which Mr. Addison has so fully and ably
expatiated upon, their reckoning may fairly be taken, in a
general estimate of its authenticity, to outweigh vastly that of
the Imperial archives ; scattered as these were by the desolations
that overtook the empire, and the removal of its seat of government at different periods. And on the other hand, if we look
into the nature of the Roman annals, we shall find no one
element which gives any security as a system, for a correct con-
servancy of their years. The reckoning of the A.U.C. had no
other method in it, but by a recurrence to the consular successions, which answered the purpose under the Republic, and so
long as the Fasti Capitolini were exposed in the Comitium, and
the registration was openly preserved in the sight of the citizens,
and yearly inscribed on its marble tables. But when that failed,
the historical records were at the mercy of every theoretic wind
that wandered through the empire, and the lists of consuls do
consequently differ in almost as many ways, as there are copies
of them in different authors.

Neither were the Olympic registrations a whit more conservative as a system of record, for they were altered to suit systems
wherever it was found necessary ; as may be seen by the adjustment of them in the list we have annexed, in those years where

the interpolated consulships occur. It seems extremely probable indeed, that much of the discrepancy which is found in the different writers of the empire, may have proceeded from misapprehensions on the true method of referring to the Olympic epoch; for diversities of opinion undoubtedly prevailed on that point; whether the years were dated from the year when the games were instituted, or the last year of the complete cycle, which was 4 years later, or the fourth celebration of the games, which was 3 years later. And this diversity of opinion was capable of leading to a duplication of the error;—for it would happen that the keeper of a register, who was zealous for the earlier and true epoch, might, under a belief that his register was defective by having its computation from the later date, when the fact was otherwise, correct his tables into a redundancy of 4 years or 3 years, according to the error he supposed to exist, in order to cure a suppositious deficiency; and so make the epoch 3 or 4 years too soon. While other emendators, taking the opposite line of correction, might set the reckoning 3 or for 4 years too late; and as the diversities of reckoning are found to reach the extent of those differences, we hold that such must undoubtedly have been the source of the error out of which they arose.

In the lists we have to refer to, this difference is plainly traceable to the full extent of that double error. In the Chronicon Paschale there are 164 consulates, back from the year of *Ulpius and Pontianus*, to the 2nd consulate of Titus; while in the list of Victorius there are 171 consulates in that interval. Cassiodorus differs, by making the number 170, or one less than Victorius. Taking the year of Ulpius and Pontianus to be the Christian year A.D. 238, these lists will, by the reckoning of the Chronicon Paschale, make the 2nd consulate of Titus in the 74th of our Lord; while the calculation of Victorius will make it fall in the 67th. But the 2nd consulate of Titus is known, by an infallible mark, to have been in the 71st year of our Lord; the year he triumphed after the taking of Jerusalem. The errors of these lists in this interval are, therefore, that there are 3 consulships omitted in that of the Chronicon Paschale,-and 4 too many inserted in that of Victorius, and 3 in that of Cassiodorus.

An examination of these lists by the light of history, discloses mistakes which satisfy these conclusions :—

Thus in the Chronicon Paschale, we detect the omission of the consulate of *Commodus and Rufus*, fifth from Titus' second consulship, well recognized in history, and found in the other lists. The consulate is also commemorated in an inscription preserved by Muratori.

In the reign of Commodus we find two other authentic consulships omitted. The first called the *Two Silani*, placed between the consulates of *Fuscianus and Silanus* on the one side, and *Commodus and Fuscianus* on the other; between which years, another elapsed, wherein the infamous minister of the emperor— (Cleander)—is said to have created 25 consuls, and himself was put to death by a tumultuous conspiracy of the people against him. The second is the consulship of *Apronianus and Bradua*, between the sixth and seventh consulates of *Commodus* himself, in the last year but one of his reign, and the year in which the Temple of Peace was burnt down.

Thus there are three authentic consulships plainly deficient in this list of the Chronicon Paschale, and augment that list to the number required between the year of Censorinus and the second consulate of Titus.

A similar investigation of the other lists will enable us, under the same light, to find the excess they manifest, beyond the true number of consulates in the same interval; that is to say, an excess of 4 in the list of Victorius, and of 3 in that of Cassiodorus.

Thus, then, in the reign of Nerva, we find the names of *Sabinus and Antoninus* in both these lists; for which there is no authority historically, and which are not contained in any other list of consuls. The course of registration at this period is so irregular in the different lists, that it may save a great deal of argument on the subject, to present our readers with an extract from the three lists of these Imperial registers of this period; and which we have disposed in the order in which they occur, in their respective tables, viz. :—

CASSIODORUS.		CHRONICON PASCHALE.	
A.D.		A.D.	
89. Asprenas and Clemens.		95. Asprenate.	Laterano.
90. Domitianus 9.	Clemens 2.	94. Domit. Aug. 13.	Clemente.
91. Nerva 2.	Rufus.	96. Domitian. 14.	Clemente 2.
92. Fulvius and Vetus.		97. Valente.	Petere.
93. Sabinus.	Antoninus.	98. Nerva Aug.	Tito Rufo 3.
94. Nerva 3.	Trajanus 3.	100. Palma.	Senecione.
95. Senecio.	Palma.	99. Trajano Augusto Solo.	
96. Trajanus 4.	Fronto.	101. Traj. Aug. 2.	Pontiano.
97. Trajanus 5.	Orfitus.	102. Traj. Aug. 3.	Peto.
98. Senecio 3.	Sura.	104. Traj. Aug. 4.	Maximo.
99. Trajanus 6.	Maximus.	103. Syriano.	Syrio.
100. Senecio 3.	Sura 2.	105. Syriano 2.	Marcello 3.
101. Urbanus.	Marcellus.	106. Candido.	Quadrato.
102. Candidus.	Quadratus.		

In these lists the irregularities are regarded as being those of Victorius and Cassiodorus; the Chronicon Paschale being held to be a correct list at this period, and the historical ones particularly otherwise. The names, therefore, of *Sabinus and Antoninus* appear to be a clear interpolation. The second instance of interpolation in these lists, occurs between the reigns of Trajan and Adrian; where a consulate of *Clarus and Alexander* is inserted, both by Victorius and Cassiodorus; which is clearly spurious. For the last consuls of the reign of Trajan were *Niger and Apronianus*, who precede this interpolation: in that consulate Trajan died in the month of August in Cilicia, while Adrian was in Syria, from whence he returned forthwith to Rome, passing through Jerusalem on his way; which, Epiphanius informs us, happened 47 years after Jerusalem was taken by Titus. In the following year *Adrian* entered upon the consulship with *Salinator* as his colleague, which is the next succeeding consulate in the lists of Victorius and Cassiodorus to the interpolated one of *Clarus and Alexander*. There can be no question, therefore, as to the spuriousness of that intermediate consulship, and it does not appear in the Chronicon Paschale.

We may pause a moment upon the statement of Epiphanius; that the first year of Adrian corresponded with the 47th year from the capture of Jerusalem; since it appears to us to confirm, in a great measure, the hypothesis that the Christian date of Censorinus is the true date. For 46 years after the capture of Jerusalem, which happened A.D. 70, will make the consulship of *Niger and Apronianus* to be in the year A.D. 116. But the list of the Chronicon Paschale makes it in the 118th year, if we count back the consulates from the year 238; there being 120 consulates in that interval. By increasing that number by two, which we have seen should be done, since the omitted consulates of the *Two Silani* and of *Niger and Apronianus* are within that interval, and must be added there to the list of the Chronicon, the consulate of Niger and Apronianus will appear of the year A.D. 116, as the authority of Epiphanius requires it to be.

To proceed with our scrutiny,—we find, between the third consulate of *Antoninus and Aurelius*, in the eighth year of the reign of Antoninus Pius, and that of *the same consuls* for the fourth time, another certainly spurious entry both by Victorius and Cassiodorus, under the names of *Gratus and Seleucus*. This consulate is not noticed by history, and is not in the list of the Chronicon Paschale, nor of Idatius. Again, in the reign of the two Antonines, Victorius has three consulships of those emperors, instead of two, which are found in the list of Cassiodorus, as well as the Chronicons; and which number history shews to be true. And lastly, in the fourth year of Alexander Severus, between the consulship of *Alexander the second time, and Marcellus his colleague*, and that of *Albinus and Maximus*, there is an interpolated entry of *Annianus and Maximus* in the two lists of Victorius and Cassiodorus; which history does not notice, and is not contained in the Chronicon.

Thus we find 5 spurious consulships in the list of Victorius, and 4 in that of Cassiodorus; the excess ought to be 4 and 3, as we have seen. But then we find an omitted entry in these lists which reduces their excessive entries to the required numbers. This is found in the reign of Adrian, where after the consulship of *Celsus and Marcellinus*, that of *Catullinus and Libo* is omitted, but found in the Chronicons. It is called by historians *Catullinus and Aper*, and is mentioned by Ammianus (Lib. 16).

These are all that we can discover of erroneous registration in these lists, and they were marked out without reference to their number in the original investigation of them; from which we think they may be depended upon as tolerably correct. All the three lists, therefore, under a proper sifting, come up to their true measures of 167 consulates between that year which was the second consulate of Titus, A.D. 71, and the consulate of Ulpius and Pontianus, in the year Censorinus wrote; being the reputed year of our Lord 238.

The knowledge we have of the exact Christian year of the second consulship of Titus, proceeds from a record by the elder Pliny of a double eclipse of the sun and moon in that consulate.[q] That writer relates that such eclipses happened within 15 days of each other, in the reign of Vespatian when the father was consul the third time, and his son the second time. These eclipses are marked in the tables of M. Pingré, preserved in the French work, *On the Art of Verifying Dates*, as having occurred on the 4th and 20th of March, A.D. 71. If that computation can be relied upon, it seems to settle the point of chronology definitively; for it is impossible any longer to doubt the corruption of the consular lists under the emperors, in the interval between that date and the age of Censorinus.

It seems a work highly worthy an age, which boasts of its enlightenment, to cast away the slander that has beset the Church for so many generations, and calls in question the age of our venerable religion. We have trusted too long to an authority which has overruled the traditions of the early Church; and given precedence to the speculations of profane chroniclers, whose works are stamped with error in all their pages, over those sacred traditions of a devotional zeal, which marked the cha-

---

q *Nat. Hist.* lib. 2, 10, 13.

racter of the early churches in their commemorative functions; and which could hardly fail, either to preserve a true record of the times that had elapsed, or to secure to the landmarks of their computations, a certainty that should never be mistaken.

To such a devotional spirit, we think we might very well confide the question implicitly; for the Christian record never varied, though held by a hundred communities, while the consular records vary in every hand they are found in. And if an impartial judge had sat over the question when the Christian reckoning was pronounced deficient, the Roman epochs ought to have been pronounced with as many beginnings as the arms of Briareus, or the heads of a Chimæra.

This subject, however, has drawn our disquisition to so great a length, that we must postpone the further pursuit of the enquiry we entered upon at the commencement, to another opportunity. All we can venture to add now, is the collateral lists of consuls, from the reformation by Cæsar to the end of the reign of Tiberius, to which we have referred in the preceding pages.

List of Roman Consuls, from A.U.C. *706 to* A.U.C. *789.*

By Dion Cassius, about A.D. 229.	By Cassiodorus, about A.D. 514.	By the Chronicon Paschale. A Provincial Register reaching to the year A.D. 629.	Observations.
C. J. Cæsar, Dict. 2, at the close of the year, Calenus and Vatinius.	Q. Fusius. P. Vatinius.	*Olympiad* 182. 1. Calinus and Vatinius.	Consular year, A.U.C. 705.
C. J. Cæsar, 3. M. Æmil. Lepidus.	C. Jul. Cæsar, 3. M. Lepidus.	2. 2. C. Jul. Cæsar, 2, alone.	True epoch of Indictions, A.U.C. 706.
C. J. Cæsar, sine conlegâ, afterwards Q. Fabius, C. Trebonius, the last day, C. Caninius.	C. Jul. Cæsar, 4. Fab. Maximus.	3. 3. C. Jul. Cæsar, 3, alone.	Year of Confusion, 446 days. A.U.C. 707 by old computation; 708 by new computation.
1. C. J. Cæsar, 5. M. Antonius. After Cæsar's death, P. Dolabella.	C. Jul. Cæsar, 5. M. Antoninus.	4. 4. C. Jul. Cæsar, 4, alone.	First year of Cæsar's Reformed Calendar. A.U.C. 709 by new computation.
2. Aulus Hirtius, C. Vibius Pansa. After their death, Octavianus Cæsar, Quintus Pedius.	C. Pansa. A. Hirtius.	*Olympiad* 183. 5. Pansa and Hirtius.	A.U.C. 710. Battle of Mutina.

By Dion Cassius, about A.D. 229.	By Cassiodorus, about A.D. 514.	By the Chronicon Paschale. A Provincial Register reaching to the year A.D. 629.	OBSERVATIONS.
3. M. Æmil. Lepidus, 2. L. Munat. Plaucus.	M. Lepidus. L. Plaucus.	2. 1. Lepidus & Plaucus.	Spurious epoch of Indictions.
4. L. Anton. Pietas. P. S. Isauricus.	P. Servilius, 2. L. Antonius.	3. 2. Antonius & Isauricus.	
5. Cn. Dom. Calvinus, 2. C. Asin. Pollio.	C. Domitius. C. Asinius.	4. 3. Albinus & Pollio.	Antigonus declared an enemy to Rome, and Herod adopted by the Senate.
6. Lucius Marcius. C. Calv. Sabinus.	L. Censorinus. C. Calvisius.	*Olympiad* 184. 4. Censorinus and Sabinus.	
7. Ap. Claud. Pulcher. C. Norban. Flaccus.	Appius Cladius. C. Norbanus.	2. 5. Pulcher & Flaccus.	
8. M. Vipsanius Agrippa. C. Canin. Gallus.	M. Agrippa. L. Caninius.	3. 6. Agrippa & Gallus.	Jerusalem taken by Herod, and Antigonus put to death.
9. L. G. Poplicola. M. Cocc. Nerva.	L. Gellius. M. Cocceius.	4. 7. Poplicola and Erva Cocceius.	
10. L. Cornuficius. Sex. Pompeius.	Sex. Pompeius. L. Cornuficius.	*Olympiad* 185. 8. Cornificius and Pompeius.	
11. M. Antonius, 2. L. Scrib. Libo.	L. Scribonius. L. Atracinus.	2. 9. Antonius & Libo.	
		3. 10. Octav. Augustus and Cicero.	First Interpolation of Chronicon Paschale.
12. Cæsar, 2. L. Volcasius. L. F. Tullus.	C. Cæsar. L. Valcatius.	4. 11. Octav. Augustus and Corvilius.	
13. Cn. Domitius. Ahenobarbus. Caius Sossius.	Cn. Domitius. C. Sosius.	*Olympiad* 186. 12. Oc. Augustus, 3, and Crassus.	
14. C. Cæs. Octavius, 3. M. Val. M. Corvinus.	C. Cæsar, 2. M. Messala.		Battle of Actium. A.U.C. 722. Sept. 2nd.
15. Cæsar, 4. M. Licin. Crassus.	C. Cæsar, 3. M. Crassus.	2. 13. Oc. Augustus, 4, and Crassus, 2. 3. 14. Ænobarbus and Sosius.	

By Dion Cassius, about A.D. 229	By Cassiodorus, about A.D. 514.	By the Chronicon Paschale. A Provincial Register reaching to the year A.D. 629.	
		4.	
16. Cæsar, 5. Sextus Apuleius.	C. Cæsar, 4. Sex. Apuleius.	15. Oc. Augustus, 5, and Apuleius.	Augustan epocl according to th Egyptian Reckon ing. Censor : D *Die Natali*, ch. 18
17. Cæsar, 6. M. V. Agrippa, 2.	C. Cæsar, 5. M. Agrippa, 2.	*Olympiad* 187. 1. Oc. Augustus, 6, and Agrippa.	
18. Cæsar, 7. Agrippa, 3.	C. Cæsar, 6. M. Agrippa, 3.	2. Oc. Augustus, 7. and Agrippa, 2.	Augustan epoc according to th Latins. Censor *ut supra.*
19. Cæs. Augustus, 8 T. Statilius Taurus.	C. A. Cæsar, 7. T. Statilius.	3. Oc. Augustus, 8, and Taurus.	
20. Augustus, 9. M. Jun. Silanus.	C. A. Cæsar, 8. M. Silanus.	4. Oc. Augustus, 9, and Silanus. *Olympiad* 188.	
21. Augustus, 10. C. Norbanus Flaccus.	C. A. Cæsar, 9. C. Norbanus.	5. Oc. Augustus, 10, and Flaccus.	
22. Augustus, 11. Cn. Calp. Piso.	C. A. Cæsar, 10. Cn. Piso.	6. Oc Augustus, 11, and Piso.	
23. M. C. Œs. Marcellus. L. Aruncius.	M. Marcellus. L. Aruncius.	7. Oc. Augustus, 12, and Aruncius.	
		8. Celsus and Tiberius.	Second Interpo lation in Chroni con Paschale.
24. M. Lollius. Q. Lepidus.	M. Lollius. Q. Lepidus.	*Olympiad* 189. 9. Lollius & Lepidus.	
25. M. Apuleius. P. Silius Nerva.	M. Apuleius. P. Silius.	10. Apuleius & Nerva.	
26. Q. Sentius. Saturninus. Q. Lucret. Vespillo.	C. Sentius. Q. Lucretius.	11. Saturninus and Lucretius.	
27. Cn. Corn. Lentulus. P. Corn. Lentulus. Marcellinus.	Cn. Lentulus. P. Lentulus.	12. Lentulus and Lentulus.	
		Olympiad 190. 13. Lentulus and Cornelius.	Third Interpola tion in Chronico Paschale.
28. C. Furnius. C. Junius Silanus.	C. Furnius. C. Silanus.	14. Fornicius and Silanus.	

By Dion Cassius, about A.D. 229.	By Cassiodorus, about A.D. 514.	By the Chronicon Paschale. A Provincial Register reaching to the year A.D. 629.	OBSERVATIONS.
29. L. Dom. Œnobarbus. P. Corn. Scipio.	L. Domitius. P. Scipio.	15. Domitius and Ænobarbus.	
30. M. Drusus Libo. L. Calpurn. Piso.	M. Drusus. L. Piso.	1. Libo and Piso. *Olympiad* 191. 1.	
31. M. Licin. Crassus. Cn. Corn. Lentulus.	Cn. Lentulus. M. Crasso.	2. Crassus and Lentulus. 2.	
32. Tib. Claud. Nero. P. Quint. Varus.	Tib. Nero. P. Quintilius.	3. Nero and Clarus. 3.	
33. M. V. Messala. Barbtuus. P. Sulp. Quirinius.	M. Messala. Pub. Sulpicius.	4. Messala and Cyrinius. 4. 5. Rubellius and Saturninus.	Fourth Interpolation in Chronicon Paschale.
34. P. Fabius Maximus. Q. Ælius Tubero.	Paulus Fabius. Quintius Ælius.	*Olympiad* 102. 6. Maximus and Tubero.	
35. Julius Antonius. Q. Fabius Africanus.	Julius Antonius. Afr. Fabius.	7. Africanus and Maximus, 2.	
36. Cl. Nero Drusus. P. Quint. Crispinus.	Drusus Nero. L. Quinitius.	8. Drusus and Crispinus.	
37. C. Marcius. Censorinus. C. Asin. Gallus.	C. Asinius. C. Marcius.	9. Censorinus and Gallus. *Olympiad* 103.	
38. Tib. Claudius, 2. Cn. Calpurn. Piso.	Tib. Nero. Cn. Piso.	10. Nero, 2, and Piso, 2.	
39. D. Lælius Balbus. C. Antistius Veter.	D. Lælius. C. Antistius.	11. Balbus and Veter.	
40. Augustus, 12. Lucius Sylla.	C. A. Cæsar, 11. L. Sylla.	12. Octavianus, 13, and Sylla.	
41. C. Calvisius. Sabinus. L. Passienus Rufus.	C. Calvisius. L. Passienus.	13. Sabinus & Rufinus.	Year of the Nativity, A.D. 1.
42. C. Corn. Lentulus. M. Val. Messala.	C. Lentulus. M. Messala.		Death of Herod. One Consulate omitted by the Chronicon Paschale.
43. Augustus, 13. M. Plautius Silvanus.	C. A. Cæsar, 12. M. Plautius.	*Olympiad* 194. 14. Oc. Augustus, 14, and Silvanus.	

By Dion Cassius, about A.D. 229.	By Cassiodorus, about A.D. 514.	By the Chronicon Paschale. A Provincial Register reaching to the year A.D. 629.	OBSERVATIONS.
44. Coss. Corn. Lentulus. L. Calp. Piso.	Cossus Lentulus. L. Piso.	15. Lentulus & Piso.	
45. Caius Cæsar. Augusti Filius. L. Æmil. Paulus.	C. A. Cæsar, 13. L. Paulus.	1. Publius Cæsar and Paulus.	
46. P. Vinicius. P. Alfenus Varus.	P. Vinicius. P. Alphenus.	2. Judicius & Varius.	
47. Lucius Ælius. L. F. Lamia.	M. Servilius. L. Lamia.	*Olympiad* 195. 3. Lamia & Servilius.	
48. Sextus Æmilius. Catus. C. Sentius Saturninus. (1.)	Sextus Ælius. C. Sentius. (1.)	4. Magnus & Valerius. (2.)	
49. L. Valerius Messala Valesus. Cn. Corn. C. Magnus. (2.)	Cn. Cinna. L. Valerius. (2.)	5. Lepidus and Arruncius. (3.)	The numbers 48, 49, and 50, are evidently transposed. The correspondent numbers are put below the names.
50. M. Æmil. Lepidus. L. Arruncius. (3.)	M. Lepidus. L. Arruncius. (3.)	6. Tib. Cæsar and Capito. (1.) *Olympiad* 196.	
51. A. Licin. Nerva. Silianus. Q. Cœcilius Metellus Cretius.	Q. Cœcilius. A. Licinius.	7. Cretius & Nerva.	
52. M. Furius Camillus. Sextus Nonius. Quintilianus.	M. Furius. Sext. Nonius.	2. 8. Camillus and Quintilianus.	
53. Q. Salpicius Camerinus. C. Popœus Sabinus.	Qn. Sulpicius. C. Poppœus.	3. 9. Camerinus and Sabinus.	
54. Pub. Corn. Dolabella. C. Junius Silanus.	P. Dolabella. C. Silanus.	4. 10. Dolabella and Silanus. *Olympiad* 197.	
55. M. Æmilius Lepidus. T. Statilius Taurus.	M. Lepidus. T. Statilius.	11. Lepidus & Taurus.	Last adoption of Tiberius, after the month of September.
56. Germanicus Cæsar. F. Cæsar. C. Fonteius Capito.	German. Cæsar. C. Fonteius.	12. Tiber. Cæsar, 2, and Scipio.	

By Dion Cassius, about A.D. 229.	By Cassiodorus, about A.D. 514.	By the Chronicon Paschale. A Provincial Register reaching to the year A.D. 629.	OBSERVATIONS.
57. L. Munatius Plaucus. C. Selius Cæsina.	L. Plaucus. C. Silius.	13. Flaccus and Silanus.	
58. Sex. Pompeius. Sex. Apuleius.	Sex. Pompeius. Sex. Apuleius.	14. Sextus & Sextus. *Olympiad* 198. 15. Pompeius Magnus and Apuleius.	Death of Augustus, A.U.C. 766, Aug. 19th. Interpolated consulate in Chronicon Paschale.
59. Drusus Cæs. Tib. fil. C. Norbanus Flaccus.	Drusus Cæsar. C. Norbanus.	1. Brutus&Flaccus. 2.	
60. F. Statilius Sisenna Taurus. L. Scribonius Libo.	Sisenna Statilius. L. Scribonius.	2. Taurus and Libo.	
61. C. Cæcilius Rufus. L. Pomponius Flaccus.	L. Pomponius. C. Cæcilius,	3. Crassus and Rufus. *Olympiad* 199.	
62. Tiber. Cæs. Augustus, fil. 3. German. Cœsar Tib., fil. 2.	Tiberius Cæsar. German. Cæsar.	4. Tiberius Cæsar, 3. Rufus, 2.	
63. M. Jun. Silanus. C. Norbanus Balbus.	M. Silanus. C. Norbanus.	5. Silanus & Balbus.	
64. M. Valer. Messala. M. Aurel. Cotta.	M. Valerius. M. Aurelius.	6. Messala & Gratus.	
65. Tib. Cæs. Augusti, fil. 4. Drusus Julius Tiber. fil. 2.	Tiberius Cæsar. Drusus Cæsar.	7. Tiberius Cæsar, 4, and Drusus. *Olympiad* 200.	
66. D. Haterius Agrippa. C. Sulpic. Galba.	D. Haterius. C. Sulpicius.	8. Agrippa & Galba. 2.	
67. C. Asinius Pollio. C. Antistius Veter.	C. Asinius. C. Antistius.	9. Pollio and Veter. 3.	
68. S. Cornelius Cethegus. L. Visellius Varro.	Ser. Cornelius. L. Visellius.	10. Cethegus & Varus.	
69. M. Asinius Agrippa. Cossus Corn. Lentulus.	M. Asinius. Cos. Cornelius.	11. Agrippa and Lentulus.	Fifteenth year of Tiberius from his last adoption, the last three months of the year. John Baptist's ministry begins.

By Dion Cassius, about A.D. 229.	By Cassiodorus, about A.D. 514.	By the Chronicon Paschale. A Provincial Register reaching to the year A.D. 629.	OBSERVATIONS.
		Olympiad 201.	
70. Cn. Lentulus. Gætulicus. C. Calvisius. Sabinus.	C. Calvisius. Cn. Gætulicus.	12. Gætulicus and Sabinus.	Fifteenth year of Tiberius during the first nine months.
		2.	
71. M. Licinius Crassus. L. Calpurn. Piso.	L. Piso. M. Crassus.	13. Crassus and Piso.	Our Lord's ministry in Judæa.
72. Ap. Junius Silanus. P. Silius Nerva.	Ap. Silanus. P. Silius.	14. Silanus and Nerva.	Ministry in Galilee and Peræa.
73. L. Rubellius. Geminus. C. Fusius. Geminus.	C. Rubellius. C. Fusius.	15. Geminus and Geminus.	Ministry in Ephraim, and death of our Lord.
74. M. V. Quartinus. L. C. Longinus.			
75. Tib. Cæsar, 5. L. Ælius Sejanus.			
76. C. D. Ænobarbus. F. C. Scribonianus.			
77. S. Sulp. Galba. L. Corn. Sulla.			
78. L. Vitellius. P. F. Persicus.			
79. C. C. Gallus. M. S. Nonianus.			
80. Sex. Pampinius. Q. Plautius.			
81. C. A. Proculus. C. P. Nigrinus.	} Death of Tiberius in this Consulate, A.U.C. 789=March 16th.		
82. M. A. Julianus. P. N. Asprenate.			

Hitcham Rectory,
    15th *Oct.,* 1855.

H. M. G.

GLORIFIED HUMANITY.

WHEN Christ had died, and had left the upper world for the purpose of meeting more closely the king of terrors, it became necessary that we should receive some assurance that he prevailed in his encounter with the last, and most fearful, evil that man has to endure, in the present dispensation of things.

We gain courage in our contest with all lesser afflictions, by knowing that our great precursor has already succeeded in the same struggle. When, therefore, we contemplate the terrible lot that awaits us all,—of yielding up our bodies to rottenness and dissolution,—we earnestly crave some information whether we have any power to emerge safe from the valley and shadow of death. And no more satisfactory answer can be given, than the one which tells us that he, who laid down his life for our sakes, could not be holden by the grave. For he burst the bonds of death, and signalized his triumph over the kingdom of darkness, by promising to those who are his, a like ability to descend into the unseen region of death, and escape from the hands of him who had the power of death.

And when he re-appeared, after his victory, it was no longer in that poor and lowly form which had been an offence, not only to his enemies, but in part at least to his disciples also. His humanity now was glorified. A great part of the veil which had concealed hitherto the divine nature of Christ was removed; and he visited his followers as a man, from whom all the disgrace and degradation consequent on Adam's transgression was cleared away. In his previous intercourse with men, he was seen as one clothed not only with humanity, but with that obscure and humble form of it which we must also wear until we pass through the great and final change. The original dispute between him and his adversaries had been, whether he should put on the glorious appearance at once, or wait until the proper time should arrive for displaying the full majesty of his presence. It was necessary, in the divine economy, that that majesty should be concealed from all, except those whose hearts were already softening under the influence of God's dealings with them. Hence, during the whole period of his ministry, when he was laying the foundation of his Church, and calling forth from the world those that were to prepare men for his future kingdom, he was seen in fashion as a man, except occasionally, as when he walked over the troubled waters of Galilee, with an unearthly halo spread around him, or when his form was transfigured, and the fashion of his face was changed, as he stood, in dazzling light, on the mount, between Moses and Elias. These glorious appearances were confined to his friends. The scribes and pharisees, together with the crowd of priests and rulers and soldiers, knew of him only as a Galilæan peasant, sometimes rising into the character of a bold prophet.

And when the necessity for his humble and offending form had passed away, and he stepped from the tomb as one who was leading captivity captive, those his enemies saw him not at all. He came only to his disciples; and he came to them as the glorious being, who could not dwell constantly with creatures of mortal mould and sinful hearts; but visited them from time to time, as angels had formerly visited the holy men of old. He passed to and fro in a mysterious manner; no one saw him come, no one knew how he went: for he had gained what Adam had lost, the perfect and normal type of humanity; which we shall hereafter gain, if we be among the glorified saints.

It is evident from the narrative, that in all the cases, when the glorified humanity was seen, there had occurred precisely the same kind of transformation which, we are expressly told, took place when he was transfigured on the mount. When he walked on the waters, the disciples did not at first recognize him, but they were troubled, and cried out for fear, supposing it had been a spirit. And, after his resurrection, even his best and dearest friends did not immediately know him; and always regarded him with a feeling of the grand and superhuman. The effect produced was not, indeed, properly speaking, an *alteration* so that none of his previous lineaments could be traced, but an *improvement*, so that a vague recollection was induced. Perhaps we cannot obtain a better idea of this effect, than by imagining it to have been similar to the result, when a man recovers from sickness to sound health. If we had never known such an one, but when he was pale and prostrated by disease, and had even passed a considerable time with him, and were afterwards to meet him, robust and ruddy, away from the accompaniments of illness, we should scarcely at first be certain of his identity; while nevertheless there might be the dim consciousness, indicating that the form was not altogether strange; until, by and bye, the tones or the gestures would recall the whole man to our memories; and complete recognition would flash across us. So was it with Christ's appearances to his disciples. At first, their hearts only burned within them, or they were affrighted by his unearthly movements. It was *by degrees*, that they came to know how truly it was the Lord.

And, furthermore, it was but natural that those who had

been most with him in his humility, should have the least difficulty in recognizing him in the glorified state.   Mary Magdalene
and Peter were much sooner able to recollect Jesus than were
Cleopas, and some of the brethren on the Galilæan mountain.

No one of earth saw Christ revive, and escape the bonds of
death.   The guard at the tomb witnessed the descent of the
angels, and the opening of the grave; but they swooned at the
terrific sight; and they did not see what no mortal eye beheld,
least of all the eyes of enemies.   We are not even informed of
the circumstances of the actual resurrection; for the evangelists
relate only what had been witnessed by themselves, or their ac-
quaintances.   They dared not mention a word of what none
could bear testimony to.   We know that he rose at some time
between the midnight of Saturday, and the dawn of Sunday;
but the first information of the event was conveyed by the faithful women, who were early at the burying-place, to render the
last sad offices of friendship to one whom they had loved so well
while alive.

The stone, which had blocked up the entrance to the chamber
of death, was removed.   The body, which they came to embalm,
and to inter with greater decency than the hasty proceedings of
Friday had permitted, was gone; and they fled with mingled
feelings of sorrow, of terror, yet of a half-awakened joy, to
bring the disciples word of what had taken place.   These came,
and satisfied themselves of the truth of what they had been told;
and departed, wondering what would next occur.

But Mary Magdalene lingered behind, and was blessed with
the first vision of the risen Christ; though, even with her perfect knowledge of him, having ministered to his wants, she did
not immediately recognize him, as he stood before her.   But
when he spoke, the well-remembered voice (which always changes
less than the features), brought him to her recollection, and she
admitted the glad impression that it was the Lord.

The eleven also, to whom he soon appeared, were struck with
awe at the majestic form which came upon them in so mysterious a manner; but they easily knew him.   Whereas the two
disciples, who were journeying to Emmaus, were some time in
his company, thinking him a stranger; although their hearts
burned within them.   Which is to be accounted for, by the supposition of their not having been so familiarly acquainted with
him.

A similar circumstance is discernible, in the appearance he
made to above five hundred brethren at once in Galilee (Matt.
xxviii. 16, and 1 Cor. xv. 6), where, it is said, some *doubted*, *i. e.*,
not disbelieved, but were in hesitation whether it were he or

not, until he drew near and spoke to them.   These must have been only beginning their discipleship.

Many other times did Jesus shew himself to the eleven, for the purpose of instructing them in the path they were to follow, when he should be parted from them.   But we are not informed exactly how often they conversed with him, before he ascended into heaven.   We only know that he communicated with them sufficiently to instruct them in the course they were to follow, after his absence; and at last, ten days before Pentecost, he led them to the summit of Mount Olivet, just outside the eastern part of the holy city.   There he laid an injunction on them to remain passive in Jerusalem, until some sign from heaven should give them authority to commence their preaching; and then his body rose up from among them, and was carried away into heaven, out of their sight; to remain, as the angel told the disciples, until the time should arrive for his final return, and until he should sit on his throne, judging the twelve tribes of Israel.

And yet, although the ascension—that is, the actual removal of Christ's bodily presence from his Church—occupies no prominent place in the sacred history, it is clear from the narrative, that occasionally he shewed himself to his followers after that event.   The martyr Stephen saw him, at the moment before his death.   St. Paul was favoured, more than once, with visions of the risen Lord.   Indeed, he grounded his claims to apostleship upon the fact of his having been so favoured.   And his language would seem to imply that there were others similarly circumstanced with himself.   It is certain that if there were new apostles (see Acts xiv. 14; Rom. xvi. 7; 1 Cor. xv. 7: 2 Cor. viii. 23; Phil. ii. 25; 1 Thes. ii. 6; Rev. ii. 2) consecrated after the ascension, they must have owed their office (according to St Paul's definition) to the privilege of having seen the Lord Jesus Christ in his glorified humanity.   And—to mention but one more instance—St. John received, in the isle of Patmos, a vision, that is especially called the Revelation of Jesus Christ; wherein it is clear that the apostle witnessed the visible presence of the mediator.

Hence, all that we can infer from the ascension is that Christ was no longer to be visibly present with men, as he had been during the period of his humility.   While men remain as they are they cannot communicate, mouth to mouth, with the glorious being who is united with the divine nature into one person. For it is a truth often repeated, and constantly urged, in the Scriptures, that no man still entangled with the sins and infirmities of Adam's race, can *see the Lord*.   The Seer of old

was indeed gifted with the power of sometimes having a part of
the veil uncovered which concealed the divine glory. Moses and
Isaiah were witnesses of this glory in part ; the three disciples
at the transfiguration were also eyewitnesses of his majesty.
The brethren, after the resurrection, shared partly in this privilege. The apostles were distinguished from all the other disciples, by having *seen the Lord*. But no man of mortal clay
could rest with him, as Peter wished to do, on the mount when
he would have set up at once the three tabernacles for their
united residence. No man, said Jehovah to Moses, may see
my full glory—*my face*—and live. He must pass into the condition of glorified humanity himself, before he could behold the
awful majesty of Jehovah. Hence, when Moses and Elias were
conversing with Jehovah at the transfiguration, it is expressly
said that they also were in glory. A change must come over
every man living, before he can meet his Lord, and share in
some visible communion with him.

Hence, we are told in the sermon on the mount, that the
pure in heart are blessed,—those who have cast away the imperfections and sins of the flesh—for they shall see God. And the
author of the epistle to the Hebrews echoes that truth, when he
urges us to follow holiness, without which no man shall see the
Lord. St. John also, in his first epistle, exhorts to purification,
for this alone will fulfil the hope of seeing the Lord as he is ;
that is, no longer in the humble form, but in the complete
glory of his majesty (1 John iii. 2).

The last named quotation, when carefully read, opens up to
us a great truth, found scattered all over the Bible—viz., that
we also shall obtain a glorified humanity. For St. John, while
acknowledging that it doth not yet appear what we shall be,
yet, knowing that we are to see him as he is, is certain that we
must be like him in that higher appearance ; for, if not, we
should not be able to witness his majesty. We cannot doubt,
therefore, that our corporeal existence, when we shall rise from
the grave, will be improved and glorified in the same kind of
way as our Master's was, when he had passed through the same
cruel road,—that is to say, we shall be like him if we see him
as he is. And this shall we do, if now, being the sons of God,
we be careful to purify ourselves as he is pure.

St. Paul teaches, in still more express language, in the
eighth chapter of the epistle to the Romans, this same hope of
the future glorification of those who are the sons of God, because
they are led by the Spirit of God. He tells us that we are to
be glorified together with Christ ; and that the creature shall be
delivered from the bondage of corruption, into the glorious

liberty of the children of God. And in still more glowing language he describes, in the fifteenth chapter of the first epistle to the Corinthians, the need of the change from corruptible to incorruptible, before we can gain by the resurrection from the dead. St. Peter also, at the beginning of his first epistle, grounds his exhortations upon the promise that we shall be partakers of the divine nature, if we escape the corruption that is in the world through lust. We shall be so conformed to Christ in his glorified state, that the apostle even speaks of our partaking of the divine nature.

But such a promise is only recorded for those who are purified by the indwelling of the Holy Spirit, which his death and merits have procured for us; we must secure that presence of God in the heart, to lead us eventually into truth, if we do not wilfully abandon the way of truth. We have that priceless operation of the Holy Ghost upon our affections, which appropriates to us the blessings of the atonement. And we have, besides, Christ in heaven, occupied in watching over and interceding for his flock on earth. Whenever our wills are directly acted on by the Holy Ghost, then, inasmuch as he, our Lord, is also God, we become spiritually united to him; and, by means of the bond of union between us, can address our prayers to him which we dared not utter, and which he could not hear, unless he were God as well as man.

While, then, we tabernacle in these fleshly bodies, we have a task before us,—to become pure and perfect. Our wills are not now in a state of absolute dependence upon God, as Christ's human will was. The holiest of us do not preserve, at all times, that sensible communion with God, which is experienced in moments of fervid prayer. And the best of us are distinguished from Jesus in that he never lost this union.

And herein, also, consists the difference between our condition now, and what it will be in the next life. At present we form a part of a vicious system, originating many of the evils in existence; and suffering many from our own faults, and from those of others. The Christian revelation completes the moral government of God, by drawing us closer and closer to him; making us, in the Scripture phrase, grow in grace; which growth implies and includes the daily dying unto sin. For as sin means separation from God, so death unto sin means communion with him. And, when the discipline is over, in God's own time, we shall depart from this abode of mingled good and evil, made capable of intimate junction with the first cause, and with no internal temptations pressing upon us. And when sin shall have ceased, death, the wages of sin, shall be everlastingly destroyed.

We shall live for ever sinless and happy, with the Holy Ghost constantly in our hearts; with no need, either of an effort from ourselves, or of any merely objective means of influence. This state was promised to the disciples when Christ declared that God's blessings would come *in that day*, independently of his intercession (John xvi. 26, 27).

We shall then, likewise, as we have said, have acquired the power of *seeing* God; not God the Father, who is ever invisible (John i. 18), but God the Son, that Person of the Trinity who manifests himself outwardly to created intelligences through the medium of the senses. We shall know God as Christ; not in the poor form of the Galilæan peasant, but with an aspect at least as glorious as that which was shewn at the transfiguration to the three; or, after the resurrection, to all the disciples. Nay, we may well believe that they did not behold the full splendor of divinity in Christ's appearance; for they were only partially purified; and in all probability none but the *perfectly* pure in heart shall have an unclouded vision of God. When, hereafter, we shall have lost every vestige of impurity, we shall see the glory of God in his face; such that no man of clay could look upon and live (Exod. xxxiii. 20).[a]

We cannot imagine any lack or hindrance whatever in our spiritual bodies, or any alloy in our happiness; when the two means of discerning God—as subject and as object—as the moral upholder and the authoritative director—as the Holy Ghost and the Son—shall be unimpaired and eternal. All the difficulties with which we now have so painfully to struggle will then have ceased for ever; and, in St. Paul's significant language, we shall know even as we are known.

We have no words that may convey anything like an adequate idea of our happiness then; eye hath not seen, nor ear heard, nor heart conceived, the things which God hath prepared for them that love him. But chiefly, let us be persuaded, we shall be happy in the utter absence of self-reliance or pride. We shall not have to walk alone; we shall rest upon the arm and lean upon the bosom of our dear Master, and live in his presence throughout the successive ages of eternity.

And let us not forget that there is but *one* way for any of us to attain to that vision and that sinless glory. First, to cast away the deceitful sense of our own self-originated righteous-

---

[a] The remarkable circumstance of the apostles seeing the risen Christ as a superhuman being; while Cleopas and his companion thought him only a man; is at once explicable by our knowledge that the eleven were more advanced disciples than were those two, and therefore able to see more of divinity.

ness. Specious as virtue of that kind may be, it can only end in misery; for it does not come from God, the author of all good. Our own efforts may only be to love and cling to Christ, for then we become changed and renewed; at last, sin is expelled from us; our hearts hold and feel God's spirit, and we rise into such natures as Christ himself wore, without spot or stain. Washed in his blood, we are whiter than snow, though we had been originally crimson.

But, on the other hand, we find in the narrative that none of Christ's enemies ever looked upon his glory. They were refused the brighter manifestation, because they had not studied and prized the lesser. They had not been rendered capable, by the discipline which Christ's friends had undergone, of being spiritually improved.

In his *humility*, our Lord was nothing more, externally, to Peter and to John, than he was to Pilate or to Caiaphas. But the infidel worldling and bigot *remained* infidel, for God's dealings with them had not softened their stony hearts. And if they had no power of seeing such glory, as the risen Christ shewed to his faithful, though yet unfinished, disciples—whence can they acquire the ability to gaze upon the transcendent and dazzling splendour which is reserved for the disciples when they shall be perfected?

These enemies are the ungodly, those whose inner souls are disjoined from God, who possess no real essential goodness; who are either isolated from the rest of the creation, or only bound with those whose master is the Evil One. And what is their end? What hope have they who scorn the effort of Omnipotence to save them? The fearful warning in the Scriptures, of a never-dying worm—of an unquenchable fire—of the wailing and the gnashing of teeth, are but glimpses of the unseen terrors of a future world, as incapable of expression, as are the unutterable joys of Christ's presence.

It is indeed true that the Gospel does no more than *allude* to the lot of the godless. For it was not the *design* of the Gospel to preach of anger, but of mercy. It is a message of love to those who embrace it; it is a mere nullity to those who reject it. And then, if this boundless, unconditional mercy produce no effect, let men say where is placed their idea of *hope*. What but the most unmitigated misery can happen to those who, gradually losing God in this life, end by utter abandonment in the next?

We are not permitted to describe the unhappiness of those who are separated from God, for it is not described in the Scriptures, otherwise than by such images as can best represent excessive misery to the human mind. The darkness, the fire, the worm, the gnashing of teeth—if not literal, are but faint shadows of what no earthly tongue dare pronounce. And however we are disposed to interpret such images, let us be sure of this—that those who are entirely disjoined from God can experience no portion of happiness whatever. Their wretchedness can be alleviated by no drop of comfort, for that would imply a still lingering connexion with God. They will be different altogether from what wicked men are in this life. For here no one is removed altogether from the influence of God, and therefore unmitigated misery is not the lot of any. But hereafter, everything they see or come near will be *godless*, and it is a matter of necessity therefore that they can see or come near nothing retaining a spark of good.

Christ shall appear, even to these, but not in the form of a glorified Lord and kind friend; but as the angel appeared to the Roman guard at the sepulchre—to terrify and prostrate. He will be the angry judge of those who do not see him as one whose features and whose tones return to the recollection—who does not come as one whom we have loved so well.

And as, with the blessed, the chief cause of their happiness will be the removal of all those hindrances and vexations which oppress them here, the ability to see as loving kindness, what, in our ignorance, we mistake for sorrows and adversities—so with the children of perdition, the veil which obscured their vision now, will then be withdrawn; and what they imagine to be honourable virtues, shall stand forth as ugly vices. The self-confident who originates his own righteousness and believes God's spirit to be needless for him, shall then discover that he was deluded in his belief, and shall then see that anything whatever (though it be called righteousness,) which does not flow from God, is miserable and unholy.

W. H. J.

EWALD'S HISTORY OF CHRIST.[a]

THE student who goes back to the literature of the Reformation, and is qualified to feel himself at home in any one part of the religious world of that period, would find himself almost equally so in any other part. He would meet, of course, with important differences of sentiment, and even antagonistic difference of principle, but he would find so much that was common, even to the most opposite parties, that he would have no difficulty in perceiving what a man of those times meant to say, and of deciding, according to the canon which he himself had adopted, that he was clearly right or clearly wrong; and if it were with the protestants of that period that he was conversing, he would find only a comparatively slight variation in the principles according to which they thought and wrote. This was perhaps owing, in part, to the circumstance that the learned of those times commonly wrote in the same language, and in a language which, even when it was living, could not *germinate* as the Greek had done, and could not so develop itself as to correspond with the developments of human thought. Cicero himself had been obliged to import a multitude of terms which could not be grown in his own language, in order to express the Greek philosophy, and the language he used was still too defective to allow him to do anything more than to exhibit, with some degree of approximation, what had been already expressed by a more powerful instrument.

Besides which, the theological writers of those times did not think themselves at liberty to depart from a certain type of ideas which already existed in one of the simplest of languages, and in a form of the Greek which was scarcely less simple, and hence the religious dialect was everywhere about the same.

It is very possible that an exactly opposite effect has been partly produced by the peculiar character of the German language, by which it is able to *grow* in almost any form and direction which an individual mind may require. Instead of having more ideas than they have language to express, we are by no means sure that our Teutonic neighbours have not more words than there are, or can be in nature, distinct and intelligible ideas

[a] *Geschichte Christus' und Seiner Zeit.* Von Heinrich Ewald. Göttingen, in der Dieterischen Buchhandlung.
The History of Christ and His Time. By Henry Ewald. Göttingen, Deiterisch. 1855.

to correspond with them, and that their language has not sometimes the effect ascribed to rhyme in verses—

> " For rhyme the rudder is of verses,
>   Which this or that way turns their courses."

We know that even in our own language speakers, yes, and
writers too, can multiply words without knowledge, a phenomenon which is in fact by no means uncommon as a humble imita-
tion of what is still more rife abroad.   This circumstance perhaps, combined with the abandonment of that theological *religio*
by which our forefathers felt themselves bound to remain within
a certain range of thought, has made the theological literature
of the day, and especially of the continent, an absolutely different
region from what it was in the 16th and 17th centuries; and the
man who may still be at home in the literature of those times,
would be obliged to look considerably about him, to discover
his whereabouts at present.   We may have been disposed to fret
a little at this, and inclined to quarrel, perhaps not unjustly,
with the fashions of the time—but, though we are far from intending to follow the devices of a perverse generation, we feel
inclined, at least just now, to find how much of old-fashioned
truth may be concealed in the grotesque forms which we see
around us and welcome as many old friends as we can in their
modern dress.

With regard to Professor Ewald, we by no means intend to
say that he is in the extreme of the fashion, though he is not an
ancient.   We can in general well understand what he means to
say.   He is in fact an independent thinker and a clear and
nervous writer.   We believe too that he is deeply impressed
with the truth and the value of the views he advocates.   But he
is still decidedly German in his religious philosophy, and valuable as many of his conclusions are, they derive none of their
soundness from the basis on which he has founded them.   The
present work is in fact the fifth volume of a series, entitled, *The
History of the People of Israel,* but it contains a distinct subject
and is, as the author himself assures us, complete in itself.   The
subjects subsidiary to the great theme to which the series is
devoted, have been discussed by him in various separate treatises
as well as in the periodical which he so ably conducts, *The Jahr-
bücher der Biblischen Wissenschaft,* and these volumes, but especially the one before us, contain the result of a long and, we
may say, a devout study of the history of revelation in reference
to its ultimate object, the glory of which is shewn by our author
to culminate in the appearance of the Messiah.   In dwelling
thus on a history in the facts of which the author has great con-

fidence, and the developments of which are so much beyond those of the common course of history, the author has been inspired by his subject and increasingly so in approaching the great conclusion. And although his mode of philosophizing is utterly different from what we believe to be true, and exhibits its weakness especially where the subjects of which he treats are of the most sublime importance, we have endeavoured, for the time, to place ourselves on his own point of view, and in doing so have been deeply interested. Instead of controverting what we believe to be the errors of the author, we think it will be more to the benefit of our readers to exhibit as far as our space will allow, and as faithfully as is consistent with great condensation, a portion of the course of thought which the author pursues in tracing the sequences of this great history.

In speaking of the antagonism of the immediate government of Rome with the modern population of ancient Israel, in this concluding part of their history, his picture of the state of things may be sketched as follows :—

At the time when the direct government of Rome was substituted for the arbitrary rule of the Herods, the country was populous, and, as far as position and wealth were concerned, respectable. The Jews preferred the security to their possessions which was afforded by a strong government; and their hopes of a national prince, in accordance with their religion, were either given up, or referred to an indefinite future. Yet, in this way, two nationalities were brought into contact essentially and extremely different. They both claimed universal dominion; and though the principle on which they claimed it differed, they both sought it with a determination unknown before. The Romans had once been grossly superstitious; they now had admitted all the gods of the nations to community with their own, merely to avoid the appearance of having hostile gods to contend with, but they had no serious thoughts about such matters, and no fear of God. On the part of the Hebrews, the claim to the world's dominion was founded on the conviction of being chosen of the true God to a higher calling among the nations than they had yet attained, and this conviction, though its object was obscured for the present, might at any time give rise, as it had often done before, to the most determined action. The Israelites had never ceased to cherish aspirations after a state of things in which their religion should attain its fulfilment. The various forms in which their government had been carried on had indeed failed, as yet, to bring this consummation about; but the continually growing hopes of Messianic times led them confidently to expect some new development to which their present circumstances especially pointed; their condition at present might be compared to what it had been in Egypt, with this difference, that there the power of heathenism was not developed, and their own religion was in its infancy, whereas now the Roman power exhibited the most developed form of heathenism, while their own religion had passed through nearly all its forms of development, and was awaiting its perfection.

Hence, the Israelites under the Romans presented the contrast of a people whose hopes depended on principles deeply seated in the soul, with one whose power was absolutely heartless and material. There were, indeed, at this time, but few in Israel who dwelt upon their religious future, as compared with those who accepted the Roman power as favourable to their worldly interests; yet the effects of this collision soon manifested themselves. Various strivings soon took place, of a religious kind, on the part of men who cared little for quiet pleasures in comparison with the higher objects which they thought it their duty to pursue. The heavy taxation to which they now became subjected, and which taught them sensibly that their nation, which ought only to belong to God, had come into the actual possession of a heathen power, excited their most determined opposition. Judas of Galilee, hence called the Gaulonite, together with Sadduc a Pharisee, became the leaders of a school which Josephus calls the fourth philosophy. These taught that God alone was their Master, and that to mention any man on earth as Lord was a guilty thing. They were not deterred by the enormous difficulties in their way; self-sacrifice was regarded by them as a merit, and they did not scruple to employ the powers of a secret tribunal on their nearest friends who thwarted them. These zealots may be compared to the leaders of ecclesiastical and political revolution, who laughed at suffering and despised death; and they were rendered desperate by the thought that the true religion must now prevail or be extinguished for ever.

Assuredly a deeper regard for the ultimate destiny, for the honour, and partly for the duty of Israel, influenced Judas and his party, than those Jews and Samaritans who were disposed to temporize with the Romans; the defects of his school were partly those of the hierarchy itself, but chiefly that they had not sought, or certainly had not found, that better principle, which a true acquaintance with their own religion might have afforded them. Josephus as a Pharisee was not qualified to give a candid judgment as to the efforts of this party, though he is right in saying that it called forth all those passions which impelled the people to their own destruction.

Though this party was put down, it was not till they had raised a feeling which could not be extinguished, and which frequently manifested itself under Pontius Pilate. In fact the spirit of the Gaulonites was the breath of life of the whole history of Israel, and if the true fulfilment of that history had not now appeared, the entire destruction of the people in this last collision with the Romans would have annihilated the aspirations of 2000 years.

We merely remark on this estimate of Judas and his party, that the author has small evidence for making it so respectable; but Ewald's system required that he should make it in some degree worthy of being the germ of the great development which was soon to appear.

There were three conditions, the fulfilment of which was previously necessary to the coming of the desired fulfilment. The *first*, that an entirely new power should appear in history; the *second*, that that power should appear in an *individual* who was himself qualified to exhibit the true religion in its perfection; the *third*, though the first in point of time, that the minds of the whole people should be directed to the coming fulfilment, and should earnestly prepare for its reception.

With regard to the *first*. It had been shewn, in Vol. II., that Jehovaism contained in it the indestructable germ of the true religion, which would necessarily bring about its own fulfilment as soon as it came into vital action; that its principles are adapted to the whole world; that it had been associated with a single people, only that in this people its power might be so established as to secure the object of its mission to the world. But that it had contracted imperfections and errors in connexion with this people, which yet, in due time, it would throw off.

The Theocracy, *i. e.*, the true religion existing and working in a single church, attained its greatest strength, historically, when associated with kingly power; but at that time a defect which appeared in it at first was allowed to gain strength, according to which outward force was appealed to, instead of that most pure and exalted love by which alone it can attain perfection.

The true religion, or the kingdom of God, as far as they are the same, certainly maintains itself now in the overthrow of the once sacred house of Israel. But though its victory over heathenism is for ever secured, its energies are not yet sufficiently concentrated, its own treasures not enough valued, nor its defects removed, to enable it to attain to its own perfection. While it is now, at length, apprehending its ancient truths with decision, and going back more and more deeply into its own sacred antiquity, it allows its theocracy to become a hierarchy, losing itself in the *prestige* of this, and is in danger of over-estimating its own sacred customs, sentiments and writings, and of ossifying in its own ancient truth. The true religion, from its commencement on earth, had always been striving to rise above itself, inasmuch as it never had been perfect. All the complaints which we meet with about the defective developments of Israel's institutions, becoming as they did more and more urgent, and the views the prophets gave of new and better formations, were all endeavours after perfection. During the course of 1500 years, indeed, endeavours, especially on the part of the prophets, to introduce reforms were never wanting, but these had never yet availed towards removing the most serious defects which existed historically. And the last of the prophets, perceiving that the present development must pass away, indicated, more clearly than had been done before, the new form in which the fulfilment must come; but perceiving that powers adequate to it were not yet present, referred it to a distant period.

The last form under which the theocracy appeared, viz., the hierarchy, being now no longer sustained by the prophets, more and more disfigured and overshadowed it, without, however, having extinguished its aspirations after perfection. The foundations of these hopes were, undoubtedly, too firmly and percep-tibly laid in the sacred writings for any doubt to be entertained, by those who studied them, as to the future of Israel; but these hopes became variously regarded, by some rejected, and by others mixed up with false notions of their own. How little Josephus made of them appears in his whole history; and the notions of Philo were equally dark. But nothing prejudiced these hopes more than the hierarchy itself. By taking a one-sided view of the past, and fixing on what once was really sacred, or was supposed to be, as the highest possible form of the religious life, they desired to fix this unchangeably on the world; neglecting the true necessities of the present, and the demands of the future, or adopting the most degraded form of expectation for what was to come. It was now seen that the hierarchy had done nothing towards the desired perfection, and supposing this the only form under which the Church could exist, men concluded that it had not yet been perfectly carried out, and it must regain the form which it had under Moses, in order to regain its efficiency and the divine favour. This was the object of the Gaulonite, viz., an absolute return to the first order of things. But the result of these efforts, exactly, was to make manifest that the hope of Israel could not thus be realized, and that nothing but some new power, qualified by its own nature to remove the evils which had accumulated in the history, could bring on the accomplishment desired.

The *second* condition was, that such new power should centre in an individual: this must be in accordance with all which had for centuries been pointed out by the prophets. They had foreseen both the manner and the form in which the perfection was to come: the human kingdom had failed to lead to the desired results; and the prophetic spirit pointed to a new David, who should be empowered to bring on the fulfilment. The true idea which this involves is, partly, that on account of the immense difficulty to be overcome, no less a hero than David himself was required; but chiefly, that such perfection must come in the *person of an individual*, who should absolutely fulfil in himself the true religion, be himself the real king of the perfect kingdom, the head of the body—the Church.

But in the meantime the house of David had sunk into the dust: under the second temple and the hierarchy, not only this, but everthing else which had been most holy, as spoken of in the Scriptures, appeared to have vanished; so that the more distinctly and confidently the prophets declared the certainty and the nearness of the fulfilment, the more the means of its accomplishment seemed to be withdrawn from the earth.

It was now however from heaven itself that the true theocracy was looked for. The ancient prophets had so clearly described the perfection as in actual existence, though concealed from the eye of sense that, since nothing earthly corresponded to this prophetic vision, and all the higher blessings of the church seemed vanished from the earth, these objects were regarded as raised to God in heaven, and the visibly holy appeared to answer to the invisible as the type to the antitype. Thus the true ark of God, the true temple, the true Jerusalem were regarded as heavenly, and expected to reappear. Thus the Messiah was looked for from heaven, and hopes which had faded from the earth were still bright in heaven. Henceforward all the hopes of Israel were centered on such a Messiah, and on this account no terms were too exalted to convey the idea of him. The minds of men struggled to find among all the most elevated ideas one which should correspond to his dignity. Such a term was the Son of God. This term had, in the higher language, been applied to the actual king of Israel. All the members of the church indeed, according to the high idea of the true religion, were sons of God, as raised to this relation by his grace, yet the true King was especially destined to this dignity as standing nearest to God and enjoying his especial favor. But, as in these

later times no earthly king could possibly answer to the exalted
language of scripture, its fulfilment, like everything else exalted
in scripture, was looked for in the Messiah. And to him this
language was applied in the highest sense of which it was capable.
The Heavenly Messiah was represented as having always existed
in heaven, as standing next the throne of God, as entrusted with
the government of the world, and as destined to visit the earth
to carry out his government. Yet the decidedly human could
not be absent from the conception of the Messiah, and this Son
of God is at the same time the original man, the original eternal
image of heavenly humanity, standing nearest to God in glory,
purity, and love.

But to complete this circle another idea was necessary. The
Heavenly Messiah, to be invested with the most complete efficacy,
must have a power resting ultimately in God himself. Hence
the title of the Word of God, or the Word, as of still higher
importance, was given him. The Word of God had always been
present among mankind more and more clearly manifested in
the Scriptures, as the light and strength of the righteous. Hence
as the revelation of God himself, the clear declaration of his
secret will, it was rightly regarded as the immediate divine power
itself, as an eternal, mysterious and yet intelligible Being,
derived from God's own existence. It coincided thus with the
conception of wisdom. And when at length this conception of a
being existing essentially in God was applied to the Messiah, and
the name itself given to him, the most perfect idea of the
Messiah was attained.

In order to make the fulfilment of all this possible, it was
necessary that there should appear an individual man so purely
holy and exalted as never man had been. Hence the Messiah
must appear in history, yet raised far above the greatest historical personage, to remove from the true religion every imperfection, to accomplish and establish everything which the holiest
had sought, and, while contending by means of purely spiritual
power derived from heaven, be able to establish his kingdom in
the face of the heathen world.

The *third* prerequisite to the fulfilment was that the people
should be prepared for his reception. It is no small proof of
the power and truth of this religion, that hopes like these,
embracing the whole world, should be projected by it, and that
it should foresee with so much certainty their fulfilment, and so
definitely point out the way in which they were to be accomplished.

But while these hopes had been perpetually rising in grandeur, the possibilities of their accomplishment seemed more and

more diminished, and they had never appeared so distant as when their fulfilment was at hand. In order to make this possible, it was necessary that the attention of men should be awakened to the real nature of the Messianic hopes. The people must be prepared to do everything on their parts and to make every sacrifice with a view to their accomplishment. The people must habituate their thoughts to the fulfilling of this hope, and to its great desirableness, with so new and deep a sincerity, as at once to seek after and to practise everything which could be done beforehand in order to pave the way for this fulfilling, and to remove every obstacle to its coming. It could only be when this was, with the utmost earnestness, attempted, and people were approaching more and more to the great difficulty itself, that the object would become more definite and the right way to it struck out: and among the thousands who had begun to make, at least a distant approach to the real task, perhaps he might be found who alone was the right person to accomplish it, and who should, in the midst of the awakened regards and closer sympathy of all, so fulfil it, as that he should do so for all as well as for himself, and find himself forthwith surrounded with an abundance of spirits who were in some degree qualified to follow him.—p. 93.

For this purpose, as the prophets had foretold, this last epoch of the history must be introduced by the reawakening of the prophetic spirit, and the reappearance of one of the great prophets was looked forward to. John the Baptist represented in fact this ancient prophet. He was the first who thought most deeply on the subject of the Messianic hopes, and he made it a vital question for the entire people. But the advance which he made, rising so wonderfully as it did above the limits of its commencement, derived its efficacy from the truth and grandeur of the hope itself. According to his view of this, he taught that the people of the coming kingdom must purge themselves from all that was corrupt and evil in the past, and that, not only as a people but as individuals, they must make ready for this appearing by a new birth: and in order to carry out his purpose he devised an entirely new instrument and sign, which should be as well the commencement as the emblem of the new life on which the people were to enter. This was baptism on a sincere profession of repentance. "Each member of the community who wished to be reckoned as worthy of the soon-expected Messiah and his salvation, must in presence of him who called for his repentance, confess his sins and promise a new life, and then by the hand of him who in God's stead received this sacred promise, he was plunged in the water as cleansed from the sins he be-

wailed, and rise again as to the new life on which he professed
to enter, and then receive the promise of divine forgiveness and
new grace."—p. 133.

It is almost self-evident that this baptism was an incom-
parably more powerful and substantial thing than that which in
a weakened form was afterwards derived from it.   In connexion
with the solemn confession and absolution, and the preparation
for the coming Messiah, this deep submersion under the hand of
a confessor was the most striking emblem which could have been
chosen for the purpose.   For a while the effect of John's ministry
was exceedingly great, multitudes flocked to him from all quarters, yet the earnest man required more than a formal profession
and fearlessly rejected those who did not appear to be worthy
recipients.   The Baptist, who knew that he was not the ancient
Elias in the literal sense, as little expected, on the same principle,
the literal descent of the Messiah from heaven.   If he held no
other view than that the corruption of the people and the delay
of the promised salvation was due solely to the power of sin, he
could not be a stranger to the hope that the one in whom he
found no trace of sin might be he who was destined, in the divine
mind, to be the Messiah, and on whom in due time all the divine
powers would descend for the accomplishment of his great work.

Nothing is so great and so wonderful in the Baptist as the
elevation and the eagerness of his hopes.   His whole mind was
directed towards eliciting the purest and the most exalted which
could be found in Israel, and which could only appear in the
Messiah.   It was thus impossible that he should fail to recognize
one who presented himself with the real characteristics of the
Messiah.   He must have been intently looking out for such an
one, and with a mind like his so well acquainted with the nature
of the Messianic hopes, and so well qualified to judge of the human
and the spiritual, he was infallibly led to a right decision.   Hence,
though he had known nothing whatever of Jesus till he was in
the midst of his active ministry, he at once recognized him as
the Messiah, and never hesitated between him and any other.
He knew assuredly that only he who was entirely free from the
power of sin could become the true Messiah, and had determined
that if any one of those who came to him for baptism was so
distinguished, he should attribute to him this divine destination
and would await the result.

We observe, with regard to the Professor's theory thus far,
that it does not appear violently objectionable.   Our readers will
see that it is intended to be what we may call, the *natural history*
of the true religion.   In the very short account which is given
of the Baptist in the New Testament, we are not supplied with

the certain means of knowing much of what his real expectations were, and there is large space for speculation. Something like the ideas which the Professor ascribes to him may have been passing in his mind, though we cannot think it likely that he should have depended upon his own discernment of the moral fitness of some one among the candidates for his baptism, for his discovery of the true Messiah, and it was to other considerations that our Lord himself appealed, when a deputation from the Baptist required of Jesus himself a declaration of what he really was.

But in the account which follows of the large share which John and his baptism had in the *elevation* of Jesus to the Messiahship, we have an illustration of what we have above remarked, that the author's philosophy most signally fails him when the subject of it is of the most sublime importance. In attempting to exhibit, as cause and effect, things which have not the most distant appearance of having any such relation, the author almost forces on one the feeling and expression of the poet—

" Quodcunque ostendis mihi sic, incredulus odi."

It is however by the following piece of philosophy that the Professor would prepare us for the phenomena which he is about to introduce, and we give it faithfully as a good specimen of this sort of thing. It will be found on p. 144.

Every truth and principle purely divine, which, entering into human history, becomes an eternal possession and an inextinguishable instinct of humanity, can only spring from its most secret bosom and come born into the world in a fixed form, by an instantaneous and deep commotion of the spirit, at the proper time. For if it be so with regard to any of the truths, though of mere perception, that they can only come forth from the individual materials of which they consist, by such a profound commotion of the spirit as thoroughly seizes and combines them, as when by strong friction a spark is excited; much more a principle which becomes a truth for men only as it has a corresponding power which strengthens and impels them to action. Such is a *religious* truth, which indeed is less a mere truth for the mind to receive than an impulsive power.

The original parts and materials of such a truth may have been long present and even for centuries acting in their individual spheres, and always tending towards each other with increasing energy; but it is only the mightiest commotion of an instant which at length brings them together, and combines them so, as that the new truth and power which is formed from them actually breaks forth like a sudden fire, and entirely fills the spirit which is adapted to receive them. All this especially applies to the instant which was the true beginning of the accomplishment of this great history. This is in fact the genuine *prophetic* or the originally creative in religion, which had now, after so long a cessation, again entered into this history with a determined power, as though it would, with one blow and with one great step, bring on the utmost which had been possible but not yet achieved, in the whole course of this history.—With deference to the good Professor, we confess that all this reminds us much more strongly of the *invention of gunpowder*, and of the "villanous saltpetre" which is doing so much havoc in the East, than of the rise on earth of the saving truths of Christianity. But we go on to the phenomena by which it is to be illustrated.

In accordance with the expectations of the Baptist, in obedience to the better impulse of the time, and as one who must himself exemplify all that was required of Israel, Jesus presented himself for baptism. On that occasion John had doubtless held long conversation with him, and had discovered in him one who entirely differed from all whom he had yet met with, and his heart must have joyfully told him, that this was he whom he had long sought in vain. Notwithstanding John's hesitation on the ground of the superiority of him who was before him, Jesus received baptism at his hand. And as in other cases the Baptist might by his observing and practised eye discern the powerful working of this transaction on the countenance of the baptised as they rose before him out of the water, and the change that was thus produced; so in the case of Jesus he must have observed that a change had come over the baptised, the purity and elevation of his nature having become more resplendent than before. He must in that instant have recognized in Jesus with certainty the character for whom he had been waiting. And if that baptism wrought on him as it had done on others, with mighty power, and thrilled through him with its cleansing efficacy, that instant must have been to Jesus also a complete regeneration, a regeneration by which he became conscious, at the call and consecration of the Baptist, of having become, as the Messiah, an entirely different person, devoted henceforth to the objects and duties of a new life.

"This sublime instant became thus the hour of the birth of Christianity; all the most elevated of sacred antiquity was concentrated in it to form a new combination, which must be the actual fulfilment, and this new thing was from this moment developed invariably and without hindrance, according to its own spirit, so largely that all the future rested upon it."—p. 161.

In speaking about the character and work of the Messiah himself, the author has employed all the power of his language.

It is indeed the *natural* history of the true religion which he is writing, and therefore nothing is to be admitted amongst the phenomena which is not *some how* to be accounted for as belonging to this; and those attributes of the Messiah which are essentially above the human, and which constitute him in the highest sense the Saviour of the world, are not ascribed to him. Yet the human character of Christ is exalted by the Professor to the utmost possible degree, to a degree in fact which far transcends every real definition of the human, and in so doing he has not scrupled to borrow largely from the divine attributes of the Saviour, to swell the fulness of his human virtues and the power of his human works. Retaining, however, for ourselves the assured conviction that the Scriptures to which he appeals, with, in general, such conviction of their historic truth, lead us necessarily to claim for the Messiah a nature and attributes infinitely above those which could appear even in the highest possible development of human history—we accept with a thankful welcome the picture which the author has given of the Son of Man.

He introduces the Messiah's work and teaching in the following manner :—The love and compassion of God towards mankind, such as the prophets had understood it, and by faith expected it, so glowed in his heart that it made his whole regal life absolutely subservient to the good of others, while yet in his deepest humiliation he constantly maintained his regal firmness and dignity. This condescension and voluntary entering into the difficulty of things being perseveringly made the law of life, comprises the larger part of the truths of religion, and while thus he shewed to all the path to serenity and delight in God, he exhibited, especially to those who would in any way exercise command, their perfect model. Hence all his occupations were directed to the establishment of this kingdom, and to this end his discourse contributed in the most important degree to his efficiency. From the first he was himself the chief evangelist— and even to the last moment of his life on earth there was no instant in which his lightest word did not come forth from the very soul of the object on which he was intent, and which did not naturally tend to illustrate that hitherto unseen object which he had introduced into the world, and which he was intent on domesticating among men.

It was not for him to teach, as a mere rabbi, by explaining whatever was true in antiquity, still less as a mere teacher in solving real or seeming difficulties. He did not indeed think himself above entertaining questions of the schools when required, nor did he disdain to recognize the more comprehensive among innumerable truths and to bring them distinctly into view. But nowhere do we meet with any thought which was less than striking, with anything that was forced in its connexion, or with anything which was foreign to his subject. His discourse varies without limit according to the circumstances of his hearers. Sometimes compressed and reserved, sometimes pouring forth with the most serene fulness and copiousness, ascending in his instruction from whatever was before him, or touching upon the most profound mysteries to unveil them, and solving the most intricate questions; uttering whatever was most tender and consoling, or the most withering rebuke. But in every aspect he is equally great, equally striking and satisfying.

Never had the deepest subjects of thought and the highest perceptions of this entire region, been declared, explained, and illustrated with such transparent clearness, and yet with such varied richness and inexhaustible fulness of representation, and at the same time with so irresistible a charm. And never had the whole creation, animate and less animate, the human and the unhuman world stood so open to an observing eye as the emblems of the invisible and unknown; as now, when even the world of the fulfilment of the Kingdom of God found in all directions the representative image of its life.

The brief and dignified certainty of the ancient divine word, as it is made eternal in the Old Testament, was here combined with the exactness and certainty of one who proved the truth by the truth itself, and with the lovely and gentle fulness of a teacher of childlike condescension, to form a whole, which neither in Israel, nor in any other ancient people had been approached before.

It is in the same general style of exalted encomium that the author speaks of our Saviour throughout the work, and had our limits allowed us we should have had pleasure in following him while he shews how the character of Christ rises in proportion to the difficulties and trials which he had to encounter till he established his victory in his death.

We shall however probably return to the subject when the last volume of the work appears, and when the views of the Professor become more distinctly expressed on some important questions which have not yet come forward. We cannot conclude however, without referring with much satisfaction to the manner in which he speaks about the documents of the Old and New Testaments, especially the latter. The idea of inspiration as it is commonly understood does not of course occur to him. But he so speaks of them as to raise them in fact unspeakably above all human writings, and as thus to admit in reality almost all which the most dependent faith requires.　　　　　　　S. T.

ON THE TRUE MESSIANIC IMPORT OF ISAIAH vii., 14—16.

לָכֵן יִתֵּן אֲדֹנָי הוּא לָכֶם אוֹת הִנֵּה הָעַלְמָה הָרָה וְיֹלֶדֶת בֵּן וְקָרָאת שְׁמוֹ עִמָּנוּאֵל : חֶמְאָה וּדְבַשׁ יֹאכֵל לְדַעְתּוֹ מָאוֹס בָּרָע וּבָחוֹר בַּטּוֹב : כִּי בְּטֶרֶם יֵדַע הַנַּעַר מָאוֹס בָּרָע וּבָחוֹר בַּטּוֹב תֵּעָזֵב הָאֲדָמָה אֲשֶׁר אַתָּה קָץ מִפְּנֵי שְׁנֵי מְלָכֶיהָ :

THESE verses form one whole : they cannot be separated : they relate to one birth—to one child. Those interpretations, therefore, which suppose two children to be referred to,—the infant Jesus, born of the Virgin Mary, in the 14th verse, and some other infant born soon after the words were spoken, in the 15th and 16th verses,—are inadmissible. Such interpretations are evidently intended to serve a purpose, and to get rid of what is accounted a grave difficulty. But Scripture must not, on any account or for any purpose be distorted and forced to give a non-natural sense. By getting rid thus of ·one difficulty, we only encompass ourselves with others still more serious.

If, therefore, these three verses speak of the same child, it is still farther evident that that child cannot be the infant Jesus. Of the child whose birth the prophet announces, it is declared, that before he shall know to refuse the evil and to choose the good, Syria and Ephraim shall be made desolate and empty. This desolation took place a few years after; the child, therefore, must have been born more than seven centuries before Christ. Various expedients, indeed, have been had recourse to with the view of removing this difficulty by those interpreters, who, mistaking the import of Matthew i. 22, suppose that, according to the Evangelist, Jesus and he alone must be the child here described. But these expedients are evidently, like the view mentioned just now, but shifts to get rid of a difficulty, and are quite incapable of carrying conviction along with them. The child of whom the words before us are spoken must have been born in the prophet's own day.

Further (for we must take yet another step in opposition to what may be called the generally received view), it is not necessary to suppose the child here spoken of to be miraculously born. עַלְמָה, the word which the prophet uses, does not necessarily mean virgin in the strict sense of that term. It means simply maiden or girl or young woman, being the feminine of עֶלֶם, *youth* (see Gen. xxiv. 43 ; Ex. ii. 8 ; Ps. lxviii. 26 ; Prov. xxx. 19) ; and though it would scarcely be employed to denote a young *married* woman, as Gesenius thinks (compare Song vi. 8, and Isa. liv. 4) ; yet it is clearly distinguished, as well in the cognate languages as in Hebrew, from הָרָה, *virgin*. Compare also the derived nouns עֲלוּמִים, the youthful period of life whether of males or females, and עֲלוּמִים, the state of virginity.

But what then shall we say of the evangelist Matthew, and how shall we reconcile the remarks just made with his interpretation of the passage? In answer to this question we would observe (and to this we crave special attention), that commentators have strangely overlooked the distinction between a sign and a prophecy, and between *the fulfilment of a sign* and *the fulfilment of a prophecy.* The passage before us is usually treated of as if it contained an ordinary prophecy. But Isaiah distinctly declares that he is giving a sign, not that he is uttering a prophecy. Now this distinction is of vast importance, and on it the whole explanation of the passage turns. If he were uttering a prophecy, then that prophecy would be fulfilled when what is uttered has actually taken place. But if he is giving a sign, then when the sign does appear, the prophet's words are not fulfilled. We have the sign, but we want the thing signified *which is the true fulfilment of the sign.* Now in the present case the prophet expressly says, "Therefore—Adonai, he will give you a sign, Behold the Alma shall conceive and bring forth a child." This birth, then, is but the sign (and not even the whole of the sign, as we shall afterwards see); and when it does take place the prophet's words are not fulfilled; we still want the thing signified. Now St. Matthew says that the words of the prophet were fulfilled in the birth of Christ. The birth of Christ, therefore, was not the sign here given, but the thing signified by that sign— the event to which the sign pointed, and in which it received its completion or fulfilment. If Christ's birth were the sign here promised, that event could not be (what St. Matthew says it was), the fulfilment of the prophetic announcement; for such an announcement is fulfilled not when the sign appears, but when the sign finds its full realization in the thing signified. So that the authority of St. Matthew, instead of necessitating an immediate reference of the words to Christ, *actually precludes such a reference.* Christ's birth was not, according to St. Matthew, the sign here promised; it was the fulfilment of the sign—the event which the sign was intended to pre-intimate and foreshadow.

Now that the ultimate fulfilment of the sign given by the prophet upon this occasion is to be found in the birth of Christ, there cannot be the slightest doubt. The prophet addresses himself to *the house of David,* and throughout he has specially in view the divine promises made to that house. The deliverance from Syria and Ephraim he regards not as standing by itself, but as preparatory to and typical of the great deliverance by the coming Christ. In the words with which he concluded his last address, "If ye believe not, ye shall not be established," there is distinct reference (as might be more fully shewn) to the prophecy of Nathan in 2 Sam. vii., that the house of David should be *established* before God for ever. And now in giving this sign, his object is to awaken faith in that great promise, and thus to avert (if that were yet possible, and it could not be possible in any other way), not only the present danger, but those far more dreadful judgments which his prophetic eye beheld impending over king and nation.

Even though it be allowed, therefore, that the sign was partially fulfilled in the expulsion or withdrawal of the forces of Syria and Israel from the Jewish territory, there can be no doubt that it had its ultimate and highest fulfilment in Christ, and that the prophet had this fulfilment specially in view.

But we think it may fairly be doubted whether the deliverance from Israel and Syria forms any part of the fulfilment at all. *That deliverance seems rather to form part of the sign, than of the thing signified.* The sign given by the prophet appears to be, not the birth of a child who should receive the name Emmanuel, but the birth of this child *taken in connexion with the events and experience of his infancy.* "*Butter and honey shall he eat,*" &c., ver. 15, 16. If this be so, how complete the fulfilment in Christ and the deliverance wrought out by him: the birth of the child shadowing forth the long predicted birth of Christ: and the deliverance of Zion prophetically connected with the birth of the child shadowing forth the far higher and more glorious deliverance which flows from the birth of Christ.

Now, let us attend somewhat more particularly to the import of the term אוֹת, here rendered sign. It is unnecessary to enumerate fully its various significations. We shall merely remark that sometimes it denotes the sign or indication of some *present* object, quality, relation or state; thus the sun and moon, the arrangements of the material world, the punishment of the wicked, are signs: sometimes it denotes the sign or memorial of a *past* transaction; thus the Passover, the censers of Korah's company, the twelve stones taken from the Jordan, are all signs: sometimes it denotes the type or pledge or portent of something *future;* thus the rainbow, the blood on the doors of the Israelites, the altar in Egypt, and Isaiah and his sons, are all called signs. Sometimes, again, the sign is a *symbolical act,* as Isaiah's walking naked and barefoot is a sign of the Egyptians being led captive (Isa. xx. 2; see Ezek. iv. 3). Farther, the sign, as well as the thing indicated by it, is not unfrequently a future event: specially is this the case when the sign is itself an event of the same sort, involving the same principle with the event of which it is the sign, and therefore itself a partial fulfilment of the prophecy which receives its complete fulfilment in that event. Thus (1 Sam. ii. 34,) the death of Hophni and Phinehas is a sign to Eli of the destruction of his whole house. Again (1 Sam. x. 7), Saul's receiving certain salutations and presents on his way home from Samuel, is a sign of his future elevation to the throne of Israel according to the word of Samuel. So (Ex. iii. 12) Moses' worshipping upon Mount Horeb after leading Israel out of Egypt, is a sign that God had sent him and would be with him till he had accomplished all he had said to him (see ver. 8). But the passage which deserves our chief attention, as throwing very great light not only on the import of this word, but on the interpretation of the whole passage before us, is the narrative contained in chap. xxxvii. of this book and repeated in 2 Kings xix.

Between that narrative and this there are many points of coincidence and also of contrast. The events it records belong to the reign of Hezekiah the son and successor of Ahaz, a prince of very different character from his father. At the point of time to which it introduces us the terror of the Assyrian arms filled the whole land, just as now, in the reign of Ahaz, Judah trembled before the anticipated assault of Syria and Ephraim. Then, as now, Jerusalem the capital city was threatened, and the monarch and his court scarce hoped to offer any effective resistance to so formidable a foe. Then, as now, a divine message was sent to the king through the medium of the same Prophet Isaiah: and the substantial import of both messages is the same, viz., that the invasion should terminate unsuccessfully—that Jerusalem should not fall—that in a short time the land should be delivered from the presence of the invading armies and these armies and their leaders overwhelmed with disaster and disgrace. And lastly then, as now, a sign was given; and it is remarkable that the sign given to Hezekiah bears a strong resemblance to the sign given on the occasion before us. "This shall be a sign unto thee, ye shall eat this year such as groweth of itself and the second year that which springeth of the same, and in the third year sow ye and reap and plant vineyards and eat the fruit thereof. And the remnant that is escaped of the house of Judah shall again take root downward and bear fruit upward. For out of Jerusalem shall go forth a remnant and they that escape out of Mount Zion. The zeal of the Lord of Hosts shall do this" (xxxvii. 30—32). The sign given is, that during that year and the next year the country would be occupied or at least threatened by the Assyrian armies, so that no regular agricultural operations could be carried on, and the population would require to subsist on the *spontaneous* products of the land, but that in the year after, all danger would cease, and the operations of sowing and reaping, of planting and ingathering, would be allowed to go on as before. *Now of what is this the sign?* Not of the withdrawal and discomfiture of the Assyrian hosts; for in that case the thing signified would precede the sign.   The sign, in fact, includes the withdrawal and discomfiture of the Assyrian hosts, which the prophet regarded (as he clearly intimates in the verses which follow,) as a type and sign of the far more complete victory and conquest reserved for Zion in the days of her promised Messiah. "For," it is added, "I will defend this city to save it for mine own name's sake and for my servant David's sake," *i. e.*, out of special regard to the promise which I have made to him and in the fulfilment of which promise my honour is involved.—Mark, then, how easily the prophet rises from the present partial and temporary deliverance to the future complete and everlasting salvation to be achieved by Christ, regarding the one as a type, a pledge, *a sign* of the other.

Now, it is so also in the case before us.   The sign given to Ahaz is substantially the same as that given to Hezekiah. Butter and honey (ver. 15,) represent those products which are not the fruit of regular cultivation, as opposed to corn and wine which are.   To say that men would subsist on butter and honey during a certain period, is just to say that during that period regular agricultural operations would cease, on account of the actual or threatened presence of superior hostile forces.   And the time fixed for the withdrawal of these forces in the present case is much the same as in the other.   It is "before the child shall know to choose the good and to refuse the evil," that is, while the child is yet in infancy : in the other narrative the period is more exactly defined, it is between two and three years. Now, comparing these two narratives, which present so many points of resemblance, we at once arrive at the conclusion that the sign promised to Ahaz and his house was not the birth of the child simply, but the happy change in the state of the land (from being allowed to lie waste to being brought under cultivation,) which was to take place during the infancy of the child. *And of what was this the sign?*   Not of the withdrawal of the armies of Israel and Syria, for that must have taken place before the cultivation of the land was resumed.   That withdrawal, therefore, is necessarily implied in and forms part of the sign. And what then was the thing signified—the fulfilment of the sign?   It was, just as in the sign given to Hezekiah, the future deliverance and glory of Zion under the Messiah.   For to awaken in the breasts of king and people faith in the certainty of this future deliverance and glory was the end of Isaiah's teaching and whole prophetic activity.

But though these two signs given on different occasions by Isaiah are thus substantially the same, they differ in form. Instead of saying simply, as was said to Hezekiah, after such and such a time the land shall be delivered and cultivation may be resumed, it is said here, a child shall be born and during the infancy of this child the land shall be delivered and cultivation resumed. Doubtless this difference is designed and the design it is not difficult to discover. The deliverance of Judah from Israel and Syria, the prophet connects with the birth of a child in order symbolically to represent the connexion of the future great deliverance with the birth of another child, the Messiah. This sign, therefore, is distinguished from the other by being more purely Messianic, by containing more distinct promise of a personal Messiah, by placing symbolically before us not only the βασιλέια (as in the other) but the βασιλεύς. Now this difference between the two signs is just what might have been anticipated. For at what period must the longing for the advent of the promised βασιλεύς have been most earnest and ardent on the part of the pious in Judah? Must it not have been at those periods, when the throne of Judah was filled by a tyrannical and ungodly prince, and when the pious, feeling by daily bitter experience that the promised seed had not yet come, longed all the more intensely for his advent? It is perhaps for this reason that under Hezekiah, Isaiah points prophetically to the βασιλεία, under Ahaz, to the βασιλεύς.

So much for the Messianic character of these verses. A question of interest, but still of subordinate interest, remains. What child was it whose birth is here so prominently set forth in immediate connexion with the deliverance of Judea from its invaders and as a type of Christ? We will not attempt to enumerate the various opinions of commentators. Perhaps this is a point with regard to which we cannot hope to arrive at a certain conclusion; nor indeed is it of very great moment that we should.

There is a close connexion between this passage and the narrative in the 16th chapter of Genesis. There we find Hagar, the handmaiden whom Sarah had given to wife to her husband Abraham, fleeing from the face of her mistress and exposed to all the perils of the wilderness. As she sat alone by a fountain of water, an angel appeared to her, commanding her to return and submit herself to Sarah, and addressing to her the following prophetic words (ver. 10, 11): "And the angel of the Lord said unto her, I will multiply thy seed exceedingly that it shall not be numbered for multitude. And the angel of the Lord said unto her, Behold thou art with child and shalt bear a son and shalt call his name Ishmael, because the Lord hath heard thy affliction," וְהִנָּךְ הָרָה וְיֹלַדְתְּ בֵּן וְקָרָאת שְׁמוֹ יִשְׁמָעֵאל. The words and forms are exactly the same as those of Isaiah in ver. 14. And the birth of Ishmael, like that of the child here promised, may be regarded as a sign, inasmuch as it was a partial fulfilment of the promise by which the announcement of his birth was accompanied, "I will multiply thy seed exceedingly,"—a promise which the poor fugitive may at first have found it hard to put faith in. But God's ways are not as man's ways; for he chooseth oftentimes the weak things of this world and things that are despised to confound those that are mighty.

It may be that the Alma here mentioned stood in somewhat the same relation to Isaiah as Hagar did to Abraham. In the beginning of the chapter we are expressly told that Shear-jashub was present by divine appointment at this conference of Isaiah with Ahaz; and if he was (as is probable,) a child of tender years, we may suppose that a maiden of the household came along with him. With this maiden the prophet may have been divinely directed to enter into the marriage relation, in the exercise of his prophetic function, as the prophet Hosea was upon another occasion, in order to raise up in his house another sign of the divine will and purpose *(compare the first three chapters of Hosea)*. This at least seems to be the most natural explanation of the insertion of the article—Behold *the* Alma. If she were a Gentile, as Hagar was, the son born to her would be a type all the more perfect of him who came to break down the wall of partition, and to unite in one spiritual body Gentile and Jew.

This union of Isaiah with the Alma, whoever she may have been, was designed symbolically to represent the union of God with his Church; as is quite evident from the chapters in Hosea just referred to. And as the prophet in such a transaction stood in the place of God, so the woman whom he took to wife must have been chosen as a fitting representative of the Church at the time when the symbolic transaction took place. Hence, Hosea is ordered to take to wife an אֵשֶׁת זְנוּנִים, because *such* the Church then was in God's sight. And so Isaiah takes to wife an Alma, a young maiden, because Zion was at that time unmarried—not having God for her husband—childless and desolate: compare liv. 1—6. "Sing, O barren, thou that didst not bear," &c.; especially ver. 4, "Thou shalt no more be put to shame: for thou shalt forget the shame of thy youth (עֲלוּמִים) and shalt not remember the reproach of thy widowhood any more.   For thy maker is thine husband." Here the two states of maidenhood and widowhood are contrasted with the married state : the former as states of affliction and shame, the latter of enjoyment and honour.   Now this passage throws great light upon the transaction before us, which we now see was intended symbolically to intimate that, as Isaiah by entering into the marriage relation with the Alma took away from her the reproach of her maidenhood (עלמה),—so God, having now become the husband of Zion, would speedily remove *her* reproach, increase her seed and clothe her with all the honour and glory belonging to the spouse of Jehovah (compare iv. 1; xxvi. 18; xlix. 14—21; l. 1; lxii. 4; lxvi. 7).   I need not point out how in the descent of the Holy Ghost upon the Virgin Mary, the promise conveyed by this symbolical marriage of Isaiah found its most perfect realization and fulfilment.

In the beginning of the next chapter we have a record of the marriage of the prophet with the Alma, and of the birth of the predicted child (viii. 3, 4).   She is there called הנביאה, the prophetess, not (we think,) because she had now become the prophet's wife, for נביאה has never that signification, but because she was in the true sense a prophetess, being the principal agent in a prophetic transaction; for that person was as truly a prophet who was divinely prompted to pre-intimate the future by act, as he or she who pre-intimated it by word.

It may perhaps be objected to the exposition which we have given, that the evangelist, in quoting from Isaiah, seems to lay peculiar stress upon the term ἡ παρθένος, as containing a pre-intimation of the miraculous birth of Christ.   *We do not think that he does.*   It seems to us quite evident that he lays the chief stress, not on the ἡ παρθένος, but on the name Emmanuel; for to that name he immediately subjoins the explanatory remark, "which is, being interpreted, God with us;" *which he would not have done had he not wished specially to direct attention to that name.*   It is, therefore, in the name Emmanuel that he beholds a pre-intimation of the miraculous birth of Christ by the power of the Holy Ghost.   Compare Luke i. 35 : "The Holy Ghost shall come on thee, and the power of the Highest shall overshadow thee, *therefore* also that holy thing which shall be born of thee *shall be called the Son of God.*"   And here we may notice that the exposition we have given furnishes a new argument for the divinity of our Lord.   Divinity is not necessarily implied in the bearing of the name Emmanuel.   That name might have been given to a child merely to intimate that at the time of his birth God had interposed in his people's behalf, and had proved himself to be *still with them.* So that, if the passage we are expounding be looked on simply as *a prophecy* fulfilled in Christ, we cannot conclusively adduce from the name Emmanuel the fact of his divinity. But if we regard the prophet, not as uttering a prophecy, but *as giving a prophetic sign* —pointing to an Emmanuel of his own day as a sign and type of another Emmanuel afterwards to appear, then it is evident that Jesus, the Antitype, in whom, according to the evangelist, the sign or type found its *fulfilment,* must have been Emmanuel, not in the restricted and humbler sense in which that name was given to the type, but in the *fullest* and highest sense ; otherwise his birth could not have been the *fulfilment* of the prophecy embodied in the typical Emmanuel of Isaiah's day. We do not adduce this as a complete proof of our Lord's divinity, but as a helping argument of great weight.

We conclude with a translation of the passage which we have been attempting to elucidate. *" Therefore, Adonai himself will give you a sign "* (you, *i. e.,* the house of David), *Behold the maiden is with child* (*i. e.,* to Isaiah's prophetic view she was so —she would certainly be so,) *and bringeth forth a son and she shall call his name Emmanuel* (his birth being a sign and pledge of the continued presence of God with his Church and of the future advent of the true Emmanuel). *Butter and honey shall he eat* (or rather shall one eat—shall be eaten—*shall be the common food,* see ver. 22, the land remaining uncultivated,) *till he know to choose the good and to refuse the bad* (till he begins to make distinction between things as pleasant and unpleasant—to be desired and not to be desired, 2 Sam. xix. 35). *For before the child shall know to refuse the bad and to choose the good, the region, of whose two kings thou art in dread, shall be an unpeopled waste* (compare viii. 4).

D. H. W.

THREE MONTHS IN THE HOLY LAND.

(Continued from the last Number, p. 48.)

CHAP. XII.—*Departure from Tiberias—Kefer Kenne—Arrival at Nazareth.*

I was up and ready to start at daybreak; but little refreshed by sleep, for the night had been oppressive and sultry: and, as if to leave on my mind a lasting impression of the climate of Tiberias, the morn withheld its cooling breath from the parched fields around, and the sky, threatening rain, was "red and low'ring."

"It will be foul weather to-day," said I to a lonely shepherd who had been waiting for the dawn by the side of his flock. "It looks like rain; what do you think?"

"Yumtir,—it will rain, and ere long too," was his reply. "Hasten, O Hadjee! and depart, for the rain from heaven will overtake thee."

And so saying, he carefully led the horse on which I was mounted through heaps of stones and ruins of fallen walls strewed around. And having brought me by the deserted gate of the town, at which neither guard nor watchman stood, he put me on the road to Nazareth. Then pointing to its windings against the hill before me, he volunteered to go back and direct my servants who were lagging behind, to follow; and with genuine Eastern courtesy, he wished me a safe journey; adding with an earnest look, "mā' salāme," "in peace."

I took leave of him with the usual farewell, "God be with thee," and put a small coin into his hand. It was evidently more than he expected; for he thanked me, poor man, as if the possession of a few pence was to form an era in his life;—and I rode on. But ere I had proceeded far on the path that rises almost immediately from the town over the hills towards Nazareth, the shepherd's words came true. For a moment, nature was, as it were, breathless. The clear note of the mountain-finch alone broke the deep silence: as deep

> ———" as of summer noon
> When a soft shower
> Will trickle soon
> A gracious rain, freshening the weary bower,"

and large, warm drops began to fall, one by one, at distant intervals, like heralds of the coming cloud; splashing the rocks

around and setting in motion the broad leaves of coltsfoot growing on the barren hill-side. But the rain soon fell in torrents;
and as my only protection against it, a brown-holland umbrella,
was left with my servants, I got thoroughly wet. I felt
refreshed, however; and when the sun emerged from behind the
passing cloud, I was not long in getting dry.

By this time I had reached the top of the pass above Tiberias,
where the path winds round a knoll, called "the hill of the
beatitudes," where our Saviour is said to have delivered his
"Sermon on the Mount;" but doubtless only to suit the convenience of easy-going travellers or of credulous pilgrims. I put,
of course, no faith in that one particular spot; but, on the other
hand, I dwelt fondly for a while on the view I was leaving
behind me and beholding then, perhaps, for the last time. I was
standing, not

———"on Bethsaida's cold and darksome height,"

but where, literally, and in the words of the sweet psalmist of
Britain,

———"over rocks and sands arise
Proud Sirion in the northern skies,
And Tabor's lonely peak 'twixt thee and noon-day light.
And far below, Gennesaret's main
Spreads many a mile of liquid plain.
(Though all seem gather'd in one eager bound.")

On my left spread the undulating landscape of Galilee, as
far back as the hills of Asher clad in evergreen oak. Above
those, the rugged outline of the mountain of Safad rose in the
distance, beyond the plain of Gennesaret, which appeared here
and there in patches between the rugged ridge of rocks that
overhang Magdala. Before me and deep below lay the tranquil
waters of the lake, streaked with the silver lines of sunbeams,
peering from behind dark overhanging clouds which enveloped
the summit of Mount Hermon and rested on the boundless table-
land of Golān and on the cliffs of Gadara. And on the water's
edge stood the ruined city of Tiberias.

Here we might muse on events past and gone without leaving
a trace on the features yet unchanged of this hallowed scene.
I saw it as it was when Canaan of old having settled on the shore
of the Great Sea, the Amorite mountaineers dwelt among these
hills, within sight of Shenir. For thus they called yon hoary
summit of Hermon, which rises over the land of the Kadmonites
and of the Hivites; from whence, even before Abraham was,
Cadmus and Hermione went forth to sow the seed of Theban
blood on the plains of Bœotia. That barren looking hill, this

side Hermon and above this lake, "the Sea of Chinneroth," looks down upon the plain where Joshua vanquished the combined forces of the kings of Hazor, of Madon, of Shimron, of Achshaph, of Chinneroth, of Dor, of the Amorites, Hivites, Perizzites, Jebusites and Hittites, that were gathered against him from all the country round, "like the sand that is upon the sea-shore, in multitude." This tract is the portion of the land of promise given to Asher, Zebulon and Naphthali; that, over the sea, fell to the lot of half the tribe of Manasseh. And that distant range of hills beyond Mount Hermon, those peaks of Lebanon hardly visible in the haze, tell of the days when they were sung by the sacred bards, as limits of the flourishing kingdom of David and of Solomon. For there stand the stupendous piles of Ba'alath, the great and renowned city; which attest to this day the glory of him who reared them as monuments of his splendid reign. But they tell also of the days of sorrow that followed, when the king of Assyria carried away captive their inhabitants; and sent in their stead others who made Zebulon and Naphthali "a land of the shadow of death;"—Galilee, a taunt and a proverb: "Art thou also of Galilee? Search and look; for out of Galilee ariseth no prophet;"—and Samaria, a term of indelible reproach. But on this land too, on Galilee, rose the Sun of Righteousness with healing in his wings; when its inhabitants, who were then "sitting in darkness, saw a great light," and rejoiced at it for a time. That light has again departed; and again darkness broods over the whole. Yet we see

> "Streaks of a brighter heaven behind
> A cloudless depth of light,"

when He will come again and visit it in glory. Lord, may we be of those who having loved thine appearing, will be found ready to meet thee at thy coming in thy kingdom!

My servants had now joined me; and casting one last lingering look on the lake, I turned round and soon found myself in the midst of very different scenery. Leaving on the left the main road which we had hitherto followed, we took a path to the right, and entered at once the meadow land of Zabulon. Here a large caravan of Arabs crossed our path on their way to the south. One or two of them stopped to speak to me; and with their greeting of peace, they asked me whither I was going. I told them; and after a few friendly words on both sides they left me to continue my journey, while their mettled steeds sniffed the wind of the plain, and prancing along in their gay trappings they soon disappeared over the brow of the hill towards Mount Tabor.

A little further on, we passed by foundations of very ancient buildings cut in the rock. Then leaving the small village of Lubiêh on a rising ground to our left, our path led us through the rich meadows of the vale of El-Buttauf, which now lay spread before us—bounded on the south by a low range of hills covered with oak and overtopped by the rounded summit of Mount Tabor;—on the west by the hills of Nazareth;—and on the north by the distant mountains of Galilee. Labourers were at work in the fields. Some were ploughing with wooden ploughs similar to the one I had noticed on the plain of Tyre. Others were sowing seed broad-cast over the rich soil of this plain, while a few women were washing their clothes in a fountain close by. The meadows through which we were passing were spangled with bright spring flowers; among which flitted the sprightly butterflies, *Pieris Daplidice and Cardamines, Colias Cleopatra, Argynnis* of various kinds, and the stately *Pap. Alexanor* basking in the sun, which now shone brightly in an almost cloudless sky. Then the sparkling bee-eater too, the brilliant roller and the friendly crested-lark—three frequent attendants of the traveller in this land, either darted in the air, flew from tree to tree by the hill-side, or tamely sauntered along our path,—all joining in their hymn of thanksgiving to him who made them. A gentle breeze waved the growing corn, and rustled among the tall grass of the plain, while fanning the pilgrim's brow to give him fresh vigour for his day. I shared the full enjoyment of nature around me, and sped onwards across the plain, towards yon undulating heights, which rise, I was told, above the city of Galilee I longed to see—above Nazareth.

In about an hour's ride along the foot of the hills which enclose this vale to the south, we reached the pretty village of Kefer Kenne. It lies against the hill, at the entrance of a narrow valley which runs north and south; and it is embosomed in rich plantations of almonds, pomegranates and ancient olive-trees. Tradition, and that too of recent date, fixes upon this village as the scene of our Saviour's first miracle at the wedding feast. I was therefore led to alight under the mulberry trees that grow by a small Greek church—an unpretending square building—erected over the very place (they say) where the miracle was wrought; and there I was requested to enter the sacred edifice and to inspect a stone water-pot—the very one also from which the wine was taken and tasted by the " governor of the feast !" And then, as if it were a matter of course, the aged priest who had shewn me over the place, asked me to add my written certificate to that of many other travellers and pilgrims—to the effect that it was even so; and that this was truly the very place and the very water-pot mentioned in Scripture. "It matters much," he said, "that you should do so, for that of late some doubt has been expressed on the subject; and travellers do not come here as much as they used to do."

"My good friend," said I to him, "to tell you the truth, I do not believe this is the place where the miracle took place, or that the thing you shewed me in the church is one of the water-pots used at the wedding feast."

"Now don't say that, Hadjee, but write. There's a good man."

"I shall only write what I believe correct, as far as I know; and I shall tell the travellers that they had better go and visit Kāna el-Jelīl, if they wish to form a more correct idea of the probable situation of Cana of Galilee."

I did so accordingly; for Kāna el-Jelīl, which is the name by which "Cana of Galilee" is mentioned in the Arabic Scriptures, and the ruins of which are still seen further to the north of El-Buttauf—has greater claims to our veneration as the site of our Saviour's first miracle, and as the birth-place of Nathaniel. But I also gave the poor man a small trifle, which reconciled him readily to my heretical notions on the subject of his relics. Before leaving the village, however, I looked about for some fragments of "water-pots," said by travellers to be found in abundance in this place, and to be a strong presumptive proof in favour of Kefer Kenne being Cana of Galilee. But they too are a myth.

The sun was past the meridian and the refreshing breeze wafted from the hills around, was for me the signal to depart. I wished the venerable priest good bye and taking leave of the church and the water-pot in it, I left Kefer Kenne for Nazareth. For there at least, I should have ample opportunity to indulge safely in associations of events endeared beyond compare to every one whose faith is in Christ. There I should study the features of a scenery with which, undoubtedly, he was familiar during the greater part of his life on earth; there I should tread the ground he must have trod. There I need not be told, "he was here, or he went there." There I can but look around, worship and give thanks.

The road, outside the village, passes by a large fountain of clear abundant water which flows into a square trough of ancient workmanship; and issuing from thence, continues to gurgle among groves of olives, pomegranates and evergreens, on its way down the narrow valley which it fertilizes as in days of old, when Zabulon rejoiced in the produce of his land. Crossing this dell, we began to ascend a rugged path on the hill opposite; now among rocks and by the edge of a deep ravine; and then winding through luxuriant crops of wheat, from whence the village of Kefer Kenne—retired although on the pilgrim's route—looked picturesque and at peace. We crossed the brow of the hill and descended into a glen on the other side, leaving the small hamlet of Er-reine against the hill on our right. Then along the narrow path that winds against the height immediately before us, through groves of almonds and of olive-trees and across meadows covered with the richest herbage, until we reached the summit of the hill; from whence, to my surprize and infinite delight, my eyes rested on the most deeply interesting view a poor sinner, servant of Christ, may be allowed to see in this world.

As I wished to remain here alone and undisturbed in order, if possible, to mark my first impressions of this scene, in a pencil sketch—and to dwell on the landscape before me, I sent onwards my servants, to pitch my tent on the spot I pointed out to them, in an olive-grove, between the church and fountain of the Virgin and the town; and there to make ready for my coming.

The spot on which I was standing, might be appropriately compared to the upper row of seats in an amphitheatre of hills which rise around the secluded town of Nazareth, as if to shelter it and to shut it out from the rest of the world. The town itself, built against the slope of the hill, facing the east and south and surrounded by thickets of prickly pear, evergreens and groves of fig, olive, and other trees—occupies, as it were, the lower tier of the amphitheatre, just above the narrow meadow plain spread in the hollow beneath and covered with rich pastures and flocks. Beyond the ridge of hills opposite, on the other side of this plain and to the south-east, arose the grassy summit of Little Hermon (Jebel ed-Duhy) and the more distant hills of Gilboah (Jelbûn), at the foot of which lies Jezreel; and behind these the horizon was bounded on the east by the hills of Bashan and of Gilead; on the south by those of Samaria and of Judea, and closed in to the west with the level heights of Carmel above Taanach and Megiddo, across the plain of Jezreel.

The air was soft and fragrant of the smell of the gum-cistus which grows here in abundance. And the hills which already cast their long afternoon shadows across the plains, appeared in a well-defined outline against the sky and left at once on the mind a clear and distinct impression of their form and relative position. The scene I beheld was a reality. I carried my thoughts back some thousand years and then saw on the landscape before me, Saul and his men repairing to the retired village of Endor at the foot of Little Hermon;—his army routed by the

Philistines and his own fall on Mount Gilboah—the stronghold
of Omri among the hills of Samaria.   Then Ahab at Jezreel—
Elisha at Shunem and on the heights of Carmel.   But dearer
still than all those is Nazareth, the city where Jesus dwelt
as a child; where he lived unknown or despised as a Galilean;
then learning obedience for our sake, by the things which he
suffered.

I could indulge in peace in thoughts of this kind, as I sat
reclining on a rock covered with moss, over against the town.
For there was no noise under the whole heaven.   Not a voice
was heard; but the familiar twitter of the lark fluttering among
shrubs of rock-rose in bloom, or under tufts of tall feather-grass.
I loved to dwell on this solemn scene.   Who, indeed, could
stand where I did, and behold the landscape I then saw, the
same as when he lived here in this peaceful retreat, without feelings too deep for utterance? without almost saying with Simeon;
"Lord, now lettest thou thy servant depart in peace, for mine
eyes have seen thy salvation;" the place where thy son my
Saviour dwelt?   He too, often looked at this beautiful scenery,
the work of his own hands; but lying under the curse of sin
which he was come to remove for ever.   He too looked at these
same flowers, and saw them as I do open their delicate form to
the hill-side breeze; he too gathered them, when as a child he
went about with his mother, the one "blessed among women."
And afterwards he noticed them as they smiled at his presence.

> "Sweet nurslings of the vernal skies,
>   Bath'd in soft airs, and fed with dew,
>   —— ye could draw th' admiring gaze
>   Of him who worlds and hearts surveys:

> "Ye felt your Maker's smile that hour,
>   As when he paus'd and owned you good;
> His blessing on earth's primal bower,
>   Ye felt it all renew'd."

For he mentions them as examples of his bountiful care;—but
only to tell us how far greater is the tenderness of his love for
those whom he came to seek, and to save from death—and who
are dearer to him than the grass of the field; even though they
be of little faith.

And these little birds, unknown, uncared for even of the
wandering shepherd, were not forgotten by him.   No! not one
of them falls to the ground without the will of his Father that is
in heaven.   And are we not better than they?

"There is not a strain to memory dear,
   Nor flower in 'sacred' grove,
There's not a sweet note warbled here,
   But minds us of thy love.
O Lord, our Lord, and spoiler of our foes,
There is no light but thine: with thee all beauty glows."

It was now time to descend the hill and to repair to my tent, which I could see in the distance, already pitched and prepared for me. The path I followed brought me at the bottom of the hill by the church of the Virgin, to the fountain at which a few women of Nazareth were come to draw water. I slaked my thirst at this spring, of which he must have drank often; and I prayed that my soul might be refreshed by the water which he alone gives; and that his words might be to me a well of water springing up into everlasting life.

The head-dress of the women struck me. It consists of a pad of black or blue cloth, in shape very much like the chin-strap of a helmet, and, like it also, fastened under the chin. That pad is covered with the whole of the money belonging to the woman. Every piece of money has a hole bored through it, and is sewn on to the pad, very much like the scales of fish. You see at once what the amount of property of the woman is; whether it be gold, as among the wealthiest, or silver, or even copper, among the poorest. Money is, in fact, worn by them as an ornament; and partly on that account, they rarely, and only when in the greatest need, part with any of it, as it spoils their ornamental head-dress at once and for all. One woman had her *asmadié*, as they call that head-dress, covered with gold coin; one or two had only coppers; while a poor-looking woman, the wife apparently of a small tradesman of the town, had on but a few pieces of money. But they were regularly arranged on each side. I then thought of the woman, who, having ten pieces of silver, lost one, of whom our Saviour tells us in his parable. How she would look for it, and how her neighbours and friends, both at the well and at home, would hear of it and see it, and rejoice with her after she had found it! For although we cannot affirm that the dress of the women was exactly the same in the days of our Saviour, it is nevertheless most probable that it was then, as it is now, peculiar to this locality. For in the East nothing changes but time.

I came to the tent and found my servants gone to the town to buy food. They returned after a short time, bringing what they had got,—eggs, a little stale butter, some bruised barley, and a few loaves of bread, with some honey. This might have been but a sorry fare at other times; I made, however, an excellent meal of it. For the great enjoyment of free and independent travel amid scenes of such intense interest, was, of itself, food to me. I required, besides, no more than that which was often my only fare,—barley-bread, a few dried figs, and a draught of clear water from some hallowed spring.

My dinner over, I left the tent in charge of my servants, and climbed the hill on which the town is built, and to the west of the one on which I had been before. I had to make my way among rocks, and by hedges of prickly pear, through meadows on which camels were grazing, to the top of the heights which overhang the town by the monument of Neby Ismaîl, and from whence my eyes ranged over a magnificent landscape. I faced the east immediately above the town, the whole of which I now surveyed;—its square, and next to it the mosque with its picturesque, but foreign minaret; a little beyond the church and convent of Terra Santa, and opposite the great khan of the town, surrounded by the town itself, built in tiers against the hill, and consisting chiefly of the low square dwellings of its inhabitants.

Beyond the hills over against me, rose the rounded summit of Mount Tabor (Jebel Tûr) and Little Hermon, at the foot of which I could distinguish the villages of Endor, Nain, and Shunem. Then Jezreel, Mount Gilboa, the mountains of Gilead, of Samaria, and of Judea, the plain of Jezreel, and beyond it the whole length of Mount Carmel. Behind me the Great Sea bounded the western horizon; and the town of Sephoris, the hills of Galilee and the far distant range of Ante-Lebanon closed the scene to the north. The sun was verging towards Mount Carmel. Taanach and Megiddo, and the bed of the river Kishon already lay deep in the shade. Bashan and Gilead appeared on the eastern horizon, in the mellow tints of an evening sky; while the nearer hills cast their long purple shadows over the sun-lit meadows of the plain. But while I was contemplating this magnificent prospect, and realizing the long-cherished hope of treading this holy ground, the sun sank behind Carmel, and soon the summits of Tabor and Hermon alone shone in his last rays, with which they seemed unwilling to part; while the whole of nature lay cold and lifeless at their feet. The shades of evening, however, gradually gained on the warm evening sky above; until the breath of eve began to stir, and the moon arose behind Mount Tabor and shed her pale but clear light over the scene; translating it as it were in a moment, from the warm brilliancy of an Eastern day, to the cool brightness of an Eastern night.

I had watched the moonbeams on the eddying wave of the Cephissus, in the dear classic land of Greece. I had listened at night to the low gurgling of the Castalian spring, as it trickles from the sides of Mount Parnassus at Delphi. I had also repeatedly sat in the gigantic temples of Thebes in the dead of night, and watched the moon rising over those awful relics of other ages, and dwelt on their past glory, when the same light shone through their sacred piles on the countless multitudes at their evening worship of the Queen of heaven. But the moon rising over Nazareth tells of other days; and the breath of eve, as it waves the grass of these hills, murmurs of other and greater glories than those of the proudest kingdom of this world. There is a look in nature which you see nowhere else; there is in the rustling of the olive-leaf at even a whisper of peace,—of "peace on earth, of good will; yea, of good will towards men," —brought by Him who dwelt at Nazareth.

I retraced my steps back to my tent, and found there an inhabitant of the town engaged in deep converse with my servants. It was Abou Nâsir, an Arab-Greek Christian and merchant in Nazareth, who had become acquainted with one of my servants during his residence at Beyrût. He had come to persuade me to repair for the night to his house in the town. He represented to me with great energy the danger I ran from a visit of Arabs, and tried to prove how much more comfortable I should be in his house than in my tent.

"Do Khawājāh! do come and lodge with me. I have a room ready for you."

"Thank you, my good friend; but I prefer by far my tent to any house in this country, and during such a fine night as this."

"But the Arabs! think of that."

"Well! I do not fear them. I have heard of their doings; but they have never done me any harm."

"As you like then! In God's keeping!"

"Yes! and always: by night as well as by day."

"But what will you do to-morrow?"

"Go to Jebel Tûr."

"You will take an escort, of course?"

"If it is to please you, I have no objection."

"To please me! Allāh yebārak fîk!—God bless you! It is indeed to please me; for it is to spare your life. I will provide it for you."

"Be it so. We start at day-break."

"In-shallāh! God willing."

So saying, Abou Nâsir left me to go home. I then sat at the door of my tent to eat my evening meal in the silence of the evening, broken at intervals by the distant voices of women at the fountain, and by the monotonous note of a scops-owl sitting on the branch of an old olive-tree behind me on the hill-side.

It was at last time to retire. I spread my bed on my carpet in the tent; and, full of gratitude for having been allowed to see this day, I began to anticipate the next, and lay down to rest.

CHAP. XIII.—*Departure from Nazareth—Mount Tabor—Endor—Nain—and Return to Nazareth.*

I started before day-break, with one servant and the 'guard' provided for me by Abou Nāsir. He was probably a friend of his, short of work, who had no objection to an easy day's work and good pay for it.

He bravely led the way on the path that winds up the hill to the east of the town, from whence we saw the sun rise from behind the ridge of wooded hills which abut on Mount Tabor, and shed abroad on the earth the light and life of his first morning rays. We continued our route against the hill-side, and soon after, we found ourselves enveloped in a thick mist, which lasted until, as the sun rose higher in the sky, the clouds dispersed, and we found ourselves near the foot of Mount Tabor. The scenery through which we passed was very varied and picturesque, and reminded me of many parks in England, as I trod the path up hill and down dale, through woods of oak *(Q. Ægilops)* and across meadows covered with rich pastures—the favourite haunt of gazelles. One started at our approach, and bounding over the mead, soon disappeared in the recesses of the forest beyond.

From this point Mount Tabor presents the remarkable appearance of a huge hay-cock, from whence it probably derives its name, of easy ascent from the north, but abrupt and rocky on the south side. Completely rounded at the top, it stands alone, and separate from a chain of hills on the north—"a high mountain apart." It is doubtless owing to this circumstance that tradition marks it as the scene of our Saviour's transfiguration, although it would appear from the gospel narrative that the event took place farther north; perhaps not far from the upper end of the sea of Galilee. Be that as it may, Mount Tabor is in itself a remarkable mountain; and for that reason it became, even in the oldest times, celebrated as one of the most notable hills in Canaan. Hither drew Barak, at Deborah's behest, before his battle against Sisera; and from hence he and his men pursued and discomfited the captain of Jabin's army. It was on the "plain of Tabor" there, at the foot of the hill, that Saul found his father's servants who were in search of him. "Tabor also and Hermon (that is, "Little Hermon" across the "plain of Tabor" opposite) shall rejoice," says the Psalmist, "when they see the glory of our God."   And its fame must have extended not only to Rhodes, that boasted of her Mount Atabyrius, but also further, even to the shores of Sicily, if olden writers tell true.

We descended into a deep ravine, and crossing near to "Daberoth," the main road from Damascus to Jerusalem, which we had left the day before, a little above Tiberias, we began to climb the mountain on the north side, where it is covered with shrubs of various kinds, among which I remarked a large quantity of storax *(Styrax officinalis L.)* in full bloom. As we rose higher, the prospect became more extended; until, from the top of the mountain, the eye soared over a wide expanse of hill and dale, of mountain and plain, of rivers and water courses, of lake and sea—embracing almost the whole of the Promised Land.   From the chain of Lebanon in the north, over the sea of Galilee and the mountains that rise around it and Mount Hermon, along the whole of Gilead and the hills of Moab at last lost in the haze, to the south; and then by the plain of Jordan, the hills of Little Hermon, of Gilboa, Samaria, Judæa, the whole of the plain of Jezreel and the course of the River Kishon, on to the level heights of Mount Carmel, and glimpses of the Great Sea, to the west.   Then the prophet's words came to mind, and I saw them true: "As Tabor is among the mountains, and Carmel is by the sea," so surely shall the word of the Lord come to pass.

I rested some time under the shade of an old oak-tree growing among the ruins of ancient churches, built on the summit of the mountain, in full enjoyment of the view and of the fine fresh air that played around the top of this noble hill.   Meanwhile, the sun had risen much higher in the sky above, and the shadows of the hills having almost disappeared, the landscape lost the freshness of its first morning look in the heat of noon.   I gathered a bunch of the scarlet-everlasting, which grows abundantly on the summit of Mount Tabor; and, having packed up my saddle-bags, we prepared to descend the hill.

The descent on the south side was by no means easy; especially at first.   Even our horses, wonderfully sure-footed as they were, found it difficult to keep their footing along the very steep and narrow track that winds down the precipitous and rocky slope of the hill.   But at last we all came to the lower slopes, and reached the "plain of Tabor," which separates this hill from Little Hermon, without any accident.   From hence, from this

high ground which connects these two mountains at their base,
flow two tributary streams; one into the Jordan, eastward, and
the other to the westward, into the "River Kishon." We crossed
the latter of these tributaries: and then, ascending the northern
slope of Little Hermon, we came to the retired and wild looking
village of Endor; the very place (even judging from the look of
it) where the witch was at home in the days of Saul. The inhabitants, startled at our arrival, crept like rabbits out of their
dwellings, for the most part excavated in the hill side. They
were, most of them, grim-looking men, descended in direct line
from their wizard ancestors; and they began to stare at me, and
handle my clothes, as if they never had before seen a traveller among them. The sheikh, or head-man of the village,
rather better behaved than the rest, yet still very free and easy
in manner, led me to their "manzīl" or shake-down. It was
a ruined dwelling consisting of the four bare and dilapidated
walls, covered in part only by a roof in which time had made
wide and frequent gaps, but which had the advantage of admitting free ventilation of air, a very necessary measure indeed, as
I found, to my cost, when they did me the honour of placing
me on a very old and dirty mat, spread on the ground, between
two far from cleanly natives; one of whom was a Nubian, whose
hair was clotted with grease, and who was, to all appearance, a
sworn enemy to water and washing.

These good people insisted on my partaking of food. I endeavoured to decline their civilities, but in vain. They asked
me what I should like to have. But, as the choice lay between
stale butter, made of sheep's milk, and eggs, I chose the latter
as the safer of the two. They, however, had never seen eggs
boiled; they only knew how to roast them as we do potatoes in
the ashes on the hearth. In the course of time, one of them
brought me a couple of these eggs in his hand. The difficulty
was to hold them; for they were very hot. I cut a round hole
in the loaf they had given me, and stuck one of the eggs in it.
They seemed much amused at the result, and watched me narrowly while I was eating, literally pulling me about, and wondering at the material of my dress. But their astonishment
knew no bounds when they saw me sketch.

"A bit of wood that writes! Mā shallāh!" said one.

"Give it me," said the sheikh, rather gruffly, snatching it
from my hand. "I shall keep it!" Remonstrance was, of
course, of no avail. They would have taken by force what I
would not give with good grace; and so I yielded.

"Give me one too!" cried another, who saw that he might
get it for asking." "Give me one too!" and so saying he

helped himself to another pencil out of my small stock of four or five.

"Wallāh! how it acts! But what is it?" asked the sheikh, "iron, or stone, inside the wood?"

I then felt a rude grasp of the hand on my left shoulder from one of the party, taller than myself, who said, "'Āti-lī kemān, wāhed! give me one also! Khawājāh 'āti-lī wallāh! give me one, Sir, I tell you!" And I was obliged, in self defence, to part with a third pencil, to my great regret.

I then thought it was high time to be gone, and I took leave of them; not altogether sorry to do so. My servant too, as well as the "guard," did not half like the look of my hosts of Endor, to whom my "guard" was especially civil. I inquired about the spring from which this village must have taken its name ('Ain-dôr), when one of the party offered to lead me to it. It is a wide circular opening in the rock on the mountain side, a little above the village; from whence flows a copious spring.

From thence we followed the path along the winding foot of the hill, sometimes among rocks covered with honeywort, or down into rocky ravines; then across meadows adorned with blue lupine, scarlet adonis, lychnis, and other bright spring flowers in abundance; and we soon reached the small and retired village of Naim, which is no other than the "city called Nain," mentioned by St Luke.

From this spot, the view, although very limited, was nevertheless full of interest. On the foreground stood the village of Naim. Here our Saviour, while journeying from place to place in the discharge of his ministry, met the poor widow weeping for her son who was being carried to his grave. Then, when he who came to bear our sorrows saw the broken-hearted mother, he "had compassion on her, and said unto her: Weep not."—There was real comfort in that voice. Those very words, coming from his mouth, relieved her aching heart, and soothed her pain. "He then touched the bier and called the dead to life, and he delivered him to his mother." It was thus he taught us here both his unbounded love and his almighty power to save, even from death.—Then, immediately below the village, stretches from east to west the undulating "plain of Tabor," which opens into that of Jezreel on the left. On the opposite side of it rises abruptly from the plain the lower range of hills of Galilee, which extend from Mount Tabor on the east, as far as the "forest of Carmel" and the steep banks of the Kishon on the west. From this point Nazareth appeared in the distance, and, as it were, nestled on high among the hills.

From Naim we descended into the plain, once covered with

the slain of Jabin's army, but now clad in rich pastures and luxuriant crops—the pride of the month of Abib in the land of Canaan. The path we followed through fields of blue lupine in bloom, spangled with the large scarlet flowers of the vernal-adonis, and with white umbelliferous plants, soon brought us to the foot of the ascent to Nazareth. In about a quarter of an hour's march we reached the top of the pass into the amphi-theatre of hills in which Nazareth lies esconced. The sun was then nearing Mount Carmel in the west, and long shadows already stretched across the plain of Jezreel at our feet. We turned round, and then descended a gentle declivity into the meadows that spread from hill to hill just below the town. Na-zareth then appeared before us, within ten minutes walk, sur-rounded by groves of olive, carub and other trees—the abode of peace and of repose. How strange that its name should ever have been an evil proverb, as if nothing good could come from thence!

The sun was set when we entered the town; and passing by the Latin church and the mosque, we repaired at once to the tent. The evening, however, was so fine that I could not abide within; but while my evening meal was being prepared, I strolled out towards the fountain of the Virgin. The women of Nazareth mustered there in numbers, every one in turn waiting to fill her pitcher at the spring. There were among them wives and daughters of some of the richest inhabitants, with head-dresses of great value, who carried their pitcher of water on their shoulder side by side with the poorest of their sex. For in the simple land of the East the sheikh's wife or his daughter fetches water, and tends her father's or her husband's flock when he cannot do it himself. As I was standing by and listening to their animated gossip,—rather more interesting than gossip is in general, from being in Arabic—and noticing the diversity of taste displayed in their dress, all made after the same pattern,—a fine-looking Arab, with a flowing beard, and conspicuous 'abaya loosely thrown over one shoulder, came to the fountain, leading his camels to watering. The scene was thoroughly Eastern and picturesque in the extreme. It was Eliezer, and the girl to whom he said, "Ya bint! 'ati-li moiyé,"—O daughter! give me some water; "w'eski el-jemāl,"—and water the camels, was Rebecca, at the well of the city of Nahor. There she was bearing on her shoulder the pitcher she had been filling at the well, and which she let down from her shoulder, saying to the camel-driver; "Eshrob!" Drink! He did not, it is true, offer her a nose-ring and gold bracelet in exchange for her services; but this incident was not requisite to bring to mind a more living picture than I then beheld of the Scripture narrative.

On my return to the tent I found Abou Nāsir, who had come to inquire after my welfare.

"Praised be God, friend, you are come back safe!" said he, with a graceful salutation. "Seen no Arabs?"

"Plenty of them, and queer-looking ones too!"

"And they have done you no harm?"

"None whatever!"

"They would, however, if they came here. You must, indeed, come and sleep at my house to-night: you really must. I particularly wish to talk to you."

"Thank you, my good friend; but let us talk here!"

"No! better at home. At all events won't you come and see us?"

"With all my heart!"

"Let us go then!" And so saying, he led the way into the town, which was not five minutes' walk from my tent. On our way thither we passed by a perpendicular rock of considerable height, which looks like an ancient quarry, on the very edge of which above many houses of the town are built. This struck me at once as "the rock" (it is the only one in the place) "on which the city was built;" and from which the hardened inhabitants attempted to throw down our Saviour. This rock, which every passer-by may see for himself, and which is most likely the locality alluded to in the sacred narrative, has nevertheless been overlooked or ignored by "sight-seers," who prefer being taken by monks and guides to a rock some two or three miles from the town; upon which, assuredly, Nazareth never was built. This seems the more inconsistent as the same local authorities mention, with assurance, "the stone on which our Saviour ate his last supper with his disciples;"—"Joseph's shop,"—"and the spot from whence the stone cell in which the angel Gabriel appeared to the Virgin Mary, was taken to Loretto;"—all within the town, and entitled, they say, to the greatest credit.

Winding our way through a narrow street, we turned to the right, and presently came to Abou Nāsir's house. The gate opened into a yard, on the right and left side of which were the kitchen and other offices, where his daughters were busily engaged in household duties when I entered. He took me at once to the opposite side of the yard, and there ushered me into the principal apartment, intended for the gathering together of the family, and for the reception of visitors. It was a large room, built in arches up to the roof. The floor was the native earth; but on the left side there was a wooden platform, raised about a foot from the ground, on which a mat was spread: here I, as guest, was asked to sit down. The servants of the establishment do not in general tread this floor; and any member of the family, as for instance, the daughters or the wife, when waiting on their father or husband, take off their shoes and leave them upon the ground before they venture to step on the mat. It was probably on a floor and matting of this kind that our Saviour sat in the house of Lazarus at Bethany. Mary then sat at his feet on the ground, like the meanest servant, unworthy as she felt herself to tread the ground on which her Lord sat at meat. There, in that humble posture, she listened to him, regardless of anything else, while her sister Martha, who "was cumbered about much serving," and careful and troubled about many things, remained in a degree a stranger to that good part which Mary had chosen, and which would never be taken from her.

Within this apartment there was on the right-hand side of the door, a railed gallery, about twelve or fifteen feet from the ground, and accessible by a staircase against the wall. It is the "reception-room" for guests at feasts. Might it not be the "upper room" (ἀνώγεων) mentioned in St. Luke xxii. 12, where our Saviour ate his last supper with his disciples? Abou Nāsir bade me go up the stairs and said, "Is it not a convenient place for friends to eat with me?" Then wishing to shew me the whole of his house, in order to tempt me to stay with him, he took me to the opposite side of the yard; and then going before me up a flight of steps outside, to the top of a part of the house, and opening the door of a room built there (ὑπέρωον),

"Now," said he, "is not this a beautiful room for you?"

"Very good, indeed! But I assure you I prefer my tent."

"Well now, sit down, I have something to say to you." And he then went on to express his earnest wish to be made English Consul for Nazareth; asking me if I could possibly promote his prospects. I replied that I regretted it was utterly out of my power to do so in any way; and that I thought the less responsibility he incurred in life, the more likely he would be to discharge it satisfactorily to himself and to others. He did not seem to enter into my views on the subject; but finding I could lend him no help, he dropped the matter for the time.

As it was getting late, I wished to return to my tent. Abou Nāsir courteously walked back with me past the town and as far as the entrance of the olive grove in which my tent was pitched. I found my servants waiting for me; and as I felt tired after my day's journey, I lay myself down and soon fell fast asleep.

CHAP. XIV.—*Departure from Nazareth—Cana of Galilee—
Sepphoris—Return to Nazareth—and home scenes there.*

Wednesday, April 20th.—I was up with the lark, and like it
too, in good spirits and ready to start on an exploring journey
to Kāna el-Jēlīl, or "Cana of Galilee," as it is supposed to be.
I retained the same guard, more as a guide than an escort, and,
taking with me my two servants, I left Nazareth.

Passing by the fountain and church of the Virgin, we ascended the hill above it, and followed the path by which we had
come from Tiberias to Nazareth, as far as Kefer Kenne. Then,
turning to the left, in a northerly direction, down the narrow
valley which is watered by the fountain outside the village, we
came, in about an hour's march, to the hamlet of Rummāneh
(or Rimmon). It is prettily situated among olive-trees on the
hill that divides the plain of El-Buttauf in its length; and from
which the pilgrim's eye rests on either side, upon richly-cultivated
land, bounded north and south by hills covered with verdure.

After a halt at this place, we came into the plain, and, crossing it in its narrowest part, we reached Kāna el-Jelīl in about
half an hour. It stands a little above the plain, on a knoll at
the foot of the hills of Esh-Shaghur, which surround El-Buttauf
on the north. Nothing of the village at present remains, but
the scattered ruins of dwellings, some of which appeared as if
they had recently been used as pens for cattle, and of no very
ancient date. The dull monotonous tint of the heaps of rubbish,
and of the rocks on which they stood, was relieved by clumps
of bright flowers, such as the scarlet ranunculus, the blue lycopsis, and various evergreens and other shrubs, among which I
remarked the viscous ononis *(O. Hispanica)* growing there in
great profusion and covered with bright yellow blossoms.

While my servants smoked their pipes under a tree at the
bottom of the hill, I sat apart on a rock above the ruins of the
village in order to study the features of the scenery before me;
—the rich plain of El-Buttauf, widening to the left, and then
closed in all round by hills above the Sea of Galilee to the east
and south, where it is surrounded by the more distant heights of
Sepphoris and of Carmel on the horizon. The Sea of Galilee is
not visible from Kāna el-Jelīl; but the cleft between the hills
to the eastward of the plain, marks the road our Saviour must
have followed when he "went down from Cana of Galilee to
Capernaum." It is expressly said that he "went down." For
although Cana is as it were on a plain, it is nevertheless much

higher than the shore of the Sea of Galilee, on which lay Capernaum. Here I opened my Syriac Gospels, and read with tenfold interest the first and second chapters of St. John, while looking at the scenery familiar to our Lord and to the disciple who was worthy—for in him there was "no guile."

We left Kāna el-Jelil, and, crossing the plain in a more westerly direction, we soon fell into the road that leads from Acco to Jerusalem, through Sepphoris and Nazareth. We joined for a while a small band of native travellers going the same way. But as they cared little for the scenery through which we were passing, I let them go before me, while I stayed behind in order to loiter awhile under the fine oak-trees that grow here on both sides of the path, and that cover the surrounding hills. The prospect was altogether lovely—fresh and fragrant of spring— yet inanimate, and as if mourning for the days that are past, in hope of better days for this land that are yet to come.

Emerging from among this oak-wood, the path brought us in a short time, through cultivated fields to the small town of Sefûrieh, or Sepphoris. It is not mentioned in Holy Scripture; but on the other hand it is celebrated in Jewish writers under the name of Tsipporis. Josephus makes frequent mention of it, and tells us that, having been rebuilt or enlarged by Herod Antipas, it became one of the largest and strongest towns of Galilee. After the destruction of Jerusalem, the great Sanhedrim is said to have been transferred to Sepphoris, which at that time was of greater note than even Tiberias itself. It is agreeably situated on a small eminence, commanding a beautiful view of the surrounding country and of the hills of Galilee, over which the snows of Hermon rise in the distance. It has a castle and a church in ruins; the latter of which is said to have been dedicated to St. Joachim and St. Ann, the parents of the Holy Virgin, who, the legend says, were natives of this town, and lived in it.

From Sefûrieh, the road winds along the bottom of a narrow valley, up the grassy slope of the hill that rises above Nazareth on the north west. We soon reached the top of that hill—for Sefûrieh is only an hour and a half from Nazareth—and we again fell into the path we had followed in the morning. The sun was nearing the horizon, and the air was so pure, the landscape so attractive, the flowers even so lovely, that I wished to tarry behind awhile. I therefore paid and discharged my "guard," and I desired my servants to go before me to the tent, which now appeared among the olive-trees below; and I sat down on a soft bed of moss and dwarf aromatic shrubs, in order

to feast my eyes once more on the sacred prospect before me.
For here I might say—

> " Mine eye unworthy seems to read
>   One page of Nature's beauteous book;
> It lies before me, fair outspread—
>   I only cast a wistful look.

> " I cannot paint to memory's eye
>   The scene, the glance, I dearest love;
> Unchang'd themselves, in me they die,
>   Or faint, or false, their shadows prove."

Everything here is fraught with greater interest than elsewhere.
Every tree, every flower, every bird, every insect even, seems
hallowed by the place in which it lives, and possesses charms
borrowed from associations which no other spot can give.   I
loved to study the details of this scenery, to acquaint myself
with the outlines of the hills as I would with the features of a
friend,—for every hill has an expression of its own; to follow
the windings of the valleys, the bed of the torrents and the
course of the streams, and even to watch

> "——— the new-born rill,
> Just trickling from its mossy bed,
> Streaking the heath-clad hill
> With a bright emerald thread,"

that flows perhaps into the Sea of Galilee, into the "ancient
River Kishon," or into the flood of Jordan that cleansed the
Syrian leper and laved the human form of Him who, through his
own righteousness, consecrated water to the mystical washing
away of sin.   Who could stand on this holy ground, and neither
hope nor fear?

I went down to my tent, and found my dinner ready.   It
was soon over; and I then sallied forth in another direction to
saunter among the hills.   While I was sketching the town from
the north, I suddenly heard sobs and then a voice of lamentation behind me.   I looked round : it was a mother weeping over
the grave of her only child.   She was a Mussulman, and wept
sore.   She wept as if she had no hope in his death.

The sun was now set, and I returned to my tent, where I
found Abou Nāsir awaiting me.   He stayed to supper with me;
and after that I accompanied him to his house, where I took
leave of him.   On my way back, I looked in at the door of a
house from whence I heard, as I passed, merry voices talking.

There was the whole family seated around the lamp (or candle), placed upon the lamp-stand (or candlestick), and literally " giving light to all that were in the house." It was the dwelling of a poor inhabitant of the town, whose "house" was "one room." So was also the house in which our Lord himself dwelt at Nazareth.—The moon was shining brightly in a cloudless sky, and the evening air waved the grass, and rustled among the leaves of the old olive-trees growing around my tent. I sat awhile at the tent door to enjoy the quiet and solemn repose of the hour, listening to the plaintive note of the friendly little scops-owl, which now for the third night perched over my tent to sing me to sleep. I rewarded it with a few fragments of meat, which I placed at the bottom of the tree on which it was sitting, and then retired for the night.

Thursday, April 21st.—Not intending to leave Nazareth to-day, I took an early walk before breakfast. On my return to the tent I found Abou Nāsir, who had come to invite me to dine with him at noon. I consented with pleasure, and walked back with him to his shop in the bazaar, where he displayed to me his wares, consisting of woollen stuffs and other such commodities. As we were not to dine till after his hours of business, I took advantage of this interval in order to saunter about the town.

One of the monks of the convent of Terra Santa was standing at the door as I passed. I entered into conversation with him, and he pressed me to visit the convent, and the other "sights" of the town. I went in to please him only: for I confess that these sorts of "sights" and the legends connected with them tended more than anything else to disturb my enjoyment of travel in this land. But here I was; and he took me at once to the Church of the convent. Presently he came to a part of the building lower than the rest. "There," said he, "there was the stone cell in which the angel Gabriel appeared to the Holy Virgin, mother of God. That cell was taken from hence to Loretto in Italy by an angel through the air."

"And you believe that, do you, my good friend?"

"Ah! ma bisogna crederlo, Signore! ma si!"

"E lei lo crede? dica pure, fra quattr' occhj," said I to him.

"Ma, si!—che so, io?"

And a good deal more in this strain, which did not convince me of the sincerity of his faith. We soon left the church; when he led the way down a narrow street, where opening the door of a modern-looking square building, "There," said he, "there is Joseph's shop!"

"Is that it, do you say?"

"Of course it is. Well then if you won't believe that, come this way."

And we went up another street, and there stopped at the door of a house, which he unlocked, and then said, pointing to a large square stone inside; "This is the stone on which our Saviour ate his last supper with his disciples!"

I really could stand it no longer; and giving him what he wanted after all—some money—I wished him good morning. He took it and went his way; and I returned to Abou Nāsir's house.

I found him awaiting me; and our meal being ready in the "upper room" (ἀνώγεων) or "gallery" within the reception room, already mentioned, he led the way to it up the flight of steps, and bade me sit down. I sat, as well as I could, cross-leg on the mat, before a table no higher than a stool, upon which the dishes were placed. These consisted of certain Eastern delicacies in the shape of "kabab" and "pilaf" of various kinds, to which I helped myself, after the fashion of my host, with my fingers; after having first, like him too, washed my hands, according to custom. The youngest daughter of Abou Nāsir waited on us, while her older sister prepared the food in the kitchen outside. Our meal over, she brought us a basin and a metal pot full of water, from which she poured some on our hands. We then rose from table; and she and her sister partook of the food after us.

Abou Nāsir went back to his shop, whither I followed him, and bought of him an 'abaya, or Arab cloak, of native manufacture, in broad stripes white and dark blue, as the only way in which I could acknowledge his kindness and attention to me.

On my way back to my tent I fell in with a party of "real" Bedouin Arabs, who had come from the plain to buy provisions at Nazareth. I purchased of one of them an "'aqāl" or tie, with which they fasten the "qafieh" around the head. It was of genuine camel's-hair, according to rule.

I put those relics in my tent, and then strolled out on horseback. But I soon returned, finding that I could explore the neighbourhood more satisfactorily on foot. I started, therefore, on a walking-tour around Nazareth; and first to the low undulating hillocks that rise a little beyond the old well, and from thence gently slope down into the meadows of Nazareth. They were clad in all the brilliancy of their spring attire—of bright scarlet adonis, deep-blue pimpernel, tender rose coloured and white flax, blue campanulæ of various kinds, white liliaceous plants, yellow marigolds, chrysanthemums, scabious, centaureæ and others in profusion, "opening their bosoms unheeded to the breeze" of noon, that waved the long grass of these fields, tenanted by quails and crickets in abundance.

After a solitary ramble of an hour or two, for the purpose of sketching Nazareth and the surrounding hills from various points of view, I returned to the town.

Not far from the khan, and in one of the streets that run parallel with the hill-side, I passed accidentally by a carpenter's shop. I looked in: he was himself apparently fifty years old, working at a plough with his son, a lad of about twelve or fourteen. This was a better image of what "Joseph's shop" must have been, than the high, dingy-looking house to which I was taken in the morning by the Italian friar. Here I felt of course deeply interested—as it were rivetted to the spot, around which so many sacred associations crowded at once. For no one could find a carpenter alone with his son at work in his shop at Nazareth, without thinking of him who was held for "the son of the carpenter" in this his own city. He too, when even a child, helped his father at his trade; learning obedience at that tender age, although himself Lord of all.

I went in, and while engaged in conversation with the carpenter, I made a sketch of his tools. They were few, simple and of rude workmanship; and but poor substitutes for (or, may be, models of) the same kind of instruments in use among us. They were an adze, a plane, a rule, a drill, a saw, a gauge, a hammer, and a pair of pincers. While at work he, like Indian workmen, used his feet as a second pair of hands, and with much dexterity.

On my way home, my attention was drawn elsewhere to a scene of home-life that brought vividly before my eyes, several allusions of our Saviour, in his intercourse with his hearers. Some women were at the oven, making and baking bread. The oven itself was exactly similar to the one I had seen at Selghair and at Magdala, which I have already described: with the addition of a pyramidal shed or covering, made of branches of trees lined outside with mud, with an opening at the top, intended as an escape for the smoke. One woman, seated on the ground, near the mouth of the oven, was heating it with dried grass and brambles, which she took from a heap by her side. I could easily recognize in the handful she held, many of the same flowers I had gathered myself in the fields, but dried up and withered. "Yesterday they were, and to day they were cast into the oven!" The scene spoke for itself. There were our Saviour's words true to the letter; and the circumstance to which he refers, enacted before me.

Meanwhile, two other women sitting close by "were at the

mill" grinding corn. The mill consists of two mill-stones, from fifteen to twenty inches in diameter, and about three or four inches thick. The nether mill-stone is a little wider than the upper one, and has a wide groove on one side cut towards the circumference, by which the corn, when ground into meal, falls from the mill. The nether mill-stone is stationary, and has in the centre a pivot of hard wood firmly fixed into it, around which the upper mill revolves, through a hole in its centre, a little larger than the pivot on which it turns. These hand-mills, the only ones in use in the Holy Land (I only saw two water-mills, of modern construction, in the whole extent of the country) are made for either one or two women. In the first case, there is only one handle fixed perpendicularly in the upper mill-stone near the edge; in the latter case, two handles are fixed, diametrically opposite to each other, also perpendicularly to the mill-stone. Then two women sit opposite to each other, with the mill between them, and put the mill in rapid motion by catching and propelling in turn each of the two handles. The corn is poured into the mill through the centre hole of the upper mill-stone, as often as required. " Two women," said our Saviour, " shall be at the mill, the one shall be taken and the other left."

While this was going on, another woman made dough of the flour ground at the mill, which she rolled into pellets the size of an orange; and then flattened them into loaves the size of a large bun. As soon as the oven was sufficiently heated and cleaned out, these loaves were stuck against the sides of it; then the lid was put upon it, and ashes heaped upon the lid until the process of baking was complete. The lid was then removed, and the loaves were taken out fit for use.

I followed a street of low houses on the flat roof of which some of the inhabitants were enjoying the cool of the evening. These houses of the poorer inhabitants, consist as I have already said, each of one room only, from eighteen to twenty feet square, and ten or twelve high. To every house there is a flight of steps outside, from the door to the roof. Several people were going up and down these steps along the street, to and from the top of their respective houses. The words of our Saviour then became plain when he says, " Let him which is on the house-top not come down to take anything out of his house," but flee at once for his life.

On going back to my tent I was agreeably surprized to find a friend I had met in Ceylon the year before. He was on his way to England; and having heard at the place where he had put up in the town, that I was at Nazareth he found me out, and came to ask me to accompany him to Mount Carmel on the morrow. We spent some time together, and after tea I walked back with him to his quarters; but as it was growing late, I returned to my tent to give directions for my intended journey to Mount Carmel; and I prepared myself for it by lying down to rest, and for the fourth night, at the song of the scops-owl perched on his favourite olive-tree.

M.

(To be continued.)

ON MIRACLES.

WARDLAW v. TRENCH, AND W. K.

In the *Journal* for April, 1854, is an able article '*On Miracles*' by W. K., mainly devoted to the refutation of Dr. Wardlaw's view and the vindication of that of Mr. Trench. I cannot but regret, that Dr. Wardlaw was not spared to vindicate his own theory, and that no abler advocate than myself has come forward to defend it. But, such being the case, the great importance of the point in question induces me to lay before your readers, and W. K. in particular (with all the deference and respect due to so able a writer), what I venture to think are fallacies in his argument, which have led him to an erroneous conclusion. I do not purpose to enter into an examination of the Article at large, nor do I undertake to defend all Dr. Wardlaw's positions. There is much in the Article in which I fully agree, and it is only on one point (though it is of fundamental importance and pervades the whole argument), on which I propose to offer any strictures; and these I shall make as few and brief as the case admits, both in order that I may not trespass on your space, and because I can refer any of your readers who may desire to see the question at issue more fully discussed to a paper in *The Christian Observer* for February and March 1848, in which I have shewn that "Morality of doctrine is not *the* criterion of miracles."

The question as between Wardlaw and Trench is thus stated by W. K. (p. 25),—"Dr. Wardlaw attaches special importance to the τέρας, and counts the σημεῖον as a necessary and certain consequence; Mr. Trench asks concerning the σημεῖον, and from it he judges of the origin and worth of the τέρας. *The one is satisfied to know, that a miracle has been wrought; the other requires to be certified of the moral teaching in connexion with it. The one tests doctrine by miracle, the other miracle by doctrine. In this difference is involved every other.*"

To this way of stating the question, Dr. Wardlaw, we apprehend, would take exception.—In the first place, a fallacy lurks
under the word 'miracle.' Take the word in the sense in which
Dr. Wardlaw uses it, and would not Mr. Trench himself be
'satisfied to know, that a supernatural *divine* authentication had
been given?' On the other hand, take it in the wider sense
which Mr. Trench gives to it, and no advocate of Dr. Wardlaw's
view could deny that some criterion would be required to distinguish divine from other miracles.—In the next place, it is
not correct to say, that "the one (Dr. W.) tests doctrine by
miracle;" for the use and authority which he assigns to miracles
is to authenticate the divine mission of him who works them,
and for this they might suffice anterior to the promulgation of
any doctrine. The truth appears to have been sacrificed here
(unwittingly no doubt) to an antithesis. And doubtless it would
not have consisted well with the view, which the writer was
about to maintain, to have stated at the outset, that 'the one
party allowed divinely-wrought miracles to be the sufficient
credentials of a divine mission,' while 'the theory of the other
precluded his admitting the sufficiency for this end of any manifestations of power (even though, if really wrought, they would
undeniably involve special interpositions of the Deity), until a
system of doctrines should have been submitted to him, and he
(an erring mortal!) had sat in judgment upon it, and decided
whether or not it was worthy of the all-wise God!'

It will be sufficiently evident from what has already been
said, that the point at issue turns on the proper definition of a
miracle. And this will be further shewn by adverting to the
origin of the question at issue between Trench and Wardlaw.
It has arisen from the necessity of distinguishing between miracles and prodigies. This, one party thinks, should be done by
narrowing the definition of a miracle, while the other, using the
term in a wider sense, would make doctrine the discriminating
test. The one would limit the meaning of the word 'miracle'
in the case in question to "*the effect of a supernatural cause,*"[a]
implying a divine agent : the other would extend it to '*the effect
of a superhuman cause,*'[b] thus including angelic and diabolic as
well as divine agencies. The question therefore resolves itself
into this:—Is GOD ALONE TO BE RECOGNIZED AS THE AGENT IN
A MIRACLE PROPER?

The affirmative of this question I have, as I believe, irre-
futably established in the paper above referred to, and I therefore do not think it necessary to go over the entire argument

---

[a] *Christian Observer*, No. 122, p. 91.   [b] *J. S. L.*, p. 33.

here. I shall content myself (after offering a few observations in confirmation of my argument), with replying to those objections of W. K. which may appear to imperil the main position, but (as I have said) not making myself responsible for every statement and argument advanced by Dr. Wardlaw.

First, then, I say, if we consider what is the fact in the present instance to be established, it will be seen to involve necessarily a *divine* agent.—A man claims to have a divine mission. Surely nothing short of a *divine* attestation of his claim can be admitted as sufficient to establish its validity. And if so, then *divine* credentials (or miracles wrought *by God)* must be necessary in the case of a revelation (which is the case in question), and no miracles of which a divine agency may not be predicated ought to be offered or received as adequate proofs.

Secondly: *Scripture* fully bears out this conclusion by attributing authority to this end to no miracles less than divine, and by claiming instant reception of a divine mission on the ground of these.

Having in the *C. O.,* pp. 156-8, adduced a great number of texts, I shall content myself now with adverting to those, the force of which W. K. has endeavoured to turn aside.

In Jno. x. 24, the Jews say to Jesus, "If thou art the Christ, tell us plainly. Jesus answered them; I told you, and ye believe not: the works which I do *in my Father's name,* these testify concerning me." . . . "If I do not the works *of my Father,* believe me not." And so again in John xiv. 10, "The Father who abideth in me, *He Himself* doeth the works. And in John xv. 24: "If I had not done among them the works which none other did, they had not had sin." If anything could appear unquestionable, it would seem to be, that the very point on which Christ here rests his appeal is, that his miracles were such as none but God the Father could work. But W. K. says (p. 42); 'Such passages are altogether inadequate to prove, that a miracle alone is a sufficient test of a doctrine, because they may include the moral end as much as the objective character." I answer;—1st, There was here no question of testing a doctrine. The question was; Had Jesus a Divine mission? And his argument was; I come from God, because I do the works of God. 2ndly, There is nothing to bear out *the supposition,* that the moral end *might* be included; but, on the contrary, enough to shew that "the works" were contemplated only as manifestations of power, both by Jesus and by his hearers,—just as they were, when the people argued, "When the Christ cometh, will he do more *signs* than these which this man hath done?" The work immediately had in view was the giving sight to a man born blind,—a work which unquestionably required the putting forth of Divine power. With regard to it the man himself argued; "Since the world began it was never known, that any man opened the eyes of one born blind : if this man were not from God he could do nothing." And when "some said : He hath a devil and is mad, others observed; These are not the sayings of one that hath a devil. Hath a devil *power* to open the eyes of the blind?" These people obviously considered, that the authorship of the work must be determined by *the degree of power* manifested in it. And so far were they from regarding *the character* of the work or "*the moral end*" as affording a test of its origin, that they saw no difficulty in the supposition, that a devil, for his own ends, might do such a good work as was the giving sight to a man born blind. While works wrought specially by God must needs be good, and have a good moral end, this goodness affords no sufficient test *to us* of their origin. Satan may make himself appear to us to be an angel of light.

Again, in John iii. 2, Nicodemus, it is evident, took the same view of what constituted a miracle in connexion with a revelation. The ground on which he was prepared to acknowledge Jesus to be "a teacher come from God" was, that "no one could have power to do those signs which he did, unless God were with him."— W. K., in order to multiply the force of this passage, remarks (p. 29) ; "Does this include merely the supernatural in power, or does it include the moral circumstances? Those miracles which Christ did were as remarkable for their ethical beauty and propriety as for their mere power. This definition, borrowed from the Jewish inquirer, is not sufficiently discriminative. It includes far too much. A man can do *nothing whatever* 'except God be with him,' and yet to call every act a miracle is to keep the name and sacrifice the thing."—Here we observe, first, that W. K.'s test of doctrine wholly fails him; for Nicodemus admitted the validity of Christ's claim on the authentication of 'the signs' *before* he knew what doctrines Jesus taught. And in consequence W. K. is compelled to have recourse again to the *hypothesis*, that "the moral circumstances" (by which he appears to explain himself to mean "the ethical beauty and propriety of the miracles") *may* be included. Now, I might allege, that this hypothesis is purely gratuitous, since we know nothing of the character of the miracles to which Nicodemus referred, being only told respecting them, that they were "*signs*" which led many to believe. True indeed it is, as I have already observed, that "the moral circumstances" attending miracles which had God for their author *could* not be otherwise than good; but such a necessary consequence or attribute could afford no adequate criterion of a miracle, even supposing it to be appreciable and available by the witnesses, neither of which it might be, and in the instance before us probably was not. I need not, however, have recourse to this method of meeting W. K.'s hypothetical argument; because, as the point in question is, What was the quality in Christ's miracles which led Nicodemus to recognize their divine origin? I may refer to his own declaration as conclusive. He himself declared, that it was *the degree of power* manifested in them, which satisfied him that they could proceed from God alone. Their "ethical beauty" or "the moral circumstances" do not appear to have entered into his thoughts.— Next, I would observe, that W. K.'s criticism upon Dr. Wardlaw's adoption of the definition of Nicodemus (an adoption not made on the ground of its being logically correct, but only as being *sufficiently* accurate *for his purpose*),—that criticism, I say with all respect, appears to me somewhat hypercritical. Dr. W. of course meant, that the declaration of Nicodemus should be taken as a definition in the sense which the latter intended it to convey, and in which it would be taken by every one who was not reduced to the necessity of drawing an argument from words rather than things. Nicodemus obviously meant, "except God be with him" *by a special or supernatural exercise of his power.* And to tie his meaning down, as W. K. does, to the grammatical signification of his words is to reduce them to what W. K. himself says they are not, "an empty truism," and truly it were "to keep the name and sacrifice the thing."—So also W. K.'s next charge against Dr. Wardlaw (p. 30) namely, that "he calls a miracle a suspension of the *known* laws of nature," appears to me to be in like manner chargeable with hypercriticism. No doubt a miracle is none the less a miracle, though we may not know it to be such. But what Dr. W. evidently had in view throughout was those wonders which may be *known by us* to be real miracles, just as W. K. himself subsequently says; "We would define a miracle *in its relation to man, with which alone we are concerned,* to be," &c. And, in order to be recognized as such by us, they must be 'suspensions of laws of nature *known to us.*'—And again W. K.'s objection (p. 29) to Dr. Wardlaw's bringing the agent into the definition has no weight against the argument itself. If the agent is (as W. K. allows that he may be) "deducible at once from the correct definition," then the practical result will be the same.

I have now advanced proofs from *reason and Scripture,* that a divine origin is rightly made a part (by implication) of the definition of a miracle. But these proofs were really supererogatory, since it would have sufficed to appeal to the *use* of the term *in the connexion in question.* The word 'miracle,' when used to denote a proof of a revelation, is taken by the generality of writers to include or imply the idea of a special *divine* interposition, and certainly this is the *prominent* idea attached to the term in its popular use and acceptation. This ought to be a sufficient justification; and those should be held to be in the wrong, who would extend the sense of the word in contravention of its received use,—more especially, when the effect really is (though they intend the contrary) to produce obscurity and increase difficulties.—And by what right or with what propriety, we may ask, do they require the adoption of their particular sense? The word may be used in three significations. 1st. To denote anything wonderful, whether an effect of man's act, or of an ordinary but rare operation of nature. 2ndly. To denote an effect produced by any being of greater power than man, such as are devils. And, 3rdly, to denote a special exercise of God's supernatural power. Now, why are we to be told, and that without proof alleged, that we must use the term in the connexion in question in the middle sense, and in *neither* of the others? And why may not the infidel object to the *partial* limitation of the second signification with as much reason as Trench and his supporters do to the *more complete* one of the first?

W. K. in seeking to elude the force of "the Scriptures cited by Dr. Wardlaw" says (p. 38); "Neither men nor spirits may be '*like unto Jehovah,* doing wonders;' but the unlikeness may be not in the *fact,* but in the *quality* of the wonders. Do we not speak correctly of *wise* men, and are not angels *wise?* Yet God is called '*only wise.'*" I admit this argument and adopt it. Allowing that it is a question 'of *the quality* of the wonders.' I contend that a *divine* revelation requires attestations of a *divine* quality : those of an *angelic* will no more meet the case than those of a *human.* The medium or angelic degree of power or wisdom will no more suffice than the first or human : the highest or divine must be put forth. And if so, it is proper to limit the term in accordance with that fact.

But again, suppose an unbeliever to demand of me, what are the chief proofs I allege in attestation of the divine origin of the Christian revelation. Am I not at liberty to say; 'Miracles, by which I intend *the effects of a supernatural cause,* implying a special interposition of the Deity?' And would a third party be justified in interposing and requiring me to include in my answer all wonders, which, it may be supposed, exceed the power of man to perform? And if I were to do so, should I not be taking up a false position, and one which would involve me in needless difficulties? How wonders wrought by the special intervention of God are to be distinguished from other wonders is another and distinct question, and one which ought not to be mixed up with that touching the proper definition of a miracle. To it the answer would be; 1st, by an inquiry whether there was sufficient reason for believing that a law of nature existed, and that there had been a deviation from it; and, 2ndly, in failure of obtaining satisfaction by this means, then it might be allowable to use any of the numerous tests that might be available (doctrine among the rest), as supplemental criteria.—But what, I may ask, would be the answer of Trench or W. K. himself to such a question as I have supposed? Would they not also answer; 'Miracles?' And in doing so, would they not on their definition be asserting, that wonders wrought by the power of the devil were the chief attestations of the Christian religion as a divine revelation? What more absurd!!!

If, after all, our opponents should still insist on the word 'miracle' being used in their sense, then (not to sacrifice the thing to its name) we must drop the word, and attain our end by using the circumlocutory phrase in its place.

I will now proceed to notice the arguments and objections of W. K.

His principal objection is, that we beg the question at the outset (pp. 29, 36 and 39). What, then, *is* the question? It must be that which lies between Dr. Wardlaw and Mr. Trench. Dr. W. says; A miracle is *per se* a sufficient attestation. Mr. T. says; A miracle is not a sufficient attestation, until it has been tested by doctrine. The difference between them obviously arises from the different significations which they give to the word miracle. The first question therefore is; What is a miracle? And if it has been proved, that it includes or involves a special *divine* interposition, then they are to blame for the *petitio principii*, who introduce it by adopting and persisting in an erroneous and too comprehensive definition. They import it, not into their opponent's real argument, but into their erroneous version of that argument. And with equal reason (as we have observed) might a *petitio principii* be objected by an infidel against them, because they do not use the word in that wider sense, which alone would be recognized by him.

But let us take W. K.'s statement of the question. He asks; "What do miracles attest?" And he then gives Dr. Wardlaw's answer to the effect, that they attest a man's claim to having a divine mission, two questions only arising with regard to them; viz., 1st, "*Is the work one which God alone can do?*" and 2ndly,

"Is it actually done?" To the former W. K. objects, that "it is a palpable *petitio principii'* to assume, that a miracle can be wrought *only by* the power of God. This indeed it would be, if it were proposed (as on W. K.'s and Trench's theory), after having alleged a miracle in proof of a claim to a divine mission, whether or not after all it was a miracle. But the advocates of this view are not guilty of any such solecism. They do not perpetrate the incongruity of having recourse to *"moral circumstances"* and religious *doctrines* to determine the nature and origin of *physical* facts. These must be established by their own proper evidences. It will be necessary only to shew, that there exists a law of nature or (to speak more properly) an uniform mode of God's acting, and that there has been a deviation from that law or mode. There will be instances, doubtless, in which it will be useful to have recourse to the moral doctrine; but such instances, if they stood alone, could not logically be adduced as proofs.—W. K. goes on (p. 36) to take exception to Dr. Wardlaw's putting what God permits on an equal footing with what he does or enjoins. Here again, I apprehend, the fallacy arises from the different senses in which they take the word 'miracle.' Dr. W. is careful to reiterate, once and again, that he is speaking of "a *real* miracle." And what he may have meant to say, or at any rate what he should have said, is, that God would no more make use of the intervention of another to make a real miracle than he would work it directly himself. And why? Because *a special act of his* would be as necessary in the one case as the other, none but himself having naturally the power to affect his laws or (more properly) his actings.

W. K. next refers to passages of Scripture, which, he thinks, would make it "exceedingly difficult to make good Dr. Wardlaw's position" (p. 37). These are the temptation of Eve, the case of a prophet giving a sign which comes to pass (Deut. xiii. 1—5), and that of the Egyptian magicians. The two last have been sufficiently examined in the *C. O.*, pp. 79, 146. With regard to the three and to all of the like kind it suffices to say, that we do not deny that morality of doctrine may have a *negative* value in some cases which may admit of doubt; but this does not constitute it an adequate, much less an universally, applicable test. It is not in any case the *natural* criterion. And when we are driven to have recourse to it among many other supplemental criteria, it is only in consequence of the limited extent of our knowledge. If we were fully acquainted with all nature's laws, we should never need any *test* of a miracle. But by reason of our ignorance many cases will arise, in which we must use all the secondary means that may be available for the

detection of counterfeits, or the more complete verification of
genuine miracles. We thus on our theory (let it be well observed) sacrifice no advantage which is possessed by our opponents, while we do not take up our position on ground, which, if
not wholly untenable, involves in needless difficulties. We care
not, for instance, to determine whether the miracles wrought by
the Egyptian magicians were effected by human or superhuman
power. Unless it could be shewn that they required *divine*
power, our position will not be in the least degree affected : nor
will there be any validity in W. K.'s inference (p. 41), "that a
miracle, or *what for all the purposes of evidence and attestation
is equivalent to a miracle*, may be wrought in support of error ;"
for superhuman miracles are not equivalent for all the purposes
of evidence to supernatural miracles. And hence, whether or
not there be reason for W. K.'s conclusion, that "Dr. Wardlaw's
entire argument falls to the ground, with everything he has built
upon it," I venture to maintain that the position which Dr. W.
has to defend remains unassailed and unassailable. And further
to shew this I will offer a few remarks on the examination which
W. K. proceeds to make of his opponent's argument.

He first quotes from Trench as follows. "A miracle does
not prove the truth of a doctrine, or the divine mission of him
that brings it to pass. That which alone it claims for him at
first, is a right to be listened to; it puts him on the alternative
of being from heaven or from hell. The doctrine must first
commend itself to the conscience as being *good*, and only then
can the miracle seal it as *divine*, &c., &c." W. K. then remarks;
"Dr. Wardlaw seems scarcely to have appreciated the meaning
of this passage which he attempts to criticize. 'If we must,
first,' he says, 'by an appeal to our "moral nature" ascertain
the doctrine to be *good*, then have we, at the same time, ascertained it to be *true ;* since no doctrine can be really and intrinsically *good* that is not *true; truth*, as to any doctrine, being
the first ingredient or element of its *goodness*.' There is," adds
W. K., "a very strange confounding here of what is good with
what is true." And, after giving examples to shew, that many
"a good thing" is not true (as that "it would be a good thing
if there were no sin"), he concludes that, "Truth is not the
only element of goodness."—Now, surely the "strange confounding" is on the part of W. K. For, does he not confound what
is *desirable* with what is *morally good?* The question between
Trench and Wardlaw is not touching 'good *things*,' but 'good
doctrines of morality or religion.' And will W. K. undertake
to shew, that a doctrine which is *morally* or *spiritually good*
(as that 'it is our duty to love God above all, and our neigh-

bour as ourselves ') is not *true ?*　Or, did Dr. Wardlaw lay down
so absurd a position, as that 'truth was the *only* element of
goodness?'　Did he not imply the very contrary in saying, that
' it is the *first* element of it?'

The next argument of W. K. (which is intended to shew,
that the Scriptures quoted by Dr. W. are inadequate) has been
refuted already.

His next is, that 'Christ's reply to the Pharisees' assertion,
that his miracles were wrought by the help of Beelzebub, admitted, or at least did not deny, the fact of the possibility of
miracles [being?] wrought by Satan' (p. 42).—Now, it certainly
admitted nothing of the kind.　And if it did not deny the fact,
the reason was, that the method adopted by our Lord was the
most ready, and in the particular case the most effectual for
refutation.　It had the nature of an *argumentum ad hominem*,
virtually saying; 'Account *on your hypothesis* for the works
being done in support of the cause of goodness and truth.'　But
the use of such an argument in such a case did not surely imply,
that this was the only or the most legitimate mode of dealing
with the objection.　And will W. K. maintain, that Christ's
not giving an explicit denial tacitly implied the possibility of *his*
miracles having been wrought by Satan; because this is what
would be implied, if anything were.　That diabolical miracles
might be wrought by devils, who would deny ?

Hitherto I have discussed this particular instance on the view
given of it by Trench and by W. K.　But I must now draw
attention to the fact, that they have altogether misrepresented
it.　It is not true, as asserted by W. K. (p. 28), that "here
was, whatever *might* have been, a testing of the miracle by the
doctrine."　It is not true, as alleged by Trench, that our Lord's
appeal was "to the whole tenour of his doctrine and his miracles,"—nor that "he repelled the accusation and derived authority to his miracles, not on account of the power which they
displayed, ... but on account of the ethical ends which they
served,"—nor yet that "he appealed to every man's conscience,
whether the doctrine to which they bore witness was not from
above."　He did *not* appeal to the character of the doctrine,
nor to "the ethical ends :" he *did* appeal to the degree of power
manifested.　The question was one touching *bodily* possession
merely.　And our Lord's argument was, that if Satan, having
sent his emissaries to take possession of a man, straightway gave
to another power to eject them (as the Pharisees alleged), such
conduct would be suicidal and necessarily subversive of his kingdom; and thence their hypothesis could not be true.　The point
of the argument lies in the absurdity of supposing that Satan

would "divide" his forces and array them against one another, and not in an incompatibility with any doctrine; for none was in any way referred to. And our Lord did not stop here. But, having disproved the Pharisees' mode of accounting for his mighty deed, he proceeded to argue, in effect, that it only remained that it was accomplished by the putting forth of a "*stronger*" *power* than that of Satan,—that, if he had entered into the strong one's habitation and despoiled him, it could only be in consequence of his being possessed of power enough to bind him. Such power could be that of God alone. Hence he "cast out devils by the finger [or spirit] of God." And "hence no doubt the kingdom of God was come unto them." So far, then, is this example from affording any support to the theory of W. K., that it is utterly subversive of it; and moreover affords the most complete proof that could be given of the truth of his opponent's view.

Fatal exceptions may be taken to W. K.'s other attacks on Dr. Wardlaw's arguments on this point. As to what comes next (p. 42), I confess I do not very clearly see the drift of it. Grammatically, W. K. asserts, that the Doctor, on his principle, must hold 'miracle' and 'doctrine' to be identical; but W. K.'s argument seems to shew, that he means 'all miracles,' and the other construction is too absurd to be admitted. Taking it, then, in the latter, I observe that the assertion is made apparently on the ground of Dr. Wardlaw's having remarked, that 'the creation of an atom is as truly a creation as the creation of a world.' Now, who would have expected to see such a statement alleged to prove the identity or equality of "all miracles" (that is, of all superhuman wonders, for in this sense the word is obviously used here by Dr. W., even as it is by W. K.)? Who does not perceive, that the above declaration affirms only the equality of acts of the same *kind*, irrespective of the effects produced? In each case a creation is *the kind of act*; but in one the product is an atom, in the other a world. And it is virtually affirmed, that these products, though so different, imply an equal amount of power in their agents, because they result from identical acts. But how does it follow that all wonders, though not necessarily implying equal power, are identical? It is true, that I may have misapprehended W. K.'s meaning, especially as I do not know what Dr. W.'s argument is, not having had the advantage of seeing his work. But if this be the case, it is wholly due to W. K.'s want of perspicuity.

W. K.'s next argument might be made to justify the Jews in their rejection of Christ. It might be turned thus. 'A prophet was to be rejected, who sought to turn away the people from Jehovah, and from his law as taught them by Moses' (p. 38). "The Jews regarded Christ as subverting the *teaching* of Moses and the prophets" (p. 42). Therefore, when "they despised him, notwithstanding his miracles," they were justified in so doing!! Does this go to shew, that doctrine is in all cases a competent test of miracles, or that we can appeal with more confidence to men's appreciation of "the teaching" than we can to their estimate of the degree of power manifested in the miracles? W. K. adds, that "Christ's reply was not an appeal to his miracles, but to his teaching; 'I came not to destroy, &c.'" Now such a perversion as this is really too bad. The words referred to were not "a reply" or "an appeal" at all. They occur in the sermon on the mount, and have no reference to any controversy, nor to miracles or doctrines.

W. K. goes on (p. 42); 'But, in fact, does not the belief in the possibility of a miracle at all depend upon certain doctrines?' —Doubtless it presupposes "the existence of a God," and his infinite power, "wisdom, and goodness." But no considerations connected therewith will establish W. K.'s following assertion, that "miracles are possible, only because it is wise that the material should subserve the spiritual," &c. On what ground is W. K. entitled thus to assign a limit to the divine liberty of action. God will necessarily do nothing *inconsistent* with wisdom and goodness; but it is "*possible,*" that he may work miracles without these being his special ends : it is as "possible," that he may have in view to manifest his *power* (Ps. cvi. 8), or even his liberty of action as his goodness. However, this matters not, so far as I can see, to the case in question; though W. K. thinks it worth while to try to establish it by a long quotation from Dr. Wardlaw. But Dr. W.'s argument goes only to shew, that there is *an* A PRIORI *probability* in favour of miracles being wrought in a supposed case. It does not prove, that any will be, or have been wrought. It is far enough from bearing out W. K.'s position, that "miracles are POSSIBLE *only*" in such cases. How then can there be in it, as W. K. asserts, "a testing of miracle by doctrine,"—much less (which is what W. K. needs to sustain his argument), a recognition that doctrine is an adequate criterion in all cases.—I feel that the space likely to be allowed me will not admit of my following W. K. further in this argument. I must therefore content myself with observing in reference to what follows on p. 43, that the fact of our being possessed of a "moral nature," capable to a certain extent of approving things that are excellent, does not prove that we are more competent to judge by a moral criterion than by physical tests,—still less, that the former is more easy of application and adapted to convince, where the opponents are sure to be ignorant, prejudiced, and averse to receive the truth. And even if it were so, the moral criterion would still not be the proper test. For, who would think of judging, whether a feat of strength proceeded from a child or giant by inquiring what were the agent's moral principles and objects, points which he might or might not have developed?

In the few remaining pages of W. K.'s article there is, as it appears to me, much misuse of terms, much want of perspicuity, much fallacious reasoning, and much undue severity in reference to Dr. Wardlaw and his erroneous representation of his statements. But these I cannot expose in detail for the reason just stated. I must confine myself to a few brief remarks on what appear to be the main props of his argument. [On the question, whether he and his friends are justly chargeable with 'reasoning in a circle' (see pp. 44, 46), I refer to the *C. O.*, p. 84.]

"*God* never rests the claim of Scripture upon miracles *alone*" (p. 44). I say, and I have shewn in *C. O.*, pp. 156-8, that Christ *does* rest his claim on miracles, as *the sufficient and alone" indispensable* evidence.—"On Dr. W.'s hypothesis, why all this appeal to our moral judgment, rather than to miracles?" It is attributable to the Divine goodness and condescension. What *ought* logically to suffice, and what *will* do so in the case of ignorant and depraved creatures who '*will* not have the light,' are very different things. Besides, are not "the five-sixths" spoken of necessarily devoted to *the teaching* of the doctrine, and is it any objection that this teaching is sometimes thrown into the form of an argument?—"No exercise of mere power will ever suffice to prove the truth or beauty of religious doctrine."[c] No doubt:—no more than 'the truth or beauty of doctrine' will logically suffice to shew who is the agent in "an exercise of mere power." But a special exercise of Divine power, or what we may be convinced is such, ought to satisfy us of the *Divine mission* of him who calls it forth.—On Dr. Wardlaw's principles, "Of what possible consequence could it be to our faith or duty, if each of the great doctrines of Christianity were proved to involve a physical or ethical *absurdity*, so long as they are found in a book attested by miracles?" (p. 45). *My* "answer" would be, that, such a thing being impossible from the nature of God,

---

[c] W. K. seems fond of collocating passages from Dr. Wardlaw's work with the view of convicting him of self-contradiction (see pp. 37, 40). Perhaps with at least equal success we might do the same by asking W. K. to reconcile with the above the following statements,—" For this (the doctrine of an immortal life) we entirely depend upon the attestation of miracles" (p. 45).—" We have nothing but miracles for our evidence of immortality " (p. 46).

either the evidence for "the absurdity" or that for "the miracles" must be fallacious.—"Dr. Wardlaw maintains, that we have no natural means of attaining to just moral conclusions," or "of knowing that a doctrine is good" (pp. 45, 46), and that "we know nothing whatever of God apart from Scripture" (p. 47). I must decline to believe, that Dr. W. means to maintain any such doctrines, until I see clear proof adduced of the fact; and then the only consequence will be, that I must think he is in error,—though not more so than W. K. will be found to be in the assertions which I have just quoted in a note, if his words are construed with equal strictness.—"Dr. Wardlaw contends, that the evidence which miracles furnish is wholly indisputable and of a mathematical certainty" (p. 47). This assertion, again, I must beg leave to doubt. I apprehend, what Dr. W. intends (if not says) is, that their evidence is *in itself* ' indisputable,' that is, it *ought* to be sufficient for conviction. But this is a very different thing from what it will be practically found to be, when presented to persons whose " affections" are *not* "in a right state," but the very reverse. And hence there will be no more difficulty, "on Dr. W.'s hypothesis, to account for the small success of Christ's ministry," than on W. K.'s.—With reference to W. K.'s next paragraph, I challenge him to name the Christian advocates, who have rested "satisfied" with adducing, what he says is " *a very small part*" of the defence of Christianity, 'the evidence of miracles.'—As to W. K.'s 'sneers' and ' sarcastic' remarks on "the elephantine unwieldiness in the merriment of this grave theologian," &c., &c.,—as to his offensive imputations to the effect, that such views as Dr. Wardlaw's tend to produce the " *spiritualism* of our day," that they are of a like nature with " *rationalism, mythism,* and the like," and that even " Strauss is, *on Dr. W.'s own principles,* more consistent and nearer the truth than himself" (p. 48),—and as to his palpable misrepresentation, that " our zealous Protestant " has left Protestantism without an answer to Newman's defence of the ecclesiastical prodigies of the early ages, leaving room ' neither for doctrine nor for *à priori* notions of God's character to test them,'—as to these, I deem them undeserving notice, though, as manifesting the *animus* of the writer, they will be of use to shew the small amount of justice and impartiality, that may be expected from him.

Inasmuch as W. K. in concluding, reiterates again and again his charge of a fundamental *petitio principii,* asserting that Dr. W. and Strauss stand upon an equal footing in that " the result in both cases depends upon a prior assumption of the probability or improbability—possibility or impossibility of a *miracle*,"[d] I will in conclusion subvert this basis of his entire argument by a summary statement of the question, and of the views of those who agree in the main with Dr. Wardlaw, and which are (I presume) those of the doctor himself. The primary question touching the evidences of Christianity is; What are the sufficient and alone indispensable evidences? Our answer is, Special attestations of the Deity, manifested either in a way of power or of wisdom. [And let us ask by the way; Will W. K. give any other answer? Will he say of the ' Deity, *and of the devil ?*'] Such attestations we designate ' the miracles,' including the prodigies commonly so called, and prophecies. If the further question be proposed; How we are to know when such miracles are wrought? we answer; By ascertaining in any given case, whether there is sufficient ground for believing, 1st, that what is commonly called ' a law of nature' exists, and 2ndly, that there has been a deviation from it. If it be objected, that there will occur cases of " superhuman " manifestations of power undistinguishable by these criteria from Divine, we reply, that in such cases we must have recourse *for the detection of pseudo-miracles,* to so many of the various supplementary tests (see *C. O.,* p. 92 ss.) as may be available in the particular case. But as to the proposed universal panacea ('moral doctrine') we deem it inadequate for various reasons (see *C. O.,* p. 76 ss.), and in particular, that difficulties of discrimination are quite as likely to arise from other causes, which it is not adapted to meet *(e. g.,* from our ignorance of nature's laws), as from that, with a view to which it has been unduly exalted. In the particular case, indeed, of miracles wrought by diabolical agency, we readily allow it to have a special use and value. But let it be remembered, that even in this its efficacy goes only to a negative extent : it serves only to detect imposture.

Whether there be in this view any " begging of the question,"—any "inconsistency of reasoning,"—anything not "more argumentative than a sneer, nor more cogent than capital letters,"—any " unbending rigidity of old fashioned orthodoxy favourable to rationalism, mythism, and the like,"—any tendency to " results far *more* negative than those by which Strauss terrified the world," — any " destructive criticism," dangerous to Protestantism,—any " over fondness for miracles, having its source in a moral and intellectual *vis inertiæ*,"—any peculiar

---

[d] " Strauss's theory is based on the assumption of the *impossibility* of a miracle." How and where does Dr. W. base his on its *improbability ?* If there be any truth in W. K.'s statement, may not the assertion be made with equal truth in reference to his own theory?

liability to difficulties and objections,—any "extreme and one-sided views," which by their reaction produce "spiritualism,"—any rendering of "five-sixths of the New Testament needless, if not ridiculous," and "the countless tomes of theological polemics" useless,—I now leave to the reader to decide.

F. B. H.

BIOGRAPHICAL SKETCH OF GIESELER, THE CHURCH HISTORIAN.[a]

By Dr. Redepenning.—*The Editor of ' Origen.'*

John Arend Gieseler, the Church historian's grandfather, himself belonged to the clerical profession. He was preacher at Lahde, and afterwards at Hartum, in the principality of Minden; having been born at Minden in 1726. He received his theological bias at Halle. 'He was zealously devoted, not indeed to Pietism proper, but yet to that practical method of treating Christianity, which had been reintroduced by Franke and Spener, and, for the rest, a loyal adherent of the Lutheran system of doctrine as laid down in the symbolical books : a very earnest, methodical, stirring man, who, however, in congenial society, could be light-hearted and cheerful enough.' I quote from the family chronicle of the Gieselers, which in this account, and in many other traits, enables us to recognize the grandsire in his descendant. The grandmother whose maiden name was Haccius, partook of her husband's pious disposition and love of order.

Both these characteristics were inherited by their son, George Christopher Frederic Gieseler, born in 1760, the father of our John Charles Louis. When this son, the eldest of ten children, was born to him, on the 3rd of March, 1793, he was preacher at Petershagen, near Minden, and at a latter period filled the same office at Werther, not far from Bielefeld ; a man of very peculiar intellectual stamp. Hard of hearing from his fifteenth year, compelled when at the university to compensate for his deafness by looking over the papers of the fellow-student sitting next to him ; then, and at a later period, almost wholly cut off from that living communion which consists in the oral interchange of thought, he was a self-taught man, who possessed in a high degree all the advantages of an education,

---

[a] Reprinted from the *Monthly Christian Spectator* for November, 1855, by permission of the Editor.

acquired by means of the most intense mental exertion, but who also could not escape from many a one-sidedness. It may be thought, that under these circumstances he ought not to have selected the clerical calling. But he seemed born for it; he was bent on that alone, and would adopt no other. Even in his eleventh and twelfth years he held public religious exercises on the Sunday afternoons in a summer-house of his father's, which were attended by a number of hearers from the village, and not without good results. On one occasion, when a boy of only thirteen, he supplied in the church the place of the schoolmaster, who had fallen sick, by leading the singing, and catechizing during the Wednesday and Sunday services in the chapel at Holzhausen. He too studied at the University of Halle, and subsequently filled several private tutorships, until, in 1790, he entered upon the above-named office in Petershagen. A man of restless activity, as conscientiously laborious in the service of his congregation as the bodily infirmity, to which reference has been made, allowed him, he has left behind him a great number of notes, chiefly relating to dogmatic theology, or, more properly speaking, theosophy and the revelation of John, as, also, to practical theology; in part, also, to the science of education, popular schools and culture. In all these was traceable a deep inner harmony, and along with much that was impracticable and erroneous, which often led to long discussions in writing with his son, much that was valuable and truly original. A great portion of these papers appeared in print, and many more are still extant in manuscript. It is to be wished that further tidings of them may see the light at some future day. For the present it will suffice to have brought forward these traits in explanation of the circumstance, that to our Gieseler, as well as to all his brothers and sisters, the freest development was permitted, inasmuch as their father deemed that only an actual mental acquisition for which one is indebted to one's own exertions. Without doubt, this method of educating his son had much to do with his great independence of spirit, by which he was already distinguished as a boy on his leaving the parental roof, and which, at a latter period, when he was a man, stood him in such good stead in so many difficult situations.

He was indebted for the earliest instructions which he received to his grandfather, who, when he was in his fourth year only, taught him, by an easy, playful method, to read fluently; and to his loving mother, whose maiden name was Berger, a woman of much practical understanding. But it was in the same year that the child lost his affectionate tutor. His father made good the loss as well as he could, but found it advisable to send him in his tenth year to the Latin school of the Orphan House at Halle. Here Niemeyer's care and interest were drawn towards him, and never afterwards deserted him. He facilitated his studies, and when they were completed, promoted him to a mastership in the Orphan House School. He had been occupied scarcely a year in this calling, when in the year 1813, he obeyed the summons of his fatherland, entered, as a volunteer rifleman, the ranks of the liberating army, and was with it before Magdeburg when the siege of that city was raised. After the peace in 1815, he returned to his mastership and two years later obtained the degree of Ph. D.; whereupon, in the same year, he became co-rector of the Gymnasium at Minden; in the year 1818, director of the Gymnasium at Cleve; and about Michaelmas, 1819, Ordinary Professor of Theology in the newly-founded university of Bonn. He had already received the degree of Doctor of Theology from that university on the 3rd of April in the same year, through the good offices of Augusti.

For this rapid success he was indebted to his *Historico-critical Essay on the Origin and Earliest History of the Written Gospels.* The assumption of a written Protevangelium as the common source whence the Synoptic Evangelists[b] drew, was set aside by this exposition, and the foundation laid by Lessing, Herder, and others, was firmly established, on which the most recent literary criticism of the Gospels still reposes. This important work of Gieseler was soon bought up in the bookshops, nevertheless, he could never bring himself to resolve on a second edition. He shrunk from the tangle of wholly groundless hypotheses, as those were in great measure which were put forward in this department, and at the same time did not deem the time come for a new decision in these questions.

His sterling philological culture is shewn by his papers in the second volume of Rosenmüller's Repertory, which have greatly enriched the grammar of the New Testament, then in its first stage. His peculiar gift in unravelling knotty problems is shewn by his article on the 'Nazarenes and Ebionites' in 'Staudlin's and Tzschirner's Archives' (Bd. iv., St. 2). And from this period it was to Church history that he almost exclusively devoted his powers and his affections. Neander's *Genetic Development of the Principal Gnostic Systems* was the occasion of his writing his searching review (in the 'Halle Literary

---

[b] Matthew, Mark, and Luke are so styled by the Germans on account of their possessing so much in common, and so serving necessarily as the basis of every evangelical *synopsis* or harmony.

Journal' for 1823), which shed much new light upon this chaos.
In the following year he commenced the publication of his
Text-book of Church History. At the same time he edited,
in association with Lücke, the *Journal for Educated Christians,*
of which four parts appeared in 1823 and 1824.

A fresh, free life then environed the youthful university on
the Rhine. The breach between the Catholics and Protestants
had not then taken place. Gratz and Seber still taught, without
hindrance, their free exegesis and dogmatic theology, and were
exposed to no attacks but those, perhaps, of Hermes; Ritter
was on terms of intimacy with Gieseler; all were of one heart
and one soul; vigorous powers wrought in mutual harmony;
this seat of learning was in the full bloom of its springtide. In
his family relations Gieseler was happy in a high degree. With
incomparable fidelity and fervour he clung to his partner, loved
by him in his early days, and too soon lost. She was of Halle,
and her maiden name was Henrietta Feist. A numerous offspring soon blessed their union, and cares increased accordingly.
But, putting his trust in God, and relying on his own capacity
for labour, untiringly active, strictly conscientious in every task,
he remained, without descending to frivolity, accessible to every
cheerful emotion.

Twelve years and a half he filled this office, principally
occupying himself as a teacher of church history, and enjoying
the confidence of his colleagues, who had just made him rector
of the university. Then Göttingen attracted him towards herself,
and certainly in no other university could he have been more
entirely in his place than here. Its fundamental character as
the patroness of the experimental and historical sciences, and
the manifold practical activity to which he was here summoned,
exactly corresponded to the bent of his own mind. A course of
life devoted solely to learned investigation would not have occupied him fully. For it is difficult to say which preponderated in
him, erudition, or the sense for practical life, and the inward
vocation for order and rule. Doubtless, in his case, both went
hand in hand; what he was in practical life, that he was also in
science; a man of clearness, precision, foresight, and conscien-
tiousness; in expression, concise, and now and then too laconic;
in every respect a character all of a piece, a man in every sense
of the word. This, too, was recognized at once, as soon as one
came in contact with him, and you placed confidence in him.
The university conferred upon him repeatedly (and in critical
times to scarcely any one else) the dignity of pro-rector, and he
was almost uninterruptedly a member of one or more of the
academical boards. If the academical legislation were to undergo

revision, or new regulations to be made, it was to his judgment that such propositions were submitted. He was a standing member of the Library Commission. The municipality of the city chose him as their orator; an office, however, which he afterwards resigned. He was curator of the Göttingen Orphan House; he had to look after numerous other benevolent founda- tions, especially bursaries. The Göttingen Academy of Sciences, of which he was a member, committed to him the awarding of the Wedemeyer prize. He was associated with Lücke as theo- logical Ephorus. But the Orphan House possessed, in an especial degree, the love of his heart. With few exceptions, he visited it every day, and, accordingly, was acquainted with every one of the children, its disposition, talents, acquirements, faults. He had advice and a friendly word for each, directed each in the choice of a calling, and long kept a watchful eye on those who had left the house. The children clung to him in return, and were visibly anxious to make a friend of him. Only in the cases of a very few orphans, whom in courageous faith he attempted to rescue, did he witness the miscarriage of his noble aims.

He devoted much time and labour to a freemasons' lodge, of which he was a member, and, doubtless, knew why he did so. At the close of his life he was exposed to a violent attack on this account, which, to be sure, will do no more harm to Gieseler's good name than to the prosperity of that society.

The interests of his country, too, lay near his heart. We see from many passages of his ' Church History of the Most Recent Times,' what were his wishes on its behalf. His opinions upon the movements of the year 1848 are scattered throughout the work, and also the hopes with which he looked calmly into the future, amidst the storms which frightened so many from their propriety.

As in the State, so also in the Church, he loved a constant and enlightened progress. He did not want to see any of the threads which bind the new to the old snapped asunder. Ac- cordingly, he declared against the so-called constituent synods contemplated by many in that year, which, in point of fact, would only, as he conceived of them, viz., as sitting in judgment upon what in future was to pass for church doctrine, have proved potent for harm. Nevertheless, they might surely have been prevented from taking such a turn; and if we reflect how many an opportunity has been let slip during the last forty years, which it is now so difficult to recall, one cannot but wish that provision for the further development of our Protestant Church system may not be again slighted; and that at least the eccle- siastical regulation and organization of the single parishes may

be proceeded with in order that when at a future period greater
doctrinal distinctness shall have been arrived at, the foundations
for the forthcoming new structure may be found to have been
already laid.

The question, whether Gieseler was a Rationalist, was answered in the negative immediately after his death by a distinguished theologian, his colleague.[c] And certainly Gieseler never
was what men commonly understand by a Rationalist. From
the beginning to the end of his literary career, he staunchly
held fast to justification by faith alone, that fundamental idea
of the Protestant doctrine. He understood by this our own
free apprehension of the Divine truth and grace communicated
to us by Christ, and manifested in him. He did not set human
reason above the divine truth given to us in Christ, but deemed
him only to be a Christian to whom Christ was the sum and
substance of all the sublimest truths in religion, truths never to
be transcended. But if, on the other hand, any wanted to deprive reason of her right and duty to appropriate this truth, to
recognize and apprehend it, to extricate it from the letter as
spirit and truth, he was a courageous and doughty champion for
this right of reason, which none may slight with impunity; a
champion for this light within us, which cannot be darkened
without the whole man's being filled with darkness.[d] In this
sense he was a Rationalist; and if, in our days, almost all who
hold to clear, logical thinking, and to an enlightened distinction
between what is really known, what is scientifically established,
and mere creations of the fancy, are wont to get that, in fact,
honourable name from their adversaries, Gieseler is fairly entitled
to that honour. To what is not uncommonly regarded as doctrinal profundity, to that empty speculation sometimes affected,
which knows nothing of the foundations in experience on which
it should be based, or which sets them aside, which, moreover,
impudently sets all logic at defiance, to this questionable art he
was no friend; and he could well afford to laugh in his sleeve,
to find that this and the other man pretended to be a speculative
theologian, without any sort of qualification. In his view,
every scientific conclusion was of value only according to the
degree of its actual certainty; and it was one of his deepest
convictions, that in the present day nothing is of greater moment
in theology than the difficult, indeed, but not quite impossible,
task of drawing the line between the Pistis (faith) and the

---

[c] Dorner, in his defence against Hengstenberg's attack upon Gieseler and Lücke,
Göttingen, 1854.

[d] Matt. vi. 22, 23 ; Luke xi. 34, 35.

Gnosis (knowledge); between that which is matter of belief, and that which is but the human working up of that subject-matter, ~~which~~ process necessarily changes with the march of the times, and is always ~~being~~ developed amidst many oscillations.

His entire treatment of church history is based on this distinction. He was only concerned to exhibit the various developments as they were. It is true, he viewed as a whole, and placed together as a whole, what was connected together; called attention to action and reaction, and gave intimation of the final issues to which things were tending; but he repudiated utterly every sort of *schematism*, after which he might have constructed the history, and all subjective arbitrariness. He started from the stand-point which he found the inquiry to have already reached, and under the guidance of the pioneers who had preceded him, he penetrated into the heart of the problem; and herein he possessed what is, in fact, a rare gift, that of rapidly discovering the path which is to lead to the goal, and of leaving untrodden every useless step. We might say that the intellectual endowments of his Westphalian fatherland, where we find so much of that practical good sense and understanding which hits the nail on the head at once, and cannot be turned aside from its aim—were his in great perfection, both in his scientific undertakings and in every-day life. On form he laid comparatively small stress, whether in reference to his style of narrative, or to his own critical investigations. He was felicitous in hitting on striking verbal conjectures, for so many of which of considerable value we are indebted to him; but, perhaps, in judging of the genuineness or spuriousness of this or that document, he allowed too little weight to matters of outward form and of diction.

Moreover, his *Church History* is not a symmetrical whole throughout as respects its plan and design; or, rather, when he came to his second volume,[e] he changed his plan. At first he counted on its extending to three volumes of about equal compass; but on its reaching the second volume, the work was enlarged to such an extent, as, in some measure, to unfit it for the purpose of serving as a text-book for prelections. From this point there commences a multiplication of the volumes, for which, again, some compensation was to be found in the cursory mode of treating the period from the Peace of Westphalia to 1814. But who has ever complained of this gradual growth of the work? Precisely in the shape which the author has given to it, it has become the mine whence so much church-historical

---

[e] Of course, the reference is to the German original.

lore has been drawn, and without which a number of new compendiums of church history would doubtless never have appeared, or, at any rate, would not have presented such copious stores of materials.

The principal portions of this work have already been characterized in another place.[f] In the history of the ancient Church, his diligence and his love were mainly given to the Greek theology, our knowledge of which has been extended to such an important degree by his monographs *On the Doctrine of Clement of Alexandria and Origen respecting the Lord's body*, as also, *On the Apocryphal Vision of Isaiah*, and *On the Doctrine of the Monophysites*, and again by his edition of the *History of the Manichæans, by Petrus Siculus*, and of the twenty-third *titulus* of the *Panoplia* of Euthymius Zygabenus. In the middle ages he has subjected to the most searching and successful inquiry, particularly the history of the Cathari, of the Waldenses, of the reformatory parties and movements before the Reformation; as also that of the *cultus*, and even many portions of the political history, in so far as it was connected with the Papacy. But the crown of his Church history is the second part of the third volume, which exhibits the development of doctrine in the Reformation age, and down to the Peace of Westphalia. On the relation to one another of the two branches of the Reformation, the German and the Swiss, on Luther's course of development, on the spiritual office and the formation of the Protestant ecclesiastical constitution, we there find expressed in the most concise form an amount of information which, as to many of the sources, is exhaustive.

To the labours by which Gieseler entered into immediate connexion with the ecclesiastical affairs of our own times, belongs his pamphlet published during the struggle between the Prussian government and the Archbishop of Cologne, which contained a statement of the concessions required from both parties in order to the restoration of a lasting peace. He published these counsels under the name of 'Irenæus.' He retained the same *nom de guerre*, when in another fugitive piece he declared against the surprising perverseness of our times, which makes loyalty to our own creeds a duty on the part of our ecclesiastical opponents, in that the Lutherans now expect the Calvinist or the Catholic to be a staunch adherent of the distinctive doctrines of their Church, which, nevertheless, he on his part rejects and eschews as soul-destroying poison. He brought out, under his own name his acute inquiry into the prophecy of Lehnin, whose foreboding

---

f In the 'Prot. Kirchenz. für das evang. Deutschl. I. (1854), No. 30.'

of ill to Prussia sounds like a warning voice amidst the dangerous complications in which that great power is now entangled.

In the affairs of the neighbouring churches, also, as those of
the Netherlands and France, Gieseler took the liveliest interest.
In the year 1840, he wrote the introduction to the publication
On the Disturbances in the Reformed Church of the Netherlands,
the author of which did not wish to be known; and in the year
1848 he gave the sanction of his name to the still more extensive
work on the *History of the Protestant Church of France from
the year* 1787 *to* 1846.   His final labour was a very elaborate
adjudication upon the prize essays of Chastel and Schmidt, *On
the Influence of Christianity upon the Social Relations of the
Roman Empire*, a question which has much in common with the
inquiry into the means of deliverance to be found in Christianity
under the pressure of the social circumstances of our own time.

This question was for him, the man of clear insight and open
heart for every existing grievance and evil, whom science did
not alienate from life, whom she rather equipped with her resources for the most varied and meritorious practical labours, a
subject of the most incessant study.   Gieseler had been taught
by manifold experience to understand the life and circumstances
of the working classes, the difficulties and privations with which
so many of them have to struggle to this hour, without any
blame on their part; and along with his strongly-developed
and manly sense of justice, he possessed a delicately susceptible
feeling for all human suffering, even when deserved.   It was he
who first founded in Göttingen a society for the relief of discharged prisoners; and he managed the affairs of the Von Hugo
charities, for which he had to draw up the statutes, and the
administration of which was in his hands so long as he lived,
with much wisdom, as we see from the numerous benevolent
purposes which are now completely and permanently answered
by its means.   Perhaps there have been few men in any period
who have been more truly helpful to others than he, or who
have rendered that help less ostentatiously, and with more sympathy and promptitude.

He possessed, in a high degree, the gift of order and of
practical plastic power, as also of the wise guidance of difficult
affairs.   He seemed born for presidency, and in the critical situation into which the university was betrayed seventeen years ago,
he proved his circumspection and firmness to the complete satisfaction of all who were capable of an unprejudiced view of the
state of the case.   Gieseler, moreover, had a liking for rule;
but, it must be added, without discovering any indication of an
ambitious spirit.   He gave his reasons, he wrought conviction,

and in instances in which he was nevertheless outvoted, he seemed for a moment to examine over again the grounds of his opinion, which, however, he seldom changed, although he was not wont to harp upon it any further. He gave his advice only when it was asked; but his sympathy and his help were often bestowed before they were sought.

He was a very faithful friend; from a man to whom he had once accorded his confidence, he did not lightly withdraw it.

The numerous honours which he obtained during his lifetime did not puff him up. At the farthest remove from every species of vanity, he possessed a noble, manly spirit of independence; he knew his worth, without being proud of it. For a just and good cause he did not hesitate about the sacrifices it might cost. He took the liveliest interest in the struggle for the maintenance of the Union Church, and rejoiced at the dawning of new light after a season of darkness, of which he was able to catch a glimpse before his departure. He felt certain that a fair and blessed new thing in the kingdom of the Lord was at hand, even if it tarried.

Giving himself plenty to do in his loyal devotedness to the well-being of Church and country, and in his loving concern for others, he was also tried himself with many cares for his own house. After the death of his first wife, which took place in 1831, soon after his removal to Göttingen, he found some compensation for this never wholly forgotten loss, in his second marriage with a relative of the deceased, Amelia Villaret, whom he selected as the future companion of his life, and the second mother of his children. This marriage, too, was unusually fruitful in offspring, and accordingly his cares for their education multiplied, as well as those for the settling in life of the sons and daughters who had grown up meanwhile. But to the last day of his life he enjoyed the richest experience of the truth and faithfulness of him who had said concerning *his* house also, ' mine eyes shall be open upon it day and night.'

On his deathbed he saw nearly all his sons and daughters, two excepted, whom distance prevented, gathered around him, and calmly took his leave of them, with stedfast confidence in God, which was the fundamental trait in his character. Sound, as few are, in body and mind till then, and consequently up to the last year of his life, which was the sixty-third of his age, a man of youthful, vigorous, and strong constitution, he succumbed only very gradually to the disease which now at length attacked him all at once with such violence. It was abdominal consumption. His robust body offered a sufficiently protracted resistance for a long while to most painful struggles, until its powers were exhausted, and a quiet, peaceable dissolution terminated his energetic life, on the 8th of July, 1854, at dawn. Three days later he was buried. Both the city and the university felt his loss with equal severity. One saw by his funeral procession that a place was vacant, which would not so soon be filled again by another with equal ability and renown.

In the history of Göttingen, of science, and of the Church, Gieseler's name will continue unforgotten. All who knew him as he was cherish his memory, thankfully and faithfully, as a precious treasure amongst their dearest reminiscences. But as for himself, though taken away from us, and painfully missed from amongst the ranks of his fellow-soldiers, fighting for the precious and noble freedom and unity of our Protestant Church, he is, nevertheless, by his works and by his life, still active in our midst, and so, like that most ancient of all God's witnesses (Heb. xi. 4), "being dead, he yet speaketh."

MATTHEW xx. 16, xxii. 14.

Matt. xx. 16.—" So the last shall be first, and the first last: For many are called but few chosen."
Matt. xxii. 14, 15.—" Then said the king, bind him hand and foot, &c. For many are called, but few chosen."

THE concluding words, found in these two different passages in the volume of inspiration, assign a reason for what precedes, or are connected with it by a γάρ casual. It is, therefore, natural to infer, that there must be something in common in the scope of the two passages, to which they are as it were a common key; and no interpretation would appear to be satisfactory, which does not establish the natural connexion between these words, and the context of both the passages in which they are found; and which does not also trace the points of resemblance, owing to which two passages, differing widely in several respects, are yet supported upon one and the same ground.

The small number of those who truly embrace the Gospel, compared to that of those to whom its invitations are extended, is supposed by many to be what is here meant; those who hear, but receive it not, being the κλητοί, those who do receive it the ἐκλεκτοί. This interpretation regards our Lord's declaration as particularly applicable to the Jews, or that, at least, they furnished the first and most striking illustration of its truth.

In favour of this view, the correspondence of the actual condition of the Jews, with the opening statement in Matt. xxii. 16, viz., the first shall be last and the last shall be first, is looked upon as conclusive. They were first or highest in spiritual privileges; and now, they are below many of the Gentiles. They were the people whom God first knew as his own; but now many other nations have flowed into the church of God before them.

In these respects, it must be admitted, that there is a coincidence between our Lord's statement, and the respective position of Jews and Gentiles at different periods of their history; and this view seems to receive further confirmation from the connexion in which a similar declaration is found in Luke xiii. 30, in which passage our Lord clearly refers to the calling of the Gentiles when he says xiii. 28, 29, "There shall be weeping and gnashing of teeth, when ye shall see Abraham, and Isaac, and Jacob, and all the prophets in the kingdom of God, and you yourselves thrust out. And they shall come from the east, and from the west, and from the north, and from the south, and shall sit down in the kingdom of God."

A closer examination, however, will perhaps shew, that there are grounds for questioning the correctness of this interpretation. Commencing with Matt. xix. 30, where a previous use of the words "*But many that are first shall be last, and the last shall be first*" is found, and viewing them in connexion merely with what precedes, and regarding the truth therein delivered by our Saviour as perfectly and completely evolved in the thirtieth verse of the nineteenth chapter, it must, it seems, be admitted, that the reversed order of final precedency expressed there, is one which applies solely and strictly to those who are not only called, but who have cordially embraced the Gospel, and who for its sake have forsaken whatever was an obstacle itself to their hearty reception of or adherence to it. It may be said, indeed, that the following context modifies this view, and that any conclusion drawn only from Matt. xix. 28—30, unconnected with the parable of the labourers in the first part of chapter xx., is partial and erroneous; but the sense of verses 28—30 seems to be complete and perfect in itself, and the structure of the whole passage tends to prove that it is so, and that the parable which forms the subject of the twentieth chapter is merely a practical illustration of what is stated in the conclusion of the nineteenth chapter.

Nor does it seem clear, that an examination of the parable itself will afford any ground for supposing that the reversed order intimated in the statement that " *the first shall be last, and the last first,*" refers either to Jews and Gentiles, or to a pre-eminence in privileges. It is an indisputed rule that doctrinal consequences are not to be drawn from all the incidental circumstances of a parable ; and this being admitted, it must be further conceded, that the greatest importance is to be attached to those which correspond most closely with its general drift, and which bear most strongly and directly upon the great truth which it is intended to illustrate. The guidance of these principles seems to lead to the conclusion, that the reversed order spoken of is one which will take place among those who will be saved, if it is not still further restricted to those who labour in the ministry ; that the priority spoken of is significant, in one case, of a pre-eminence in future glory, and in the other of a precedence or priority in the time of their entering into the church, and that the reason of this is, that *the called are many, but the chosen are few.*

That a reversed order of precedence and its grounds are the truths which the parable is intended to illustrate, is evident from the connective γάρ with which the parable is introduced, and the causative γάρ which concludes it with a repetition of that truth.

The apostle Peter had asked our Lord what he and his fellow apostles should receive, who had forsaken all and followed him, evidently referring to a future reward. In reply to his question our Saviour had declared, that they should hereafter sit on twelve thrones of Israel, referring as clearly to the future judgment, and the reward laid up hereafter. But he adds, "*many that are first shall be last, and the last first.*" The simple and unconstrained connexion of this verse is with those which immediately precede, and the interpretation which it at once suggests to us is, that all who have followed Christ shall derive immeasurable advantages from their choice ; that those who have been eminent in labour and usefulness, as for instance, the apostles, will be eminent in glory ; but that many who have been first in one sense will be last in another, while those who have been last in the former, will be first in the latter sense. To illustrate this feature in the divine dealings with those who shall be thus rewarded, and to vindicate God's justice in the manner of dispensing rewards, our Saviour introduces the parable of the householder, going out to hire labourers into his vineyard.

From the character of the parable thus chosen, in which labourers are the conspicuous object, it would not be unnatural to conclude, that our Saviour's immediate object was to reconcile the apostles themselves to the manner in which the rewards of his kingdom would be distributed.   At the same time, there is no positive argument for restricting it to them, and not including within it all his disciples.   But the evening and the payment of their hire, point, not to a time of entering upon labour, not to a time of vocation into the church, but to a time of rest from labour, and of reaping its fruits; or, in other words, to the time indicated in those verses of the nineteenth chapter which the parable is intended to illustrate, the time of future and eternal reward.

The reward also of all without exception, and in a particular order, corresponds as closely with the interpretation which connects the declaration in verse 30, that the *first shall be last and the last first, with* verses 28 and 29, and which maintains that the inverted order is one which will take place among those who have forsaken whatever opposed their adherence to the Gospel and followed Christ; or that, among those who have done so, there will be a gradation and order of reward, and that this order will, in many cases, be the opposite of a particular order in which they formerly stood in some other respect.

The parallel passage in St. Mark affords no argument for any particular interpretation being introduced in exactly the same connexion in which it is found in St. Matthew.   The only remaining passage in which the words *The first shall be last and the last first* occur, is Luke xiii. 30, and this has every appearance of indicating the time of future judgment and reward. It is the time, like that in the parable of the bridegroom, when the door has been shut—when Abraham, and Isaac, and Jacob, and all the prophets shall be again seen; and many from the east, and west, and north, and south, shall come and sit down with them, while others shall be thrust out, and among these last shall be the unbelieving Jews.   It is the time when, in consequence of this awful decision, there shall be weeping and gnashing of teeth, &c., many of which things cannot, without great violence, be predicated of any time whatever, but that of future and final judgment, and reward.

In opposition to this, the only argument that seems capable of being adduced is, that it cannot be supposed that there will be any murmuring or discontent among those who shall be admitted to eternal felicity; and that, consequently, the day of reward cannot be intended, nor can the blessed be the persons among whom this inverted order of rewards will take place. But a due regard to the proper interpretation of a parabolical illustration will shew, that this is altogether an insufficient argument to oppose to such numerous and strong indications of the scope of our Saviour's words.

Those parts of the passage in which our Lord speaks without figure, point clearly to the time of reward, and this circumstance itself should make us very cautious in opposing to a literal statement any incidental part of a figurative illustration. But when, in addition to this, the main scope of the illustration corresponds with the literal and positive truths to which it is subservient, a single circumstance in the parable which may not correspond is altogether an inadequate foundation for controverting the sense, which the literal declaration and the main features of the figurative tend to establish.

The object was to give some idea of the nature of the precedency which should hereafter take place, in opposition, in many instances, to a previous order, in which its subjects had stood; and to vindicate God's justice in the transaction. To accomplish this latter particular, nothing could be more natural than to *suppose* exception to be taken to God's manner of dealing, and to suggest an objection that would not really be made at the time, in order to remove dissatisfaction which would be very likely to spring up in the minds of the early disciples, at being told that many who should enter the vineyard after them in time, might, and that some would, acquire greater eminence in glory than they should.

The objection was necessary to introduce the answer. To remove a present scruple, or danger of dissatisfaction, a future discontent was imagined, and its unreasonableness exposed : nor can this be made a ground for asserting that there will really be any discontent at the time to which the parable refers, or for controverting the whole drift of the passage.

The kingdom of Christ has, like every other, a subordination of its various subjects; like every other body, a relative arrangement of its several members; and for this purpose our Saviour has given it prophets, evangelists, &c., &c. But, unlike other kingdoms which are of this world, its rewards are not to be attained here; its various subjects, in whatever period they have lived, shall hereafter be re-assembled, and shall then, and not until then, receive their final reward. Such being the case, it is natural to suppose, that, as there will be not only amongst its members at large, but also among those who have occupied prominent positions, various degrees of faithfulness and excellence, as peculiar seasons in the church's history exhibit brighter transcripts of the Redeemer's glory than others, so will there be, at times, bright and shining stars, chosen to exercise a particular influence, and to occupy positions of more than ordinary difficulty, danger, or usefulness in the church. An earthly sovereign may, at any time, reward his servants according to the order in which they entered upon their office, and would do so justly; but all the subjects of Christ's kingdom, in all its successive ages, must be assembled before their respective position in the future state of reward can be determined; and all the eras in the history of the church must roll over before their comparative importance or peculiar character can be decided. That there are seasons in her history of more intense interest and brighter glory than others, and persons chosen to occupy proportionably more prominent positions, and to exercise more powerful influences than others, cannot be questioned. The deluge, the call of Abraham, the Exodus of the Israelites, the return from captivity, the appearance of our Lord, the calling of the Gentiles, the future restoration of the Jews, are seasons of peculiar interest, and as it were crises in the church's condition. Noah, Abraham, Moses, Elias, and John the Baptist, the apostles, and especially Peter, John, and Paul, are instances of chosen instruments for peculiar times, and of men who shall hereafter be as eminent in glory over multitudes who preceded them in the time of their admission to the church, as they have been in the position which they have occupied, and the influences they have exercised on the general welfare and extension of the church at large.

The interpretation which is thus suggested is not to be confounded with that which regards the ἐκλεκτοί as those who excel simply in character, without reference to a choice on God's part. On the contrary, it recognizes a selection and choice, and that of a very marked character; such a choice as that which selected Abraham and Moses, separated Jeremiah to his office before his birth, exercised its influence upon John the Baptist while he was yet unborn, and by its overpowering influence converted the persecuting Saul into a most zealous and laborious apostle of the faith which he once sought to destroy. This interpretation takes as one of its strong grounds the greatly distinguishing influences exercised upon these chosen instruments, and the extraordinary means employed in fitting them for their position, or leading them to occupy it. These shining stars, these luminaries of the church must be few; for all cannot be prophets, or evangelists, or teachers; much less can many be greatest in the particular class to which they belong. To qualify them for stations of more than ordinary importance and influence, more than ordinary gifts must be vouchsafed, more than ordinary grace must be shewn. And this interpretation affords a clue to the force of the declaration that many are called, but

few chosen, where it occurs in the parable of the man without a
wedding garment. His sin and folly consisted in presuming to
think that in his case the king would depart from his ordinary
course, and would make him an exception to a general rule—
that he should experience and might reckon upon, not only the
gracious acceptance vouchsafed to the other guests notwithstanding their unworthiness, but upon such a departure from the conditions and obligations connected with his admittance as would
mark him out as an especial favourite, and give him an importance in the eyes of those around him.   But he was soon convinced of his error. God has his chosen instruments, and in
their selection and preparation for their peculiar office and position, he vouchsafes to them extraordinary influence and very
peculiar favour; but these persons are few indeed compared to
the body of his church, and he who presumes on the strength of
this, or upon any other ground, to expect to be admitted except
upon God's general terms, and in the diligent use of his appointed means,—who presumes so far upon the riches of God's
mercy as to expect exceptions from the general rule of God's
dealing in his favour—will assuredly be disappointed; for the
called are many, the chosen but few.

    It has been, and it may be maintained, that the expression,
"*many are called, but few chosen,*" in the parable of the wedding
feast, refers not to the latter circumstances of that parable; viz.,
the exposure and rejection of the man without a wedding garment, but to the persons who refused to come in contradistinction to those who did; but none of the circumstances of the
parable harmonize with this view.   In the first place, if the word
"chosen" is regarded as significant of any peculiarity in the
circumstances of the calling, it is much more applicable to the
guests who refused than to those who accepted the invitation.
They were the chosen guests, the persons whom the king selected
as most agreeable to himself; and the others were called in consequence of their refusal. The number who eventually sat down
was as large as that originally invited, so that if the whole who
were invited were the called, and those who accepted the invitation were the chosen, the latter could scarcely be called few in
comparison with the former. It is further opposed to the interpretation, that those who accepted the invitation were the chosen,
in the sense of persons peculiarly selected, that one of them
was clearly and evidently not so; but was, on the contrary,
immediately challenged, upon the entrance of the king, as a
person who was unfit, and a subject not for choice but rejection.

    Of the four places in which it is stated that "*the first shall
be last and the last first,*" there is only one from which any

direct inference can be drawn in favour of the view which regards
the relative position of the Jews and Gentiles as intended,
namely, Luke xiii. 30; but, even in this connexion, the preponderance is against it. Our Saviour's previous words enforce two
things, the necessity of diligence and labour in religion, or of
striving to enter in at the strait gate, and the futility of resting
on mere outward privileges, whether on the part of Jews or
Gentiles, or the certainty of the rejection of all who, resting on
these, continue workers of iniquity. The rejection of the Jews
who did so, and the exaltation of the Gentiles who did not, is
indeed introduced, but not in such a manner as to indicate that
our Lord had any intention of intimating a reversion in the
position of the Jews as a nation; but merely that many of the
Gentiles should be admitted to sit with Abraham in the kingdom,
while those who trusted in outward privileges, which the Jews at
large did, should be cast out.

The form of connexion also between "*the first shall be last,
and the last first,* with what precedes it in this place (Luke xiii.
30), is not such as to favour such an interpretation. Had such
been the sense intended, the words which would have conveyed
it most clearly, and which are elsewhere used where the connexion is indisputable, would have been, "*So* the first shall be
last, and the last first." Our Saviour had declared that the
Jews, or such of them as trusted in outward privileges, should
be cast out, but that many should come from the East, &c. If
the declaration which follows is in any way significant of the
inversion of the relative position of the Jews and Gentiles, the
proper connective particle to signify what was a repetition in
other words of this truth, or an illustration of it, would have
been that used in Matt. xx. 16, namely, ὄντως. As this is not
the connective used in Luke xiii. 20, there can be no ground for
asserting that what follows, or the statement—"*And behold,
there are last that shall be first, and there are first which shall be
last* "—conveys the same meaning as the declaration "*So* the
last shall be first," &c. On the contrary, the introductory expression, *And behold,* is an appropriate phrase to signify the
intimation of another and a distinct truth, not a repetition or
illustration of one just revealed.

Another difference in the form of the expression is also
worthy of consideration, as coinciding with that already noticed.
It is not said, *And, Behold, the* first, but And behold *there are*
first, which shall be last and last first, intimating clearly a partitive arrangement among those who should sit down in the kingdom of God. But the time of partition had been so definitely
marked between Jew and Gentile, that if they had been the

respective parties intended, the natural expression to signify a repetition or illustration would have been as in Matt. xx. 16, ὄντως. Indeed the modification and connexion of these words compared with those in the other passages in which they occur is just such as would naturally have been adopted to prevent a misconstruction in this passage by applying them to the case of Jews and Gentiles. In Matt. xx. 1, where they indubitably apply to the labourers in the parable immediately preceding, it is said, *So* the first shall be last and the last first: in Matt. xix. 30, and Mark x. 31, where a partitive or reversed arrangement of one preceding class, namely, those who had forsaken all or much for Christ, it is said, *"But* many that are first shall be last and the last first;"* but in Luke xiii. 30, where two classes had been mentioned, and there was, consequently, a danger of referring the partition or classification intimated by these words to the previously mentioned classes, and of regarding the statement as merely a repetition of a truth already stated, or an illustration of it, a form of expression, strongly calculated to shew that a new and important truth is to be made known, and to intimate another classification, or one which will take place among those who will sit down in the kingdom of God is used, viz., *And Behold there are* last that shall be first, &c.

It is also opposed to the application of the words "the last shall be first," &c., to the relative position of Jews and Gentiles, that the word many refers more correctly to many individuals of one class as opposed to the rest of that class than to one nation in contradistinction to others. The unbelieving Jews would never enter; the believing Jews would enter among the first and at parallel times with the Gentiles. If, therefore, we regard believers generally as the persons spoken of, it cannot be said that the Gentiles precede the Jewish converts in time; although larger numbers of the Gentiles have flowed into the church up to the present time, and we have ground for believing that large numbers of the Jews will hereafter do so; for even this latter conversion of the Jews is, we have every reason for supposing, to be the precursory or preparatory step to the conversion of all the rest of the world, or to the bringing in of the fulness of the Gentiles. If this is true, it cannot be said that the Jews will, upon the whole, or embracing their history from the beginning to the end of time, be the last either in time or in privilege.

May it not also be matter for enquiry, how the declaration *"that many are called but few chosen,"* can, by any simple or unconstrained, or well-established, connexion of cause and effect, be made the ground or reason why the first shall be last and the last first, in the sense of an inverted order in the respective position of Jews and Gentiles? An inverted order of precedency has nothing to do with number, and cannot in any way be dependent or consequent upon it. An inverted order of precedency can as readily take place or be arranged among five thousand as well as among fifty; and, in this respect, therefore, it would make no difference if all the Jews who had been invited to embrace the Gospel had done so, or if both they and the Gentiles had universally listened to its invitations, or if very few of either or of both had done so. In all these cases the inverted order of precedence of the two classes of people would have been equally practicable; nor does it appear at all clear how anything like a proper sequitur can be established between the proposition, that many are called but few chosen, and a mere inverted order of position between Jew and Gentile or any other distinct classes.

An interpretation which refers this order to one class and which regards the chosen as prominent characters in that one class, places the subject in a very different position, and establishes a simple, clear, and strong connexion of consequence between the number and the consequent order. The chosen persons—the great luminaries—those who are selected to fill stations of peculiar importance in critical, or even ordinary periods of the church's history, over whom, to prepare them for their position, more than ordinary measures of providential and gracious influence are exercised—to whom larger and more abundant supplies of wisdom, energy, and love are vouchsafed, and greater and distinguishing degrees of divine forbearance, superintendence, and privilege are shewn, must be few; and, being dispersed over the various eras of the church's history, those who have appeared in her latest periods must take precedency in the day of reward, over those who have appeared before them in time, but who have been called to occupy less influential positions; and this will in a less marked degree extend to all who shall be considered worthy to enter into the joy of their Lord.

The structure of the parable of the labourers is strongly in favour of this interpretation. The householder is represented as going out not merely *twice*, as would naturally have been the case, had the Jews and Gentiles been intended, by these calls at different hours, but several times, namely at the first, second, sixth, and ninth hours; and, in accordance with this feature in the parable, the current of ancient interpretation attaches to it the following opinions.

1st. That they who were called at the first hour, were Adam

and Eve, Enoch and Noah; they at the second, Abraham and the Patriarchs; they at the sixth, Moses and the Jews; they at the ninth, the prophets: or, secondly, it is supposed that it relates to the several ages of man, and to those who are called at earlier or later stages of life. Both these views seem to agree in this, that they regard those among whom this inverted order takes place, as all of one class, in this respect, that they are all rewarded, the rejected man of course excepted, which does not affect the subject, as his exclusion could not make the many few. On this account both these interpretations seem to be more consistent with the tenor of the parable, and with the natural signification of the language, than that which refers it to the Jews and Gentiles.

But, independently of some others, there are two objections to these interpretations, which appear insuperable; and from which that now proposed is not only quite free, but, in reference to which, it presents a marked contrast, if not a direct opposition.

According to both the above views, we must either regard all who are called as also chosen; or else suppose that those who have been called last, viz., the prophets, or otherwise, those who have been called latest in life, will be rewarded first, or have the most favour shewn to them; and that all the rest will follow in a regular gradation according to their lateness in life, or the lateness of the period in the church's history in which they live. This indeed would correspond most minutely with the circumstances of the parable; but that our Sáviour did not intend it to be thus applied is evident both from what precedes the parable, namely, not that *they* or that *all* who are first shall be last, but that *many* shall be so, and from the known facts of the case. They which are alive shall not prevent or anticipate the dead in the day of reward; nor can we possibly suppose that the gradations of reward or of favour shewn will proceed in an order, exactly, and in every case, the reverse of that in which men appear in the world, or of the time of life when they entered the church, *e. g.*, that the prophets should precede Moses, and Moses precede Abraham, &c., either in the time, or greatness of the reward; or that Samuel, Jeremiah, John the Baptist, or Timothy, should be amongst the very last either in their reception into glory, or in the degree of favour shewn to them, simply because they were devoted to God from their very youth.

Both these interpretations either draw no line of distinction between the called and chosen, or else lead to one the very reverse in many cases not only of what we should suppose, but of what we know will actually take place. The present interpretation not only draws a line of demarcation which

gives to the word *"chosen,"* in contra-distinction to *"called,"*
the fullest significancy of which it is susceptible in the sense
of selected, peculiarly distinguished, most highly-favoured or
privileged, the subjects of extraordinary favour and of communications of more than ordinary grace in all its branches,
but one which makes the reversed order of precedence such
as we should naturally expect, and such as we know will
hereafter prevail. Thus, for instance, the apostles are said by
our Saviour to have reaped that whereon they bestowed no
labour, and to have entered upon the labour of others, yet they
shall sit on twelve thrones judging the twelve tribes of Israel.
John the Baptist appeared long after the last of the purely
Jewish prophets, yet he was among the greatest. Paul entered
long after the other apostles upon his office, yet he had the
greatest favour shewn to him, and the most overwhelming influence exercised to bring him to submit to the Redeemer's yoke.
He was also in labours the most abundant, and was permitted
to behold, during his life, the glories of the third heaven.

There is another circumstance which may have some weight
in the support of the arguments already adduced, as giving some
reason to conclude that this was the sense in which our Saviour's
words were understood by those who heard them ; and that the
order of precedence among Christ's disciples at the day of
reward, and especially among those who had laboured in his
church, was what was signified. The application of the children
of Zebedee, through their mother, follows the words under consideration very closely ; from which it may be inferred, that the
declaration which precedes the assurance, that the twelve apostles should sit upon the twelve thrones, led to the train of
thought which induced them to seek that they might sit one
upon his right hand and the other on his left; and that the
intermediate words that the first should be last, &c., refer to
that subject of our Saviour's declaration, and to their consequent
petition ; or that these three circumstances are closely connected
in time and in import, and in their indication of what was
uppermost in the minds of the apostles, and consequently the
subject of our Saviour's reply.

The answer given to Zebedee's children also harmonizes with
this view. Their application was made as it were at the meridian of the church's history : but all the ages embraced within
her term of militancy must elapse, and all the labourers must be
assembled before their respective positions can be assigned.

The subject of the petition of the sons of Zebedee was not
our Lord's then to give, nor could he, as the suffering Saviour,
or as a king who embraced in his regard the various successive

eras of his kingdom, and the numerous servants who should, at widely distant intervals of time and place, be required and chosen by him to occupy pre-eminent positions, anticipate the time when they should all be assembled to share his triumph and his glory : nor could he shew a partiality for any particular persons, or any particular time, to the prejudice of those great principles which guide him through his universal dominion, or to a diminution of the interest of that era which will concentrate in itself the interest of all other eras—the great day of final assembly and reward.

The interpretation advocated in these remarks may be attended with difficulties which have not occurred to the writer, but it seems to combine the following advantages. It draws a clear and broad line of demarcation between the *called* and the *chosen,* and assigns to the latter term as powerful a signification in the sense of peculiarly selected as the advocates of any other interpretation could desire. It establishes a simple and unconstrained causal connexion between the two clauses, or the protasis and apodosis of Matt. xx. 16, by shewing how the first being last and the last first, springs naturally from the circumstance that many are called but few chosen. It furnishes a ground upon which the two passages in which the declaration that many are called but few chosen is spoken of as a cause of what precedes, may, in common, be made to rest, or viz., common cause for the rejection of the guest without a wedding garment, and for the inverted order of future reward, or that they, in whose behalf peculiar privileges and distinguished favour are exhibited, are few in proportion to those who are called in the ordinary method of God's dealing with the body of his people—that, for this reason any person who presumed to *expect* any such distinction or departure from God's general manner of dealing will, like the guest who entertained similar expectations, be cast out, and that, for the same reason, many who are first in order as to their time of entrance and of labour in God's church, will be later in the order of eminence or glory. It establishes an order such as might be expected from the nature of the case, and such as we know will, to some extent, prevail. It preserves the connexion between the different parts of the context, or the statements of our Lord and their figurative illustration, and harmonizes with the circumstances of the parable, with a solitary exception which is naturally accounted for, if it is not shewn to have been necessary to the modifications. *And Behold there are* first, &c. *But many* that are first, &c. *So the first shall* be last, &c., assigns a proper and due significancy, and agrees with what we know to have been the subject which, at that time,

occupied the minds of the apostles, namely, the consummation
of our Saviour's kingdom, and the position which they would
occupy in it.   This seems satisfactorily proved by the question
of St. Peter, which elicited these words from our Saviour, and
by the petition of Zebedee's children and their mother, which
was offered up on the same occasion.

R. K.

JAPANESE TRANSLATIONS OF THE NEW TESTAMENT.

AT a time when the empire of Japan is likely to be open to
commercial—and, let us hope, also to missionary—enterprise,
it may not be out of place to say one word on the subject of
the translations of Holy Scripture in Japanese, for the purpose
of drawing the attention of Japanese scholars to that subject in
particular.

There are, we believe, as yet, only two versions in existence,
one by the late Dr. Gutzlaff, and another by Dr. Bettelheim,
late resident missionary at the Loo-Choo islands.   The translation by Dr. Gutzlaff contains the whole New Testament.   Of
this, St. John, the Acts of the Apostles, and the Epistles of St.
John, have alone been printed; the rest exists only in MS.
The whole work is at present, we think, in this country.   Its
size is crown 4to.; it is neatly written, and the printed portions
are the counterpart of the MS., except that the printed characters are less elegant than the MS. ones; but it is executed in a
clear, legible manner.

Unfortunately, however, owing to the source from whence
Dr. Gutzlaff borrowed his knowledge of Japanese, the language
and style of his version are not likely to prove acceptable to the
educated men of Japan.   The style is rather vulgar; or perhaps
it is a dialectic deviation from the pure and elegant Japanese,
which alone finds favour with a vast class of people in that peculiar country.   Chinese being much studied in Japan as the classical
language, from which the Japanese syllabic system of writing
has been borrowed, a two-fold language may be said to be
spoken there—one with a considerable admixture of Chinese
words, the other with very little indeed of that idiom.   These
two kinds of style—the one high, the other low—are again subdivided into various shades of language, partaking more or
less of one or of the other, exactly as it also is in China, and

indeed in most countries where education is not general. Hence a great difficulty meets the translator at the outset—it is the choice of the style that will at the same time both please the educated and be well understood by the common people. But this, we need not say, demands a greater knowledge of the language than translators are willing to acknowledge. For there is a wide stretch between sufficient knowledge for a creditable " exercise" in a language, and the ability necessary for a good rendering of the " WORD OF GOD ;" though, unhappily, these two distinct requisites have often been thought identical.

The result as regards Dr. Gutzlaff's version is, that the whole of it has not yet been printed ; but, as mentioned above, only detached portions of it, which did not, we think, meet with a cordial reception among Japanese readers.

As an improvement upon Dr. Gutzlaff's version, a fresh translation of the New Testament into Japanese was undertaken by Dr. Bettelheim, at the Loo-Choo islands. We do not know that more than the four gospels have been completed, but the MS. of these was for some time at the Depository of the British and Foreign Bible Society, where we were liberally allowed to make extracts from it. It was subsequently sent back to Hong-Kong, where the Gospel of St. Luke has been printed from it, as a trial only. A copy of it was kindly sent us by the Bishop of Victoria, by one of the last mails ; and it is to this version in particular,—while it is on its trial,—that we are anxious to draw the attention of Japanese scholars, in order that, if possible, it may ultimately go forth as a true representative of its inspired original.

The size of the MS. (and of the printed portion, which is a counterpart of the MS.) is common 4to. It is in Chinese and Japanese. First comes a paragraph in Chinese, and then its translation into Japanese. This plan presents several advantages : it gives the classical Chinese (as rendered by Dr. Medhurst and his coadjutors at Shanghaë) to the learned Japanese, while it presents to the less educated a translation of it in their own tongue.

But as the MS. was both incorrectly and inaccurately written, so also is its printed counterpart. The MS. was written by a very unskilful hand, and perhaps also by different hands, some of the syllabic characters being disfigured, or even illegible. And as it was copied and cut on the blocks at Hong-Kong, by Chinese workmen, probably ignorant of Japanese, we need scarcely say that inaccuracies in the printed specimen are in greater number even than in the MS. The columns (or lines) are too close : and as the words are frequently badly divided (one word in two or two words in one), its appearance is rather confused, and the reading of it is rendered difficult on that account. It should have been printed in columns more spaced (like St. Paul's Epistle to the Romans in Loo-Chooan, or like Dr. Gutzlaff's version) ; but as it now stands, we do not think that even natives could find it an easy book to read.

We know that in Japan the orthography is far from being fixed or settled, owing to there being more than one syllable in their so-called alphabet representing the same sound, or at least being pronounced alike; so that some words are occasionally written with *i, wi*, or *fi*, or *hi*, for *i—o, wo, ho*, or *go*, for *o—e, ye, be*, or *he*, for *e*, etc. But, at all events, in the same work the mode of spelling should be the same. In Dr. Bettelheim's translation, however, the same word is often spelled differently. The syllables *müh* and *mi, mo*, or *me, ba, ga, da, sa, pa, ta, te*, and several others, are constantly interchanged; but this may be partly owing to the difficulty a German ear frequently finds in detecting the difference between some of those sounds.

As we have read the Japanese Gospel of St. Luke, as yet, only once through, it would be unfair towards the learned translator, and very inconsiderate and unwise on our part, to attempt now a *critical* notice, which we may reserve for a future occasion, when we shall have had more leisure to do Dr. Bettelheim ample justice. It is enough for the present to say that the work, in its actual state, is not fit for distribution in Japan as a worthy rendering of the WORD OF GOD. Even a superficial survey of its execution shews that, while it possesses much merit, and does its author credit, considering the difficulties under which he laboured, yet it does not bear the requisite stamp of scholarship. The choice of fit words to render the original (English, we suppose,) often seems to have been made without sufficient care. At other times the style savours more of Chinese than of true Japanese character, and reads more like a rendering into Japanese characters of the Chinese symbols by the side of it. We do not speak of *words* only, for it is often necessary to adopt that plan, but of *sentences* also, which do not harmonise well with others of Japanese stamp. The style is wanting in uniformity. It appears also (though it may look presumptuous in us to say so) that the rules of grammar are not always adhered to; and we cannot but think that in the use of particles and of postpositions especially (on which the Japanese language hinges in a great measure), the translator has followed his own impression of their relative meaning and place in a sentence, rather than a thorough knowledge of the position they ought by right to hold in purely idiomatic language.

It seems also that Chinese words have frequently been interwoven with the text, without any necessity. The Japanese have pure words of their own for father, mother, heaven, &c., without giving them in Chinese in the Japanese text. This remark applies also to verbs, adjectives, and other parts of speech; perhaps it is that the translator is a better Chinese than Japanese scholar. But since the two languages are essentially distinct, though more or less amalgamated together in different writings, it would seem that they should be no more blended into one than is strictly conformable to good taste and to sound scholarship; so as to leave to each language its distinctive character untouched.

But the fault of thus needlessly borrowing terms from the language reckoned the higher of the two, is common to most translators who either are not masters of the language into which they translate, or are not above making a show of their information. For instance, in Turkey, Persia, India, &c., it is with the greatest difficulty you can procure a teacher who will teach his language in its characteristic purity. He will insist on bringing in his own knowledge of Arabic or of Sanscrit; so that if you attempt to converse in the language thus learned, you are listened to by few, and understood by fewer still. Thus, too, translations—of Holy Scripture especially—are frequently made, in a language which, whatever name it may bear, ends at last in becoming a dialect of the " translator's own." This is the more to be guarded against, as, however pleased we may be ourselves with our own proficiency, and even wonder it does not appear so to others also, we have to translate the WORD OF GOD—not our own ideas, but the WORD OF GOD—for people whose ear is as keen as our own, and often much keener, too; whose taste for calligraphy and for certain terms and turns of phrase is at least quite as well trained as ours is likely to be.

A fair knowledge of a language, therefore, that may answer almost every purpose for even familiar conversation, is not alone sufficient for the faithful rendering of GOD's inspired Word. The choice of *fit* terms to convey correct ideas of Him and of His eternal Truth, demands more than a mere knowledge of a certain amount of words. It requires deep thought and profound study. For instance (and although we could not, perhaps, at present, offer a fit substitute), we do not think that the Japanese rendering of the word *cross*, by Dr. Bettelheim, in Luke xiv. 27, is at all likely to convey to heathen readers a correct idea of what is required of a " disciple of Christ." The expression he uses is, I see, partly taken from the Chinese original, and given in the Japanese text in Chinese characters, accompanied with the Japanese reading.

It is " a beam like the letter +" (ten).   Surely this and such renderings require modification ere they can impart to heathen (or even to Christians) a correct idea of our Saviour's searching words.

There are also other inaccuracies in Dr. Bettelheim's version. A word—even a portion of a verse—is sometimes repeated twice ; while at other times they may be omitted.   The whole of St. Luke vii. 17, is left out altogether.

It is of such vital importance that the natives of Japan, who are about to open their eyes, almost for the first time, to the light of God's truth, should receive it at our hands pure, that science and scholarship could not be turned to a higher and more worthy object, than to the revision and improvement of the translation of the New Testament intended for Japan.   Let us hope that additional knowledge will be brought to bear upon it, in order that Dr. Bettelheim's labours may bring forth wholesome fruit to the glory of GOD, for whom he has worked.

S. C. MALAN.

CORRESPONDENCE.

⁎ The Editor begs the reader will bear in mind that he does not hold himself
responsible for the opinions of his Correspondents.

WHO WAS DARIUS THE SON OF AHASUERUS, OF THE SEED OF THE MEDES?—DANIEL IX. 1.

Sir,—Your correspondent G. B., in the last number of your *Journal*, p. 163, has offered some observations on a paper of mine, now published in the *Journal of the Royal Asiatic Society*, entitled "Chronology of the reigns of Tiglath-pileser, Sargon, Shalmanezer, and Sennacherib, in connexion with the phenomenon seen on the Dial of Ahaz."

It is not my intention here to offer any objections to his remarks as far as they relate to the subject of the shadow on the dial, which I am content to leave to the judgment of your readers, more especially of those skilled in astronomy, within whose province it lies to determine the physical possibility or otherwise of the suggested solution of the phenomenon. My object now is, to draw attention to a series of chronological notes appended to the letter of your correspondent, in which he has endeavoured to defend the paradoxical opinion, that "Darius the son of Ahasuerus, of the seed of the Medes," was identical with Cyaxares the son of Astyages, and, in doing so, to overthrow the system of dates which I have adopted. This conclusion I have ventured to designate "a hopeless contradiction," as little satisfactory indeed to my mind, and as absolutely contradictory, as regards titles, as if Darius the son of Ahasuerus had been identified with Alexander son of Philip.

Your correspondent, however, is by no means disturbed by the contradiction. On the contrary, so reasonable and acceptable does this sort of conclusion appear to him, that in a postscript he reminds us that there are two similar cases of supposed identification resulting from the same chronological view of this period of Bible history, viz., that Ahasuerus of the book of Ezra was the king known by the name of Cambyses, and Artaxerxes, or Artashastha of Ezra, the king commonly called Smerdis or Bardes.

Your correspondent has fairly and clearly stated the popular view of the chronology; and if his dates are correct, I do not object to the accuracy with which he has drawn his unsatisfactory conclusions. But I do dispute the correctness of the common mode of reckoning which he adopts, as regards this period of Egyptian, Persian, and Babylonian history: and I ask for no other proof of the impossibility of this reckoning being correct than the facts with which he has provided me, viz., that four kings of Media and Persia, living within a period of about eighty years, who undoubtedly bore the titles in their own country (in Greek orthography) of Astyages, Cyaxares, Cambyses, and Smerdis or Bardes, should of necessity be identified, by means of this reckoning, with four kings whose names are written by contemporary sacred historians, acquainted both with their persons and titles, Ahasuerus, Darius, Ahasuerus, and Arta-shastha. I have no hesitation in pronouncing that a scheme of chronology which produces such results must be absolutely false. Your correspondent has reduced it to an absurdity : and the proper verdict to be pronounced over it is—"*felo de se.*"

Nevertheless it is due to your correspondent, who has fairly and for-cibly explained the popular view of the subject, that I should follow him seriatim through his several chronological arguments : premising only that as the generally received reckoning is in his favour, and I am disputing the correctness of that reckoning, he should be careful to abstain from making the received opinion the foundation of an argument, in answer to direct proof tending to subvert the received dates—an error which he has fallen into at the outset of his observations.

Your correspondent begins by attacking my date for the first year of Nebuchadnezzar, viz., B.C. 578. As this is a fundamental date in my arrangement, I shall be content to withdraw from the subject altogether, whenever it shall have been proved to be materially incorrect. Till then I look upon it as established, and shall use it as a foundation from which to compute other dates. It is arrived at

1st. By fixing the reign of Sennacherib, by a series of arguments, contained partly in the paper examined by your correspondent, partly in my "*Sacred and Profane Chronology,*" independently of the eclipse in the third year of his reign, the applicability of which is not yet confirmed, as running from B.C. 692 to 667, and then counting eighty-eight years, with the Chaldean historians, "from Sennacherib to Nebuchodonosor," which brings me to the year B.C. 578 or 579 for the first year of Nebu-chadnezzar.

2nd. From the consideration that the first year of the reign of Nebu-chadnezzar fell after the final destruction of Nineveh : that Nineveh was destroyed after a siege which lasted some length of time, and which was begun by Cyaxares after the eclipse of Thales B.C. 585 ; and that his first year could not therefore much precede the year B.C. 578.

3rd. Because Nineveh was destroyed exactly twenty-eight years after the reign of the last king of the Assyrian line, viz., Sardanapalus; and history informs us that Sardanapalus was the same as Nabopalassar, whose reign is fixed by an eclipse, either in his fifth or seventh year, as ending about the year B.C. 606 or 608. And twenty-eight years counted from that time brings us again to about B.C. 579 or 578.

4th. Because Abydenus informs us that the father of Nebuchadnezzar (Nabopalassar) was still living after the expulsion of Sardanapalus from Nineveh ; and Berosus, that Nabopalassar reigned twenty-nine years at Babylon before his son's accession, which deducted from B.C. 606 or 608 again leads us to about the year B.C. 578.

5th. Because Demetrius, contemporary or nearly so with Berosus, tells us that the nineteenth year before the capture of Jerusalem, or the first year of Nebuchadnezzar, was B.C. 578.

This date your correspondent observes, "appears to contradict the Egyptian chronology." He then goes on to state, that "the generally received dates of the accession and death of Pharaoh Necho are B.C. 619 and 603; but that Dr. Hincks thinks it certain that the first year of Necho II. corresponded to B.C. 612, and that he died in the sixteenth year of his reign B.C. 597-6.

Now, if Dr. Hincks and the received dates may be relied upon, it correctly follows, as argued by your correspondent, that Nebuchadnezzar, who smote the army of Pharaoh Necho, must have begun to reign not later than B.C. 597-6; that the capture of Jerusalem in his nineteenth year could not be dated later than 577; that Demetrius must be in error in placing that event in B.C. 560; and that the twenty-eight years of Scythian dominion over Asia, which took place in the reign of Psammetichus the predecessor of Necho, could not have commenced later than B.C. 613. Thus by one master-stroke would the whole fabric of dates which I have adopted be destroyed.

Nevertheless the question still remains for consideration, Are the received dates in Egyptian chronology, and is the opinion of Dr. Hincks, for whose learning and authority I have the greatest respect, to be implicitly relied upon? Glad indeed should I be if either Egyptian chronology, or that of any other nation might be assumed as an infallible criterion, by which to test the correctness of concurrent lines of reckoning. But there is none, I submit, less to be relied upon for this purpose than the Egyptian.

All Egyptian reckoning is founded upon some assumed date for the conquest of Egypt by Cambyses. This date by modern chronologists is generally placed in the year B.C. 525. Dr. Hincks, Lepsius, and Bunsen propose to place the date two or three years earlier, *i.e.*, in 527 or 528; all proceeding on the assumption that Cambyses reigned only eight years, as stated by Herodotus. Ctesias, however, who wrote after Herodotus, and had better opportunity of informing himself, asserts that Cambyses reigned eighteen years, and this view seems to have been adopted by many of the earliest chronologists. The Armenian copy of Eusebius,[a] in transcribing the dynasties of Manetho the Egyptian annalist, writes, "Cambyses in his fifteenth year (B.C. 515), reigned over Egypt for three years," making the length of his reign eighteen years. Clemens Alexandrinus makes the length of the reign of Cambyses nineteen years.[b] Syncellus, who appears to allow only eight years to Cambyses, places the conquest of Egypt in the first year of the sixty-sixth Olympiad=B.C. 516, which coincides with the fourteenth year of his reign, counted from the true date of his accession B.C. 529, and which, added to four years which he gives him in Egypt, makes eighteen years. Africanus, in transcribing the dynasties of Manetho, writes, "Cambyses, in the *fifth* year of his reign (which Dr. Hincks proposes to read *ninth*, θ for ε), over Persia, reigned over Egypt for six years," together eleven years. He reckons, however, 169 current years from the first year of Tarcos, or Tirhakah, as king of Egypt, to the conquest of Egypt by Cambyses. Now if we adopt the reading of Dr. Hincks, and not his reasoning, and place the conquest of Egypt in the ninth year of Cambyses=B.C. 521, the year in

---

[a] Aucher, p. 106.   [b] Clemens Alex., *Strom.* i.

which Darius Hystaspes probably seized the throne of Persia during his absence, and count 169 current years upwards, we come to the year B.C. 689 as the first year of Tirhakah; being the very year which I have found to be that in which Sennacherib fought against him, when he came out to assist the helpless Sethos, whom we may reasonably suppose to have been superseded by him in that year, or soon after. Thus with great exactness confirming my dates, instead of refuting them.

Again, Manetho, according to Africanus, counts seventy-six current years from the last of Psammetichus to the conquest by Cambyses, which counted upwards from B.C. 521 brings us to the year B.C. 596, about two years earlier than that which I have ascertained on other grounds to be the last year of Psammetichus, not to B.C. 612, the date which your correspondent has adopted. Lastly, I have published my reasons for believing that the ten years deducted erroneously by Africanus from the reign of Necho, should be deducted from the reign of Amosis, who reigned for some years during the life of Apries, after which correction the death of Necho would fall, when counted from B.C. 521, two years earlier than I place it. My belief is that Egypt was conquered by Cambyses in the year B.C. 519 or 518. Certain it is that the earliest chronologists are in favour of a date later, rather than earlier, than B.C. 520. Nothing certain, therefore, can at present be determined with regard to the date of the conquest of Egypt; and to those who would resort to Egyptian chronology as an infallible measure of time, I may not unreasonably apply the words of Rabshekah, "thou trustest to the staff of this bruised reed, even upon Egypt, on which if a man lean it will go into his hand and pierce it."

Your correspondent next objects to my proposed date, B.C. 511, as that of the conquest of Babylon by Cyrus, which necessarily follows upon the adoption of the fundamental date, B.C. 578, as that of the first year of Nebuchadnezzar. He refers to the eclipse observed at Babylon in B.C. 523, which fixes indisputably the seventh year of Cambyses; and, relying upon Persian history as related by Herodotus, observes, "Cyrus must have died cir. B.C. 530, and could not, therefore, have reigned at Babylon in B.C. 511." Now here lies the strength of your correspondent's position, and that of all chronologists who place the thirty years reign of Cyrus as running from B.C. 559 to 530. Eclipses afford the most accurate and satisfactory data upon which to found a chronological computation. No one has ventured to doubt that the eclipse of B.C. 523, marks the seventh year of Cambyses. And if we may rely therefore upon the history of Cyrus, related by Herodotus, the conclusion of your correspondent is indisputable. But how unsafe and uncertain must this position appear to any one really anxious to fix with accuracy the dates of events about this period. Herodotus has also given us a very interesting account of the history of the Medes, who came into collision with the Assyrians, Lydians, and Persians before the fall of their empire. He tells us that Cyaxares the father of Astyages fought a battle with the Lydians, which was terminated by a solar eclipse, the date of which is definitively fixed by astronomers to the year B.C. 585. Cyaxares reigned for some years after this date, and recaptured Nineveh: his son Astyages then reigned for thirty-five years; and after the conquest of Astyages, Cyrus reigned thirty years. So that Cyrus could not have died less than about seventy years after the eclipse, or earlier than B.C. 515. And if we place the death of Phraortes (called Arphaxad in the Book of Judith) in the twelfth year of the last Assyrian king, B.C. 614, and accept the traditional date, which accords with it, for the fall of Astyages, B.C. 539, as preserved in the Astronomical and Ecclesiastical Canon, the death of Cyrus would not have taken place according to the Median reckoning till the year B.C. 509, where, whether rightly or wrongly, it is placed by the Ecclesiastical Canon. Herodotus, therefore, is clearly at variance with himself; and as it is impossible to move the date either of the eclipse of B.C. 585, or 523, we are compelled to condemn either his Median or Persian history as erroneous. It is the fashion to set aside without hesitation the Median account, and to declare that Herodotus was mistaken in placing the eclipse of Thales at the time of the Lydo-Median war. Who that has examined the difficulties in reconciling sacred and profane chronology about this period, can be satisfied with so arbitrary a decision? The rational mode of proceeding is, to test the two discordant histories, by comparing them with other authentic and contemporaneous history. Now we have already alluded to a series of contradictions of what has been recorded by contemporaneous sacred historians, involved in the adoption of Herodotus' account of Persian history, which alone is sufficient to cause the rejection of the reckoning founded upon it. While on the other hand we shall find that the Median account is consistent, for the most part, both with fixed astronomical data, and with all that has been recorded of Ahasuerus, Cyrus, Darius and Artaxerxes in the Books of Daniel and Ezra. When, moreover, we are told by Herodotus himself, that two other histories of Cyrus were current in his days, besides that which he has adopted, that he was not cognizant of the existence of Cyaxares, whose name is recorded on the rock at Behistun, and by Xenophon, and find that both Ctesias and Xenophon who followed him, have contradicted his statements in many most material points, I come without hesitation to the conclusion that Herodotus, with the most honest intention of recording the truth, has made an erroneous selection as regards the history of Cyrus, and that your correspondent's Persian reckoning, founded on an implicit reliance upon Herodotus, is as little to be relied upon as his Egyptian.

Your correspondent next applies the test of Babylonian chronology to disprove my dates. He refers to the eclipse which fixes the fifth year of Nabopalassar the father of Nebuchadnezzar to the year B.C. 621, and observes, " that it is utterly inconsistent with the testimony of ancient history to suppose that this Nabopalassar ceased to reign on the joint thrones of Babylon and Nineveh in B.C. 606, on account of the Scythian eruption into Asia, and that he was afterwards again reigning at Babylon in 579 in conjunction with his son Nebuchadnezzar."

The eclipse of B.C. 521, again forms a firm foundation for a chronological argument. The reasoning, however, or rather assertion which follows, is quite inconclusive. It is a bold assertion to declare that the above conclusions are inconsistent with ancient history. The testimony of ancient history is against, not in favour of, your correspondent's assertion.

Historians, ancient and modern, are agreed in assigning twenty years to the reign of Sardanapalus, and the ordinary view of the date of this king, collected from ancient history, is, that he ceased to reign in B.C. 606. The first twenty years of Nabopalassar also, as fixed by the eclipse in his fifth year, are found to be concurrent with the twenty years of Sardanapalus. Assyrian monuments, still extant, inform us that Babylon was subjected to Assyria by Sennacherib, and Scripture informs us that the Assyrian king Esarhaddon carried captives to Babylon. It is no violation therefore of these most authentic ancient records, but in conformity with them, to suppose that Sardanapalus and Nabopalassar, who reigned together over the same, or parts of the same, united kingdom, may have been the same king. Alexander the Polyhistor, who professes to have copied from Berosus, asserts that Sardanapalus and Nabopalassar were one and the same. Thus far then, ancient history supports the idea that Nabopalassar ceased to reign at Nineveh in B.C. 606. I will now draw the attention of your correspondent to a short, yet significant, statement of Syncellus, being the result of his study of ancient historians, which I doubt not he will recognize as asserting, though obscurely, the fact of the identity of Nabopalassar and Sardanapalus. Syncellus[e] informs us that there were forty-one Assyrian kings, "from Belus the first, to Macoscolerus the forty-first, called also Sardanapalus, as many eminent historians, such as Polybius, Diodorus, Cephalion, Castor and others, agree in asserting." Now if we alter the Greek termination, eros, into the Assyrian termination, asser, we shall read Macoscolassar, called also Sardanapalus. This Macoscolassar, I think, will be recognized as a corruption of Nabopalassar; and, if so, there is the further testimony of four ancient historians to the fact attested by Polyhistor, and confirmatory of the conclusion that Nabopalassar ceased to reign at Nineveh in B.C. 606.[d]

Again Cleitarchus, an historian more ancient than Berosus, informs us that Sardanapalus survived the loss of the throne of Assyria, and died at a great age. Abydenus tells us that the father of Nebuchadnezzar was contemporary with the king who succeeded Sardanapalus at Nineveh. And Berosus tells us that Nabopalassar reigned at Babylon twenty-nine years, and was too infirm for war in the last years of his reign; and these twenty-nine years, counted from his expulsion from Nineveh, bring us to about the year B.C. 578, a few years after the eclipse of 585, as we are led to expect. So that, in fact, the testimony of ancient history is in favour of Nabopalassar having reigned till B.C. 579; while the ancient historian Demetrius, whose authority is lightly put aside in the next paragraph of your correspondent, goes direct to the fact, in affirming that Nebuchadnezzar began to reign in the year B.C. 578.

Having thus pointed out the unsoundness and insecurity of your correspondent's reasoning, founded upon the received view of Egyptian,

---

e Dindorf's Edit., vol. i., p. 271.
d Eusebius has transmitted a still more corrupt reading of the title in *Thonos-Concoleros.*

Persian, and Babylonian history, let us now proceed to the main subject of our inquiry, viz., who was Darius the son of Ahasuerus of the seed of the Medes, that mysterious yet mighty king who reigned over 120 provinces of Media and Persia, and was yet unknown to Herodotus, Berosus, or any other historian, unless referred to by them as Darius the son of Hystaspes.

The passage in the Book of Daniel, where this king is mentioned, I propose to read according to the interpretation in the margin of our Bibles, thus, "In the first year of Darius the son of Ahasuerus of the seed of the Medes, *what time* he was set over the realm of the Chaldeans, in the first year of his reign: I Daniel understood by books the number of the years whereof the word of the Lord came to Jeremiah the prophet that he would accomplish *seventy years in the desolations of Jerusalem.*" The repetition of the year of the reign here is remarkable, and appears to me to be used for the purpose of marking emphatically that this was not the first year of the king's accession to the throne, when we know that Babylon had revolted from Cambyses and was not yet subdued, but his first year, when he took the government of Babylon into his own hands, that is to say, when he was about sixty-two years old. This first year also over the Chaldeans is fixed, as being about the time when Jerusalem had been desolate nearly seventy years, "to fulfil the word of the Lord by the mouth of Jeremiah, until the land had enjoyed her sabbaths: for as long as she lay desolate she kept sabbath, to fulfil threescore and ten years" (2 Chron. xxxvi. 21).

Bearing in mind these distinguishing characters, let us first consider who was Ahasuerus of the seed of the Medes, from whom Darius claims his descent. Cyaxares and Astyages are the only kings of Media about the time in question who can be supposed to represent Ahasuerus. That Cyaxares, and not Astyages, is the king alluded to by Daniel, appears :—

1st. Because we know, through Herodotus, that Nineveh was overthrown by Cyaxares I.; and the Book of Tobit speaks of Nineveh having been overthrown by Ahasuerus. So that, according to early Jewish authority, the titles are the same.

2nd. Because Cyaxares and Acksueres are identical, dropping the first syllable of the first name.

3rd. Because in the rock inscription at Behistun, two pretenders to the throne of Media, in the reign of Darius son of Hystaspes, lay claim to that throne, as "of the race," not of Astyages, but of U-wakh-shatara, or Cyaxares, as Rawlinson renders the title. These two pretenders, therefore, testify that the Medes themselves looked to the family of Cyaxares for the rightful owner of the crown.

Whoever the Darius of Daniel may have been, if he took the throne by virtue of his Median descent, as seems to be implied, he must, in consistency with the rock inscription, have claimed it as "of the race of Cyaxares," son of Astyages, who was last on the throne of Media. The strict logical conclusion therefore, if the word "son" is to be interpreted in the most confined sense, is, that which was come to by Sir Isaac Newton, viz., that Cyaxares the Mede had a son called Darius, who took the kingdom by right from his father.

If so, let us next consider the time when this supposed Darius must have begun to reign over the Chaldeans. Daniel tells us that it was when he was about sixty-two years old, and also when Jerusalem had lain desolate nearly seventy years (keeping Sabbath). Now Jerusalem became desolate in the nineteenth year of Nebuchadnezzar, or B.C. 560, counting from the fundamental date, B.C. 578, or first of Nebuchadnezzar; and as seventy years counted from 560 would expire in B.C. 491, the first year of Darius must have been about 492 or 493. But at this date we know that Darius the son of Hystaspes was reigning over the whole Persian empire, including the Chaldeans; so that on the supposition that Darius was literally the son of Cyaxares, we must suppose two great kings, bearing the same title, and with co-extensive dominions, to have been reigning together, which is too hard for belief.

The difficulty of the position is equally apparent, independently of dates, when we consider that the prophet Zechariah tells us, that three score and ten fasts had been kept by the Jews in commemoration of the destruction of the temple, in the fourth year of a king called Darius; and that it is "altogether certain," as your correspondent observes, that this Darius of the second temple was the son of Hystaspes. So that seventy fasts, counted from the burning of the temple, end in the fourth year of the mighty king, Darius Hystaspes; and seventy years counted from the desolation of Jerusalem, end soon after the beginning of the reign of another mighty king, Darius, son of Ahasuerus; each claiming sovereignty over the Chaldeans, which is incredible. But when, in addition to this, we are told by the prophet Daniel that the sixty-second year of the age of Darius the son of Cyaxares lies seventy weeks, or 490 years, before the coming of the Messiah; and we know from history that Darius the son of Hystaspes was about sixty-two years old[e] in the year B.C. 493, or 490 years before the birth of Christ, the conclusion is irresistible, that Darius the son of Ahasuerus, of the seed of the Medes, is one and the same king with Darius the son of Hystaspes; and that this latter king, who was Persian on the father's side, was also either lineally descended from Cyaxares I., king of Media, or had married a lineal descendant of Cyaxares II., and so, in common Eastern latitude of speech, was styled also "son of Cyaxares."

Your correspondent objects, that Cyaxares had but one daughter, and that she was married to Cyrus; and he "cannot admit, therefore, that Darius also married a daughter of this Cyaxares." Where, I would ask, is the difficulty? Was it not a common practice in the East for usurpers to marry the wives of monarchs that they succeeded or dethroned? And why may not Darius have married the widow of Cyrus? Darius, we know, strengthened his title to the throne of the empire in the female

---

[e] I take this opportunity of correcting an inadvertency in my former paper, where I stated, that according to Ctesias, Darius died at the age of seventy. I ought to have written seventy-two. Referring the reader to Mr. Airy's observations on the eclipse which occurred in the year of the Battle of Salamis (*Philosoph. Trans.*, 1853), I am of opinion that Darius lived into the year B.C. 484, having reached the age of seventy-two full years. So that in the year B.C. 493 he would commence his sixty-second year, "being about three score and two years old."

line, by marrying Atossa the widow of Cambyses, and also by marrying the widow of Smerdis his brother. He had the same inducement also to marry the widow of Cyrus, son-in-law of Cyaxares, a more youthful bride than either of the former, according to Xenophon, and in whom was vested the title to the Median throne. There is no difficulty, I repeat, in supposing that Darius may have married a daughter of Cyaxares, and that possibly his only offspring.

The conclusion that Ahasuerus and Cyaxares are the same title, leads to important consequences from which we cannot shrink. The inscription at Behistun speaks of Cyaxares as the king of Media, from whom all claimants to that throne drew their titles in the days of Darius. The Book of Esther inform us, that Ahasuerus or Cyaxares reigned over the Medes and Persians and 127 provinces, about the period of the captivity of the Jews at Babylon—Mordecai, who was carried captive in the reign of Jechoniah, being in attendance on him—and not long, therefore, before the reign of Darius. And Xenophon speaks of Cyaxares having reigned over the empire of the Medes and Persians after the death of Astyages. These three, therefore, must be one and the same king. This triple evidence of the existence of such a king, who was unknown to Herodotus, tends much to lower our estimate of the Persian account of that historian; and the value of that of Xenophon, who gives so circumstantial an account of his actions, is equally enhanced. Cyaxares must have reigned upwards of fourteen years after the death of Astyages. And it must have been the daughter of this king in whom the title to the empire of the Medes was vested, whose hand Darius sought in marriage, and so became his son-in-law, or son, according to the Eastern mode of expression.

Now the Targum on the Book of Esther asserts that Darius of the second temple, or Darius Hystaspes, was the son of this Ahasuerus or Cyaxares, in conformity with the Book of Daniel. That, "son of" Cyaxares, signifies no more than of the family or race of Cyaxares by descent, I think may be proved from the same invaluable testimony to which we have referred, viz., the inscription at Behistun.

The two usurpers, Phraortes and Martes, who claimed the Median throne, it will be there seen, set up their titles, not as sons of Cyaxares, but as of "the race of Cyaxares." If Cyaxares had a son, that son would have been heir to the throne: and no usurper would have ventured to claim except as representing that son. Thus we find Gomates and Veisdates, each calling himself Bardes son of Cyrus; and Niditabelus and Aracus, each setting up as Nabochodrossor son of Nabonidus. The expression "of the race of Cyaxares," implies, therefore, that Cyaxares had no son, as Xenophon declares; and the two imposters untruly, and Darius truly, must have claimed connexion with Cyaxares through the female line.

Thus I have shewn,—

1st. That Ahasuerus is the same as Cyaxares.

2nd. That "son of Ahasuerus," is equivalent to the expression, "of the race of Cyaxares."

3rd. That "Darius the son of Ahasuerus," who began to reign over the Chaldeans when about sixty-two years old, and 490 years before the birth of Christ, is the same as Darius the son of Hystaspes, who was about sixty-two years of age in the year 490 before the birth of Christ.

I will not trespass upon you by answering more than one more of your correspondent's arguments at present. He remarks that Darius the son of Hystaspes came to the throne about the year B.C. 521. This I am not disposed to deny. Also that Assyria, Media, Lydia, Armenia, Egypt, and Tyre, were included under one vast empire at that time. With the exception of Egypt, I believe this statement to be correct. "But if Darius," he says, "was the mighty king of Persia, and monarch of the vast Medo-Persian empire at that time, it seems clear beyond all question that Cyrus could not have been king of Persia and Babylon in B.C. 511."

In reply, I would observe, that Darius, though on the throne, was not monarch of the Medo-Persian empire so early as the year B.C. 521. Cyrus we know, was "great king," according to Herodotus, and this is equivalent to "king of kings," implying that subordinate kings reigned under him during his supreme sovereignty. Accordingly, the prophet Daniel, in the third year of Cyrus, king (βασιλευς) of Persia, speaks of the prince (αρκων) of the kingdom of Persia, as a person of independent and great authority. Cyrus himself had been king of Media, while Cyaxares was sovereign of the empire of the Medes and Persians. It is not sufficient, therefore, to shew that Darius began to reign in B.C. 521, in order to prove that Cyrus could not properly have written, in B.C. 511, "The Lord God of heaven hath given me all the kingdoms of the earth." If Cyrus came to the throne before he came to the empire, why may not the same have been the case with Darius? Fortunately we have the means of proving, on the most indisputable authority, that there was a time when Darius did not claim to be "king of kings," or sovereign of the empire, but styled himself simply king of the province of Persia.

In the *Journal of the Royal Asiatic Society,*[f] there is a series of Persian inscriptions, found at Persepolis, relating to Darius, and translated by Colonel Rawlinson. Most of these inscriptions begin in the usual style, "I am Darius, the great king, king of kings." In some of them he styles himself "supporter of this great world," and the provinces which he had added to Persia are generally referred to and enumerated. There is one inscription, however, which throughout is of a very different character, and which must have been written earlier than the rest. It begins, "The great Ormazd, who is the chief of the gods, he established Darius king . . . says Darius the king. This province of Persia, which Ormazd has granted me, which is illustrious, abounding in good horses . . . from the enemy feareth not. May Ormazd protect this province from slavery." Now this is not the style of Cyrus in his first year of empire, nor the style of Darius when ruler over the provinces, but of a far humbler tone. He is here described as the ruler of the single province of Persia, and the vaunt that it fears no enemy, and the prayer that it may be protected from slavery, savours more of a position of doubtful independence, than of the position of one who might style himself "supporter of this great world," or of one "feared by the provinces." I look

---

f Vol. x., part 3, p. 271—313.

upon this inscription as affording the most distinct evidence that Darius was once merely king of the province of Persia, of which Persepolis perhaps was the seat of government—that he was not, at the time of writing this inscription, king of Babylon—and that he must then have been subordinate to some greater king who was sovereign of the empire. The argument of your correspondent, therefore, that Darius became king in B.C. 521, does not prove that he may not have been subordinate to Cyrus in B.C. 511, or that he may not have taken the government of the province of Babylon into his hands in B.C. 493, when about sixty-two years of age.

On the other hand the indubitable testimony of the rock to the existence of Cyaxares as king of Media, and of the inscription at Persepolis of the inferior character of the early kingdom of Darius, are alone sufficient to demonstrate the hopeless nature of that chronology which rests upon the assumption, that after Astyages, Cyrus for thirty years, after Cyrus, Cambyses for eight years, and after Cambyses, Darius for thirtysix years, were sole monarchs of the vast Medo-Persian empire.

I. W. BOSANQUET.

Claysmore, 5th November, 1855.

THE GENESIS OF THE EARTH AND OF MAN.

THE strictures of R. S. P. in your last require from me a somewhat more extended reply than would have been necessary if he had treated my argument with greater courtesy. I regret if I have anywhere misunderstood his language, and that he has so much mistaken my spirit. Remembering then that I have a great question before me, and that I not only myself profess to be a sincere believer in the Holy Scriptures, but that R. S. P. also is prepared to accept the teachings of the same sacred volume, I shall proceed with the task which I have undertaken. My hope is to speak ἐν πραΰτητι σοφίας, but R. S. P. must not complain if I not only differ from him, but give my reasons for so doing. Before I enter upon the discussion, I wish to assure your correspondent that I am neither a Chiliast nor a Neologian, and that my views are such as are generally termed orthodox. I do not subscribe to the traditional interpretation of the Bible because it is such, nor as such, but I desire to lay down as my fundamental principle, the words of the apostle,—' Prove all things : hold fast that which is good.' Very sorry should I be to disparage prophecy, or to set one part of Scripture above or against another, for ' all Scripture is given by inspiration of God, and is profitable,' &c.

The biblical revelation is either of facts or of principles ; both of which are beyond the reach of unassisted reason. But the Bible is more than a divine revelation ; it is an inspired record. In the former case the writers were supplied with the materials, and guided in the arrangement of them ; in the second, they were directed in the selection of materials, and guided in their arrangement. Thus while there was a diversity of operations there was one Spirit. In the first case, the writers appear to have been furnished with their materials by vision and by suggestion : by vision frequently in the giving of prophecies, and by suggestion in other instances. When the inspiration was by vision, it seems to be generally if not always so stated, but in other cases nothing is said—there may be a few exceptions.

Now where are we to place the different narrations contained in the early chapters of the Book of Genesis? the account of the creation for instance? In the absence of all direct testimony, and of any analogous case, I must maintain, certainly not among visions. To assume that the revelation of Gen. i. was by vision, is to my mind, fanciful, unsatisfactory and unnecessary. I very much question whether Moses was its author in any proper sense, and am disposed to think his task was the compilation, correction and arrangement of pre-existing documents out of which the Book of Genesis was composed. This however in no way affects the character of the cosmogony of the Bible. The verity of this as a historical narrative of the creation of all things by God, it seems is unquestioned, and it now appears that the chief difference between R. S. P. and myself (so far as I know) is respecting the *modus inspirandi*. I shall therefore dismiss this first question, and advance to the second, upon which your correspondent has his doubts, and I trust, that what I shall say, will contribute to the removal of those doubts, and draw from him a declaration against the doctrine of Pre-Adamites. In the Number for January, 1855 (p. 484), the question is stated to be, ' Whether the human species be referrible to different origins.'[a]

In taking the negative of this question a second time I may run the risk of repeating myself, but this I trust you will excuse. I shall first endeavour to remove the objections which have been taken to my views by R. S. P. and the anonymous writer of the pamphlet quoted by him.

I. The case of Cain (Gen. iv. 14—17) presents several difficulties as,—

a. The mention apparently of other men, ' whoever finds,' ' whoever slays,' &c. These expressions have reference not only to that time, but to the future, and as we know neither the exact period and population of the earth when Cain killed his brother, we can base no argument upon the occurrence of such phrases.

b. Cain went and dwelt in the land of Nod. It is certain he must have dwelt somewhere, and the name given to the locality in which he settled proves that it had not that name certainly before, as it alludes so pointedly to the exile of Cain.

c. Cain was married, and it is thought he could not have married his sister for two reasons; first, it is against a positive divine law, and secondly unnatural. To which it is added, that it would make the race of incestuous origin.

I reply to the first. The law quoted (Lev. xviii. 9) was not promulgated

---

[a] I think the question ought to have been, ' Whether the human species be referrible to one origin,' such being the apparent teaching of the Bible.

at that time; and when R. S. P. accuses me of denying the immutability
of God's laws, when I say, it appears to me that Cain married his sister,
he forgets that many of God's laws have been local in their obligation,
and temporary in their duration; and also that necessity knows no law.
To the second I answer, that however unnatural such marriages may
seem, they have been allowed and frequent in many parts and periods.
To the third I reply in the words of old Edward Simson (*Chron. Cath.*),
"Eam quidem ipsius sororem fuisse necesse est ut fateamur: Neque id
pro incesto est habitum, quia erat necessarium ad generis propagationem."
The Rabbins say Cain married his twin sister, as also did Abel.

d. Cain builded a city.

It is not said how long it was before this city was built, nor is it said
how large it was. For the latter we all know that the Hebrew עיר was
often nothing but a mere settlement, occupied by a handful of inhabitants.

II. The Adamites, &c.

a. "Adam, whenever it occurs after the death of the man to whom
the name is first applied, properly signifies the Adamites, just as Israel, in
the like case, properly signifies the Israelites."

To this I object, and repeat that while sometimes we could render
Adam Adamites, very frequently we could not without manifest impropriety. But to be more explicit, 1. the word אדם originally denoting the
first man with reference to the material of which he was formed, and *its*
colour, came to be used in a more extended sense. In this more extended
sense of a collective or Gentile noun, it frequently occurs. But it also
denotes an individual man, and except in reference to Adam, appears to
have no intermediate signification. Like the word *man* in English when
undeclined, it denotes either some one man, or all men; as you cannot
say two man, so you cannot say *two Adam.* Indeed, R. S. P. himself
admits that "Adam may very properly be sometimes used to signify man,
or men." 2. The word cannot always with propriety denote Adamites
as distinguished from others; so to render the word would often mar the
sense and be opposed to the scope of a passage. Who, for example, will
say that the כל־בשר of Gen. vii. 21, does not include the entire species?
or that in Job v. 7 אדם is to be used in the limited signification of Adamite? Was the universal dominion assigned to אדם in Ps. viii. 5, the
peculiar privilege of one race of men? and are the sins of the בני־אדם in
Ps. xiv. 2, the sins of merely a portion of the human species? or, to quote
no more, when Jehovah says "I made the earth and created man (אדם)
upon it, my hand stretched out the heavens, &c." Are we to suppose
that there is mention but of one tribe or stock of man out of several?
Surely in all these cases and in many more, the answer is plain. By
Adam or the Adam we must understand the whole human race.
Secondly, a proper name used as a Gentile noun does *not* regularly take
the article except when it is defined and limited by some other word.
The rule is, that it should be without. Again, the signification of the
word Adam, compared with Adamah (the ground, earth), suggests the
same conclusion, when taken in connexion with the Latin *homo* and
humus. Compare also בנה to build, with בן a son, δέμω to build, with

δέμας the human form.[a] And again, Gen. ii. 5, which says "man was not" prior to the creation recorded immediately after, clearly shews what is meant by the word *Adam*. To say there were men, but none who tilled the soil, *i. e.* who were civilized, is an assumption contrary, first, to the very strong declaration involved in this text; and secondly, to all the deductions of learning and science, which place the civilization anterior to all barbarism.

b. The sons of God are distinguished from the daughters of *Adam*, or of the *Adamites*.

By the sons of the gods, as the anonymous author understands this expression, I suppose he thinks a different race is meant from that of Adam. True, "the sons of God" is in antithesis to "daughters of men," but not in the way supposed. Sons are opposed to daughters, as men to women, unless "sons" denotes servants: and God or gods is opposed to man. But where do we find any trace of idolatry before the flood? the "sons of the gods" can therefore hardly mean idolaters. It is most improbable that the Hebrew writer would have employed in reference to idolators, supposing he had meant it, an expression which has been consecrated to the worshippers of the one living and true God. But even if idolaters are meant, it is no proof that they were not descendents from Adam. According to my opponents, by intermarriage, the race of Adam lost its distinctive character at the outset by the marriage of Adam's sons and daughters with the pre-Adamite sinners. To plead for their separateness now seems impossible. The expression sons of God occurs in Job i. 6; ii. 1; (xxxviii. 7) in all which places I am inclined to think the meaning is "ministering spirits," good or bad, and what is said of the verb יִתְיַצֵּב sometimes meaning to oppose or confront, by no means weakens my opinion, because it often occurs when so such idea is intended: (see particularly Ex. xxxiv. 5; Num. xi. 16; Zech. vi. 5; Prov. xxii. 29; 2 Chron. xi. 13; 2 Sam. xviii. 30, &c.) Again, in the Old Testament God frequently calls his servants his sons, while in the New Testament it is their peculiar appellation. I therefore take it, that sons of God in Gen. vi. 2, means the servants of God. The only other explanation for which much can be said, is that it means the great and noble, as distinguished from mean and base, but I must prefer the other. The daughters of men would then denote common and worthless women.

c. The Nephilim, or giants.

Suppose the Nephilim were giants, is it any proof that they were not descended from Adam? The stature of the earlier inhabitants of the world is by many supposed to have been much greater than at present. But as we have no proof that the Nephilim did not descend from Adam, it is gratuitous to say they did not. If it be answered that we read of Nephilim in the book of Numbers, and that therefore they survived the flood; I ask where? There is a notoriously false account of the land and its inhabitants, made by the spies, for which the heaviest judgments descended upon them, but I know of no other, and can I, dare I, build

---

[a] To this comparison above given add *vir, virtus,* גְּבַר גְּבוּרָה.

my faith on this? Perhaps some will object again with R. S. P. that this passage is to be taken in connexion with others. But there are no others (save Gen. vi. 4) in which the Nephilim are mentioned. If it still be objected, "the might of Goliath and his kinsmen, the size of Og's bed or coffin, and the like, prove the existence of a giant people (the Rephaim) who were connected with the antediluvian Nephilim, I answer first, Goliath was a Philistine, and Og an Amorite, and if they were at the same time connected with the Rephaim (of Gen. xiv. 5) how is it shewn that they belonged to the Nephilim of Gen. vi. 4? Moreover, as it respects the Anakim, who stand in the same category, I refer your readers to Joshua xiv. 15, where we read that "Arba was a great *man* among the Anakims," in which place the Hebrew has הָאָדָם *ha-Adam* for one of the Anakim. Now if one of the Anakim was an *Adamite*, as it is now said we may render the word, the probability is that they were all Adamites, which is what we maintain. Now in Num. xiii. 33 the "Nephilim" are called the "sons of Anak of the Nephilim," the previous passage, therefore, by which we prove the Anakim to have descended from Adam, by implication proves the same of the "Nephilim." We go further, and remark that the Emim equally with the Anakim, are referred to the Rephaim in Deut. ii. 11, and are thus disposed of in the same way. So of the rest. If הָאָדָם denotes peculiarly a descendant of Adam, we must admit that all these tribes belong to them. That they do not belong to any race which survived the flood over and above those included in the ark, must be admitted on the faith of Gen. vi. to xi; and 1 Pet. iii. 20 ; and 2 Pet. iii. 5, 6.

3. The next argument for pre-Adamites is derived from some allusions to the Gentiles, Gen. x. 5, 32; Deut. xxxii. 8. No special treatment is required, in this case, as it is admitted that they are "reconcileable with the general opinion as to the unity of the human race."

4. The distinction between Ish and Adam.

Upon this enough has been already said incidentally, but if not it may suffice to remark, that the same person is called both Ish and Adam, that in Hebrew poetry both words are used in the same sense in the same sentence, on the principle of parallelism, and often merely, it would seem, to vary the form of expression.

As I am unwilling to occupy too much of your valuable space, I will now proceed to give a number of facts all bearing upon this subject, which, though they are not new, will I trust be of some service.

In Acts xvii. 26 it is said that "God made of one blood all nations of men for to dwell on all the face of the earth." I formerly thought this taught merely the unity of man's nature, or at most the unity of the species. More mature consideration, however, has convinced me that it means more, and teaches the CONSANGUINITY OF MEN. Not forgetting "blood," αἵματος, is here wanting in some copies, I may assume the genuineness of the present reading, and observe that I can find no instance wherein the word has so extensive a significance as "nature" or "species." Not unfrequently it denotes a race=γένος, in its literal sense, as the descendants of a common stock, the offspring of one root. Thus the well-known passage in Homer,

Ταύτης τοι γενεῆς τε καὶ αἵματος εὔχομαι εἶναι.
Il., ζ, 211.

And again,

Κήδιστοι τελέθουσι μεθ' αἷμά τε καὶ γενὸς αὐτων.
Od., θ, 583.

And again,

Εἰ ἐτεόν γ' ἐμός ἐσσι, καὶ αἵματος ἡμετέροιο.
Od., π, 300.

So Pindar,

Αἷμ' ἀπο Σπαρτᾶς.
Nem., xi.

And Sophocles,

Βλαστὼν ἂν αἰσχύνοιμι τοὺς πρὸς αἵματος.
Ajax, 1305.

In a similar sense is *sanguis* used in Latin: the *Auctor sanguinis* of Virgil has many parallels; so also we speak of "consanguinity," of "blood relationship." But everywhere when the word *blood* is used, either in Greek, Latin, or English, in this way, it denotes natural relations.

Again, we have no trace of pre-Adamites except we regard as such the Autochthones and aborigines of the ancients; but where is the monument or the genuine history which will carry us back to those times? Nothing either above or underground has been discovered to attest their existence. The state of arts and science and the progress of civilization all seem to speak of man as a recent comer. The extent of the world's population and the spread of letters require no longer period for man's sojourn.

But we have better evidence; all history and tradition represent the principal nations as having an origin foreign to their own country. This is true of Europe, Asia, Africa, America, and even of Polynesia. China herself is no exception to this; and it is worthy of remark that these traditions generally point towards that portion of the world from which Holy Scripture records that the nations of the earth went forth after the flood. As to physical differences, laws, customs, &c., they multiply and change; yet it is true that many tribes have undergone no perceptible alteration for many ages, except when removed to other latitudes, and not always even then.

So languages continually change, as Horace observed long ago,

" Multa renascuntur, quæ jam cecidere, cadentque
Quæ nunc sunt in honore vocabula, si volet usus,
Quem penes arbitrium est et jus et norma loquendi."

In considering languages in connexion with the unity of the human race, we, as believers in Holy Scripture, are bound not to ignore the miraculous confusion of tongues recorded in the Book of Genesis. It is probable that then every nation carried away with it fragments of the original language, fragments of their common customs, and fragments of their primitive religious beliefs and ceremonies. Some of these may still remain, but many are no doubt lost. Objections may be raised against resemblances of language, traditions, customs and such like, but we think they furnish striking testimonies for the common origin of all men.

The length to which I have already written renders it impracticable for me now to give you some of those resemblances in words, customs, traditions and laws which I had intended to give. I nevertheless believe them to be so many links in that chain by which every man is bound to Adam as the head and father of humanity. I think such an amount of evidence can scarcely be accumulated for any other historical fact narrated in the Bible (as I believe) as can be collected to prove the oneness of the human family; and on a subsequent occasion I shall be happy, if you or your correspondents desire it, to give a specimen of the class of proofs to which I refer. For the present I must be content to say what I have said. Hitherto I have mainly laboured to shew that the arguments for pre-Adamites are not unanswerable, but that even the strongest of them may be met. I have secondly endeavoured to point out some of the passages of Scripture upon which I base my belief that Adâm was the first man; but I have not exhausted the list. Thirdly, I have referred to certain facts apart from the Bible which can be gathered from the whole world, and which taken together confirm the faith of our fathers on this matter. Other evidence from the moral and physical nature of man can be adduced, and I trust will be adduced if necessary.

In conclusion let me say that, if anything in this paper hurts the feelings of R. S. P., it was not intended.

B. H. C.

THE PASSAGE OF THE RED SEA.

To the Editor of "The Journal of Sacred Literature."

DEAR SIR,—Will you allow me to add a few words only to the article of H. H. B. in "vindication of the translation of Ex. xv. 8," which I have just perused in your last number. I will limit myself to a hint or two in corroboration of the Authorized Version.

H. H. B. is right in calling attention to the word נֶעֶרְמוּ *coacervatæ sunt*, since it is intimately connected in meaning with נֵד in the next line, which is only as it were a repetition of the first, only in a loftier style. I will not quote from lexicographers which are in everybody's hands, but only remark that although this niph. (נֶעֶרְמוּ) of עָרַם is ἅπαξ λεγ, its meaning of "condensing," "gathering in a heap," is entirely borne out, not only by its derivative עֲרֵמָה, "a heap" (of corn), which occurs frequently in Holy Scripture, but also by the concurrent witness of the cognate dialects.

Thus נֶעֶרְמוּ is rendered in the Peschito by the Ethp., ܐܬܟܰܫ, and in St. Ephraem[a] by the Pe., ܟܰܫ, which he explains by ܐܬܟܰܫ .ܐܘ ܟܰܝ .ܐܘ ܘܰܐܣܝ ܘܚܰܩܠܐ ܡܟܢ, "either, the waters were gathered in a heap;" ܒܩܣܘܡܐ ܐܝܟ ܡܣ ܕܘܙ ܠܐ, "or, that like water-skins (filled and tied up) they stood erect in the midst of their flow;" an image familiar to every traveller

---

[a] L.c., Opp., vol. i., p. 216.

in the East, where water-skins, when filled and tied up at the mouth, *stand erect* by the side of the well until they are carried away. The Samaritan Version also agrees with the Syriac in rendering נֵד by אשור, while the Arabic reads, تعرّمت المياه, "the waters were gathered in a heap." One of the meanings of عرم in Arabic, as in Hebrew, is "condensing, gathering up into a heap," we have, e.g., on the authority of the Qamûs, Djeuhari and the Qoran, not only عرمة, i.q., Heb. עֲרֵמָה, "a heap (of corn or of stones)," but also عرم, sing. عرمة, "a dyke, a wall built in order to stem a river or a flood." Thus in Qor. Sur., xxxiv. 16, we are told that the Sabæans were visited with سيل العرم, "a river that overflowed and threw down its dykes," an expression which has become proverbial in Arabia. נֵד then, would be well rendered by "were gathered together in a heap," like a wall or a dyke.

As to the second line, נֹזְלִים נָצְבוּ, I do not wish to call to my aid any help (such as Indo-Germanic philology) not known to the venerable translators of the Authorized Version. It will be far better to explain the Hebrew text by the text itself, and with no other assistance than that text to shew that the rendering "the floods stood upright as an heap" is *strictly correct*. I believe that the meaning of נצב *niph.* implied in this verse is that of "standing *upright and erect*" (and it would be difficult to stand otherwise) like a person, a statue, or a wall.

A) literally;

a) like a *man* (1 Sam. x. 23), when "Saul וַיִּתְיַצֵּב בְּתוֹךְ הָעָם stood (*erect*, no doubt) among the people, he was higher than any one of the people from his shoulders and upward."

Moses' sister, וַתֵּתַצַּב מֵרָחֹק, stood (probably on tip-toe) afar off, to wit what would be done to him."

The three men who came to Abraham (Gen. xviii. 1) were, נִצָּבִים, "standing before him," who, while sitting, had to raise his eyes in order to see them.

In like manner, the angel withstood Balaam (Numb. xxii. 23, 31, 34) with a drawn sword in his hand, which he could not have wielded except when (נצב) "standing."

So also Balak (וַיִּתְיַצֵּב) "stood" (doubtless *upright*) by his sacrifice (Numb. xxiii. 4), &c.

β) like *soldiers* (Judges xviii. 16) נִצָּבִים, "standing by the entering of the gate."

γ) like *a watchman* (נִצָּב כֹּל־הַלֵּילוֹת) "standing on the look-out whole nights."

δ) like *servants* (נִצָּבִים) "standing around their king" (1 Sam. xxii. 6).

ε) like a man *praying*. Hannah said, "I am the woman that stood (הַנִּצֶּבֶת) by thee here" (1 Sam. i. 26).

ζ) like a *gate* hung on its hinges (Jos. vi. 26, and 1 Ki. xvi. 34). Hiel of Beth-el (הִצִּיב דְּלָתוֹת) "set up the gates" of Jericho, &c.

η) like a *monument;* "Jacob (וַיַצֵּב מַצֵּבָה) set up a pillar," &c. (Gen. xxxv. 14 ; 2 Ki. xvii. 10).

θ) like an *altar.* Jacob (וַיַּצֶּב־שָׁם מִזְבֵּחַ) "set up there an altar," &c. (Gen. xxxiii. 20).

ι) like a *ladder.* Jacob saw a ladder (מֻצָּב) "set up on the earth, and the top of it reached to heaven" (Gen. xxviii. 12).

κ) like a *tree* (Judges ix. 6).

λ) like a *heap of stones,* which they (וַיַּצִּבוּ עָלָיו) "laid upon Absalom" (2 Sam. xviii. 17).

We also find צב (1.) as synonymous with עמד (עַמּוּד, a pillar, a column) e.g., 2 Sam. xviii. 30. הִתְיַצֵּב—וַיַּעֲמֹד. (2.) As following the act of *rising,* e.g., Gen. xxxvii. 7, where Joseph's sheaf (קָמָה—וְגַם־נִצָּבָה) "was risen—and even standing" (*erect* of course). So also men (Ex. xxxiii. 8) קָמוּ—וְנִצְּבוּ (and Numb. xvi. 27, &c.) (3.) As distinguished from יָשַׁב, "to sit" (Ex. xviii. 4).

B) figuratively, צב means to stand high, over and above as chief, Lord, &c., e.g., 1 Sam. xxii. 9 ; Ps. lxxxii. 1 ; cxix. 89.

כְמוֹ־נֵד, "as an heap," (Auth. Ver.) נֵד (like נָאַל, מַה, גֵּר), is part. K. of the onomatop. v. נָד, נוּד (Ar., ناد, "to nod" the head when falling asleep). These roots have the meaning of "wandering," "agitating to and fro," like corn when winnowed with the shovel-fan (as in the East). Hence נֵד is that corn thus winnowed, which is always put "as an heap" on one side of the threshing-floor, and is then called נֵד קָצִיר (Is. xvii. 11) "the heap of harvest (produce)." [Gesenius (Thes. l. s.), I see, hesitates and differs; but he had never been in the East, and had not seen it repeatedly, as I have.] נֵד then, is "a solid heap," composed of small moveable particles, like wheat or stones, which are "gathered" "as an heap" (comp. Arab. in Dial. of Yemen, ند, "a high hill.") It is thus beautifully applied to the "waters" of the sea which "God (כֹּנֵס כַּנֵּד) gathers as an heap" (Ps. xxxiii. 7), and which he הִצִּיב "caused to stand" or placed (כְמוֹ־נֵד) "as an heap" (Ps. lxxviii. 13), so that they (נִצְּבוּ) "stood" *high* and *erect,* like a wall or a dyke, on either side, when God (בָּקַע יָם) "rent or split" the sea, to make his people pass; or when he divided the river Jordan (Jos. iii. 13, 16), the waters of which (קָמוּ־וַיַעַמְדוּ) "stood still, like a pillar" (נֵד־אֶחָד) "in one heap," until the multitude having gone through, set foot on the promised land of Canaan.

מִלִּים, "the floods" (Auth. Ver.), quite correct. For אָלַל both in the Hebrew and in the cognate dialects, means "to flow" like water, "to distil" like dew, perfume, or words from the mouth, &c. Here the part. pres. K. is taken in a substantive sense, as is often the case: and it is applied exactly like "flood," not to whatever is "*actually flowing,*" but to whatever is by nature *liquid,*—especially to water. In like manner then, as "flood," which properly means "an overflow;" "crystal wave," which contradicts itself; "tide," which is a phenomenon of nature, &c., are used in poetry for "water;" so also מֵל, מִלִּים. For instance, in Ps. lxxviii.

16 we read that God "brought streams (מִלִים) out of the stony rock," and
the waters "gushed out" and "ran down like rivers ;" so also Jer. xviii. 14,
and Song of Solomon, iv. 15, where נִלְים is rendered by "streams;" while in
Is. xliv. 3, it is translated "floods ;" and in Ps. lxxviii. 44, by "rivers."
But as we find the word "flood" applied poetically to "still water," so
also do we read in Prov. v. 15, that the pl. נִלְים is said of the water in a
well, which assuredly does *not* flow. For the same difference which
existed of old between מֹאר "a well," and עַיִן "a fountain," still distin-
guishes a بِير and a عين throughout that part of the East where Arabic is
spoken.   بِير and מֹאר is a well properly so called, as at Beer-sheba, Beeroth,
&c., while عين is a fountain of "living" or "gurgling" water, which
flows above ground where it sparkles like "an eye" (عين), as at 'Ain-dor,
'Ain-gedi, &c. The idea of "flowing" then, though inherent in נִלְים, is,
we see, not always attached to it, any more than it is to "flood." In
this passage, therefore, the idea of "motion" or "flowing" does not
necessarily belong to נִלְים, which, though "liquid," may like "flood"
stand as "still" as water at the bottom of a well. "Flood," I conclude
then, is a correct rendering of נִלְים ; and נָצְבוּ כְמוֹ־נֵד נֹזְלִים is well translated,
"the floods stood *upright* as an heap."

As no objection is made to the third line, קָפְאוּ תְהֹמֹת בְּלֶב־יָם, I will not
refer to it beyond merely pointing out that it completely overthrows the
theory of those who would explain away this miracle by the natural phenomenon of a neap-tide, however extraordinary, and the whirling of the
same wind half round the compass. For תְהוֹם, pl. תְּהֹמֹת, means nothing
else in Scripture than "the deep;" great depth (said three of four times)
of the *earth*, and (about thirty times) of the *sea*. No metonomy consistent with the dignity of the inspired text could apply תְּהוֹם to so shallow
a surface of the sea, as to recede completely by natural and ordinary
means. It means ἄβυσσος, ἄβυσσοι πηγῶν κάτωθεν ; and it was "through
the deep" that God led his people as an horse in the wilderness, dividing
the water before them to make himself an everlasting name" (Is. lxiii.
12). Had it been otherwise, had the local circumstances been what some
persons would fain represent them, the people might have been led round
a portion of the gulf said to have been so shallow as to become dry by the
force of the wind alone. But it was not God's purpose, and there was of
course a reason for it.

The Theocratic government of the Israelitic community did not fairly
begin, until, having been brought out of Egypt by God with a mighty
hand and stretched-out arm, they found themselves comparatively isolated
in the wilderness. They then became "the people of God," the קָהָל or
ἐκκλησία ἐν τῇ ἐρήμῳ, over which God ruled, as Lord and King, supreme.
He brought them to that state by a miracle, and he constituted them his
"church in the wilderness" by a rite. He wrought the miracle by natural agencies miraculously subservient to his almighty counsel, when he
ordered his קָדִים or "shurqieh" (شرقية, ريح شرقية, *east*-wind, not *south*, as
H. H. B. says) a hot, unhealthy wind to blow, until (וַיִּבָּקְעוּ הַמָּיִם) "the

waters were divided" or split asunder. Then the people went through the way made for them, and trod the deep dry-shod, with the waters, "to them (וַחֹמָה רִימָיָם וּמִשְׂמָאלָם) a wall on their right hand and on their left." They were fairly buried in the depth of the waters which arose on each side over and above their heads; "they were," as the Holy Apostle tells us, "baptized in the cloud and in the sea;" from whence they came out outwardly and ostensibly a distinct and peculiar people. That initiative and necessary rite could not have been administered in any other way to that multitude; nor could they have been "buried unto death" to Egypt but by the circumstantial features of the whole miracle as it is related by the inspired writers.

And this is proved by the remarkable difference between that miracle, and the somewhat similar one of the passage of the Jordan, which was the setting aside of the insuperable barrier that kept back the "church in the wilderness" from the Promised Land. In this case, the waters (יִכָּרֵתוּ) "were cut," so as to form only "one heap" to the right of the people, and to allow the stream to flow downwards to the left into the Dead Sea. The bed of the river was then dry; and while the floods in a heap on the right threatened death and destruction, not one man of the "people of God" perished, while walking through what would have been a grave but for the ark of the covenant and their Chief and Saviour, 'Jesus' the Son of Nun.

Having thus briefly shewn from the Hebrew text alone that the Authorized Version is correct, and that its adversaries give proof of rather more love of novelty than scholarship, it might not be necessary to consult the ancient versions of Scripture. As, however, it may interest those of your readers who differ from Miss F. Corbaux to inquire into the sense given by the principal versions to the passage criticised by that lady, I will briefly state their meaning in English.

I. The Peschito, as I have already remarked, reads (Walton's Polyglot),—"By the wind of thy presence the waters were gathered together in a heap; the floods arose and stood still as it were in water skins (reading מאד for נד); the depths were coagulated in the heart of the sea."

II. The Targum Onkelos reads (Walton's Polyglot),—"And by the word of thy mouth the waters acted wisely (reading נשמו in the K. sense of *callidus fuit*); the floods stood like a wall; the depths were coagulated in the heart of the sea."

III. The Samaritan Version reads (Walton's Polyglot),—"And by the wind of thy wrath the waters were gathered together in a heap; the floods (arose or) stood up like a surrounding wall; the depths were coagulated in the heart of the sea."

IV. The Vulgate reads (Walton's Polyglot),—"Et in spiritu furoris tui congregatæ sunt aquæ: stetit unda fluens, congregatæ sunt abyssi in medio mari."

V. The Septuagint reads (Walton's Polyglot),—"Καὶ διὰ πνεύματος τοῦ θυμοῦ σου διέστη τὸ ὕδωρ· ἐπάγη ὡσεὶ τεῖχος τὰ ὕδατα· ἐπάγη τὰ κύματα ἐν μέσῳ τῆς θαλάσσης."

VI. The Arabic Version reads (Walton's Polyglot),— "And by the wind of thine anger the waters were gathered together in a heap; and the mass of waters stood still and erect like mountains; and the depths of water were coagulated in the heart of the sea."

VII. The Armenian Version reads (Venice Ed., 1805-45),—"And by the wind of thine indignation the waters were rent asunder; the waters were congealed like a wall; the waves were congealed in the midst of the sea."

VIII. The Sclavonian Version reads (St. Petersburgh, 1821, 4to.)—" By the spirit of thy fury the water was divided; the waters became concrete like a wall; and the waves were concrete in the midst of the sea."

IX. The Ethiopic Version reads (Octat. Æthiop. Ed., Dillman, l.c., Psalt. Ludolfi, p. 320),—"And the water stood up by the wind (or spirit) of thy wrath; and the water stuck together like a wall; and the flood (or storm) became coagulated in the midst of the sea."

X. The Coptic Version reads (Tuki. Psalt., p. 426, Ed. Rom., 1740),—And by the spirit of thy wrath the water stood still; the waters rose high like a wall; the billows were coagulated in the midst of the sea."

S. C. MALAN.

The Vicarage, Broadwindsor, July 24th.

ON THE ASSYRIAN INSCRIPTIONS.

SIR,—I observe, from several articles in your excellent Journal, that the great importance of the Assyrian antiquarian discoveries is becoming daily more appreciated by biblical scholars. There exists at the same time in the minds of many a very considerable degree of doubt and hesitation with respect to the reality of the alleged discoveries. This scepticism does not apply to the details merely, but extends to the very root and foundation of the whole system. Indeed, some writers have not hesitated to come forward in print and boldly aver their belief that the whole thing is a delusion, and that Colonel Rawlinson and Dr. Hincks have completely deceived, first themselves, and then the world, with regard to a long series of statements of the highest historical and literary importance which they have confidently and repeatedly put forward.

The question is one undoubtedly of the highest importance. Allow me to occupy a few pages with the consideration of it. As my excuse for so doing, I may state that I have devoted a considerable amount of time and attention to the subject, which is certainly a difficult one, but from the singularity and great importance of its results fully repays the labour of enquiry.

The first difficulty which strikes many thinking minds is the following: It is admitted (and a most extraordinary and unexampled fact it is) that both the language of the Assyrian inscriptions, and the characters in which it is written, were altogether unknown some twenty years ago. "How then," it is argued, "were they at all discoverable? There is nothing to begin with. You may suggest an alphabet, and having by means of it reduced the inscriptions into legible words, you may then suggest a meaning for those words, but however clear the meaning which seems to evolve itself from your sentences, it is a fallacious result and nothing more: because you are reasoning in a circle. Your alphabet cannot support your language, because itself wants proof and support, and has no other than the words of that very language which you yourself have invented to suit it."

Such I take it, is a fair statement of the argument. Your correspondent, "Scrutator," puts it well in the following words (page 190 of your last number) :—

"To the uninitiated the interpretation of these mysterious legends appears like what is called in algebra an indeterminate problem, or a single equation, containing two unknown quantities, which admits of an indefinite number of solutions. Given the *language*, it is easy to see how the characters might be discovered, or if the characters be given one might hope at length to master the language; but when we are equally ignorant of the language and its symbols, where shall we find a limit to assumption and conjecture?"

I will now mention another circumstance which has added to the doubt and perplexity already prevailing on the subject. A rival system of interpretation has been proposed by Mr. Forster, which is not merely different from that of Hincks and Rawlinson, but totally and irreconcileably opposite to it. Where Rawlinson thinks he reads the great names of Darius and Xerxes, Sennacherib and Nebuchadnezzar, with chronicles of great works and mighty wars, there Forster declares there is nothing whatever of the kind to be found: no such names, and no such events, but that what is really contained in the Assyrian inscriptions are mere trivialities, recording unimportant circumstances which occurred to the architect of these buildings, or to some of his workmen. To give an example of this new system of interpretation. There is a sentence which occurs fifty-eight times in the Behistun inscription. It is invariably translated by Rawlinson "Darius Rex dicit." But your correspondent, "T. M.," whose paper will be found at p. 371 of your last volume, assures us that Mr. Forster's translation runs as follows :—

"A cut-short man engraving many captives fastened by a single rope, by cutting and striking with a mallet."

"Consequently," says T. M., "this sentence describes the engraver himself." Your correspondent further goes on to say, that after some consideration, on the whole he prefers the system of Mr. Forster to that of Hincks and Rawlinson.

The question then is, which of these rival theories is the true one? or is there any ground for believing either of them?

Few persons have sufficient leisure to study the Cuneiform writings very carefully themselves. The interest however which is attached to the subject is daily increasing, and I believe there are many biblical scholars who desire to know, without going very deeply into the subject themselves (at least not at present), whether there are any *primâ facie* reasons for believing in the truth of Colonel Rawlinson's interpretations?

To this question then I would reply, in the first place, that the clearness and consistency of the numerous passages, and the long historical narratives translated by Rawlinson, afford in themselves no slight presumption that he cannot be greatly or altogether mistaken as to the meaning of these ancient records. Granting it however to be possible that an intelligent enquirer might be so far swayed by a predetermined idea as to think he was reading a long and consecutive history of the life of Darius, when in fact the incriptions which he held in his hand contained no mention of that monarch, yet there are monuments of another nature, which allow no play to the imaginative faculty, and which admit of only one interpretation. Colonel Rawlinson states that he has found an Assyrian tablet containing the squares of all the natural numbers from 1 to 60, and he has published a portion of this tablet. (Notes on the early history of Babylonia, p. 4.)

This establishes the truth of the system, so far as the explanation of the numerals is concerned, beyond the possibility of doubt.

What interpretation could possibly be given of this table of square numbers on the Forsterian hypothesis? But this evidence relates to the numerals alone, and therefore will not assist us beyond a certain point. If then the explanations of the Assyrian historical records depended upon the single testimony of Colonel Rawlinson, it might be fairly said that, knowing the fallibility of human judgment, they should not be too implicitly relied on. But such is not the fact. For several years, and almost from the first discovery of the Assyrian inscriptions, two rival scholars have been separately engaged in the work of interpretation, and some of the chief discoveries are due to the sagacity of each. And each of them, far from acquiescing indolently in the other's opinions, has always shewn a disposition to criticize and examine them narrowly. The result of their long and careful examination has however been a substantial agreement as to the nature, sense and meaning of the inscriptions, the pronunciation of the words, and the almost complete revivification as it were of a long and totally forgotten language. An individual scholar might perhaps be misled by his fancy in such an enquiry, but it is quite impossible that two intelligent men, enquiring independently, should agree respecting the syllabic value of one or two hundred crabbed and complicated symbols, and a vast number of words and sentences formed out of such syllables, and also as to the true intent and meaning of long historic statements contained in those phrases of a nearly unknown language, if there were no real basis of truth on which they had each separately reared their edifice. It will be observed that the argument depends upon this fact, namely, that Hincks and Rawlinson were independent enquirers, each knowing little or nothing of the results which the other had obtained, which I believe was the case. For instance, while one of these scholars, studying the subject in Ireland, discovered that the name written on a certain marble obelisk, was " Jehu son of Omri," the other made the same discovery at Baghdad. Is it not then *primâ facie* most probable that that name really exists on the monument? Would it not be a strange circumstance if both scholars were deceived? I give this merely as one instance, though an important one, of entire agreement between these independent enquirers. But there are many such, too numerous to mention.

Let me now advert to another point. I have myself, for my own satisfaction, pursued to a considerable extent this branch of study, and have had many opportunities of comparing my own translation of words and phrases with those contained in the previously published works of Hincks and Rawlinson, and I have frequently found a satisfactory agreement. But it may be said, the opinions of the disciple are often unconsciously influenced by those of the master, even when he supposes he is thinking independently. I will therefore give an instance which is free from any such objection, and will, I think, convince biblical students and others that there is no kind of illusion or deception in this matter. Your readers are aware that certain trilingual inscriptions of Xerxes and Darius have been found, written in the Persian, Scythian and Assyrian languages, in order that all the inhabitants of that vast empire might understand them. Some years ago, Colonel Rawlinson translated most of these from the Persian language, and published his translation in the *Journal of the Royal Asiatic Society*, vol. x., part iii. (1847). But at that time the Assyrian language was wholly unknown to him, consequently he left the Assyrian writing untranslated. Some months ago I took up one of these trilingual inscriptions, of moderate length, and without looking at Rawlinson's version, I essayed to translate the *Assyrian* writing, which I found I could easily accomplish. Not having as yet studied the old Persian, I was of course quite unaware of the meaning of the Persian writing, and could not therefore be in any way influenced or led astray by having it before me. On comparing afterwards my version of the Assyrian with Rawlinson's version of the Persian writing, I found an almost perfect agreement. As a *primâ facie* argument, in reply to the doubts and hesitations of certain scholars, I think I may venture to offer the above as satisfactory.

As an appendix to the foregoing remarks, I beg leave to offer a few observations on the great inscription of Nebuchadnezzar which is preserved at the India House. It consists of ten columns, averaging about sixty or seventy lines each, written very clearly, and in excellent preservation. The characters are of the complicated and ornamental form which was used by the Babylonians. This inscription was sent to England in the year 1801, and engraved in 1807, but its contents remained a mystery until very recently. It appears from the literary intelligence contained in your last Number (p. 227), that last July, Colonel Rawlinson presented a literal English version of this interesting monument to the Royal Asiatic Society, which will be published in their Transactions.

I have not seen Rawlinson's translation, but having myself, last summer, translated several passages of the inscription, and found them to be very interesting, I beg leave to subjoin them here for the sake of comparison, as I am desirous that the correctness of this system of interpretation should be tested in every possible way, feeling sure that it rests on a basis of truth. I will give my translation of only a small portion of the inscription. Let it be compared with Rawlinson's translation when the latter is published. I shall be found, no doubt, to have erred in many things, and shall stand corrected; but if only one half of the lines I have translated shall closely correspond in meaning to Rawlinson's version, how can any candid enquirer doubt that the system reposes on true principles of interpretation? But first I must state, that though I have not seen his version, I had the pleasure of hearing a lecture delivered by Colonel Rawlinson at the Royal Institution, in May last, upon the subject of his Assyrian discoveries, in the course of which he gave a general outline of the meaning of this great inscription, viz., that it contained an account of various great public works executed by Nebuchadnezzar at Babylon. One point then mentioned by Colonel Rawlinson struck me as particularly interesting, viz., the splendid confirmation which the inscription supplies of the truthfulness of the old historian Berosus, who has recorded in his history the vain boast of Nebuchadnezzar, " that he had built the temple of Babylon in fifteen days." Colonel Rawlinson assured us that his vainglorious boast is actually contained in this inscription which has come down to our own times in such a fortunate state of preservation. Such a coincidence deserves to be regarded as something wonderful.

Wishing to satisfy my own curiosity, and convince myself, if I could do so, of the truth of this discovery, I examined my copy of the great inscription, and had no difficulty in finding the passage to which Colonel Rawlinson referred. It stands at the bottom of the eighth column, and its sense is assuredly very clear and satisfactory, as I will endeavour to shew. Before, however, quoting the original words of the inscription, I will first refer to some previous passages which contain the same words, and will therefore help to determine their meaning. At the end of the seventh column we find these four lines :

wesharsitu	I constructed it ?
in kupri u agurri	in bitumen and brick (and)
wezakkir-su	I finished it ?
khursanish	completely.

From this passage it is evident that *we sharsitu* must be a verb with a meaning of "building" or "constructing." Next I must refer to the following passage, which will be found at the end of the fourth column. The king relates how he adorned and finished :—

" the temple of —— and the temple of ——,
" the two great shrines of Babylon,
" which Nabopollassar, king of Babylon, my father,
" erected, but did not complete."

The original words must be quoted :

ibusu	he constructed,
u la weshaklilu	but did not complete; (or),
	did not cover in
sibir-sun	their roofs.

To come now to the important passage which confirms the truth of the statement of Berosus, it stands as follows (end of column 8) :

wesharsitu risi-su	I erected its walls ;
wezakkir khursanish	I finished it completely
ina 15 tamu	in 15 days
sibir-su weshaklilu	its roof I covered in.

With the exception of *risi* and *tamu*, all these words have occurred before in the passages I previously adduced. The Assyrian numeral which corresponds to our *fifteen* is given with the greatest distinctness, and as to the important word *tamu* (days), it is very frequent in the Assyrian inscriptions, but is usually written *tami*.

From an examination of this passage I naturally proceeded to study the remaining parts of the inscription, and found that many portions of it were easily intelligible, and contained much curious matter, of which however Colonel Rawlinson will doubtless soon give us a full explanation.

To begin with the beginning of the inscription, the first column commences with the two following lines:—

| 1. Nabukudrussur | Nebuchadnezzar, |
| 2. sar Babel | king of Babylon. |

It is to that great monarch therefore that this inscription relates. The next lines imply, I think, that he was a devoted worshipper of the gods Marduk and Nebo (written Nabiuv), and adored or honoured *iluti-sun* (their divinities). The inscription then refers to the building of the two great temples, which appear to have been among the greatest ornaments of Babylon. The first of these I cannot read, and therefore I will denote it as "temple X." But the other reads, "temple of Zida or Seyda," that is, in my opinion, the planet Jupiter, or Good Fortune. (See Gesesius's *Lexicon.*)

These two temples then, Beth X. and Beth-Seyda were erected by the king at Babylon. At line 16, we find Babel u Barzipa. Here we have mentioned together the two great capitals of Nebuchadnezzar's kingdom, Babylon and Borsippa, which, though very near together, yet appear (like Paris and Versailles) to have been rivals in splendour.

The king then calls himself

19. Zanin Beth X. u Beth Seyda	the builder of those temples; (or), their careful guardian.
20. bal asharidu	the eldest (or beloved) son
21. sha Nabupalussur	of Nebopolassar,
22. sar Babel anaku	king of Babylon, I am.

After some intermediate verses we find

| 30. sha Marduk Bel reb Il bani-ya | of Marduk the great Lord, the god my creator (or, the star which ruled over my birth). |

For Marduk was the planet Mars. Line 34, the god Nebo is said to be

| 34. naram sarruti-ya | supporter? of my kingdom. |

We read soon afterwards

| 37. in Zida sib-ya Kinu | in Zida and in Kinu, my place (or, which I built?) |
| 38. aramu bulukhti iluti-sun | I exalted the sacred rites of their divinities. |

I cannot explain the grammatical construction of line 37, nor why *Beth* (temple) is twice omitted. But it will be seen by reference to column 3, line 38, that the temples of Zida and Kinu are there mentioned together. If the former is the planet Jupiter, I think it likely that the latter is the planet Saturn, *Chiun*, mentioned in Amos, chap. v., 26.

In line 48, Nebo is called * * * * of heaven and earth, perhaps, ruler of heaven and earth. In line 61, we find the king uttering a prayer to his guardian deity, Marduk, but I cannot make out exactly where this prayer begins.

61. anaku rubu mazira-ka	I, the chief of thy worshippers
63. atta taban annima	thou hast created me;
64. sarruti kishat nisi	the kingdom ——
65. tadipanni	thou hast given me?

In the meaning of line 63 I have followed Dr. Hincks (see the last Number of this Journal, p. 144). But verse 65 is a mere conjectural translation of my own. The prayer continues

69. belluta-ka shriti	thy exalted greatness.
70. bulukhti iluti-ka	the sacred rites of thy divinity.
71. supsha in sib-ya	I set up? in my dwelling-place.

We will now proceed to the second column. The king is no longer praying to Marduk, but speaks of him in the third person (see line 3) as " Marduk, chief of the gods." The word used here for " chief " or " eldest " is *sikh* or *sheikh*, which resembles the Arabic *sheikh*, the chief or elder of a city, but I suppose this is accidental.

The last quoted lines now again recur, but in the *third person* thus :—

6. belluta-tzu shriti	*his* exalted greatness.
7. bulukhti iluti-su	the sacred rites of *his* divinity.
8. weshashkin in sib-ya	I set up in my dwelling-place.

Further on we find

15. iahtu tiamti eliti	from the upper tiamti.
16. adi tiamti shapliti	unto the lower tiamti.

Referring to the extent of the buildings and constructions. I rather think that *tiamti* signifies the right bank of the river, but am not confident about it. In line 30, we read of gold, silver, and precious stones. Then follows a description of the adornments of the great temple at Babylon which I have called " Temple X," which is called in line 41, " the great sanctuary of his divinity." I therefore presume it was the principal temple of the city.

At line 43 follows an account of the adornment of another temple, which may be called " Temple Y," which is called " the *papakha* of the great chief of the gods, the God Marduk." I propose to translate *papakha* " the shrine," although doubtfully.

It is then said : " Its *walls* (?) were covered with gold brilliant as the *sun* (?). The word for " gold," *khurassu*, is very remarkable. Both Hincks and Rawlinson (if I mistake not) have pronounced it to be the origin of the Greek χρυσος. The description then continues, line 49,—

49. With lapis lazuli and marble
50. The *walls* (?) of the temple I covered.

The word " I covered " is in the original *weshalbish*.

The king then states (line 51) that he made three gates, splendid as the sun, the last of the three belonged jointly, as it seems, to the two temples before mentioned, viz., the Temple X and the Temple of Seyda. If so, they must have been situated near together.

At line 57 a date occurs, viz., "day the eighth, and day the eleventh." I apprehend this relates to the celebration of some festival at the temples on those days.

Column the third opens with a curious symbol, apparently a crown. The king says: "The royal crown, the divine crown of the chief of the gods, the god Marduk, which the former king had made in silver, I covered with *namri* of gold." These may be plates of gold, or perhaps *spots* or *spangles*. The latter version is less probable in itself, but is suggested by the analogy of the Hebrew *Namr* (pardus maculatus). The phrase for "I covered it," weshalbish-zu (line 7), it will be observed, is the same as before. He then says, as I think (line 9), that he gilt (khurassu rusha) the sacred vessels (hunuti) of the Temple of X.

At line 16, precious slabs (agurri illiti) of lapis lazuli are brought for the decoration of this same temple.

He then passes on to the Temple of Y, and speaks of *rishati* of some precious wood. "Sha ishtu mate Labanan gushur? illiti upla," (which from the land of Lebanon and its precious forests I brought) ana zululu (to be the *beams?*) of the temple of Y, the shrine (*papakha*) of his supreme divinity" (line 25).

This high epithet, applied to the Temple of Y, agrees perfectly with what went before (col. II., line 43. Indeed the consistency with which all the parts of this long inscription cohere together and support each other is most satisfactory.

Observe in passing the epithet "precious" (illiti) applied to the forests of Lebanon. "Upla" is a very common word, it always signifies "I brought home." The *zululu* are then adorned and covered with golden *namri* and the precious *nisik* stone. He then speaks of the city of Borsippa (line 36), and says—

38. Beth-Zida Beth-Kinu	the Temple of Jupiter (?) and the Temple of Saturn (?)
39. in kirbi-su weshopish	in the midst of it I erected.
and "with silver, gold, and *nisik* stone	
43. weshaklil sibir-su	I covered its ceiling.

Then follows: the beams (zululu) of the shrine (papakhat) of Nebo, with gold I covered (weshalbish), "but the *zululu* of the Temple of Y, I covered (weshalbish), with *namri* of silver.

In Porter's *travels* there is a copy in the cursive character of this part of the inscription. This copy substitutes for *weshalbish* (line 45) the word *wekhallilu*, which is therefore of the same meaning. The fact is, that *khalil* is the Hebrew ללכ *perfecit, coronavit*, whence *wekhallilu*, "I covered." But the *causative* conjugation inserts *sha*, and the word then becomes *weshaklil*, "I caused to be covered," *vide supra*, line 43. Similarly *lebesh* is the Hebrew word שבל (to clothe) but in the *causative* conjugation it takes the syllable *sha* and becomes *weshalbish*, "I caused to be clothed." Similarly *epish* "to build," "to erect," has the causative form *weshopish*, "I caused to be erected" (see line 39), and *sib* "to dwell" has the causative *weshasib*, "I caused to dwell," that is, "I located inhabitants in a certain place;" a verb of very frequent occurrence. Many other instances of rich adornment of the temples are then specified, and at line 65 we read, if I am not mistaken, that the king erected at Borsippa the Temple of the Seven Planets, adorned with slabs of precious lapis lazuli (line 69).

In column IV. we have a most full and important account of the temples erected by Nebuchadnezzar at Babylon and Borsippa. The list commences in line 7 with a temple dedicated to "the chief of the gods, the god Marduk." Line 14 we have "the Temple of Makh? and the Temple of . . . . unto the god Makh? who ruled over my birth. In Babylon I made."

The name of this god is doubtful, but whatever it was, the temple had the same name.

Line 18, "Unto the god Nebo protector? of the kingdom, the temple of . . . . . . his temple in Babylon, in bitumen and brick (eptik pitik-su) I constructed its building."

Then at line 25, "Unto the god Bel-tzu, the *mudammik* of my *idati*, the temple of marble, his temple in Babylon I made." The next clause, line 29, is of a very similar construction. "Unto the god . . . . . who is the . . . . . of my . . . . the temple of . . . . his temple in Babylon, of bitumen and brick (shakish ebus) skilfully I made." Then comes, at line 35, "Unto the god Yem, the *mushashkin* of the *kanik* in my *mada*, the Temple of Namakan? his temple in Babylon I built" (abnu).

The sculptor purposely varied almost every time the phrase for "I built," as well as the adverb "skilfully," "richly," "nobly," &c., &c., with which it is generally accompanied. It will be observed that almost all these Babylonian adverbs end with the syllable *ish*.

The god Yem was one of their chief deities, he probably corresponded to the Jupiter Tonans of the Romans.

At line 38 we have, "Unto the goddess Gula the *ekirat* and *gamilat* (observe the female ending) of my *nabishti*, the Temple of Sabel and the Temple of Kharrish-Zula, those two temples which are in Babylon, in bitumen and brick (ashmish abnu) skilfully I built."

The Temple of Sabel I am disposed to render "the Temple of Cybele," or "the Temple of the Sibyl." I have long ago advocated in another work the connexion of the two latter mythological names, and this great goddess *Gula* was probably identical with Cybele. I do not recollect, however, to have found any mention of such a goddess as "*Gula*" in any author of antiquity. The idea has occurred to me therefore, that it may have been pronounced "*Shula*," identical with one of the names of the Sibyl, for if I mistake not, Mr. Cureton has shewn that the old Syriac MSS. in the British Museum instead of *Sibulla* use the contracted form *Sula* or *Shula*. Moreover the Babylonian Sibyl was famous, we may therefore not unreasonably expect to find the name in some shape or other on the Babylonian monuments.

The king next dedicates (line 44) a temple to another god at Babylon, and then (line 49) a temple at Borsippa. Then follows (line 52) the following important dedication: "Unto the goddess Gula, the Queen of my

...... the Temple of Gula, the Temple of Tila, and the Temple of Ziba-tila, those three great shrines which are in Borsippa, I erected."

This goddess must evidently have been one of the greatest objects of the national worship, since she had three temples in the single city of Borsippa, besides her two great temples in Babylon (see col. iv., l. 40). She was the same as the moon, and the great Babylonian goddess Nanaia. See Rawlinson's Notes on the early history of Babylonia (p. 24), who says that it may be proved "by a host of examples," that all these three goddesses are the same.

Line 57 continues, "Unto the god Yem *mushashnin* of the . . . . in my land, his temple in Borsippa skilfully I made (ashmish abnu).

Then at line 61, "Unto the god Bel-tzu, the *nashtap* of my *damikhti*, the Temple of Tianna, his temple in the vicinity of the Temple of Seyda, splendidly I built (namrish ebus).

In the next lines (66, &c.) which conclude column iv. and commence column v., I have doubtfully rendered the divine name as Belus or Bel.

> 66. "Imgur-Bel and Nimitti-Bel
>   the two great shrines of Babylon
>   which Nabopolassar king of Babylon
>   my father, my progenitor,
>   erected but did not cover their roofs.....
>   he had dug the canal (khiritzu yekhru
>   with two walls in bitumen and brick
>   he had constructed its mound " (kibir-su.

It will be observed that in these last lines I have availed myself of the translation suggested by Dr. Hincks in the last number of this Journal.

In line 8 there is mention made of the river Euphrates, but it is expressly said (line 10) that the works his father had begun there *(la weshaklilu)* "he did not complete." These great works therefore were left for his son Nebuchadnezzar to accomplish, and I venture, though with much diffidence, to offer the following translation of line 21.

> 21. "Then I, his eldest son, standing in his place
>   Imgur-Bel and Nimitti-Bel
>   The two high places of Babylon
>   I completed them" (weshaklilu).

Very elaborate architectural descriptions appear to fill the rest of this column, in which the two high places of Imgur-Bel and Nimitti-Bel are again mentioned.

In column vi. the king completes the canal and mound which we were before told had been left unfinished by his father *(vide* line 30), and he executes a similar work at Borsippa (line 58, 60).

This column ends with the name of Nebuchadnezzar, which is the commencement of a very interesting passage, of which I will venture upon the following translation.

"Nebuchadnezzar King of Babylon, who made the great god Marduk to be the guardian god of his city Babylon, *anaku,* "I am he." The Temple of X and the Temple of Seyda I made as bright as the rays (?) of the sun. The shrines of the supreme deity daily *(tamish)* I adored— panama .... valtu tamu valluti (in the former times) aki .... pali (the years) of Nabopolassar my exalted father (abi ali-ya) king of Babylon, that great king (sar madut) who is gone (alik) to the abode (sha ilu) of the Gods." Or in other words, "The spirit of the great king my father has ascended to the realms of glory, but I have continued to worship the gods with zeal, as he did in his days."

Proceeding to column 8, line 43, there seems to have been in Imgur-Bel, the great shrine of Babylon, a statue or chapel of the god of war (il takhazi, see line 42, or perhaps we should pronounce takhaziel).

The passage is obscure to me. It is a series of *negations*. I think the king says it had been left unfinished :—

" zuzu su la enu	zuzu ejus non fuit . . .
. . . . su la wenish	corona ejus non fuit . . .
palaga su la eskier	palaga ejus non fuit . . .

He then adds : "kumuratsish astakhima," which may mean "bene vel splendide perfeci."

In column ix., line 12, we have "kaspa khurassu," that is, silver and gold, written at full length. They are usually expressed by symbols. Further on, line 43, we have "Wedannin (I consecrated?) the city of Babylon, *khursanish* (completely) unto the god Marduk my lord;" and then after a line, 46, which I do not understand, follows, at line 47, a prayer to Marduk.

"O Marduk, great chief of the gods, *rubu mustarkha* (great creator?) *atta taban annima*—thou didst create me, *sarruti*—the kingdom, *tadipanni* —thou gavest me?" The prayer then continues : "O Marduk I have exalted thy star, and it shines brightly over thy city Babylon (kima napshati eli ir-ka Babel), aramu bulukhti iluti-ka—(I have exalted the sacred rites of thy divinity) ashitiniku billut-ka (I have adored (?) thy godhead) Zanin kala makhazi-ka—(I am the guardian of all thy temples) or it may be their *builder*, but I think *zanin* usually signifies a shield."

This is evidently a solemn dedication of the city of Babylon to its protecting deity, and when fuller understood will probably be found to be expressed in lofty and glowing language.

This remarkable monument abounds with notices of the architecture of the temples and other great public works in Babylon and Borsippa, and will enable us to form some idea of the splendor of those ancient cities.

Lacock Abbey, October, 1855.   H. F. Talbot.

P.S. I forgot to mention at the commencement of this essay, that there is another class of evidence which cannot fail to interest biblical scholars. The Assyrian language is allied to the Hebrew, although not very closely, and whenever the meaning of an Assyrian word can be guessed from the context with something like certainty, it is always worth while to look in the Hebrew lexicon, and see if that word occurs in the same sense in Hebrew. If it does so it is very satisfactory, as it must be obvious that mere chance could not often produce such a coincidence. I will give an instance or two to illustrate my meaning.

In plate 151 of Botta's great work, Sargina king of Assyria makes war on Merodach Baladan king of Chaldea, and assigns for a reason the *wickedness* of that monarch " who had reigned over Babylon twelve years *with impiety* [literally, " without heaven "], and had burned and.... the images of the gods."

In this passage after " he burned" followed *yeshbur* or *ishbur*, a word unknown to me, but the context led me to the meaning. What could the impious monarch have done to the sacred images besides burning them? Most likely he *broke* them also. I assigned therefore to *yeshbur* the provisional interpretation of "he broke." Then since the initial vowel is the sign of the third person singular, the root of the word will be *sheber* or שבר. Turning, therefore, to this root in Gesenius's *Lexicon*, p. 980, I found it there immediately, viz., שבר, *fregit*.

I will observe in passing that the historical fact here mentioned, possesses considerable interest in itself. Was then Merodach Baladan an iconoclast? Had he seen the inanity of the gods of the Gentiles, and was that the reason why he sent so courteous an embassy to Hezekiah, whom he probably knew to be like himself, no worshipper of idols?

I will give another example, from an inscription of Xerxes, which is written on the rock of Van. A copy will be found in Vol. xviii. of the *Journal Asiatique* (see plate ii., No. xi.) The monarch says: "My father Darius built his house nobly in the name of Oromasdes. He gave command to erect a tablet (ana epish sis), but never wrote anything on it (u la eli val esthur). Afterwards I gave a command (upki anaku bilemi altakan) to inscribe the tablet (ana shadari sis). Most part of this has been translated by Rawlinson, p. lxxix. But in transcribing the Assyrian writing, he omits altogether the word *sis* or *shish*, which corresponds to "tablet." This omission shews that he had no confidence apparently that *sis* could be the true pronunciation of the Assyrian word; and therefore he preferred to give no transcription of it. Nevertheless, on referring to Gesenius's *Lexicon*, we shall find at once שש *sis*, marmor candidum, which must be the very word; for what material can be more proper for a "tablet" than white marble?

Many other instances might be given, but these may suffice for the present.

SIDONIAN SARCOPHAGUS AND INSCRIPTION.

To the Editor of the Journal of Sacred Literature.

DEAR SIR,—You have already given in No. II of *The Journal of Sacred Literature*, p. 481, some account from an American publication of the remarkable sarcophagus of a Sidonian King, which was discovered near Saida (the ancient Sidon) in January last, and on which are contained many lines in the ancient Phœnician characters. I now beg to send you some further particulars on the same subject, as I was myself one of the first in England, who was informed of this very interesting discovery, and who immediately afterwards took much trouble in trying to secure the monument itself for the British Museum.

On February 17th of this year, my friend and correspondent, the Rev. J. L. Porter, writing to me from Damascus, added at the end of his letter, a short notice of this extraordinary sarcophagus. He wrote thus, " I have now to inform you of one of the most important discoveries, which has been made in this country for a long time. Some weeks ago, a beautiful sarcophagus of stone was accidentally exhumed at Sidon. The lid was sculptured into the form of a full length human figure, and upon it were found twenty-two lines of an inscription in well-preserved Phœnician characters. A dispute, however, arose between some European consular agents as to the possession of this rare treasure, and an appeal being made to the Pacha, he ordered the sarcophagus to be re-buried, and a guard placed over the spot, and appointed a commission of four Moslems, four native Christians, and four Europeans, to try the case. Before it was covered up, a friend of mine at Sidon succeeded in copying the inscription, and I have written requesting him to transcribe it for me. I do not know whether he will do so; but if he do, I shall feel great pleasure in sending it to you."

I wrote on March 9th, the day after I received the above letter, to Damascus, requesting Mr. Porter to procure a copy of the inscription for me from his friend at Sidon, and I observed to him "one would suppose that it was the sarcophagus of some great personage."

My next step was to endeavour to obtain the monument itself by a prompt application, through friends, to Government, urging an immediate order to be sent to our authorities in Syria to secure it. This was readily done, and Government authorized its being obtained at even a large price. Then, not long afterwards, there appeared a statement in the papers, copied from a Smyrna Newspaper, that the Sultan, to put an end to the contest which had arisen between the French Consul and other parties at Sidon for this precious sarcophagus, had ordered it to be shipped to Constantinople, whither it was on its passage. Conceiving this report to be true, I urged another friend well acquainted with matters and the embassy at Constantinople to write, and try to procure it from the Turkish Government for our National Museum, which was also quickly done. From the very first account I received of it, I feared that France would be beforehand in gaining possession of this most interesting monument of Phœnicia; because, as far as I could learn, England had no active Consul in that part of Syria. Before leaving London in last June, I attended a meeting of the Society of Antiquaries on May 17th, at which was presented a lithograph copy of the Phœnician inscription in twenty-two lines, but without any attempted translation. It was communicated, through the President, by Dean Milman, who had received it from America, from our late minister, the Hon. Edward Everett.

I heard nothing more of this subject, until the meeting of the Syro-Egyptian Society, on the evening of the 13th instant, when I had the gratification of hearing Dr. A. Benisch read a translation of some of the Phœnician lines in English, compared with Hebrew and German versions of them. From his account, all these translations agreed in the main points, though the name of the King Ashmonezer, was by some called Ashmonedo, doubts of course arising as to the accuracy of certain words in the different copies, and which Dr. Benisch conceived could be decided by examining a correct rubbing from the sarcophagus itself. The following day, November 14th, I procured a copy of Dr. Dietrich's work entitled *Zwei-Sidonische Inschriften, eine Griechische aus Christlicher Zeit, und eine altphönicische Königsinschrift*, which was published at Marburg about the end of last August, and read with pleasure the German translation of the Phœnician lines which Dr. Benisch had so ably noticed the previous evening. Being the first meeting of the Royal Society of Literature for the ensuing session, I took the opportunity of giving a short *vivâ voce* account of what had been done with respect to this noble monument, as well as of my own humble efforts in trying to obtain possession of it for the British Museum, and of briefly reading portions of Dr. Dietrich's translation of what he properly terms the " old Phœnician King's inscription," and likewise of alluding to some of Dr. A. Benisch's statements.   Now, singularly enough, on the very next day, I met with the last number of the *Revue Archéologique* for the 15th October, 1855, and which I found to contain at p. 430—4, a paper entitled *Le Sarcophage d'un Roi de Sidon ;* but from the concluding lines of it, I was very sorry to read, what I had always suspected would be the result of the claims for the possession of this sarcophagus, viz., that the Duke de Luynes had obtained it, and had presented it to the French Government for the Museum at the Louvre.   My consolation, however, is twofold : first, that it is committed to the good custody of our neighbours and allies ; and second, that it has arrived so near to our own shores.

From the first portion of the paper in the *Revue*, it seems that M. Perretié, Chancellor of the Consulate of France at Beyrut, claiming the sarcophagus, had at length obtained it; but no mention is made of its having been sent to Constantinople, which was probably only a ruse. The same account goes on to say, that the commander of the sloop of war La Sérieuse was ordered to convey it to France with all expedition. It describes the monument itself as composed of black basalt, and in shape like an Egyptian mummy-case, and of which the sculptured head, with its large head-dress, alone remained ; it wears a rich and wide collar, worked in relief, at each end of which a head of the sacred hawk is seen.   Nearly the whole height of it is covered with an inscription in twenty-two lines, written in well preserved Phœnician characters. A second inscription, in like letters still more perfect, but only repeating, with some variations—the two first rows of the former—occurs around the head of the corpse at its outer extremity.

The French narrative of the discovery of this tomb appears not to be correct; at least, the date varies from that given to me by Mr. Porter, and also from that related by Dr. Dietrich.   It continues, " it was the 20th of February, 1855, when M. Perretié, having undertaken some excavations in a piece of ground a short distance to the south of Saida, received the news that his agent had just found a sarcophagus."   The German notice says, the " sarcophagus was found in a rock-sepulchre in January of this year by some country people, who were seeking for gold ; and this quite coincides with Mr. Porter's statement, which is, that it was exhumed " some weeks ago," *i. e.*, some weeks before the day (February 17th) in which he wrote to me.

Mr. Porter never accomplished his desire of sending me a copy, or a rubbing, of the Phœnician inscription; and I think the friend at Sidon, to whom he alluded, is very likely the American missionary, the Rev. Mr. Thomson, to whom Dr. Dietrich has dedicated his work as "the discoverer," and first sender of it to Germany. The gentleman, who transmitted the copy to America, appears to be another American missionary, the Rev. Dr. Van Dyck. And I must observe—as a matter somewhat remarkable, that no separate copy, or rubbing even, was ever forwarded (as far as I can hear) from Syria to any scholar in England.

Mr. Thomson sent his copy early to the Chevalier Bunsen, from which Dr. Dietrich made his translation and philological remarks.

Plate II. of the Doctor's learned work gives the twenty-two lines of the inscription in Phœnician characters; and Plate III. represents the same transcribed into Hebrew. Dr. Dietrich also adds two translations; one p. 31—33, which is literal, and follows the twenty-two lines of the original; but the other (p. 35—37) is disposed in a different manner, and is divided into two parts.

I here subjoin my translation, as accurately as I could render it, from the first of those German versions, only observing that the Doctor remarks, that in lines 16 and 17, owing to an injury or flaw in the marble, some gap occurs.

(Line 1)"In the month Bul, in the fourteenth year of my reign, King Aschmunezer King of the Sidonians,

(2) of the son of the King Tabnith, King of the Sidonians, speaks King Aschmunezer, King of the Sidonians, saying: I have decreed,

(3) when I sink in sleep (at), the end of (my) days, then (may there be) rest, reverence of the Dead. And (when) I lie in this stone-coffin and in this grave,

(4) in the place, which I have built, founding an ornament of the whole kingdom. And (let) no one open this tomb, or

(5) seek for treasure by us, since by us no treasure shall have been placed, and take not away the stone-coffin of my tomb, and injure not

(6) the lower part of this tomb with a lid of a second tomb. Whenever a person sells our grave, let it be as a curse to him, we banish him out of the whole kingdom, and

(7) Every one, who here opens the lid of this tomb, or who takes away the stone-coffin of my tomb, or who injures the lower part

(8) of this tomb, may God place him without a tomb among the manes, and he shall not be buried in his grave, may God place him without son and seed;

(9) instead of his sleep may he tremble before the Mighty one, before the Holy one, before the Future one. The glorious King, who would reign among us after our

(10) departure from the dominion—when there is a person, who here opens the lid of this tomb, or who takes away

(11) this stone-coffin—him this King curses. When a person violates (it), may God make him to be weak (and) to starve, to totter and

(12) to break, by injury and curse in the life under the sun, as one whom it is not fit to pity.—I have decreed, when I sink in sleep, the end

(13) of (my) days, then (may there be) rest,—reverence of the dead. I, even I, Aschmunezer, King of the Sidonians, son of the

(14) King Tabnith, the King of the Sidonians, son's son of the King Aschmunezer, King of the Sidonians, and my mother Amaschtoreth,

(15) Priestess of Aschtoreth, our Lady, the Queen, Daughter of King Aschmunezer, King of the Sidonians, we who have built this House

(16) for us (from the foundations) in Sidon, in the land on the sea, and we have led away the Bostrat from hence, very high, and we

(17) we who have built a house of the mother (from the very ground) situated on

the side (of the steps ?) upon the mountain, and the building itself is very lofty, and we, we who have built (a) temple,

(18) for Elon the Sidonian in Sidon in (the) land on (the) sea, a temple for Baal of Sidon, a temple for Aschtoreth there on the height : henceforth let the Lord the King give us

(19) the ornament and the beauty of thê countries, in the noble garden, which is in our Dominion, according to the measure of the greatness, which I performed, and may he protect us from

(20) on high the borders of the Land, in order to fortify every Sidonian for ever, founding the ornament of the whole kingdom. And let no one open my lid,

(21) nor remove my lid, and injure not the under-part of this tomb, and take not away the stone-coffin of my tomb, and let him not exclude us from

(22) Elon, from the Holy one, from God, and make abominable this realm. And the person who violates (it), let (him) be cursed in eternity."

The next translation I have made from the version in French, as published at p. 432—4, *Rev. Archéol.*, which will be found to differ in many parts from the preceding,

"In the month of Bul, the fourteenth year of my reign, to me Esmunazar, King of the Sidonians, son of the King Thebunath, King of the Sidonians, the King Esmunazar speaks, and says :—

In the midst of my feasts and of my perfumed wines, I am taken away from the assembly of men to pronounce a lamentation, and to die, and to rest, laid down in this coffin, in this tomb, in the place of sepulture which I have built.

By this lamentation, I adjure every royal race and every man : that no one opens this funereal bed ; that no one searches the asylum of the faithful, for there are some images of the Gods among the faithful.

That no one takes off the lid of my coffin ; that no one builds upon the top of this funereal bed, the top of the bed of my sleep, although any one shall tell (him) ; listen not to those who are humbled (in death). For every royal race and every man who shall open the monument of this funereal bed, whether they take off the lid of this coffin, or they build upon the monument which covers it over, may they not have any funereal bed reserved for them amongst the Rephaim (shades) ; let them be deprived of sepulture ; may they not leave after them either son, or posterity ; may the Alonim (the great gods) put them aside in the infernal regions.

If it is a royal race, may his cursed crime fall on his children even to the extinction of their posterity.

If it is a (private) man who opens the top of this funereal bed or who carries away the lid of my coffin and the corpses of the royal family, this man is a profaner.

That his stem neither put forth any roots nor bear any fruit ; let him be marked with reprobation among those living under the sun.

Because, I worthy of pity, am taken away in the midst of my banquets and of my perfumed wines in order to quit the assembly of men and to pronounce my lamentation, afterwards to die.

I repose here, verily, I Esmunazar, King of the Sidonians, son of the King Thebunath, King of the Sidonians, son of the King Esmunazar, King of the Sidonians, and with me my mother Ammastoreth, who was Priestess of Astarté in the palace of the Queen, daughter of the King Esmunazar, King of the Sidonians, who had built the temple of (the) Alonim, the temple of Astarté at Sidon, maritime town ; and both have consecrated some magnificent offerings to the Goddess Astarté. Moreover with me repose Onchonna, who had built, in honour of Esmun, the holy God, Ene-Dalila in the mountain, and had offered me some magnificent presents, and Onchanna, who had built some temples to the Alonim of Sidon, at Sidon, maritime town, the temple of Baal-Sidon, and the temple of Astarté, glory of Baal. So that (in requital of his piety), the lord Ado Milchom gave us the towns of Dora and Japhia, with their vast territories of wheat which are below Dan, pledge for the possession of the strong places that I have founded and which he had limited, as the bulwarks of our frontiers secured to the Sidonians for ever.

By this lamentation, I adjure every royal race and every man: that they neither open, nor overthrow the top of my tomb ; that they do not build upon the edifice which covers his funereal bed ; that they do not carry away my coffin of my funereal bed for fear the Alonim should put them aside (among the dead). Otherwise may that royal race (and), those men profaners, and their posterity be destroyed for ever."

Lastly, as to the age of this most ancient royal sarcophagus, it is doubtless very difficult to form any tolerably correct opinion. Although the Duke of Luynes, judging from its shape and proportions as compared with those made in Egypt, during the period from the 19th to the 26th dynasties, thinks it may be referred to about the time of Nebuchadnezzar. The names of "Ashtoreth," the "Priestess of Ashtoreth," and the expressions "The Temple of Ashtoreth," and the "Temple of Baal of Sidon," are of considerable interest, and carry one directly to those very early Heathen Deities of the Holy Land, which are mentioned in the Old Testament.

Since writing the above, I have met with the *Journal of the American Oriental Society,* vol. v., No. 1, New York, 1855, which has been very recently published, and only received about three weeks since in England, and have the pleasure to send to you a few additions to my former communication on the inscribed sarcophagus from Sidon, in order to render it more complete, and to enable the readers of *The Journal of Sacred Literature* to compare two other English translations of the Phœnician lines that have been made in America with those two which I have already given.

From Professor E. E. Salisbury's paper on the "Phœnician Inscription of Sidon" (at p. 227-243), in that journal, I have learnt the day on which the sarcophagus was discovered near Sidon, was January 19th last; that its lid is estimated at about eight feet in length by four feet in width, and that the missionary who actually copied the inscription from the monument itself, previous to its reinterment, is Dr. Van Dyck. Also, it appears that the Rev. Mr. Thomson corrected it by another "examination of the original," and that he had "sent his copy to Chevalier Bunsen, who placed it in the hands of Dr. Dietrich" for publication; consequently, the inscription, as published in the German work, is clearly the most to be relied upon. Professor Salisbury writes the name of the Sidonian king, Eshmun'iyed; and he thinks that of his mother, Amashtoreth, is a contracted form of Amatashtoreth—meaning "the handmaid of Ashtoreth" (or Ashtaroth, or Astarte.) Eshmun is considered as a Phœnician deity.

The Professor observes, "a comparison of this inscription with those collected by Pococke in Cyprus, to which Gesenius assigns an age not long posterior to Alexander at the latest, shews it to be older, paleographically considered, certainly not more recent, than those. To this is to be added, that one of those very inscriptions of Cyprus reads אשמניעד, To Eshmun'iyed, giving us the same name as that of the king on whose sarcophagus the inscription of Sidon appears ; and considering the well-known intimate relations between Sidon and Cyprus, it seems not unlikely that the same person is intended.[a] And he concludes by saying, "it seems most pro-

---

[a] But from lines 13 and 14 of the Sidonian Inscription there are two Eshmun'iyeds

bable that the era of this inscription is the rebuilding of Sidon, between B.C. 350 and 320; and, as it is dated in the year 14, it may be set down as very near the truth, that it belongs to the latter half of the generation intervening between the destruction of Sidon in the time of Artaxerxes, and its surrender to Alexander."

I here insert Professor Salisbury's interpretation, but which I cannot think is either very literal, or exact:—

" Line 1. In the month Bûl, in the year fourteen, 14, departed the King's king Esh mun'iyed, King of the Sidonians,

(2) Son of King Tabnîth, King of the Sidonians. Speaks King Eshmun'iyed, King of the Sidonians, saying, I have been carried away,

(3) I have been swallowed up (by Sheol) within my covert; there is an end of burthens within my vestibule; and I am reposing in my enclosure and in my sepulchre,

(4) in a place which I have built. My imprecatory prohibition in conjunction with all the kingdoms (is as follows): And let no man open my place of repose,

(5) nor scrutinize, within my place of sleep, how it is with men within the place of sleep, nor take away the enclosure of my place of repose, nor remove

(6) the inner part of my place of repose. If thou enterest my place of repose, although a man who judgest like El, mayest thou hear a judgment by all the kingdoms.

(7) and as for every man who shall open the entrance of my place of repose, would that he who shall take away the enclosure of my place of repose, would that he who shall remove the inner part of my place of repose,

(8) let there not be prepared for any one whomsoever a place of repose in the society of the Rephaim, and let him not be buried in a sepulchre, nor let there be prepared a son for any one whomsoever, and let it be ill with him below.

(9) Let whosoever is refractory have a judgment by the holy gods in conjunction with the kingdom, through the head-rule of the son of the King of the Sidonians over the kingdoms.

´(10) Would that that man who shall open the entrance of my place of repose, would that he who shall take away my enclosure,

(11) I pray that he may have experience of this saying. Would that the man who kills,—let there not be prepared for any one whomsoever a field of sweet peace

(12) in the midst of the high places of the Light, among those living under the sun, after the manner in which I am resting. I have been carried away, I have been swallowed up (by Sheol) within my covert;

(13) there is an end of burthens within my vestibule. As for me, me Eshmun'iyed, King of the Sidonians, son of

(14) King Tabnîth, King of the Sidonians, grandson of King Eshmun'iyed, King of the Sidonians, and my mother Amashtoreth,

(15) priestess of Ashtoreth our lady, the queen, daughter of King Eshmun'iyed, King of the Sidonians, lo, we have built the house of

(16) the gods, the house of judgment, of the land of the sea; and we have established the (house of) Ashtoreth—let the name of the Light be exalted! and it is we

(17) who have built the house of my mother, wide spread, rich, the light of the midst of the hill, and my abode—let the name of the Light be exalted! and it is we who have built the temples of

(18) the gods of the Sidonians, in Sidon, the land of the sea: the temple of Baal-Sidon, and the temple of Ashtoreth—the name of Baal (be exalted)! and until the Lord of Kings shall give to us

(19) the delectableness and beauty of the land of Tyre, the garden of the plain country, we have taken possession for Marathus of the fortifications which she made, and we have added to

---

—grandson and grandfather—mentioned. This name, or, as others have rendered it, Ashmunyyer, Ashmunezer, or Esmunazar, may possibly be a common name of the Kings of Sidon.—J. H.

(20) the citadels of the borders of the land, in order to protect all the Sidonians for ever. My imprecatory prohibition in conjunction with all the kingdoms (is as follows): And let no man open my entrance,

(21) nor pull down my entrance, nor remove the inner part of my place of repose, nor take away the enclosure of my place of repose. Let whosoever is refractory have a judgment

(22) by these holy gods, and let the kingdoms cut him off, him, and the man who kills ; so that it may be ill with them for ever."

The same journal presents (at p. 243-259) another memoir on "The Sidon Inscription, with a Translation and Notes, by Wm. W. Turner." This, as well as the preceding, gives a "Hebrew Transcript" of the twenty-two Phœnician lines; and the translation into English as made by Mr. Turner, and which I have here transcribed, is evidently more accurate, and corresponds better with Dr. Dietrich's German version (which I have translated in my previous communication) than the former by Professor Salisbury.

" (1) In the month Bûl, in the year fourteen, the thirteenth anniversary of the king, King Ashmunyyer, King of the Sidonians,

(2) son of King Tabnith, King of the Sidonians, spake King Ashmunyyer, King of the Sidonians, saying:

(3) I, son of the molten sea-god, have received a wound from the hand of Mithumbenel, I am dead, and am resting in my sepulchre and in my grave,

(4) in the place which I built. My curse to every kingdom and to every man. Let him not open my resting-place, and

(5) let not a son of liars seek that I destroy a son of liars, and let him not remove the sepulchre of my resting-place, and let him not take

(6) the fruit of my resting-place (or) the cover of the resting-place where I sleep. Yea, if men speak to thee, hearken not to thy enticer. Any kingdom or

(7) any man who shall open the cover of my resting-place, or who shall remove the sepulchre of my resting-place, or who shall take the fruit of my

(8) resting-place, let them not have a resting-place with the shades, and let him not be buried in a grave, and let them not have a child, and let it go ill

(9) because of them, and let the holy gods terrify them, even the kingdom with the ruling prince ; wholly cutting

(10) them off, even the kingdom or that man who shall open the cover of my resting-place, or who shall remove

(11) my sepulchre. Neith shall know of that matter. Yea, a man that slayeth they shall have no dwelling in peace. Good is

(12) the judgment from on high ! Behold in life, as I was resting beneath the sun, I, son of the molten sea-god, received a wound

(13) from the hand of Mithumbenel; I, the king, am dead. I, Ashmunyyer, King of the Sidonians, son

(14) of King Tabnith, King of the Sidonians, grandson of King Ashmunyyer, King of the Sidonians, and my mother Emashtoreth,

(15) priestess of Ashtoreth, our lady the Queen, daughter of King Imanyyer, King of the Sidonians, behold we built the temple

(16) of the gods, the temple of Justice, by the sea—and justice is the support of the stars ! There shall they be worshipped; and we

(17) who have built a temple for the peoples, behold our guilt shall be diminished thereby, and there shall my children worship. And we who have built temples

(18) to the god of the Sidonians, in Sidon, the land of the sea, a temple to Baal-Sidon, and a temple to Ashtoreth the glory of Baal, to us Lord Milcom giveth a city

(19) the desire and beauty of the earth, our glorious delight, which is in the dwelling of our deity, to stretch out the fortresses which I have made ; and they have been constructed

(20) on the border of the land, to strengthen all the Sidonians for ever. My curse to every kingdom and to every man :   Let him not open my cover,

(21) and not remove my cover, and let him not take the fruit of my resting-place, and not remove the sepulchre of my resting-place. As for them, those

(22) holy gods shall humble them ; and they shall cut off that kingdom and the man that slayeth, that it may be ill with them for ever."

Mr. Turner notes that the month Bul is interpreted in 1 Kings vi. 38, to be " the eighth month." He also writes the name צמתשא Ashmunyyer, and he adds that " on No. 17 of the inscriptions found by Pococke at Citium is the name Eshmun'-yyed, meaning *quem Æsculapius restituit ;* this might also be read Eshmun'yyer,—*quem Æsculapius suscitavit.*" Eshmun—'Εσμοῦν, צמשא being considered as the Phœnician Esculapius.

On the word Alonim, in the plural, which occurs in my translation from the French, and Elon (or Alon) in the singular, which is seen in that from the German, Mr. Turner observes, " we have here a gratifying confirmation of the genuineness of the Plautian Punic text, this being clearly the alonim of the Pœnulus, on which the scholiast Sisenna remarks, ' *alon* linguâ Punicâ esse *deum.*' "

On the temple of Ashtoreth it is worthy of note, that, " according to Movers (*Die Phœnizier,* i., 602, 605), a large temple of Astarte, in Sidon, is spoken of both by Achilles Tatius, and by Lucian." The usual interpretation of Baal and Astarte is, that the former signifies the sun, and the latter the moon—the two supreme celestial bodies. The last was, from a most early period, the favourite deity at Sidon : the verses 5 and 33, of chap. xi., 1 Kings, especially call " Ashtoreth the goddess of the Zidonians."   And I may state that Mr. Porter, in his new work, *Five Years in Damascus* (vol. ii., p. 106), gives a woodcut of a colossal head of Ashtoreth, bearing a sort of radiated crescent on the forehead, which is sculptured in strong relief, as discovered by him near a small temple of great beauty, at the ruins of Kunawât, the ancient Kenath, situated a little to the west of Gebel Hauran. And concerning the Lord Milcom, mentioned also in 1 Kings, xi. 5-33, he is held by many to be the Mars of Phœnicia, and is identified with Moloch.

The Phœnician inscriptions that have hitherto been found, are separated by Dr. Movers (*vide Phönizien,* in Ersch and Grüber's *Encyklop.,* p. 425) into two classes, or divisions—1st, the older and purer, which includes the legends on the coins of Phœnicia, and the inscriptions from Citium, Marseilles, &c., which also presents the archaic type of Phœnician characters ; and, 2nd, the more corrupt division comprising the inscriptions from Numidia, Sardinia, the northern coast of Africa, &c., and in which the characters and the language itself are mixed, or altered, by barbaric additions, or corruptions, derived from those localities. And Mr. Turner refers the present inscription to the first of these divisions, and he well observes, " its interest is greater, both on this account, and as being the first inscription, properly so called, that has yet been found in Phœnicia proper, which had previously furnished only some coins and an inscribed gem."   And again, he adds, " the inscription before us confirms the opinion, held since the discovery of that of Marseilles, that the Phœnician language in its purity, besides a slight tinge of Aramaism, differs but little from the Biblical Hebrew."

But, with respect to the date of the inscription, Mr. Turner is induced "to place it before the conquest of Alexander, namely, as early as the middle of the 4th century B.C." And whether or not we all agree with him in assigning to it so comparatively recent a period, still we must all agree in "the hope" that more true Phœnician monuments and sarcophagi, inscribed with the names and histories of the Sidonian kings and royal personages, may yet be disinterred from the rock sepulchres and ruins belonging to ancient "Sidon, in the land on the sea."

I remain, dear Sir, yours faithfully,

8, *Serjeant's Inn, London, Nov.* 21, 1855.   JOHN HOGG.

MELITO OF SARDIS AND HIS REMAINS.

DEAR SIR,—In *The Journal of Sacred Literature* for January last there appeared "An Unpublished *Apology*, ascribed to Melito of Sardis." This was succeeded in April, by a second paper entitled "Melito of Sardis and his Remains." The latter included such fragments of the author as I had been able to collect. Having for myself found and copied such of these remains as exist in the Syriac, with no previous knowledge of their existence, I thought proper to put them forth in an English dress. In so doing, I never dreamed of infringing upon the prerogative of another; my only object was to give a plain version of the fragments, with such facts and observations as seemed of sufficient interest to justify their publication. These papers appeared anonymously, and were introduced with no flourish of trumpets, nor ostentation. I find, however, that very recently the Rev. W. Cureton, in his *Spicilegium Syriacum*, has made some very severe animadversions upon myself in reference to these documents.

As I feel that justice has not been done me, I am constrained to take some notice of the matter. I regret any errors into which I have fallen, and am glad to have them corrected, but the tone of Mr. Cureton's observations must be deprecated as unworthy of a man in his position—a man who could afford to be generous to so obscure an individual as myself. What he has said has given to my papers a prominence which they did not aspire to, and an importance which they did not claim.

Not only to myself, but to you and your readers, is it due that I should speak, and I therefore, with your permission, will do so.

Mr. C. says that my translation "appears to be the attempt of some young man who at present has but a very imperfect acquaintance with the language, as well as with what has been done in Syriac literature of late," which is perfectly true. He proceeds, "or he could hardly have been ignorant that my volume was in the press." I was not ignorant that he had printed a volume of selections from the Syriac, but as he had not made its contents public, how can I be blamed for not knowing them? Why, they are culled from no fewer than 604 volumes of Syriac MSS.; and now they appear, they occupy just fifty pages! He adds that he has pointed out some of my errors, but could not undertake to notice them all. This is all very well, but *I* undertake to say that he has left no important variation from his own version unnoticed. He subjoins what he calls "a specimen of this author's version," which consists of six or eight sentences, and parts of sentences, selected from the whole, and consisting of the worst renderings I have given.   And this is what he calls a specimen!   As to what he says about my deserving encouragement, and his advising me to follow Horace's advice, "nonumque prematur in annum," it must go for what it is worth.   I fear, however, that he has not always courted such encouragement, nor followed such advice.

I cannot say that Mr. C. has derived any benefit from the version he so much deprecates, but I recommend your readers to compare the two,— mine with his.   It is certain I received no advantage from his translation; and mine has the merit, if no other, yet of being the first into English. Nor is it unworthy of notice that he has failed to add a single sentence to the Melitonian fragments.   As for the other contents of his work, I have been long acquainted with them all, except a short passage on p. 40 of the translation.   The treatise of Bardesanes in particular was copied and translated by me long ago, although my version is still unpublished.

The fifty references with which Mr. C. honours my translations from Melito may, for convenience, be divided into three classes.

1. Those in which he is himself in error.
2. Those in which my errors can be readily accounted for.
3. Those in which I am clearly and unaccountably wrong.

All these variations are not of equal consequence, and indeed many of them are of so little moment, that they may be omitted in my examination.   All together, they fail to weaken faith in the general accuracy of my translation, and to shew that I did not do the very little which I professed.   If every instance of free translation, including that of active verbs by passives, or even of masculines by feminines, and singulars by plurals, and their converse, is to be set down as a proof of my ignorance, and a grammatical blunder, Mr. C. will not himself escape the charges which he has heaped upon me, as I mean to shew before I conclude.

I now proceed to consider a few of the cases.

1. Those passages in which Mr. Cureton himself makes erroneous statements.   My references will be to those pages of his volume upon which the notes occur.

P. 86. "Evidently not knowing the difference between ܣܘܠܩܐ and ܣܠܩ."   This difference is not uniform, as appears from Acts xiii. 39, where the word has the sense which I have given to it here.

P. 88. "Revenue," thus Mr. C. renders the word which M. Renan and myself (and with no small reason, for it is the regular plural of a common Syriac word,) have translated "decrees."   But Mr. C. makes it a pure Latin word, *fiscum*.

Ib. "Acte."   So Mr. C., where I have "Ecate," I knew, of course, that Attica was anciently called *Acte*, but rejected the meaning, because of the pointing which the word has in the MS., and which, here and elsewhere, Mr. C. has *omitted* in his printed text.

P. 90. "While he was hunting wild boars."   Such is the rendering here given of a passage of some difficulty.   Mr. C. has here made *two* or *three* mistakes for the *one* in the MS.   There we read plainly ܒܚܙܝܪܐ

with the pointing, by which, no doubt, by a slip of the pen, ܣܵܪ݁ܕܵ is meant, but our unerring translator turns it into ܣܵܐܕ, or ܣܵܐܕ, "hunting!" He then, without reason, save that the story seemed to require it, translated ܡ̇ܪܘ "wild boars," instead of deriving it from the same root as ܡ̣ܪ, *a furrow*, and giving it some such meaning as "wounds," which I have done. And lastly, he renders ܣܒܠܒ ܚܡ ܡ "while he was hunting." Surely I have seldom done worse.

Ib. "Nuh." The MS. reads plainly ܟܘܣ. Here again Mr. C. has omitted the pointing, which is what I have given; and he has made that *plain* which is not so. I therefore refuse to endorse this rendering of the word,

P. 91. "Cuthbi. The MS. reads most plainly ܟܚܟܘܠܐ." In the MS. *two* vowel points are given: Mr. C. prints but one of them; and the final *yud* is so small, as to be almost imperceptible.

Ib. "The secret parts." This is my rendering of a word which Mr. C. translates "passage." Hear him: "It committed violence and attacked the passage of every one who was passing by in all that place." Now compare mine: "Which injured and afflicted the secret parts of every one who passed through all the place." Judge which is the more rational. I read the word ܟܡ̣ܙܘܠ, but Mr. C. makes it ܟܚܡܙܘܠ. An examination of the MS. has failed to convince me that the tautology and feebleness of Mr. C.'s version is correct; and I maintain my own on other grounds.

P. 92. "Impalpable." Here Mr. C. commits as stupid a blunder as any of mine. He says ܟܣܐܡ݁ܪ݁ܣ is "*by transposition for* ܟܣܐܡ݁, *from the root* ܪ݁ܐܡܣ, *and not from* ܪ݁ܐܡܣ, *as M. Renan has taken it in translating 'nec commovetur.'*" Surely the "veriest tyro" must know that no such transposition could occur. And any one may see that "immutable" is as appropriate an epithet of divinity as "impalpable." My reading is wrong, from an error in my copy; but M. Renan is correct.

P. 96. "That we may prove to your love." Of this very singular idiom I was ignorant, when I wrote my translation, but I have since met with another example of it in an account of some Persian martyrs who suffered about A.D. 524, and which begins thus: "Again we make known *to your love.*" So far I give up my version; but what right has Mr. C. to insinuate what he does, in saying, "The veriest tyro in Syriac surely knows that ܣܘܒܠ means 'love,' from the root ܟܚܣ?" ܣܘܒܠ also means a "debt," and then that for which one is condemned; and hence my rendering. Cf. Col. ii. 14.

Ib. "Meliton, Bishop of the city of Attica." Apart from the absurdity of the "*city* of Attica," which Mr. C. very lamely endeavours to account for, there are some other things in the note, which require to be pointed out. He says that I "assume" that there is some confusion between the names of Meliton and Meletius. I shall shew in the next note that my assumption has the best of reasons for it. He asserts again that a Syrian writer would no more make a blunder in spelling Antioch, than an educated Englishman in spelling London, when, in his own extract from Eusebius it is written both ܠܝܘܬܝܐ and ܠܝܘܬܝܐ, yet both cannot be correct.[a] Again, he says Meletius could hardly have been generally styled Bishop of Antioch. But he was; and such is he called, not merely by modern writers such as Cave, &c., but he is so styled in his funeral oration by Gregory of Nyssa, both in the Greek original and in the Syriac translation in our Museum.[b] Fourthly, he says "the word Attica is unquestionably right," but my next note will shew that it is unquestionably wrong. Fifthly, he says Meletius of Sebastopolis was present at the Council of Nice,[c] and refers to Valesius on Euseb. vii. 32, in support of his assertion. Now it happens that Valesius quotes this statement from Philostorgius, *merely to deny it*, on the faith of Athanasius.

P. 98. "B. H. C., in support of his assertion above, has not hesitated to turn *Meliton* into *Melitus*, and *Itica* or *Ittica* into Antioch." Indeed: Mr. C. here unwittingly does me a favour; he produces a case in which the name of the "great city Antioch" is spelled wrong. The fact is that this fragment of Melito occurs in two places, with different headings. Mr. C. has given one, and I have given the other, of which *he was ignorant*; I therefore give the heading of it, for his satisfaction, and for yours.

ܘܪܡܐ ܠܐ ܣܟܝܠܘܬ ܐܘܣܒܣ ܐܝܟܕܘ ܡܟܝܠ ܕܝܠܐ.

I shall not add a word of comment upon this, but only say that Mr. C. will find it in *Add. MSS.*, No. 14,532, *f.* 12, *a.*, and cannot translate it differently from me.

I have passed over a number of minor matters, such as Mr. C.'s gratuitous guesses for me, and his putting "Dionysius" for Dionysus, in his translation, and proceed to the next class of offences, viz.:

2. Those in which my errors can be readily accounted for.

For the sake of brevity I shall not particularize many of these—not that I am unwilling to do so, but to avoid being tedious. In several instances a single letter in a word has been variously read in the MS. by Mr. C. and myself. In some such cases I am evidently wrong; but this must be put down to the account of my eyesight, which, at the time I made these extracts, was injured by over-application. Again, errors have

[a] As it respects erroneous spelling, the very volume from which the last extract is taken (No. 14,533) will furnish a score of examples in the case of proper names. And I may remark that in my researches into these MSS. I have met with such extraordinary instances of bad spelling, that I have concluded that some of the MSS. were either written by men ignorant of the language, or by mere copyists, who knew how to write, but not how to read. Mr. C. himself maintains that the scribe thought Attica was a city! yet does not believe he could misspell Antioch!

[b] See *Add. MSS.*, No. 12,165.

[c] I have a copy of a most ancient list of those who were present at the Council of Nice. The MS. is in the Nitrian Collection, and was written between A.D. 491 and 501. The name of Meletius is not contained in it. The Meletius whose name is connected with the Council of Nice, was Meletius of Lycopolis, founder of the Meletian sect.

arisen from the hasty manner in which my transcript was written; and in translating from it, I have confounded similar forms and letters, but I put this to the account of my handiwork, which is so far defective. Again, in copying the original, in some cases a single word, and in a few instances a whole line, was dropped, owing to ὁμοιοτελευτα, a thing to which few transcribers are strangers. All the cases under this head resemble one or other of these, with the exception of such as involve conjecture, in which Mr. C. has been sometimes more successful than myself.[d]

I have already denied that free translations are errors, in a version such as mine professed to be. I now give two or three examples.

P. 86. "Light [without envy is given to all of us that we may see thereby; and if, when light] has arisen upon us, any one closeth his eyes that he may not see, his course is to the ditch." I have put in brackets the words which I had omitted in my copy. The difference of rendering at the close is a matter of opinion.

Ib. "That also the Sybil has said respecting them." This is a passage which Mr. C. says I have rendered in a marvellous manner. I leave this, and simply observe, first, that this is a passage in which my conjecture failed and Mr. C.'s succeeded, if it be a conjecture; secondly, that he grossly errs in saying ﺟﺎﻣ could not come from the verb ﺟﻟ, because close to it in the dictionary we have ﺟﻣﺎﻋ from ﺟﻣﻟ. My rendering of the verb is better than Mr. C.'s parsing of the sentence. I rendered the verb as indefinite, quite as grammatically as some others would have done in like cases. The verb ﺍﺿﻳﺏ in Rev. ii. 13 will partly meet my case; and the recognized rule of rendering neuter verbs sometimes as passives, may also help it.

P. 88. "Of such as worship." Here I mistook my own copy, but not as Mr. C. supposes.

P. 91. "Thracian Magus." This was an unfortunate guess, where no conjecture was needed.

Ib. "Hadran." Here, as in the case of Zuradi, my copy was defective. Mr. C. gives me a rebuke for rendering the former "they honour;" but I shew below that he has done the same, or worse, with no excuse.

P. 96. "While he was esteemed a servant he denied not the worship." I have here made a blunder in translation, by overlooking the fact that ﺣﺏ takes the preposition ﺏ after it; and I read ﺟﺣﺑﺍ for ﺣﺻﺍ.

P. 97. "Thou wast reclining on a soft bed." This is one of my ugliest blunders, and yet one of the simplest. I read in my MS. ﻧﺣﺳﺍ for ﺟﺣﺳﺯ.

These may suffice as specimens, and there are more like them, but I think it will be seen that my error of errors lay in not reading my printed proof by the original MS. I now proceed to the last class.

4. Those in which I am clearly and unaccountably wrong. Of these

---

[d] If Mr. C. will allow me, I will make one guess for him—it is that the "Hadibite," or rather "Hadibitess," of p. 44 means an inhabitant of *Adiabene.* The initial ﺏ is no objection, as we have Aleppo, &c., formed in a similar manner.

there are but few, as, for instance, where I have put "shall be made alive" for "shall lament," "crucifixion" for "cross," "shearer" for "flock," and "sun" for "earth," and some more upon which I need not dwell. My readers will understand how possible such errors are.

Wherein I am wrong I freely own my errors; and while I ask the forbearance of your readers, I wish them to understand that I mean to do better another time. For the present, I can only say that what little I have done I have done alone, without encouragement, honour, or remuneration, and almost without notice. Mr. Cureton is the first to reward me for what I have done. Therefore, as my Mæcenas, I hereby commit his name to posterity; and as the veteran who, having borne the heat and burden of the day, "encourages" the "young man" to enter upon the ripened field and gather in the grain!

Here I could willingly close, but the truth must be told, that even Mr. C. himself has committed a few small blunders, and some large ones. I now allude to places in which there is no personal reference to me, but where I meet with illustrations of the adage, *humanum est errare*. These I would never have pointed out, but as I have been put into one scale, Mr. C. must go into the other. For his translations in general, they are not always more readable than my own; and in individual cases he has often given a dubious rendering, and sometimes a positively erroneous one. Not that his errors are like mine, either in magnitude or importance; they are like the sins of the saints, "splendid sins," happy deviations merely for the sake of variety! However, such as they are I present your readers with a few, as "specimens" of this Rhadamanthine translation.

Pref. p. vi. "He has made use of it as *a means* of concealing his own error, and took it from the doctrine of the Church." Read "He used it as an *artifice* to cover his error, and took it *from us*, from the doctrine of the Church." We also have the participle ܣܘܒܠ rendered "assumes," *i. e.*, *takes up*, but the word means what is *laid down;* to say nothing of the affectation of strange forms of verbs and nouns which meet us here.

P. 1. "He created *mankind*, and willeth that you should do that which you are commanded." Here "men" is rendered "mankind," and the words "by this" are *omitted*. *Ib.*, "Holily," read "righteously;" "give me an answer," read "return me a reply."

P. 2. "Draweth near to the way of truth without obstinacy needeth not be ashamed, because he will certainly give great pleasure," read "draweth near to the way of truth without *contentiousness*, is not condemned and put to shame." *Ib.*, "participate with thee," read "agree with thee." *Ib.*, "we, for our part, shall have spoken without any ill-feeling," read, "we utter our own (sentiments) without envy." *Ib.*, "any other man," for "another man."

P. 3. "a *ship* which another man steereth," read "a *chariot* which another driveth." So, just after, for "the ship, whether it be well steered and guided," read, "the chariot, whether it be well *drawn* and driven." *Ib.* (and many times elsewhere), the simple word "freedom" is rendered "freewill."[e] *Ib.*, "creatures," read "things."

---

[e] It really means "liberty," as opposed to "necessity." And in this sense Bardesanes uses the two words ܚܐܪܘܬܐ and ܥܒܕܘ in this treatise.

P. 5. "Their force of energy," read "force and precision."

P. 7 (and frequently), the verb اِذْنَ *to desire* is rendered by the word "pleased." *Ib.*, "he is not pleased to be seen by every man," for "he desires to be seen by no man." *Ib.*, "we ought plainly to understand that the *unrestrained ardour* of love is called lust," read "plainly we are bound to understand that the *counterfeit* of love is called lust." *Ib.*, for "if all men acted with *the* one mind," read, "if all men cherished one opinion," or "were of one mind."

P. 9. "in the eating," read "in meats," the word being a feminine-noun plural. P. 10, for "abandoned," read "contemned;" for "in one will," read "in one mind;" for "a vain plea" read "a vain word;" and for "practise deceit, or poisoneth, or curseth," read "practiseth deceits, or is a poisoner, or a curser." P. 11, "Fortune." Throughout سِلْهَا is thus rendered, when Fate, or necessity, would be a more literal and appropriate term. *Ib.*, "they are true, because men speak after the *fashion* which they see," read "*Now* they are true, because men speak according to the *phenomena* which they witness." *Ib.*, "they mistake," read "they lie." P. 12, "do not inherit," for "do not retain."

P. 13 presents us with this: "Fortune is an order of procession which is given to the Powers and Elements by God, and according to this procession and order, intelligences are changed by their coming down to be with the soul, and souls are changed by their coming down to be with the body, &c." I beg you to observe that here Mr. C. has some of my worst mistakes. He renders the words سِلْهَا مَخْدَ "intelligences are changed." Here, first, مَخْدَ is not "intelligences;" مَخْدَ might have had that meaning. Then we have a verb (if it be a verb) in the feminine made to agree with the aforesaid noun, which is masculine, and followed by a masculine pronoun. And again, this verb, which *must* be active, from its form (which would be *pael*), is rendered as a passive. Moreover, the same word and the same form of it, is, in the *next* clause of the same sentence, translated as a feminine, but again as a passive. I might repeat what Mr. C. has elsewhere said of me, that if سِلْهَ be a verb it is the *first* plural "we change," and not "they are changed." My copy of the treatise reads سِلْهَ مَخْدَ, but I have not verified it, and I shall leave Mr. C. to consider his version of this passage, and ask whether the whole of it does not require revision. In the same sentence, "bodies" is rendered "the body"—a plural by a singular; a little lower, for "hinders" read "afflicts;" and correct the strange idiom and defective translation, "the pleasure of the both heads."

P. 14. "these sects" for "this sect." P. 15. "to believe," the text has "to be persuaded"—active put for passive. P. 17. "Laws of the Brahmins, &c.," and "Another law which is in India." These inscriptions are in the wrong place in the MS., but Mr. C. here restores them without a remark. Lower down he allows a similar case of error to remain, and does not see it.

P. 18. "The country of the Parthians and in Egypt." Here Mr. C.

mistranslates ܩ‍‍ܰ‍ܕ by Parthians, who are called ܩ‍‍ܳ‍ܕ‍ܩ just below; and he omits ܩ‍ܰ‍ܩܳ‍ܩ "And in Parthia." He has thus lost a country, but I cannot now stop to attempt its recovery.[f] On p. 21, we have "adulterers" for "adulteresses." P. 22, "laws of"—the MS. reads, "laws of the Greeks." *Ib.*, "laws of the Orientals." Mr. C. has not observed that this inscription is in the wrong place, and should come after l. 10. P. 28, "For the purpose of deceit," read "for an instrument (*or* means) of deceit." P. 29, "But it is known, because those men are distant from the intercourse of men they are many in the manners of their living." This is Mr. C.; Bardesanes says, "But the thing is known, because these men are removed from intercourse with many men by their modes of living;" which at least has the credit of being intelligible.

P. 31, "In Syria and in Edessa men used to cut off their foreskins to Tharatha, but when Abgar the king was converted to Christianity, he commanded that every one that cut off his foreskin should have his hand cut off. And from that day, and up to this hour, no man cutteth off his foreskin in the country of Edessa." Here we have a version which looks baldly literal, but such is not the fact. First, ܩ‍‍ܰ‍ܕ‍ܩ is the word which we have seen above I read in Melito, and rendered "secret parts;" its meaning is not *præputium*, but *virilitas*, and hence *virilia*. Secondly, that *mutilation* is meant and not *circumcision*, is plain from many authorities, *e. g.*, Arnobius, (b. v., c. 6, &c.;) Lucian, *De dea Syra*, c. 15, and Sallust. Phil., *De diis et mundo*, pp. 14, 84, &c. Thirdly, instead of "Abgar the king was converted to Christianity," Bardesanes merely says, "Abgar the king believed."

The previous are a portion of those I have noted in Bardesanes alone, and may serve as a "specimen" of what the book contains. I shall omit the rest of the volume with a remark or two, on as many points. Why does Mr. C. translate the word "passover" by that of *Easter ?* For "its novelty and strangeness," p. 61, he has "its recent and strange production." "Heard *not* the voice of the Sirens:" *not* is omitted from the Syriac text. Why at p. 65 is ܩ‍‍ܰ‍ܩ‍ܩ translated "forgotten," a meaning which the word has not? and why, at p. 70, is "hunger" translated "thirst?" At p. 73, he renders ܩ‍‍ܰ‍ܩ‍ܩ "thy part in the world;" the MS. probably reads ܩ‍‍ܰ‍ܩ‍ܩ "thy labour." At p. 74 "because of the laws," is put for "because of the *new* laws ;" and at p. 76 we read, "For we have shewn our truth that we have no vice in an empire," a translation which is certainly wrong, and gives no good sense. The sentence is not plain, but I suggest that the writer means to say, "we have shewn our true opinion, or truly, that we find no fault with the government, but are content to remain in the kingdom and to promote its welfare."

There are a few passages in Melito to which I might refer, but the length to which I have gone deters me, and I submit those which I have

---

[f] *Parthin* or *Parthyin* here is probably *Parthyene*, named by Pliny as a region, but I cannot speak positively.

pointed out to the opinion of such as are qualified to judge. More especially am I moved to this, by the fact that I have a few more little things of a different description to lay before you.

When Mr. C. published the *Corpus Ignatianum*, why did he leave out of it several Ignatian fragments of which I have a note, and to which he has made no reference?

When Mr. C. furnished Chevalier Bunsen with a list of the fragments of Hippolytus contained in the Syriac MSS., why did he mention but a fourth of the entire number?

When Mr. C. published his *Spicilegium*, why did he omit one fragment of Bardesanes which I have, however brief? This fragment is headed "The names of the signs of the Zodiac according to Bardesanes."

In my notes on *Add. MS.*, No. 17,192, I have met with this fol. on 282, "History of the holy and beloved Man John the Evangelist, who preached and taught and baptized, *by the help* of our Lord Jesus Christ, in the city of Ephesus. Mr. Cureton has "with the *baptism*" for "with the help."[g]

When Mr. C. published the *third* part of the *Ecclesiastical History of John of Ephesus*, why did he not say, that besides the two volumes mentioned by him, others contain a large portion at least, of the *second* part of John's History? In fact seven or eight of the volumes contain large extracts from his writings, yet Mr. C. makes no mention of any but two.

I now wish it to be understood, that not many more *discoveries* are to be made in these MSS., because, with the exception of liturgies and some others, I have gone over every accessible volume, and made a note of its contents, and of the authors, down to the minutest fragments. I have the names of some two hundred authors, and references to several thousands of treatises and parts of treatises contained in this noble collection.

The foregoing observations will shew that it is not obscure and anonymous authors alone who err.

"Indignor, quandoque bonus dormitat Homerus,"

and the more because in this instance, when dealing with me, Mr. C. has forgotten the rules of literary courtesy. He who is himself conscious that he may err, should be lenient towards the failings of another. To remind Mr. Cureton of this has been my aim, whether I have succeeded or not, time will shew. Of this, however, I am sure, that in this case less of honour will redound to the critic for his asperity, than of dishonour, while the object of his remarks will no doubt be stimulated to greater exertions to secure accuracy and completeness in future, with regard to everything he does.

In conclusion, I again express my regret that so many faults have crept into my contributions, and offer to you and your readers my "apology" for the same. You will, I am sure, give publicity to my reply, and I shall be content to abide by the decision of yourself and of

---

[g] See *Corpus Ign.*, Intr., p. xxxiii.

all who can enter into the merits of the case. One consolation I have, yea, a second, that in what I did I never sought to benefit myself but the cause of truth, and in what I now say I seek no more than a fair and honest representation of facts.[A]

I remain, dear Sir, yours very truly,
B. H. C.

London, November 22, 1855.

AGE OF DAVID.

DEAR SIR,—In page 41 of the April number of *The Journal of Sacred Literature,* the following passages occur:—"We cannot assign a less number than seventy as the years of David's life;" and "presuming him to have been from thirty to thirty-five years old when he ascended the throne." The writer of the article in which these passages occur, appears to have overlooked the precise information contained in 2 Samuel, v. 4: "David was thirty years old when he began to reign, and he reigned forty years."

I am, &c.

Southgate, Sept. 24, 1855.
H. B.

LORD ARTHUR HERVEY "ON THE GENEALOGIES OF OUR LORD."

DEAR SIR,—Will you permit me to point out to your correspondent, Lord A. Hervey, the following particulars in the descent of the family of *Caleb,* who, as the father of Salmon and the houses of *Hebron, Bethlehem,* and other families of the tribe of *Judah,* affords a fair parallel *but in the way of contrast,* to that of *Ram,* the father of Salmon, and the house of David. Both families are from Pharez, the first-born of the two sons of Judah, for of his house there were three branches: *Jerameel,* the eldest; *Ram,* the second; *and Caleb,* the third and youngest.

The descent of this Caleb down to the time of the exodus is very plain; viz.,—Pharez, Hezron, Caleb, in three descents; by whose second wife Ephrath came Hur, Uri, Bezaleel, in three descents, all recognized in the early events of the wilderness. From Hur also came a younger *Caleb,* who must have been the faithful SPY, and called, in that history, the son of Jephunneh, though that was certainly a patronymic of the

---

[A] I wish it to be distinctly understood that I have not pointed out all the errors into which Mr. C. has fallen; and yet it is due to him to say that his errors do not prevent his version from being generally faithful, any more than mine lead to the same result in my own case. I have no wish to pluck even a leaf from the laurels of Mr. C., who merits all he wears.

house, and belonged equally to his grandfather, the son of Hezron, as we may see in 1 Chron. iv. 15.

The lines of descent of these two "*Calebs*" are shewn in the subjoined table, side by side with the "Legal Genealogy" of "*Ram*," upon which Lord A. Hervey builds his argument, and from whose stock came the house of David. The "line" of the eldest brother Jerameel, will be noticed separately hereafter;—

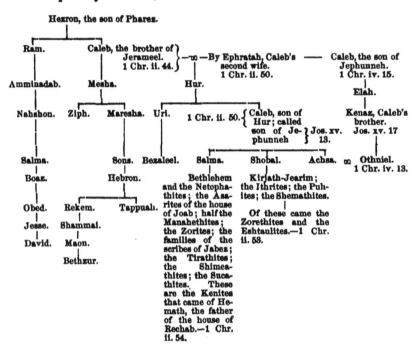

These genealogies bring Hebron, Bethlehem, and Kirjath Jearim on the same descending line, and denote the settlement of those families in the land of Canaan in that generation. The line above them is that of Salmon and Salmon, in the two genealogies of Ram and Caleb; and these, we may observe also, were the contemporaries with Bezaleel, the artist of the tabernacle.

Then will your correspondent be content to take the Salmon of this descent for the same person as the Salmon of the Book of Ruth, which is there counted next in legal ascent from Boaz. The legal genealogy, it is true, puts them in that connexion; but *Boaz bought the* inheritable right in the heiress of the youngest branch of the three sons of Hezron, from her nearer relative; which could only apply to a descendant in the eldest line; Boaz himself being of the second. It is impossible to say how the legal descent would be framed in such a case; and it is obviously not by the natural descent.

It will not fail to strike your correspondent that the descents, both from the principal line of Caleb, and from that which comes through

Hur, break off simultaneously at the names of Hebron, Bethlehem, Kirjath-Jearim and the other old families of the Holy Land, and denote as plainly as possible, by their immediate position below the line of *Bezaleel,* that the settlement of those houses, as they were found existing in the time of David (down to which the genealogies certainly reach) took their origin at that period.   For could these names of towns have sprung up after, or collaterally even with that of Boaz, who was the son of Salmon in the fourth ascending line above David, as the legal genealogy represents it ?

In the history of Ruth the whole generic description of Elimelech, who was of the generation next above Boaz, and so on a line with Salmon, *refers to his being a native of these old settled towns,* and the iteration of that description forbids the possible application of it in a proleptical way.   The story says "that Elimelech the husband of Naomi, was a man of Bethlehem-Judah;" and of his wife and sons, "that they were Ephrathites of Bethlehem-Judah" (Ruth i. 1, 2).

There is not a doubt that this account was meant to be strictly descriptive of the family stock of Elimelech, to shew that he was of the house of Hezron, through Caleb, by his second wife Ephrath; and this designation was by reference to his abode.   The family must, therefore, have belonged to *old settlements* of those names at that date; and they must have been new ones at the date of that Salmon who was the contemporary of Bezaleel.   All the names of these lines about the age of *Bezaleel* are, in effect, the names of the old settlements of the land of Judah, and bespeak the period of their establishment, as plainly as the names of Virginia and Carolina do the time, when those provinces of the new world were first settled upon.   *Ziph, Maresha, Gazez, Tappuah,* and *Maon,* all found in this pedigree, are, like the names I have already quoted, the names of towns in the lot of Judah, mentioned in their first settlement by Joshua (chap. xv. 35, 44, 47, 54, and 55).

There may be, perhaps, some little difficulty in these genealogies, arising from the designation of the elder Caleb as the son of Jephunneh, and the father of Achsa, the daughter who was given as a reward to Othniel for the capture of the city of Kirjath-Sephar (Josh. xv. 16).   For while the history of the spies calls that Joshua, who was one of the spies, the son of Jephunneh (Numb. xiii. 6), the genealogies of the 1st Chron. designates the elder Caleb by the same descent; as appears in the annexed pedigree of Othniel.   But the generations are fixed in their position by the notice in Joshua, "that Othniel was the son of Kenaz, who was the brother of Caleb, Achsa's father."   It is quite impossible that Caleb, the son of Hezron, should be that Caleb, that is so spoken of; for Hezron was one of the 70 persons of Jacob's family, who accompanied the patriarch into Egypt, and his son could not have had a daughter to give in marriage at an interval from that event of 265 years.

As to the name of Achsa, it is quite probable it belonged to the daughters of both generations; yet the elder Caleb, it is not impossible, might have been alive at the exodus, for he was in the fourth generation from Jacob, the parent stock which came into Egypt; and the promise of

God to Abraham was that the children should be brought out of their bondage in the fourth generation (Gen. xv. 16). Those descents will coincide with the family of Moses and Aaron in the following way :—

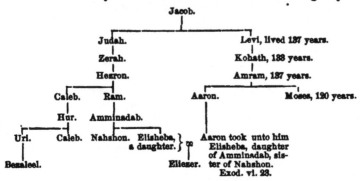

In this table the younger Caleb, Nahshon the captain of the host of Judah, Elisheba the wife of Aaron, and Uri the father of Bezaleel the artist are all upon the same line of descent.

But this Nahshon, who was the ruler of the Host of Judah in the exodus, is taken by Lord A. Hervey as the natural grandfather of Boaz, because the "legal descents of his line" so represent the genealogical succession of the headship of the house. The other genealogies, however, shew this to be impossible. Those I have instanced indicate very plainly that between the generations of the wilderness and the more recent progenitors of the house of David a great chasm must have existed, sufficient to *allow of the establishment of the townships of Judah* as *patronymial names* by *long prescription;* and if such is inferrible from these "*generic descents,*" the same is shewn distinctly in the descent of the eldest son of Hezron, Jerameel, whose generations down to David number 24; for they are as follow :—

Judah, 1; Pharez, 2; Hezron, 3; Jerameel, 4; Onan, 5: Shammai, 6; Nadab, 7; Appaius, 8; Ishi, 9; Sheshan, 10; Ahlai, a daughter, given to Jarha the Egyptian, 11. From them Attai, 12; Nathan, 13; Zabad, 14; Ephlal, 15; Obed, 16; Jehu, 17; Azariah, 18; Helez, 19; Eleazah, 20; Sisamai, 21; Shellum, 22; Jekamiah, 23; Elishama, 24; —all successive descents (1 Chron. ii. 85—41).

Taking 23 of these generations as extending from the entering into Egypt to the death of David, at the common estimate of 30 years to a generation, they will extend to 690 years; while the chronology shews an interval of 691 years.

I would beg to point out to your correspondent also, the coincidence in point of time of the name of Salma in the two descents of Ram and Caleb, and that all the "*local names*" are in immediate sequence to that generation, both in the principal and collateral branches of the house of Caleb; and I would ask whether these things do not indicate a course of descent in the "*Legal Genealogies,*" different altogether from the natural descent; and governed by some laws of computation which are not known to us, but are clearly marked in their effects.

Upon this point perhaps I may be permitted to observe, that it has always appeared to myself, that the legal genealogies have had their entire foundation upon the chronological periods: that their object was to mark the intervals of time between the epochs through a series of descents, which had a specific value; and so, by the sums of such descents recording the intervals. By way of illustration, suppose the laws of "legal succession," genealogically, in that dispensation that lay between the exodus and the temple, recognized generations of 70 years, according to the full period of life mentioned by David; then, for a period of 700 years, the genealogists must mark the distance of the epochs by a suitable course of the generations somehow concocted, whatever the number of the natural descents. To do this it seems quite accordant to the reason of the matter, that they should select the required generations from the two extremes of the natural line, so as to make sure of the root and last branches in their proper association. But this hypothetical case is that which exactly answers the reality we are considering: for the period between Judah and the death of David is about 700 years, and the generations are ten.

The object of these "legal tables" was evidently threefold;—the families, the epochs, and the intervals;—and the system which is thus manifested, appears sufficient to keep all these in a proper and true association. The system is the same as that of the Roman indictions, and was intended to preserve a true register of time, by counting by large cycles instead of by a mere succession of years; only the Jewish reckoning is made subservient to the preservation of the genealogical connexions of the houses of that people. There has always appeared to myself great difficulty in these legal genealogies; and before this idea as to their formation presented itself, they appeared more as the shreds of the real successions, than the full and genuine pedigrees of descent by the natural line; they dip and are lost, if I may so say, like the stratifications of the earth; so that the croppings out of families appeared in different ages, without any apparent recognition of the intermediate generations. In the case before us, we have one such outcropping of the royal race in the age of the Exodus and the four descents of Ram, Amminadab, Nahshon, and Salma; and another outcropping of the same family in the age of the Judges, in the four descents of Boaz, Obed, Jessi and David; the intermediate descents being hid from our cognizance by a superincumbent history.

If we try this system of "*Periodic Generations*" by the genealogies of St. Matthew, we shall find it answer, if we vary the years of the generations or the "*Time of Life*." Thus the generations from Abraham to David, says that Evangelist, are 14: count by 70 years to a generation and to the epochs of the two extremes, and there will be 70×14 or 980 years; and 980 years is the true interval between Abraham and David; taking the year B.C. 1017 as the last of David, being the year he established the foundation of the New Temple by the purchase of its site from Aurauna the Jebusite, and probably the year before Solomon's adoption.

It cannot be denied that a change took place in the "*Time of Life*" of these patriarchal families at the period of the Egyptian captivity, and the

epoch of the Exodus. Whether the other families of the earth lived to
such great ages as the Elders of Israel, may be doubted; for the address
of Jacob to Pharaoh is framed in language, that evinces a distinction in
his own family in that respect,—" The days of the years of my pilgrimage
are an hundred and thirty years : few and evil have the days of the years
of my life been, and have not attained to the days of the years of the life
of my fathers" (Gen. xlvii. 9). The ages of all the families of Levi down
to Moses betoken the continuance of that gift of life, which was bestowed
upon the family of Noah after the flood: "Yet his age shall be 120
years " (Gen. vi. 3), as may be seen by the preceding pedigree of that
house, where the ages are marked. The 24 descents from Hezron,
through his eldest son Jerameel, shew however, as plainly, that the long-
lived patriarchal race had entirely vanished in that family; while the
"legal generations" of that age were, as we have shewn, certainly of 70
years; for that is indicated both by the 10 generations quoted from
Ruth of the descents from Pharez to David; and by the 14 generations
quoted from St. Matthew, of the descents from Abraham to David. The
natural generations had at that time degraded 30 years as the 24 generations of Jerameel indicate, which fill up the interval by that cycle.

A reference to this change in the " Time of Life " may perhaps enable
us to explain the anomaly of the promise to Abraham ' that his seed should
return out of Egypt in the fourth generation,' in connexion with the two
series of years assigned to the length of that bondage; namely, the 430
years, to which period the Book of Exodus affirms, the sojourning of the
people in Egypt had extended (Ex. xii. 41), and the 215 years, which was
the actual period of the captivity. For the 430 years undoubtedly refers
to the visit of Abraham and Lot into Egypt in the year B.C. 1921; from
which some relics of their faith may have remained behind, which probably
formed the root of these " mixed multitudes," which we are told accompanied the house of Israel out of Egypt. These were the Lean-to's or
sects of the true household, and formed part of the " *Hosts of the
Lord*," by which name the people of the Exodus are denominated.

But this 430 years must not extend beyond the fourth generation;
for such is the promise; " in the fourth generation they shall come hither
again." Then, taking the Noahic term of life of 120 years as applicable
to this dispensation, three full generations will extend to 360 years; but
the interval between 1921 and the Exodus is 430 years: wherefore 70
years of that term would have fallen beyond the three full generations, and
so been within the fourth. But the entrance into Canaan 40 years afterwards would also still be within the fourth generation; for that would fall
in the 470th year from B.C. 1921, whilst four full generations would extend to 480 years. So that, the return would be 10 years short of four full
generations and fairly within the fourth, according to the promise.

Applied to the shorter period of the actual servitude or 215 years, plus
the 40 years in the wilderness, the promise can only be brought within the
fourth generation, by taking the shorter term of life of 70 years mentioned
by the Psalmist. For three full generations of 70 years will amount to
210 years; so that the coming out of Egypt would be 5 years within the
fourth, the captivity being 215 years: while the entering into Canaan 40

years afterwards, would be 45 years towards the 70 of the fourth generation; leaving 25 years wanting of the four full generations. But 25 years was the period occupied by Joshua in settling the tribes in their new inheritance, and so would reach to the last year of the fourth generation, in which last year the complete return of the children would be effected.

The first fourteen generations of St. Matthew's genealogy count, as we have seen, by these cycles of 70 years, and by that order of counting fill up the historical interval. But it is clear the other two series of generations cannot count by that "time of life:" for the whole period from the last year of David to our Saviour's birth is only 1017 years, and to his death 1050. The "*time of life*" must therefore have suffered another shortening in that interval; for St. Matthew states that from David to the carrying away into Babylon "was 14 generations." But from the year B.C. 1017, when David built the altar of Araunah, to the year B.C. 597, when the captivity was about the mean point of being effected, is only 420 years; and if that is the interval of fourteen generations, it will give 30 years to a generation; for 30×14 is 420. And from the carrying away into captivity to Christ, says the same evangelist, is fourteen generations; which, counted from the last epoch, would be 597. But as that sum cannot be divided by fourteen it will not answer the hypothesis; yet added to the 33 years of our Lord's life, it will amount to 630 years, which will divide by 14 into the number 45.

But the sabbatical period of the captivity may perhaps be counted in this series; for in the denunciation of the captivity it is said, that it should be in one of its phases; "that the land might fulfil its sabbaths so long as it lay desolate" (Lev. xxvi. 34; 2 Chron. xxxvi. 31). The 70 years sabbatical captivity may therefore be presumed to count with the week unsabbatized of the 420 years; which would be 6 days of 70 years, and added to the 420 years will make 490; and so coincide with the 70 weeks of Daniel. But there is another 70 years of captivity, which cannot be counted in this way, and may be omitted *in toto* as a true captive period; and so not within the genealogies. For we find that the period from the captivity, B.C. 597, to the year B.C. 457, which was the year when Ezra made the people put away their strange wives, and properly closed the events of the captivity and its penal separation from God, is exactly 140 years, or two 70 years; and from that year to the death of our Lord is the prophetic 7 weeks of Daniel, or 490 years, viz., $457 + 33 = 490$, and this seems to answer all the legal conditions, as far as we may collect them from the Levitical Law.

There is a simpler way of putting the case, however, by saying that from the year David built the inaugural altar of the temple, to the death of our Lord, that is, from B.C. 1017 to A.D. 33, there is an interval of 1050 years. Deduct 70 for the blotting out of the captive generations, and there will remain 980 years, or two series of 490 years each, containing 14 generations of 35 years; being the exact half of the first 14 generations of St. Matthew, which we have seen were generations of 70 years.

I venture to offer these suggestions to your correspondent, whose own views appear to be so fairly put, and in themselves so reasonable, that they are deserving of every consideration. In considering the circumstances I have stated, however, whether he agrees or disagrees with the conclusions drawn from them, he will I trust see reason for believing that the "Legal Genealogies" of the "Heads of Israel," must have been framed by some law which was not confined to the mere natural succession of the families.

On other points connected with this genealogy I could wish your correspondent would refer to 1 Chron. xxiv. 3, 4, for a probable explication of Judges xx. 28, to which he refers: the reading being, I think, of the same kind, and intimating the line of priesthood only, who stood before the ark at that time: but the date of the event referred to is by no means certain, and might have happened at an early period of the Judges. With reference to the statement, that 1 Sam. i. 1, shews "*Zuph*," the fifth generation above Samuel, as the probable settler at Ramathaim-Zophim after the exodus, he will find the *natural pedigree* of that family at 1 Chron. vi. 34; where there are 10 generations shewn between "*that Zuph*" and Korah, who was in the wilderness, *and whom your correspondent takes for the grandfather* of "*Zuph.*" But the genealogy of the "*Heads of that family*," the house of Eleazar, has like the genealogy of David, the *same "legal descents" as that of David* himself for the same intervals; that is to say, it has 28 descents from Abraham to the Babylonian captivity, divided into two fourteens at the name of Amariah, the second above Zadok, who was priest at the later part of David's life; and of whom therefore Amariah might have been the precursor at the period of his birth; of which he may assure himself by referring to 1 Chron. vi. 1, 14.

On the other grounds of his theory for shortening the interval between the exodus and the succession of the house of David, I have no opportunity of judging, not having yet met with his book: but so far as concerns his arguments from the legal genealogy of the house of David, I think he rests his opinion upon unreliable grounds.

H. M. G.

Hitcham Rectory, 22nd October, 1855.

ON THE DIFFICULTY AS TO THE TIME WHEN THE CURE OF THE BLIND NEAR JERICHO WAS PERFORMED.

To the Editor of the "Journal of Sacred Literature."

Dear Sir.—Your correspondent, J. A.,[a] objects to my conjectural emendation of the text in the accounts, given by Matthew and Mark, of the cure of the blind near Jericho on two grounds. First, that it is not admissible because ἐισπορευομένων would not agree with ἀπὸ Ἱεριχὼ: next, that it would not agree with the text of Luke (ἐν τῷ ἐγγίζειν).

---

[a] *J. S. L.* Oct. p. 192.

The incompatibility is undeniable, but I did not think it necessary to repeat the explanation I had given elsewhere, because it was foreign to the subject of which I was treating.—The explanation I gave in my *Dissertation on the Origin of the Gospels*[b] is as follows.—After shewing that EK might easily be a misreading of EIC, which is admitted, I added, "If, therefore, the transcriber of the passage in Matthew has left out an "iota," and perceiving his error, has inserted it, he would unconsciously alter the word into one of a directly opposite meaning. *The next transcriber* seeing the following word to be εἰς, which would contradict the preceding word, would, to make sense of it, be obliged to change it into ἀπὸ."

The great difficulty of this mode of explanation is, that the reading in question occurs in the parallel passages of two Gospels, for we cannot suppose that the same error and the same correction should happen twice —nor did I; I attributed the change in Mark to what may be called the process of assimilation, borrowing the term form the following just observation of Mr. Alford. "Few readers are at all aware to what an extent the process of *assimilating the parallel places* in the Gospels has gone. It is in *these* that by far the greater number of various readings is invariably found."[c]

With regard to the next remark, that Luke does not say, "As they were going in to Jericho," but "as they drew near" (ἐν τῷ ἐγγίζειν), I confess, I cannot see any contradiction between Luke's statement and the conjectural one; nor can I see how De Wette's rendering removes the difficulty, because St. Luke explicitly states that, after the miracle, our Lord entered Jericho and passed through it (xix. 1). He must, therefore, have meant to state that it took place before entering; whereas, by the received reading, both Matthew and Mark as explicitly state that it was after leaving Jericho.

JAMES SMITH.

THE NITRIAN PALIMPSEST OF ST. LUKE'S GOSPEL.

SIR,—I wish to inform those who are interested in critical studies, *why* I have not as yet carried out my intention of editing and publishing the text of these valuable fragments.

I communicated such an intention to several some years ago; and amongst others to Professor Tischendorf. To carry out this design I was in London for many weeks of the summer of 1854, and I investigated almost every legible letter of these Palimpsest fragments. Having thus prepared the text for publication, I made my arrangements for the use of the types cut for Woide's edition of the *Codex Alexandrinus*, and since employed by Mr. Cureton in editing the Homeric portion of the same Palimpsest; all was agreed also with a publisher, and a fac simile was prepared for lithographing.

---

[b] p. 299.   [c] Vol. i., 2nd Edit., Proleg., p. 77.

As I found that there were questions occasionally which required to be answered as to particular points, in the last autumn I re-examined the MS.; but just as this was *completed*, so that all was in a fit state to go into the printer's hands, I received a letter from Professor Tischendorf, informing me that it would be useless for *me* to go on with my edition as *he* was going to publish this MS. himself in a new volume of *Monumenta Sacra*, and nothing which appeared in *England* could compete with what would be published at Leipsic.

I therefore pause; if Professor Tischendorf publishes these fragments with the exactitude which characterized his earlier works, my proceeding will be needless:—but if on the other hand he does this with as little accuracy as some of his *later* publications exhibit, then I shall consider the path to be clear before me, for publishing the text of this MS., together with *the historical account of the examination of Palimpsest MSS.*, which I had proposed giving.

As to the manner in which Professor Tischendorf has recently edited such obscure documents, I may refer, with regard to *his own Palimpsest*, to *The Journal of Sacred Literature* for July last (p. 451). Also I may mention that in his recently published *Anecdota Sacra et Profana*, he gives a professedly complete collation of one of his MSS. (now sold to the British Museum), containing the Book of Acts. This collation in the course of a few consecutive chapters contains oversights.

Thus, ch. ii. 3, for ἐκάθισεν of the common text, he gives καὶ ἐκάθισεν (rightly); but without noticing the omission of the following τε.

Ch. ii. 18, the reading of the MS. ἐνυπνίοις is unnoticed.

Ch. iii. 1, stands thus, "Elz., ἐπὶ τὸ αὐτὸ δε Πέτρος. Cod., Πέτρος δὲ." Thus it seems as if ἐπὶ τὸ αὐτὸ were quite omitted; whereas in fact the words are (as in some other valuable documents) joined to the end of the preceding chapter (omitting τῇ ἐκκλησίᾳ).

Ch. iii. 21, Tischendorf gives the reading of the MS. as being ἀπ' αἰῶνος αὐτοῦ instead of ἀπ' αἰῶνος of the common text; whereas in fact the variation is a transposition of ἀπ' αἰῶνος before αὐτοῦ προφητῶν.

These are specimens of the kind of oversights in Tischendorf's *recent* works; and if such should appear in his edition of the Nitrian Palimpsest, then I shall think it my place to carry out my long announced intention.

I remain, yours very truly,
S. P. TREGELLES.

6, *Portland Square, Plymouth.*
Dec. 12, 1855.

*La Sacra Bibbia, contenente il vecchio ed il nuovo Testamento. Ver-
sione secondo la traduzione di Giovanni Diodati, diligentemente e
partitamente riveduta ed emendata, sugli originali Ebraico e Greco,
Con referenze ; ed illustrata da carte geographiche, da Sommarii
cronologici e da tavole delle monete, dei pesi, e delle misure.*
Londra : (Society for promoting Christian Knowledge) Bagster,
e figliuoli, stampatori. 1855.

FOR circulation in Italy there have been hitherto *two* translations of
the Holy Scriptures available for use; that of Diodati, and that of
Martini; the former being the Protestant version, the latter the
Roman Catholic. The basis of that of Diodati was, of course, the
inspired originals, while that of Martini was avowedly taken from the
Clementine Vulgate, and it has been from time to time rather ostentatiously announced that the version was made in all respects conformable " to the doctrines of the Holy Catholic Church, as defined by the
Council of Trent."

To those who desired to put into the hands of Italians an honestly
executed translation of Holy Scripture, the path was plain and easy ;
the version of Diodati was the only one which they could properly
employ ; for how can those who value Holy Scripture themselves as
being the inspired revelation of God, wittingly put into the hands of
Roman Catholics a translation which has been designed of set purpose
to teach doctrines which have *not* been revealed, and which has been
altered so as *not* to convey the truths taught by prophets and apostles?

And yet Martini's translation has been circulated by Protestants :
this has been in part through inadvertence, and in part from principles
of supposed expediency having unduly swayed the mind. It has
been said that a Roman Catholic translation must of necessity be better
suited to a Roman Catholic population ; just as if the object which we
had in view in putting into men's hands the Word of God in any
form, was to uphold them in their errors ; and to give them the
supposed sanction of the Holy Ghost himself, in favour of doctrines
and practices which the true Word of God absolutely condemns. It
was also said that the Roman Catholic version was probably the only
one which the Italian population *would willingly* receive, and that the
language of that of Diodati was in many respects harsh, ungrammatical,
or obscure.

Now as to these two latter points, it is a simple fact that it is only
within the last few years that there has been anything like an opening
on an extended scale, to introduce the Scriptures into Italy at all ;
but since inquiry has been aroused, there has been a demand for the

Scriptures amongst those who have at all learned their value as being the revelation of God, and as pointing out God's way of giving pardon and acceptance to men, not through their own works or deservings, but through the atoning sacrifice and perfect merits of Jesus Christ, apprehended by the soul through faith. In this manner many have learned to prize the Word of God, and the more purely it could be placed in their hands, so much the better was it for them.

It is not to be denied, that *if* a man refuse to receive an honestly made Protestant version, there *may* be cases in which a Romish translation may be wisely put into his hands; but not as being the pure Word of God, but only *as a Romish version*, yet still containing *much* that is true and good. Though many passages, here and there, are altered so as to give a kind of support to most Romish doctrines, yet this is not done so systematically as to pervert all that teaches God's way of salvation, and the freeness of the mercy which shines forth in the cross of Jesus Christ.

When the version of Diodati found, in recent years, a new and unparalleled circulation in Italy, the defects which had been previously pointed out continued to be felt. The Italian ear, especially amongst the cultivated Tuscans, is sensitive in the extreme as to any harshness or impropriety of language; and thus the version of Diodati was valued in spite of certain serious drawbacks. It was intelligible, but not agreeable. But the want of elegance, which was felt to characterize Diodati, by no means led the Italians to desire to adopt the version of Martini; they wished not to sacrifice truth to external attractiveness.

For some time it was rumoured that a revision of Diodati had been undertaken by one of those Italians, who had been exiled from his native land for the profession of the simple Gospel of Jesus Christ. In the reports which reached our ears, from time to time, as to this work, it seemed to be understood that the object was to remove from Diodati those words and phrases which are now harsh or scarcely intelligible to the Italian (or at least the Tuscan) ear, and to avoid all that was ungrammatical and harsh, substituting pure Tuscan phraseology for the somewhat peculiar expressions employed at times by Diodati. Thus the *translation* from the originals would have continued to be that of Diodati, on whom alone would have rested the responsibility of giving the true meaning of the Hebrew and Greek, while in those places in which the language of Diodati was not retained, the reviser would be responsible for giving better and more accurate Italian.

The appearance of the volume before us furnished certain data on which a judgment might be formed respecting the plan of the revision, and the mode in which it has been carried out.

It was evident on the first inspection of the volume, that *far more* had been accomplished than might have been anticipated from anything which we had previously heard; but as the book made its appearance without any preface or introductory statement, it was only by an examination of many parts, that we could rightly learn how much had been accomplished. The *title* was the only intimation of these things. *How* the plan was extended we are not informed, but one thing is certain, that competent scholarship was brought to bear on the undertaking, so that it is *really* "diligently and particularly revised and emended, according to the Hebrew and Greek originals;" and *besides* this, an amount of knowledge of textual criticism is shewn, such as would have been creditable to the biblical studies of a scholar of this country, if engaged in Bible translation or Bible revision. Unhappily the work of Bible translation amongst us, is far too much confined to giving a version based only on the common text, as if the critical labours of three centuries were ignored, and as if it were of less importance to translate Holy Scripture from the *best copies*, than would be the case if some common book were under consideration.

In this Italian Bible passages and words, which, though in the common Greek text, are known by critical scholars to rest on *no* sufficient authority are boldly thus designated, and in this manner the evil is avoided of putting before men, as the Word of God, that which we have every reason to believe forms no part of that inspired word.

This feature of this revised Italian Bible is, of course, far more obvious in the New Testament than in the Old; the reason why this *must* be the case, is the far greater advance which textual criticism has made with regard to the Greek than the Hebrew Scriptures. This has arisen from the *materials* in the former case being so much better known, so much more abundant, and from their leading us so much nearer to the time when the New Testament itself was written.

Before giving examples from the New Testament, as to the manner in which the text has been critically treated, it may be right for us to inform our readers that we have no greater means than they have of judging what the principles are on which the editor has proceeded. It was with surprise that we saw that he had entered into the domain of criticism; and it was wholly unexpected to observe that he had given in many passages results far more correct than some timid editors amongst ourselves would have done.

For instance, the whole of the passage in 1 John v. 7, of the nongenuine character of which there can be but one opinion amongst critical scholars, is here put entirely in italics, as being no part of the genuine text.

So, too, the words of Philip to the Ethiopian and his reply, in Acts viii. 37. In Acts xxiv. 6, &c., where the best authorities make the speech of Tertullus so much more concise than it is in the common text, the editor has made no change in the passage itself; but in the *margin* he has indicated how the middle of verse 6 should be joined to the middle of verse 8, omitting the whole of verse 7, and the latter half of the preceding verse, and former half of the following. In Acts xv. 34, there is noted in the margin, "Questo verso manca in molti testi antichi." In Acts xx. 28, "la chiesa di Dio" stands in the text, with, however, a reference to "del Signore" in the margin.

The latter part of Acts ix. 5, and the former part of the next verse are suitably noted in italics.

After the full expression of critical judgment shewn in the passages already specified, no one will be surprised to hear that other passages are treated with a similar commendable boldness. Thus at John vii. 53, there is the note, " Questo verso, e anche, cap. viii. 1—11, mancano in molti testi antichi." In this the editor sufficiently shews his own judgment ; and those who differ from him have no cause to complain, because he has simply stated a well-known and important fact. And if the common readers of the New Testament are not put in possession of such information in a right and proper way, they are *sure* to have such things brought before them by those who would seek to discredit all objective certainty in Holy Scripture.

In John v. 3, this note is placed in the margin, " Questa ultima clausola, insieme col verso 4, manca in vari testi antichi;" information of which the reader *ought* to be apprized.

We will now give *continuously* some of the *critical* information which the margin or italics of this edition so concisely brings before the reader's eye, together with the words of the *text* when needful.

Matt. i. 25.—*text*, " Finchè ebbe partorito il γ suo figliuol primogenito;" margin, " γ un figliuolo."

„   v. 44.—The clauses, the genuineness of which is impugned by such good critical authorities, are marked as omitted in the marginal form of the text.

„   vi. 1.—text, " limosina ;" marg., " giustizia."

„   vi. 13.—The doxology is given in italics, as not genuine.

„   vii. 14.—text, " Quanto è stretta la porta" (following critical authorities) ; marg., " Perciocche," etc.

„   viii. 31.—text, " permettici d'andare ;" marg., " mandaci."

„   ix. 8.—text, " maravigliarono ;" marg., " temettero."

„   ix. 13.—εἰς μετάνοιαν of the common text is passed by in the margin.

„   x. 3.—text, " e Lebbeo, chiamato per soprannome Taddeo ;" marg., " e Lebbeo : *altri esemplari*, e Taddeo."

„   x. 8.—The words " suscitate i morti," are passed by in the marginal reading ; this rests, however, on very imperfect critical evidence.

„   x. 10. The reading ῥάβδον is followed in the textual rendering, while ῥάβδους is in that of the margin.

„   xi. 1.—text, " mando due γ dei suoi discepoli ;" marg., " γ per i suoi," etc.

„   xi. 8.—" vestito di vestimenti morbidi," in the text ; while *vestimenti* is put in different characters in the margin, as a word not found in good authorities.

„   xii. 6.—The masculine reading μείζων is expressed by " alcuno" (maggior) in the text, while the critical reading μεῖζον in the neuter, is represented by " cosa" in the margin.

„   xii. 8.—text, " Signore del Sabbato ;" marg., " eziandio del

Sabbato" (the common Greek reading, opposed by the critical editors).

Matt. xiii. 22.—text, "di questo secolo;" marg., "del secolo."

" xiii. 43.—The doubtful authority of ἀκούειν is intimated in the margin.

" xiii. 44.—So, too, as πάλιν in this verse; and in

" xiii. 51.—Λέγει αὐτοῖς ὁ Ἰησοῦς, and κύριε.

" xiv. 9.—text, "Ed il re se ᵝne attristò: ma pure per i giuramenti:" marg., "ᵝattristato, per i," etc.

" xv. 4.—text, "Iddio ha comandato in questa maniera;" marg., "detto, Onora," etc.

" xv. 6.—text, "il comandimento;" marg., "la parola."

" xv. 8.—Ἐγγίζει μοι and τῷ στόματι αὐτῶν καί are marked in the marginal reading as omitted, as they *must* be on critical grounds.

" xvi. 3.—"Ipocriti, ben sapete" stands in the text, the former of which words is omitted in the margin.

" xvi. 4.—So, too, the word "profeta" in this place.

" xvi. 13.—The margin indicates the omission of με in some authorities.

" xvi. 28.—The text has "che alcuni di coloro che son quì presenti non;" the marg., "vi sono alcuni quì presenti che non;" so as to represent the different readings of the Greek.

" xvii. 11.—Πρῶτον, of the common Greek text, is marked in the margin as omitted.

" xviii. 10.—The first "nei cieli" is omitted in the margin.

" xviii. 11.—marg., "Questo vers. manca in vari exempl. antichi."

" xviii. 14.—text, "Padre vostro;" marg., "mio."

" xviii. 15.—"Contro a te," marked in the margin as omitted.

" xviii. 29.—"Ai piedi," similarly noted: also "tutto."

" xviii. 35.—So, too, "i suoi falli" here.

" xix. 16.—"Buono," omitted in margin.

" xix. 17.—text, "Perchè mi chiami buono? niuno è buono, se non un solo, cioe, Iddio;" marg., "Perche mi domandi intorno al bene? un solo è buono."

" xix. 20.—"Fin dalla mia giovanezza," omitted in margin.

" xix. 24.—text, "regno di Dio;" marg., "regno dei cieli."

" xix. 29.—"O moglie," omitted in margin.

:) " —"cento cotanti," text; "molti," margin.

" xx. 6.—Ἀργοὺς, of the common text, omitted in the margin.

" xx. 7.—So, too, the last clause of this verse.

" xx. 16.—And here all the words after "ultimi."

" xx. 17.—"Discepoli," similarly marked.

" xx. 22, 23.—The clause καὶ τὸ βάπτισμα κτλ, in each of these verses is omitted in the margin.

" xx. 26.—"Sia vostro ministro," text; "sara," margin.

" xx. 34.—Αὐτῶν οἱ ὀφθαλμοί, omitted in margin.

" xxi. 4.—ὅλον, similarly marked.

Matt. xxi. 30.—text, "al secondo ;" marg., "all 'altro."

„ xxi. 31.—text, "il primo ;" marg., " L'ultimo. *c.* colui che ultimamente v'andò., ver. 29" (where " ultimamente " is in the margin).

„ xxi. 44.—marg., " Questo verso manca in alcuni esemplari."

„ xxii. 30.—Τοῦ Θεοῦ, marked in margin as omitted.

„ xxii. 44.—" Per scannello dei tuoi piedi," text ; " disotto a tuoi," margin.

„ xxiii. 3.—Τηρεῖν, marked as omitted in margin.

„ xxiii. 4.—So also καὶ δυσβάστακτα.

„ xxiii. 5.—So also τῶν ἱματίων αὐτῶν.

„ xxiii. 7.—So also ῥαββί 2°.

„ xxiii. 8.—" Rettore," text ; "Dottore," margin.

„ xxiii. 11.—" Sia vostro ministro," text ; " sara," margin.

„ xxiii. 14 (13 of the Stephanic text).—" Questo verso manca in vari testi antichi."

„ xxiii. 19.—Μωροὶ καὶ, marked as omitted.

„ xxiii. 21.—text, " l'abita ;" marg., " l'abitava."

„ xxiii. 26.—καὶ τῆς παροψίδος, marked as omitted.

These passages have been taken from a continuous portion of the New Testament, in order that they may fairly exhibit the various kinds of alteration of the text which have been noted. The critical reader will see that in this Italian Bible, the dicta of no one reviser of the Greek text have been followed, but the editor appears to have exercised a judgment of his own. In many of the cases specified, we should fully agree with him ; several of the places marked are at least doubtful ; and in some few we should wholly differ from his estimate of the results of evidence. As one point of the last-mentioned kind, we may mention the name of *Jesus* prefixed to Barabbas in Matt. xxvii. 16, 17, which here appears in the margin. The evidence for this addition is, we consider, wholly insufficient ; and in part, even what has been stated in its favour is based on misapprehension.

We do not specially discuss the alterations made in the Italian phraseology : it belongs rather to those to whom that tongue is vernacular to do that. We do, however, observe the absence of some of those long, harsh, and obscure words, " conciosiacosache," and the like, which have hitherto made the Epistle to the Romans and other parts difficult to read.

That those who value the Word of God in Italy, will gladly receive this revised version, prepared, as it has been for them, at the expense of the Society for promoting Christian Knowledge, is a thing that we cannot doubt. And with regard to others, it has been found by experience, that a version is not rejected by the Italians because of its being *Protestant ;* and thus if they have hitherto received Diodati's (and such is the fact) in spite of any peculiarity of language, how much more will the Bible before us meet their wishes and requirements.

We are glad that the Society for Promoting Christian Knowledge has not been withheld from the publication of this Bible through any considerations connected with its *critical* character. There are many in this country who are afraid if any question respecting the rendering or reading of a passage of Holy Scripture is discussed at all; and thus they would go on for ever not only using themselves, but also putting before others, through new translations, sentences and words, which, as they have the fullest opportunity of knowing, are no part of Holy Scripture. They wish to exclude all attention to such facts, fearing lest harm should arise from the discussion, and deprecating the thought that uncertainty should be at all attached to the text of God's Word. But what is the consequence? We continually find the advocates of scepticism and the deniers of the authority of Holy Scripture, well-informed enough on points which Christians, whether learned or unlearned, ought to regard as their own proper sphere : and thus so far from the end being gained that the timid objectors to discussion have hoped for, the result really is, that the impression made on bystanders is, that the advocates of Christianity have felt that there is a weakness as to their own cause in particular parts; and that they only disguise this, by keeping the subject out of sight.

We shall be truly glad if the manner in which critical results are brought forward,—concisely, clearly and correctly,—in this Bible, may be a precedent to be followed by other editors in this country. Of one thing at least we are sure, that if this Bible does obtain a proper circulation in Italy, it will cause the real state of the text of Holy Scripture, and the true results of honest criticism, to be better known by straw-plaiters in Tuscany, than they are by many a learned doctor in England.

Patriarchy ; or the Family: its Constitution and Probation. By JOHN HARRIS, D.D., Author of "The Pre-Adamite Earth," "Man Primeval," &c. London: Partridge, Oakey, and Co., 1855. 8vo. pp. 548.

THE title of this work is at once suggestive of the importance of the subject, and of an assurance that it will be treated in an efficient and practical manner. Dr. Harris's former productions have prepared us for patient research, careful analysis, and the useful application of whatever proceeds from his pen; and we are not disappointed in the present instance. As to the subject he has submitted to discussion, both its relation to past times and dispensations, and its bearing on the present and future well-being of mankind, combine to invest it with high interest and much dignity. We have long felt that the great principles of natural and revealed religion, embodied in the word PATRIARCHY, have been placed too much in abeyance in the present age, overshadowed and injured, in our conceptions, by the still nobler edifice of Evangelical truth, which is rather intended to protect and honour them. We therefore feel we are discharging a pleasant duty in giving this volume all the publicity in our power.

Dr. Harris's design is *historical* as well as *ethical*, and this really divides the work into two parts, although they are not kept formally distinct from each other. The *first* part is devoted to the laws or method of the domestic constitution; the *second* indicates the stages and changes through which the Patriarchal community may have passed in the course of its probationary history. The object kept in view by the author, is to link the present work with his two former ones, *The Pre-Adamite Earth*, and *Man Primeval*, the three thus giving the natural history of mankind both in relation to nature and grace. This is a fine and worthy design, though we fear the comprehensiveness of it will make it slow in exerting that practical influence which we wish to see extended. We will give first an analysis of the contents, and then add some observations on some points which appear to us of greatest importance.

The whole work is divided into four Parts. Part I. is entitled "The Divine Method," and contains sixteen chapters. It is by far the largest portion of the book, occupying 416 pages, or four-fifths of the whole. A connexion is first instituted between man in a state of innocence and his position after the fall:—

"By the creation of man the earth itself may be said to have been transfigured; for its new inhabitants consciously radiated the divine image. In his constitution, his dominion, and his far-reaching relations, he stood forth the embodiment of a divine idea,—'the type of him that was to come.' His probation raised the earth into a scene of moral government. Sinai itself was anticipated, and even surpassed in him; for his constitution was a living court of divine judicature. His temptation announced that he had joined the solemn march of events in the government of God at a period when the great conflict between good and evil had already begun; and that, as a moral agent, he could not but take part in it. His first sin may be regarded as a foreshadowing, for all time, of the kind of contest he would be likely to wage;—presuming on his sufficiency for himself, he brought his will into selfish collision with the supreme will. And the first great lesson taught him by experience—that the well-being of the creature lies in loving obedience and dependence—may be regarded as a prophecy of the *moral* of man's entire history. Henceforth, no second fall of man, as a sinless being, is possible. His probation, in this sense, can never be repeated."—p. 1.

The Family constitution was now, in a deep and solemn sense, to be placed on probation. Patriarchy was established as a system expressly arranged and adapted by God himself to the wants of his erring creatures; having in it sufficient elements for stability and happiness, if man should be obedient to its laws; yet, like the state of paradise, admitting of abuse, deterioration, and decay. By itself, this form of government was adapted only to an early stage of civilization, but, "in the exact proportion in which it fulfilled its divine design, it would have prepared the way for a larger form of government; a form, for example, akin to that of the Jewish Theocracy." The character of such a tentative provision is acutely discerned, and much wisdom is exhibited as distinguishing all its arrangements. It is then shewn that the means of divine manifestation in the preceding stage of man's history are continued under the Patriarchy, and that the economy of the family is *remedial*. This leads to the consideration of the first promise, and of sacrifice, as a unique institution, and associated with *mediation.*

The government of the family being thus established by God himself, its development is exhibited as it took place on the theatre of the antediluvian world. Chapters four, five, and six, are devoted to this subject, which is handled in a very masterly manner ; and a field of thought, very apt to be presided over by the fancy, is submitted to a well-regulated judgment. It is true, that the world before the flood has but few documents to inform us of its condition ; but enough is made known in the origin of its society, its progress, and its fate, to lead to a mental re-construction of its grand and principal features. If a physiologist can produce all the unknown parts of a *megatherium* from a single bone, because he understands the laws of organic life, it should not be considered an impracticable task to give form and shape to antediluvian society from the few records of it which present themselves in history. Dr. Harris thinks that the dispensation then existing allowed of miracles, and that the deluge must be contemplated as connected with such a præter-natural system of events, which, however, as in the case of the miracles in the time of our Saviour, allowed of the scepticism of the irreligious. A passage here will exhibit the mode in which the author works up the intimations of Scripture, and makes them illustrate his subject.

" One part of the Divine procedure there is, however, which appears to deserve distinct remark—the prediction of a Deluge. In reference to that event, the antediluvian sceptic would probably object, as the scoffer of ' the last days' will do, relative to another catastrophe, saying, ' where is the promise of his coming ? for since the fathers fell asleep, all things continue as they were from the beginning of the creation. All observation and experience are against such an event. Nature is uniform in her operations. The laws of the human mind compel my disbelief. I reject the prediction as unreasonable.' Now, here the first error lay in confounding that inner circle called the course of nature, with that larger outer circle—the course of providence, which preceded nature and encompasses it ; which originated it, employs it, and at distant intervals adds to it, or modifies it at pleasure. That no similar event had taken place from the time of the Adamic creation might have been true. But, is that sufficient to prove that nothing like it ever will or can occur ? Experience is, in this sense, against everything till it occurs. Before the first family existed, the experience of Adam was against its existence. Indeed, during the first ages of the human dispensation, events were, and from the nature of the case, must have been, constantly occurring for the first time. The existence of man himself was contrary to all that had previously taken place on the earth. If the proposition that nothing will take place, but what has taken place is to be admitted, it must be because it is a principle of the Divine Being ; and if it be such at present, it must ever have been such ; and if it has ever been such, even before creation began, no creation could ever have taken place. There was no precedent for the creation of a world, any more than there is now said to be for its destruction. Thus, the objection becomes an intellectual absurdity. The fact is, however, that the root of the error lay, as in the case of the scoffers of the last days, not in the intellect, but in the state of the affections. ' For this they *willingly* are ignorant of'—that the existence of man himself, and of all those material laws on the stability of which they rely, were once unknown to the universe, and owe both the time and manner of their existence entirely to the will of God. It may suit the purpose of the sceptic indeed, to reason from the analogy of a thousand years ; but why, if he assume to be a man of enlarged and comprehensive views, will he not rather reason from the analogy of *ten* thousand years? Of this he is *willingly* oblivious. It suits not his purpose."—p. 181.

This extract will shew the correctness of our remark, that Dr. Harris's design is partly *historical*. On this feature it is not our purpose to dwell, but will pass on to the more *ethical* portion of the volume, merely observing, however, that the general reader will probably find the former the more interesting of the two. We wish expressly to convey the idea which the work has given us, of great originality in its views of the remote period of the world's history to which it refers. Let us now accompany the author in the course he further pursues, and convey, by quoting the heads of the Chapters, some outline of the picture he so powerfully and effectively fills up: laws which the relations of the family constitution pre-suppose;—obligations consequent on the relations and laws of the domestic constitution; the well-being of the domestic constitution measured by the discharge of its obligations; the order of the laws of the family constitution implied in its well-being; the subordination implied in the order and well-being of the domestic constitution; the law of influence implied in the order, well-being, and design of the family constitution; dependence of the family constitution, and of the remedial system which underlies it, on the good pleasure of God; ultimate facts and necessary truth involved in the dependence of the domestic constitution; the constitution of the family, and of the means of mercy, in analogy with every preceding part of the Divine conduct.—It will be seen how comprehensive these topics are, and how capable they are, in their treatment, of exhausting the subject to which they relate. Everything of importance concerning the family appears to be touched upon by the author, in a learned and satisfactory manner. There is the precision of a learned disquisition, without its dryness; scientific details are brought under the reader's notice, but clothed often in a truly poetic dress, so that he is instructed by means of appeals to his judgment and his heart. We must give some extracts to prove the correctness of our remarks, for by no other means do we feel able to do justice to the volume. The first is on the numerical proportion of the sexes.

" It may be expected that the sexes will be found to be *numerically* related. For it is only in this way that the social, intellectual, and moral claims of the sexes can be equally respected. Consequently, the peace, happiness, and well-being of the husband and wife can only thus be secured. Accordingly, not only were one man and one woman created at first for each other, but the same numerical proportion has been maintained substantially ever since. No science has yet traced the laws by which this result is attained. We can only perceive that untold myriads of particular incidents must have been placed and sustained in exquisite adjustment in order to produce it. This numerical relation of the sexes, then, is as much an indication of the Divine Will respecting the proportion in which they are to be united in marriage, as the distinct constitution of each is, that they are to be united at all. If the one intimates this purpose that they should be united, the other denotes that the union is to be limited to individuals, who are to be exclusively united to each other for life. And thus the appointment of nature coincides with the laws of social happiness and of morality; and all these arrangements harmonize with the great end of creation, the Divine manifestation."—p. 194.

The following is a beautiful picture of the close relation of the babe and its mother :—

"From the time the independent existence of the child commences, these relations, or their effects, begin to operate in a new manner, and innumerable others are added to them. At first, the child is almost as dependent on the mother for sustenance, as it was prior to its birth; while every strong emotion of the mother affects the condition of the child, through the medium of its natural nourishment, much more deeply than it does the mother herself. Her bosom is its first paradise. Her face the first object on which its wandering eye learns complacently to settle. Her tones lull it to repose, and mingle with its dreams—with its being. Her eye discourses with its infant mind, while yet words are, to it, mere inarticulate sounds. Her every movement gives to it a new sensation. And thus at the moment of its birth, its education begins, and from that moment never knows a pause."—p. 199.

The above will shew how attractive is the style in which Dr. Harris presents mere common-place truths; the following is in a higher didactic strain, illustrating the fact, that "filial affection rises to the love of God."

"The order in which the love of the child graduates is from the stage of instinctive love to moral affection, and from this to the love of its heavenly parent. Desirous as the parents may be to lead its affections up at once to the creator, the previous stages of the path must first be passed through. For awhile, the maternal care is the only providence it knows; and the father's experience [is to it] a world of grand enterprise, and of power unlimited. In vain it strives to climb the height of his knowledge—his virtual omniscience; nor can it conceive of a diviner guarantee than his promise. To see its parents bend in worship, and to hear them speak with holy awe of their father in heaven, is itself solemn and suggestive as a ladder set up from earth to heaven. The wise discipline, too, which leads the parent kindly to repress its selfish desires, and constantly to aim at its moral welfare, invariably begets in return the highest order of filial love and confidence; evincing the power of the child to discriminate between instinctive and moral affection, and preparing it to embrace that heavenly parent of whom the earthly is but an imperfect representation. And let the parents remark, that, from the moment they begin to point their child to God as an object of reverence and love, they are pursuing the certain course for augmenting its moral affection for themselves; while its intelligent love for them is a valuable means and a pledge for its ascending to the love of God."—p. 352.

How obvious is this truth, yet how almost constantly ignored or forgotten! Schemes without number are yearly asking for public approval and support in relation to the education of the various classes of society, especially the lower, but how little effort is made to bring things into the divinely appointed channel in which alone the work can be properly accomplished! Although the vast system of Sunday School instruction is really an infringement on the natural law above indicated—a less evil certainly than parental neglect, yet still an evil —how little pains are taken to bring that which is "out of course" into harmony again! to affect society at large through the home and the parent! We merely glance at this subject, for we cannot now enter upon it; nor are we sure that we could find a patient hearing if we were to discuss it. The religious public have taken upon them-

selves to place the human and imperfect Sunday School system into
the rank of divine ordinances, and will scarcely hear of a defect in
their idol. But time is teaching the lesson which men are so unwilling to learn; and a state of things, deteriorating year by year, will
at length shew the folly of beginning at the wrong end, and being
wiser than God.——Closely related to this subject is the section,
"Home Education a law," which we gladly quote:—

"If the infant human being is introduced by a divine ordination into the
bosom of the family, it is implied that all the requisites for the development of
his constitution exist there; and they exist there for the express purpose of his
receiving the gradual and orderly development necessary to his well-being; and
no part of this divine arrangement, delicate and complicated as it is, can be
tampered with, without incurring proportional evil. Home education is a law
of nature; and to send the child forth from the circle into which the hand of
God hath led it, must be a violation of that law. Plausible reasons may be
assigned for such a step—and for what can they not? "Cosmopolitanism," says
Chalmers, "in particular, has endeavoured to substitute a sort of universal
citizenship in place of the family affections—regarding these as so many disturbing forces." Lycurgus may take the new-born infant from its parents,
with a view of propagating a sound and superior race. Plato may abolish the
family in his *Republic*, on the plea of reducing multiplicity to unity, and of
drying up one of the sources of division among men. And Aristotle may advocate the same procedure, in order to escape the difficulty of placing women on a
footing with free men, as if they were "by nature capable of the same virtues."
Or society itself may come to be in a state which may render it difficult to
pursue any other course; and the evils resulting from it to the individual may
be of subtle operation; and those resulting to the family and the community
may ask a considerable time and an extended scale for their development, and
may be even partially disguised and neutralized by counteracting agencies; but
if domestic education be a duty devolved on the parents by God, it is untrans-
ferable by man."—p. 242.

The second Part of the work treats of "The law of change: or,
history of the probation of the family;" and, although it is principally
confined to the Sethites and their gradual apostacy, the picture drawn
is applicable to all dispensations and all ages. Three sentences, as
titles of subjects, will suggest the importance of this part of the
work:—The ultimate design of the family lost sight of; Family sins
became customs; Education misunderstood and parental restraint lost.
The last sentence, to our minds, exactly describes the crying evil of
our day. We can only give the headings of parts three and four:—
The reason of the method and of the history, and, The ultimate end of
the family probation and economy as a means of divine manifestation.
These chapters are short, but highly valuable and important. The
whole work, we think, supplies a want in our literature, and most
worthily and effectively too. The treatise is truly a philosophical one,
penetrated in every part by the spirit of our holy religion, and having
close practical bearings on social problems now agitated among us.
It will be read eagerly by the cultivated portion of the public, but we
fear that, unless cast into a new shape, it will not answer the purposes
we wish it to subserve. Having provided a work like this for the
higher class of readers, and, in doing so, having become familiar with
all the details of the subject, can we recommend Dr. Harris to draw

up a small volume for arousing the masses to the neglected duties of the family constitution?—We will conclude with a portion of the close of the volume, which most graphically and powerfully describes the fate of the antediluvians:—

"But what a manifestation of the Divine forbearance had it led to; for by what long travail in sin had man reached his fearful climax! Every sinful man that had lived had tried the patience of God in "his own way;" in a manner different from all the rest. Every godless family had varied the great experiment on his long-suffering. What lessons, warnings, and significant intimations, each man of many centuries had unconsciously sown broad-cast as he walked through life; and what vital seeds, numerous as the spores shed in autumn, had others unconsciously scattered in his path—to be all trodden into the general mire! What myriads of children had come, age after age, bringing with them traces of their Divine origin and mission, to be all wrought up into the great organization of evil! What an amount of resistance man must have offered to Divine remonstrances and restraints, in order to break through them all! What miseries he had been content to endure in his prolonged hostility against God! What misrepresentations, caricatures, of the Divine Being had come to pass for portraits! What perversions of humanity, for normal man—the image of God! What object in nature had he not wrested from its rightful purpose, and selfishly appropriated? What law of the family constitution had he not violated, and what violation had he not misnamed liberty—an improvement on the Divine plan? What sins did that constitution make possible which he had not perpetrated? What promise or possibility of amendment was there at any point of the process which had not been waited for, and which he had not disappointed? What interposition of mercy which he had not turned into an occasion for new acts of presumption? What delay of judgment, from which he had not taken heart to believe that no excess of depravity will ever arouse the Divine displeasure? Of all the evil which his state admitted, what stage of evil had he not passed through, and what depths had he not reached? Yet of what regret was he conscious, except that he could not descend deeper; that the laws of his nature, and the limitation of even his many-centuried life, placed bounds to his powers for evil which he could not exceed? But that which he could not perpetrate he could imagine, and, having exhausted the present and the actual, what worlds of possible evil and Titanic daring did not his imagination create and revel in? For, 'God saw that the wickedness of man was great in the earth, and that every imagination of the thoughts of his heart was only evil continually.' In addition to the wrecks of a Divine economy which he had strewn around him, there were undeveloped powers of evil within him; springs which only wanted room to uncoil, in order to desolate other worlds. And all this was ever present to the Divine eye, standing side by side with the possible heaven which might have occupied its place. Yet, for all this, the Divine forbearance proves itself sufficient."—p. 528.

Faith in God and Modern Atheism Compared, in their Essential Nature, Theoretic Grounds, and Practical Influence. By JAMES BUCHANAN, D.D., LL.D., Divinity Professor in the New College, Edinburgh, and author of "Comfort in Affliction," &c. Edinburgh: James Buchanan, Jun., 1855. 2 vols. 8vo. pp. 912.

THIS work is the substance of a series of Lectures prepared by the author, when Professor of Apologetic Theology. It has been written, he says, under an impression, which growing experience has only tended to deepen and confirm, "that a crisis is impending in the religious history of this country, such as will put the faith of many in the most elementary principles of Divine truth to a very severe and perilous test." He thinks that while there is much profession, or, as we should say, much *talk* about religion, there is, beneath the surface of society, a deep under-current of dark and troubled thought, a restless spirit of inquiry, an uneasy sense of doubt, a conscious dissatisfaction with existing beliefs, which, whether openly avowed or secretly cherished, reveals itself too clearly both in our philosophy speculations, and our popular literature. We may state, that a careful study of the volumes convinces us that the author has the first requisite of a safe physician; he knows the nature and extent of the evil he proposes to cure; our conviction is also equally strong, that he is well acquainted with the only appropriate and effectual remedies.

The following is a slight sketch of the plan pursued by Dr. Buchanan in these volumes. The whole work is divided into four sections. I. Statement of the evidence for the Being and Perfection of God, in eight chapters, which exhibit very lucidly and at sufficient length, the proof from the fact of existence, from the existence of mind, from the phenomena of conscience, from the marks of design in nature, and from the vestiges of the historic fact of creation. The selection of natural phenomena required to illustrate these positions, displays at once competent knowledge, and the power of discreet selection and right application. II. Examination of the rational principles which are involved in the process of proof, containing four chapters on the Metaphysics of Theism, the principle of Causality, the doctrine of final causes, and Kant's critique of the proofs of Natural Theology. III. Modern Atheism, and the Theories which have been applied in support of it. This is a section of great value, and examines with much acuteness the principal hypotheses, or mere dogmatic statements of modern sceptics. These are the Theories of Cosmical, Physiological, Social, and Ecclesiastical Development; of Pantheism; of Materialism; of Government by Natural Laws; of Chance and Fate ; of Religious Liberalism; of Secularism; and of Certitude and Scepticism. Pantheism and Secularism are well treated, in reference to existing phases of scepticism. IV. The Uses and Defects of the Natural Manifestation of God ; in which the way is prepared for the assertion of the necessity of Revelation. Our limits quite forbid us giving anything like a full description of the contents of this truly valuable work. We recommend it to our readers, in the full confidence that they will be as much edified and entertained as ourselves by its perusal.

New Testament Millennarianism: or, the Kingdom and Coming of Christ, as taught by Himself and his Apostles: set forth in eight Sermons preached before the University of Oxford in the year 1854 ; at the Lecture founded by the Rev. John Bampton, Canon of

Salisbury. By the Hon. and Rev. S. WALDEGRAVE, M.A., Rector of Barford St. Martin, Wilts, and late Fellow of All Souls' College. London: Hamilton and Co. 1855. 8vo. pp. 700.

WE hail with much satisfaction every attempt which is made to stem the current of crude, false, and injurious doctrine on the subject of what is yet future in the Christian dispensation. Books lately published on the End of the World, the Number of the Beast, and kindred topics, are sufficient to corrupt the principles of those who are *weak in faith,* and who, instead of *doubtful disputations,* need the pure milk of the Word that they may grow thereby. The speculations to which we refer are too much tolerated, because they appear in the garb of piety and of deference to Holy Writ; but they are really as perilous as confessedly infidel publications; and, in our opinion, lead ultimately to infidelity, when their specious predictions are found to be only lying vanities. Poisons differ in their external phenomena; some being nauseous, and others conveying no unpleasant ideas to the senses; yet they are all equally dangerous to life. So false doctrine is not the less perilous because it uses Scripture language, and professes to occupy itself in unfolding Scripture mysteries.

Mr. Waldegrave's Bampton Lecture is the most important work which has been published for some time, on the subject of the *orthodox* views of the kingdom and coming of Christ. An earnest piety pervades every line; a full acquaintance with the subject is everywhere displayed; and the true doctrine of Scripture is exhibited with learning and much discrimination. The form of sermons somewhat interferes with the compact form which we could wish such a treatise should assume, yet, on the other hand, it gives occasion for important practical reflections, and appeals to the heart and conscience. To all who wish to be furnished with a sensible antidote to the subtle poisons of the school of the modern prophets, and to look for the coming of Christ as the fathers of the Church, with some few exceptions, have done, we can confidently recommend this handsome volume.

---

1. *The Apocalypse fulfilled in the consummation of the Mosaic economy and the coming of the Son of Man;* an answer to the "Apocalyptic Sketches," and "The End," by Dr. Cumming. By the Rev. P. S. DESPREZ, B.D., late Evening Lecturer of the Cathedral Church, Wolverhampton. Second Edition. London: Longmans. 1855. 8vo. pp. 528.
2. *The Testimony of Jesus is the Spirit of Prophecy; or, All pure prophecy terminated in the Advent of Christ and the establishment of Christianity.* By G. L. STONE, B.A., Incumbent of Rossett, Denbighshire. London: Whittaker and Co. 1854. 24mo. pp. 104.

BOTH these works are the result of a re-action against the absurdities of the spirit of soothsaying, which infects the visible church to an alarming extent. There is reason to fear that an extreme of folly in

H H 2

affirming may beget the opposite one of *denying* :—"*Incidit in Scyllam, cupiens vitare Charybdim.*" We do not say that either Mr. Desprez or Mr. Stone have fallen into this error, for, while we do not agree with all their opinions, we think they have done good service by calling attention to some serious and prevalent errors. We have before noticed the work of Mr. Desprez, of which this is a greatly enlarged and improved edition. In the present preface he says—

"He desires to express his sense of the importance of the present subject of enquiry, both in itself and in its consequences. If he is right, the expositions of the Apocalypse, with which, alas, hundreds of pulpits are now resounding, must be as utterly at variance with truth and Scripture as they are with reason and common sense; and views like those advocated in Dr. Cumming's *End of the World*, must be as false and presumptuous as they are deficient in argument, and in a due consideration of the rules of biblical interpretation. If he is wrong, it is incumbent on those in authority to expose his error, and not to suffer heresy to stalk through a second edition unreproved."

The argument of Mr. Stone proceeds somewhat on the principles of prophetical interpretation adopted by the late Dr. Samuel Lee. Mr. Stone states that the learned Professor was more indebted to Calvin for his views than he appeared to be aware of; and that Grotius and Hammond, Bossuet and Calmet, also "immensely helped towards the same conclusion." As the work is a very small one, our readers can easily study it for themselves.

---

1. *Internal Evidences of the Genuineness of the Gospels.* Part I., "Remarks on Christianity and the Gospels, with particular reference to Strauss's *Life of Jesus.*" Part II., "Portion of an unfinished work." By ANDREWS NORTON. Boston : Little, Brown and Co. London: Trübner. 1855. 8vo. pp. 326.

2. *A Translation of the Gospel, with Notes.* By ANDREWS NORTON. Boston: Little, Brown and Co. London: Trübner. 1855. 2 vols. 8vo. pp. 1020.

NOTHING written by Andrews Norton can be unworthy of notice; and where his peculiar opinions are not concerned, he discourses learnedly and sensibly on matters of biblical science; but, unfortunately, his opinions *do* often intrude. In the translation of St. Matthew, for instance, the two first chapters entirely disappear, contrary to the rules of textual criticism, as laid down by almost all scholars, some Unitarians and German Neologists excepted. We may observe in passing that these volumes are printed in a style which would be thought splendid in England, and which is quite novel in connexion with the American press.

Introduction to the Book of Genesis, with a Commentary on the open-ing portion. From the German of Dr. Peter Von Bohlen, late Professor of Oriental Literature in the University of Königsberg. Edited by JAMES HEYWOOD, M.P., F.R.S. London: John Chap-man. 1855. 2 vols. 8vo. pp. 668.

IT is rather too bad to have all Von Bohlen's monstrous sceptical fig-ments thrust upon the English public, without a word to intimate that they have long ago been blown into the air by competent scholars. All our readers will regret that Mr. Heywood should have lent him-self to give currency to such mendacious attacks on inspiration as the following :—

"The object of the first work, the Pentateuch (called from its general contents *Torah,* or *Law,* or *Learning*), is to trace the earliest origin of the people from the darkest antiquity, even from the creation of the world; to present a short summary of their history before the legislation of Moses; to ascribe all the legal enactments of their system to Moses; to interweave these enactments with their own traditions; and thus, by a strange mistake of the narrator, to refer the very laws and institutions which expressly relate to Canaan, to a period anterior even to their settlement in the country: (vol i., p. 16). . . . . The records of all religious systems, in all times and in every nation, are so favoured by their peculiar position, that the popular views they contain become sacred in the eyes of their professors under the influence of early education, and cannot be viewed without prejudice, or thoroughly understood except by those beyond their pale; and the Hebrew nation, whose whole literature was early stamped as divine, and transferred as such to Christianity, has been far from escaping the ordinary consequences; the whole of their history has, in fact, been utterly perverted and completely misunderstood, because the mythic element has been raised, in the progress of time, to the rank of the historical, and mistaken zeal for the interests of religion has in consequence fettered for centuries the spirit of philosophical enquiry: (p. 19). . . . The Pentateuch, as we have seen, is ac-quainted with the art of writing [and, therefore, must be of far later origin than the historic period referred to Moses,] and assumes its existence in Egypt, as is implied in the signet-ring of Pharaoh. This assumption, however, does not advance us a single step towards proving the high antiquity of the art; nor can we deduce such an argument from the assumption, in order to apply it again, afterwards, in support of the antiquity of writing. When we examine the history of the Hebrews down to the period of the Kings, it appears so tradi-tionary and fragmentary as to put the existence of writing entirely out of the question. This art was probably introduced by slow degrees among some indi-viduals of more than ordinary acquirements, and most likely remained for a long time in the hands of a few, till at a later period it was generally dissemi-nated by the agency of the priesthood: (p. 40). . . . . In conclusion [of an examination of the Miracles of Moses], we derive from the examination of these various narratives this certain result, that they are not contemporaneous history, but the pure legends of a later date. A king so silly as the Egyptian Pharaoh of the Book of Exodus is nowhere to be found except in popular fables; and Moses, to use the gentlest expression the case will admit, would have certainly exposed himself to the suspicion of self-deception among contemporaries so fami-liar with Egypt, if he had endeavoured to pass off as miracles the ordinary phenomena of nature, which could, besides, have exercised no influence on Goshen: (p. 67). . . . . The derivation of Jehovah in Exodus is, however, in complete accordance with the general practice of the Pentateuch in the explana-tion of names: for in this case the Deity himself is represented as supplying the interpretation of his title; but that interpretation is evidently adapted to the conceptions of a much later period, and is of much too abstract a nature for the national deity of a very early period. It was reserved for after bards and prophets to give this extension to his character."—p. 153.

----

1. *Examination Questions upon Bishop Pearson's Exposition of the Creed, to assist the Theological Student in making his Analysis, and in testing his knowledge of that important work. With additional notes on points of interest.* By C. A. SWAINSON, M.A., Principal of the Chichester Theological College. London: J. W. Parker. 1855. 18mo. pp. 156.
2. *The Analogy of Religion to the Constitution and Course of Nature: also Fifteen Sermons preached in the Chapel of the Rolls' Court.* By JOSEPH BUTLER, D.C.L., Bishop of Durham. With a Life of the Author, a copious Analysis, and Notes and Indices. By JOSEPH ANGUS, D.D., Author of the Bible Hand-book, &c. The whole designed for the use of students and others. London: the Religious Tract Society. 1855. 12mo. pp. 574.

MR. SWAINSON has conferred a great boon on theological students by this careful analysis of an author who cannot be studied without great profit. Although the volume is small, it is the result of great labour and well applied learning. The notes treat on many points of deep interest to Christian truth.

The new edition of Butler is furnished with very valuable appliances for assisting to the right and easy comprehension of his great argument. Dr. Angus has worked at his subject with great diligence, and his labours will doubtless be fully appreciated by a large class of readers.

Internal History of German Protestantism, since the middle of Last Century. By CH. FRED. AUG. KAHNIS D.D., Professor of Theology in the University of Leipzig. Translated from the German by the Rev. THOMAS MEYER, Hebrew Tutor in the New College, Edinburgh. Edinburgh: T. & T. Clark. 1855. 18mo. pp. 330.

PERHAPS in nothing are general readers of theological literature more perplexed than in ascertaining the *status* of German writers, and the amount of authority which should be allowed to their opinions. Many guides exist in scattered publications, but they are not always accessible, and when possessed, are not complete. In this small volume the various bearings of the schools of German Protestants are clearly indicated, and the labours of Dr. Kahnis and his translator will, we are sure, confer an important benefit on a large class of the English public. The position of the author is thus stated by Mr. Meyer:—

"While thus willing to bear my share of the responsibility for the translation of this book, I must decline to be throughout identified with the author. Dr. Kahnis is a Lutheran divine, belonging to the High Church section of that denomination, who, in their views of the Church and the sacraments, come pretty near the opinions entertained by the Ultra High Church party in the

Anglican Church, and who, imagining themselves to be in possession of *the* truth, speak often in rather a disparaging manner of other evangelical denominations, and have revived the exclusiveness and fanaticism of bygone centuries against the Reformed Church. Dr. Kahnis's *views* on these subjects lie before us in a doctrinal monograph, *Die Lehre vom Abendmahl.* While, in the book before us, he is strictly impartial in representing the facts, he sometimes allows his peculiar Lutheran views to come out in judging of the events of the last years. It would have been easy to remove or alter these few passages; but altogether apart from the consideration, that by so doing I should have misrepresented the Author, I thought that this very circumstance would impart additional interest to the book. For, in this his Lutheranizing tendency, our Author does not by any means stand isolated. This ultra-Lutheranism, on the contrary, is now in the ascendant in Germany, sweeping, like a powerful tide, everything before it. How little soever we in this country may approve of these sentiments, they express the opinions of a large number of leading divines in Germany, and thus throw light upon the present religious condition of that country."

Characters of most of the names which have figured in theology, of the German schools, will be found in this very useful work, from Leibnitz and Wolff, to Tholuck, Neander, and Hengstenberg.

The Suffering Saviour: or, Meditations upon the last days of Christ upon Earth. By the Rev. F. KRUMMACHER, D.D., Chaplain to the King of Prussia. Translated under the express sanction of the Author by SAMUEL JACKSON. Edinburgh: T. & T. Clark. 1855. 8vo. pp. 490.

PERHAPS this is the most finished of the works of the well-known author. It abounds with fine pictures of the life presented in the New Testament, from the most immaculate example of our blessed Lord, down to the dark conduct and fate of Judas. An extract referring to the latter will convey some conception of the style and nature of the volume:—

"The whole circle of the guests at Bethany are deeply touched by Mary's significant act. Only in the case of one does its sweet harmony sound as discord; only one of them with repugnance rejects the grateful odour. Oh, we imagine who it is! No other than the unhappy Judas, the child of darkness. Never, probably, has frigid self-love stood in such horrible contrast with warm and sacred affection, as was the case here, in the cold and really offensive expression, 'Why this waste? Why was not this ointment sold for three hundred pence, and given to the poor?' Alas, how deeply is the miserable man already fallen! 'The poor?' O thou hypocrite! As if the reason was unknown to his Master why he would rather have the ointment sold. 'For three hundred pence!' He knows how to value the spikenard, but is unable to appreciate the love that provided it, for he is wholly destitute of such a feeling.

"O let the example of Judas serve as a warning to any of my readers, who betray a strong inclination to mistake the love of a soul like Mary's to her Saviour; and when it is manifested, can speak of it with a certain inward disgust and bitterness; and if not of waste, yet of enthusiasm, cant, hypocrisy, &c. Know, that on such occasions, a slight similarity to the features of the traitor Judas passes over the face of your inner man. You have need to be most carefully upon your guard, not to let that which you feel at such moments extend itself till it gradually makes you brothers of the traitor. O, when once the scales fall from your eyes—and God grant that this may be the case ere long!—and your souls awake from their Pharisaic dreams at the awful thought of eternity; when pursued by the curse of the law, terrified at the judgment to come, and sorely pressed by death, the king of terrors, you learn to thank and praise the Almighty that, as a last resource, the bleeding arms of Jesus still stand open to you: you will then no longer knit your brows, when you meet with one who has presented his whole heart to the Lord; nor feel repugnance at the fervour with which Asaph exclaims, 'Whom have I in heaven but thee, and there is none upon earth that I desire besides thee!' O no; you will then weep, in secret, penitential tears that you could ever have so mistaken the most precious thing on earth, the love of Christ, and lament with us that we do not love him as we ought."

Theological Essays: reprinted from the Princeton Review. First Series. With a Preface by the Rev. PATRICK FAIRBAIRN, D.D. Edinburgh: T. & T. Clark. 1855. Large 8vo. pp. 576.

IT appears that these papers have excited great interest in America, and that there has been a considerable demand for them in this country. To those who value the metaphysics of theology, this reprint will be acceptable. Dr. Fairbairn says that "for an exact and discriminating knowledge of the peculiar doctrines of Calvinism, and of the fundamental grounds on which they rest, of the false admixtures on the one side, and the dangerous concessions on the other, with which at successive periods they have been associated, and of the relations in which they stand to a true and false philosophy, the essays under consideration could not easily be surpassed." The papers are on the following subjects: The Rule of Faith—the Sonship of Christ—the decrees of God—the Early history of Pelagianism—Original Sin—the doctrine of Inspiration—Melancthon on the nature of Sin—Doctrines of the Early Socinians—the Power of contrary choice—the Inability of Sinners—Sacerdotal Absolution—Regeneration—Sanctification—Transubstantiation—Sabbath Observance—Transcendentalism—Cause and Effect, and a few others.

Christ and other Masters: an Historical enquiry into some of the Chief Parallelisms and contrasts between Christianity and the Religious systems of the ancient world. With special reference to prevailing difficulties and objections. By CHARLES HARDWICK, M.A., Fellow of St. Catharine's Hall, Divinity Lecturer at King's College, and Christian Advocate in the University of Cambridge. Part I. Cambridge: Macmillans. 1855. 8vo. pp. 168.

THE object of this work, only commenced in the present part, is one of great importance, treating as it does of what has exerted much influence, for good or evil, in various ages of the Church. Mr. Hardwick, in a preliminary paper on "The Religious tendencies of the present age," points out the bearing of the subject on certain opinions of our own day, and proposes to make his design meet objections often raised:—

"The order I propose to follow in discussing the religious systems where minute comparison has been thought desirable, is this:—*The Religions that arose and still prevail in Hindostan and some adjoining countries. The Religions of Mexico, of China, and the Southern Seas.* Both these groups appear to have always been entirely external to the sphere of Hebrew influence. *The Religions of Ancient Egypt and Persia.* These, it is alleged, have both at different periods actually modified the development of thought among the Hebrews; the first, during their long residence in Egypt; the second, during the Babylonish captivity. *The Religions of Ancient Greece and Rome.* With these the planters of Christianity were brought into immediate contact at the very opening of their work, and over these they won a triumph in the first five centuries of the present era. *The Religions of the Saxon, Scandinavian, and Slavonic tribes.* Among these tribes the principles of heathenism appear to have been strongest; and some of them in fact were not converted to Christianity for a thousand years after its promulgation."

The Clergyman's Instructor ; or, a Collection of Tracts on the Ministerial duties. Sixth Edition. Oxford: at the University press. 1855. 8vo. pp. 482.

SOME years ago the Delegates of the Oxford Press published the first edition of this volume, in pursuance of a plan adopted by them "of assisting the parochial clergy, either by reprinting some of the more scarce and eminent treatises of our English divines, or by editing in a more convenient form such documents as, though necessary to be referred to by those in holy orders, were before accessible only in works of great magnitude and expense. The circulation of five editions of this collection gives a pleasing idea of the accomplishment of much good in a private unostentatious way. This sixth edition is somewhat altered from the former, and contains the following treatises :— Herbert's Priest to the Temple, Jeremy Taylor's Rules and Advices, Bishop Burnett's Pastoral care, Dr. Sprat's Discourse to the Clergy, Bishop Ball's Companion for Candidates for Holy Orders, Bishop Gibson's Directions to the Clergy, Archbishop Hort's Instructions to the Clergy, Bishop Wilson's Parochialia, Archbishop Howley's Letter to the Clergy, and Bishop Kaye's Charge.

Te Ika a Maui; or, New Zealand and its Inhabitants, illustrating the Origin, Manners, Customs, Mythology, Religious Rites, Songs, Proverbs, Fables, and Language of the Natives. Together with the Geology, Natural History, Productions, and Climate of the Country; its state as regards Christianity; Sketches of the principal Chiefs, and their present position. With a Map and numerous Illustrations. By the Rev. RICHARD TAYLOR, M.A., F.G.S., many years a Missionary in New Zealand. London: Wertheim and Macintosh. 1855. 8vo. pp. 504.

NEW Zealand affords perhaps the most satisfactory instance, in modern times, of the power of Christianity over a whole people, and this alone renders any account of the place highly interesting. But, apart from this, the country has numerous attractions for the lover of nature and

the student of humanity, and has engaged the attention of philan-
thropists from its discovery to the present day. Mr. Taylor gives the
fullest account yet published of the whole island, and has provided a
volume with all the attractions of romance heightened by truthfulness
in every particular. The plates illustrative of the Fauna and Flora
of New Zealand are very beautiful, and numerous wood engravings
scattered through the work give vivid sketches of the arts, costumes,
and manners of the people.

Letters of John Calvin. Compiled from the original Manuscripts, and
    edited with historical notes by Dr. JULES BONNET. Translated
    from the French Language by DAVID CONSTABLE. Edinburgh:
    Constable and Co. 1855. Vol. I. 8vo. pp. 484.

THE character of Calvin, as a scholar and theologian, has long been
freed from some thick mists which gathered round it when he was
merely viewed as the head of a party; a justification attributable to
the more extensive study of his published works. In the same way
his personal excellencies will be developed by the extensive series of
letters, now first presented to the public. Both the original editor
and the translator have discharged their duties with an affectionate
fidelity, and the English work is an important addition to our literature.
The first letter of this volume is dated Noyon, 14th May, 1528; and
the last, Geneva, 13th August, 1545. The collection is to occupy
four volumes. Among Calvin's correspondents in this volume are
Bucer, Daniel, Bullinger, Farel, Viret, Myconius, Melancthon, and
the Queen of Navarre.

---

*America. A Sketch of the Political, Social, and Religious Character
    of the United States of North America.* In Two Lectures, delivered
    at Berlin by Dr. PHILIP SCHAFF. Translated from the German.
    New York: Scribner. London: Trübner. 1855. 12mo. pp. 316.

ALL who have read Schaff's history of the Apostolic Church will
approach any of his productions with an eager curiosity, and the
present volume will not disappoint their expectations. With a great
power of discernment of character, and a keen view of the bearings
and relations of religious parties and questions, he describes his adopted
country in a candid and faithful manner; indicating faults and excellencies as they severally come under his notice.

---

*The Rational Creation; an Enquiry into the Nature and Classification
    of Rational Creatures, and the government which God exercises over
    them.* By the Rev. J. BRODIE, Monimail. Edinburgh: Constable.
    1855. 12mo. pp. 356.

THIS is a well-written treatise, furnishing in every page abundant food for thought. The author thus explains his design in the Introduction.

"An intelligent study of the philosophy of the human mind, and a sincere belief in the doctrines of revelation, have by many been looked upon as directly opposed to each other, and by many more have been regarded as distinct and dissimilar. On the one hand, those who have treated of the science of the human mind have seldom referred to the statements of Scripture in support or illustration of their views, and some of them seem to look on the Christian religion as a vain superstition; on the other hand, the expounders of Holy Writ make but few appeals to the conclusions of philosophers, and some of them seem to shrink from the speculations of science, as if the taint of infidelity adhered to all who venture to intermeddle with them.

"In the following treatise we purpose to pursue a course equally distant from either extreme. We shall begin by inquiring into the nature and constitution of man, the only member of the rational creation with which natural science is conversant, as they are made known to us by reason and observation; we shall, in the next place, examine the account which Revelation gives us not only of man, but of other classes of intelligent creatures, and shall then proceed to consider the nature and work of the Redeemer, who is man in union with God, and the influence which He exerts on the whole intelligent creation as the instructor and governor of all."

Tropologia ; a Key to open Scripture Metaphors, in Four Books. To which are prefixed Arguments to prove the Divine authority of the Holy Bible. Together with Types of the Old Testament. By the Rev. BENJAMIN KEACH. Ireland : The Industrial Printing School, Bonmahon. London : W. H. Collingridge. 1855. Large 8vo. pp. 1032.

THE writer of this ponderous volume was a Baptist divine of considerable eminence in the seventeenth century. This is the most popular of his productions, and had become very scarce until the appearance of this edition, which enables the admirers of this species of writing to gratify themselves at a small cost. There is much information scattered through the work, such as was obtainable two hundred years ago, but not always truthful. For instance, in describing swine, the author states that they love dirt, and will often eat till they burst, neither of which positions is correct. From the size of the volume it will be readily believed that Scripture metaphors are illustrated very minutely, and the work, besides having some intrinsic value, is a curious example of the racy and diffuse theological writing of the age of the author. The book is well printed, and an interest attaches to it as having been executed by the inhabitants of a retired Irish village.

The whole Evidence against the Claims of the Roman Church. By SANDERSON ROBINS, M.A., Rector of St. James's, Dover. London : Longmans. 1855. 8vo. pp. 522.

SOME time back we briefly noticed a work of Mr. Robins somewhat similar to the present, which indeed is an enlarged and perfected form of the same argument. It is rightly stated by the author that the controversy with Rome turns, at the present day, on the claim of papal supremacy, so that if the futility of that dogma can be proved, the whole superstructure of Romanism falls to the ground. The special errors of that system, such as purgatory, the mass, indulgences, and the worship of the dead, are all dependent on the great generic false-hood of the supremacy of the see of St. Peter; and although past experience does not promise much success to an exposure of that delu-sion, however complete, it is proper that Protestant theologians should still reiterate the arguments against it, and place them before the public in every possible variety of forms. Mr. Robins gives the first place, of course, to the Holy Scriptures, as the great storehouse of weapons in this controversy; but he is too wise to confine himself to that alone. Romanists do not allow that Scripture testimony is the only one, and therefore if we will still treat it as such, we never can overturn their assumptions. They appeal to antiquity, and so must we, if we wish to gain the respect of the candid Papist, or to avoid the sneers and triumphant sarcasms of the unscrupulous one.

It is evident that to meet this question fully, the whole field tra-versed by the Romanist must be familiar to the Protestant; so that the former may not be allowed to entrench himself in any inaccessible position. We must give our adversaries credit for great learning and research, and qualify ourselves by the same acquisitions, before we can successfully grapple with them. The old writers of the Reforma-tion period were mighty in the recondite lore demanded for the proper discussion of Papal supremacy, and from the stores gathered by them modern controversialists have been too often content to draw. But this vicarious learning is not enough—we must have recourse to the fountain-heads whence our forefathers drew their information, and apply to any which they overlooked or neglected. On this subject the observations of Mr. Robins are very appropriate, and we gladly record them here :—

" It will not suffice to take down the weapons which have been hanging on the wall for centuries ; they will not fit our hands, nor suit the present warfare. And we shall gain little by using the authorities, from whatever sources they may be derived, which have descended as an heirloom from one generation of controversialists after another, unless we are prepared to answer some im-portant questions connected with them. Who were the writers ? in what con-text are the passages to be found ? on what occasions were they written ? under what circumstances ? are they neutralized by any statement made by the same person elsewhere ? Grievous damage has often been done to a good cause by the inaccuracy of second-hand quotations. Cardinal du Perron is said to have been first alienated from the reformed religion through the erroneous citations of the fathers by Philip de Mornay. We must go to the same sources of infor-mation, and much in the same spirit as our forefathers. . . . Want of prepara-tion for the controversy has told fearfully for Rome. Its strength lies in the unlearnedness of the age, and has kept pace with the decline of ecclesiastical studies. It has always been the same. As long as the argument from Scrip-ture and antiquity was familiar, the papal cause seemed desperate: the intel-ligent people of Germany, the English, the Scotch, and other great nations of the North were lost irrecoverably; while the French Church paid but half allegiance, and was again and again on the verge of separation."

It will be seen that Mr. Robins knows what is demanded for the successful treatment of his subject, and we think he has diligently qualified himself for the task proposed.   His work is careful and learned, and, at the same time, characterized by much temper and moderation in its tone.   We can only now indicate the general contents of the volume, assuring our readers that they will find here full and reliable information on the important topic treated of.   There are eight chapters, with the following general headings:—The Evidence of Scripture; the Testimony of the Ancient Church; the Origin and Progress of the Usurpation; Forgeries and Corruptions of Documents; Failure of the Succession in the Roman Church; Want of Unity in Doctrine; the Council of Trent; the Claim of Infallibility.

The Gospel in Ezekiel, Illustrated in a Series of Discourses.   By the Rev. THOMAS GUTHRIE, D.D. Edinburgh: A. and C. Black.   1855. 12mo.   pp. 436.

THE Sermons here given are twenty-two in number, each having a text taken from the Book of the Prophet Ezekiel.   Considered as pulpit addresses, they have much eloquence and a bold slashing style of address which no doubt made them effective in delivery, and will render the reading of them pleasant to many classes of devout persons. Beyond this, they have no pretensions, and it is therefore a pity that such a title should be chosen as seems to confer upon these Sermons the character of a treatise in divinity.   To ascertain how far God's purposes in his revelations to Ezekiel harmonize with the gospel dispensation would have been an excellent subject for discussion; but Dr. Guthrie does not undertake such a task.   He merely takes texts from Ezekiel, and then from his own subjective ideas treats them *as if they were the Gospel.*   There is room for fancy in this process, but it is not a truthful one: it leads astray the superficial reader, and confers no benefit on one who is thoughtful.

An Exposition of the Epistle to the Hebrews, with Preliminary Exercitations.   By JOHN OWEN, D.D.   Edited by W. H. GOOLD, D.D. Vols. VI. and VII.   Edinburgh: Johnstone and Hunter.   1855.

THESE two volumes complete the work, which is executed in every respect in a most satisfactory manner.   We hope the publishers will now be able to proceed as successfully with their promised new edition of the works of John Howe.

The Way of Salvation; a series of Discourses by the Rev. ALBERT BARNES.   Edited by the Rev. E. HENDERSON, D.D.   London: Knight and Son.   1855.   12mo.

THESE sermons have all the good qualities and all the faults of the

Author's other numerous productions. The volume is greatly praised, *cum grano*, by Dr. Henderson, and that must stand in the place of any lengthened critique on our part.

The Family Commentary on the New Testament: with notes; adapted to the use of Family Worship, and made into short readings By the Rev. J. RAVEN, M.A. London: James Blackwood. 1855. 8vo. pp. 640.

WITHOUT any pretensions to learning, these comments accomplish what they promise. There is a sound discretion pervading them; a healthy tone of piety, which adapts them well for use in the family circle.

The Book of Genesis, according to the Version of the Septuagint. Translated into English, with notices of its omissions and insertions, and with notes on the passages in which it differs from the Authorized Translation. By the Hon. and very Rev. H. E. J. HOWARD, D.D., Dean of Lichfield. Cambridge: Macmillan, 1855. 12mo. pp. 286.

IT appears that the University of Cambridge have appointed the Septuagint Version of Genesis as a subject for examination for the candidates for honours in Theology in the spring of the present year—1856; and that the Dean of Lichfield has been somewhat regulated by that fact in the publication of this very useful volume. The translation is very literal, and the notes are of a kind to suggest to a student what is to be done in the department of sacred learning before him, and what should be his aim and his qualifications. While there is much learning, it is made subservient to the proposed object, and not ostentatiously displayed. We recommend to all who would enter successfully on the cultivation of the sacred literature of the Old Testament, to begin with this volume, and they will find their knowledge of both the Hebrew and Greek Scriptures greatly increased as they follow the guide thus prepared for them.

The New Testament Quotations, collated with the Scriptures of the Old Testament, in the original Hebrew and the Version of the LXX., and with the other writings, Apocryphal, Talmudic, and Classical, cited or alleged so to be. With Notes and a complete Index. By HENRY GOUGH. London: Walton and Maberley. 1855. 8vo. pp. 346.

THIS must become a classical work in sacred literature. The subject of which it treats has often been discussed with more or less precision: but the present writer leaves nothing to be wished for in the full and perspicuous exhibition of all the available materials. The quotations are displayed under the following heads :—I. Quotations from the Old

Testament; II. Alleged quotations from Apocryphal books; III. Supposed quotations from ancient Jewish writings, together with some examples of the use of Jewish proverbs and forms of speech; IV. Quotations from Greek poets, &c. The volume is one to which we hope to give a more full consideration, but which, in the meantime, we cordially bring before our readers. It is beautifully printed.

Corporis Hæreseologici Tomus Primus, continens Scriptores Hæreseologicos minores Latinos. Edidit Francis Œhler. Berolini : apud A. Asher et socios. 1855. London : Nutt. Large 8vo, pp. 434.

THE author proposes to embrace in eight volumes, of which this is the first, all the principal works which have been written on heresies. This portion furnishes,—I. Philastrii sive Philastri Liber de Hæresibus; II. Augustini Liber de Hæresibus; III. Anonymi Scriptoris Liber, quo XC. enumerantur Hæreses. This writer is called Prædestinatus by J. Sirmondus in an edition printed at Paris in 1643; IV. Anonymi Scriptoris Libellum adversus omnes Hæreses, quod vulgo Tertulliano adscribebatur; V. Pseudo-Hieronymi Indiculus de Hæresibus; VI. Isidori Hispalensis Catalogi; VII. Pauli Catalogus; VIII. Honorii Libellus; IX. Gennadii Liber. The whole of these are edited with prolegomena and notes of a very important character, and it will be at once seen by the student of Church history how very valuable and curious the whole collection must be. We hope the other parts will appear without any unnecessary delay.

The Doctrine of the Greek Article, applied to the criticism and illustration of the New Testament. By the late Right Reverend THOMAS FANSHAW MIDDLETON, D.D., Lord Bishop of Calcutta. With Prefatory Observations and Notes by HUGH JAMES ROSE, B.D. New Edition. London : Rivingtons. 1855. 8vo. pp. 552.

IT will be sufficient to call attention to a new and very elegant edition of a work so well known to Biblical scholars.

Devotional Verse for a month, and other brief pieces. By THOMAS DAVIS, M.A., Incumbent of Roundhay, Yorkshire. London : Hamilton and Co. 1855. 24mo. pp. 198.

MR. DAVIS knows well how to touch the poetic lyre with taste and judgment; and, which is more important, to make all its sweet music do honour to religion, to which music and poetry have always been handmaids. Let our readers judge for themselves.—

"I SHALL BE SATISFIED, WHEN I AWAKE, WITH THY LIKENESS."—Psalm xvii. 15.

I.

" 'Tis sweet to wake at early morn,
Refreshed and glad, when faint and worn
We laid us down at Even :
How sweet when last we sink to rest,
Pallid and spent—amid the blest
To wake in Heaven !

II.

" On earth, at Morning's dawn, once more
Restored to strength, that strength is o'er
When Evening comes again :
In Heaven renewed, our Angel powers
Shall yield not to a few brief hours ;
But fresh remain.

III.

" On Earth, though we may wake and smile
With new-born joy, a little while,
And tears may tell our woe:
In Heaven, who once with joy awake,
Shall still unceasing bliss partake,
As ages flow.

IV.

" Who then that knows Thy Power and Will,
Atoning, Lord, from every ill
To shield him and to save,
Would shun the swift approaching close
Of this frail being—and repose
Within the grave ?

"ARE THEY NOT ALL MINISTERING SPIRITS SENT FORTH TO MINISTER FOR THEM WHO
SHALL BE HEIRS OF SALVATION."—Heb. i. 14.

I.

" How lonely seems above the mountain's crest
Yon single Star, towards which a heavy cloud
Steadily floats, as it would soon invest
Her twinkling lustre, and in darkness shroud !
But ah ! sweet Star, that cloud to thee
Is beauteous as a silver sea,
On which the Empress of the night
Sheds softly down her crystal light ;
And, though to us thou seem alone,
Not she upon her fulgent throne
Did ever look around on starry Heavens more bright.

II.

" So oft the chosen of the Lord appear
To one who dwells afar beneath the skies ;
Compassed with clouds they seem so dark and drear,
The gazer's heart can scarce but sympathize ;
While they discern but in the blue
Serene around each lovely hue,
That in the Autumnal Even glows,
Where sinks the bright Sun to repose ;
And, while to other eyes they seem
Lonely and sad, a golden gleam
To them encircling hosts in radiant beauty shews.

*The Church Psalter and Hymn Book, containing the Psalter, together
with the Canticles,·pointed for chanting: four hundred Metrical
Hymns, and six responses to the Commandments ;* the whole united
to appropriate chants and tunes, for the use of congregations and
families, by the Rev. WILLIAM MERCER, M.A., Incumbent of St.
George's, Sheffield, assisted by JOHN GOSS, Esq., Organist of St.
Paul's Cathedral, London. Second Edition. London : Nisbet. 1855.
Small 4to. pp. 304.

THIS is the most comprehensive book of the kind we have ever seen,
and will be found of special use in families. In every case words
accompany the music ; a convenience which will be appreciated in
social singing as well as in public worship. Another recommendation
is the extreme cheapness of this well-printed and handsome volume.

Parables of our Lord illustrated by John Franklin. London : John
Mitchell, Bookseller to the Queen. 1855. Folio.

THIS exquisite volume contains twelve plates, illustrating as many
Parables. They are designed by Franklin, and, we presume, engraved
by him ; the text is executed in Old English, in red ink, and engraved
by Becker's patent process on steel. The entire work is printed by
Mc Queen. We have seldom experienced so much pleasure from a
work of art, professedly illustrating Biblical subjects, as this has
afforded us, and our thanks are due to all the parties concerned in its
production. Christmas will have passed when this notice meets the
eye of our readers, but it will still be the season for making presents,
and we can conceive of none more appropriate than this. The artist
has caught the spirit of the sacred narrative, and made all his drawings breathe the air of holiness and devotion in their principal characters. The representations of our Lord appear to us highly beautiful ; wrought up, we should think, by a hand which considers it an
honour to consecrate its best power to the "Man of sorrows." We
may specify two of the engravings as of peculiar interest. "The
Faithful Servant" is an illustration of St. Luke xii. 42—48, "Who
then is that faithful and wise steward," &c. It represents the celebration of the Lord's Supper by two ministers, one in the beauty of
youth, the other in a green old age. Around are groups of communi-
cants, some partaking, others drawing near ; and behind the assembly,
just entering by a door, is our Lord, in the act of blessing the whole.
"Dives and Lazarus" are portrayed in a manner faithful at once to
Scripture and to Oriental manners. The portly rich sinner is eagerly
carving the viands on his table, attended by many domestics and by a
band of musicians. Lazarus and his canine friends are below. The
countenances of all concerned are highly expressive, as is the case
with all that are introduced into the work.

Robert's Sketches of the Holy Land, &c.; with historical and descriptive notes by Dr. Croly. Parts XIV. and XV. (a double number). London; Day and Son.

THIS fine work is regularly going on to completion, and we invite all our readers who have not seen it, to do so; as without such an inspection they can have no idea of the value and cheapness of it.

The Journal of the Royal Asiatic Society, Part II. of Vol. XV., (J. W. Parker and Son), is just published, and is of very peculiar interest. It contains the following articles: "Memoir on the Scythic version of the Behistun Inscription," by Edward Norris, Esq.; "Notes on the Early History of Babylonia," by Col. Rawlinson: "Notes on the ruins of Muqeyer," by J. E. Taylor, Esq.; "Chronology of the Reigns of Tiglath Pileser, Sargon, Shalmanezer, and Sennacherib, in connexion with the Phenomenon seen on the Dial of Ahaz," by J. W. Bosanquet, Esq.; "Topography of Nineveh, illustrative of the Maps of the chief Cities of Assyria," &c., by Felix Jones, Commander, Indian Navy; "On the Orthography of some of the later Royal Names of Assyrian and Babylonian History," by Colonel Rawlinson; and other valuable papers. The number is illustrated by three large maps, and many engravings.

The Encyclopædia Britannica. Vol. IX. Edinburgh: A. & C. Black. 1855.

THIS volume bears evidence of the anxiety of the proprietors to give all the information down to the time of publication; by which the work takes its place at the head of its class, as well as on other grounds. Among the articles are Ephraem Syrus, by Rev. H. Burgess, LL.D.; Episcopacy, by Dr. Gleig; and Foster, the Essayist, by J. E. Ryland, M.A.

The Ferns of Great Britain; illustrated by JOHN E. SOWERBY; the descriptions by CHARLES JOHNSON, Esq., Botanical Lecturer at Guy's Hospital. London: Sowerby. 1855. Large 8vo. pp. 90, and 50 coloured portraits.

No recreation from severer studies is more pleasant and invigorating than the cultivation of flowers, or the general practice of horticulture. We and very many of our readers know this from actual experience, and we need therefore make no excuse for bringing this interesting volume under their notice. It is intended as an aid to the less scientific observers and admirers of natural productions, and tells all that is necessary to be known respecting the Fern tribes, equally curious in their habits and beautiful in their forms. They may be grown almost anywhere, by the possessor of a large domain who can give a tropical climate to the exotic varieties, or by the inhabitant of a crowded city in his garden of a few yards square. Every particular as to soil and treatment is here given; and the faithfully drawn portraits will form a sure guide to anyone disposed to make a collection. "The Fern Allies," a similar work, is in the course of publication.

INTELLIGENCE,

BIBLICAL, EDUCATIONAL, LITERARY, AND MISCELLANEOUS.

The Number of Jews in the known world.—It is a most difficult task to form a correct estimate of the number of Jews in the known world. Jost and Lew-isohn give some grounds upon which calculations can be formed; and a statement was published some twenty years ago, which has been much relied on by many; but all, whose special attention has been directed to the subject, concur in thinking the numbers given too small. Milman has also paid much attention to the subject; and to these various authorities I am indebted for the following statistics. The grand total of the various estimates differs from 3 to 6,000,000. At the present time there are from 5 to 6,000,000, in all probability; but, even in Europe, a close approximation to the truth is most difficult: how much more so must it then be in Africa and Asia, where we have no statistical data to go upon, and where the habits of the people are essentially nomadic?

In Africa, but little is known of their numbers; they are found along the whole coast from Morocco to Egypt; they travel with the caravans into the far interior, and, as has been already stated, they exist in great numbers in Ethiopia and Abyssinia.

In Egypt, 150 families alone inhabit that once magnificent city, Alexandria, which occupies so sanguinary a pre-eminence in Jewish history, where the blood of the devoted race has flowed like water, and where their wealth ever excited the rapacity of their Macedonian tyrants. In Cairo there are 2,500, including several Karaite families. The Weïmer statement gives the following numbers as those of the Jews of Africa: in Fez and Morocco, 300,000; Tunis, 130,000; Algiers, 30,000; Habesh, 20,000; Tripoli, 12,000; Egypt, 12,000. Total, 504,000.

It is impossible to assign a limit to the number of Jews in Asia. The total given by the Weïmer authority is three quarters of a million; but we can form no correct idea of the extent to which they are to be met with in China and the far interior, where undoubted traces of them are known to exist. In Malabar, there are about 1,000; Bokhara, 2,000 families; and Balkh, 150. In Persia, they number close upon 4,000 families; their chief communities are at Ispahan, Shiraz, Kashaan, and Yezd; they groan under the most oppressive tyranny, and are subject to the heaviest exactions.

In Palestine, of late years, they have much increased; it is said that 10,000 inhabit Safet and Jerusalem, and among them are many Karaites. In Arabia, the Bene-Khabir still maintain their Jewish descent and faith: in Yemen there are nearly 20,000. Damascus counts seven synagogues and four colleges; Mesopotamia and Assyria, the ancient seats of the Babylonian Jews, are still occupied by 5,300 families, exclusive of those in Bassora and Bagdad.

In the Turkish dominions, irrespective of Barbary, their number is estimated at 800,000: in Asia Minor they are numerous and fanatical. There are 40,000 in Constantinople: they are at perpetual variance with the Greeks, and sangui-nary tumults are of no unfrequent occurrence. Adrianople numbers 800 families, with thirteen synagogues; Salonica 30,000, with thirty synagogues. This has ever been one of the great strongholds of Judaism. In the mountains of the Crimea there are 1,200 Karaites. In the Russo-Asiatic dominions of Georgia and Circassia they are numerous; but an exact estimate is wanting. In Georgia some of them are serfs attached to the soil; and some among the wild tribes of the Caucasus are bold and marauding horsemen, like their Tartar compatriots.

But the great seat of modern Judaism is the ancient kingdom of Poland, including Moravia, Moldavia, and Wallachia. In Austria there are 68,000; in the Prussian territory 50,000; which is about the number in the rest of Germany. There are many Jews in Denmark and Sweden : they enjoy freedom of commerce and the protection of Government. In Copenhagen, in the census of 1819, their number was 1,492; in the Netherlands there are 80,000; in France from 60,000 to 65,000. In Spain there are few or none; Gibraltar has 3,000 or 4,000. In Italy their numbers are considerable; Milman estimates them at 100,000, but this is exaggerated; in the Austrian possessions in Italy they are also numerous; and they abound in Mantua, Tuscany, and the States of the Church. In Great Britain there are from 30,000 to 40,000; they are entitled to every privilege of British subjects, except certain corporate offices and seats in Parliament, from which they are excluded by the act which requires an oath to be taken "on the faith of a Christian." A struggle is at the present time going on, with regard to this last remnant of exclusion; and there can be no doubt, however acrimoniously it be supported, that its days are numbered, and that, ere very long, the Jews will have the full and unrestricted rights that are enjoyed by every other class of British subjects.

In America, which was the first to accord to them such privileges, there were about 6,000 twenty years ago; this number, it is known, is amazingly increased at the present day; but correct statistics are wanting.—*Extract from past Bible History of the Jews.*

The Codex Vaticanus.—A proposition by a correspondent of *The Times*, to perpetuate valuable Biblical MSS. by Photography, has led to some interesting information on the *Codex Vaticanus*, from which we extract the following :—

" Sir,—About a year and a half ago, when in Rome, I had the honour of an introduction to the celebrated scholar the Cardinal Angelo Mai. In the course of conversation, he asked some questions as to the state of the *Codex Alexandrinus* in the British Museum; and, on my remarking on my disappointment at not being able to see the *Codex Vaticanus* at the great library, he explained that it was in consequence of his being engaged in preparing an edition of it himself, and that it was, of course, obliged to be kept at his palace. The learned Cardinal proceeded to open a large strong chest, from which he took an elaborately-worked iron coffer, containing this most precious manuscript. Observing that the greater part that had been published was unsatisfactory and contradictory, he said that he was occupying his leisure by editing it page by page, line by line, letter by letter; that he had entertained serious thoughts of having a fount of type cast in *fac-simile*, in the same manner as Dr. Woide had for the *Codex Alexandrinus*, but the difficulties were so great he had abandoned the idea. I then suggested the making a *fac-simile* of the whole in lithography, page by page, as Mr. Arden had done for the *Orations of Hyperides* he discovered at Thebes."

*   *   *   *   *

" Besides Mr. Thoresby's letter, which you have so kindly given, I have received several anxious inquiries from gentlemen who take an interest in this important matter, and in consequence I venture once more to trespass, as shortly as I can, upon your valuable columns.

" In answer to Mr. Thoresby's inquiry, I suppose the MS. has now most probably been returned to the Vatican since the cardinal's decease. Every precaution there is taken against fire, and as the floors are all either of marble, or the composition called *pavimento vineziano* (a sort of marble mosaic), and as the little fire that is wanted there is generally supplied by portable *bracieri* (the ancient *foculus*), there is not much fear of accident in this way.

" I cannot say whether or not the authorities are favourable to the publication of the MS.; the cardinal evidently was at work upon it alone and unassisted; he did not consider his exertions part of his public duties, but a labour of love of his own.

" Could I have foreseen that that great man would have been so soon taken from us, I should have endeavoured to have noted down as full an account as possible of the MS. It formerly had been, I was told, separated into two volumes; when I saw it it formed one large thick octavo. It is incomplete at the beginning and end, having lost about half the book of Genesis and nearly all the

Apocalypse. This last is supplied by another hand, in cursive Greek, of the date probably of the 10th century. As I remember, it contains one or two of the smaller books of the Apocrypha, but not the books of the Maccabees.

"The Gospels and Epistles seem, as nearly as I could judge, to be tolerably complete. The celebrated verse in the First Epistle of St. John, as is well known, is not in the text. I saw nothing of the Epistles of Barnabas, Polycarp, Clemens Romanus, the Pastor of Herman, nor any of the writings of that period.

"I asked particularly whether it was known that the MS. had come under the notice of the Complutensian editors, when Cardinal Mai said it was universally believed at Rome that every MS. of any value whatever, through all Italy, had been carefully examined by Cardinal Ximenes or his assistants; that knowing, even as early as the time of Origen, the Greek text had been corrupted by the Gnostics, and later by the Arians, that scholar had made the most careful selection he could from these MSS., and he had borrowed and conveyed them to Alcala for the purpose of collation, and for correcting his celebrated *Polyglott*, and with the intention of afterwards returning the MSS. to their respective owners; that it was generally stated, after the publication of the *Polyglott*, the most precious MSS., by the error of a servant, were sold, instead of a quantity of waste paper—some say to a maker of fireworks; and it is for this reason there is such a paucity of early *codices* of the sacred Scriptures.

"With regard to the date, the cardinal pointed out a note at the end of one of the books—a sort of colophon—which states it was transcribed A.D. 70; but this, I venture to observe would prove that the Christian era was used as a means of computation even before the siege of Jerusalem. He considered, however, the MS. could not be later than the middle of the second century.

"In reply to questions as to the Orations of Hyperides—the notes and illustrations were by the Rev. Churchill Babington, the fac-similes by Messrs. Netherclift and Durlacher; they shew the smallest mark and every flaw in the papyrus, and are equal, if not superior, to the best fac-similes of the French. The book was published by subscription, and I believe is now very scarce. Mr. Arden, no question, has the lithographic stones, and with his usual courtesy, would, no doubt, permit some copies to be taken off.

"With many thanks for the kind communications of several photographers, I fear it would be necessary to reduce the page so much to get a clear image in the camera that the text would be scarcely legible. A quarto page of uncial Greek, reduced to three or four inches square, would, I fear, be of little practical utility. It would, however, be very easy to try the experiment on some other MS. I fear, also, it would be necessary to strain the page and get it perfectly flat, or the curl of the vellum would alter the focus and distort the image. Once more apologizing for taking up so much of your valuable columns,

"I have the honour to be, sir,
"Your obliged and faithful servant,
"ARTHUR ASHPITEL.

"2, Poet's Corner, Westminster Abbey, Nov. 23rd."

"Sir,—In common with many others, I feel a very deep interest in the proposition of Mr. Thoresby, that the New Testament portion of the Vatican MS. should be photographed.

"I may, perhaps, be allowed to add some particulars to what has already appeared in your columns, partly in correction of what has been stated, and partly in reply to inquiries that have been made.

"The New Testament is not now a separate volume, but it and the Septuagint are all bound in one; and this is as it should be, for they are all one MS.

"The *Codex* exhibits no trace of intentional mutilation. It is true that the Epistles of St. Paul to Timothy, Titus, and Philemon are wholly wanting, as well as the Apocalypse, so far as the ancient writing is concerned; but this arises from the MS. having been injured at both ends, so that in the beginning the greater part of Genesis is gone, and in the New Testament the old writing breaks off in Hebrews ix. As the pastoral epistles, in the arrangement of old

Greek MSS., stand after that to the Hebrews, they are thus of necessity wanting. Not so, however, the Catholic Epistles, which occupy their usual Greek location, after the Acts and before Romans.

"A later hand has remedied the defects in part, after a manner, by prefixing the missing part of Genesis, inserting a portion lost from the Psalms, and adding the latter part of the Hebrews, and the Book of Revelations.

"If the testimony of one who has examined and collated personally almost every known Greek MS. of the New Testament, is needed to shew the importance of this proposed step, then let me add, that I believe that the carrying out of Mr. Thoresby's proposition would be one of the greatest services that could be rendered to textual criticism; and no one could feel more deeply obliged to him than myself. In my *Account of the Printed Text of the Greek New Testament* (page 156) I have mentioned the pains and trouble which I took in the hope of obtaining the readings accurately of this most important MS.

"The MS. ought to be examined as well as photographed; because the manner in which the letters have been traced over again by a later hand is such that here and there implicit dependence on the photographed copy might lead to inattention as to the faint, pale, original reading.

"If any one who used the photographed copy were properly on his guard, by such places having been noticed, then the work proposed by Mr. Thoresby would be satisfactory in the extreme.

"I saw at Cambridge, about a month ago, a beautiful photograph of one page of the *Codex Augiensis* lying in the MS. itself, in the library of Trinity College.

"Your obedient servant,
"S. P. Tregelles,
"6, Portland Square, Plymouth, Nov. 23rd."

[In reference to Mr. Ashpitel's communication, our readers need scarcely be informed, that the story of the rocket-maker of Alcala is now pretty well known to be a fable.—Ed. *J. S. L.*]

Assyrian Antiquities.—At a meeting of the Asiatic Society, Nov. 17, the Assistant Secretary read a paper by Capt. Ormsby, of the Indian Navy, upon the "Epigraphs of the Nimrûd Obelisk." It will be in the remembrance of those who have followed the course of Assyrian discovery, that Col. Rawlinson, six years ago, read at a meeting of the Society a translation of the inscription upon this obelisk, which was printed in the early part of the year 1850, detailing the expeditions undertaken by the king who erected the monument, during thirty-one years of his reign. Around the obelisk there were five series of sculptured figures, all representing processions of objects presented to the king by conquered potentates, as tributes of their submission to his power. In the the translation above mentioned, Col. Rawlinson merely gave general notices of the articles thus presented, which consisted, as he said, of "gold and silver, pearls and gems, ebony and ivory; perhaps also of rare woods, or aromatic gums, or metals; and of horses and camels, the latter being described as beasts of the desert with double backs." The object of Capt. Ormsby's paper was to particularize the articles of tribute thereon represented; in doing which he availed himself of all that had been published when the translation of Col. Rawlinson appeared, and shewed that he was an independent worker in the field of Assyrian research, with the laudable ambition to which we should be glad to see more learned men making a claim. The date of the obelisk is placed by Capt. Ormsby about the year 868 b.c.; the king having defeated Benhadad of Syria in his eleventh year, and Hazael in his sixteenth year, and having reigned sixteen years of that campaign, as recorded on the monument. He then proceeds to analyze the words contained in the epigraphs over each row of figures by philological arguments which need not be given here. The results of his reading give, as the translation of the first epigraph, the following words:—"The tribute received from Shena, King of Gozan, silver, gold, precious stones, bright copper vessels, horses for the king, camels, ivory." The second epigraph he reads:—

"Tribute of Jehu, the son of Beth-Omri; silver and gold, gold vases for the ceremony of the Solstice, gold rings or seals, gold and pearls, brilliants, ointment, and oil of Sheba." Capt. Ormsby pronounces the features of the tribute-bearers on this row to be "graphically Jewish," thus corroborating the reading which ascribes the tribute to one of the kings of Israel. The third is, a "Tribute received from the foreign country—camels, ivory, elephants, apes, white bulls, rhinoceroses." The fourth:—"Tribute of Sutadan of Shekai—silver, gold, pearls, gold ingots, oil of Sheba: all choice articles of * * * ." The fifth, which closes Capt. Ormsby's paper, he reads:—"Tribute of Barhagrada of the Shetni (the Cherethiti of the Bible)—silver, gold, precious stones, copper ingots, copper cups, wood of Sheba."

Syro-Egyptian.—Nov. 13.—Dr. J. Lee in the chair.—The chairman exhibited some Papyri, which had been arranged by Mr. Bonomi and Mr. Heath. Mr. Sharpe read on them the name of Rameses II., and believed that they merely contained religious formulæ of that epoch.—The chairman also exhibited photographs of monuments and other subjects, taken in Egypt by Miss Selina Harris. Mr. Ainsworth gave some details of the discovery of a Sarcophagus with Phœnician inscription on it at Sidon, as also descriptive details concerning the same. Dr. Benisch read a translation of the inscription by the Rabbi Isidor Kelisch, with remarks upon the mode of decipherment. This translation was compared with others made by Dr. Dietrich, of Marbug, by the Duc de Luynes in Paris, and by Mr. W. Turner and E. E. S. in the Journal of the American Oriental Society. Archdeacon Raymond observed upon the slight discrepancies exhibited by three different translations, that we had succeeded in deciphering in the present day that which had already, in the time of Homer, been given up as a lost language. Mr. Hogg gave an account of the efforts which he had made, as Foreign Secretary to the Royal Society of Literature, to secure this valuable monument to the British Museum, but which had not been attended with success. Mr. Sharpe made a communication respecting the important discovery made by Zumpt, of Pagan evidence to the effect that Cyrenius *was* Governor of Syria (only employed in Cilicia) at the time of our Saviour's birth, as stated by St. Luke the Evangelist.

Druidical Remains.—Having learnt, on a recent tour through the Highlands that there were some "Curious Stones" to be seen at Castle Leys, about three miles south-west from Inverness, I proceeded thither, and with the assistance of the residents on the spot soon found the object of my search. The "Druids' Temple," as it is styled, stands on a woody knoll, within a corn-field, at some distance from the high road, so as to elude the observation of the passing stranger. It is, besides, so overgrown with copse and furze, as to shew that it is not often visited, and also to render its thorough exploration a matter of no small trouble. It consists of two concentric circles of boulders; within the inner of which there is another assemblage of stones, arranged in no regular order; and, without the exterior circle, a hugh pillow towards the west. The *outer* circle is seventy yards in circumference, and contains (exclusive of the pillar) fifteen stones of different sizes,—those on the north side being blocks of, I should think, from twelve to fifteen tons in weight, placed at equal distances; those on the other sides being mostly smaller, and placed more irregularly, so as to convey the impression that many of them are fragments, and that the original number was much less than it now is—probably not exceeding ten. Some are erect, others prostrate. The *inner* circle contains thirty boulders, nearly equal in dimensions, (although those to the south and west are somewhat larger than the others,) and about one quarter of the size of those in the outer ring, placed in close juxtaposition, like a string of beads, except at three points, —two towards the east, and one on the west side, the opening at which probably constituted the entrance; and most of them erect and entire, apparently in the same position as when first set up. Within this inner circle, as I have said, and somewhat nearer its western edge, there is a confused collection of ten stones, of the same size as those immediately around them, (or perhaps I should say twelve, as two of the thirty composing the ring are lying *behind* their neighbours at the entrance). It is just *possible* that they may have formed the supports of a "cromlech," of which the two stones lying near the west opening may have formed the table; but appearances favour their having formed an interior *screen* behind the entrance, as four of them are still lying close together in a line. The great "Dallan" (as the Irish call them) or pillar is (8 feet 7 inches) nearly three yards high, and five yards in girth, having nearly the form of a prism, with one of the edges turned towards the east. Such pillars, as is well known, frequently occur in the vicinity of cromlechs, and in the *centre* of circles, such as that described. I forbear to speculate on the origin and design of such monuments. The late Dr. Kitto appended valuable remarks on the subject to successive chapters in 'The Pictorial History of Palestine,' In which the reader will find a very extensive collection of *facts;* while his theory has at least the merit of reconciling all the other hypotheses deserving of attention.—*Athenæum.*

THE SCOTCH UNIVERSITIES.

" *To the Editor of the Times.* Sir,—Observing in an article of *The Times* of the 22d of November that you state "the fact is that the salaries of the professors being absurdly small, it is a matter of much importance to increase the number of their students, each paying a fee; hence, there is no limit to the admission of freshmen; there is no entrance examination; in the Greek classes the professor has to begin with the alphabet, and he actually ' poaches on the schools,' " I beg leave to enclose a list of the salaries now received by the professors, fully proving your statement. Yours, &c., STATIST.

" SALARIES OF PROFESSORS AT SCOTCH UNIVERSITIES.

	Edinburgh.	Glasgow.	Aberdeen.			
			St. Mary.	St. Salvador & St. Leonard.	King's.	Marischal.
	£.	£.	£. s. d.	£. s. d.	£. s. d.	£. s. d.
Principal	...	...	93 0 0	55 11 0	20 0 0	60 0 0
Prof. of Ecclesiastical History	100	...	86 1 8	...	...	50 0 0
„ Hebrew	80	...	86 1 8	...	...	...
„ Divinity	80	...	86 1 8	...	*12 0 0	53 0 0
„ Greek	80	...	86 1 8	55 11 0	10 8 8	43 16 8
„ Mathematics	80	62	...	55 11 0	...	43 16 8
„ Rhetoric and Belles Lettres	100	...	...	...	...	...
„ Civil History	...	...	...	55 11 0	..	43 16 0
„ Physic	...	75	...	...	...	...
„ Medicine	...	75	...	55 11 0	10 8 8	100 0 0
„ Materia Medica	...	100	...	...	...	...
„ Humanity	80	25	...	55 11 0	10 8 8	200 0 0
„ Logic	80	11	...	55 11 0	...	...
„ Moral Philosophy	80	11	...	55 11 0	10 8 8	†43 16 8
„ Natural Philosophy	80	21	...	55 11 0	10 8 8	43 16 8
„ Civil Engineering	...	275	...	...	...	...
„ Civil Law	...	...	...	...	10 8 8	...
„ Medical Jurisprudence	100	...	...	...	...	...
„ Midwifery	...	50	...	...	...	...
„ Oriental Languages	...	20	...	...	...	33 0 0
„ Chymistry	...	200	...	...	...	210 0 0
„ Botany	100	100	...	...	...	...
„ Anatomy	...	‡30	...	...	...	150 0 0
„ Pathological Surgery	100	...	...	...	...	...
„ Surgery	100	75	...	...	...	100 0 0
„ Astronomy	300	50	...	...	...	...
„ Natural History	100	150	...	...	...	...

* £150 additional. † And Logic. ‡ And Botany.

"King's College has an additional allowance of £700 per annum to the Principal and Professors."

Archbishop Tenison's Library.—"Sir,—While the question of public libraries is being mooted, may I ask you to direct the attention of the public to that fine old library, founded by Archbishop Tenison about 1695, to supply what he then considered a deficiency of 'any one shop of a stationer fully furnished with books of various learning within the precinct of the city and liberty of Westminster.'

"I stepped into this library yesterday by accident, and on inquiry of the curator, the Rev. Philip Hale, what formalities were necessary to be admitted there, he informed me that all who resided within the precincts of the liberty of Westminster had a right, and all strangers like myself were welcome to come at any time. But when I exercised this right what a spectacle presented itself. I stood in a room, well-proportioned, built by Sir Christopher Wren, surrounded by books of the fathers of the English church, 5,000 in number, rotting and mouldering like their authors in their graves. I was told that for the last two years the heat of summer and the damp of winter had done their worst upon these ancient and valuable relics of a past age—works which in some hands would be considered priceless. There lies Bacon's Note-book, and various other MSS. of his, buried amid a heap of dust. Can nothing be done to rescue these noble works from their present sepulchre? The trustees cannot even afford money to pay for firing and light, so I left my dusty friends to their fate for a while with a sad heart. On leaving the house I stepped accidentally into the school-room, which forms the basement floor. That, too, was untenanted, and I was informed that, although there were a few scholars still on the foundation, the trustees had refused to elect more, and the school would be closed at the end of the year. What are the Charity Commissioners about in St. James's Square? A reply to this question may be elicited if you will favour me by inserting this letter from

"Your obliged, N. H. R.
"*To the Editor of the Times.*"

A New Map of the Holy Land, constructed by C. W. M. Van de Velde, late Lieut., Dutch R.N., Chevalier of the Legion of Honour, from his own surveys in 1851 and 52; from those made in 1841, by Majors Robe and Rochfort Scott, Lieut. J. F. A. Symonds and other Officers of Her Majesty's Corps of Royal Engineers; and from the results of the researches made by Lynch, Robinson, Wilson, Burckhardt, Seetzen, &c., is on the eve of publication.

Lieut. Van de Velde has made known to the public, in the narrative of his travels,[a] that he went in 1851 to the *Holy Land,* with the design of making as accurate a Map of that most interesting country as the means of a private individual, and the present condition of the land and its inhabitants, would permit.

As the construction of such a Map would of necessity take a long time, the author thought it expedient to publish first the incidents and experiences of his journey, along with the discoveries of ancient sites, enlarging somewhat on the geographical and topographical details of those places which were as yet little or not at all known, so far as his simple narrative would admit. He has, in his narrative, also expressed his intention of collecting his geographical information into a separate memoir, which will accompany his map.

Lieut. Van de Velde is happy to announce that his geographical labours on Palestine are now completed, and that the Map is already in the engraver's hands. At the same time, he would observe, that all the difficulties which present themselves in the execution of such a work, are not yet overcome. The publication of so large a Map requires the outlay of a very large capital; and he therefore owes it to himself to ascertain the extent of such a risk, by inviting

---

[a] *Narrative of a Journey through Syria and Palestine.* Two vols. 8vo.

contributions towards it.	Particulars can be obtained of Messrs. Williams and Norgate, Henrietta Street, Covent Garden.

Shortly will be published an " Essay upon the State of the Metallurgical Arts in Ancient Times, from the allusions to these Arts in the Old Testament, compared with our present knowledge of the same arts," by James Napier, Esq., F.C.S., &c., &c.

The new number of *Zeitschrift für die bisterische Theologi* (*dated* 1856), contains a valuable and interesting paper (160 pp.) on the Ignatian Epistles, by R. A. Lipsius; he confirms greatly Mr. Cureton's conclusions.

*_** It will be seen that important Intelligence has been anticipated in the department of *Correspondence.*

NEW WORKS PUBLISHED DURING THE LAST QUARTER.

FOREIGN.

Arnoldi (M.)—Commentar zur Evangelium der heil. Matthäus. (Commentary on St. Matthew's Gospel.) Trier, 8vo.

Renan (Ernest).—Histoire générale et Système comparé des Langues Sémitiques. Ouvrage couronné par l'Institut. Première partie. Histoire générale des Langues Sémitiques. Paris: Imprimé, par autorisation de l'Empereur, à l'Imprimerie impériale. 8vo, pp. viii, 500.

Bressauvido (Ildefonse de).—Instructions morales sur la doctrine chrétienne. Five vols. Lyons, Paris, 12mo.

Breviarum Romanum ex decreto SS. concilii Tridentini restitum, &c. Paris, 12mo.

Bunsen (Von Christian Carl Josias).—Die Zeichen der Zeit. Briefe an Freunde über die Gewissensfreiheit und das Recht der Christlichen Gemeinde. ("Signs of the Times. Letters to friends concerning Freedom of Conscience and the Right of Christian Congregations." By Christian Charles Josias Bunsen.) Part II. Leipzig, F. A. Brockhaus.

Christenfreude in Lied und Bild (A Collection of Hymns and Spiritual Songs, with woodcuts). Leipzig, 8vo.

Commentar zu Koheleth und dem hohen Liede von R. Samuel ben Meir, &c. Leipsic, 8vo, pp. xii. 68. ("Commentary upon Ecclesiastes and the Song of Solomon.")

Coquerel (Athanase).—Cours de religion chrétienne. Third edition. Paris, 12mo.

Cornelius (C. A.)—Geschichte der Münsterichen Aufruhrs, &c. (The Insurrection of the Anabaptists in Munster, in Three Books.) Leipzig, 8vo.

Elster (E.)—Commentar über der Prediger Salomo. (Commentary on the Book of Ecclesiastes.) Göttingen, 8vo.

Glossaire, Dictionnaire des locutions obscures et des mots vieillis qui se rencontrent dans les Œuvres de Jean Calvin. Paris, 8vo.

Hecht (Em.)—Israels Geschichte, &c. (History of the Jews from the close of the Bible to the present day.) Leipzig, 8vo.

Hoffmann (Dr. W.)—Ueber den rechten Gebrauch der Bibel in Kirche, Schule und. ("On the proper use of the Bible in the Church, the Household, and the School-room.") 12mo.

Huther (Dr. J. E.)—Kritisch-exegetisches Handbuch über die drei Briefe des Johannes. Auch unter dem Titel: Kritisch-exegetischer Commentar über das Neue Testament. Dr. A. H. W. Meyer. Fourteenth Part. Göttingen, 8vo.

Hymni Latini medii ævi. E codd. MSS. edidit, et adnotationibus illustravit, Franc. Jos. Mone, archivii Carlsruhensis præfectus. Tomus tertius. Hymni ad Sanctos. Friburgi Brisgoviæ (Freyberg). 8vo, pp. iv. 580.

Krummacher (F. W.)—Predigtweisen, &c. (Manner in Preaching: a Lecture on the subject, How far the Clergy should study the taste of their hearers in their Sermons.) Berlin, 8vo.

Leonhardi Hutteri compendium locorum theologicorum.   Addita sunt
excerpta ex Jo. Wollebii et Ben. Pictetí compendiis ed. A. Twesten. Berlin, 8vo.

Lepsius (Dr. Von R.)—Das Allgemeine Linguistische Alphabet, Grund-
sätze des Uebertragung fremder Schriftsysteme, und bisher noch ungeschriebener Sprachen;
in Europäische Buchstaben ("Universal Linguistic Alphabet, or principles for the reduction
of strange systems of writing, and hitherto unwritten languages into European Characters.")
Berlin, 8vo, pp. 64.

Lhomond (M.)—Doctrine chrétienne, in forme de lectures de piété, où l'on
expose les preuves de la religion, &c.   New edition.   Paris, 12mo.

Liebner (Dr. T. A.)—Introductio in Dogmaticam Christianam.   Part. 1, 2.
Berlin, 4to.

Lippner (G. F. W.)—Sulamite, oder das Lied der Lieder.. (The Song of
Songs.   Translated for the first time for the last eighteen centuries from figurative into intelligible language.) Nürnberg, 8vo.

Marche (J. P.)—La Croix du Pasteur.   Paris, 8vo.

S. Caroli Borromæi instructionum fabriciæ ecclesiasticæ et supellectitis
ecclesiasticæ libri duo.   New edition.   Paris, 12mo.

Schliephake (Dr. F. W. Th.)—Die Grundlagen des sittlichen Lebens.
Wiesbaden, 8vo.

Seyffarth (Von Dr. Gust.)—Grammatica Ægyptiaca.   Erste Anleitung
zum übersetzen Altägyptischer Literaturwerke; nebst der Geschichte des Hieroglyphen-
schlüssels.   Mit. 92 Seiten lithographien.   Gotha: G. A. Perthes.   London: Williams and
Norgate.   8vo, pp. xlvi. 120 & 92. ("Egyptian Grammar.   First Introduction to the Translation of Ancient Egyptian Literature; with a History of the Interpretation of Hieroglyphics,
and 92 pages of Lithographs.")

Ταμιεῖον τῶν τῆς καινῆς διαθήκης λέξεων; sive, Concordantiæ omnium
vocum Novi Testamenti Græci.   Primum ab Erasmo Schmidio editæ, nunc, secundum critices
et hermeneutices nostræ ætatis rationes, emendatæ, auctæ, meliori ordine dispositæ, curâ
Caroli Hermanni Bruder, Ph.D., A.A., LL.M.   Lipsiæ: sumptibus et typis Caroli Tauchnitii.
Editio stereotypa altera.   4to.   London, Nutt.

Theologische Schriften der Alten Ægypten, nach dem Turiner Papyrus,
zum ersten male übersetzt von Dr. Gustav Seyffarth.   Gotha.   London: Williams and Norgate.   8vo, pp. viii. 120. ("Theological Writings of the Ancient Egyptians, after the Turin
Papyrus," translated for the first time by Dr. G. Seyffarth.)

Uhlemann (Auctore M. A.)—Linguæ Copticæ Grammatica, in usum
Scholarum Academicarum scripta, cum Chrestomathia et Glossario.   Insertæ sunt observa-
tiones quædam de veterum Ægyptiorum Grammaticâ.   Lipsiæ, T. O. Weigel.   8vo, pp. viii.
168.

Une vie de Chanoine au XVIIe siècle.   Chalons, 8vo.

Zwilling (Louis).—Doctrine Biblique de la mort du Christ.   Strasbourg,
8vo.

ENGLISH.

A Plain Commentary on the Four Holy Gospels, intended chiefly for
devotional reading.   In 7 vols. fcap. 8vo.

Barnes (Rev. Albert).—The Way of Salvation, illustrated in a series of
Discourses.   Revised by the Rev. E. Henderson, D D.   12mo, pp. 486.

Bloomfield (Rev. S. J., D.D.)—The Greek Testament, with English
Notes, Critical, Philological, and Exegetical, especially adapted to the Use of Theological
Students or Ministers.   Two vols., 8vo, pp. 900, 908.

Buchanan (James, D.D., LL.D.)—Faith in God and Modern Atheism
compared, in their Essential Nature, Theoretic Grounds, and Practical Influence. Two vols.
8vo, pp. 924.

Craig (Rev. R., A.M.)—The Man Christ Jesus. Small 8vo, pp. 378.

Davidson (S., D.D., LL.D.)—Hebrew Text of the Old Testament, revised
from Critical Sources; being an Attempt to present a Purer and more Correct Text than the
received one of Van der Hooght, by the aid of the best existing Materials; with the principal
Various Readings found in MSS., Ancient Versions, Jewish Books and Writers, Parallels,
Quotations, &c. &c. 8vo, pp. 228.

Freeman (Rev. Philip, M.A.)—The Principles of Divine Service; an
Inquiry concerning the true manner of understanding and using the order for Morning and
Evening Prayer, and for the administration of the Holy Communion in the English Church.
8vo, pp. 436.

Gill (John, D.D.)—An Exposition of the Book of Solomon's Song. Imperial 8vo, pp. 394.

Gough (Henry).—New Testament Quotations, collated with the Scrip-
tures of the Old Testament in the original Hebrew and the version of the LXX.; and with
the other writings, Apocryphal, Talmudic, and Classical, cited or alleged so to be. With
Notes, and a complete Index. 8vo, pp. 346.

Guthrie (Rev. Thomas, D.D.)—The Gospel in Ezekiel, illustrated in a
Series of Discourses. Crown 8vo, pp. 436.

Hardwick (C., M.A.)—Christ and other Masters: an Historical Inquiry
into some of the Chief Parallelisms and Contrasts between Christianity and the Religious
Systems of the Ancient World; with Special Reference to Prevailing Difficulties and Objections. Part I. 8vo, pp. 168.

Harrington (E. C., M.A.)—Rome's Pretensions Tested: a Sermon
preached at the Cathedral Church of St. Peter, Exeter, Nov. 5, 1855. With Notes and copious
References. 8vo, pp. 48.

Harvey (Richard, M.A.)—The Sabbath, or Rest the Right of every Man.
A Sermon preached in the Chapel Royal, St. James's, on Sunday, July 1, 1855. 12mo, pp. 22.

Howard (Hon. and Very Rev. Henry E. J., D.D.)—The Book of Genesis,
according to the Version of the LXX., translated into English, with Notices of its Omissions
and Insertions, and with Notes on the Passages in which it differs from our Authorized
Translation. Crown 8vo, pp. 228.

Jackson (John, D.D., Bishop of Lincoln).—A Charge delivered to the
Clergy of the Diocese of Lincoln at his Primary Visitation, in October, 1855. 8vo, pp. 46.

Jeremie (J. A., D.D.)—A Sermon preached before the University of Cam-
bridge, on Sunday, July 1st, on the occasion of the death of the Rev. J. J. Blunt, late Margaret
Professor of Divinity. 8vo, pp. 24.

Jowett (Benjamin, M.A.)—The Epistles of St. Paul to the Thessalonians,
Galatians, Romans: with Critical Notes and Dissertations. In 2 vols.

Kay (W., D.D.)—The Promises of Christianity: an Essay. 8vo, pp. 132.

Krummacher (Rev. F., D.D.)—The Suffering Saviour: a Mediation on
the last days of Christ upon Earth. Translated, under the express sanction of the Author,
by Samuel Jackson. 8vo, pp. 490.

Milner (Rev. Joseph, M.A.)—The Essentials of Christianity theoretically
and practically considered. Edited by Mary Milner. 18mo, pp. 316.

Mueller (Max).—Proposals for a Missionary Alphabet, submitted to the
Alphabetical Conferences held at the Residence of Chevalier Bunsen, in January, 1854. 8vo,
pp. 58.

Oakley (Rev. C.E., B.A.)—The English Bible and its History: a Lecture
delivered in the School-room at Tortmouth-court, Gloucestershire, Jan. 23, 1854. A new
edition, published by request. 24mo, pp. 68.

Pagani (Very Rev. John Baptist).—The End of the World, or, the Second
Coming of our Lord and Saviour Jesus Christ. 12mo, pp. 372.

Raven (Rev. T., M.A.)—The Family Commentary on the New Testament;
with Notes adapted to the Use of Family Worship, and made into Short Readings. 8vo,
pp. 640.

Samuel (Lord Bishop of Oxford, &c., &c.)—The Principles of the English
Reformation. A Sermon preached on Monday, Nov. 5, 1855, before the University of Oxford,
at St. Mary's Church. Published by request. 8vo, pp. 28.

Schnorr's Bible Pictures.—English edition, printed from the original
wood blocks. Parts I. and II.

Scudamore (W. E., M.A.)—England and Rome. A Discussion of the
Principal Doctrines and Passages of History in Common Debate between the Members of the
Two Communions. 8vo, pp. 508.

Scudamore (W. E., M.A.)—The Communion of the Laity. An Essay,
chiefly Historical, on the Rule and Practice of the Church with respect to the Reception of the
Consecrated Elements at the Celebration of the Holy Eucharist. 8vo, pp. 136.

Sinclair (Ven. Archdeacon).—British Eloquence of the Nineteenth Century.
Sacred Oratory, First Series.—Sermons of Eminent Living Divines of the Church of England,
contributed by the Authors. With an Introductory Charge on Preaching. 12mo, pp. 360.

Stewart (Dugald).—Outlines of Moral Philosophy. With a Memoir of
the Author, Explanatory Notes, and an Appendix of Questions, by the Rev. John Jordan,
M.A. 18mo, pp. 286.

Taylor (Rev. Richard, M.A., F.G.S.)—Te Ika a Maui; or, New Zealand
and its Inhabitants, illustrating the Origin, Manners, Customs, Mythology, Religion, Rites,
Songs, Proverbs, Fables, and Language of the Natives.

Waldegrave (Hon. and Rev. Samuel, M.A.)—New Testament Millenna-
rianism : or, the Kingdom and Coming of Christ as taught by himself and his Apostles : set
forth in Eight Sermons, preached before the University of Oxford, in the year, 1854, at the
Lecture founded by the late Rev. John Bampton, Canon of Salisbury. 8vo, pp. 702.

Westcott (Brooke Foss, M.A.)—A General Survey of the History of the
Canon of the New Testament during the First Four Centuries. Crown 8vo, pp. 618.

END OF VOL. II.

Walton and Mitchell, Printers, 24, Wardour Street, Oxford Street.

INDEX

VOLUME THE SECOND.

Lightning Source UK Ltd.
Milton Keynes UK
UKHW010740261118
332983UK00009B/926/P

9 781527 657045